Economic Interdependence and Flexible Exchange Rates

Economic Interdependence and Flexible Exchange Rates

Edited by
Jagdeep S. Bhandari
and
Bluford H. Putnam

with
Jay H. Levin

Foreword by
Rudiger Dornbusch

The MIT Press
Cambridge, Massachusetts
London, England

This book was set in Times New Roman by Asco Trade Typesetting Ltd., Hong Kong, and printed and bound by Halliday Lithograph in the United States of America.

Library of Congress Cataloging in Publication Data

Main entry under title:

Economic interdependence and flexible exchange rates.

  Bibliography: p.
  Includes index.
  1. Foreign exchange—Addresses, essays, lectures. 2. International economic integration—Addresses, essays, lectures. 3. Economic stabilization—Addresses, essays, lectures. I. Bhandari, Jagdeep S. II. Putnam, Bluford H. III. Levin, Jay H.
HG3852.E26 1983   332.4′562   82-14830
ISBN 0-262-02177-3

Contents

Foreword   ix
Rudiger Dornbusch

Preface   xvii

1

Flexible Exchange Rates, Prices, and the Role of "News":
Lessons from the 1970s   3
Jacob A. Frenkel

I

Exchange Rate Determination   43

2

Exchange Rate Economics: Where Do We Stand?   45
Rudiger Dornbusch

3

Monetary and Portfolio-Balance Models of Exchange Rate
Determination   84
Jeffrey A. Frankel

4

Balance of Payments and the Foreign Exchange Market:
A Dynamic Partial Equilibrium Model   116
Pentti J. K. Kouri

5

Exchange Rates in a Global Monetary Model with Currency Substitution and Rational Expectations   157
Victor A. Canto and Marc A. Miles

II

Energy and International Adjustment   177

6

Oil and the Dollar   179
Paul Krugman

7

Energy and Growth under Flexible Exchange Rates: A Simulation Study   191
Jeffrey Sachs

8

Oil, Disinflation, and Export Competitiveness: A Model of the "Dutch Disease"   221
Willem H. Buiter and Douglas D. Purvis

III

Policy Interdependence   249

9

Monetary and Fiscal Policy with Flexible Exchange Rates   251
William H. Branson and Willem H. Buiter

10

Exchange Market Intervention Policies in a Small Open Economy   286
Stephen J. Turnovsky

11

**Policy Interdependence under Flexible Exchange Rates:
A Dynamic Analysis of Price Interactions**   312
Willard E. Witte

12

**A Model of Stabilization Policy in a Jointly Floating Currency
Area**   329
Jay H. Levin

13

**Reserve Requirements on Eurocurrency Deposits: Implications
for the Stabilization of Real Outputs**   350
Dale W. Henderson and Douglas G. Waldo

14

**The Choice of an Invoice Currency in International
Transactions**   384
John F. O. Bilson

15

**International Trade, Indebtedness, and Welfare Repercussions
among Supply-Constrained Economies under Floating Exchange
Rates**   402
Bryce Hool and J. David Richardson

IV

Simulations   425

16

**International Transmission under Pegged and Floating Exchange
Rates: An Empirical Comparison**   427
Michael R. Darby

17

**Tariff and Exchange Rate Protection under Fixed and Flexible
Exchange Rates in the Major Industrialized Countries**   472
Alan V. Deardorff and Robert M. Stern

18

**Economic Change and Policy Response in Canada under Fixed
and Flexible Exchange Rates**   500
Malcolm D. Knight and Donald J. Mathieson

List of contributors   531

Index   533

Foreword   Rudiger Dornbusch

This book brings together a rich collection of essays on the economics of stabilization and transmission of disturbances under flexible exchange rates. The obvious diversity, in both modeling and the issues addressed, suggests that the area is alive and moving and indeed is far from settling down to a consensus. How does the work reported in this volume differ from the Keynes-Cassell view of the 1920s, the Robison-Haberler-Machlup tradition of the 1930s and 1940s, and the Meade-Fleming-Mundell tradition of the postwar years? After all it is on their shoulders that we have been standing to get a better view.

Keynes and Cassell dealt with PPP (purchasing power parity). The Robinson-Haberler-Machlup tradition was very much one of the inter-war period, concerned with the currency experience of the hyperinflations of the twenties, the marginalist revolution and the employment concerns of the thirties. It was a relative price-oriented theory of the current account and employment and a monetarist theory of long-run trends. It was in no way a theory that could deal with issues of short-run macroeconomic dynamics and the important role of the international mobility of capital.

It is my impression that there was relatively little work on the question of capital mobility and its role in exchange rate theory, although studies by Nurkse, Pollack, and Kindleberger, looked at from the perspective of today's models, must be thought highly insightful. For example, Charles P. Kindleberger, *International Short-Term Capital Movements* (New York: Columbia University Press, 1937) notes, "The fact that the franc is weak when the chamber of deputies is sitting or when an unbalanced budget is announced is due to the fact that the French public fears uncontrolled inflation and begins to export capital. In part, of course, it is due to the fact that foreign exchange dealers in other parts of the world expect such a reaction and accentuate it by selling the franc short at such time" (p. 106).

The remark surely comes close to present-day Minnesota-style thinking on the budget, inflation, and exchange rates.

The Meade-Fleming-Mundell tradition represents a major break with previous exchange rate modeling in three respects. First, exchange rate modeling is placed in the context of an explicit or formal general equilibrium model. Second, the relevant model is quite explicitly a macroeconomic model. Third, because exchange rate determination is discussed in a macroeconomic context, it becomes obvious that interest rate and exchange rate determination are intimately linked. This is a dramatically different perspective from earlier work, in which capital movements and their incidence on the exchange rate where treated as if they had no effect on the equilibrium in asset markets. In part this reflects the partial equilibrium tradition of earlier work; in part the difference in approach reflects the progress derived from the Hicksian IS-LM paradigm.

The Meade-Fleming-Mundell approach achieved the major breakthrough in exchange rate modeling. The next twenty years have seen valuable additions, but these were primarily issues of realism and extension, not of a conceptual kind. Mundell himself, Black, and Argy-Porter introduced in a formal way exchange rate expectations into modeling and thus led the way for today's Mundell-Fleming models.

Of course, the idea of exchange rate expectations has also been used in a very fruitful way in more monetarist models, more along the line of Kindleberger's quoted remark. The most insightful paper here is surely Mussa's 1976 discussion of exchange rate formation. The setting is one in which the money supply process is stochastic and individual money holders have to guess whether innovations in money reflect noise or changes in trend. The model thus draws attention to the role of "news" in exchange rate determination.

In another development the current account was made an important part of exchange rate economics. Tower and Floyd, and later Branson, Dornbusch, and Kouri, drew attention to the fact that unbalanced current accounts give rise to external asset accumulation, thereby introducing an exchange rate dynamics beyond what derives from short-run macroeconomics. This is , of course, the international counterpart of the Lerner-Silber argument that an unbalanced budget is a source of macroeconomic dynamics.

The actual experience with flexible exchange rates has been surprising in many respects and has had an important influence on exchange rate economics. The single most important fact, I believe, is that the flexible rate system has managed to achieve the real depreciation of the dollar in the early 1970s. In the transition to flexible rates the dollar has undergone a lasting *real* depreciation relative to the 1960s of 25 percent, thus making up for the growing overvaluation that had come about in the postwar period in consequence of high European and Japaneses growth in productivity. The second important achievement of the flexible rate system has been to cope with the financial consequences of the oil shock in a manner that has made much of the discussion of world financial programming quite redundant.

Beyond these two sturdy facts the record is wide open and under consideration. There have come up, among other issues, the following: dirty floating; massive intervention; sterilized intervention; virtuous and vicious circles; exchange market-based disinflation policy; real exchange rate problems of material exporters; real exchange rate problems of countries undergoing inflation stabilization; instability in third (small) countries deriving from variability in the exchange rate between major currency areas; reserve demand under floating; and international asset diversification and her little sister, currency substitution. The experience with flexible rates has not only brought up these new problem areas—or dramatized them, to the extent that they were already familiar from the Canadian or interwar experience—it has also provided the data with which to take theories to the mat.

This is not the place to review in any detail the entire menu that this book offers or to ask where, between overview and simulations, the main dish is. There is room, though, to comment on a few of the papers, if only to highlight how much the work reported here is novel, controversial, and plain interesting.

A good starting point is the Canto-Miles paper on currency substitution. The paper shows that with a diversified *currency*, portfolio liquidity service technology and relative user costs determine the composition of money holdings by currency denomination and, given supplies, the relative price of monies. Changes in the user cost because of current or prospective changes in relative money supplies or in technology exert an immediate impact on the exchange rate. The formulation is of particular interest in at least two respects. First, it offers a microeconomic foundation for currency composition based on a production function for liquidity or transactions services. More important, the paper offers a sufficently sharp formulation of the currency substitution hypothesis to place it in contrast with the monetary approach. The monetary approach contemplates substitution between home money and *all* other assets treated as a composite asset—foreign bonds, stocks, goods, and home bonds alike. Increased rates of home money expansion, because they raise inflation, reduce real money demand, leading to substitution toward all other assets, thus inducing a once-for-all depreciation. This velocity change of the monetary approach would appear the same as the change in money proportions of the currency substitution model. The currency substitution model comes into its own in pointing to a microeconomic underpinning for the derived demands for currencies. In doing so it will, of course, have to reckon with the economies of scale issue that Swoboda took as the basis of the vehicle currency phenomenon.

"Exchange rates are determined in asset markets (not in the foreign exchange market)" has been the central proposition of much of the work in the 1970s. Kouri's paper addresses that issue by proposing a foreign exchange market or balance of payments-based theory of exchange rate determination. Here current accounts and capital flows are reconciled with each other by an equilibrium exchange rate. The reader will ask whether this is the asset market model, ingeniously restated, or is it an altogether different theory? Consider the following simple model of the exchange rate. There are two assets, home money and a real asset with a fixed world real rate of return. The home country is small and PPP holds all the time. Real money demand is proportional to the value of real assets, and monetary equilibrium obtains continuously:

$$M/E = \theta a, \tag{1}$$

where M/E is the real money supply, having imposed PPP, and a is the value of real asset holdings. The rate of accumulation of external assets is equal to the current account, which in turn depends on real wealth $a + M/E$:

$$a = CA(a + M/E). \tag{2}$$

Finally the current account-determined rate of asset accumulation must equal the planned rate of addition to real assets consistent with asset market equilibrium, over time, or, by differentiating (1) with respect to time,

$$\dot{a} = a(m - e), \tag{3}$$

where m and e are the growth rate of nominal money and the percentage rate of depreciation, respectively. Combining (2) and (3) to ensure payments balance yields Kouri's acceleration hypothesis:

$$e = m - \frac{CA}{a}. \tag{4}$$

Depreciation thus equals monetary growth adjusted for the current account. We have used a traditional asset market/monetarist/current account model of the 1976 Kouri vintage to derive the key equation of a foreign exchange market theory of the exchange rate. It surely is not a model in which capital flows, divorced from the conditions of stock equilibrium, establish the exchange rate. Kouri's paper opens up this important question, which no doubt will remain an active research item for some time to come.

Jeffrey Sachs offers a piece of research the ambition of which is matched only by its accomplishment: a multilateral, intertemporal, rational expectations maximizing model of production (with energy), trade, lending, and accumulation. The monster is slain by first-order conditions, multiple shooting, and simulation and reveals the time paths of optimally adjusting ecomonies (with some short-run macrofriction as gravy). The work very firmly establishes that macrodynamics of open economies in an intertemporal setting, using simulation, is a highly fruitful exercise. More strikingly, it draws attention to the fact that accumulation and lending are processes concurrent with labor market and expectations adjustments and must therefore be part of any sensible dynamics. The Sachs paper thus shows us the blueprint of a Project Link of the 1980s.

The question of multilaterial trade and lending is also addressed in Paul Krugman's paper. A few sleights of hand and there is a model of OPEC, the United States, and Germany, focusing on the determination of the exchange rate as it is influenced by OPEC's marginal spending patterns and the marginal pattern of portfolio preferences. In the short run, portfolio preferences dominate, as OPEC spending lags behind the oil bonanza; but in the long run, trade patterns exert their dominant influence on equilibrium exchange rates. The model is highly suggestive and, its simplicity notwithstanding, makes an important case for multilateral exchange rate theorizing.

The same concern for a realistic modeling of the exchange rate implications of oil disturbances is at the center of the Buiter-Purvis paper. Drawing on the experience of the United Kingdom, the paper shows that inflation stabilization and oil discovery make difficult bedfellows. This is an important line of research, not in innovating on a conceptual front, but in actually showing in a precise manner what oil does to the real exchange rate and employment and which monetary-fiscal mix optimally achieves disinflation.

In a world of dirty floating the issue of exchange rate strategies obviously arises. Turnovsky addresses that question in asking where, in the spectrum between fixed and flexible rates, a country should place itself.

The answer is that there is no general case for full flexibility, not even when disturbances are monetary and originate abroad. More important, even the traditional case for intervention policy, following a rule of leaning against the wind, is questioned and shown inferior in some circumstances. Turnovsky's paper is a good example of the important insights to be gained from setting stabilization and exchange rate issues in stochastic macroeconomic models.

The implications of joint floating for adjustment to disturbances originating within the currency area and to external disturbances are the topic of Jay Levin's paper. This is, of course, a question that goes back to Mundell's "optimum currency area," wherein it is argued that fixed relative prices within the union (and labor mobility) combined with external relative price flexibility is an optimal arrangement for suitably integrated areas. The European Monetary Arrangement in fact is a currency area, and its labors make Levin's analysis particularly topical.

Among the simulation studies I would draw attention in particular to those of Deardorff-Stern and Knight-Mathieson. The Deardorff-Stern study enquires into the effects of tariff changes under flexible exchange rates. This is a question that had been posed by Harry Johnson, who in an effective protection context looked at the effects of tariffs on exchange rates, real income, and protection. The Deardorff-Stern paper, although regrettably lacking in much of the detail of the model closure, at least in its conclusions attests to the critical importance of exchange rate effects for effective protection and indeed for the ranking of protected sectors. Once again the multilateral aspects of exchange rate problems come very much into their own.

The Knight-Mathieson paper presents a complete macroeconometric model of the Canadian economy. In the tradition of recent work at the International Monetary Fund (IMF) the model is a disequilibrium variant with a pervasive monetary disequilibrium spillover effect. The traditional transmission channels of the open economy are carefully modeled to include demand, price, and interest rate linkages. Money is endogenous, and exchange rate policy is represented by an intervention function. The entire model is driven by adaptive inflationary expectations. Much of the model is congenial even if one doubts the pervasive spillover of money and the modeling of inflation expectations. But one wishes that the model would go further in respect to the budget, nonmonetary financial assets, and the term structure of interest. If money exerts spillover effects, should the same not be true for the stock market or debt finance, and if so, what are the implications for output, inflation, and the exchange rate? It is, I believe, particularly in the area of fiscal policy and debt finance that the economics of flexible rates are in need of some further analysis. This, of course, is well recognized and advanced in the Buiter-Branson paper.

I have only commented on some features of some of the papers offered in this volume, hoping thereby to give an idea of how far the field has moved and in what directions. But of course there is much more in the volume: Frenkel's impressive empirical study; disequilibrium economics by Hool and Richardson; Jeffrey Frankel's money demand-based work on exchange rate equations; Bilson's model of trade invoicing in support of Grassman's law; Witte's discussion of price interactions in integrated markets; Henderson-Waldo's discussion of Eurocurrency markets; and Darby on Mark IV. It is quite apparent that flexible exchange rates is the largest common denominator of these studies; but in a broader sense they fit together in their shared concern for finding a useful way to think about how open, integrated economies hang together and how much scope there is for stabilization policy.

Preface

The origins of this book date back to a chance meeting between us in Atlanta, Georgia, in November of 1979. We agreed that the time had come for a new collection of essays devoted to the general topic of economic interdependence under floating exchange rates. As world markets have evolved from national markets into an internationally efficient system, the ability of governments to isolate their economies from international disturbances has decreased dramatically. Furthermore, the costs of economic isolation, sometimes referred to as independence, have risen as well. That is, in today's highly integrated world economic system, government authorities must come to terms with the economic interdependence of the system.

As a practical matter, this challenge to national economic policymakers affects different countries in different ways. Japan, for example, is finding that more openness is required of its capital markets, and a capital and exchange liberalization program is being formulated there. In Europe, interdependence has often been highlighted by exchange rate movements, as countries that have attempted to "go their own way" have been disciplined by the market. In recognition of these constraints, various formal arrangements, such as the European Monetary System, were constructed.

For the United States, the critical importance of monetary and exchange rate policy for domestic inflation was underscored by the events of 1977–1980, when a large depreciation of the US dollar (1977/78), following expansive policies, ignited a sustained rise in inflation (1979/80). This increase in inflation was severely underestimated by virtually all "domestic" forecasters because they failed to grasp the full implication of exchange rate depreciation, even for the United States, in an integrated and interdependent world economic system.

We looked at works written in the last three years on theoretical and applied international economics and found that much had happened that had not yet been examined. After all, ours was one of the most rapidly developing disciplines in economics. We decided to put together a book emphasizing these issues, a book that represented several different schools of thought in both theoretical and empirical work. We invited several scholars of what we believed to be different persuasions to participate in the volume. The response far exceeded our expectations.

As manuscript drafts arrived, it was clear that the book would have a fairly specific structure. The final product keeps the organization we first believed suitable. First Jacob Frenkel presents a broad-based overview of the functioning of flexible exchange rates in the 1970s. Part I consists of papers of general appeal related to exchange rate determination; they are by Dornbusch, Kouri, Frenkel, and Canto and Miles. Part II deals exclusively with a subject that has become a household term— imported oil. Papers by Sachs, Krugman, and Buiter and Purvis comprise this section. Part III includes papers by Branson and Buiter, Turnovsky, Levin, Henderson and Waldo, Witte, Bilson, and Hool and Richardson. A common theme of these papers is the policy implications of economic interdependence under flexible exchange rates. The final section contains empirically relevant pieces by Darby, Knight and Mathieson, and Deardorff and Stern. These papers have implications for the debate on the international transmission of economic disturbances.

It is difficult to undertake a project of this kind without incurring intellectual debt. We would like to thank Jay Levin, whose contribution and support as consulting editor was far beyond the call of duty. Rudiger Dornbusch generously agreed to write the foreword, and others, especially Jacob Frenkel, were supportive throughout the duration of this undertaking. We are also grateful to all our contributors for their patience and understanding in coping with our many requests.

Jagdeep S. Bhandari
Bluford H. Putnam

Economic Interdependence and Flexible Exchange Rates

1

Flexible Exchange Rates, Prices, and the Role of "News": Lessons from the 1970s

Jacob A. Frenkel

Recent experience with flexible exchange rate systems has led to renewed interest in the operation of foreign exchange markets as reflected in many recent studies of the principal determinants of exchange rates. The 1970s witnessed dramatic alteration of the international monetary system from a regime of pegged exchange rates, which had prevailed for about a quarter of a century (since the Bretton Woods conference), into a regime of flexible (though managed) rates. As a consequence of the emergence of the new legal and economic system traders, national governments and international organizations were confronted with new economic problems, choices, and instruments. During the 1970s exchange rates fluctuated widely and inflation rates accelerated. The international monetary system had to accommodate extraordinarily large oil-related shocks that affected trade flows in goods and assets. Huge oil payments had to be recycled. Uncertainties concerning future developments in international politics

An earlier version of this chapter was prepared for a Conference on Stabilization Policy: Lessons from the 1970s and Implications for the 1980s, sponsored by the Federal Reserve Bank of St. Louis and the Center for the Study of American Business at Washington University held at the Federal Reserve Bank of St. Louis on 19–20 October 1979. The present chapter is a somewhat abridged version of Frenkel (1981b). I am indebted to Lauren J. Feinstone for helpful suggestions and efficient research assistance and to the National Science Foundation grant SOC 78-14480 for financial support. I have benefited from useful comments by Andrew Abel, William Branson, Sebastian Edwards, Stanley Fischer, Craig S. Hakkio, Edi Karni, Paul Krugman, Leonardo Leiderman, Robert E. Lucas, Jr., Allan Meltzer, Michael L. Mussa, Sam Peltzman, Nasser Saidi, and Roland Vaubel as well as of participants in seminars held at the NBER, Columbia University, New York University, Harvard University, the University of Virginia, the University of Rochester, Oxford University, Tel Aviv University, and the International Monetary Fund. This research is part of the NBER's Program in International Studies. The views expressed are those of the author and not necessarily those of the NBER, Inc.

reached new heights and the prospects for the world economy got gloomier. These developments placed unprecedented pressures on the markets for foreign exchange as well as on other asset markets. They were associated with a large slide in the value of the US dollar and resulted in speeding up the creation of new institutions like the European Monetary System, which provided the formal framework for the management of exchange rates among members. The increased interdependence among countries and the realization that exchange rate policies by one national government exert influence on other economies have also induced legal responses from international organizations. For example, in late April 1977 the Executive Board of the International Monetary Fund approved the details of the second amendment to article IV of the amended Articles of Agreement dealing with the principles and procedures for surveillance of exchange rate policies of member countries.

These developments provide the background for this chapter, which is intended to sum up the relevant evidence bearing on a set of related questions and to present a brief survey of key issues and lessons from the experience with floating rates during the 1970s. The main orientation of the paper is empirical and the analysis is based on the experience of three exchange rates involving the dollar/pound, the dollar/french franc, and the dollar/DM. Section 1.1 provides an analysis of the efficiency of foreign exchange markets by examining the relation between spot and forward exchange rates. The extent of exchange rate volatility is also examined. This analysis of the foreign exchange markets sheds light on several questions, including (i) whether exchange rates fluctuate "excessively," (ii) whether speculation in the foreign exchange markets is destabilizing, (iii) whether there is "insufficient" speculation in the foreign exchange markets, (iv) whether there is evidence for market failure in the sense that there are unexploited profit opportunities. These issues are significant in assessing the performance of floating rates as well as in evaluating the need for government intervention in the foreign exchange markets. The analytical framework that is used for interpreting the volatility of exchange rates and the association between spot and forward rates is the modern theory of exchange rate determination. Within this framework exchange rates are viewed as the prices of assets that are traded in organized markets and, like the prices of other assets, are strongly influenced by expectations about future events.

The relation between exchange rates and interest rates is analyzed in Section 1.2. One of the key issues that is raised in this section is the distinction between anticipated and unanticipated changes in rates of interest. As an analytical matter this distinction is important because the modern approach to exchange rate determination implies that exchange rates are strongly influenced by "news," which by definition is unpredictable. Therefore, it is unanticipated rather than anticipated changes in interest rates that should be closely associated with changes in exchange rates. This prediction is tested empirically.

Section 1.3 analyzes the relation between exchange rates and prices by examining the patterns of deviations from purchasing power parities. The main point that is being emphasized is that there is an important intrinsic difference between exchange rates and national price levels. Exchange rates are more sensitive to expectations concerning future events than national price levels. As a result, in periods which are dominated by "news" that alters expectations, exchange rates are likely to be more volatile and departures from purchasing power parities are likely to be the rule rather than the exception. The analysis of the relation between exchange rates and prices is relevant for assessing whether the flexible exchange rate system was successful in providing national economies with an added degree of insulation from foreign shocks, and whether it provided policymakers with an added instrument for the conduct of macroeconomic policy. The evidence regarding deviations from purchasing power parities is also relevant for determining whether there is a case for managed float. Section 1.4 contains concluding remarks.

1.1 The Efficiency of the Foreign Exchange Market and the Movement of Exchange Rates

1.1.1 The Efficiency of the Foreign Exchange Market
One of the central insights of the monetary (or the asset market) approach to the exchange rate is the notion that the exchange rate, being a relative price of two assets, is determined in a manner similar to the determination of other asset prices and that expectations concerning the future course of events play a central role in affecting current exchange rates.[1]

If the foregin exchange market is efficient and if the exchange rate is determined in a fashion similar to the determination of other asset prices, we should expect current prices to reflect all currently available information. Expectations concerning future exchange rates should be incorporated and reflected in forward exchange rates. To examine the efficiency of the market, I first regress the logarithm of the current spot exchange rate, $\ln S_t$, on the logarithm of the one-month forward exchange rate prevailing at the previous month, $\ln F_{t-1}$, as in equation (1):[2]

$$\ln S_t = a + b \ln F_{t-1} + u_t. \tag{1}$$

If the market for foreign exchange is efficient, so that prices reflect all relevant available information, then the residuals in equation (1), u_t, should contain no information and therefore should be serially uncorrelated. Further, if the forward exchange rate is an unbiased forecast of the future spot exchange rate (as should be the case under an assumption of risk neutrality), then the constant term in equation (1) should not differ significantly from zero[3] and the slope coefficient should not differ significantly from unity. I examine three exchange rates: the dollar/pound, the dollar/franc, and the dollar/DM. Equation (1) was estimated using monthly data for the period June 1973–July 1979. (Data sources are listed in the appendix.) The beginning of the period was set so as to concentrate on the experience of the current exchange rate regime (following the initial post-Bretton Woods transition period). The resulting ordinary least squares estimates are reported in table 1.1. Also reported in table 1.1 are additional regressions, which will be analyzed shortly. As may be seen for the dollar/DM exchange rate, the hypotheses that (at the 95 percent confidence level) the constant term does not differ significantly from zero and that the slope coefficient does not differ significantly from unity cannot be rejected. These hypotheses are rejected for the dollar/franc exchange rate and are rejected (marginally) for the dollar/pound exchange rate. The joint hypotheses, however, that the constant is zero *and* that the slope coefficient is unity, cannot be rejected at the 95 percent level for the dollar/pound and the dollar/DM exchange rates and at the 99 percent level for the dollar/franc exchange rate. The test statistics for testing the joint hypotheses are reported in the column headed by F in table 1.1. These results are relevant for assessing whether the forward rate is an unbiased forecast of the future spot rate. We turn next to the question of efficiency.

It was argued above that in an efficient market, expectations concerning future exchange rates are reflected in forward rates and that spot exchange rates reflect all currently available information. If forward exchange rates prevailing at period $t - 1$ summarize all relevant information available at that period, they should also contain the information that is summarized in data corresponding to period $t - 2$. It thus follows that including additional lagged values of the forward rates in equation (1) should not greatly affect the coefficients of determination and should not yield coefficients that differ significantly from zero. The results reported in table 1.1 are consistent with this hypothesis; in all cases the coefficients of $\ln F_{t-2}$ do not differ significantly from zero and the inclusion of the additional lagged variables does not improve the fit. Most important, in all cases

Table 1.1
Efficiency of foreign exchange markets—monthly data: June 1973–July 1979 (standard errors in parentheses)[a]

Dependent variable ln S_t	Estimation method	Constant	ln F_{t-1}	ln F_{t-2}	R^2	s.e.	D.W.	F	m
Dollar/pound									
	OLS	0.033 (0.017)	0.956 (0.024)		0.96	0.027	1.72	1.86	
	OLS	0.031 (0.018)	1.047 (0.116)	−0.088 (0.113)	0.96	0.027	1.94		
	IV	0.030 (0.018)	0.961 (0.025)		0.95	0.027	1.74		2.01
Dollar/franc									
	OLS	−0.237 (0.078)	0.843 (0.051)		0.79	0.029	2.23	4.83	
	OLS	−0.225 (0.082)	0.706 (0.117)	0.146 (0.117)	0.79	0.029	1.90		
	IV	−0.236 (0.080)	0.844 (0.053)		0.78	0.030	2.24		2.26
Dollar/DM									
	OLS	−0.023 (0.027)	0.971 (0.032)		0.93	0.032	2.12	0.51	
	OLS	−0.019 (0.028)	0.913 (0.119)	0.063 (0.122)	0.93	0.032	1.96		
	IV	−0.021 (0.027)	0.973 (0.032)		0.93	0.032	2.10		0.91

a. s.e. is the standard error of the equation and R^2 is the coefficient of determination; in the case of instrumental variables estimation the R^2 was computed as $1 - \text{var}(\hat{u}_t)/\text{var}(\ln S_t)$. The F-statistic tests the joint restriction that the constant equals zero and the slope equals unity. The test statistic is distributed as $F(2, 71)$. Critical values for $F(2, 71)$ are 3.13 (95 percent) and 4.92 (99 percent). The instrumental variable (IV) estimation method is used in order to allow for the possibility of errors in variables arising from using ln F_{t-1} as a proxy for the expected future spot rate; the instruments are a constant, time, time squared, and lagged values of the dependent and the independent variables. The m-statistic which tests for the absence of errors in variables is distributed χ^2 with 2 degrees of freedom. The critical value for $\chi^2(2)$ is 5.99 (95 percent).

the Durbin-Watson statistics are consistent with the hypothesis of the absence of first-order autocorrelated residuals, and an examination of higher order correlations (up to 12 lags) shows that no correlation of any order is significant.[4]

To examine further the relation between the various exchange rates we note that one of the assumptions underlying equation (1) was that the forward exchange rate measures the unobservable value of the *expected* future spot exchange rate. This assumption provided the justification for using equation (1) instead of the explicit specification of the rational expectations hypothesis that is embodied in equation (2):

$$\ln S_t = E_{t-1} \ln S_t + \varepsilon_t, \tag{2}$$

where $E_{t-1} \ln S_t$ denotes the expected (logarithm of the) spot exchange rate for period t based on the information available at period $t-1$. If, however, the forward exchange rate at $t-1$ is a "noisy" proxy for the expected future value of the spot rate (i.e., it measures it with a random error), then we obtain

$$a + b \ln F_{t-1} = E_{t-1} \ln S_t + v_{t-1}, \qquad E(v_t) = 0, \tag{3}$$

and substituting equation (3) into equation (2) yields

$$\ln S_t = a + b \ln F_{t-1} + (\varepsilon_t - v_{t-1}). \tag{4}$$

In this case the error term in equation (1) would be $u_t = \varepsilon_t - v_{t-1}$, the assumption that the covariance between $\ln F_{t-1}$ and u_t is zero would entail a specification error, and the application of the ordinary least squares (OLS) procedure would yield biased estimates due to the classical errors in variables bias.

In order to examine the possibility that the OLS estimates may be subject to the errors in variables bias, one needs to test the hypothesis that $\text{cov}(u_t, \ln F_{t-1}) = 0$. This test follows the specification test outlined by Hausman (1978).[5] To perform the test, equation (1) was estimated by applying the OLS procedure as well as by using an instrumental variables (IV) estimation method. Under the null hypothesis of no misspecification, the OLS coefficients vector $\hat{b}_0$ is an efficient and an unbiased estimate of the true coefficient vector. Under the alternative hypothesis of misspecification, the vector $\hat{b}_0$ is biased and an unbiased coefficient vector $\hat{b}_1$ can be obtained by applying an instrumental variables estimation procedure. The test statistic relevant for testing the null hypothesis can be written as

$$m = (\hat{b}_1 - \hat{b}_0)'(\text{var}\,\hat{b}_1 - \text{var}\,\hat{b}_0)^{-1}(\hat{b}_1 - \hat{b}_0), \tag{5}$$

where $\text{var}(\hat{b}_1)$ and $\text{var}(\hat{b}_0)$ denote the variance-covariance matrices of $\hat{b}_1$ and $\hat{b}_0$, respectively. Under the null hypothesis m is distributed (in large samples) as χ^2 with two degrees of freedom. Table 1.1 reports the results of estimating equation (1) by applying the instrumental variables estimation method. As may be seen, for all exchange rates the two vectors of coefficients $\hat{b}_1$ and $\hat{b}_0$ are very close. For example, for the dollar/pound exchange rate the constants are 0.033 and 0.030 and the slopes are 0.956 and 0.961; consequently, the resulting m statistic is 2.01, which is well below 5.99—the critical value of $\chi^2(2)$ at the 95 percent confidence level. The m statistics corresponding to the other exchange rates are also below this critical value. It is concluded, therefore, that the use of the forward exchange rate as a proxy for expectations does not introduce a significant errors in variables bias, and thus the use of the OLS estimation procedure seems appropriate.[6]

The principal conclusions that may be drawn from the previous discussion are that the behavior of the foreign exchange market during the 1970s has been broadly consistent with the general implications of the efficient market hypothesis.

1.1.2 Exchange Rate Movement: Volatility and Predictability

As is well known, during the same period exchange rates have been very volatile. The standard errors of the monthly percentage changes of the three exchange rates have been about 3 percent per month. Further, the standard errors of the regressions in table 1.1 indicate that the forecasts of future spot exchange rates based on the forward rates are very imprecise; the standard errors of the equations are about 3 percent per month.

These characteristics of price changes (volatility and unpredictability) are typical of auction and organized asset markets. In such markets current prices reflect expectations concerning the future course of events, and new information which induces changes in expectations is immediately reflected in corresponding changes in prices, thus precluding unexploited profit opportunities from arbitrage. The strong dependence of current prices on expectations about the future is unique to the determination of durable asset prices; it is not a characteristic of price determination of nondurable commodities. The strong dependence of asset prices on expectations also implies that periods which are dominated by uncertainties, new information, rumors, announcements and "news," which induce frequent changes in expectations, are likely to be periods in which changes in expectations are the prime cause of fluctuations in asset prices. Further, since the information which alters expectations must be *new*, the resulting fluctuations in price cannot be predicted by lagged forward exchange rates which are based on past information.[7] Therefore, during such periods, one should expect exchange rates (and other asset prices) to exhibit large fluctuations. When the prime cause of fluctuations is new information, one may expect that lagged forward exchange rates (which are based on past information) are imprecise (even though possibly the best unbiased) forecasts of future spot rates.

To gain further insights into the implications of this perspective on

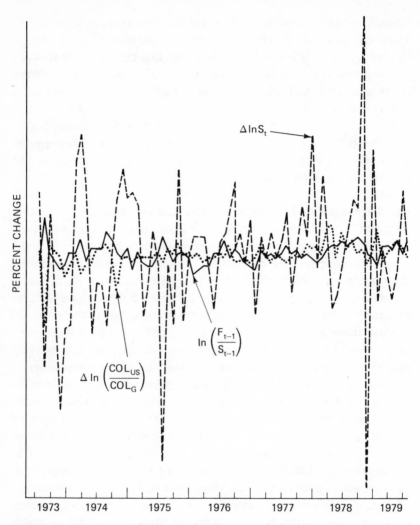

Figure 1.1
Monthly percentage changes of the US/German consumer price indices
$[\Delta \ln(COL_{US}/COL_G)]$ of the dollar/DM exchange rate ($\Delta \ln S_t$), and the monthly
forward premium $[\ln(F_{t-1}/S_{t-1})]$: July 1973–July 1979.

the relation between predicted and realized changes in exchange rates, figure 1.1 presents plots of predicted and realized percentage changes in the dollar/DM exchange rate where the predicted change is measured by the lagged forward premium. Also presented in this figure are the differentials in national inflation rates, which are discussed in section III. The key fact which emerges from this figure is that predicted changes in exchange rates account for a very small fraction of actual changes.[8] This phenomenon is also reflected in the comparison between the variance of actual and predicted changes in exchange rates; the variance of monthly percentage changes in exchange rates exceeds the variance of monthly forward premia by a factor that is larger than twenty.[9] This fact suggests that the bulk of exchange rate changes seem to be due to "new information" which, by definition, could not have been anticipated and reflected in the forward premium or discount which prevailed in the previous period. A similar pattern also characterizes the dollar/french franc and the dollar/pound exchange rates.

This view of the foreign exchange market can be exposited in the following simple model.[10] Let the logarithm of the spot exchange rate on day t be determined by

$$\ln S_t = z_t + bE_t(\ln S_{t+1} - \ln S_t),\tag{6}$$

where $E_t(\ln S_{t+1} - \ln S_t)$ denotes the expected percentage change in the exchange rate between t and $t + 1$, based on the information available at t, and where z_t represents the ordinary factors of supply and demand that affect the exchange rate on day t. These factors may include domestic and foreign money supplies, incomes, levels of output, and so forth. Equation (6) represents a sufficiently general relation which may be viewed as a "reduced form" that can be derived from a variety of models of exchange rate determination. These models may differ in their emphasis of the determinants of $z(t)$, but they all are likely to share a similar reduced form.[11] Assuming that expectations are rational in that equation (6) applies to expectations of future exchange rates, it follows, by forward iteration, that

$$E_t \ln S_{t+j} = \frac{1}{1 + b} \sum_{k=0}^{\infty} \left(\frac{b}{1 + b}\right)^k E_t z_{t+j+k}.\tag{7}$$

Thus, the current exchange rate ($j = 0$) and current expectations of future exchange rates ($j > 0$) are linked because both depend on expectations concerning the future z. The strength of the link depends on the magnitude of b which characterizes the dependence of the current ex-

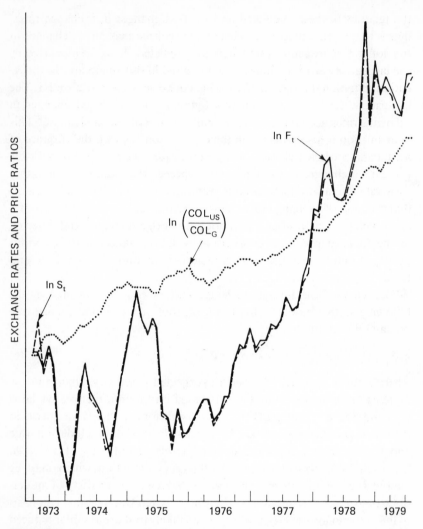

Figure 1.2
Monthly observations of the dollar/DM spot ($\ln S_t$) and forward ($\ln F_t$) exchange rates and the ratio of the US/German cost of living indices [$\ln(COL_{US}/COL_G)$ (scaled to equal the spot exchange rate at the initial month)]: June 1973–July 1979.

change rate on the expected percentage change thereof.[12] The presumption is that due to profit opportunities from arbitrage this link is strong at least for the exchange rates expected in the near future. Hence, the current exchange rate, $\ln S_t = E_t \ln S_t$, should be closely linked to the current expectation of the next period's exchange rate, $E_t \ln S_{t+1}$, which in turn should be closely linked to the exchange rate expected for the following period, $E_t \ln S_{t+2}$, and so on.

In order to examine this hypothesis, I present in figure 1.2 plots of spot and contemporaneous forward exchange rates for the dollar/DM, and a similar pattern characterizes the other two rates. Also presented is the ratio of national price levels discussed in section III. If the dominant factor underlying changes in rates is new information which alters views about current and expected future exchange rates by approximately the same amount, then one should expect a high correlation between movements of spot and forward rates. This fact is clearly demonstrated by figure 1.2, where it is seen that spot and forward exchange rates tend to move together and by approximately the same amount (the vertical difference between the two rates corresponds to the percentage forward premium or discount on foreign exchange). The correlations between the spot and the forward exchange rates for the three pairs of currencies exceed 0.99 and the correlations between the corresponding percentage changes of the spot and forward rates exceed 0.96. The high correlation between movements in spot and forward rates is expected since the two rates respond at the same time to the same flow of new information (which is presumed to affect the rate for more than one period). In general, the details of the relation between spot and forward exchange rates depend on the time series properties of the z in equation (7) and in particular on whether the new information is viewed as permanent or transitory.[13]

The comovement of spot and forward rates is evidence of the close link between current and expected future exchange rates which is illustrated by equation (7). This characteristic is typical of the foreign exchange market and is also shared by prices of many assets and commodities traded in organized markets. The recent pattern of gold prices provides a useful example of this general principle. Table 1.2 reports the spot and the futures prices of gold as recorded recently in the International Money Market (IMM) at the Chicago Mercantile Exchange on five consecutive days. The two key facts which are illustrated by this table are (i) the extent of day-to-day volatility in gold prices and (ii) the general uniformity

Table 1.2
Futures price of gold on consecutive days—daily data: 1 May 1980 – 7 May 1980[a]

Delivery date	Price (per ounce) and change from previous day									
	1 May	Change	2 May	Change	5 May	Change	6 May	Change	7 May	Change
1980 May	516.0	14.4	511.0	−5.0	519.0	8.0	506.5	−12.5	512.0	5.5
June	517.0	10.5	575.5	−1.5	523.7	8.2	510.3	−13.4	516.0	5.7
September	536.0	10.5	533.5	−2.5	540.7	7.2	527.0	−13.7	531.5	4.5
December	554.0	9.5	551.0	−3.0	558.0	7.0	541.5	−16.5	547.0	5.5
1981 March	571.5	9.5	568.0	−3.5	574.7	6.7	557.0	−17.7	561.5	4.5
June	588.5	10.5	585.0	−3.5	591.0	6.0	571.5	−19.5	576.0	4.5
September	605.3	10.3	602.0	−3.3	607.0	5.0	585.5	−21.5	590.0	4.5
December	622.0	11.0	619.0	−3.0	623.0	4.0	599.5	−23.5	604.0	4.5
1982 March	638.5	11.5	636.0	−2.5	693.0	3.0	613.5	−25.5	618.0	4.5

a. These prices are settlement prices at the International Money Market (IMM) at Chicago Mercantile Exchange as reported in the *Wall Street Journal* 2 May – 8 May 1980.

by which these changes are reflected in the price of gold for immediate delivery as well as in the prices for the eight future delivery dates.

Another feature which is revealed by figure 1.2 is that the contemporaneous spot and forward exchange rates are approximately equal, thus indicating that the market's best forecast of the future spot rate is (approximately) the current spot rate. This phenomenon reflects the fact that, as an empirical matter, exchange rates have followed (approximately) a random walk process. For such a process current prices are indeed the best forecasts of future prices. (And to the extent that the exchange rate had some drift, the above statement should be interpreted in reference to that drift.) It is relevant to note, however, that while the random walk phenomenon seems to correspond to the actual paths of exchange rates, it does not reflect a theoretical necessity.

The final characteristic of the foreign exchange market is that generally (though not always) there is a positive correlation between the expected depreciation of the currency (as measured by the forward premium on foreign exchange) and the spot exchange rate.[14] This positive correlation may be rationalized by noting that currencies which are expected to depreciate are traded at a discount in the forward market and, on average, these currencies also command a lower foreign exchange value in the spot market.[15] This relation is embodied in the specification of equation (6) and is interpreted further in the next section.

1.2 Exchange Rates, Interest Rates, and Innovations

1.2.1 Exchange Rates and Interest Rates: The Broad Facts

It is useful to recall the analysis which predicts a negative association between the rate of interest and the exchange rate. According to that analysis a higher rate of interest attracts foreign capital, which induces a surplus in the capital account of the balance of payments and thereby induces an appreciation of the domestic currency (i.e., a *lower* spot exchange rate). Another variant of this approach states that the higher rate of interest lowers spending and thus induces a surplus in the current account of the balance of payments, which results in a *lower* spot exchange rate. A third variant claims that the higher rate of interest implies (via the interest parity theory) a higher forward premium on foreign exchange; and to the extent that at a given point in time the forward exchange rate, which represents the expected future spot rate is predetermined by past history, as would be the case under the adaptive expectations hypothesis (which is clearly rejected by the evidence on the comovements of spot and forward rates), the required rise in the forward premium will be brought

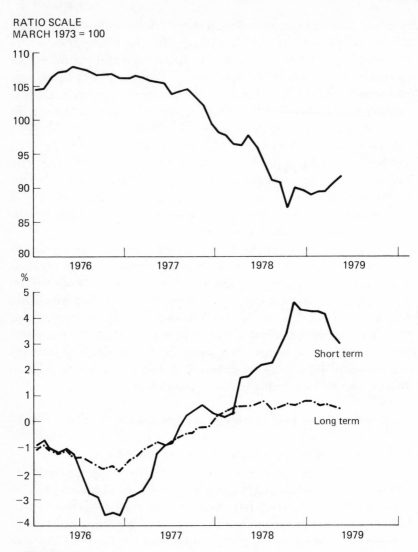

Figure 1.3
Weighted average foreign currency value of the US dollar (top) and US-foreign interest rate differentials (bottom). Source: Mudd (1979).

about by a *lower* spot rate (i.e., by an appreciation of the domestic currency). Whatever the route, by ignoring the distinction between nominal and real rates of interest, this approach predicts a *negative* relation between the rate of interest and the spot exchange rate (or, alternatively, a positive relation between the rate of interest and the foreign exchange value of the domestic currency).

While such a prediction might be appropriate for noninflationary environments, it might be entirely inappropriate for inflationary environments (like the one prevailing in the United States during the 1970s). In such periods variations in rates of interest are most likely to be dominated by variations in inflationary expectations rather than by liquidity effects associated with changes in the ratio of money to bonds. In such an environment the rate of interest is expected to be *positively* correlated with the exchange rate. The broad facts are consistent with this hypothesis. For most of the 1970s the rise in the rate of interest in the United States (relative to the foreign rate of interest) has been associated with a rise in the spot exchange rate (i.e., with a depreciation of the dollar) rather than with a fall in the spot rate. Figure 1.3 illustrates the point by plotting the foreign exchange value of the US dollar against the interest rate differential. As is evident, the higher (relative) rate of interest in the United States has been associated with a higher exchange rate (i.e., with a lower foreign exchange value of the dollar). It is relevant to note, however, that since mid-1979 this relation reversed itself.

The positive association between the rate of interest and the exchange rate in the context of the US dollar and the inflationary environment can be accounted for by the monetary (or the asset market) approach to the exchange rate, which puts a special emphasis on the influence of the expectations on current exchange rates.[16] For example, according to the monetary approach, a rise in the domestic (relative) rate of interest, which is dominated by a rise in the expected (relative) rate of inflation, induces a decline in the demand for real cash balances; for a given path of the nominal money supply asset market equilibrium requires a price level which is higher than the price which would have prevailed otherwise. When the domestic price level is linked to the foreign price through some form of purchasing power parity, and when the path of the foreign price is assumed to be given, the higher domestic price can only be achieved through a *rise* in the spot exchange rate (i.e., through a depreciation of the currency).[17]

This explanation of the positive association between interest rates and exchange rates has an intuitive appeal in that it implies that in an inflationary environment a relatively rapid rise in prices is associated with high *nominal* rates of interest as well as with a depreciation of the currency in terms of foreign exchange. This relation is embodied in equation (6), which states that an expected depreciation of the currency (which in our case is associated with inflationary expectations and high nominal rates of interest) results in an immediate depreciation.[18] The reversal of the relation between the U.S. interest and the external value of the dollar which has taken place since mid 1979, indicates that currently the prime cause for the fluctuations in U.S. interest rates is not variations in inflationary expectations but rather variations in the *real* rate of interest which are occasioned by the large U.S. budget deficit.

The foregoing analysis also provides the explanation for the observation (which was noted in section 1.1.2) that generally there is a positive correlation between the forward premium on foreign exchange and the level of the spot rate. Since during inflationary periods the spot rate is expected to be positively correlated with the interest rate differential and since, according to the interest parity theory, that differential must equal the forward premium on foreign exchange, it follows that during inflationary periods the forward premium is also expected to be positively correlated with the level of the spot rate.[19]

1.2.2 Exchange Rates and News
One of the central implications of the rational expectations hypothesis is that unanticipated events "news" play a predominant role in affecting real variables and asset yields. This implication is embodied in many expositions of modern macroeconomics and its empirical content has been the subject of numerous recent studies.[20] In the context of exchange rate determination the discussion in section 1 and in particular the contributions by Mussa (1977, 1979a) and Dornbusch (1978) emphasized that the predominant cause of exchange rate movements are "news" which could not have been anticipated.[21] Expressing the spot exchange rate at period *t* as the sum of factors which were anticipated from the past as well as factors which represent "news," Dornbusch (1978) decomposes the effects of "news" into those which alter the expected future spot rate between the last period and the present and those which lead to a reassessment of the one-period interest rate differential starting at the present, that is, "news" about the term structure. Both of these white noise serially uncorrelated components play a role in determining the spot exchange rate in Dornbusch's analysis.

The evidence presented in section 1 suggests that the forward rate summarizes the information that is available to the market when the forward rate is being set, and in equation (3) it was assumed that the expected exchange rate can be written as $a + b \ln F_{t-1}$ plus a serially uncorrelated error. We may therefore express the spot rate at period t as a function of factors which have been known in advance and are summarized by the lagged forward rate, as well as a function of the "news":

$$\ln S_t = a + b \ln F_{t-1} + \text{"news"} + w_t. \tag{8}$$

In what follows, this notion is applied to an empirical analysis of the role of "news" as a determinant of the exchange rate. The key difficulty lies in identifying the variable which measures the "news." Since quite frequently it is difficult to observe and quantify the "news," it is convenient to examine the relation between the exchange rate and a variable whose time series is likely to *manifest* the "news" promptly. Assuming that asset markets clear fast and that the "news" is immediately reflected in (unexpected) changes in the rates of interest, equation (8) may be written as

$$\ln S_t = \underbrace{a + b \ln F_{t-1}}_{\substack{\text{"expected} \\ \text{exchange rate"}}} + \underbrace{\alpha \big[(i - i^*)_t - E_{t-1}(i - i^*)_t \big]}_{\text{"news"}} + w_t, \tag{9}$$

where the bracketed term denotes the innovation in the (one-month) interest differential and $E_{t-1}(i - i^*)_t$ denotes the interest differential which was expected to prevail in period t based on the information available at $t - 1$. The expected interest rate differential was computed from a regression of the interest differential on a constant, on two lagged values of the differential and on the lagged forward exchange rate $\ln F_{t-1}$.

As was argued, the association between exchange rates and interest rates is likely to be positive during periods in which most of the variations in nominal rates of interst are dominated by variations in inflationary expectations—a characteristic which seems to fit the inflationary environment of the 1970s. Under such circumstances, when the unexpected interest differential reflects "news" concerning inflationary expectations, the coefficient α in equation (9) is likely to be positive.[22] Table 1.3 reports the two-stage least squares estimates of equation (9) for the three exchange rates over the period June 1973–July 1979.[23] As may be seen, in all cases the coefficients of the expected interest differential are positive and in the case of the dollar/pound exchange rate the coefficient is statistically significant. In order to varify the importance of using the series of innova-

Table 1.3
One-month interest rate differentials and exchange rates; instrumental variables—monthly data: June 1973–July 1979 (standard errors in parentheses)[a]

Dependent variable ln S_t	Constant	ln F_{t-1}	$(i - i^*)_t$	$[(i - i^*)_t - E_{t-1}(i - i^*)_t]$	s.e.	R^2	D.W.
Dollar/pound	0.021 (0.020)	0.965 (0.026)	−0.152 (0.118)		0.028	0.95	1.69
	0.031 (0.017)	0.959 (0.024)		0.432 (0.181)	0.026	0.96·	1.78
Dollar/franc	−0.024 (0.181)	0.992 (0.124)	−0.462 (0.324)		0.034	0.71	2.21
	−0.246 (0.077)	0.837 (0.051)		0.245 (0.167)	0.029	0.80	2.17
Dollar/DM	0.004 (0.064)	0.997 (0.064)	−0.180 (0.394)		0.033	0.93	2.12
	−0.022 (0.026)	0.972 (0.031)		0.413 (0.347)	0.031	0.93	2.05

a. Interest rates are the one-month (annualized) Euromarket rates. The expected interest rate differential $E_{t-1}(i - i^*)$, was computed from a regression of the interest rate differential on a constant, two lagged values of the differential, and the logarithm of the lagged forward exchange rate. The two-stage least squares estimation method was used. The instruments for the interest rate differential were a constant, two lagged values of the differential, and the logarithm of the lagged forward exchange rate; the instruments for the unexpected differential were a constant, Durbin's rank variable, and the logarithm of the lagged forward exchange rate. $(i - i^*)_t$ denotes the actual interest rate differential, where i is the rate of interest on securities denominated in US dollars and i^* the rate of interest on securities denominated in foreign currency. $[(i - i^*)_t - E_{t-1}(i - i^*)_t]$ denotes the *unexpected* interest rate differential. s.e. is the standard error of the equation. A quasi-R^2 was computed as $1 - \text{var}(\hat{u}_t)/\text{var}(\ln S_t)$.

Table 1.4
One-month interest rate differentials and exchange rates; instrumental variables—monthly data: June 1973–July 1979 (standard errors in parentheses)[a]

Dependent variable $\ln S_t$	Constant	$\ln F_{t-1}$	$(i - i^*)_t$	$[(i - i^*)_t - E_{t-1}(i - i^*)_t]$	s.e.	R^2	D.W.
Dollar/pound	0.018 (0.017)	0.969 (0.022)	-0.156 (0.100)	0.562 (0.191)	0.023	0.97	1.81
Dollar/franc	-0.136 (0.112)	0.915 (0.076)	-0.312 (0.209)	0.547 (0.282)	0.031	0.75	2.19
Dollar/DM	0.002 (0.044)	0.996 (0.045)	-0.173 (0.286)	0.599 (0.457)	0.032	0.93	2.07

a. Interest rates are the one-month (annualized) Euromarket rates. The expected interest rate differential $E_{t-1}(i - i^*)_t$ was computed from a regression of the interest differential on a constant, two lagged values of the differential, and the logarithm of the lagged forward exchange rate. The two-stage least squares estimation method was used. The instruments were a constant, two lagged values of the interest differential, Durbin's rank variable of the unexpected differential, and the logarithm of the lagged forward exchange rate. $(i - i^*)_t$ denotes the actual interest rate differential, where i is the rate of interest on securities denominated in US dollars and i^* the rate of interest on securities denominated in foreign currency. $[(i - i^*)_t - E_{t-1}(i - i^*)_t]$ denotes the *unexpected* interest rate differential. s.e. is the standard error of the equation. A quasi-R^2 was computed as $1 - \mathrm{var}(\hat{u}_t)/\mathrm{var}(\ln S_t)$.

Table 1.5
Twelve-month interest rate differentials and exchange rates; instrumental variables—monthly data: June 1973–July 1979 (standard errors in parentheses)[a]

Dependent variable ln S_t	Constant	ln F_{t-1}	$(i - i^*)_t$	$[(i - i^*)_t - E_{t-1}(i - i^*)_t]$	s.e.	R^2	D.W.
Dollar/pound	0.027 (0.019)	0.960 (0.025)	−0.083 (0.147)		0.027	0.95	1.71
	0.031 (0.017)	0.959 (0.024)		0.887 (0.291)	0.025	0.96	1.81
Dollar/franc	−0.152 (0.155)	0.904 (0.107)	−0.230 (0.320)		0.030	0.77	2.32
	−0.246 (0.077)	0.837 (0.051)		0.729 (0.342)	0.029	0.80	2.10
Dollar/DM	−0.012 (0.063)	0.982 (0.063)	−0.074 (0.395)		0.032	0.93	2.11
	−0.022 (0.026)	0.972 (0.031)		0.979 (0.663)	0.031	0.94	2.07

a. Interest rates are the twelve-month Euromarket rates. The expected interest rate differential $E_{t-1}(i - i^*)$, was computed from a regression of the interest differential on a constant, two lagged values of the differential, and the logarithm of the lagged forward exchange rate. The two-stage least squares estimation method was used. The instruments for the interest differential were a constant, two lagged values of the differential, and the logarithm of the lagged forward exchange rate; the instruments for the unexpected differential were a constant, Durbin's rank variable, and the logarithm of the lagged forward exchange rate. $(i - i^*)$, denotes the actual interest rate differential, where i is the rate of interest on securities denominated in US dollars and i^* the rate of interest on securities denominated in foreign currency. $[(i - i^*)_t - E_{t-1}(i - i^*)_t]$ denotes the *unexpected* interest rate differential. s.e. is the standard error of the equation. A quasi-R^2 was computed as $1 - \text{var}(\hat{u}_t)/\text{var}(\ln S_t)$.

Table 1.6
Twelve-month interest rate differentials and exchange rates: instrumental variables—monthly data: June 1973–July 1979 (standard errors in parentheses)[a]

Dependent variable $\ln S_t$	Constant	$\ln F_{t-1}$	$(i - i^*)_t$	$[(i - i^*)_t - E_{t-1}(i - i^*)_t]$	s.e.	R^2	D.W.
Dollar/pound	0.024	0.965	−0.087	0.978	0.022	0.97	1.82
	(0.016)	(0.021)	(0.121)	(0.286)			
Dollar/franc	−0.180	0.884	−0.184	0.915	0.029	0.79	2.16
	(0.118)	(0.181)	(0.245)	(0.432)			
Dollar/DM	−0.013	0.981	−0.063	1.031	0.031	0.93	2.08
	(0.053)	(0.054)	(0.338)	(0.752)			

a. Interest rates are the twelve-month Euromarket rates. The expected interest rate differential $E_{t-1}(i - i^*)_t$ was computed from a regression of the interest differential on a constant, two lagged values of the differential, and the logarithm of the lagged forward exchange rate. The two-stage least squares estimation method was used. The instruments were a constant, two lagged values of the interest differential, Durbin's rank variable of the unexpected differential, and the logarithm of the lagged forward exchange rate. $(i - i^*)_t$ denotes the actual interest rate differential, where i is the rate of interest on securities denominated in US dollars and i^* the rate of interest on securities denominated in foreign currency. $[(i - i^*)_t - E_{t-1}(i - i^*)_t]$ denotes the *unexpected* interest rate differential. s.e. is the standard error of the equation. A quasi-R^2 was computed as $1 - \text{var}(\hat{u}_t)/\text{var}(\ln S_t)$.

tions in the interest differential, table 1.3 also reports estimates of regressions which replace the innovations by the actual series of the interest differential. In all cases the coefficients of the actual interest differential do not differ significantly from zero. Table 1.4 describes analogous two-stage least squares estimates of regressions which include both the actual interest rate differential and the innovation in the differential.[24] Again, in all cases the coefficients on the actual differential do not differ significantly from zero, while the coefficients on the innovations are all positive and are significant for the dollar/pound and the dollar/franc exchange rates.

One possible interpretation of the positive coefficient on the (unexpected) interest differential may be given in terms of the prediction of the monetary approach to the exchange rate, in which case the estimate of the coefficient α in equation (9) might be interpreted as an estimate of a structural parameter. Under an alternative interpretation the innovations in the interest differential belong in equation (9) only as far as they *manifest* "news" which is relevent for exchange rate determination. If, for example, the dominant element of "news" was variations in inflationary expectations, then one could also use the innovations in other time series as long as they reflect this relevant "news." To examine this possibility the same regressions as in tables 1.3 and 1.4 were estimated using the 12-month interest differential and the results are reported in in tables 1.5 and 1.6. As before, in all cases the coefficients on the actual differential do not differ significantly from zero, while in all cases the coefficients on the innovations in the differential are positive and significant for the dollar/pound and the dollar/franc exchange rates.[25]

On the whole the record shows that during the 1970s exchange rates and the interest rate differential have been associated positively, thus indicating that during that inflationary period the same factors which induced a rise in the interest differential also induced a rise in the spot exchange rates. Furthermore, consistent with the hypothesis that current changes in exchange rates are primarily a response to new information, the evidence shows the importance of the innovations in the interest differential.

The principle that current exchange rates already reflect expectations concerning the future course of events implies that unanticipated changes in exchange rates are primarily due to innovations. Since the empirical work suggests that most of the actual changes in exchange rates are unanticipated, it follows that most of the actual changes in exchange rates are due to "news." In the present section this principle was applied to the analysis of the relation between exchange rates and interest rate differentials. The principle, however, is general. For example, it implies that the relation between a deficit in the balance of trade and the exchange rate depends crucially on whether the deficit was expected or not. A deficit that was expected may have no effect on the exchange rate since the latter already reflected these expectations. In contrast, an unexpected deficit in the balance of trade may contain significant new information that is likely to be accompanied by large changes in the exchange rate.[26] This distinction might be useful in interpreting the weak and unstable relation between the balance of trade and the exchange rate without having to rely on explanations like the J curve or on variable import and export elasticities.

1.3 Exchange Rates and Prices

One of the striking facts concerning the relation between prices and exchange rates during the 1970s has been the poor performance of the predictions of the simple versions of the purchasing power parity doctrine. The originators and proponents of the purchasing power parity doctrine (Wheatley and Ricardo during the first part of the nineteenth century and Cassel during the 1920s) have viewed the doctrine as an extension of the quantity theory of money to the open economy. By now the consensus seems to be that, when applied to aggregate national price levels, purchasing power parities can be expected to hold in the long run if most of the shocks to the system are of a monetary origin which do not require changes in relative prices. To the extent that most of the shocks reflect "real" changes (like differential growth rates among sectors), the required changes in sectoral relative prices may result in a relatively loose connection between exchange rates and aggregate price levels. The experience during the 1970s illustrates the extent to which real shocks (oil embargo, supply shocks, commodity booms and shortages, shifts in the demand for money, differential productivity growth) result in systematic deviations from purchasing power parities. As illustrated in figure 1.1, short-run changes in exchange rates have not been closely linked to short-run differentials in the corresponding national inflation rates as measured by consumer price indices. Furthermore, this loose link seems to be cumulative. As illustrated in Figure 1.2, divergences from purchasing power parities, measured in terms of the relation between exchange rates and the ratio of consumer price indices, seem to persist.

The link between prices and exchange rates is illustrated in table 1.7, which reports the results of regressions of the various exchange rates on the corresponding ratios of wholesale and of cost of living price indices. As may be seen, the results of the regressions which involve the US dollar are

Table 1.7
Purchasing power parities: instrumental variables—monthly data: June 1973 – July 1979 (standard errors in parentheses)[a]

Dependent variable ln S_t	Constant	$\ln(P_W/P_W^*)$	$\ln(P_c/P_c^*)$	s.e.	D.W.	ρ
Dollar/pound	0.712 (0.149)	0.165 (0.507)		0.027	1.63	0.963
	2.982 (2.978)		1.070 (0.897)	0.029	1.66	0.998
Dollar/franc	−1.521 (0.027)	0.184 (0.374)		0.029	2.26	0.863
	−1.570 (0.047)		−1.070 (0.817)	0.029	2.30	0.901
Dollar/DM	−0.900 (0.018)	1.786 (0.230)		0.034	1.69	0.739
	−0.908 (0.175)		2.217 (0.263)	0.031	1.96	0.759
Pound/DM	−1.668 (0.041)	0.821 (0.144)		0.027	1.60	0.895
	−1.666 (0.048)		0.965 (0.197)	0.027	1.57	0.909
Franc/DM	0.863 (0.143)	−0.026 (0.487)		0.020	1.61	0.981
	0.602 (0.048)		1.180 (0.327)	0.019	1.48	0.929

a. ln S_t denotes the logarithm of the spot exchange rate; $\ln(P_W/P_W^*)$ and $\ln(P_c/P_c^*)$ denote, respectively, the logarithms of the ratios of the wholesale price indices and the cost of living indices. The Cochrane-Orcutt iterative technique with two-stage least squares estimation method was used; the instruments are a constant, time, time squared, and lagged values of the dependent and independent variables. s.e. is the standard error of the equation.

extremely poor. For the dollar/pound and the dollar/franc exchange rates the estimates of the coefficients of the price ratios are insignificant, and for the dollar/DM exchange rate the estimates differ significantly from unity. In contrast, the results of the regressions of exchange rates that do not involve the US dollar or the US price level (the pound/DM and the franc/DM exchange rates) are superior; except for the wholesale price indices in the franc/DM regression, all the coefficients are highly significent, and the elasticities of the exchange rates with respect to the various price indices do not differ significantly from unity.

The vast difference in the performance of the regressions for the various currencies can be explained by noting that first, due to transport cost, purchasing power parities are expected to hold better among the neighboring European countries than among each of these countries and the United States; second, changes in commercial policies and nontariff barriers to trade seem to have been more stable within Europe than between Europe and the United States; third, within Europe the snake agreement and later on the European Monetary System have resulted in a reduced degree of intra-European flexibility of exchange rates; and fourth, there seem to have been large changes in the equilibrium *real* exchange rate between the US dollar and the European currencies.[27] It should be noted, however, that to some extent the overall poor performance of the purchasing power parities doctrine is specific to the 1970s. During the floating rates period of the 1920s, the doctrine seems to have been much more reliable.[28]

The preceding discussion accounted for the persisting deviations from purchasing power parties in terms of changes in real factors which affect equilibrium relative price structure. It should be noted, however, that even in the absence of such changes there is a presumption that, at least in the short run, exchange rate fluctuations would not be matched by corresponding fluctuations of aggregate price levels. The discussion in section 1 emphasized that in periods which are dominated by "news" which alters expectations, exchange rates (and other asset prices which are traded in organized markets) are expected to be highly volatile. Aggregate price indices, on the other hand, are not expected to reveal such a degree of volatility since they reflect the prices of goods and services which are less durable and therefore are likely to be less sensitive to the news which alters expectations concerning the future course of events. It follows therefore that in periods during which there is ample "news" which causes large fluctuations in exchange rates there will also be large deviations from purchasing power parities.[29]

The difference between the characteristics of exchange rates and national price levels is also reflected in their time series properties and is fundamental for interpreting the deviations from purchasing power parities. The monthly changes in exchange rates exhibit little or no serial correlation, while national price levels do exhibit a degree of serial correlation. The "stickiness" exhibited by national price levels need not reflect any market imperfection, rather, it may reflect the costs of price adjustment which result in the existence of nominal contracts of finite length. Likewise, it may reflect the results of confusion between relative and absolute prices and confusion between permanent and transitory changes. This difference between the time series properties of exchange rates and prices is reflected in the low correlation between the practically

Table 1.8
Mean absolute percentage changes in prices and exchange rates—monthly data:
June 1973–July 1979[a]

Country	Variable WPI	COL	Stock market	Exchange rates against the dollar Spot	Forward	COL/COL$_{US}$
United States	0.009	0.007	0.037	–	–	–
United Kingdom	0.014	0.012	0.066	0.021	0.021	0.007
France	0.011	0.009	0.054	0.020	0.021	0.003
Germany	0.004	0.004	0.030	0.024	0.024	0.004

a. All variables represent the absolute values of monthly percentage changes in the data. WPI denotes the wholesale price index and COL the cost of living index. Data on prices and exchange rates are from the IMF tape (May 1979 version). The stock market indices are from *Capital International Perspective*, monthly issues.

random month-to-month exchange rate changes and the serially correlated differences between national rates of inflation.

The different degrees of volatility of prices and exchange rates are illustrated in table 1.8, which reports the average absolute monthly percentage changes in the various exchange rates and prices. As is evident, the mean absolute change in the various spot exchange rates has been about 2 percent per month (and even slightly higher for the changes in the forward rate). The magnitudes of these changes have been more than double the magnitudes of the changes in most of the various price indices as well as in the ratios of national price levels. For example, the mean monthly change in the cost of living price index was 0.4 percent in Germany, 0.7 percent in the United States, 0.9 percent in France, and 1.2 percent in the United Kingdom. These differences are even more striking for the detrended series.

The notion that exchange rates have been volatile is clearly illustrated by figure 1.1 and by table 1.8. The comparison of the magnitudes of the changes in the exchange rates with the magnitudes of the changes in the price indices and in the ratios of national price levels may suggest, according to a narrow interpretation of the purchasing power parity doctrine, that exchange rate fluctuations have been "excessive." The previous discussion, however, has emphasized that exchange rates, being the relative prices of assets, are fundamentally different from the price indices of goods and services and therefore are expected to exhibit a different degree of volatility, in particular during periods that are dominated by "news." An alternative yardstick for measuring the degree of exchange rate fluctuations would be a comparison with prices of other

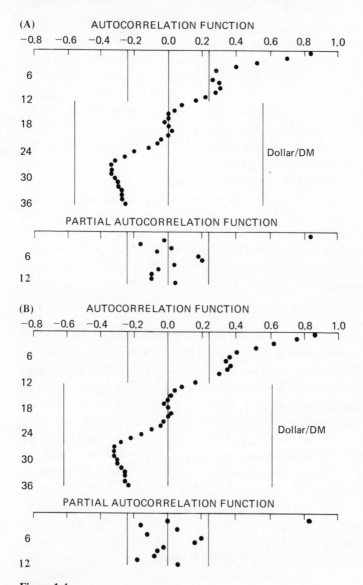

Figure 1.4

(*A*) The dollar/DM: deviations from PPP with wholesale price indices. (*B*) The dollar/DM: deviations from PPP with cost of living price indices.

assets. Indeed, while exchange rate changes have been large relative to changes in national price levels, they have been considerably smaller than changes in the prices of other assets like gold, silver, many other commodities that are traded in organized markets, and common stocks. For example, table 1.8 also reports the mean absolute monthly percentage change in stock market indices. As may be seen, the mean monthly change in these indices ranged from over 3 percent in Germany to over 6 percent in the United Kingdom. By these standards it is difficult to argue that exchange rates have been excessively volatile.

Given the short-run deviations from purchasing power parities, it is relevant to explore whether these deviations tend to diminish with time or tend to persist or even grow in size. In order to examine the patterns of the deviations, the autocorrelation functions and the partial autocorrelation functions of these deviations for the wholesale and the cost of living price indices have been computed. The deviation from purchasing power parities during month t is denoted by Δ and is defined as

$$\Delta_t = \ln S_t - \ln(P/P^*)_t. \tag{10}$$

Figure 1.4 illustrates the patterns of deviation for the dollar/DM exchange rate, and a similar pattern characterizes the deviations from purchasing power parities for the other two exchange rates. In all cases the autocorrelation function tails off at what seems to be an exponential rate and in all cases the partial autocorrelation function shows a spike at the first lag. This pattern seems to indicate (as might have been expected on the basis of the time series properties of exchange rates and price indices) that the deviations from purchasing power parities follow a first-order autoregressive process. It is noteworthy, however, that in all cases the value of the autoregression term is about 0.9, indicating the possibility that the series may not satisfy the stationarity requirement. To allow for this possibility the autocorrelation functions and the partial autocorrelation functions of $\Delta_t - \Delta_{t-1}$, that is, of the first difference of the deviations from purchasing power parities, have also been examined. The results indicate that these differences are serially uncorrelated and thus imply that the deviations Δ_t follow a random walk process. In view of this possibility it is concluded that the deviations from purchasing power parities seem to follow a first-order autoregressive process but that the data do not provide sufficient evidence to reject the alternative hypothesis of a random walk.[30]

1.4 Concluding Remarks

This chapter examined some aspects of the operation of flexible exchange rates. The analysis was based on the experience of the 1970s. The principle conclusions which may be drawn from the empirical work are

1. In spite of the extraordinary turbulence in the markets for foreign exchange, it seems that to a large extent the markets have operated efficiently. It should be emphasized, however, that the concept of "efficiency" that is being used in this context is somewhat narrow in that it only refers to the notion that the markets do not seem to entail unexploited profit opportunities. A broader perspective should deal with the social cost of volatility in terms of the interference with the efficiency of the price system in guiding resource allocation as well as with the cost of alternative outlets for the disturbances that are currently reflected in the volatility of exchange rates. As for the choice among alternative outlets for the disturbances, one may argue that since the foreign exchange market is a market in which risk can be bought and sold relatively easily, it may be reasonable to concentrate the disturbances in this market, rather than transfer them to other markets, such as labor markets, where they cannot be dealt with in as efficient a manner.

2. The high volatility of exchange rates (spot and forward) reflects an intrinsic characteristic of the relative price of monies and other assets that are traded in organized exchange. The price of gold and the price of stocks, as well as exchange rates between national monies, depend critically on expectations concerning the future course of events and adjust rapidly in response to new information. In this perspective the exchange rate (in contrast with the relative price of national outputs) is being viewed as a financial variable which is determined in a macroeconomic setting.

3. During inflationary periods variations in nominal rates of interest are dominated by changes in inflationary expectations; as a result, high nominal rates of interest are associated with high exchange rates (a depreciated currency). This relation was supported by the empirical work. Since mid-1979 the relation between the rate of interest and the exchange rate reversed itself. This reversal indicates that since mid-1979 the main cause for fluctuations in the rate of interest was fluctuations in the real rate rather than in inflationary expectations.

4. The asset view of exchange rate determination implies that "news" is among the major factors which influence changes in exchange rates. In this context the key finding was the dependence of exchange rate changes

on the unexpected changes in the rates of interest. This finding is in accord with the analytical prediction that current exchange rates already reflect current expectations about the future, while changes in the current exchange rates reflect primarily changes in these expectations which, by definition, arise from new information.

5. The experience of the 1970s does not support the predictions of the simple version of the purchasing power parity doctrine which relates the values of current measured prices to current exchange rates. The empirical work showed that deviations from purchasing power parities can be characterized by a first-order autoregressive process.

6. One of the key analytical insights that is provided by the monetary (or the asset market) approach to the exchange rate is that exchange rates reflect not only current circumstances but also those circumstances which are expected to prevail in the *future*. This anticipatory feature of the exchange rate (which is emphasized by Mussa, 1979b) does not characterize (at least to such a degree) the prices of national outputs, which reflect to a large extent *present* and *past* circumstances as they are embedded in existing contracts. Consequently, periods which are dominated by large and frequent changes in expectations are likely to be periods in which the future is expected to differ greatly from the present and the past. Under such circumstances one may expect to find frequent deviations from purchasing power parities when the latter is computed using current prices. These deviations reflect the intrinsic difference between asset prices and national price indices.[31]

7. Since commodity prices do not adjust fully in response to exogenous shocks, it seems that intervention in the foreign exchange market which ensures that exchange rates conform with purchasing power parities would be a mistaken course of policy. When commodity prices are slow to adjust to current and expected economic conditions, it may be desirable to allow "excessive" adjustment in some other prices. Further, changes in real economic conditions requiring adjustment in the equilibrium *relative* prices of different national outputs occur continuously. An intervention rule which links changes in exchange rates rigidly to changes in domestic and foregin prices in accord with purchasing power parity ignores the occasional need for equilibrating changes in relative prices.

Data Appendix

1. Exchange rates   The spot exchange rates are end-of-month rates obtained from the IMF tape (May 1979 version, updated to July 1979 using

the November 1979 issue of the *International Financial Statistics*) obtained from the International Monetary Fund.

The forward exchange rates are end-of-month rates for one-month maturity. The forward rates for the UK pound and the DM for the period June 1973–June 1978 are bid prices obtained from the International Money Market (IMM). For the period July 1978–July 1979 they are sell prices obtained from the *Wall Street Journal*. The forward rates for the French franc for the period June 1973–July 1974 are bid prices calculated from the *Weekly Review* publication of the Harris Bank, which reports the spot rate and the forward premium; in each case the closest Friday to the end of the month was chosen. For the period August 1974–June 1978 the rates are bid rates obtained from the IMM, and for the period July 1978–July 1979 they are sell prices obtained from the *Wall Street Journal*.

2. Prices   The wholesale and cost of living price indices are period averages obtained from the IMF tape, lines 63 and 64, respectively.

3. Rates of interest   All interest rates are 1-month Eurocurrency rates obtained from the *Weekly Review* of the Harris Bank. In all cases the figures used correspond to the last Friday of each month.

4. Stock markets   The stock market indices correspond to the last trading day of the month. The sources are *Capital International Perspective*, Geneva, Switzerland, monthly issues.

Notes

1. For collections of articles summarizing this approach see the *Scandinavian Journal of Economics*, no. 2, 1976, and Frenkel and Johnson (1978).

2. For an application of the same methodology in analyzing the efficiency properties of the foreign exchange market during the German hyperinflation of 1921–1923 see Frenkel (1976, 1977, 1979). For an application to other exchange rates during the 1920s see Frenkel and Clements (1981); for an application to the 1920s and the 1970s see Krugman (1977); for an interesting analysis using time series and cross-section data see Bilson (1981); for an analysis of market efficiency using novel econometric techniques see Hakkio (1979) and Hansen and Hodrick (1980); and for surveys see Levich (1978, 1979).

3. More precisely, if (assuming risk neutrality) the forward rate measures the expected value of the future spot rate, then the constant term in the logarithmic equation (1) should be $-0.5\sigma_u^2$; see Frenkel (1979). The statement that under risk neutrality the forward rate equals the expected future spot rate neglects the effects of the stochastic elements in prices. As an empirical matter this neglect does not seem to be consequential; see Frenkel and Razin (1980).

4. Since $ln\, F_{t-1}$ is highly correlated with $ln\, S_{t-1}$ the Durbin-Watson statistic may

not be appropriate since equation (1) is very similar to a regression of $ln\ S_t$ on its own lagged value. Durbin's h-statistic reveals however that the residuals are serially uncorrelated at conventional confidence levels.

5. This test was recently applied by Obstfeld (1978) to the analysis of the foreign exchange market during the 1970s and by Frenkel (1980a, b) to the analysis of the foreign exchange markets during the 1920s.

6. The efficiency of the foreign exchange market can also be analyzed from a different angle, as in Frenkel (1980b). Consider the equation

$$x_t = \alpha_0 + \alpha_1 t + \sum_{i=1}^{n} \beta_i x_{t-i} + \gamma \pi_{t-1} + w_t,$$

where x_t denotes the percentage change of the spot exchange rate ($ln\ S_t - ln\ S_{t-1}$); π_{t-1}, the forward premium on foreign exchange ($ln\ F_{t-1} - ln\ S_{t-1}$); t, time; n, the number of lags; and w, an error term. If π_{t-1} summarizes all available information concerning the future evolution of the exchange rate, then *given* the value of the forward premium π_{t-1}, the past history of the percentage change of the exchange rate should not "help" the prediction (i.e., the past history should not be viewed as Granger-causing future changes), and the joint hypotheses that α_0, α_1, and β_i are zero and that γ is unity should not be rejected. The results of applying these tests to the three exchange rates for various numbers of lags as well as to the pooled data base of the three exchange rates show that the null hypothesis cannot be rejected at the 95 percent confidence level since the values of the various F-statistics fall well below the corresponding critical values. It is noteworthy, however, that the power of this test is low and that the joint hypothesis that α_0, α_1, β_i and γ are zero could also not be rejected. The difficulties in "explaining" the percentage change of the exchange rate in terms of past values of various variables reflect the fact that like the prices of other assets which are traded in organized markets, changes in exchange rates are dominated by "news" which by definition could not have been incorporated in past changes or in the lagged forward premium. For a further elaboration see the following section.

7. The analysis of the role of "news" in determining current exchange rates and in explaining forecast errors from the forward rate has been made forcefully by Mussa (1976a, b, 1977, 1979a) and Dornbusch (1978). The large degree of volatility is also analyzed by McKinnon (1976), who attributes it to insufficient speculation.

8. These and the following empirical regularities are analyzed in detail in Mussa (1979a). See also Frenkel and Mussa (1980).

9. For an analysis of the relation between the variances of series of predictions and series of realizations see Shiller (1979) and Singleton (1980).

10. The following paragraph draws on Frenkel and Mussa (1980).

11. See, for example, the comprehensive econometric model of Fair (1979).

12. A result of this general form is derived in Mussa (1976a). The unique role of expectations is also emphasized by Black (1973), Dornbusch (1976c, 1978), Kouri (1976), and Bilson (1978). In general the value of b may be viewed as the relevant parameter for determining whether a specific commodity [whose pricing rule is described in terms of equations like (6) and (7)] may be viewed as an asset. The higher is the value of b for a given commodity, the larger is its asset attribute.

13. New information might be "permanent" when the relevant horizon is a month, while it might be transitory when the relevant horizon is a year. In that case the correlation between the spot exchange rate and the contemporaneous 1-month forward rate is likely to be high, while the correlation between the spot rate and the 12-month forward rate is likely to be low. The perceived permanence of the new information can be inferred from the correlation between the spot and the various maturities of the forward rate. As expected it is generally found that this correlation diminishes with the maturity of the forward contract.

14. This correlation is exhibited in the fuller version of this paper in Frenkel (1981b).

15. It is noteworthy that since the forward premium (like the rate of interest) and the exchange rate are dimensionally incommensurate, their association raises questions that are familiar from the discussions of the Gibson paradox. In a separate paper I intend to examine the relation between exchange rates and the forward premium (or the interest differential) in light of the various explanations of the Gibson paradox.

16. For theoretical developments and applications of the approach see, for example, Dornbusch (1976a, b), Kouri (1976), Mussa (1976a), Frenkel (1976), Frenkel and Johnson (1978), Frenkel and Clements (1981), Clements and Frenkel (1980), Bilson (1978), Hodrick (1978), and Frankel (1979).

17. It should be emphasized that this explanation of the positive association between the rate of interest and the exchange rate *does not* rely on a rigid form of the purchasing power parity theory. It only requires that domestic and foreign price levels, when expressed in terms of the same currency, are positively correlated. The evidence from the 1970s is consistent with this requirement; see Frenkel (1981a).

18. The traditional prediction of a negative relation between interest rates and the exchange rate could in principle be rationalized under the assumption that it concentrates on the short-run liquidity effects of monetary changes. It should be emphasized, however, that in an inflationary environment, like the one prevailing in the United States, the applicability of this rationalization is very limited. The short-run liquidity effect is emphasized in Dornbusch (1976b). The role of inflationary expectations in dominating exchange rate developments is emphasized in Frenkel (1976). Frankel (1979) and Edwards (1979) attempt to integrate these two factors.

19. For evidence on the robustness of the interest parity relation see Frenkel and Levich (1977).

20. See, for example, Barro (1977) and Fischer (1980).

21. See also Bilson (1978), Frenkel and Mussa (1980), Isard (1980), and Longworth (1980).

22. In general, of course, the sign of the coefficient α depends on the source of the variation in the interest rate.

23. In all cases the lagged forward exchange rate was included as an instrument in order to obtain consistent estimates; see Nelson (1975). Adding lagged values of the percentage changes of the domestic and the foreign money supplies as determinants of the expected interest differential and adding the current values of the percentage change of the money supplies as instruments for the unexpected interest

differential did not affect the results in any material way. In order to obtain consistent estimates the assumption that is being made in the regressions reported in tables 1.3–1.6 is that in forming expectations concerning the interest differential, individuals look only at the lagged forward premium and at past values of the differential. An alternative way to compute the expected differential would use data on the term structure of interest rates. Since data on the differential of two-month rates are not readily available, this computation would require interpolations.

24. The difficulties in obtaining instruments for data that are innovations are obvious since, by virtue of being "news," it is unlikely that variables which characterize the history can serve as good instruments. The difficulties are acute in cases in which a variable and its expected value appear in the same regression in which case consistent estimates require the use of an instrument that is contemporaneous with the innovation and is exogenous (see McCallum, 1979). Thus, in addition to a constant and the lagged forward exchange rate, Durbin's rank variable was used as an instrument for estimating the innovations in the interest rate differential.

25. To allow for the possibility that the exchange rate equation includes both the short- and the long-term interest rates, where, as suggested by Frankel (1979), the former captures liquidity effects and the latter captures expectations effects, equation (9) was also estimated using the innovations in both the 1-month and the 12-month interest differential on the right-hand side. Since the two sets of innovations are highly collinear, none of the coefficients differed significantly from zero. In this context it is also noteworthy that the 12-month interest rate contains elements of the 1-month rates due to the characteristics of the term structure of interest rates. As a result, coefficient estimates from regressions which use both rates, like those in Frankel (1979), must be interpreted with great care.

26. For a further elaboration on the relation between exchange rates and the current account see Kouri (1976), Branson (1977), Branson, Halttunen, and Masson (1977), Dornbusch and Fischer (1980), and Rodriguez (1980). For a special emphasis on the role of innovations in the trade balance see Mussa (1979c), and for empirical evidence see Hakkio (1980) and Dornbusch (1980). It should be noted that the empirical work on the association between exchange rates and current account innovations faces some difficulties since, in contrast with data on financial variables like interest rates, data on the current account are not available at short intervals. Furthermore, findings on the association between exchange rates and current account innovations should be interpreted with care since rather than reflecting the sensitivity of exchange rates to "news," they might just reflect invoicing practices according to which US exports are invoiced in terms of US dollars, while imports are invoiced in terms of foreign currencies.

27. The failure of the regression of the franc/DM exchange rate on the ratio of the wholesale price indices is explained in terms of the large changes in the French intersectoral relative prices; for an elaboration see Frenkel (1981a).

28. For evidence see Frenkel (1976, 1978, 1980a) and Krugman (1978).

29. On this see Mussa (1979a). It is noteworthy that the emphasis in the text has been on the words large *fluctuations*; this should be contrasted with periods during

which there are large *secular* changes in the exchange rate (like the changes which occurred during the German hyperinflation). During such periods the secular changes do not stem necessarily from "news" and need not be associated with deviations from purchasing power parities.

30. If the deviations follow a random walk process, then they do not entail (ex ante) unexploited profit opportunities. For a study of the deviations from purchasing power parities see Roll (1979). For an analysis of equilibrium deviations from purchasing power parities see Saidi (1977). It may be noted that the main difference between accepting the AR(1) rather than the random walk hypothesis relates to the economic interpretation of the two alternative processes. The random walk process implies that deviations from purchasing power parities do not tend to diminish with the passage of time, while the stable AR(1) process implies that there are mechanisms which operate to ensure that in the long run purchasing power parities are satisfied. For the purpose of forecasting the near future, however, there is very little difference between using the AR(1) process with an autoregressive coefficient of 0.9 and using the random walk process.

31. It is interesting to note that this phenomenon was recognized by Gustav Cassel— the most recognized proponent of the purchasing power parity doctrine—according to whom, "The international valuation of the currency will, then generally show a tendency to anticipate events, so to speak, and become more an expression of the internal value that the currency is expected to possess in a few months, or perhaps in a year's time" (Cassel, 1930, pp. 149–50).

References

Barro, Robert J. (1977). "Unanticipated Money Growth and Unemployment in the United States." *American Economic Review* 67:101–15.

Bilson, John F. O. (1978). "Rational Expectations and the Exchange Rate." In *The Economics of Exchange Rates: Selected Studies*, edited by Jacob A. Frenkel and Harry G. Johnson. Reading, MA: Addison-Wesley.

Bilson, John F. O. (1981). "The 'Speculative Efficiency' Hypothesis." *Journal of Business* 54:435–51.

Black, Stanely W. (1973). "International Money Markets and Flexible Exchange Rates." Princeton Studies in International Finance, no. 32, Princeton University.

Branson, William H. (1977). "Asset Markets and Relative Prices in Exchange Rate Determination." *Sozialwissenschaftliche Annalen* 1:69–89.

Branson, William H., Halttunen, Hannu, and Masson, Paul (1977). "Exchange Rates in the Short Run: The Dollar-Deutschemark Rate." *European Economic Review* 10:303–24.

Cassel, Gustav (1930). *Money and Foreign Exchange After 1914*. London: Macmillan.

Clements, Kenneth W., and Frenkel, Jacob A. (1980). "Exchange Rates, Money and Relative Prices: The Dollar-Pound in the 1920's." *Journal of International Economics* 10:249–62.

Dornbusch, Rudiger (1976a). "Capital Mobility, Flexible Exchange Rates and Macroeconomic Equilibrium." In *Recent Issues in International Monetary Economics*, edited by Emil Claassen and Pascal Salin. Amsterdam: North-Holland.

Dornbusch, Rudiger (1976b). "The Theory of Flexible Exchange Rate Regimes and Macroeconomic Policy." *Scandinavian Journal of Economics* 78:255–75. Reprinted in *The Economics of Exchange Rates: Selected Studies*, edited by Jacob A. Frenkel and Harry G. Johnson. Reading, MA: Addison-Wesley, 1978.

Dornbusch, Rudiger (1976c). "Expectations and Exchange Rate Dynamics." *Journal of Political Economy* 84 (December 1976): 1161–76.

Dornbusch, Rudiger (1978). "Monetary Policy under Exchange Rate Flexibility." In *Managed Exchange-Rate Flexibility: The Recent Experience*. Federal Reserve Bank of Boston Conference Series, no. 20.

Dornbusch, Rudiger (1980). "Exchange Rate Economics: Where Do We Stand?" *Brookings Papers on Economic Activity* 1:143–85.

Dornbusch, Rudiger, and Fischer, Stanley (1980). "Exchange Rates and the Current Account." *American Economic Review* 70:960–71.

Edwards, Sebastian (1979). "A Simple Monetary Model of Exchange Rate Determination in the Short Run—Some Preliminary Results for the Peruvian Experience 1950–1954." Unpublished manuscript, University of Chicago.

Fair, Ray C. (1979). "A Multicountry Econometric Model." National Bureau of Economic Research Working Paper Series, no. 414.

Fischer, Stanley (ed.) (1980). *Rational Expectations and Economic Policy*. Chicago: University of Chicago Press.

Frankel, Jeffrey A. (1979). "On the Mark: The Theory of Floating Exchange Rates Based on Real Interest Differentials." *American Economic Review* 69:610–22.

Frenkel, Jacob A. (1976). "A Monetary Approach to the Exchange Rate: Doctrinal Aspects and Empirical Evidence." *Scandinavian Journal of Economics* 78:200–24. Reprinted in *The Economics of Exchange Rates: Selected Studies*, edited by Jacob A. Frenkel and Harry G. Johnson. Reading, MA: Addison-Wesley, 1978.

Frenkel, Jacob A. (1977). "The Forward Exchange Rate, Expectations and the Demand for Money: The German Hyperinflation." *American Economic Review* 67:653–70.

Frenkel, Jacob A. (1978). "Purchasing Power Parity: Doctrinal Perspective and Evidence from the 1920's." *Journal of International Economics* 8:169–91.

Frenkel, Jacob A. (1979). "Further Evidence on Expectations and the Demand for Money During the German Hyperinflation." *Journal of Monetary Economics* 5:81–96.

Frenkel, Jacob A. (1980a). "Exchange Rates, Prices and Money: Lessons from the 1920's." *American Economic Review* 70:235–42.

Frenkel, Jacob A. (1980b). "The Forward Premium on Foreign Exchange and Currency Depreciation during the German Hyperinflation." *American Economic Review* 70:771–75.

Frenkel, Jacob A. (1981a). "The Collapse of Purchasing Power Parities During the 1970's." *European Economic Review* 16:145–65.

Frenkel, Jacob A. (1981b). "Flexible Exchange Rates, Prices and the Role of 'News': Lessons from the 1970's." *Journal of Political Economy* 89:665–705.

Frenkel, Jacob A., and Clements, Kenneth W. (1981): "Exchange Rates in the 1920's: A Monetary Approach." In *Development in an Inflationary World*, edited by M. June Flanders and Assaf Razin. New York: Academic Press.

Frenkel, Jacob A., and Johnson, Harry G. (eds.) (1978). *The Economics of Exchange Rates: Selected Studies*. Reading, MA: Addison-Wesley.

Frenkel, Jacob A., and Levich, Richard M. (1977). "Transaction Costs and Interest Arbitrage: Tranquil versus Turbulent Periods." *Journal of Political Economy* 85:1209–26.

Frenkel, Jacob A., and Mussa, Michael L. (1980). "The Efficiency of Foreign Exchange Markets and Measures of Turbulence." *American Economic Review* 70:374–81.

Frenkel, Jacob A., and Razin, Assaf (1980). "Stochastic Prices and Tests of Efficiency of Foreign Exchange Markets." *Economics Letters* 6:165–70.

Hakkio, Craig S. (1979). "Expectations and the Foreign Exchange Market." Unpublished PhD Dissertation, University of Chicago.

Hakkio, Craig S. (1980). "Exchange Rates and the Balance of Trade." Unpublished manuscript, Northwestern University.

Hansen, Lars P., and Hodrick, Robert J. (1980). "Forward Exchange Rates as Optimal Predictors of Future Spot Rates: An Econometric Analysis." *Journal of Political Economy* 88:829–53.

Hausman, Jerry A. (1978). "Specification Tests in Econometrics." *Econometrica* 46:1251–72.

Hodrick, Robert J. (1978). "An Empirical Analysis of the Monetary Approach to the Determination of the Exchange Rate." In *The Economics of Exchange Rates: Selected Studies*, edited by Jacob A. Frenkel and Harry G. Johnson. Reading, MA: Addison-Wesley.

Isard, Peter (1980). "Expected and Unexpected Changes in Exchange Rates: The Role of Relative Price Levels, Balance-of-Payments Factors, Interest Rates and Risk." Federal Reserve Board, International Finance Discussion Papers, no. 156.

Kouri, Pentti J. K. (1976). "The Exchange Rate and the Balance of Payments in the Short Run and in the Long Run: A Monetary Approach." *Scandinavian Journal of Economics* 78:280–304.

Krugman, Paul (1977). "The Efficiency of the Forward Exchange Market: Evidence from the Twenties and the Seventies." Unpublished manuscript, Yale University.

Krugman, Paul (1978). "Purchasing Power Parity and Exchange Rates: Another Look at the Evidence." *Journal of International Economics* 8:397–407.

Levich, Richard M. (1978). "Further Results on the Efficiency of Markets for

Foreign Exchange." In *Managed Exchange Rate Flexibility: The Recent Experience*, Federal Reserve Bank of Boston, Conference Series, no. 20.

Levich, Richard M. (1979). "The Efficiency of Markets for Foreign Exchange." In *International Economic Policy: Theory and Evidence*, edited by Rudiger Dornbusch and Jacob A. Frenkel. Baltimore: Johns Hopkins University Press.

Longworth, David (1980). "An Empirical Efficient-Markets Model of Exchange Rate Determination." Unpublished manuscript, Bank of Canada.

McCallum, Bennett T. (1979). "Topics Concerning the Formulation, Estimation, and Use of Macroeconometric Models with Rational Expectations." Unpublished manuscript, University of Virginia.

McKinnon, Ronald I. (1976). "Floating Foreign Exchange Rates 1973–74: The Emperor's New Clothes." In *Institutional Arrangements and the Inflation Problem*, edited by Karl Brunner and Allan Meltzer. Vol. 3 of the Carnegie-Rochester Conference Series on Public Policy, a Supplementary Series to the *Journal of Monetary Economics*.

Mudd, Douglas R. (1979). "Do Rising U.S. Interest Rates Imply a Stronger Dollar?" *Federal Reserve Bank of St. Louis Review* 61:9–13.

Mussa, Michael (1976a). "The Exchange Rate, the Balance of Payments and Monetary and Fiscal Policy under a Regime of Controlled Floating." *Scandinavian Journal of Economics* 78:229–48. Reprinted in *The Economics of Exchange Rates: Selected Studies*, edited by Jacob A. Frenkel and Harry G. Johnson. Reading, MA: Addison-Wesley, 1978.

Mussa, Michael (1976b). "Our Recent Experience with Fixed and Flexible Exchange Rates: A Comment." In *Institutional Arrangements and the Inflation Problem*, edited by Karl Brunner and Allan Meltzer. Vol. 3 of the Carnegie-Rochester Conference Series on Public Policy, a Supplementary Series to the *Journal of Monetary Economics*.

Mussa, Michael (1977). "Exchange Rate Uncertainty: Causes, Consequences, and Policy Implications." Unpublished manuscript, University of Chicago.

Mussa, Michael (1979a). "Empirical Regularities in the Behavior of Exchange Rates and Theories of the Foreign Exchange Market." In *Policies for Employment, Prices, and Exchange Rates*, edited by Karl Brunner and Allan Meltzer. Vol. 11 of the Carnegie-Rochester Conference Series on Public Policy, a Supplementary Series to the *Journal of Monetary Economics*.

Mussa, Michael (1979b). "Anticipatory Adjustment of a Floating Exchange Rate." Unpublished manuscript, University of Chicago.

Mussa, Michael (1979c). "The Role of the Trade Balance in Exchange Rate Dynamics." Unpublished manuscript.

Nelson, Charles R. (1975). "Rational Expectations and the Estimation of Econometric Models." *International Economic Review* 16:555–61.

Obstfeld, Maurice (1978). "Expectations and Efficiency in the Foreign Exchange Market." Unpublished manuscript, MIT.

Rodriguez, Carlos A. (1980). "The Role of Trade Flows in Exchange Rate Determination: A Rational Expectations Approach." *Journal of Political Economy* 88:1148–58.

Roll, Richard (1979). "Violations of Purchasing Power Parity and Their Implications for Efficient International Commodity Markets." In *International Finance and Trade*, vol. 1, edited by Marshall Sarnat and Gikorgio P. Szego. Cambridge, MA: Ballinger.

Saidi, Nasser (1977). "Rational Expectations, Purchasing Power Parity and the Business Cycle." Unpublished manuscript, University of Chicago.

Shiller, Rober J. (1979). "Do Stock Prices Move Too Much to be Justified by Subsequent Changes in Dividends?" Unpublished manuscript, University of Pennsylvania.

Singleton, Kenneth J. (1980). "Expectations Models of the Term Structure and Implied Variance Bounds." *Journal of Political Economy* 88:1159–76.

I
EXCHANGE RATE
DETERMINATION

2

Exchange Rate Economics: Where Do We Stand?

Rudiger Dornbusch

This chapter takes as its frame of reference the experience with floating exchange rates and seeks to explain, in the light of today's theories, the pattern of exchange rate movements and policy responses.

The main lessons that emerge from the analysis concern the inadequacy of the monetary approach as a complete theory of exchange rate determination, the central role of the current account in influencing exchange rates, the suggestion that there is a deutsche mark shortage and, finally, the conclusion that an interest rate policy not oriented toward the external balance has aggravated exchange rate instability.

2.1 Exchange Rate Theories and Empirical Evidence

There are basically three views of the exchange rate. The first takes the exchange rate as the relative price of monies; the second, as the relative price of goods; and the third, the relative price of bonds. I regard any one of these views as a partial picture of exchange rate determination, although each may be especially important in explaining a particular historical episode. Still, it is useful to approach exchange rate theory not from the complex perspective of an all-encompassing model, but rather from the vantage point of a sharply articulated, partial model. The monetary approach is a good place to start. Although in the opinions of some of its proponents it represents a quite complete theory of the

An earlier version of this chapter appeared in *The Brookings Papers on Economic Activity* 1: 1980.

I am grateful for comments from members of the Brookings panel and from Stanley Fischer. Robert E. Cumby made many suggestions and provided generous research assistance. Financial support was provided by a grant from the National Science Foundation.

exchange rate, I will expand it to a more general theory by relaxing some of the special assumptions that are required if it is to stand on its own.

2.1.1 The Monetary Approach

At the outset of flexible rates in the 1970s, the literature emphasized a monetary interpretation of exchange rate determination.[1] Most versions of the monetary approach assume strict purchasing power parity (PPP). Exchange rates move promptly in order to maintain the international linkage of prices. Thus there is no room for changes in the terms of trade. With e denoting the logarithm of the home currency price of foreign exchange, and p and p^* denoting the logarithm of home and foreign prices, respectively, PPP implies[2]

$$e = p - p^*, \tag{1}$$

where here and throughout the paper variables in lowercase (except interest rates) represent logarithms.

The next step in the monetary approach is to take prices as determined by domestic nominal money supply and real money demand. With real money demand depending on real income and the nominal interest rate, the expression becomes

$$p = m - ky + hi,$$
$$p^* = m^* - ky^* + hi^*, \tag{2}$$

where

$m = $ logarithm of nominal money,
$k = $ income elasticity of real money demand,
$y = $ logarithm of real income,
$h = $ semilogarithmic interest response of real balances,
$i = $ nominal interest rate.

Combining equations (1) and (2) yields the exchange rate equation of the monetary approach:

$$e = m - m^* + h(i - i^*) - k(y - y^*), \tag{3}$$

where coefficients are assumed to be equal for all countries.

The model establishes that relative changes in money supply, interest rate, and real income affect the exchange rate. An increase in the money supply at home leads to an equiproportionate depreciation. Because an increase in domestic real income raises the demand for real balances and thus leads to a fall in domestic prices, it induces an offsetting exchange appreciation. Relatively higher domestic interest rates, by contrast,

Table 2.1
Inflation and currency appreciation in major industrial countries, 1973–1979 (annual average, in percent)

| | Measure | |
Country	Consumer price inflation	Appreciation on the dollar
United States	8.5	–
Other major industrial countries[a]	9.4	1.4
Canada	9.2	−2.6
France	10.7	0.7
Germany	4.6	6.4
Japan	9.9	3.6
United Kingdom	15.6	−2.4

Source: International Monetary Fund, *International Financial Statistics*, vol. 33 (March 1980), series ahx for exchange rates and series 64 for prices.
a. These series are weighted averages of the respective individual series for the five foreign countries. The relative weights are derived from the International Monetary Fund's multilateral trade model. They are: Canada—0.2405, France—0.1640, Germany—0.2340, Japan—0.2160, and the United Kingdom—0.1440.

reduce the demand for real balances, raise prices, and therefore bring about an exchange depreciation.

There are two ways to test the monetary approach. One recognizes that instantaneous PPP is an essential part of the monetary approach and directly tests whether PPP prevails. The second examines the explanatory power of econometric equations specified like equation (3).

There is ample evidence accumulating that this assumption is *not* warranted. Not only does the short-term exchange rate deviate from a PPP path, but there are also cumulative deviations from that path that show substantial persistence. This is clearly brought out by table 2.1, which shows annual inflation rates for consumer prices in the United States, five other major industrial countries, and a trade-weighted index of those countries. The table also shows the average annual appreciation of the foreign currencies relative to the dollar, bilaterally and as a group. Contrary to PPP theory, *real* exchange rates have not remained constant. The striking fact is that during the period from 1973 to 1979, the annual rate of inflation in the United States averaged about 1 percentage point less than in the group of foreign countries, yet the dollar has depreciated at an average rate of over 1 percent a year.[3] There has thus been an average annual change in relative price levels adjusted for exchange rate movements (or a *real* depreciation of the dollar) of more than 2 percentage points. This substantial rate of real depreciation should attract attention and study rather than being confined to the error term. The evidence of table 2.1 is also reflected in figure 2.1, which shows that the International

INDEX, 1975 = 100

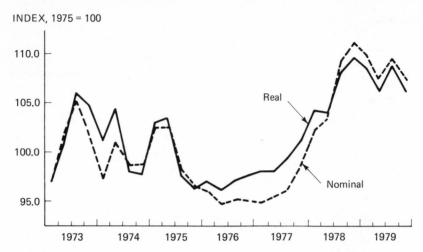

Figure 2.1
International Monetary Fund's effective exchange rate of the dollar, nominal and real, 1973: 1–1979: 4. The data are quarterly averages. Source: International Monetary Fund, *International Financial Statistics*, various issues. The real and nominal rates are the inverses of, respectively, the index of relative wholesale prices (series 63 110) and the nominal effective exchange rate index (series amx).

Monetary Fund's multilateral nominal and real effective exchange rates of the dollar have moved together. Figure 2.2 illustrates how the nominal effective exchange rate has departed from, rather than simply offset, inflation differentials.[4]

The alternative approach to testing the monetary theory relies on evidence from regression equations. The empirical evidence reported in table 2.2 tests the explanatory power of the theory as specified by equation (3), using the dollar-mark exchange rate. The explanatory variables are relative nominal money supplies, relative real income levels, and nominal long-term and short-term interest differentials.

The long-term interest differential appears in the exchange rate equation either because, in addition to short-term interest rates, long-term rates measure one of the alternative costs of holding money or because they are taken as a proxy for anticipated inflation differentials. In either view, a rise in the domestic long-term interest rate differential leads to a reduction in real money demand and thus to higher prices and depreciation.[5]

The theory suggests that a rise in domestic relative income induces appreciation and that an increase in domestic interest rates induces depreciation. Equation 2-1 in table 2.2 tests this theory with quarterly

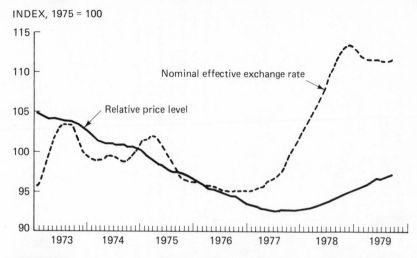

Figure 2.2
Relative price level and nominal effective exchange rate in the United States,
January 1973–September 1979. The data are seven-month centered moving
averages. The nominal effective exchange rate is calculated as a weighted average
of the index of five foreign countries, as described in table 2.1, note a. The relative
price level is calculated as the ratio of the US index of consumer prices to a
weighted index of consumer prices in the five countries, with weights equal to
those used in calculating the exchange rate. Sources: Nominal effective exchange
rate—same as table 2.1: and prices—*Business Conditions Digest*, various issues,
series 320, 732, 733, 735, 736, and 738.

data, with coefficients constrained to be equal for all countries. It offers
little support for the monetary approach. Only a small fraction of the
variance in the exchange rate is explained, and there is a high (0.88)
estimated coefficient of serial correlation. Although interest rates have
the expected sign and are significantly different from zero, the coefficient
of relative monies is actually negative, but it is insignificant.

The coefficient of relative monies in the remaining equations is constrained to unity. Equations 2-2 and 2-3 differ in sample period and
demonstrate the instability of equation (3). For the complete sample
period the equation has negligible explanatory power. Equation 2-4
allows for lagged adjustment in real balances by introducing the lagged
dependent variable as an explanatory variable.[6] Only the lagged adjustment term appears significant in this formulation.

The evidence on PPP and the econometric evidence reported here
leave little doubt that the monetary approach in the form of equation (3)
is an unsatisfactory theory of exchange rate determination. The key link

Table 2.2
Equations explaining the monetary approach to exchange rate determination, using the dollar-mark exchange rate, 1973:2–1979:4 and subperiod[a]

Equation and sample period	Independent variable						Summary statistic			
	Constant	$(e + m^* - m)_{-1}$	$m - m^*$	$y - y^*$	$(i - i^*)_S$	$(i - i^*)_L$	R^2	Durbin-Watson	Standard error of estimate	Rho
2-1 1973:2–1979:4	5.76 (2.81)	–	-0.03 (-0.07)	-1.05 (-0.97)	0.01 (1.90)	0.04 (2.07)	0.33	1.83	0.05	0.88
2-2 1973:2–1978:1	4.82 (2.51)	–	1.00	-0.93 (-0.90)	-0.00 (-0.29)	0.07 (5.94)	0.66	1.69	0.04	0.06
2-3 1973:2–1979:4	4.63 (2.12)	–	1.00	-0.76 (-0.66)	0.01 (1.62)	0.04 (1.82)	0.08	1.80	0.05	0.99
2-4 1973:2–1979:4	0.23 (0.12)	0.83 (8.26)	1.00	0.16 (0.17)	0.01 (1.36)	0.01 (0.67)	0.88	1.85	0.05	–

Sources: Exchange rate—Board of Governors of the Federal Reserve System, *Federal Reserve Statistical Release*, G.5, "Foreign Exchange Rates," various issues; US money supply—Board of Governors of the Federal Reserve System; German money supply—International Monetary Fund, *International Financial Statistics*, various issues, and Deutsche Bundesbank; real income—Organisation for Economic Co-operation and Development, *Main Economic Indicators*, various issues; and interest rates—Morgan Guaranty Trust Company of New York, *World Financial Markets*, various issues.

a. The equations were estimated using quarterly data. The independent variables are e—logarithm of the dollar-mark exchange rate; m—logarithm of the money supply (M_1), seasonally adjusted; y—logarithm of gross national product at 1975 prices, seasonally adjusted at annual rates; i_S—yield on representative money-market instruments; and i_L—yield on domestic government bonds. An asterisk denotes a variable for Germany. The numbers in parentheses are t-statistics.

between the exchange rate and PPP fails to hold, and any reasonable model must include a theory of real exchange rate determination.

The monetary approach was an important stepping stone of empirical research in international monetary economics and a plausible, if bold, hypothesis. Together with the asset market approach, it reflected a reaction to elasticity models of the exchange rate and, in that respect, was a substantial contribution. Both approaches share the partial equilibrium view that exchange rates are determined by the conditions of stock equilibrium in the asset markets. They ignore other factors important to a general equilibrium analysis. I turn next to a broader model that reintroduces the more traditional aspects of exchange rate determination—the current account, wealth effects, expectations, and relative prices.

2.1.2 A General Model of Exchange Rates

If strict PPP is abandoned, the way is clear for a broad approach to modeling exchange rate determination. A first step here is the traditional Mundell-Fleming model that remains, with some adaptations, the backbone of macroeconomic models of the exchange rate.[7] This model assumes that domestic prices are fixed in each home currency so that the exchange rate sets the terms of trade or the price of domestic goods relative to imports. Capital is fully mobile internationally and, with perfect substitutability between home and foreign securities (ignoring exchange rate expectations), interest rates are equalized internationally. Output is demand determined.

Suppose, in this setting, that monetary expansion occurs at home. The resulting decline in interest rates leads to an international differential that brings about an incipient capital outflow. The exchange rate depreciates and, with elasticity conditions satisfied, demand shifts toward domestic goods. The induced increase in output leads to a rise in income and money demand until equality among international interest rates is restored at a higher level of output with a lower real exchange rate.

An expansion in demand for home output arising from fiscal policy or an exogenous shift in demand leads to an increase in income and money demand, and hence a tendency for interest rates to increase. The induced capital inflows bring about exchange rate appreciation, a loss in competitiveness, and hence a deterioration in the current balance that dampens or offsets the expansion. This result is clearly a curiosity, and I return to it below.

An extended Mundell-Fleming model can be derived by relaxing five key restrictive assumptions: fixed prices, the fully demand-determined level of output, the absence of exchange rate expectations, the absence of a role for the current account in exchange rate determination, and the perfect substitutability of domestic and foreign securities. The first three assumptions are readily relaxed.[8]

Rational expectations and long-run neoclassical features such as full employment are included in the extended Mundell-Fleming model. The increase in demand again brings an immediate nominal and real appreciation that restores demand to the full employment level through an offsetting deterioration in the current account, and monetary expansion leads to an immediate depreciation of the nominal and real exchange rate. Moreover, the exchange rate must overshoot, depreciating proportionately more than the expansion in money, if asset markets adjust more rapidly than goods markets. The domestic interest rate falls relative to those abroad, and asset markets will be in balance only if the exchange rate initially overshoots, so that there are corresponding expectations of currency appreciation.[9]

The extended Mundell-Fleming model is a first approach to expanding exchange rate theory in the absence of PPP that allows for short-run real effects of monetary disturbances and that permits the possibility of permanent changes in relative prices in response to changes in the pattern of world demand. By introducing rational expectations, the model focuses on "news" as the determinant of unanticipated changes in the exchange rate. Over time the exchange rate follows a path delineated by interest differentials. News about monetary developments or the state of demand bring about immediate changes in the level and path of the exchange rate. These ideas can be incorporated by distinguishing between actual and anticipated depreciation, $\dot{e}'$ and $\dot{e}$, respectively. With perfect asset substitutability, the actual rate of depreciation is the sum of anticipated depreciation, which equals the nominal interest differential, $i - i^*$, and the effect of news, which is given by the difference between actual and anticipated depreciation,

$$\dot{e}' = (i - i^*) + (\dot{e}' - \dot{e}). \tag{4}$$

The relevant news in this model is changes in monetary conditions and in the demand for domestic output.

The model retains the uncomfortable property that *any* increase in demand for home output, whether through fiscal expansion or increased net exports, leads to nominal and real appreciation because the only role of the current account is as a component of demand. Imbalances in the current account have no medium-term feedback on the economy, either

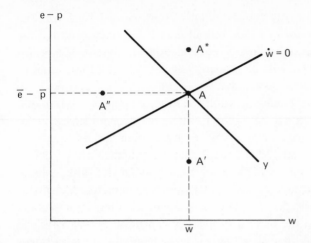

Figure 2.3

in goods markets or in asset markets. The analysis can now be expanded to introduce the role of the current account.

Suppose that in the goods market demand for home output depends not only on income and the terms of trade but also on real wealth. A rise in real wealth would be expected to increase real spending and demand for domestic goods. A rise in wealth thus creates an excess demand, which, to maintain output at full employment, would have to be offset by the expenditure-shifting effect of a real exchange rate appreciation. In figure 2.3 the y schedule is seen as the combination of real exchange rates—defined as the ratio of the price of imports to domestic goods imports—and the level of real wealth w, which is consistent with output at full employment.[10]

The current account is balanced along the schedule $\dot{w} = 0$. With more wealth there is increased spending and thus a tendency for an external deficit. To restore external balance, the real exchange rate must depreciate, thus shifting demand from foreign goods toward home output, and thereby restoring external balance. Accordingly, the external balance schedule is positively sloped; points above the schedule correspond to a surplus and points below to a deficit. Furthermore, a surplus implies net acquisition of claims on the rest of the world and hence growing real wealth; the converse is true for a deficit.

The extended framework is helpful in identifying the long-run equilibrium of the economy, its determinants, and some of the factors that affect the dynamics. The diagram shows that long-run equilibrium occurs for real variables—real wealth and the terms of trade or real exchange rate. At point A, demand for domestic output is at full employment and the current account is in equilibrium, or, equivalently, income equals expenditure. In the background is the monetary sector that specifies the price level and the nominal exchange rate.

The expanded model makes possible the immediate interpretation of a demand shift or increase in net exports. With a permanent increase in net exports there is an excess demand for domestic goods and an equal surplus. To restore internal and external balance simultaneously, at that is required is nominal and real appreciation. A demand shift thus leads to an instantaneous real and nominal appreciation to a point like A', with no further adjustments needed. By contrast, a rise in spending on both home and traded goods in the pattern of average expenditures will leave the equilibrium composition of spending unchanged, and thus only leads to a change in long-run wealth at point A''. Over time the economy will reduce its stock of assets until spending has declined sufficiently for the initial real exchange rate to be reestablished. The adjustment process depends, of course, on the interaction between goods markets and the monetary sector.

The uncomfortable fact remains that even in this model there is a short-run tendency for an expenditure increase to induce appreciation. The reason is, once again, that the increase in demand leads to a rise in income and thus to higher money demand and increased interest rates. Because the long-run real *and* nominal exchange rate are unchanged, higher interest rates are only compatible with equilibrium in the international capital market if there is the expectation of depreciating currency. That expectation will arise through an initial real and nominal appreciation. Thus in the diagram above the real exchange rate would appreciate in the short run to a point like A'. Over time, as the stock of assets is reduced through the current account deficit and demand falls, the real exchange rate depreciates until point A'' is reached. An immediate appreciation is again implied when the dynamics are governed by short-run price stickiness and rational expectations in asset markets.

Expansionary fiscal policy will only lead to an initial depreciation of the nominal and real exchange rate if, in addition to the expectation of an unchanged long-run *real* exchange rate, the expectation of a nominal depreciation is introduced. There is good reason for such an assumption if one considers a fiscal expansion as one that is accommodated by an expansion in nominal money so that the nominal interest rate is unchanged. And it is the only way to generate this result in the model. With an accommodating nominal money expansion, the expectation of a higher long-run level of prices with unchanged terms of trade leads to an immediate depreciation of the real exchange rate to a point like A^* in the figure. At A^*, assuming smooth adjustment, there is a current account deficit (the $\dot{w} = 0$ locus shifts leftward, as does the y schedule) combined with an output expansion. From A^* the economy moves toward A''; wealth declines, and the real exchange rate appreciates to restore the initial terms of trade.

The final exercise to be considered is a sustained increase in the rate of money creation. The expectation of higher long-run inflation, and of the induced increase in velocity, implies a one-time rise in the cost of foreign currency. With rational expectations, the currency immediately depreciates before prices rise and the economy moves to a point like A^* in the figure. But because in the long run the real exchange rate and real wealth are unchanged, and because the real depreciation induces a current account surplus at A^* (this time the schedules remain the same), a clockwise adjustment occurs until the economy returns to point A. Output is initially above full employment in the adjustment process as a consequence of the overdepreciation; assets are accumulated through the current account; and the real exchange rate appreciates. The current account surplus and the income expansion are, of course, only transitory, as is the real depreciation.

I have described a fairly eclectic general equilibrium model of goods markets and asset markets, expectations, and current account adjustment. The model is capable of accounting for some of the exchange rate experience in the United States, in particular, the transitory deviations from PPP, permanent changes in the real exchange rate, and jumps of exchange rates in response to new information. This latter phenomenon is a key feature of the model and implies that, because of the differential speed of adjustment in goods markets and asset markets, even purely monetary disturbances have transitory real effects.

2.1.3 Testing the News

In this section I offer some tests of the exchange rate model developed. I showed there that unanticipated changes in aggregate demand or in net exports affect the equilibrium exchange rate. In particular, an accommodated increase in demand leads to depreciation and a current account deficit; an unanticipated increase in net exports leads to an appreciation. A monetary expansion induces depreciation, income growth, and a transitory current account surplus.

Perhaps the central implication of the rational expectations model is that it must be tested in "news form." With the assumption that asset markets are efficient, all available information is immediately embodied in asset prices and exchange rates. If one disregards for now the possibility of a risk premium, deviations of exchange rates from the path implied by interest differentials are thus entirely due to news.[11]

The extended model first distinguishes news of three kinds as important determinants of unanticipated changes in exchange rates: news about the current account, cyclical or demand factors, and interest rates. To test this model empirically, I use the definition of unanticipated depreciation as the difference between the actual depreciation and interest differentials, $\dot{e}' - (i - i^*)$. The theory suggests that an unanticipated surplus in the current account leads to appreciation, while an unanticipated increase in demand that is accommodated will lead to depreciation. Denoting news about the current account, cyclical movements, and interest rates as CAE, CYC, and INN, respectively, the equation becomes

$$\dot{e}' - (i - i^*) = \alpha_0 - \alpha_1 CAE + \alpha_2 CYC - \alpha_3 CYC^* + \alpha_4 INN, \qquad (5)$$

where in the absence of a risk premium, α_0 is expected to be zero.

As measures of the current account and cyclical news I use the official forecast errors of the Organisation for Economic Co-operation and Development, which publishes biannual six-month forecasts for current account balances and real growth of major industrial countries.[12] Combined with the subsequently realized current account balances and growth rates, these forecasts yield time series data for the news shown in the explanatory variables. Because these forecasts are prepared through multilateral intergovernmental consultation, they are broadly representative of informed opinion about growth and current account balances.

Consider next the unanticipated depreciation, $\dot{e}' - (i - i^*)$, for the nominal effective exchange rate of the dollar (defined in table 2.1). The monthly series is shown in figure 2.4, together with the series for anticipated depreciation given by $i - i^*$ (both expressed as annual percentage rates). As the figure clearly illustrates, unanticipated changes constitute nearly all the actual variation in exchange rates.

Regression equations explaining unanticipated depreciation of the dollar against a trade-weighted mixture of other currencies are shown in table 2.3. Equation 3-1 explains the unanticipated depreciation of the dollar by the current account and cyclical errors. The cyclical errors for the United States and five foreign countries are constrained to be of equal and opposite sign in this equation. The equation accounts for much of

PERCENTAGE POINTS

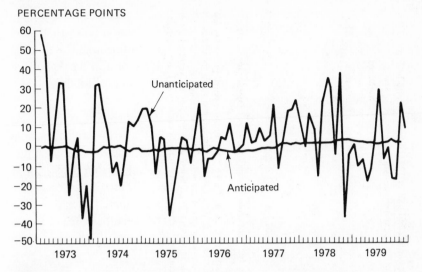

Figure 2.4
Anticipated and unanticipated depreciation of the dollar, February 1973–January 1980. Sources: Exchange rate—same as table 2.1: and interest rates—same as table 2.2. The data are monthly, expressed at annual percentage rates. The unanticipated depreciation of the dollar is the difference between actual depreciation of the dollar and anticipated depreciation. The exchange rate is the nominal effective exchange rate described in table 2.1, note a. Anticipated depreciation is measured by short-term interest differentials between the United States and a trade-weighted average of the interest rates of five foreign countries. The weights equal those used in calculating the exchange rate.

the unanticipated depreciation, and evidence of serial correlation does not appear in the errors. The coefficients do have the expected signs. The coefficient on the current account news is significant. An unanticipated current account surplus in the United States of $1 billion is worth half a percent of appreciation. The coefficient on the cyclical forecast error indicates that unanticipated growth leads to depreciation. But it is not significantly different from zero. Perhaps this reflects the fiscal expansion phenomenon discussed.

Equations 3-2 and 3-3 include unanticipated changes in interest rates. Ideally the term structure of interest rates should be used to measure innovations; but here, because of the complexity of deriving such series, residuals from an autoregression of the short-term interest differential have been used. The equations show that unanticipated increases in short-term interest differentials appear with a positive coefficient that is significant. The interest differential may reflect a causal role for unanticipated

Table 2.3
Equations explaining unanticipated depreciation of the nominal effective exchange rate of the dollar, second half of 1973 through second half of 1979[a]

Equation	Independent variable					Summary statistic			
	Constant	CAE	CYC	CYC*	INN	R^2	Durbin-Watson	Standard error of estimate	Rho
3-1	3.5 (1.88)	−0.49 (−2.62)	1.86 (1.35)	−1.86	—	0.41	2.13	6.2	—
3-2	2.7 (1.69)	−0.31 (−1.82)	0.47 (0.33)	−0.78 (0.57)	13.33 (1.99)	0.63	2.03	5.5	−0.24
3-3	3.1 (2.47)	−0.27 (−2.19)	—	—	13.79 (2.53)	0.61	2.13	5.1	−0.28

Sources: Forecast and actual current account balances and real output growth—Organisation for Economic Co-operation and Development, OECD Economic Outlook, various issues; exchange rate—same as table 2.1, and interest rates—same as table 2.2.
a. The dependent variable, unanticipated depreciation of the dollar, is described in figure 2.4 caption. CYC and CYC* are unanticipated growth in real output of, respectively, the United States and a trade-weighted average of the five foreign countries in table 2.1. Unanticipated growth is the difference between the OECD's six-month forecast and realized growth. The data are seasonally adjusted annual rates of growth. CAE is the forecast error for US current account balances, using the OECD's forecasts. The data are measured in billions of dollars, seasonally adjusted. INN denotes the residuals from an autoregression of short-term interest differentials between the United States and a trade-weighted average of five foreign countries. Trade-weighted variables use the weights in table 2.1, note a. The numbers in parentheses are t-statistics.

Table 2.4
Equations explaining unanticipated depreciation of the dollar-yen and dollar-mark exchange rates, second half of 1973 through second half of 1979[a]

Country and equation	Independent variable						Summary statistic			
	Constant	CAE	CYC	CYC*	INN	RES	R^2	Durbin-Watson	Standard error of estimate	Rho
Japan										
4-1	-3.81 (-0.45)	1.35 (4.21)	-2.63 (-4.03)	1.27 (1.13)	-	-	0.73	2.11	8.7	0.75
4-2	0.60 (0.27)	1.40 (5.70)	-1.71 (-2.12)	1.71	13.0 (2.03)	-	0.82	2.09	8.0	-
4-3	-0.29 (-0.08)	1.39 (4.43)	-2.45 (-2.81)	2.45	-	-2.14 (-0.73)	0.71	1.85	9.1	0.32
Germany										
4-4	2.29 (1.22)	1.38 (1.93)	-0.53 (-0.76)	-	26.1 (3.51)	-	0.62	2.22	7.6	-0.40
4-5	1.37 (0.42)	1.01 (1.50)	-	-	13.0 (1.36)	-	0.32	2.09	10.2	-
4-6	1.80 (0.51)	1.10 (1.48)	-	-	-	-0.52 (-0.13)	0.19	2.01	11.1	-

Sources: Exchange rates and interest rates—same as table 2.2; and forecast and actual current account balances and real output growth—same as table 2.3.
a. CAE and CYC represent forecast errors for current account balances and real output growth in Japan or Germany. In the equations for both countries CYC* represents forecast errors for real output growth in the OECD countries. INN denotes the residuals from an autoregression of the US-Japanese or US-German short-term interest rate differential. RES denotes the residuals from a regression of US-Japanese or US-German short-term interest differentials on differentials between the United States and the respective country on long-term and short-term interest rates, unemployment rates, and inflation rates, with all explanatory variables lagged one period. CYC and CYC* are seasonally adjusted annual rates of growth; and CAE is seasonally adjusted, in billions of dollars. In equations 4-2 and 4-3 the coefficients of cyclical errors are constrained to be equal and opposite in sign. The numbers in parentheses are t-statistics.

changes in the term structure, inflation news, or cyclical effects as suggested by a comparison of equations 3-1 and 3-2 in table 2.3.

Table 2.4 presents similar equations for the dollar-mark and dollar-yen exchange rates. Consider first the case of Japan. Equation 4-1 shows quite strikingly the role of current account errors and cyclical errors. An unanticipated surplus in the Japanese current account leads to dollar depreciation or yen appreciation. A cyclical expansion in Japan induces a yen depreciation. Both the coefficients of CAE and CYC are significantly different from zero. The equation explains a large portion of the unanticipated depreciation. Unlike equation 3-3 for the United States in table 2.3, the constant terms are not significantly different from zero.

Equations 4-2 and 4-3 include interest rate news. The innovations in equation 4-2 are from an autoregression of the interest differential. In equation 4-3 the interest variable is residuals from an interest differential equation. The roles of the two interest rate innovations are quite different. The former have a significant positive coefficient reducing the magnitude and significance of the cyclical effects; the latter, which are more nearly orthogonal to cyclical effects, appear with a negative and insignificant coefficient. The same pattern is observed in the equations for Germany.

Unlike the dollar-yen exchange rate, unanticipated movements in the dollar-mark rate are not dominated by news about cyclical or current account events. Unanticipated improvements in the current account of Germany leads to a dollar depreciation, but the coefficient on the current account and cyclical innovations variables are not significantly different from zero. Innovations from an autoregression of interest differentials do play a part in explaining exchange rate movements in equation 4-4. But in 4-6 the residuals from a reaction function for the interest differential, which is discussed below, turn out to be insignificant. I argue there that portfolio shifts may well be the explanation for these results.

The empirical analysis confirms that unanticipated real and financial disturbances bring about unexpected movements in the exchange rate. To that extent, the preceding theory is confirmed. Whether the size of exchange rate movements stands in reasonable relation to the disturbance remains an open question. Clearly the answer depends not only on the structural parameters, including trade elasticities, but also on the expected persistence of the disturbance. The more persistent the disturbance, other things being equal, the larger the required change in the real exchange rate.

2.1.4 Portfolio Diversification and the Deutsche Mark Shortage

The analysis so far has largely excluded portfolio balance and its implications for exchange rates. The models considered share the assumption of perfect substitutability of home and foreign securities on a depreciation-adjusted basis, thus leaving no room for shifts in wealth or relative asset supplies to affect the balance in asset markets. I now depart from this assumption to see what insights a broader treatment of portfolio choice will yield.

A starting point is the hypothesis that money demand depends not only on income, the conventional transactions variable, but also on wealth. Shifts in wealth induced by current account imbalances create monetary imbalances leading to adjustments in long-run price level expectations and thus to exchange rate movements. This effect does not presuppose imperfect asset substitutability, although it is entirely compatible with it. With perfect mobility of capital, this specification of money demand implies that the real money demand of a country with a surplus rises while it falls abroad. The relative price level of the country with a surplus declines and, therefore, exchange rates for given terms of trade tend to appreciate.[14]

The results, of course, follow from a strong assumption about distribution effects. Monies are treated as nontraded assets, the demand for which is affected by an international redistribution of wealth. In the absence of an empirically significant wealth effect on money demand, this theory probably does not go very far in explaining exchange rates.

An alternative and more persuasive role for portfolio effects arises in the context of imperfect asset substitutability. With uncertain real returns, portfolio diversification makes assets imperfect substitutes and gives rise to determinate demands for the respective securities and to real yield differentials or a risk premium.[15]

The portfolio model provides an explanation of the unanticipated mark appreciation that is only poorly accounted for by the current account and cyclical innovations. I argue that the system of flexible exchange rates and the macroeconomic policies and disturbances have created an incentive for portfolio diversification, that the mark would occupy a large share in an efficiently diversified portfolio, and that the resulting portfolio shifts or capital flows account for some of the unanticipated appreciation.

Table 2.5 shows the realized means and variances of the *real* returns on assets denominated in different currencies. The real yield in each instance is the nominal short-term interest rate plus the depreciation of the dollar relative to the particular currency, thus creating dollar returns,

Table 2.5
Means, variances, and covariances of real returns in four major industrial countries, 1973:3–1979:2 and subperiod[a] (percentage points)

Statistic	1973:3–1979:2				1976:1–1979:2			
	United States	Germany	Japan	United Kingdom	United States	Germany	Japan	United Kingdom
Mean	−2.48	0.55	0.94	−0.98	−3.54	3.74	4.31	2.49
Variance or covariance								
United States	139.7	–	–	–	49.7	–	–	–
Germany	−26.9	98.3	–	–	−9.9	48.8	–	–
Japan	34.6	36.5	320.3	–	−55.8	−32.6	350.1	–
United Kingdom	2.7	22.1	−16.9	214.0	−1.7	−11.4	−97.2	336.3

Sources: Interest rates and exchange rates—same as table 2.2; and price index for manufactures in world trade—United Nations, *Monthly Bulletin of Statistics*, various issues.

a. Real returns are calculated as the nominal short-term interest rate, plus the depreciation of the dollar relative to the country's currency, minus the rate of inflation of the price index of manufactures in world trade. The data are quarterly averages.

less the rate of inflation of the dollar price index of manufactures in world trade. The real return data thus are comparable and appropriate for an investor that does not have a particular local habitat.

Concentrating on the 1976/79 period, note that both the mark and the dollar are relatively stable (low-variance) assets and that their returns are negatively correlated. The dollar has a negative mean return, while the mark has a positive one.

In principle, an efficiently diversified portfolio is a wide-ranging one, including bonds, amusement parks, old-age homes, and so on. In practice, investors develop a narrow portfolio, highly concentrated in home securities with a small range of international claims. Suppose, to make a point, that only dollars and marks are part of the portfolio of international assets. What would be their respective shares? The relevant model of utility-maximizing portfolio diversification shows that the share of mark assets, using the distribution of returns of table 2.5, is 56 percent. This corresponds to a 50 percent share of bonds denominated in makrs in the minimum-variance portfolio plus a 6 percent share in a speculative mark position.[16] The speculative position in marks, motivated by the differential in mean real yields, is quite small because of the large variance of the nominal rate of depreciation that makes speculation risky. The share in the minimum variance portfolio is substantial, though, because the mark is an attractive asset—it has a relatively low variance of the real yield and a negative covariance with the dollar. The exercise, while merely an illustration, does suggest that the mark has characteristics that should make it play a large role in portfolios, and indeed, an even greater role as an international asset than was the case in the 1960s or early 1970s.

The argument may overstate the case in a number of ways. First, the realized returns may not equal the return distribution that investors anticipate. This is even more true if much of the differential in mean real returns reflects unanticipated mark appreciation.[17] Second, other currencies may enter the portfolio, some with features more attractive than those of the mark. Third, international differences in consumption patterns may bias the portfolio shares away from those implied by the return distribution of table 2.5. Each of these arguments has some force, although none of them necessarily suggests a lower mark share in an international portfolio.[18]

The main point is simply that the transition to flexible rates has quite decisively changed the structure of real returns confronting international investors—central banks, firms, or households. With the new return structure, and by virtue of size, the mark should occupy a large share of portfolios, much larger than would have been expected in 1970–1973, before the period of flexible exchange rates. Investors can be expected to make a gradual transition to the new diversification pattern. But, as the poorly understood process of substitution from M_1 to negotiable-orders-of-withdrawal (NOW) accounts and money market funds in the United States suggests, little is known about the dynamics of portfolio adjustment.

As the substitution process takes place, the mark will tend to appreciate unless there is an offsetting increase in the relative supply of assets denominated in marks. Such an increase could be created through deficit finance, arising from sterilized exchange rate intervention, or take the form of Carter bonds (bonds issued by the US government denominated in marks). In fact, as I show below, there has been a large increase in the relative supply of these assets because of larger German deficits. Sterilized intervention has made up a further part of the increased demand. The remainder has been met by appreciation of the mark, revaluing the share of marks already existing in international portfolios.

A first implication of the portfolio model then is to help identify a shortage of marks. The adjustment process to the new role of the mark as an international asset has brought about a curious reversal of the old intermediation view of the US balance of payments. Germany has been showing a sustained short-term capital account surplus with a direct investment and portfolio investment deficit. Germany displays the pattern typical of the United States when the dollar took an increasing role in international portfolios after the restoration of currency convertibility in the late 1950s.

2.1.5 Relative Asset Supplies, Wealth, and Exchange Rates

I now explore the portfolio model further to see whether there are implications that reinforce or put in question the conjecture discussed above, that for given asset supplies and wealth the structure of real returns implies a shift in portfolios toward assets denominated in marks, thus explaining the persistent appreciation of the mark.

The portfolio-diversification model implies a relation between the nominal interest differential, the expected rate of depreciation, and the risk premium R:

$$\dot{e} = i - i^* + R\left(\frac{EV^*}{V + EV^*}, \frac{W^*}{W + W^*}\right), \tag{6}$$

where

E = level of domestic currency price of foreign exchange,
W = level of wealth,
V = supply of nominal debt.

The risk premium in equation (6) is an increasing function of the relative supply of assets denominated in foreign currency, $EV^*/(V + EV^*)$, and a decreasing function of foreign relative wealth.[19] What matters for the risk premium are the relative supplies of *outside* bonds (net assets of the private sector) denominated in the two currencies, independently of the issuing source.[20] Risk is here a question of the variability of real returns due to uncertain inflation and exchange rate depreciation, not a question of default. Note also that the relative wealth term will give rise to a risk premium only to the extent that there are differences in consumption patterns *and* that there is variability in the *real* exchange rate.

Suppose now that interest rates and anticipated rates of depreciation are given, perhaps determined by, the monetary sector of the more general model. The risk-premium model has implications for the relations among wealth, asset supplies, and the exchange rate. In particular, the model implies that an increase in foreign relative wealth, say arising through a cumulative foreign current account surplus, will bring a relative increase in the demand for securities denominated in foreign currency. The resulting disequilibrium in the asset market is resolved by an appreciation of the foreign currency that revalues existing stocks of securities denominated in foreign currency. This must be an unanticipated wealth redistribution; otherwise, speculators would have anticipated the jump in the exchange rate.

Unanticipated changes in the relative supplies of securities likewise affect the exchange rate. For example, an unanticipated fiscal deficit that expands the supply of bonds denominated in foreign currency leads to a depreciation of the foreign currency, which restores portfolio balance at unchanged yields. (In general, exchange rates and asset yields are jointly determined.)

The risk-premium model has served as the basis for extensive research attempting to explain exchange rate movements by changes in relative wealth (using changes in net foreign assets as a proxy) and in relative asset supplies.[21]

The model has had mixed results in empirical tests, largely because of the difficulty in developing measures of relative nominal outside assets and relative nominal wealth. Part of the problem may also have been the use of actual versus unanticipated variables. Given these difficulties, the existing results must be considered very tentative. Even so, the risk-

Table 2.6
Current account balances and net borrowing in Germany, and ratios of German to US debt, 1973–1979 (billions of deutsche marks, except as noted)

Item	1973	1974	1975	1976	1977	1978	1979
Current account balance	12.3	25.5	8.5	8.6	9.8	17.6	−9.0
Net government borrowing	6.1	10.8	36.4	20.0	21.7	27.4	25.1
Ratio of German to US government debt (percent)							
Measured in dollars	6.7	8.5	9.5	10.7	12.7	15.7	17.8
Measured in respective currencies	18.0	20.5	24.8	25.4	26.6	28.7	30.8

Sources: Government debt and borrowing—International Monetary Fund, *International Financial Statistics*, vol. 33 (May 1980), series ae, series 84 and 88, and series 88, pp. 164, 166 and 404, respectively; and current account balances—Deutsche Bundesbank, *Monthly Report of the Deutsche Bundesbank*, vol. 32 (March 1980), p. 70.

premium model is of interest because it offers, through the wealth channel, a role for the current account to affect exchange rates. At the same time, this model introduces a potential link between deficit finance and exchange rates through the relative supply of assets. It thus supplements the extended Mundell-Fleming model and offers alternative channels through which current account and fiscal innovations can affect the exchange rate. Indeed, the equations reported in tables 2.3 and 2.4 may well reflect in part the effects of the risk-premium model.

2.1.6 Mark Appreciation
The risk-premium model may help explain the mark appreciation of recent years. In table 2.6, I report the German current account balance, net public sector borrowing, and the ratio of German to US debt (valued both in dollars and in the respective currencies). The first point to note is that since 1975 the current account has been entirely dominated by the fiscal deficit. The demand for mark assets created by the redistribution of wealth toward Germany through the current account must have been met quite amply by the deficit finance. The German debt has increased much more rapidly than that of the United States. Thus if a risk-premium view were taken, one would expect the mark to show a cumulative depreciation, not an appreciation.

The risk-permium model suggests that a demand shift toward assets denominated in marks has dominated the downward pressure on the exchange rate arising from the combination of changes in relative wealth and the relative supplies of mark assets. Given the attempt to attain optimal diversification, the mark was appreciating because of an insufficient creation of mark assets.[22]

The risk-premium model has one further implication that has relevance for the equations in tables 2.3 and 2.4. The existence of a risk premium implies that not all the difference between interest differentials and actual depreciation is unanticipated; part corresponds to the risk premium and only the residual represents news. Thus equation (4) becomes

$$\dot{e}' - (i - i^*) = (\dot{e}' - \dot{e}) + R$$

$$= news + risk\ premium. \tag{7}$$

The risk premium accordingly can account for a significant constant or for serial correlation in the equations above.[23]

2.2 The Flexible Exchange Rate System

I now examine some key features of the system of flexible exchange rates to form a judgment about its shortcomings and the possibilities for reform. Has the system been critically defective? In this section I investigate some firmly established working characteristics of the system, including intervention, interest rate policies, current account adjustment, and current account financing. The issues are whether intervention policies have been designed to frustrate real exchange rate adjustment; whether interest rate policies were significantly restricted by actual or potential exchange rate developments; and finally, whether current account imbalances have been sustained and officially funded rather than adjusted and financed through capital flows.[24]

I show that the capital mobility problem is summarized by the observation that when the current account gets bad the capital account gets worse. The reason is that interest rate policies are oriented toward internal balance, which aggravates the exchange rate consequences of cyclically unsynchronized movements in economic activity in the world economy.

2.2.1 Official Intervention
The reported changes in official reserve holdings have increased sharply during the 1970s. Have intervention policies had systematically stabilizing characteristics?

Figure 2.5 shows an adjusted series for changes in US net liabilities to foreign official reserve agencies. The figure indicates sizable swings in intervention, which were larger than the swings in the US current account. I present equations on the determinates of intervention in table 2.7.

BILLIONS OF DOLLARS

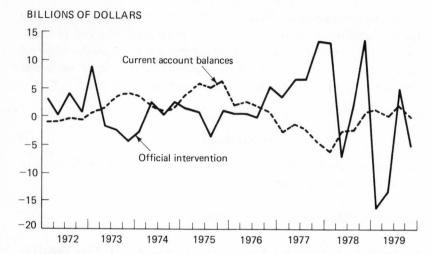

Figure 2.5
Current account balances and official intervention in the United States, 1972: 1–
1979: 4. The official intervention series is the change in official reserve holdings,
adjusted to exclude the accrual of interest earnings. Interest earnings were
estimated as the market yield on US three-month Treasury bills times the lagged
stock of official reserve holdings. The stock of reserve holdings was cumulated
from its level of $63.2 billion in 1972: 4, using the series on changes in official
reserve holdings. Sources: Current account balances and changes in official
reserve holdings—*Survey of Current Business*, vol. 59 (June 1979), pp. 38–41,
lines 38, 57, 61, and 79; and US Treasury bill rate—Board of Governors of the
Federal Reserve System.

Given the size of reserve holdings and the level of nominal interest rates,
much of the reported increase reflects the accrual of interest earnings
rather than active market intervention. I thus use as a dependent variable
an adjusted series that subtracts from changes in reserves an amount
equal to the US Treasury bill rate times the lagged stock of reserves.
This series is measured as a fraction of lagged reserves. Equations 7-1
and 7-2 use unanticipated depreciation rates to explain US net liabilities
to foreign official holders. With a policy of 'leaning against the wind,"
foreign central banks would acquire dollars through intervention whenever the dollar showed unanticipated depreciation. The equations strongly
support that view, although only a small fraction of the variance is
explained.

Equation 7-2 suggests that unanticipated depreciation of 1.0 percentage
points (at an annual rate) leads to a cumulative intervention of 0.4
percent of foreign net claims on the United States, which at current levels

Table 2.7
Estimates of the determinants of intervention in Germany, Japan, and major industrial countries, 1973:3–1979:4[a]

Country and equation	Independent variable					Summary statistic			
	Constant	$\dot{e}_u$	$\dot{e}_u(-1)$	U	$\dot{p}$	R^2	Durbin-Watson	Standard error of estimate	Rho
Major industrial countries									
7-1	1.01 (103.8)	0.003 (3.25)	—	—	—	0.31	2.01	0.05	—
7-2	1.00 (104.8)	0.003 (3.22)	0.001 (1.68)	—	—	0.38	1.81	0.05	—
Germany									
7-3	0.96 (22.4)	0.003 (3.99)	—	0.018 (1.88)	−0.007 (−1.89)	0.54	2.00	0.06	−0.15
Japan									
7-4	0.97 (50.5)	0.004 (4.41)	—	—	—	0.44	1.94	0.10	—

Sources: US official intervention—same as figure 2.5; German and Japanese official intervention—International Monetary Fund, *International Financial Statistics*, various issues, series 1d.d; US Treasury bill rate—same as figure 2.5; unanticipated depreciation of the dollar—same as figure 2.3 for the United States, and table 2.4 for Germany and Japan; prices—same as figure 2.2; and German unemployment—Organisation for Economic Co-operation and Development, *Main Economic Indicators*, various issues.

a. The dependent variable is the change in reserves net of interest earnings as a fraction of the lagged stock of reserves. Interest earnings are estimated as the market yield on US three-month Treasury bills times the lagged stock of reserves. In equations 7-1 and 7-2, $\dot{e}_u$ is the unanticipated depreciation of the nominal effective exchange rate of the dollar described in table 2.1, note a. In equations 7-3 and 7-4 it is the unanticipated depreciation of the dollar-mark and the dollar-yen exchange rates, respectively. The symbols U and $\dot{p}$ denote unemployment rates and inflation rates. The major industrial countries are Canada, France, Germany, Japan, and the United Kingdom. The numbers in parentheses are *t*-statistics.

of foreign net reserve holdings is about $600 million. The constant term of 1.0 suggests that the absolute size of intervention is growing along with nominal reserve holdings.

Equation 7-3 considers German intervention policy. There is more evidence of leaning against the wind. Unanticipated depreciation of 1 percentage point, at an annual rate, leads to an intervention at 1979 reserve levels of about $140 million. Interestingly, macroeconomic conditions affect the level of German intervention. A high rate of unemployment increases the rate of intervention, while high inflation reduces intervention. With more unemployment, authorities use intervention to slow down real dollar depreciation to achieve a "beggar-my-neighbor" effect. With faster inflation, unanticipated dollar depreciation is opposed less strongly in order to achieve a reduction in inflationary pressure or to avoid imported inflation. The coefficients on the cyclical variables suggest a policy that goes significantly beyond leaning against the wind.[25] I found no evidence of real exchange rate targets.

Equations of the form reported in table 2.7, which use unanticipated depreciation to explain reserves adjusted for interest earnings, are more successful than actual reserve changes and actual depreciation. This can be interpreted to mean that nominal interest payments roughly maintain the stock of real reserves in the face of dollar depreciation. Unanticipated depreciation as the explanatory variable is compatible with a PPP evolution of nominal exchange rates and with an adjustment of real exchange rates that is dampened, but not offset, by intervention.

There also is strong evidence of leaning against the wind in the equations for Japan. Unanticipated dollar depreciation again appears as the relevant determinant. The size of the reaction coefficient is similar to those reported for Germany and for the rest of the world. For Japan, however, there is no evidence of cyclical influences on intervention policy.

The intervention equations support the view that monetary authorities largely aimed their operations at smoothing unanticipated movements in the exchange rate. For Germany, the presence of cyclical variables also suggests an element of beggar-my-neighbor policy in exchange intervention.

2.2.2 Interest Rate Policies
The sensitivity of exchange rates to monetary policy interferes with the ability of monetary policy to achieve a noninflationary real expansion. Lowering interest rates leads to exchange rate depreciation and faster

Table 2.8
Estimates of the determinants of the German-US and the Japanese-US interest rate differentials, 1973:2–1979:4[a]

Country and equation	Independent variable						Summary statistic			Rho[b]	
	Constant	$\dot{p}^* - \dot{p}$	U^*	U	$(i^* - i)_{-1}$	$\dot{e}_u$	R^2	Durbin-Watson	Standard error of estimate	(1)	(2)
Germany-US											
8-1	1.86 (1.4)	0.20 (2.29)	−0.97 (−2.24)	0.45 (1.2)	0.57 (3.91)	—	0.82	1.89	1.3	—	—
Japan-US											
8-2	−0.58 (−0.2)	0.14 (3.97)	−5.15 (−3.84)	2.45 (6.4)	—	—	0.73	1.71	1.1	0.57	—
8-3	1.72 (1.0)	0.12 (3.42)	−6.42 (−6.71)	2.50 (10.4)	—	0.03 (3.23)	0.90	1.80	0.9	0.27	—
8-4	1.84 (1.5)	0.09 (2.54)	−3.51 (−3.39)	1.14 (2.9)	0.53 (4.01)	—	0.96	2.03	1.0	0.07	0.53

Sources: Short-term interest rates—same as table 2.2; prices—same as figure 2.2; unanticipated depreciation—same as table 2.4; and unemployment rates—same as table 2.7.

a. The dependent variable is $i^* - i$, the short-term interest rate differential between the two countries; $\dot{p}^* - \dot{p}$ is the inflation differential; U is the unemployment rate; and $\dot{e}_u$ is unanticipated depreciation of the dollar. An asterisk denotes a variable for a foreign country. The numbers in parentheses are t-statistics.

b. First- and second-order autocorrelation corrections, respectively.

inflation through rising import prices. Exchange rate sensitivity thus steepens the Phillips curve when monetary policy is used to affect real output. It is not possible to determine whether the worsened trade-off has significantly reduced the use of monetary policy as an instrument. What can be investigated is whether interest rates have shown the cyclical pattern associated with domestic stabilization, declining during a recession and increasing with inflation. One can also ask whether exchange rate depreciation exerted a significant effect on interest rate policy.

Table 2.8 reports regression equations for the German-US and Japanese-US differential in short-term interest rates. The differential is used on the assumption that international cyclical movements have not been closely synchronized. The German-US differential in nominal interest rates is explained by the current inflation differential, unemployment in the respective countries, and the lagged nominal interest rate differential. Higher inflation differentials are reflected in a higher nominal interest differential. An increase of 1 percentage point in the German unemployment rate leads to a decline of about 2 percentage points in the nominal interest differential. It cannot be established that the flexible rate system did not weaken the use of countercyclical monetary policy. But the evidence is that relative interest rates continued to have a clearly cyclical pattern.

In the German-US case, I found no evidence for either monetary growth targets, intervention, or exchange depreciation as a significant influence on interest differentials.[26]

Equations 8-2–8-4, explaining the Japanese-US interest rate differential, provide more evidence of a cyclically stabilizing pattern of nominal interest rates. Higher inflation differentials lead to higher nominal yield differentials. Higher unemployment in Japan reduces the relative Japanese interest rate, while higher unemployment in the United States raises it.

Unlike the German-US case, the equations for Japan show high serial correlation of errors and are reported with rho corrections. Unanticipated depreciation is introduced in equation 8-3 and shows a significant coefficient but with the wrong sign—higher dollar depreciation leads to an increased spread in favor of Japan. The variable may represent joint errors in the interest and exchange rate equations; or it may merely pick up lagged adjustment effects, as equation 8-4 suggests.

From the interest rate evidence it seems apparent that, whatever limitations on monetary policy may exist, interest spreads internationally have had the cyclical pattern called for by stabilization objectives. To that extent, at least, there is no clear demonstration that the flexible exchange

Table 2.9
Current account balances as a percent of GNP for four industrial countries, 1960–1973 and 1973–1979 (percentage points or correlation)

| | Statistic | | |
Period and country	Mean	Standard deviation	Serial correlation
1960–1973			
United States	0.4	0.4	0.58
Germany	0.7	0.9	0.41
Japan	0.5	1.2	0.39
United Kingdom[a]	0.1	1.1	0.37
1973–1979			
United States	0.1	0.6	0.28
Germany	1.0	0.9	−0.11
Japan	0.5	0.9	0.61
United Kingdom[a]	−0.9	1.8	0.62

Source: Organisation for Economic Co-operation and Development.
a. The output measure is gross domestic product.

rate system has limited the use of instruments. Furthermore, there is no evidence that interest rates have been systematically affected by intervention or exchange rate targets.

2.2.3 Current Account Adjustment and Capital Flows

The next question is whether the flexible exchange rate period has been one of persistent and large current account imbalances with exchange rate movements exerting relatively little impact to restore balance. Table 2.9 shows means, standard deviations, and serial correlation of current account for four major industrial countries. The 1960–1973 period of fixed exchange rates is compared with that of flexible exchange rates, 1973–1979. No substantial change in current account behavior is apparent. Imbalances did not become more persistent, and, in particular, the United States did not have a persistent deficit.

The surprise of the last few years, if anything, is the fact that current account imbalances are not at all the "sticky mass" that Keynes thought they were. Instead, the large effect of variations on current accounts and the responsiveness of trade flows and direct investment to real exchange rates lead to a view of great flexibility in all important dimensions of the balance of payments.

How have current account imbalances been financed? In particular, to what extent have the large swings in current accounts been financed by

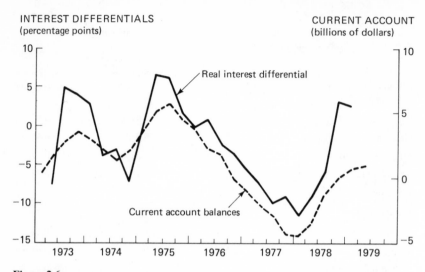

INTEREST DIFFERENTIALS
(percentage points)

CURRENT ACCOUNT
(billions of dollars)

Figure 2.6
Current account balances and real interest differentials for the United States,
1973: 1–1979: 4. The data are three-quarter centered moving averages. The real
interest differential is the difference between the real interest rate for the United
States and a trade-weighted average of five foreign countries, using the weights in
table 2.1, note a. Real interest rates are calculated as described in table 2.5, note a.
Sources: Current account balances—same as figure 2.5; real interest differentials
—same as table 2.5.

stabilizing private capital flows? As figure 2.5 shows, exchange market
intervention in the dollar, both transitory and cumulative, has been
subtantial compared to current account imbalances, frequently exceeding
the latter by a large margin. In fact, rather than financing those imbalances, net capital flows add to them. Deficits are accompanied by net
capital outflows and surpluses by net inflows. In 1977 and 1978, for
example, the United States ran current account deficits of about $14
billion, while the holdings of foreign official reserve agencies increased
by $35 billion and $32 billion, respectively. In net terms the foreign
private sector's claims on the United States were reduced at a rate of
more than twice as great as the US deficit. In 1979, in turn, the US current
account was nearly balanced; central bank intervention, this time in
support of foreign currencies, amounted to nearly $16 billion.

It appears that interest rate policy, adjusted for depreciation, was not
at all geared toward financing current account imbalances and stabilizing
exchange rates. On the contrary, the independent pursuit of interest rate
policy, together with current account surprises, has given rise to exchange

rate instability, capital flows, and intervention. This has led to a clear positive relation between the US current account and the return on US assets, which is illustrated in figure 2.6. When the United States was in deficit, the return on dollar assets, adjusted for depreciation, was negative. Conversely, when the United States showed a surplus, the return differential, adjusted for depreciation, was positive.

A coherent story emerges from combining the evidence in figure 2.6 with that for intervention, exchange rate determination, and portfolio selection. Current account surprises give rise to unanticipated fluctuations in the exchange rate. There is no offset through interest rate policy and, accordingly, real interest differentials worsen for the deficit country. The unanticipated depreciation leads central banks to intervene in support of the depreciating currency, and the adverse depreciation-adjusted interest differential leads portfolio holders to shift from the depreciating currency.

Central bank intervention provides the umbrella for portfolio holders to shift their portfolios in response to anticipated interest differentials. Sterilization of the intervention implies that central banks can largely pursue their interest rate policy, albeit at the cost of larger and more dramatic intervention operations.

2.3 Exchange Rate Flexibility and the Capital Mobility Problem

The preceding review of theory and empirical evidence indicates the fundamental problems that confront the design of an exchange rate and payments system. The system must meet conflicting needs. On the one hand, it should have flexible real exchange rates to provide for adjustment of current account imbalances through channels besides deflation or protection. On the other hand, short-term disturbances in the real sector should be largely accommodated at unchanging real exchange rates so that unnecessary variability will not be introduced in the allocation of resources. This accommodation requires a mechanism that ensures the financing of current account imbalances, cyclical or otherwise, through capital flows. Furthermore, financial disturbances should be substantially accommodated through asset management—trading one debt for another —and should not affect real activity or the real exchange rate. This requires institutional arrangements that make possible large-scale sterilized intervention or the issuance of debt denominated in foreign currency.

In the 1960s governments opted for an exchange rate regime with fixed nominal exchange rates, full accommodation of financial disturbances through pegging of exchange rates, and a lack of effective medium-term adjustment in the real exchange rate. When the dollar became overvalued under this regime, it led to the collapse of the system of fixed exchange rates and has left observers with the impression that a flexible real exchange rate is an essential part of a viable exchange and payments system. The large disparity of current inflation rates among countries and the imprecision in estimating their respective underlying trend rates of inflation make it difficult to formulate viable rules for pegging nominal rates, even if there could be agreement on the appropriate real exchange rate.

Once it is accepted that the medium-term real exchange rate should be flexible and that tight pegging of nominal rates is infeasible, the range of options is reduced to a form of floating rates. There does remain, however, a dimension of choice that may add to the stability of the macroeconomy and that concerns the treatment of capital flows. Should capital be free to move in response to expected yields and risks, or should it be immobilized? James Tobin has summarized one main concern about complete freedom of capital movements: "Under either exchange rate regime the currency exchanges transmit disturbances originating in international financial markets. National economies and national governments are not capable of adjusting to massive movements of funds across the foreign exchanges, without real hardship and without significant sacrifice of the objectives of national economic policy with respect to employment, output, and inflation."[27]

Tobin proposes "to throw some sand in the wheels of our excessively efficient international money markets."[28] Specifically, he advocates placing an internationally agreed, uniform, proportional tax on all spot conversions of one currency into another. The tax would reduce the round trip return on international portfolio shifts, and thereby open up an interest spread that would leave monetary authorities more freedom. The proposal would virtually eliminate short-term capital flows and allow the basic balance, in conjunction with intervention, to determine the exchange rate. Relieved of the need to cope with massive short-term capital flows, interest rate policy would be freer to address domestic objectives, and exchange rates would presumably be more stable.

The Tobin tax proposal presumes that the failure of private short-term capital flows to finance current accounts adds to exchange market instability and to the need to intervene. Although capital flows have largely failed to play a financing role, they have forced major changes in real exchange rates whenever government policies failed to aim for cyclical coordination and a dampening of external imbalances. Thus capital flows definitely promoted current account adjustment, although possibly exaggerating exchange rate instability.

It is not certain in what way the Tobin tax would work to stabilize exchange rates. There would be less incentive to move capital internationally in response to small yield differentials; but then the basic balance and the extent of central bank intervention would govern the exchange rate. Rather than leaning against the wind, central banks would have to take a view of exchange rates and become rate setters. Would they want to maintain nominal exchange rates or would they adjust real exchange rates in response to current account imbalances?

There is a second, and perhaps more serious, objection to the proposal. Suppose a country does not have the reserves to finance a transitory current account imbalance and thus wishes to use interest rate policy to attract capital. Clearly such a country would now have to increase interest rates by more than it would in the absence of the tax. The country would suffer the burden of financing the deficit and the Tobin tax. There is, of course, an alternative. The country could bring about a sufficiently large depreciation that the expectation of future depreciation would be reduced or eliminated; then with unchanged interest rates there would be a sufficient expected yield differential to attract capital inflows. But again, the country would be paying for the "sand in the wheels."[29]

The welfare economics of the Tobin proposal is not without question. From the standpoint of utility maximization, the choice of an optimal portfolio ranks on a par with the ability to choose one's preferred diet. To the extent that the portfolio cannot be efficiently diversified solely from home securities—and this would surely be the case for small countries—the tax is as disturbing an intervention as a tariff.

Once the principle of free capital flows is accepted, there remains the issue of how to live with them. Capital flows should operate in a stabilizing manner to finance transitory current account imbalances while allowing real exchange rate changes to cope with medium-term adjustment in the current account balance. It is, in fact, not possible to identify what part of a current account balance it is appropriate to finance and what part requires adjustment. The proper policy rule for stabilizing real exchange rates when confronted with short-term and financial disturbances, without affecting the medium-term adjustment of real rates, is the following: A country with a growing current account deficit (particularly one that occurs in the process of unsynchronized cyclical movements) would both raise its real interest rate and intervene by leaning against the wind. The analysis of the present paper shows that only half the rule has, in fact, been pursued: intervention policy has leaned against the wind, but interest rate policy has been the opposite of what is recommended here.

Notes

1. See the collection of papers in *Scandinavian Journal of Economics*, vol. 78, no. 2 (1976), pp. 133–412; the papers collected in Frenkel and Johnson, eds. (1978), Bilson (1978), and Frenkel (1980), (1979).

2. Throughout the paper an asterisk denotes a foreign variable.

3. The comparison here is based on consumer prices; it holds, in general, for other price indexes also.

4. Throughout the remainder of this paper the nominal effective exchange rate is this trade-weighted index of the five foreign countries of table 2.1, rather than the International Monetary Fund's published multilateral trade-weighted index.

5. For further discussion of the roles of long-term and short-term interest differentials, see Frankel (1979).

6. For further discussion see Dornbusch (1979), Frankel (1979), and Hooper and Morton (1979).

7. For an exposition and further references, see Dornbusch (1980).

8. See Dornbusch (1976a) and (1980a).

9. The model is made up of the condition of monetary equilibrium,
$$m - p = ky - hi;$$
the condition of equalization of interest rates, adjusted for anticipated depreciation $\dot{e}$,
$$i = i^* + \dot{e};$$
and the condition of equilibrium in the goods market,
$$y = a(e - p) + u,$$
where it is assumed, for expository simplicity, that there is no direct effect of interest rates on aggregate demand. The rate of inflation (relative to trend) is determined by the output gap, $y - \bar{y}$; that is, $\dot{p} = b(y - \bar{y})$. The model determines at a point in time the level of output and the exchange rate, as well as the rate of inflation and depreciation, as a function of prices. Shifts in demand, shown by shifts in u, lead to immediate offsetting changes in the real exchange rate.

10. In terms of note 9, the equilibrium condition in the goods market now becomes $y = J(e - p, w, u)$, where w denotes the level of real wealth and a rise in real wealth increases demand for home output. Real balances are excluded from the definition of real wealth. The current account is equal to the rate of change of real wealth $\dot{w}$; that is, $\dot{w} = H(e - p, w, y, v)$, where v is a shift parameter. The current account improves with real depreciation but deteriorates with an increase in income or wealth as both induce increased spending. For a more complete model along these lines see Dornbusch and Fischer (1980).

11. The idea of testing rational expectations models in news form is familiar from the work of Robert J. Barro in macroeconomics. In the context of exchange rate problems the idea is rapidly becoming accepted. See in particular Dornbusch (1979), Isard (1979), Dooley and Isard (1979), and Mussa (1979) as well as references given there.

12. See Organisation for Economic Co-operation and Development, *OECD Economic Outlook*, various issues.

13. Frenkel reports regressions of the level of the exchange rate on lagged forward rates, interest differentials, and interest innovations, the last appearing with a positive coefficient. He attributes the positive coefficient to inflation news. See Frenkel (1982). In my equations the introduction of inflation news yields a negative, insignificant coefficient.

14. This variant of the current account theory of exchange rates is emphasized in Dornbusch (1976b) and Kouri (1976a).

15. This line of research has been particularly pursued in Branson (1977) and Branson, Halttunen, and Masson (1977). See also Porter (1979), Dooley and Isard (1979), Obstfeld (1979), Kouri and de Macedo (1978), and Dornbusch (1975).

16. Let w be the initial level of real wealth; r and r^*, the random real returns on home and foreign securities; and x, the portfolio share of foreign securities. End-of-period wealth then is random and equal to $\bar{w} = w(1 + r) + xw(r^* - r)$. Utility is a function of the mean and variance of end-of-period wealth:

$$U = U(\bar{w}, s_{\bar{w}}^2).$$

The mean and variance of wealth are defined as

$$\bar{w} = w(1 + \bar{r}) + xw(\bar{r}^* - \bar{r}),$$
$$s_{\bar{w}}^2 = w^2[(1 - x)^2 s_r^2 + x^2 s_{r^*}^2 + 2x(1 - x)s_{rr^*}],$$

where a bar denotes a mean. Maximizing utility with respect to x yields the optimal portfolio share

$$x = \frac{(\bar{r}^* - \bar{r}) + \theta(s_r^2 - s_{rr^*})}{\theta s_n^2},$$

where $\theta = U_2 w/U_1$ is the coefficient of relative risk aversion, s_{rr^*} is the covariance of real returns, and

$$s_n^2 \equiv s_r^2 + s_{r^*}^2 - 2s_{rr^*}$$

is the variance of the nominal rate of depreciation. The first term, $(\bar{r} - \bar{r}^*)/\theta s_n^2$, corresponds to the speculative portfolio share in marks and depends on the mean real yield differential and the variance of the nominal rate of depreciation. The second term represents the hedging, or minimum-variance, portfolio that depends only on variances. For further discussion, see Dornbusch (1980b) and the references cited there.

17. Table 2.5 cannot strictly be used to establish the case for diversification since the data reflect both the "fundamentals" *and* the effect of the alleged portfolio diversification. To the extent that the incidence of the latter was unanticipated, the reported means and variance are not those the asset holders had in mind and accordingly cannot be used to establish the case for portfolio diversification. In a short

time-series for the flexible exchange rate system there is no apparent way of extracting the fundamentals, nor is it possible to tell how serious the discrepancy has been between previous beliefs and ex post returns.

18. Kouri and Macedo (1978, p. 129) found an optimal mark share of 37 percent in a multiple-currency portfolio with local habitats. See, too, the analysis in Fellner (1981).

19. The risk premium can be written as

$$R = \theta \left[s_n^2 \left(\frac{EV^*}{V + EV^*} - \beta \right) - s_q^2 (\phi - \phi^*) \frac{W^*}{W + W^*} \right],$$

where V is domestic currency outside bonds, and W is domestic nominal wealth; s_n^2 and s_q^2 are the variances of the rates of nominal and real depreciation; θ is the coefficient of relative risk aversion; $\phi - \phi^* \geq 0$ equals the difference between domestic and foreign expenditure shares of domestic goods; and β is the minimum-variance portfolio share defined in note 16. For a derivation, see Dornbusch (1980b).

20. Frankel and Kouri emphasized that the risk premium involves outside assets independent of the issuer. See Frankel (1979) and Kouri (1976b).

21. Early work, in particular Branson, Halttunen, and Masson (1977), gave particular emphasis to the current account, taking wealth to be represented by the cumulative current account. A more balanced treatment that recognizes the central role of asset supplies, as opposed to the distribution effects induced by current account imbalances, is found in Obstfeld (1979) and Martin and Masson (1979).

22. The data in table 2.6 understate the increase in these assets because they omit items such as Carter bonds or debt created through sterilized intervention.

23. Cumby and Obstfeld do find evidence of a risk premium in weekly data for all major currencies. See Cumby and Obstfeld (1981).

24. For an extensive discussion see the papers by Artus and Young (1979), Goldstein (1980), and Kohlhagen (n.d.).

25. On intervention policy and specifically "leaning against the wind" see Wonnacott (1958), Tosini (1977), Artus (1976), Quirk (1977), Longworth (1979), and Black (1980).

26. For further evidence see Tirole (n.d.).

27. Tobin (1978).

28. *Idem.*

29. While I argue against the Tobin tax in its worldwide application, I do think there is a forceful case for the tax in isolated instances. I particularly note the example of the United Kingdom, where the differential adjustment speed of interest rates and inflation, in response to the stabilization policy, has led to a vast real appreciation. A real interest equalization tax is warranted to repel capital inflows and thus maintain a more nearly constant real exchange rate in the adjustment of prices to lower inflation. For a further discussion see Liviatan (1979) and Dornbusch (1980a, chapter 12).

References

Artus, J. A. (1976). "Exchange Rate Stability and Managed Floating: The Experience of the Federal Republic of Germany," *IMF Staff Papers* 23, July, 312–33.

Artus, J. R., and J. H. Young (1979). "Fixed and Flexible Exchange Rate: A Renewal of the Debate," *IMF Staff Papers* 26, December, 654–98.

Bilson, John F. D. (1978). "The Monetary Approach to the Exchange Rate: Some Empirical Evidence," *IMF Staff Papers* 25, March, 48–75.

Black, S. W. (1980). "Central Bank Intervention and the Stability of Exchange Rates," *Seminar Paper* 136, University of Stockhom, Institute for International Economic Studies, February.

Branson, W. H. (1977). "Asset Markets and Relative Prices in Exchange Rate Determination," *Sozialwissenschafter Annalen* I, 69–89.

Branson, W. H., Hannu Halttunen, and Paul Masson (1977). "Exchange Rates in the short Run: The Dollar–Deutschmark Rate," *European Economic Review* 10, December, 303–24.

Cumby, Robert E., and Maurice Obstfeld (1981). "Exchange Rate Expectations and Nonimal Interest-Differentials: A Test of the Fisher Hypothesis," *Journal of Finance*. 36, June, 697–703.

Dooley, Michael P., and Peter Isard (1979). "The Portfolio Balance Model of Exchange Rates," *International Finance Discussion Paper* 141 (Federal Reserve Systems), May.

Dornbusch, R. (1975). "A Portfolio Balance Model of the Open Economy," *Journal of Monetary Economics* 1, January, 3–20.

Dornbusch, R (1976a). "Expectations and Exchange Rate Dynamics," *Journal of Political Economy* 84, December, 1161–76.

Dornbusch, R. (1976b). "Capitol Mobility, Flexible Exchange Rates and Macroeconomic Equilibrium," in E. Claasen and P. Salin eds., *Recent Issues in International Monetary Economics*, vol. 2 (Amsterdam, North-Holland), pp. 261–78.

Dornbusch, R. (1979). "Monetary Policy Under Exchange Rate Flexibility," in Federal Reserve Bank of Boston, *Managed Exchange Rate Flexibility: The Recent Experience*, Conference Series, 20, pp. 90–122.

Dornbusch, R. (1980a). *Open Economy Macroeconomics* (New York: Basic Books).

Dornbusch, R. (1980b). "Exchange Risk and the Macroeconomics of Exchange Rate Determination," unpublished manuscript, MIT, April.

Dornbusch, Rudiger, and Stanley Fischer (1980). "Exchange Rates and the Current Account," *American Economic Review*, December.

Fellner, William (1981). "The Bearing of Risk Aversion on Movements of Spot and Forward Exchange Relative to the Dollar," in J. S. Chipman and C. P. Kindleberger eds., *Flexible Exchange Rates and the Balance of Payments: Essays in Honor of Egon Sohmen* (Amsterdam: North-Holland).

Frankel, Jeffrey A. (1979). "On the Mark: A Theory of Floating Exchange Rates Based on Real Interest Differentials," *American Economic Review* 69, September, 610–22.

Frankel, J. A. (1979). "The Diversifiability of Exchange Risk," *Journal of International Economics* 9, August, 379–93.

Frenkel, Jacob A. (1979). *Papers and Proceedings of the American Economic Association*, May, 235–42.

Frenkel, Jacob A. (1980). "Exchange Rates, Prices and Money: Lessons from the 1920's," *American Economic Review* 70, May.

Frenkel, Jacob A. (1982). "Flexible Exchange Rates Prices, and the Role of 'News,'" this volume, chapter 1.

Frenkel, Jacob A., and Harry G. Johnson (eds) (1978): *The Economics of Exchange Rates: Selected Studies*, (Reading, MA: Addison-Wesley).

Goldstein, M. (1980). *Have Flexible Exchange Rates Handicapped Macroeconomic Policy?*, Special Papers in International Economics, 14, Princeton University International Finance Section, June.

Hooper, P., and J. Morton (1979). "Fluctuations in the Dollar: A Model of Nominal and Real Exchange Rate Determination," *Board of Governors of the Federal Reserve, System, Discussion Paper*, October.

Isard, Peter (1979). "Expected and Unexpected Changes in Interest Rates," *International Finance Discussion Paper* 145 (Federal Reserve Systems), June.

Kohlhagen, S. W. (n.d.). "The Experience with Floating: The 1973–1979 Dollar," University of California, unpublished manuscript.

Kouri, P. J. K. (1976a). "The Exchange Rate and the Balance of Payments in the Short Run and in the Long Run: A Monetary Approach," *Scandinavian Journal of Economics* 78, no. 2, 280–304.

Kouri, P. J. K. (1976b). "The Determinants of the Forward Premium," *Seminar Paper* 62, University of Stockholm, Institute for International Economic Studies, August.

Kouri, P. J. K., and J. B. de Macedo (1978). "Exchange Rates and the International Adjustment Process," *Brookings Papers on Economic Activity* 1, 111–50.

Liviatan, N. (1979). "Neutral Monetary Policy and the Capital Import Tax," unpublished manuscript, Hebrew University, October.

Longworth, D. J. (1979). "Floating Exchange Rates: The Canadian Experience," Ph.D. dissertation, MIT.

Martin, J. P., and P. R. Masson (1979). "Exchange Rates and Portfolio Balance," *Working Paper* 377, National Bureau of Economic Research, August.

Mussa, Michael (1979). "Empirical Regularities in the Behavior of Exchange Rates and Theories of the Foreign Exchange Market," in Karl Brunner and Allan H. Meltzer, eds., *Policies for Employment Prices and Exchange Rates*, Carnegie-Rochester Conference Series on Public Policy (Amsterdam), vol. 11, pp. 9–57.

Obstfeld, M. (1979). "Capital Mobility and Monetary Policy Under Fixed and Flexible Exchange Rates," Ph.D. dissertation, MIT.

Porter Michael G. (1979). "Exchange Rates, Current Accounts and Economic Activity—A Survey of Some Theoretical and Empirical Issues," Board of Governors of the Federal Reserve System, *Discussion Paper*, June.

Quirk, P. J. (1977). "Exchange Rate Policy in Japan: Leaning against the Wind," *I.M.F. Staff Paper* 24, November, 642–64.

Tirole, J. (n.d.). "Exchange Rate Expectations and Monetary Policy: A Structural Approach for France, Germany, U.K.," unpublished manuscript, MIT.

Tobin, J. (1978). "A Proposal for International Monetary Reform," *Cowles Foundation Discussion Paper* 506, Yale University, October.

Toshini, P. A. (1977). *Leaning against the Wind: A Standard for Managed Floating*, Princeton Essays in International Finance 126, International Finance Section, December.

Wonnacott, P. (1958). "Exchange Stabilization in Canada 1950–4: A Comment," *Canadian Journal of Economics and Political Science* 24, May, 262–65.

3

**Monetary and
Portfolio-Balance
Models of Exchange
Rate Determination**

Jeffrey A. Frankel

3.1 The Asset-Market View of Exchange Rates

The theoretical literature on the "asset-market" view of exchange rates
has been expanding voluminously in recent years. The popularity of this
view may be attributed to the compelling realism in today's world of both
its distinguishing theoretical assumption and its distinguishing empirical
implication. The theoretical assumption that all asset-market models
share is the absence of substantial transactions costs, capital controls, or
other impediments to the flow of capital between countries, an assumption which will here be referred to as perfect capital mobility. Thus the
exchange rate must adjust instantly to equilibrate the international demand for stocks of national assets—as opposed to adjusting to equilibrate
the international demand for flows of national goods as in the more traditional view. The empirical implication is that floating exchange rates will
exhibit high variability, variability that exceeds what one might regard as
that of their underlying determinants.

But beyond this common point, the asset-market models diverge down
a bewildering complexity of routes. Synthesis models and comprehensive
surveys are notably lacking. Furthermore, the specific empirical implications of the various theories conflict with observed events, as well as with
each other. Econometric attempts to relate the theory to recent data have

An earlier version of this chapter was presented at the World Congress of the Econometric Society, Aix-en-Provence, France, 29 August 1980, and also appeared as
NBER Summer Institute Paper 80–7.

This material is based upon work supported by the National Science Foundation
under Grant No. SES-8007162, and further supported by a research grant from
the Institute of Business and Economic Research at the University of California,
Berkeley. I would like to thank Brian Newton, Charles Engel, Eric Fisher, and
Allen Berger for research assistance, and to thank Peter Kenen and Hali Edison
for very useful comments and suggestions.

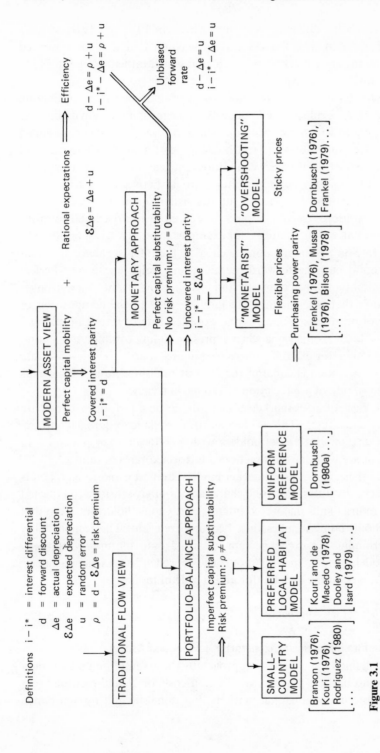

Figure 3.1
Exchange rate models and assumptions.

foundered on the dollar depreciation, which, in 1977 and 1978, was too highly correlated with the US current account deficit to be explained readily by the asset-market approach, and which rather seemed to fit the more traditional approach.

This chapter proposes a taxonomy of asset-market models of floating exchange rates, as illustrated in figure 3.1. The most important dichotomy is according to whether or not domestic and foreign bonds are assumed to be perfect substitutes in asset-holders' portfolios. It is important to note the distinction between capital mobility, as the term is used here, and substitutability.[1] Perfect capital mobility between countries means that actual portfolio composition adjusts instantaneously to desired portfolio composition. Assuming no risk of default or future capital controls, perfect capital mobility implies, for example, covered interest parity: The interest rate on a domestic bond is equal to the interest rate on a similar foreign bond plus the forward premium on foreign exchange.[2] Perfect substitutability between domestic and foreign bonds is the much stronger assumption that asset holders are indifferent as to the composition of their bond portfolios as long as the expected rate of return on the two countries' bonds is the same when expressed in any common numeraire. It would imply, for example, uncovered interest parity: The interest rate on a domestic bond is equal to the interest rate on a foreign bond plus the *expected* rate of appreciation of foreign currency.[3]

In one class of asset-market models, domestic and foreign bonds are imperfect substitutes. This is the "portfolio-balance approach" to exchange rates, in which asset holders wish to allocate their portfolios in shares that are well-defined functions of expected rates of return.[4]

In the other class of asset-market models, domestic and foreign bonds are perfect substitutes: Portfolio shares are infinitely sensitive to expected rates of return. Thus uncovered interest parity must hold. But given that it does hold, bond supplies then become irrelevant. The responsibility for determining the exchange rate is shifted onto the money markets. Such models belong to the "monetary approach" to exchange rates,[5] which focuses on the demand for and supply of money.

3.2 The Monetary Approach

3.2.1 The Flexible-Price ("Monetarist") Monetary Model
We have defined the monetary approach by the assumption that not only are there no barriers (such as transaction costs or capital controls) segmenting international capital markets, but domestic and foreign bonds

are also perfect substitutes in investor demand functions. In essence, there is only one bond in the world.

As the starting point within the monetary approach we begin with the model that also makes the analogous assumption for goods markets: Not only are there no barriers (such as transportation costs or trade controls) segmenting international goods markets, but domestic and foreign goods are also perfect substitutes in consumer demand functions. In essence, there is only one good in the world.

This assumption, of course, implies purchasing power parity: The domestic price level is equal to the foreign price level times the exchange rate. Large short-run failures of purchasing power parity have been observed empirically.[6] But the assumption can be useful in certain contexts, for example, hyperinflation. And, in any case, the model that assumes one world good as well as one world bond is a powerfully simple prototype that will serve as a point of departure for more sophisticated models.

If perfect price flexibility is considered the crucial characteristic of monetarism, then the best name for the variety of monetary model that assumes purchasing power parity is the "monetarist model."[7] It has been developed by Frenkel [1976, 1977, 1980], Mussa [1976], Girton and Roper [1977], Hodrick [1978], and Bilson [1980a, b].

The fundamental equation in the monetary approach is a conventional money demand function:

$$m = p + \phi y - \lambda i, \tag{1}$$

where

$m \equiv$ log of the domestic money supply,
$p \equiv$ log of the domestic price level,
$y \equiv$ log of domestic real income,
$i \equiv$ the domestic short-term interest rate,
$\phi \equiv$ the money demand elasticity with respect to income,
$\lambda \equiv$ the money demand semielasticity with respect to the interest rate.

We assume a similar money demand function for the foreign country:

$$m^* = p^* + \phi y^* - \lambda i^*$$

where asterisks denote foreign variables and the parameters are assumed the same in both countries. Taking the difference of the two equations gives us a relative money demand function:

$$(m - m^*) = (p - p^*) + \phi(y - y^*) - \lambda(i - i^*). \tag{2}$$

The one-bond assumption gives us uncovered interest parity:

$$i - i^* = \mathscr{E}(\Delta e) \tag{3}$$

where $\mathscr{E}(\Delta e) \equiv$ the expected depreciation of domestic currency. We combine (2) and (3) and solve for the relative price level:

$$(p - p^*) = (m - m^*) - \phi(y - y^*) + \lambda\mathscr{E}(\Delta e). \tag{4}$$

The one-good assumption gives us purchasing power parity:

$$e = p - p^*, \tag{5}$$

where $e \equiv$ log of the spot exchange rate, defined as the price of foreign currency in terms of domestic. A consequence is that expected depreciation is equal to the expected inflation differential:

$$\mathscr{E}(\Delta e) = \mathscr{E}(\Delta p) - \mathscr{E}(\Delta p^*). \tag{6}$$

We combine (5), (4), and (6) to obtain the monetarist equation of exchange rate determination:

$$e = (m - m^*) - \phi(y - y^*) + \lambda(\mathscr{E} \Delta p - \mathscr{E} \Delta p^*). \tag{7}$$

Equation (7) says that the exchange rate, as the relative price of currency, is determined by the supply and demand for money. An increase in the supply of domestic money causes a proportionate depreciation. An increase in domestic income, or a decrease in the expected inflation rate, raises the demand for domestic money and thus causes an appreciation. The equation has been widely estimated econometrically.

Assume that expectations are rational and the system is stable. Assume further that income growth is exogenous (for simplicity equal to zero, so $y - y^* = \bar{y} - \bar{y}^*$), as it usually is in monetarist models. Then the expected inflation rate is equal to the rationally expected monetary growth rate. A benchmark specification of the money supply process is that monetary growth follows a random walk. Then the rationally expected future relative monetary growth rate, and thus the last term in equation (7), is simply the current relative monetary growth rate, which we will represent by $\Pi - \Pi^*$:

$$e = (m - m^*) - \phi(\bar{y} - \bar{y}^*) + \lambda(\Pi - \Pi^*). \tag{8}$$

As an alternative to the benchmark specification, a very restrictive special case occurs when we specify the *level* of the money supply, rather than the change in the money supply, to be a random walk. Then the expected relative rate of monetary growth, $\Pi - \Pi^*$, is zero. The level of the exchange rate is perfectly correlated with the level of the relative money supply. But in today's world the existence of secular inflation and its effect on money demand cannot be ignored.[8]

On the other hand, one could generalize beyond the benchmark case of a random-walk specification for money growth. More sophisticated specifications of the money supply process have appeared in monetarist exchange rate models by Mussa [1976], who distinguishes between transitory and permanent monetary disturbances, and Barro [1978], who distinguishes between anticipated and unanticipated disturbances.

3.2.2 The Sticky-Price ("Overshooting") Monetary Model

As mentioned, purchasing power parity may be a good approximation in the long run, but large deviations appear in the short run empirically. The existence of contracts, imperfect information, and inertia in consumer habits means that prices do not change instantaneously but adjust gradually over time.

We now retain the monetary approach's one-bond representation of financial markets but relax the monetarist model's one-good representation of trade. This gives us a class of models in which changes in the nominal money supply are also changes in the real money supply because prices are sticky, and thus have real effects, especially on the exchange rate.

The sticky-price class of monetary models begins with the well-known analysis of perfect capital mobility by Mundell [1963]. Mundell abstracts from expectations, so that uncovered interest parity (3) becomes a simple equality between the domestic and foreign interest rates. In a money demand equation like (1), the combination of a fixed price level and an interest rate tied to the world rate means that a monetary expansion causes a large instant depreciation in the currency: Export demand has to be stimulated sufficiently for the increased income to raise money demand to the level of the new higher money supply *without* lowering the domestic interest rate below the foreign one.

A number of authors have introduced a nonzero expected rate of depreciation into the Mundell model.[9] They argue that as long as the expected future spot rate is less than unit-elastic with respect to the current spot rate, a monetary expansion will not cause as large an increase in the exchange rate and income as in the Mundell model. This is because it is possible for the domestic interest rate to fall below the foreign one without inducing an infinite capital outflow.

At first Argy and Porter [1972] and Dornbusch [1976a] specified expectations adaptively. But then Dornbusch [1976b] offered a model in which expectations are specified rationally. In this model purchasing power parity does hold in the long run, so that a given increase in the money supply raises the exchange rate proportionately as in the monetarist model, but *only* in the long run. In the short run, because prices are sticky, a monetary expansion has the liquidity effects of the Mundell model. The interest rate falls, generating an incipient capital outflow, which causes the currency to depreciate instantaneously *more* than it will in the long run; it depreciates just enough so that the rationally expected rate of future *appreciation* precisely cancels out the interest differential. The phenomenon just described is known as "overshooting" of the spot rate. In its honor, this paper will use the name "overshooting model" for the sticky-price monetary approach to distinguish it from the monetarist (flexible-price monetary approach) model.[10]

The overshooting model retains the money demand function (1) and uncovered interest parity condition (3) essential to the monetary approach. It replaces the instantaneous purchasing power parity condition (5) with a long-run version:

$$\bar{e} = \bar{p} - \bar{p}^*, \tag{9}$$

where bars over variables signify a relation that holds in the long run. Thus the monetarist exchange rate equation (7) is replaced by a long-run version:

$$\bar{e} = (\bar{m} - \bar{m}^*) - \phi(\bar{y} - \bar{y}^*) + \lambda(\overline{\mathscr{E}(\Delta p)} - \overline{\mathscr{E}(\Delta p^*)}). \tag{10}$$

Precisely as we did in the monetarist model, we assume that expectations are rational and the system is stable; for simplicity, income growth is exogenous (or random with mean zero); and as a benchmark specification, monetary growth follows a random walk. It then follows that the relative money supply, and in the long run the relative price level and exchange rate, are all rationally expected to follow paths along which they increase at the current rate of relative monetary growth $\Pi - \Pi^*$. Equation (10) becomes

$$\bar{e} = (m - m^*) - \phi(y - y^*) + \lambda(\Pi - \Pi^*). \tag{11}$$

It remains only to specify expectations. In the short run, when the exchange rate deviates from its equilibrium path, it is expected to close that gap with a speed of adjustment θ. In the long run, when the exchange rate lies on its equilibrium path, it is expected to increase at $\Pi - \Pi^*$:[11]

$$\mathscr{E}(\Delta e) = -\theta(e - \bar{e}) + \Pi - \Pi^*. \tag{12}$$

We combine (12) with the uncovered interest parity condition (3),

$$i - i^* = \mathcal{E}(\Delta e) \tag{3}$$

to obtain

$$e - \bar{e} = -(1/\theta)[(i - \Pi) - (i^* - \Pi^*)]. \tag{13}$$

The gap between the exchange rate and its equilibrium value is proportional to the real interest differential. Intuitively, when a tight domestic monetary policy causes the nominal interest differential to rise above its equilibrium level, an incipient capital inflow causes the value of the currency to rise proportionately above *its* equilibrium level.

Now we combine (11), representing the long-run monetary equilibrium path, with (13), representing the short-run overshooting effect, to obtain a general monetary equation of exchange rate determination:

$$e = (m - m^*) - \phi(y - y^*) + \lambda(\Pi - \Pi^*)$$

$$- (1/\theta)[(i - \Pi) - (i^* - \Pi^*)]. \tag{14}$$

As the basis for econometric estimation, equation (14) is identical to the monetarist equation (8) but for the addition of a fourth explanatory variable, the real interest differential. This variable should show up in a regression with a zero coefficient if the monetarist model is correct; the economic interpretation would be that the speed of adjustment θ is infinite.

As we did in the last section, we can depart from the benchmark specification of the money supply process by considering the simple special case when the *level* of the money supply, rather then the *change* in the money supply, is a random walk. Then the expected long-run inflation differential $\Pi - \Pi^*$ is zero. This is precisely the context in which this model was originally developed by Dornbusch. Equation (14) becomes

$$e = (m - m^*) - \phi(y - y^*) - (1/\theta)(i - i^*). \tag{15}$$

The Dornbusch equation (15), like the monetarist equation (8), can be viewed as a nested model which can be tested econometrically by estimating equation (14).

Again as in the last section, one could also depart from the benchmark specification by considering a more general money supply process. More sophisticated specifications of the money supply process have appeared in Dornbusch-type models by Rogoff [1979], who distinguishes between transitory and permanent monetary disturbances, and Wilson [1979] and Gray and Turnovsky [1979], who distinguish between anticipated and unanticipated monetary disturances.

3.2.3 Empirical Application of the Monetary Approach

Five years or so after exchange rates began to float in 1973, a number of empirical studies of the period appeared.[12] These studies tended generally to support the implications of the monetary approach against those of the traditional flow approach: a coefficient on the relative money supply which is positive or—more precisely—unity, and a coefficient on relative income which is negative and interpretable as the income elasticity of money demand. However, the empirical basis for a choice between the flexible-price and sticky-price variants of the monetary approach was less clear-cut. When the United Kingdom was one of the two countries whose exchange rate was studied, Bilson [1978a] and Hodrick [1978] found the interest differential to show the significant positive coefficient that is implied by the flexible-price model represented by equation (8). But Hodrick [1978] found the German interest rate to show the significant negative effect on the mark/dollar rate that is implied by the sticky-price model represented by equation (15). Estimation of equation (14)—Frankel [1979b]—supported the general monetary model for the mark/dollar rate from July 1974 to February 1978. The coefficient on the short-term interest differential was significantly less than zero, as in the sticky-price model, while the coefficient on the expected long-run inflation differential was significantly greater than zero, as in the flexible-price model.

In 1978 the dollar depreciated sharply. The depreciation prompted increasing political criticism of the noninterventionist policies of the US government and did not come to an end until the November package of increased monetary restraint and direct intervention to support the dollar. Much of the criticism, such as that appearing in repeated *Wall Street Journal* editorials, subscribed to the monetary model. In this view the declining price of dollars was simply due to the rapid increase in the supply of dollars "spewing forth from Federal Reserve printing presses." The behavior of the Bundesbank and the performance of the mark were pointed to as paragons of monetary restraint and its rewards. Unfortunately for this theory, German monetary growth in 1978 was, and has been for some years, actually *higher* than US monetary growth. The reason for the surprisingly high rate of monetary growth in Germany, ironically, was the strength in the value of the mark against the dollar. The Bundesbank resisted this appreciation by buying dollars, without sterilizing the reserve inflow, and thus caused the German money supply to swell.

Empirical studies that tried to update the monetary equation to include the events of 1978 and 1979 were quite unsuccessful from the viewpoint of all versions of the model.[13] The only coefficient to appear statistically significant was that on the expected inflation differential. The coefficient on the relative money supply actually appeared with the incorrect sign, attesting to the mystery of a mark that went up in price even as it was increasing in relative supply.[14]

In 1980 the traditional Keynesian correlation between the interest rate and the value of the dollar strongly reemerged. Both exhibited two sharp peaks centered on April and December. Table 3.1 reports an update of the monetary equation through December 1980. When we correct for serial correlation, the coefficient on the interest differential rejoins the coefficients on the expected inflation rates in appearing statistically significant. This new evidence would tend again to support the general sticky-price form of the monetary model, equation (14). However, the insignificant (or in one case significant but of the wrong sign) coefficient on the money supplies and relative income continue to cast doubt on the monetary model in all forms.

If the money supplies are endogenous, because of either the existence of central bank reaction functions or disturbances in money demand, then the estimates reported in the first row of table 3.1 are not consistent. One remedy is to impose the constraint of a unit coefficient on the relative money supply, in effect moving the endogenous variable to the left-hand side of the regression equation. The results of such regressions (not reported here) are no better than the unconstrained regression.

3.3 The Portfolio-Balance Approach

3.3.1 The Effect of the Current Account

The other popular explanation for the decline of the dollar in 1978, besides US monetary growth, was the large US current account deficit. The old-fashioned view that the level of the exchange rate must clear the current account had been refuted by theorists who pointed to the existence of high capital mobility and by practitioners who pointed to the fact that until the end of 1977 the dollar's trade-weighted value was quite high despite a record current account deficit. But more recently, the correlation between current account deficits and exchange rates has been undeniably strong, not only in 1978 when the dollar depreciated and the currencies

Table 3.1
Estimation of monetary exchange rate equation (14): dependent variable—log of mark/dollar rate[a]

Sample	Technique	c	gml − usmlb	gy	usy	gi − usi	gΠ	usΠ	R^2	D.W.	$\hat{\rho}$
7401–8012	OLSQ	3.229	−0.835[b]	−0.885[c]	0.289	−0.190	4.717[c]	−3.932[c]	0.93	0.92	
		(0.570)	(0.158)	(0.255)	(0.195)	(0.300)	(0.813)	(0.301)			
	CORC	3.283	−0.770[b]	−0.382	−0.199	−0.698[c]	3.485[c]	−3.444[c]	0.95		0.67
		(1.018)	(0.268)	(0.271)	(0.240)	(0.328)	(1.187)	(0.539)			
7402–8011	FAIR	2.453	−0.503	−0.167	−0.222	−1.465[c]	7.244[c]	−4.877[c]	0.94		0.66
		(1.217)	(0.335)	(0.319)	(0.294)	(0.516)	(2.081)	(0.755)			

a. Definitions: gml − usmlb ≡ log of relative money supply, Germany/U.S. (M1B); gy, usy ≡ log of real income levels (proxied by industrial production), Germany and United States, respectively; gi − usi ≡ nominal interest differential (short-term money market rates, per annum basis); gΠ, usΠ ≡ expected inflation rates (proxied by average CPI inflation over preceding twelve months); OLSQ, ordinary least squares; CORC, iterated Cochrane-Orcutt; FAIR, Fair's method of correcting for possible endogeneity of gi − usi, gΠ, and usΠ (instrumental variables are the German and US ratios of outstanding government bonds to monetary base, and the German and US long-term government bond interest rates) in the presence of serial correlation (current and lagged values of all endogenous and included exogenous variables are added to the list of instruments). (Standard errors are in parentheses.)
b. Significant at the 95% level and of the incorrect sign.
c. Significant at the 95% level and of the correct sign.

of the surplus countries, Germany and Japan, appreciated, but also in 1979 and 1980 when the pattern was reversed.

There are three main lines according to which current account developments can be argued to affect the exchange rate, without reverting to the traditional flow theory of foreign exchange. The first begins by observing that current account developments have been largely dominated by oil. One could argue within the monetary approach that, because the United States produces oil while Germany and Japan produce none, or else because world oil trade is actually transacted in dollars, the sharp increase in world oil prices that took place in 1979 raised the demand for the dollar at the expense of the mark and yen, much as did the increase that took place in late 1973. On the other hand, financial commentators have often argued more loosely that oil price increases actually *hurt* the dollar because the United States had not yet decontrolled domestic oil prices or else because US political prestige is at stake in the Middle East.[15]

The second line of argument begins by observing that the release by the government of unexpected figures on the trade balance or current account appears to have large immediate "announcement effects" on the exchange rate. In some versions the current account figures reveal new information about shifts in the long-run terms of trade. But the important point is that only the unexpected component of the current account has a large effect, the expected component having already been taken into account by the foreign exchange market.[16]

The third line of argument begins by observing that the counterpart of a current account surplus is a transfer of wealth from foreign residents to domestic residents. The increase in domestic wealth can, in turn, appreciate the currency through any of three channels. First, it can raise domestic expenditure as in the well-established Modigliani consumption function, and thus raise domestic income and the transactions demand for domestic money. Second, it can raise the demand for domestic money directly if wealth enters the money demand function and domestic money is not held by foreigners. Third, if domestic bonds and foreign bonds are imperfect substitutes and domestic residents have a greater tendency to hold wealth in the form of domestic bonds than do foreign residents, the increase in domestic wealth will raise the demand for domestic bonds. Each of these effects might claim a role in a comprehensive model, but we will focus on the last of the three and refer to it as the "portfolio-balance" effect, giving us the second major branch in figure 3.1.[17]

3.3.2 The Portfolio-Balance Equation

We retain our assumption that there are no barriers segmenting international capital markets, but we relax the assumption that domestic and foreign bonds are perfect substitutes. Thus investors allocate their bond portfolios between the two countries in proportions that are functions of the expected rates of return.

There are many reasons why two assets can be imperfect substitutes: liquidity, tax treatment, default risk, political risk, and exchange risk. However, at the level of aggregation relevant for most macroeconomic models (see note 2), and under our assumption of perfect international bond markets, the last of these is the most important. We assume that there is only one respect in which domestic and foreign bonds differ: their currency of denomination. Investors, in order to diversify the risk that comes from exchange rate variability, balance their bond portfolios between domestic and foreign bonds in proportions that depend on the expected relative rate of return (or risk premium):

$$B_j/EF_j = \beta_j(i - i^* - \mathscr{E} \Delta e). \tag{16}$$

Here B_j is the stock of domestic-denominated bonds held by investor j; F_j, the stock of foreign-denominated bonds held; and E, the exchange rate. β_j is a positive-valued function; for concreteness let it be $\exp[\alpha_j + \beta_j (i - i^* - \mathscr{E} \Delta e)]$.[18] An increase in the interest differential or a fall in the expected rate of depreciation induces investors to shift their portfolios out of foreign bonds and into domestic bonds. (Note that B_j and F_j can be negative, which will be the case if agent j is a debtor.)

We assume at first that all active participants in the market have the same portfolio preferences, as represented by the function β. This assumption allows us to add up individual asset demand functions into the aggregate asset demand equation (17):

$$\frac{B}{EF} = \beta(i - i^* - \mathscr{E} \Delta e), \tag{17}$$

where

$$B \equiv \sum_{j=1} B_j \quad \text{and} \quad F \equiv \sum_{j=1} F_j.$$

B and F are the *net* supplies of bonds (domestically denominated and foreign denominated, respectively) in the market. If one market participant is in debt to another, the asset and liability will cancel out. All that matters are the supplies of *outside* assets in the market.

A relation like (17) between asset supplies and expected rates of return is not by itself a theory of exchange rate determination, as Dooley and Isard [1979] have pointed out. Even if the interest rates are omitted or taken as exogenous, expectations must be specified. For example, if either the expected rate of depreciation $\mathscr{E} \Delta e$ or the expected future exchange rate $\mathscr{E} e_{+1}$ is determined, then the exchange rate is uniquely determined.[19] But specifying that expectations are formed *rationally* is not sufficient to determine the exchange rate uniquely; as in so many rational expectations problems, the assumption of stability is also required. The simplest possible portfolio-balance model would specify static expectations: $\mathscr{E} \Delta e = 0$. Then the exchange rate is simply determined by relative bond supplies and the interest differential:

$$e = -\alpha + \beta(i - i^*) + b - f, \tag{18}$$

where $b \equiv \log B$ and $f \equiv \log F$. Equation (18) is estimated below.[20]

So far we have not been very precise about the definitions of B and F. If the market consists of the whole world, and residents of all countries have the same portfolio preferences, then "the supplies of outside assets in the market" include only government-issued liabilities held by the private sector.[21] In (17) B must be interpreted as net domestically denominated government indebtedness and F as net foreign-denominated government indebtedness. B and F will be the same as domestic and foreign government debt, respectively, under the assumption that governments issue debt denominated exclusively in their own currencies.[22]

The proposition that residents of all countries have the same portfolio preferences implies that the indebtedness of residents of one country to residents of the other has no effect. This proposition holds in several recent finance papers—Grauer, Litzenberger, and Stehle [1976]; Frankel [1979a]; Fama and Farber [1979]; and Dornbusch [1980a]—and is represented by the "uniform preference" branch of portfolio-balance models in figure 3.1. These papers derive the asset demand functions as the outcome of maximization of expected utility by risk-averse agents. The proposition that all agents have the same portfolio preference follows from the assumption that they all consume the same good, or basket of goods.[23]

This interpretation of equation (17) contrasts with macroeconomic models of portfolio balance that take asset-demand functions as given. The majority of these models, though they maintain our assumption that no barriers discourage residents of any country from participating in the world market, make the assumption that domestic residents are the only ones who *wish* to hold domestically denominated assets.[24] The domestic country is assumed to be too small for its assets to be of interest to foreign residents.

One motivation for this assumption is to simplify the accounting—it allows the identification of a capital inflow or outflow with an increase or decrease in the supply of foreign assets in the home market by assuming away the problem of currency of denomination of the capital flow. The second motivation for the assumption is that, under floating exchange rates, it leads to the result that a current account deficit causes a depreciation of the home currency, since the counterpart to the current account deficit is a capital inflow: The reduction in the supply of foreign-denominated assets in the market leads to a rise in their price in terms of domestic currency.

Thus as an alternative to (17), we aggregate (16) over all domestic residents only:

$$\frac{B_H}{EF_H} = \beta_H(i - i^* - \mathscr{E}\,\Delta e), \tag{19}$$

where B_H is defined as the sum of all domestic bonds held by home residents (identical to B, under the small-country assumption), F_H is defined as the sum of all foreign bonds held by home residents (equal to the accumulation of past current account surpluses under the small-country assumption), and β_H is the asset-demand function shared by all home residents. Assuming static expectations, the exchange rate equation is

$$e = -\alpha_H - \beta_H(i - i^*) + b - f_H, \tag{20}$$

where $b \equiv \log B$ and $F_H \equiv \log F_H$.

The small-country assumption—the assumption that foreign residents do not hold domestic bonds—is particularly unrealistic if the domestic country is the United States. One alternative is to assume that the *foreign* country is the small country—that domestic residents do not hold foreign bonds. Then (20) is replaced by

$$e = -\alpha_F - \beta_F(i - i^*) + b_F - f, \tag{21}$$

where b_F is defined as the log of domestic bonds held by foreign residents (equal to the accumulation of past foreign current account surpluses under the small-country assumption).[25] Equations (20) and (21) are estimated below.

A realistic portfolio-balance model for large countries must recognize that residents of both countries hold assets issued by both countries. But the (cumulated) current account will still have the expected effect on the exchange rate, provided domestic residents wish to hold a greater proportion of their wealth as domestic assets and foreign residents wish to hold a greater proportion as foreign assets. (Such models are classified under the name "preferred local habitat" in figure 3.1.[26]) This is because the current account will redistribute world wealth in such a way as to raise net world demand for the surplus country's assets, thus raising the price of its currency. We would have to specify a separate asset-demand function for foreign residents:

$$\frac{B_F}{EF_F} = \beta_F(i - i^* - \mathscr{E}\,\Delta e), \tag{22}$$

where $\beta_H \geqslant \beta_F$ for all values. Equations (19) for the home country and (22) for the foreign country could each be solved independently for the exchange rate and regressed in logarithmic form, were data on B_H, B_F, F_H, and F_F available. Unfortunately, data on the four-way breakdown—who owns how much of which asset—are difficult to obtain. Only the two-way breakdowns can be attempted: between domestically and foreign-denominated bonds ($B \equiv B_H + B_F$ versus $F \equiv F_H + F_F$) and between domestically and foreign-held wealth ($W_H \equiv B_H + EF_H$ versus $W_F \equiv B_F + EF_F$).

The nonlinear nature of (19) and (22) prevents solving for the exchange rate as a function of B, F, W_H, and W_F. However, the signs to be expected in such a relation are clear. An increase in the supply of foreign bonds F lowers their relative price E. An increase in the supply of domestic bonds B raises E. An increase in foreign wealth W_F raises the overall world demand for foreign assets and thus raises their relative price E. Finally, an increase in home wealth W_H raises the overall world demand for domestic assets and thus lowers E.

Table 3.2 presents regressions of the dollar/mark exchange rate against the interest differential and bond supplies, which are tests of the portfolio-balance approach under static expectations. Calculation of the net supplies of domestically and foreign-denominated assets requires correcting outstanding treasury debt for exchange intervention by central banks—as mentioned in note 22.[27] In addition, each country's monetary base is subtracted from the supply of its assets to arrive at the supply of its interest-paying bonds. Kouri [1978] argues that all nominally fixed assets should be included in the portfolio, whether interestpaying or not. Proponents of the currency-substitution model argue in effect that *only*

Table 3.2
Estimation of portfolio-balance equations—log of dollar/mark rate, January 1974–October 1978[a]

Asset preferences	Technique	c	usi − gi	usb	gb	usf	gf	R^2	D.W.	$\hat{\rho}$
1. Uniform worldwide	OLS	−0.485 (0.215)	−0.472 (0.579)	−0.798[b] (0.122)	+0.916[b] (0.116)			0.78	0.46	
	CORC	+0.733 (0.971)	−0.387 (0.461)	−0.343[b] (0.173)	+0.431[b] (0.089)			0.94		0.97
2. US bonds held only by US residents	OLS	−6.391 (0.831)	0.240 (0.643)	−0.393[b] (0.098)		+1.255[b] (0.217)		0.71	0.29	
	CORC	−10.312 (3.202)	−0.248 (0.525)	−0.117 (0.171)		+1.639[b] (0.524)		0.92		0.95
3. German bonds held only by German residents	OLS	−1.530 (0.223)	1.920[b] (0.598)		+0.224[b] (0.062)		−0.096 (0.105)	0.61	0.23	
	CORC	+0.632 (1.041)	−0.311 (0.426)		+0.154 (0.106)		−0.521[b] (0.162)	0.94		0.96
4. General case	OLS	−5.648 (0.881)	−1.595[c] (0.491)	−0.607[b] (0.105)	+0.893[b] (0.102)	+1.330[b] (0.226)	−0.295[b] (0.096)	0.87	0.61	
	CORC	−5.620 (2.497)	−0.699 (0.431)	−0.188 (0.106)	+0.271 (0.147)	+1.174[b] (0.423)	−0.463[b] (0.149)	0.95		0.94

a. Definitions: usi − gi ≡ interest differential (short-term money market rates, per annum basis); usb ≡ log of net supply of dollar bonds to the private sector, calculated as US Treasury debt + cumulative Federal Reserve sales of dollar assets in foreign exchange intervention (inferred from Fed international reserves without valuation changes) − dollar assets held by other central banks − US monetary base; gb ≡ log of net supply of mark bonds to the private sector, calculated as German Treasury debt + cumulative Bundesbank sales of mark assets in foreign exchange intervention (inferred from Bundesbank international reserves without valuation changes) − mark assets held by other central banks − German monetary base; usf ≡ log of net supply of foreign bonds to the US private sector, under the (unrealistic) assumption that dollar assets are held only by US residents and that all capital flows are denominated in marks, calculated as the cumulation of (expressed in marks) the US current account − Federal Reserve purchases of foreign assets in foreign exchange intervention + sales by other central banks of foreign assets for dollars; gf ≡ log of net supply of foreign bonds to the German private sector, under the (unrealistic) assumption that mark assets are held only by German residents and that all capital flows are denominated in dollars, calculated as the cumulation of (expressed in dollars) the German current account − Bundesbank purchases of foreign assets in foreign exchange intervention + sales by other central banks of foreign assets for marks. (Standard errors in parentheses.)
b. Significant at the 95 percent level and of the incorrect sign.
c. Significant at the 95 percent level and of the correct sign.

moneys should be included in the portfolio.[28] But regressions based on these alternatives were no more successful than those, based on supplies of bonds alone, reported in table 3.2.

Row 1 is an estimation of equation (18): the portfolio-balance model when residents of all countries have uniform asset preferences, so that the worldwide distribution of wealth via current accounts is irrelevant and government bond supplies are all that matter. Row 2 is an estimation of equation (20), the "domestic small-country" model, in which the relevant stock variables are the supply of domestic government bonds and the supply of foreign bonds to domestic residents, with the United States defined as the domestic country. Row 3 is an estimation of equation (21), the "foreign small-country" model, in which the relevant stock variables are the supply of foreign government bonds and the supply of domestic bonds to foreign residents, with Germany defined as the foreign country. Row 4 uses all four stock variables: the supplies of both domestic and foreign bonds and the cumulated current accounts of both countries.[29] This regression includes each of the first three as special cases.[30]

The results are very poor for the portfolio-balance models. The coefficients on all four stock variables are always of the incorrect sign and usually appear significantly so.

3.4 A Synthesis of the Monetary and Portfolio-Balance Equations

In section 3.2.1 we presented the simple monetarist model of exchange rates which assumes one world bond (i.e., perfect capital substitutability, implying uncovered interest parity) and one world good (i.e., perfect price flexibility, implying purchasing power parity). The result was the monetarist equation in which the exchange rate is determined by the relative money supply, relative income, and the expected inflation differential:

$$e = (m - m^*) - \phi(y - y^*) + \lambda(\Pi - \Pi^*). \tag{8}$$

In section 3.2.2 we relaxed the price flexibility assumption. In empirical terms, we simply added the real interest differential to the other three explanatory variables:

$$e = (m - m^*) - \phi(y - y^*) + \lambda(\Pi - \Pi^*)$$
$$-(1/\theta)[(i - \Pi) - (i^* - \Pi^*)]. \tag{14}$$

In this section we extend the synthesis process by relaxing the perfect substitutability assumption.[31] We integrate the monetary models, as represented by equation (14), with the portfolio-balance models, as represented by equation (17):

$$B/EF = \beta(i - i^* - \mathcal{E}\,\Delta e). \tag{17}$$

In logarithmic form (17) becomes

$$b - e - f = \alpha + \beta(i - i^* - \mathcal{E}\,\Delta e). \tag{23}$$

We repeat the expectation equation (12):

$$\mathcal{E}(\Delta e) = -\theta(e - \bar{e}) + \Pi - \Pi^*. \tag{12}$$

By adding and subtracting the nomial interest differential, we see that (12) implies that the exchange rate deviates from its long-run value by an amount proportional to the real interest differential and the risk premium:

$$e - \bar{e} = -(1/\theta)[(i - \Pi) - (i^* - \Pi^*)] + (1/\theta)[i - i^* - \mathcal{E}\,\Delta e]. \tag{24}$$

We substitute in equation (11) for the equilibrium exchange rate:

$$e = (m - m^*) - \phi(y - y^*) + \lambda(\Pi - \Pi^*)$$
$$-(1/\theta)[(i - \Pi) - (i^* - \Pi^*)] + (1/\theta)[i - i^* - \mathcal{E}\,\Delta e]. \tag{25}$$

In the monetarist model, purchasing power parity (6) ensured that the real interest differential was zero and uncovered interest parity (3) ensured that the risk premium was zero, so that equation (25) reduced to (8). The sticky-price monetary model relaxed the first condition but maintained the second, so that (25) reduced only to (14).

The synthesis of the monetary and portfolio-balance equations is accomplished simply by relaxing the second condition. We replace uncovered interest parity (3) with the imperfect substitutability condition (23). Now the exchange rate deviates from its equilibrium value not only because sticky goods prices create a real interest differential, but also because imperfect bond substitutability creates a risk premium. We substitute (23) into (25), getting bond supplies into the exchange rate equation in place of the unobservable risk premium:

$$e = (m - m^*) - \phi(y - y^*) + \lambda(\Pi - \Pi^*)$$
$$-(1/\theta)[(i - \Pi) - (i^* - \Pi^*)] + [1/(\theta\beta)][b - e - f - \alpha]. \tag{26}$$

Finally, we solve for e:

Table 3.3
Implied regression coefficients of competing exchange rate equations[a]

e against	$(m - m^*)$	$(y - y^*)$	$(i - i^*)$	$(\Pi - \Pi^*)$	$(b - f)$
Traditional flow view	+	−			
Modern asset view					
Monetary approach					
Monetarist equation (8)	+	−	+	+	
Overshooting equation (15)	+	−	−		
Real interest differential equation (14)	+	−	−	+	
Portfolio-balance approach (18)		−			+
Synthesis asset equation (27)	+	−	−	+	+

a. Definitions: $e \equiv$ log of exchange rate; $m - m^* \equiv$ log of relative money supply; $y - y^*$ $\equiv$ log of relative income; $i - i^* \equiv$ nominal interest differential; $\Pi - \Pi^* \equiv$ expected inflation differential; $b - f \equiv$ log of relative bond supply.

$$e = \frac{\alpha}{\theta\beta + 1} + \frac{\theta\beta}{\theta\beta + 1}(m - m^*) - \frac{\theta\beta\phi}{\theta\beta + 1}(y - y^*)$$

$$+ \frac{\beta(\theta\lambda + 1)}{\theta\beta + 1}(\Pi - \Pi^*) - \frac{\beta}{\theta\beta + 1}(i - i^*) + \frac{1}{\theta\beta + 1}(b - f). \quad (27)$$

In empirical terms we have simply added the relative bond supply to the monetary equation (14) as a fifth explanatory variable.

Equation (27) is intended to synthesize many varieties of asset-market model, monetary as well as portfolio balance. Since it contains the individual competing models as special cases, it provides a framework for evaluating them empirically. Table 3.3 summarizes the coefficient signs implied by the various models in a regression of equation (27). The implications of the various models are so conflicting that one would think that regression could hardly help but reject some models in favor of others.

Table 3.4 reports the regression of equation (27). The results are similar to those in tables 3.1 and 3.2. The coefficients of the variables from the monetary equation—the relative money supply, relative income, interest differential, and inflation differential—are usually correct in sign. However, when we correct for serial correlation, most of them lose their significance. The coefficient of the relative bond supply, in the uniform-preference and German small-country version, appears significant but of the *reverse* sign from that hypothesized in the portfolio-balance model.

An examination of the data on dollar and mark bond supplies readily reveals the problem with tables 3.2 and 3.4. During a period when the dollar/mark rate rose on average, the dollar bond supply (like the dollar

Table 3.4
Estimation of synthesis exchange rate Equation (27)—log of dollar/mark rate, January 1974–October 1978[a]

Technique	c	usmlb − gml	usy − gy	usi − gi	usΠ − gΠ	usb − gb	usb − usf	gb − gf	R^2	D.W.	$\hat{\rho}$
1. OLS	0.086 (0.131)	−0.751[b] (0.136)	0.357 (0.190)	−1.588[c] (0.550)	2.657[c] (0.530)	−0.578[b] (0.121)			0.86	0.56	
CORC	−0.260 (0.230)	−0.011 (0.358)	−0.133 (0.224)	−0.396 (0.502)	0.852 (0.766)	−0.398[b] (0.091)			0.94		0.97
2. OLS	−0.520 (0.090)	−0.388 (0.226)	−0.281 (0.229)	0.706 (0.595)	5.559[c] (0.597)		0.419[c] (0.115)		0.83	0.84	
CORC	−0.674 (0.256)	0.190 (0.416)	−0.355 (0.255)	0.156 (0.570)	0.773 (0.928)		−0.184 (0.194)		0.92		0.98
3. OLS	−0.772 (0.086)	−0.687 (0.116)	−0.220 (0.167)	−0.491 (0.420)	4.480[c] (0.371)			0.284[b] (0.041)	0.89	0.76	
CORC	−1.103 (0.186)	0.050 (0.314)	−0.056 (0.208)	−0.358 (0.465)	1.851[c] (0.691)			0.313[b] (0.052)	0.95		0.92

a. Definitions: see tables 3.1 and 3.2. (Standard errors are in parentheses.)
b. Significant at the 95 percent level and of the incorrect sign.
c. Significant at the 95 percent level and of the correct sign.

money supply) did *not* increase as fast as its mark counterpart. The problem can be traced to foreign exchange intervention: Foreign central banks rapidly increased their holdings of dollar assets in order to keep their own currencies from appreciating against the dollar. As Hooper and Morton [1982] point out, one cannot use a current account deficit within the portfolio-balance model to explain a currency depreciation if the deficit is more than offset by exchange intervention on the part of foreign central banks.

To the extent that this intervention was sterilized, its failure to maintain the value of the dollar is evidence against the portfolio-balance approach and in favor of the monetary approach.[32] As noted in section 3.2.3, the purchases of dollars by foreign central banks *were* allowed to increase their money supplies. However, the relative German monetary base did not increase anywhere nearly as quickly as the relative German net bond supply. While 1978 remains a mystery for both models, the updated results in table 3.1 appear promising enough, at least in comparison to the disaster of table 3.2 and 3.4, tentatively to justify a return of attention to the monetary approach.

Notes

1. This distinction between capital mobility and substitutability is made precise by Dornbusch and Krugman [1976]. Earlier references to it appear in Girton and Henderson [1976], Girton and Roper [1976], and Dornbusch [1977]. The distinction is far from universally accepted (for example, Mundell [1963] implicitly took perfect mobility to require perfect substitutability), but is useful.

2. Empirical tests have shown covered interest parity to hold to a high degree of approximation, at least in the Eurocurrency market. See, for example, Frenkel and Levich [1977]. Covered interest parity holds less well if the interest rates used refer to treasury bills, commercial paper, or other financial securities that differ from the forward contract with respect to tax treatment, default risk, or other factors. However, at the level of aggregation relevant for most macroeconomic models we speak only of "the" interest rate, abstracting from distinctions such as that between the 30-day Eurodollar interest rate and the 30-day treasury bill rate. This paper presumes that level of aggregation and presumes covered interest parity.

3. It is difficult to test uncovered interest parity empirically because expectations are not observable. Uncovered interest parity (and, by implication, perfect substitutability) can be tested *jointly* with market efficiency by examining the ex post excess return on domestic currency. The excess return is defined as the interest differential in excess of ex post depreciation, or alternatively (given covered interest parity) as the forward discount in excess of ex post depreciation. Under the joint null hypothesis, the ex post excess return should be random; the forward rate should be an unbiased predictor of the future spot rate (see figure 3.1).

Most such tests take the perfect substitutability component of the joint hypothesis as given and interpret the results as evidence on efficiency. See for example Cornell [1977], Cornell and Dietrich [1979], Frankel [1980], and Frenkel [1977]; the literature is surveyed by Levich [1979] and Kohlhagen [1978]. But a few such tests take the market efficiency component of the joint hypothesis as given and interpret the results as evidence on substitutability. See Stockman [1978], Cumby and Obstfeld [1979], and Frankel [1982b].

4. Some of the many examples are Allen and Kenen [1980]; Black [1973]; Branson [1976]; Branson, Halttunen, and Masson [1977]; Calvo and Rodriguez [1977]; Dooley and Isard [1979]; Dornbusch [1980a]; Flood [1979]; Girton and Henderson [1977]; Girton and Roper [1976]; Kouri [1976a, 1978]; Kouri and deMacedo [1978]; McKinnon [1976]; Porter [1979]; Tobin and deMacedo [1980]; and Rodriguez [1980]. The antecedents are the portfolio-balance approach under fixed exchange rates, as represented by Branson [1968], and the portfolio-balance model in a closed economy, as represented by Tobin [1969].

5. Examples are Frenkel [1976, 1977, 1980], Mussa [1976], Dornbusch [1976a,b], Girton and Roper [1977], Bilson [1978a,b], Hodrick [1978], and Frankel [1979b].

6. Officer [1976] surveys the literature on purchasing power parity. Some recent empirical studies are Isard [1977], Genberg [1978], and Krugman [1978].

7. This distinction between the monetary approach to exchange rates and the more restrictive monetarist model follows the distinction made by Whitman [1975] in the theory of fixed exchange rates between the monetary approach to the balance of payments and the more restrictive "global monetarist" model. (In the past— Frankel [1979b]—I have used the term "Chicago model" for what I am here calling the monetarist model.)

8. Little, if any, published monetarist work asserts this restrictive special case, the monetarists having long ago relaxed the quantity theory of money to study the effect of expected inflation on money demand.
A recent paper by Caves and Feige [1980] that purports to test "the monetary approach to exchange-rate determination" uses as its criterion the unusual proposition that the exchange rate is entirely explainable by the past history of the money supplies. Even the most extreme monetarist proponent of the monetary approach recognizes the importance of fluctuations in real income.
In a further confusion, Caves and Feige claim that proponents of the monetary approach "have failed to recognize that one of the consequences of an efficient foreign exchange market is to eliminate the possibility of directly observing a systematic relationship [between] exchange rates and past supplies of national monies. If the foreign exchange market is efficient, all monetary effects on exchange rates will be contemporaneous" [1980, p. 121]. But as is well known, market efficiency requires not that changes in the spot rate be independent of past variables such as money supplies, but that changes in the spot rate *in excess of the interest differential* (or forward discount) be independent of past variables. In any monetary model except the restrictive special case described above, the past history of the money supply may contain information on changes in the spot rate without violating efficiency. In the benchmark monetarist model, for example, the interest differential

and the rationally expected change in the spot rate are each equal to the relative rate of expected monetary growth; actual changes in the spot rate will be independent of past money supply *changes*, not *levels*. In the Dornbusch overshooting model, changes in the spot rate are not independent of either past money supply changes *or* levels.

9. See Mundell [1964], Argy and Porter [1972], Niehans [1975], and Dornbusch [1976a,b].

10. The version that follows is based on Dornbusch [1976b] as generalized in Frankel [1979b] to include the case of secular inflation. (In that paper I used the term "Keynesian model" for what I am here calling the overshooting model. We should also note that overshooting is possible in other models, as shown by Flood [1979].) Investigations of the overshooting properties of the Dornbusch model include Mathieson [1977] and Bhandari [1981].

11. In the appendix to Frankel [1979b], it is proved that the form of exchange rate expectations specified in (12) is rational, assuming an additional equation in which the price level adjusts in the short run in response to excess goods demand (itself a function of relative prices, and possibly income and the real interest rate) and increases in the long run at the secular inflation rate (Π).

12. For example, Bilson [1978a,b], Hodrick [1978], Dornbusch [1978], Kohlhagen [1979], Frankel [1979b], and Driskill [1981].

13. For example, Dornbusch [1980], and an earlier version of the present paper.

14. The unexplained fall in demand for dollars relative to marks may be associated with the observed unexplained downward shift in the US money demand function known as "the mystery of the missing money."

15. Krugman [1980] identifies OPEC's asset-holding and importing preferences between the United States and Europe as the key determinants of the effect of oil price increases on the value of the dollar. Obstfeld [1980b] is typical of a number of papers that emphasize oil's role as an intermediate input and are primarily relevant for small countries.

16. For example, Hooper and Morton [1982], Isard [1980] and Dornbusch [1980b].

17. The expenditure channel is represented by Dornbusch and Fischer [1980]. Wealth enters the money demand function in Dornbusch [1976c] and Frankel [1982a]. Both effects are present in Turnovsky and Kingston [1979]. The strategy of attempting to "put the current account back" into the asset-market models through the portfolio-balance effect is made explicit by Kouri [1976a], Kouri and deMacedo [1978], Hooper and Morton [1982], Porter [1979], Dooley and Isard [1979], and Rodriguez [1980]. Dornbusch [1980b] mentions all three wealth effects (pp. 154–57, 164, and 164–68, respectively), but emphasizes the imperfect substitutability effect as "more persuasive."

18. If portfolio-balance behavior is the outcome of the maximization of expected utility by risk-averse investors, then we are implicitly assuming in (16) that the variances of currency values, and covariances with other forms of real wealth, are stationary over time. Only the expected rate of return is assumed to vary.

19. If the expected future exchange rate is $\overline{\mathscr{E}e_{+1}}$, then the solution for the current exchange rate, in log form, is

$$e = -\frac{\alpha}{1 + \beta} + \frac{1}{1 + \beta}(b - f) + \frac{\beta}{1 + \beta}(\overline{\mathscr{E}e_{+1}} - (i - i^*)).$$

20. Kouri [1976a] considers the alternatives of static and rational (or perfect foresight) expectations.

21. If government-issued assets are not considered net wealth by the private sector because they imply off-setting liabilities in the form of future taxation, the Ricardian principle, then the possibility arises that the net supply of outside assets to the world market is zero. If there are no outside assets (including real assets) then exchange risk is completely diversifiable. Under these very special circumstances, investors will consider domestic and foreign bonds perfect substitutes in market equilibrium because they can always cover any exchange risk on the forward market *without* paying any risk premium; the perfect substitutability assumption holds despite risk aversion. (The argument is made in Frankel [1979a]. For an empirical test of perfect substitutability based on equation (17) see Frankel [1982b].)

22. Of course many small countries do sometimes issue debt denomination in foreign currencies, and even the United States began to do so with its Carter notes. (The Roosa bonds of the 1960s do not count because they were held by foreign governments rather than citizens.) In empirical work, any such debt must be counted according to its currency of denomination. A bigger problem is central bank behavior. Purchases of domestically denominated assets in foreign exchange intervention (by foreign as well as domestic central banks) must be subtracted from treasury debt to arrive at the proper measure of the net supply of domestically denominated assets to the private market.

23. At the opposite extreme, Solnik [1974] derives asset-demand functions as the outcome of maximization by agents who consume only goods produced in their own countries.

24. Branson [1976], Kouri [1976a], Flood [1979], Branson, Halttunen, and Masson [1977], Porter [1979], Dornbusch and Fischer [1980], and Rodriguez [1980], among others, assume that domestic assets are not held by foreigners.

25. Shafer [1979] assumes that the foreign country is the small country, that is, the foreign accumulated current account surplus is the supply of domestically denominated bonds.

26. A small but growing number of models allow the foreign preference for holding domestic assets to be less than the domestic preference and yet greater than zero. In the category of finance models that derive asset-demand functions from expected-utility maximization are Kouri [1976b] and Kouri and deMacedo [1978] and the appendix to Dornbusch [1980a]. The necessary assumption at first appears to be only that the foreign preference for consuming domestic goods is less than the domestic preference and yet greater than zero. However, Krugman [1981] shows in a continuous-time stochastic model that it is also necessary that the coefficient of relative risk-aversion be greater than one.

In the category of macroeconomic models of portfolio balance which take asset-demand functions as given are Dooley and Isard [1979] and parts IV and V of Allen and Kenen [1980]. Henderson and Rogoff [1981] use such a model to investigate the possibility that negative holdings of foreign assets cause dynamic instability (a possibility that in a small-country context concerns Branson, Halttunen, and Masson [1977] and Obstfeld [1980a] among others).

27. These calculations become especially difficult after October 1978 because of the issuing of Carter notes by the Treasury, the holding of foreign exchange reserves valued at current exchange rates by the Federal Reserve, and the turning over of reserves to the European Monetary System by the Bundesbank. For this reason the data sample used in tables 3.2 and 3.4 ends in October 1978. Data sources were the *Federal Reserve Bulletin* and the *Bundesbank Monthly Report Statistical Supplements*. Data and details of the calculations are available on request.

28. The term "currency substitution" was originated by Girton and Roper [1981] to describe the allocation of market portfolios between domestic and foreign money. Other examples are Barro [1978] and Calvo and Rodriguez [1977]. In many of the theoretical models, only the use of the words "money" or "currency" distinguishes them from the other portfolio-balance models, which use the words "bonds" or "assets." But one might argue, following note 21, that, to the extent that government debt implies future tax liabilities to pay it off, high-powered money is the only true outside asset, and thus the only asset able to create nondiversifiable exchange risk for the private market.

Presumably if only money is included in the asset measures, the interest rates do not belong in the equation. Some currency substitution models, such as Miles [1978], use interest rates as the opportunity cost of money, thus hypothesizing a *positive* coefficient in the exchange rate equation. It is difficult to distinguish such an equation from the reduced form of the monetarist model (7), in which national moneys are held only in their own countries but bonds and goods are perfect substitutes across countries.

Branson, Halttunen, and Masson [1977, 1979] include bonds in their theoretical model, in addition to money, and use them to solve out the endogenous interest rate. However, they restrict the empirical estimation to money supplies under the rationale that the effect of an increase in the supply of domestic bonds on the exchange rate is ambiguous: The resulting increase in the interest rate has the opposite effect from the increase in total domestic assets. Porter [1979] does the same. Dooley and Isard [1979] restrict their asset measures to bonds throughout, which strategy table 3.2 follows.

29. Of course, if the world really consisted of only two countries, one country's current account would be the negative of the other and row 4 would be subject to perfect multicollinearity. However, there are many wealth holders not residing in either Germany or the United States.

30. Branson, Halttunen, and Masson [1977, 1979] regress the exchange rate against all four stock variables although their theoretical discussion is based on the small-country model. Such an equation cannot be rationalized by the assumption that both the United States and Germany are small countries, aside from the unrealism of such an assumption, unless the current account and intervention figures that enter into usf and gf are cumulated in terms of some third currency such as the

SDR. This method of calculation produces results no better than those in table 3.2.

One possible rationale for such an equation is that it is a log-linear approximation to the two-country relation described after equation (22).

31. Hooper and Morton [1982] and Isard [1980] integrate the risk premium into the monetary equation in a very similar fashion. For a more theoretical synthesis of the portfolio-balance model and the sticky-price monetary model, see Henderson [1980].

32. In the monetary approach, foreign exchange intervention affects the exchange rate *only* to the extent that it is nonsterilized, that is, allowed by the central banks to affect the money supplies. Girton and Henderson [1977], p. 169, and Obstfeld [1980a, pp. 142–43], illustrate this point in portfolio-balance models as the special case in which domestic and foreign bonds are perfect substitutes.

References

Allen, Polly, and Kenen, Peter (1980). *Asset Markets, Exchange Rates, and Economic Integration.* New York: Cambridge University Press.

Argy, Victor, and Porter, Michael (1972). "Forward Exchange Market and the Effects of Domestic and External Disturbances under Alternative Exchange Rate Systems." *IMF Staff Papers:* 503–28.

Barro, Robert (1978). "A Stochastic Equilibrium Model of an Open Economy under Flexible Exchange Rates." *Quarterly Journal of Economics.* February: 149–64.

Bhandari, Jagdeep (1981). "A Simple Transnational Model of Large Open Economics." *Southern Economic Journal.* April.

Bilson, John (1978a). "The Monetary Approach to the Exchange Rate: Some Evidence." *IMF Staff Papers* 25. March: 48–75.

Bilson, John (1978b). "Rational Expectations and the Exchange Rate." In *The Economics of Exchange Rates.* Edited by J. Frenkel and H. G. Johnson. Reading, MA: Addison-Wesley.

Black, Stanley (1973). "International Money Markets and Flexible Exchange Rates." *Princeton Studies in International Finance* no. 32. March.

Branson, William (1968). *Financial Capital Flows in the U.S. Balance of Payments.* Amsterdam: North-Holland.

Branson, William (1976). "Asset Markets and Relative Prices in Exchange Rate Determination." IIES Seminar Paper no. 66, Stockholm. December.

Branson, William, Halttunen, Hannu, and Masson, Paul (1977). "Exchange Rates in the Short Run: The Dollar-Deutschemark Rate." *European Economic Review* 10, no. 3: 303–24.

Branson, William, Halttunen, Hannu, and Masson, Paul (1979). "Exchange Rates in the Short Run: Some Further Results." *European Economic Review* 12, no. 4. October: 395–402.

Calvo, Guillermo, and Rodriguez, Carlos (1977). "A Model of Exchange Rate

Determination under Currency Substitution and Rational Expectations." *Journal of Political Economy* 85, no. 3. June: 617–26.

Caves, Douglas, and Feige, Edgar (1980). "Efficient Foreign Exchange Markets and the Monetary Approach to Exchange-Rate Determination." *American Economic Review* 70, no. 1. March: 120–34.

Cornell, Bradford (1977). "Spot Rates, Forward Rates and Exchange Market Efficiency." *Journal of Financial Economics* 5. Reprinted in *International Financial Management*. Edited by D. Lessard. Boston: Warren, Gorham and Lamont. 1979.

Cornell, Bradford, and Dietrich, J. K. (1979). "The Efficiency of the Market for Foreign Exchange under Floating Exchange Rates." *Review of Economic Statistics* 60, no. 1. February.

Cumby, Robert, and Obstfeld, Maurice (1981). "A Note on Exchange-Rate Expectations and Nominal Interest Differentials: A Test of the Fisher Hypothesis." *Journal of Finance* 36. June.

Dooley, Michael, and Isard, Peter (1979). "The Portfolio-Balance Model of Exchange Rates." International Finance Discussion Paper no. 141, Federal Reserve Board. May.

Dornbusch, Rudiger (1976a). "The Theory of Flexible Exchange Rate Regimes and Macroeconomic Policy." *Scandinavian Journal of Economics* 78, no. 2. May: 255–79. Reprinted in J. Frenkel and H. Johnson, eds., *The Economics of Exchange Rates*. Reading, MA: Addison-Wesley. 1978.

Dornbusch, Rudiger (1976b). "Expectations and Exchange Rate Dynamics." *Journal Political Economy* 84, no. 6. December: 1161–76..

Dornbusch, Rudiger (1976c). "Capital Mobility, Flexible Exchange Rates and Macroeconomic Equilibrium." In *Recent Developments in International Monetary Economics*. Edited by E. Claasen and P. Salin. Amsterdam: North Holland.

Dornbusch, Rudiger (1977). "Capital Mobility and Portfolio Balance." In *The Political Economy of Monetary Reform*. Edited by R. Aliber. London: Macmillan & Co.

Dornbusch, Rudiger (1978). "Monetary Policy Under Exchange Rate Flexibility." In *Managed Exchange Rate Flexibility*, Federal Reserve Bank of Boston Conference Series. Reprinted in D. Lessard, ed., *International Financial Management*. Boston: Warren, Gorham and Lamont. 1979.

Dornbusch, Rudiger (1980a). "Exchange Risk and the Macroeconomics of Exchange Rate Determination." MIT. April. [Published in 1982 in *The Internationalization of Financial Markets and National Economic Policy*. Edited by R. Hawkins, R. Levich, and C. Wihlborg. Greenwich, CT: JAI Press.]

Dornbusch, Rudiger (1980b). "Exchange Rate Economics: Where Do We Stand?" *Brookings Papers on Economic Activity* 1:143–94. Adapted for this volume, chapter 2.

Dornbusch, Rudiger, and Fischer, Stanley (1980). "Exchange Rates and the Current Account." *American Economic Review* 70, no. 5. December:960–71.

Dornbusch, Rudiger, and Krugman, Paul (1976). "Flexible Exchange Rates in the Short Run." *Brookings Papers on Economic Activity* 3:537–75.

Driskill, Robert (1981). "Exchange Rate Dynamics: An Empirical Investigation." *Journal of Political Economy* 89, no. 2. April:357–71.

Fama, Eugene, and Farber, Andre (1979). "Money, Bonds and Foreign Exchange." *American Economic Review* 69, no. 4. September: 639–49.

Flood, Robert (1979). "An Example of Exchange Rate Overshooting." *Southern Economic Journal* 46:68–78.

Frankel, Jeffrey (1979a). "The Diversifiability of Exchange Risk." *Journal of International Economics* 9. August:379–93.

Frankel, Jeffrey (1979b). "On the Mark: A Theory of Floating Exchange Rates Based on Real Interest Differentials." *American Economic Review* 69, no. 4. September:610–22.

Frankel, Jeffrey (1980). "Tests of Rational Expectations in the Forward Exchange Market." *Southern Economic Journal* 46, no. 4. April:1083–1101.

Frankel, Jeffrey (1982a). "The Mystery of the Multiplying Marks: A Modification of the Monetary Model." *Review of Economics and Statistics*. August.

Frankel, Jeffrey (1982b). "A Test of Perfect Substitutability in the Foreign Exchange Market." *Southern Economic Journal*. October.

Frenkel, Jacob (1976). "A Monetary Approach to the Exchange Rate: Doctrinal Aspects and Empirical Evidence." *Scandinavian Journal of Economics* 78, no. 2. May: 200–224. Reprinted in J. Frenkel and H. Johnson, eds., *The Economics of Exchange Rates*. Reading, MA: Addison-Wesley. 1978.

Frenkel, Jacob (1977). "The Forward Exchange Rate, Expectations, and the Demand for Money: The German Hyperinflation." *American Economic Review* 67, no. 4:653–70.

Frenkel, Jacob (1980). "Exchange Rates, Prices and Money: Lessons from the 1920s." *American Economic Review* 70, no. 2. May:235–42.

Frenkel, Jacob, and Levich, Richard (1977). "Transactions Costs and Interest Arbitrage: Tranquil versus Turbulent Periods." *Journal of Political Economy* 85, no. 6:1207–24. Reprinted in D. Lessard, ed., *International Financial Management*. Boston: Warren, Gorham and Lamont. 1979.

Genberg, Hans (1978). "Purchasing Power Parity under Fixed and Flexible Exchange Rates." *Journal of International Economics* 8. May:247–76.

Girton, Lance, and Henderson, Dale (1976). "Financial Capital Movements and Central Bank Behavior in a Two-Country, Short-Run Portfolio Balance Model." *Journal of Monetary Economics* 2:33–61.

Girton, Lance, and Henderson, Dale (1977). "Central Bank Operations in Foreign and Domestic Assets under Fixed and Flexible Exchange Rates." In *The Effects of Exchange Rate Adjustments*. Edited by P. Clark, D. Logue, and R. Sweeney. Washington: US Government Printing Office, pp. 151–79.

Girton, Lance, and Roper, Don. 1977. "A Monetary Model of Exchange Market

Pressure Applied to the Postwar Canadian Experience." *American Economic Review* 67, no. 4. September:537–48.

Girton, Lance, and Roper, Don (1981). "Theory and Implications of Currency Substitution." *Journal of Money, Credit and Banking.* 13, no 1. February: 12–30.

Grauer, F. L. A., Litzenberger, R. H., and Stehle, R. E. (1976). "Sharing Rules and Equilibrium in an International Capital Market under Uncertainty." *Journal of Financial Economics* 3, no. 3.

Gray, M., and Turnovsky, S. (1979). "The Stability of Exchange Rates Dynamics under Perfect Myopic Foresight." *International Economic Review* 20, October: 643–60.

Henderson, Dale (1980). "The Dynamic Effects of Exchange Market Intervention: Two Extreme Views and a Synthesis." In H. Frisch and G. Schwödiauer, eds., *The Economics of Flexible Exchange Rates,* Supplement to *Kredit und Kapitol* (Heft 6). Berlin: Duncker and Humblot, pp. 156–209.

Henderson, Dale, and Rogoff, Kenneth (1981). "Net Foreign Asset Positions and Stability in a World Portfolio Balance Model." Federal Reserve Board International Finance Discussion Paper no. 178.

Hodrick, Robert (1978). "An Empirical Analysis of the Monetary Approach to the Determination of the Exchange Rate." In *The Economics of Exchange Rates.* Edited by J. Frenkel and H. Johnson. Reading, MA: Addison-Wesley, pp. 97–116.

Hooper, Peter, and Morton, John (1982). "Fluctuations in the Dollar: A Model of Nominal and Real Exchange Rate Determination." *Journal of International Money and Finance* 1, 1. April.

Isard, Peter (1977). "How Far Can We Push the 'Law of one Price'?" *American Economic Review* 67. December: 942–48.

Isard, Peter (1980). "Factors Determining Exchange Rates: The Roles of Relative Price Levels, Balances of Payments, Interest Rates and Risk." Federal Reserve Board International Finance Discussion Paper no. 171. December.

Kohlhagen, Steven (1978). *The Behavior of Foreign Exchange Markets—A Critical Survey of the Literature.* N.Y.U. Monograph Series in Finance and Economics.

Kohlhagen, Steven (1979). "On the Identification of Destabilizing Speculation." *Journal of International Economics,* 9: 321–40.

Kouri, Pentti (1976a). "The Exchange Rate and the Balance of Payments in the Short Run and in the Long Run: A Monetary Approach." *Scandinavian Journal of Economics* 78, no. 2. May: 280–304.

Kouri, Pentti (1976b). "The Determinants of the Forward Premium." Seminar Paper 62, University of Stockholm. August.

Kouri, Pentti (1978). "Balance of Payments and the Foreign Exchange Market: A Dynamic Partial Equilibrium Model." Cowles Foundation Discussion Paper no. 510, Yale University. November. Also appearing in this volume, chapter 4.

Kouri, Pentti, and de Macedo, Jorge (1978). "Exchange Rates and the International Adjustment Process." *Brookings Papers on Economic Activity* 1: 11–50.

Krugman, Paul (1978). "Purchasing Power Parity and Exchange Rates: Another Look at the Evidence." *Journal of International Economics* 8, no. 3. August: 347–407.

Krugman, Paul (1980). "Oil and the Dollar." MIT, June. Also appearing in this volume, chapter 6.

Krugman, Paul (1981). "Consumption Preferences, Asset Demands, and Distribution Effects in International Financial Markets." NBER Working Paper no. 651. March.

Levich, Richard (1979). "On the Efficiency of Markets for Foreign Exchange." In *International Economic Policy*. Edited by R. Dornbusch and J. Frenkel. Baltimore: Johns Hopkins University Press, pp. 246–66.

Mathieson, Donald (1977). "The Impact of Monetary and Fiscal Policy under Flexible Exchange Rates and Alternative Expectations Structures." *IMF Staff Papers*. November: 535–68.

McKinnon, Ronald (1976). "Floating Exchange Rates, 1973–74: The Emperor's New Clothes." In *Institutional Arrangements and the Inflation Problem*. Edited by K. Brunner and A. Meltzer. Carnegie-Rochester Conference Series on Public Policy, vol. 3. New York: American-Elsevier.

Miles, Marc (1978). "Currency Substitution, Flexible Exchange Rates and Monetary Independence." *American Economic Review* 68, no. 3. June: 428–36.

Mundell, Robert (1963). "Capital Mobility and Stabilization Policy under Fixed and Flexible Exchange Rates." *Canadian Journal of Economics and Political Science* 29, no. 4. November: 475–485. Adapted in R. Mundell, *International Economics*. New York: Macmillan. 1968.

Mundell, Robert (1964). "The Exchange Rate Margins and Economic Policy." In *Money in the International Order*. Edited by J. C. Murphy. Dallas.

Mussa, Michael (1976). "The Exchange Rate, the Balance of Payments, and Monetary and Fiscal Policy under a Regime of Controlled Floating." *Scandinavian Journal of Economics* 2. May: 229–48. Reprinted in J. Frenkel and H. Johnson, eds., *The Economics of Exchange Rates*. Reading, MA: Addison-Wesley. 1978.

Niehans, Jurg (1975). "Some Doubts about the Efficacy of Monetary Policy under Flexible Exchange Rates." *Journal of International Economics* 5. August: 275–81.

Obstfeld, Maurice (1980a). "Portfolio Balance, Monetary Policy, and the Dollar-Deutsche Mark Exchange Rate." Columbia U. Discussion Paper 62. March.

Obstfeld, Maurice (1980b). "Intermediate Imports, the Terms of Trade, and the Dynamics of the Exchange Rate and Current Account." *Journal of International Economics* 10(4): 461–80.

Officer, Lawrence (1976). "The Purchasing Power Parity Theory of Exchange Rates: A Review Article." *IMF Staff Papers* 23. March.

Porter, Michael (1979). "Exchange Rates, Current Accounts, and Economic Activity." Federal Reserve Board. June.

Rodriguez, Carlos (1980). "The Role of Trade Flows in Exchange Rate Determination: A Rational Expectations Approach." *Journal of Political Economy.* 88, no. 6. December: 1148–58.

Rogoff, Kenneth (1979). "Anticipated and Transitory Shocks in a Model of Exchange Rate Dynamics." Chapter 2 of Ph.D. dissertation, MIT.

Shafer, Jeffrey (1979). "Flexible Exchange Rates, Capital Flows and Current Account Adjustment." Federal Reserve Board. October.

Solnik, Bruno (1974). "An Equilibrium Model of the International Capital Market." *Journal of Economic Theory* 8, no. 4: 500–24.

Stockman, Alan (1978). "Risk, Information, and Forward Exchange Rates." In *The Economics of Exchange Rates.* Edited by J. Frenkel and H. Johnson. Reading, MA: Addison-Wesley, pp. 193–212.

Tobin, James (1969). "A General-Equilibrium Approach to Monetary Theory." *JMCB* 1. February: 15–29.

Tobin, James, and deMacedo, Jorge Braga (1980). "The Short-Run Macro-economics of Floating Exchange Rates: An Exposition." In *Flexible Exchange Rates and the Balance of Payments: Essays in Memory of Egon Sohmen.* Edited by J. Chipman and C. P. Kindleberger. New York: North-Holland.

Turnovsky, S., and C. Kingston (1979). "Government Policies and Secular Inflation Under Flexible Exchange Rates." *Southern Economic Journal* 47: 389–412.

Whitman, Marina V. N. (1975). "Global Monetarism and the Monetary Approach to the Balance of Payments." *Brookings Papers on Economic Activity* 3: 491–536.

Wilson, Charles (1979). "Anticipated Shocks and Exchange Rate Dynamics." *Journal of Political Economy* 87, no. 3. June: 639–47.

4

Balance of Payments and the Foreign Exchange Market: A Dynamic Partial Equilibrium Model

Pentti J. K. Kouri

The modern theory of flexible exchange rates appears to have no connection with actual market processes. There is no explicit treatment of the sources of supply and demand in the foreign exchange market and no explicit analysis of how supply and demand interact in that market to determine the exchange rate. In part this is because such details are hidden in the background of general equilibrium models; but in part it is because analysis has been reduced to terms that bear no connection to supply and demand in the foreign exchange market. An example of the latter is the monetarist theory of exchange rate determination according to which "the exchange rate is a relative price of two monies and as such is determined by the relative supplies of these monies on the one hand and the relative demands for these monies on the other" (see Frankel, 1976; Mussa, 1976; and Bilson, 1978). This cannot be a statement about supply and demand in the foreign exchange market because, as mentioned, they derive from demands for and supplies of all kinds of assets and goods and services. In fact holdings of foreign money are so small that the direct effect of changes in money demand or supply on the exchange rate must be insignificant. Rather, such shifts affect the exchange rate through their effect, *ex ante*, on capital movements and other components of the balance of payments.

In many of the recent models, including Dornbusch (1976), it is assumed that all other assets but monies are perfect substitutes. In such models

This chapter extends and refines in part an earlier paper entitled "Capital Flows and the Dynamics of the Exchange Rate," Seminar Paper No. 67, Institute for International Economic Studies, University of Stockholm, December 1976. The chapter was first written while I was in the Finnish army. At that time the work was supported by a grant from the Yrjo Jahnsson Foundation. I wish to thank the Jahnsson Foundation for this support, and also the Ford Foundation for their support in 1979/80. I also wish to thank Jorge de Macedo for many helpful discussions.

balance of payments pressures have no effect on the exchange rate, which can deviate from its purchasing power parity, or long-run equilibrium, value only to the extent that monetary conditions permit differences in interest rates, as is shown in Kouri and de Macedo (1978). These models cannot, however, explain observed movements in exchange rates in recent years because these movements have been far in excess of differences in inflation rates even if allowance is made for anticipated differences in future inflation rates as reflected in interest rate differentials. The models of perfect substitutability simply assume away market pressures that could account for the observed behavior. As one example, they cannot explain the tendency of the currencies of surplus countries to appreciate and those of deficit countries to depreciate continuously in real terms. This stylized fact of recent years cannot be explained either by the "textbook" partial equilibrium model, based on Bickerdike (1920), Robinson (1937), and Machlup (1939, 1940). In that model the capital flow account is independent of the exchange rate—in fact, it is treated as a transfer payment. This implies that *ex ante* shifts in the current account or in the capital flow account give rise to once-and-for-all adjustments in the exchange rate. Furthermore, shifts in the trade balance *ex ante* have no effect on the current account *ex post* because the *ex post* current account is determined independently of the exchange rate.

The purpose of this chapter is to develop a dynamic supply-demand model of the foreign exchange market, consistent with the modern general equilibrium approach—given the assumption that prices or quantities in other markets are exogenous. The burden of balance of payments adjustment is thus assumed to fall on the exchange rate alone.

It is assumed that the foreign exchange market clears continuously, as indeed it almost does. Therefore, at a given time only stock demands for and supplies of foreign exchange derived from stock transactions on the capital account matter in determining the short-run equilibrium value of the exchange rate. This is similar to the liquidity preference theory of interest rate determination, or the theory of the determination of the demand price of capital assets in terms of stocks rather than flows. It is also consistent with the general equilibrium "asset market approach" to international monetary economics that determines all of these prices simultaneously by conditions of stock equilibrium.

Given the short-run equilibrium value, the exchange rate must change *per unit of time* in such a way as to equilibrate flow demands for and supplies of foreign exchange derived from capital flows on the one hand and current account transactions on the other. Capital flows are functions of the rate of change of the exchange rate because the *stock* demand for foreign assets is a function of the level of the exchange rate. Therefore in order for the foreign exchange market to stay in equilibrium, domestic currency must depreciate whenever the current account is in deficit (in excess of "normal deficit") and appreciate whenever the current account is in surplus (in excess of "normal surplus"). This *acceleration hypothesis* accords well with the behavior of the major currencies in recent years.

In long-run equilibrium the real exchange rate is constant and is determined by the condition that the current account is at its normal level, which is taken to be zero in this analysis.

4.1 Capital Account and the Exchange Rate: Short-Run Equilibrium in the Foreign Exchange Market

The foreign exchange market is but one of many interconnected financial markets. Its special nature is that intermediation and arbitrage between financial markets in different currency areas must go through it: To invest abroad in excess of their current holdings of foreign assets domestic residents must first acquire foreign currency in the amount of their planned investment; to add to their asset holdings in the domestic economy foreign residents must similarly first acquire domestic currency in the foreign exchange market. Demand for and supply of foreign currency, or what comes to the same, demand for and supply of domestic currency *at a given time* can thus be derived from domestic demand for foreign assets in excess of already existing holdings on the one hand and foreign demand for domestic assets in excess of existing holdings on the other. This description must be qualified when domestic residents lend to foreign residents in domestic currency or when foreign residents lend to domestic residents in foreign currency: This case is analyzed separately in appendix 3.

Consider now how domestic demand for foreign assets and foreign demand for domestic assets depend on the exchange rate. For this purpose assume that prices and rates of return of all assets in the domestic economy are exogenously given in domestic currency, and that prices and rates of return of foreign assets are exogenously given in foreign currency. Thus all domestic assets can be aggregated into a single "domestic asset" whose price for a foreign investor is the foreign currency price of domestic currency; and similarly all foreign assets can be aggregated into a single foreign asset whose price for a domestic investor is the domestic currency price of foreign currency, *ceteris paribus*.

Portfolio theory suggests that, given total domestic marketable wealth, domestic residents want to hold some fraction of it in foreign assets, this fraction depending on expected returns and risk characteristics of domestic and foreign assets.[1] Therefore, taking prices of foreign assets as exogenous in foreign currency and the stock of domestic marketable wealth as exogenous in domestic currency, it follows that domestic demand for foreign assets is a declining function of the price of foreign currency with elasticity of minus one.[2] By the same reasoning, demand for domestic assets by foreign residents is a declining function of the price of domestic currency in terms of foreign currency with elasticity of minus one. This simple result linking stock transactions on the capital account to the level of the exchange rate has not, surprisingly, been noted in the literature. Thus in a recent paper on foreign exchange market intervention John Williamson (1976) states that "in striking contrast [to the current account] there are rather few reasons for expecting the capital account to depend on the *level* of the exchange rate, but compelling reasons for expecting it to depend on the expected change in the rate."[3] Similarly in his well-known paper on flexible rates Dornbusch (1976) assumes away the dependence of capital account transactions on the level of the exchange rate with the assumption of perfect substitutability between domestic and foreign assets, except for money. Therefore the exchange rate is indeterminate in his model in a system of dual exchange rates, when the capital account is isolated from the trade account.[4]

4.1.1 The Formal Model of Short-Run Equilibrium

To develop the model formally let F_0 be the stock of foreign assets held by domestic residents at time 0 valued in foreign currency, and let G_0 be the stock of domestic assets held by foreign residents at time 0 valued in domestic currency. F_0 and G_0 are both given at the initial moment. In contrast, the *desired holdings* of foreign assets by domestic residents F^d and of domestic assets by foreign residents G^d are subject to choice. Let s be the domestic currency price of foreign exchange. Then $F^d - F_0$ is the stock demand for foreign exchange derived from domestic excess demand for foreign assets (in excess of initial holdings) and $(G^d - G_0)/s$ the stock supply of foreign exchange derived from foreign excess demand for domestic assets. Momentary equilibrium in the foreign exchange market is then defined by

$$(F^d - F_0) + (I^d - I_0) = (G^d - G_0)/s, \tag{1}$$

where

I_0 = initial stock of central bank's foreign exchange reserves,

I^d = desired stock of foreign exchange reserves,

$I^d - I_0$ = central bank's purchase of foreign exchange at time 0.

With fixed exchange rates change in reserves, $I^d - I_0$ is the residual that equilibrates the foreign exchange market; with clean floating $I^d - I_0$ is zero and the exchange rate adjusts to equilibrate private demand and supply. Between these two extremes there are other types of regimes which can be specified by appropriate characterization of intervention behavior. In the present paper we restrict the analysis to floating with no systematic intervention.

Next we need to specify the asset demand functions. Let V be the value of domestic marketable wealth in domestic currency and V^* the value of foreign marketable wealth in foreign currency. Then, with reference to earlier discussion,

$$F^d \cdot s = f(R, R^* + \pi, z)V, \qquad G^d/s = g(R - \pi, R^*, z)V^*, \tag{2}$$

where

R = nominal rate of return on domestic assets in domestic currency,

R^* = nominal rate of return on foreign assets in foreign currency,

π = expected rate of change in the domestic currency price of foreign currency,

z = vector of other determinants of international investment.

Substituting these demand functions in equation (1) above and setting $I^d - I_0$ equal to zero, we get the condition of short-run equilibrium in the foreign exchange market with no intervention:

$$f(R, R^* + \pi, z)V/s - F_0 = g(R - \pi, R^*, z)V^* - G_0/s. \tag{3}$$

The left-hand side gives the stock demand for foreign exchange at time 0 derived from desired domestic purchases of foreign assets at time 0. It is illustrated by the downward sloping DD schedule in figure 4.1. The right-hand side gives the stock supply of foreign exchange derived from desired foreign purchases of domestic assets at time 0. It is illustrated by the upward sloping SS schedule in figure 4.1. Short-run equilibrium in the foreign exchange market, which clearly is unique, obtains at the intersection of these demand and supply schedules at A_0. As the schedules are drawn no transactions take place at the equilibrium exchange rate s_0 because initial asset holdings just happen to equal desired asset holdings. This does not mean, however, that the exchange rate is indeterminate, for a small increase in the price of foreign currency would bring forward an excess supply of foreign exchange; and a small decrease, an excess demand

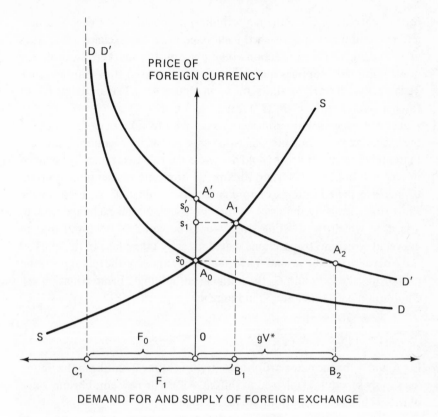

Figure 4.1
Short-run equilibrium in the foreign exchange market.

for foreign exchange. Thus, although no transactions take place, potential transactions keep the exchange rate at s_0. It is clear then that short-run equilibrium is not only unique but also stable. It will be assumed from now on that the foreign exchange market is always in short-run equilibrium.

Suppose now that domestic residents want to increase their holdings of foreign assets for some reason—for example, because of an increase in foreign interest rates. In figure 4.1 the demand schedule shifts to the right, to $D'D'$, by OB_2 at the initial exchange rate s_0. If the central bank pegged the exchange rate at s_0, it would, of course, lose reserves in that amount. With no intervention, domestic currency instead depreciates to s_1. This enables domestic residents to increase their foreign asset holdings by OB_1—which is equal in value to the additional purchases of the now cheaper domestic assets by foreign residents (measured in foreign currency). Once the new equilibrium position has been reached, and by assumption it is reached instantaneously, the exchange rate stays at s_1 and again no transactions take place in the market (ignoring for now "marginal" supplies and demands coming from flow transactions). Technically, the origin shifts to B_1 in figure 4.1: The initial stock of foreign assets is now $C_1 B_1$ (F_1) rather than $C_1 O$ (F_0).

It is not necessary for transactions actually to take place in order for the exchange rate to change, as is the case above. For example, suppose that foreign residents do not hold domestic assets, a case typically assumed in recent literature. Then an attempt by domestic residents as a group to increase their holdings of foreign assets would only succeed, in the short run, in raising the price of foreign assets, or the exchange rate, to a level at which the existing stock would be willingly held and thus to a level at which no transactions would actually take place in the market.

To develop the above analysis formally, let f and g be the initial portfolio proportions, and F_0 and G_0 the initial asset holdings. From equation (3), equilibrium exchange rate, s_0 in figure 4.1, is given by

$$s_0 = \frac{fV + G_0}{gV^* + F_0}. \tag{4}$$

Let f_1 and g_1 be the new portfolio properties at time 0 (unlike in the figure, the supply schedule is allowed to shift at well). The new equilibrium value of the exchange rate, s_1 in figure 4.1, is then

$$s_1 = \frac{f_1 V + G_0}{g_1 V^* + F_0}. \tag{5}$$

At this new exchange rate, asset holdings are

$$F_1 = f_1 V / s_1, \qquad G_1 = g_1 V^* s_1. \tag{6}$$

F_1 and G_1 become the new initial conditions. If nothing changes after the shift from (f, g) to (f_1, g_1) at the initial moment, the exchange rate will stay at s_1 with no transactions taking place thereafter. To check this apply formula (4) again to the new situation:

$$s_1' = \frac{f_1 V + G_1}{g_1 V^* + F_1} = \frac{f_1 V + g_1 V^* s_1}{g_1 V^* + f_1 V / s_1} = s_1, \tag{7}$$

which confirms that the exchange rate will indeed stay at s_1.

Figure 4.2 illustrates the effect of a once-and-for-all sale of foreign exchange by the central bank. The market is initially in equilibrium at A_0 with exchange rate s_0. The central bank sells foreign exchange in the

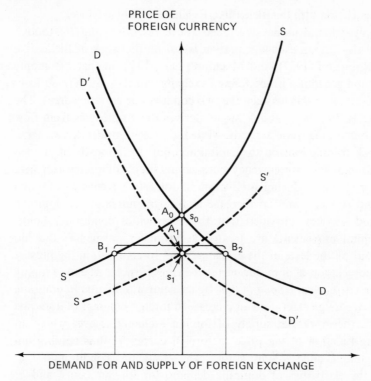

Figure 4.2
Effect of a once-and-for-all sale of foreign exchange by the central bank.

amount B_1B_2 ($= \Delta I_0$), thus forcing the price of foreign currency down
to s_1. At this new exchange rate, B_1A_1 of the decline in central bank
reserves finances an increase in domestic holdings of foreign assets,
while the rest, A_1B_2 in the figure, finances a reduction in foreign holdings
of domestic assets. The exchange rate will not return to s_0 immediately
as the central bank leaves the market; instead it stays at s_1 because the
initial conditions change, thus shifting the demand and supply schedules
so that they intersect at s_1. From equation (1) the new equilibrium
exchange rate s_1 is

$$s_1 = \frac{fV + G_0}{gV^* + F_0 + \Delta I_0}. \tag{8}$$

This formula is useful because it shows the limited possibilities that
central banks have to influence the exchange rate when official reserves
are only a small fraction of private asset holdings.

4.1.2 Comparison with the Bickerdike-Robinson-Machlup Model

The supply-demand model developed above resembles the "textbook" model of the foreign exchange market based on the work of Bickerdike (1920), Robinson (1937), and Machlup (1939, 1940) in that the supply and demand schedules in the foreign exchange market are derived from economic transactions between the two countries or currency areas. The difference is that the textbook model derives these schedules from flow transactions on the trade account, while the present model derives them from stock transactions on the capital account. In the textbook model, depreciation of domestic currency increases net supply of foreign exchange *per unit of time* by inducing a reduction in domestic purchases of foreign goods and services, and an increase in foreign purchases of domestic goods and services, provided that the "elasticities condition" holds, while capital movements are treated as "transfer payments" that do not depend on the level of the exchange rate. In contrast, in the present model depreciation of domestic currency brings forward an excess supply of foreign currency *at a point in time* by inducing a reduction in domestic holdings of foreign assets and an increase in foreign holdings of domestic assets. Furthermore, net supply of foreign exchange is everywhere an increasing function of the price of foreign currency; thus equilibrium is both unique and globally stable. The elasticities condition is met because the elasticities of domestic demand for foreign assets, and of foreign demand for domestic assets with respect to the exchange rate are both equal to one in absolute value. (See, however, the discussion in appendix 1.)

If there was a dual exchange rate system with capital account transactions going through one market, market A, and current account transactions, including interest payments going through another market—market B—the model developed above would be a complete partial equilibrium model of market A, while the Bickerdike-Robinson-Machlup model would be a complete partial equilibrium model of market B. Market B would be linked to market A because the net inflow or outflow of interest income would have to be effected through exchange rate adjustments in market B. In a unified floating rate system there is, as it were, also a feedback from market B to market A because the initial conditions on which equilibrium in market A depends change whenever the current account is different from zero. We now turn to study this dynamic process.

4.2 Interaction between the Current Account and the Capital Account: The Dynamics of the Exchange Rate

To study the dynamics of the foreign exchange market we make two simplifying assumptions initially: first, there is no inflation or real growth in either country; and second, all interest earnings on foreign assets are spent on imports. The first assumption implies that current account must be zero in long-run equilibrium, while the second assumption implies that the long-run equilibrium value of the exchange rate, associated with zero current account, does not depend on the level or direction of international investment. The reason for these assumptions is to abstract from the complex problems of intertemporal transfer whose satisfactory treatment requires general equilibrium analysis.

4.2.1 A Special Case

We begin the analysis with the special case, typically assumed in recent literature, in which foreign residents do not hold domestic assets. Short-run equilibrium condition (3) then becomes

$$F \cdot s = f(R, R^* + \pi, z)V, \tag{9}$$

where π is still set equal to zero. This equilibrium condition is illustrated by the FF schedule in figure 4.3b. With initial stock of foreign assets equal to F_0, initial equilibrium obtains at A_0 with exchange rate s_0.

The stock of foreign assets changes whenever the current account is different from zero, or

$$\dot{F} = B(s; y), \tag{10}$$

where B is current account surplus in foreign currency and y is a vector of determinants of the current account, including domestic and foreign prices and activity levels. Equations (9) and (10) together with the initial condition $F = F_0$ define the complete dynamic partial equilibrium model of the foreign exchange market.

Assume first that the current account is everywhere an increasing function of the price of foreign currency, as illustrated by the BB schedule in figure 4.3a. At the initial exchange rate s_0 the current account is in surplus by B_0. Thus, thereafter the stock of foreign assets increases and domestic currency appreciates as the market converges to long-run equilibrium at A^* with exchange rate s^* and stock of foreign assets F^*. If, instead, the stock of foreign assets was initially above its long-run level, the price of foreign currency would be below its long-run equilibrium

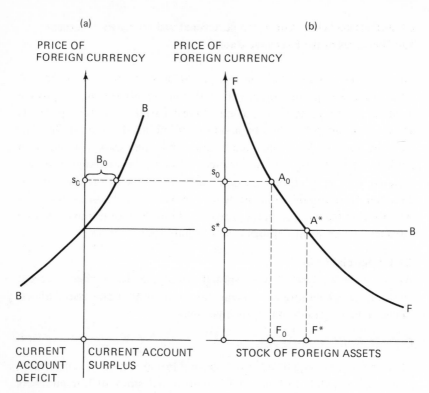

Figure 4.3
Interaction between current and capital accounts 1: a special case.

value, and the market would converge to equilibrium at *A** along *FF* from the right-hand side with domestic currency depreciating and the current account in deficit. It is thus evident that, given the monotonicity of the *BB* schedule, long-run equilibrium is both unique and globally stable.

The dynamics of the foreign exchange market, illustrated in figure 4.3, is consistent with observed exchange rate behavior in recent years with the currencies of surplus countries appreciating and those of deficit countries depreciating in excess of differences in inflation rates. It is useful to restate this implication of the model as the *acceleration hypothesis*: Domestic currency appreciates whenever the current account is in surplus and depreciates whenever it is deficit.

4.2.2 Multiple Equilibria and Dynamic Instability
Consider next the possibility that long-run equilibrium is not unique because the current account is not a monotonic function of the exchange

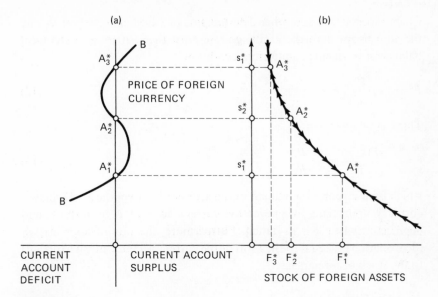

Figure 4.4
Interaction between current and capital accounts 2: multiple equilibria.

rate. Figure 4.4 gives an example in which there are three long-run equilibria, namely, A_1^*, A_2^*, and A_3^*. Of these, only A_1^* and A_2^* are stable. Which one of these the market will converge to depends on where it starts. As is indicated in figure 4.4a, it converges to A_1^* if it is initially on the right-hand side of A_2^*, and to A_3^* if it is initially on the left-hand side of A_2^*; and it stays at A_2^* if it happens to be there. With multiple equilibria, the foreign exchange market is thus dynamically unstable in that perturbations may move it from one equilibrium to another, unlike the case above, in which it always ended in the same long-run equilibrium.

Before considering the general case it is illuminating to derive the results of the above analysis in a slightly different way. In order for the foreign exchange market to stay in equilibrium after the initial moment, the exchange rate has to change per unit of time in such a way as to equilibrate the net flow supply of foreign exchange from current account transactions with the net flow demand for foreign exchange from marginal additions to domestic holdings of foreign assets, or capital outflow for short. But capital outflow is a function of *the rate of change* of the exchange rate; that is,

$$\dot{F}^{\mathrm{d}} = -f\frac{V}{s}\frac{\dot{s}}{s}, \tag{11}$$

where expectations and other determinants of f are held constant. Along the adjustment path the exchange rate must then satisfy a "dynamical balance of payments equilibrium condition":

$$\dot{F}^{\mathrm{d}} = -f\frac{V}{s}\frac{\dot{s}}{s} = B(s; x). \tag{12}$$

This can be rewritten

$$\frac{\dot{s}}{s} = -\frac{sB(s; x)}{fV} = -\frac{B}{F}, \tag{13}$$

which is an algebraic statement of the acceleration hypothesis: Domestic currency appreciates whenever the current account is in surplus, and depreciates when it is in deficit. Furthermore, the rate of appreciation (depreciation) is equal to the ratio of the current account surplus (deficit) to the stock of foreign assets.[5]

4.2.3 The General Case
To build on the previous section it is useful to rearrange short-run equilibrium condition (3) in the form

$$f(R, R^* + \pi, z)V/s - g(R - \pi, R^*; z)V^* \equiv NFA^{\mathrm{d}} = NFA^{\mathrm{s}}$$

$$\equiv F_0 - G_0/s. \tag{14}$$

The right-hand side can be interpreted as net supply of foreign assets and the left-hand side as net demand for foreign assets.[6] These two schedules are illustrated by the FF and SS schedules in figure 4.5. The FF schedule corresponds to the FF schedule in figures 4.3 and 4.4; they are the same when foreign residents do not hold domestic assets. Unlike in the special case, however, net stock of foreign assets is not predetermined at a given time—its value in foreign currency increases as domestic currency depreciates. For any exchange rate excess demand for foreign exchange at a given time can be read as the horizontal distance between the FF and DD schedules (see figure 4.1). Excess demand is zero at A_0, which is the same short-run equilibrium position as A_0 in figure 4.1.

Given its initial value s_0, the exchange rate must change in such a way as to equilibrate the current account with "marginal" net outflow of capital. Net outflow of capital is a function of the rate of change of the exchange rate; that is,

$$CF = \frac{\dot{G}^{\mathrm{d}}}{s} - \dot{F}^{\mathrm{d}} = \left(gV^* + f\frac{V}{s}\right)\frac{\dot{s}}{s} = \left(F + \frac{G}{s}\frac{\dot{s}}{s},\right) \tag{15}$$

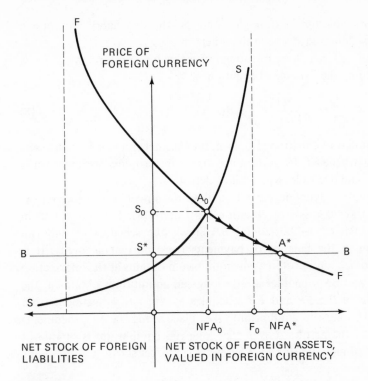

Figure 4.5
Interaction 3: the general case.

where $\dot{G}^d/s = gV^*(\dot{s}/s)$ = inflow of capital and $\dot{F}^d = -f(V/s)(\dot{s}/s)$ = outflow of capital.[7]

For the foreign exchange market to stay in flow equilibrium, it is then necessary that the exchange rate satisfies the dynamical balance of payments equilibrium condition:

$$CF = \left(gV^* + f\frac{V}{s}\right)\frac{\dot{s}}{s} = B(s; x),$$ (16)

where B is the current account surplus in foreign currency as before. This can be written

$$\frac{\dot{s}}{s} = -B(s; x)/\left(f\frac{V}{s} + gV^*\right),$$ (17)

which is simply the "acceleration equation." Thus the rate of appreciation (depreciation) of domestic currency is equal to the ratio of the current account to the level of international investment as measured by the sum of domestic holdings of foreign assets on the one hand and foreign holdings of domestic assets on the other.

Change in the net stock of foreign assets, valued on foreign currency, is governed by the dynamical equation

$$N\dot{F}A = -f\frac{V}{s}\frac{\dot{s}}{s} = \frac{f(V/s)}{f(V/s) + gV^*}B(s; x), \tag{18}$$

which is similar to equation (11). In particular, net stock of foreign assets is constant whenever the current account is in zero, increases when it is in surplus, and decreases when it is in deficit.

The complete dynamic partial equilibrium model of the foreign exchange market consists of equations (14) and (18). It is illustrated in figure 4.6, where the horizontal BB line is the schedule of long-run equilibrium in the balance of payments (zero current account). It is assumed to be unique.[8] Short-run equilibrium obtains at the intersection of the FF and SS schedules at A_0; long-run equilibrium obtains at the intersection of the FF and BB schedules at A^*; and adjustment from short-run to long-run equilibrium takes place along the FF schedule as indicated by the arrows. Given that long-run equilibrium is unique, it is clearly also globally stable; Wherever the market starts, it always ends there.

4.2.4 Comparative Dynamics
We now apply the model to study the dynamic response of the foreign exchange market to (i) a decline in foreign demand for domestic assets; (ii) a once-and-for-all purchase of foreign exchange by the central bank; and (iii) an increase in domestic demand for imported foreign goods and services. Except for the analysis in figure 4.7 it is assumed that long-run equilibrium is unique.

Figure 4.6 illustrates the dynamic response of the foreign exchange market to a decline in foreign demand for domestic assets from an initial situation of long run equilibrium at A_0. The FF schedule shifts to the right to $F'F'$: At the initial exchange rate there is excess supply of domestic currency and thus excess demand for foreign currency in the amount $A_0 A^*$. Short-run equilibrium is restored as domestic currency depreciates to s'_0. Foreign residents are able to reduce their holdings of domestic assets immediately to the extent that domestic residents reduce their holdings of the now more expensive foreign assets. They are able to do so over time by importing more from and exporting less to the domestic economy, in effect by gradually exchanging their assets for goods and

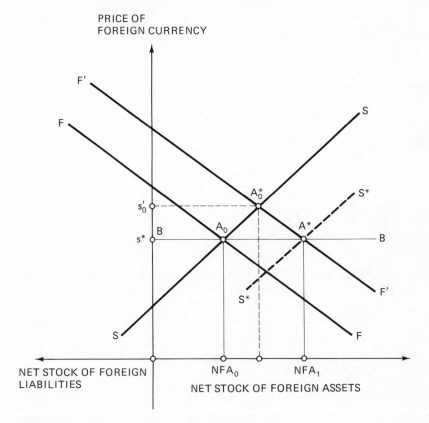

Figure 4.6
Dynamic response 1: effect of a decline in foreign demand for domestic assets.

services. As is shown in figure 4.6 the exchange rate eventually returns back to its "normal" level s^*.

The cumulative current account surplus in the course of the adjustment process is approximately equal to A_0A^*: The initial excess demand for foreign exchange in the amount A_0A^* translates over time into an equal cumulative current account surplus.[9]

One can interpret the capital account disturbance as a once-and-for-all financial transfer payment that is effected over a period of time through surpluses in the current account brought about by transitory depreciation of the domestic currency. The time it takes the foreign exchange market to effect such capital transfers depends on the level of trade in relation to the level of asset holdings on the one hand and the exchange rate

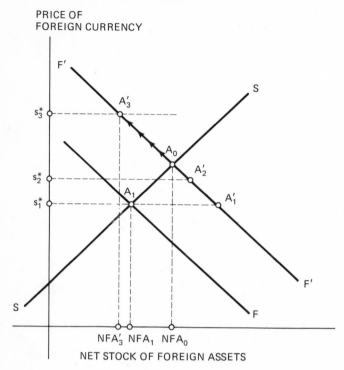

Figure 4.7
Dynamic response with multiple equilibria.

elasticity of the current account on the other (see appendix 1 and in particular table 4.1).

When long-run equilibrium is unique, as above, the exchange rate effect of a capital account disturbance is only transitory. With multiple equilibria, however, the effect may be permanent because the market may move from one equilibrium to another in response to a disturbance. Figure 4.7 illustrates such a possibility. There are three possible long-run equilibrium values of the exchange rate, namely, s_1^*, s_2^*, and s_3^*, of which only s_1^* and s_3^* are stable. The market is initially at A_1 with exchange rate s_1^* and net stock of foreign assets NFA_1. Reduction in foreign demand for domestic assets shifts the FF schedule to the right to $F'F'$. To restore equilibrium, domestic currency depreciates to s_0, which is above the exchange rate associated with the unstable equilibrium, namely, s_2^*. Therefore the exchange rate will not come back to s_1^*, but instead increases to s_3^*. Thus there is a permanent decline in the value of domestic currency and a period of *deficits* in the current account which may in fact cause the

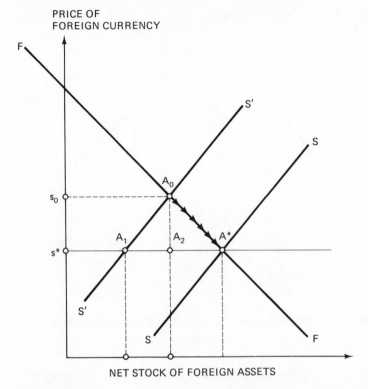

PRICE OF
FOREIGN CURRENCY

NET STOCK OF FOREIGN ASSETS

Figure 4.8
Dynamic response 2: effect of a once-and-for-all purchase of foreign exchange by
the central bank.

net stock of foreign assets to decline in the long run. Thus with multiple
equilibria, it is difficult to infer whether observed currency depreciation
is caused, *ex ante*, by "capital outflow" or an adverse shift in the trade
balance, because, as the example shows, *ex ante* "capital outflow" may
turn into *ex post* "capital inflow."

Consider next the response of the market to a once-and-for-all purchase of foreign exchange by the central bank. This is shown in figure
4.8 as a leftward shift of the SS schedule by $A_1 A^*$ at the initial exchange
rate s^*, assumed to be the long-run equilibrium exchange rate. The *ex
ante* excess demand of $A_1 A^*$ is eliminated by depreciation of the domestic
currency to s_0. At this exchange rate, $A_2 A^*$ of the increase in the central
bank's foreign exchange reserves comes from domestic residents who
reduce their holdings of foreign assets by this amount, and the rest from
foreign residents who supply foreign exchange in the amount $A_1 A_2$ in
order to increase their holdings of domestic assets. Over time, however,

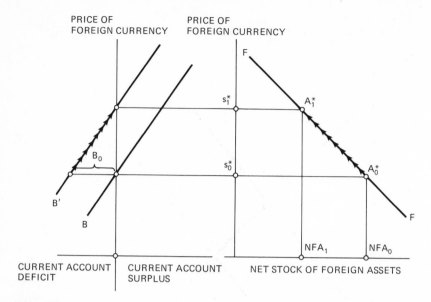

Figure 4.9
Dynamic response 3: effect of a permanent increase in the domestic demand for
foreign goods.

the purchase of foreign exchange translates to an exactly equal cumulative
surplus in the current account, and after the initial depreciation domestic
currency appreciates back to the same long-run equilibrium level. The
initial impact of intervention on the exchange rate depends on the size
of the central bank's purchase of foreign exchange in relation to total
international investment, while the duration of the impact depends on
the strength of the induced current account response, as is clear from
earlier analysis.

To conclude this section we show in figure 4.9 the response of the
foreign exchange market to a permanent increase in domestic demand
for imported goods and services. In the textbook model such shift would
cause an immediate depreciation of domestic currency with no change in
the current account balance which is determined *ex post* by the capital
flow account independently of the exchange rate. In contrast, in figure 4.9
the increase in import demand causes an equal increase in the current
account deficit at the initial moment (B_0). Domestic currency depreciates
to its new long-run equilibrium value s_1^* only gradually as successive,
although diminishing, current account deficits are financed by reductions
in domestic holdings of foreign assets on the one hand and increases in

foreign holdings of domestic assets on the other. The total cumulative current account deficit resulting from the increase in import demand is approximately equal to $NFA_1 - NFA_0$.

4.2.5 Balance of Payments Equilibrium with Inflation

We have assumed so far that there is no inflation in either country. Suppose now that prices in the domestic economy are increasing at a constant rate π_p and prices in the foreign country at constant rate π_p^*. The rate of change of the price of foreign currency in long-run equilibrium is then $\pi_p - \pi_p^*$. Even in the absence of real growth the current account is not zero in long-run equilibrium: In order to maintain a constant real stock of foreign assets domestic residents must purchase new assets at the rate of $\pi_p^*(F/p^*)$ in real terms, where (F/p^*) is the real value of domestic holdings of foreign assets in long-run equilibrium. Similarly, foreign residents must purchase new domestic assets at the rate of $\pi_p(G/p)$ in order to keep the real value of their holdings of domestic assets constant, where G/p is the real value of foreign holdings of domestic assets in long-run equilibrium. The current account surplus is thus equal to $\pi_p^*(F/sp^*) - \pi_p(G/p)$ in the units of domestic output. If the balance of payments accounts were properly measured this notional surplus of the current account would instead be counted as outflow of interest income: in real terms, net inflow of interest income would be $(R^* - \pi_p^*)(F/sp^*) - (R - \pi_p)(G/p)$. If we continue to assume that real interest earnings are spent on imports, the above analysis still applies to the real exchange rate $s(p^*/p)$ and the real, or inflation adjusted, balance of payments. A satisfactory treatment of inflation as well as of real growth requires, however, an analysis of its own. For this reason we continue to assume in the following that there is no inflation or real growth.

4.3 Implications of "Rational" Speculation in the Foreign Exchanges

In this section we study the implications of "rational" speculative behavior for the dynamics of the foreign exchange market. Such behavior is technically interpreted as perfect foresight, that is, $\pi = \dot{s}/s$, in contrast to the assumption of stationary expectations maintained so far. The analysis is limited to the special case in which foreigners do not hold domestic assets because space does not permit satisfactory treatment of the general case. For the same reason, long-run equilibrium is assumed to be unique.

The dynamic partial equilibrium model of the foreign exchange market is now defined by the following two differential equations:

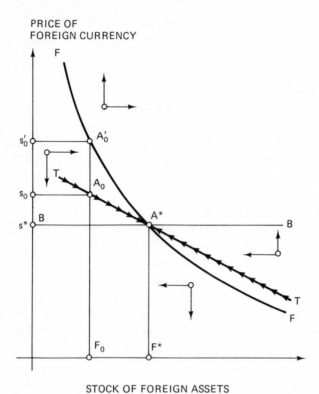

PRICE OF
FOREIGN CURRENCY

STOCK OF FOREIGN ASSETS

Figure 4.10
Rational expectations equilibrium.

$$f\left(R, R^* + \frac{\dot{s}}{s}, z\right)\frac{V}{s} = F \qquad \text{[see equation (9)],} \qquad (19)$$

$$\dot{F} = B(s; x). \qquad (20)$$

The dynamics of this system can be studied with the aid of figure 4.10. The *FF* schedule, defined by setting $\dot{s}/s$ equal to zero in equation (18), gives for each stock of foreign assets the exchange rate that is consistent with no expected appreciation or depreciation. It is the same as the *FF* schedule in figure 4.3. As the arrows indicate, domestic currency must be expected to appreciate at any point above the *FF* schedule and depreciate at any point below it for such a point to be an equilibrium point. The dynamics of the stock of foreign assets can be determined with the aid of the *BB* schedule, defined by setting $\dot{F}$ equal to zero in equation (20) [see equation (23) in appendix 1]. As indicated by the arrows, the stock

PRICE OF
FOREIGN CURRENCY

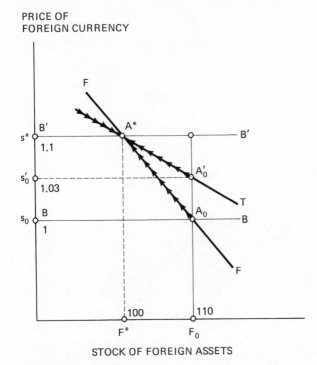

Figure 4.11
Effect of an unanticipated increase in domestic demand for foreign assets under rational expectations 1.

of foreign assets increases above the BB schedule and decreases below it. Inspection of the direction of movement in each of the four regions separated by the FF and BB schedules reveals that there is only one path along which expectations are continuously realized such that it takes the market to long-equilibrium at A^*. This is the "rational expectations" path and it is illustrated by the TT schedule in the figure. With initial stock of foreign assets equal to F_0 the equilibrium value of the exchange rate consistent with "rational expectation" of subsequent appreciation is s_0, in comparison with s_0' that would obtain with stationary expectations [see figure 4.3]. How the market could reach s_0 and stay on TT, which is the only path that takes it to long-run equilibrium, is an open question and an answer will not be attempted here.

4.3.1 Comparative Dynamics
The response of the foreign exchange market to *unanticipated permanent disturbances* with rational expectations differs from the response pattern

PRICE OF
FOREIGN CURRENCY

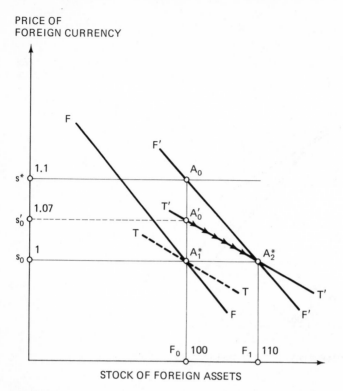

Figure 4.12
Effect of a permanent unanticipated increase in domestic demand 2.

with stationary expectations only in that the short-run effect of capital account disturbances on the exchange rate is weakened while the short-run effect of trade account disturbances on the exchange rate is strengthened.

Figure 4.11 illustrates response to an increase in domestic demand for foreign assets on an initial situation of long-run equilibrium with exchange rate s_0 and stock of foreign assets F_0. The exchange rate jumps to s_0' from s_0, which is consistent with equilibrium under stationary expectations. Thereafter, the market converges back to equilibrium at A^* along the TT schedule. The analysis of appendix 1 and appendix 2 permits a quantitative illustration. The numbers reported in the figure give an example with $\alpha = 0.50$ and $\beta = 1$. The initial impact of the trade account disturbance on the exchange rate is to increase it from 1 to 1.03. The average exchange rate for the first year is 1.04, compared to 1.02 under stationary expectations. However, the market reaches long-run equilibrium faster under stationary expectations than it does under rational expectations—from table 4.4 the market reaches 1.09 in 4.6 years under stationary expectations and only in 6 years under rational expectations. The cumulative current account deficit along the adjustment path from A_0 to A^* is 10 units. From table 4.6 the deficit is 3.1 in the first year, compared to 3.9 under stationary expectations. This example shows that when the level of international investment is high in relation to trade flows, permanent shifts in the trade account give rise to long periods of deficits or surpluses in the current account associated with continuous currency depreciation or appreciation, *ceteris paribus*.

Figure 4.12 illustrates the response of market to a permanent increase in domestic demand for foreign assets in an initial situation of long-run equilibrium at A_1^* with exchange rate s_0 and stock of foreign assets F_0 ($s_0 = 1$, $F_0 = 100$). The FF schedule shifts to $F'F'$ and the TT schedule to $T'T'$. Rational expectations equilibrium obtains initially at s_0' and thereafter the market converges to long-run equilibrium at A_2^* along the TT schedule. Using the same parameter values as in the above example ($\alpha = 0.5$, $\beta = 1$), s_0' is equal to 1.07. Average exchange rate in the first year is, from table 4.7, 1.06, compared to 1.08 under stationary expectations. However, the exchange rate reaches 1.09 only in 6 years under rational expectations, compared to 4.6 years under stationary expectations (table 4.4). This is also the time it takes the market to effect 90 percent of the total transfer of $F_1 - F_0$.

4.3.2 Market Response to Anticipated Disturbances

As an efficient speculative market, the foreign exchange market responds to disturbances when they are anticipated rather than when they occur: Disturbances that have been correctly discounted in advance have no effect when they actually occur. Using another terminology, the market responds only to new information. In this section we show the effects of permanent capital account and trade account disturbances when they are anticipated in advance.

Figure 4.13 shows market response to an anticipated central bank purchase of foreign exchange at some future date T. The market is initially in equilibrium at A_0 with exchange rate s^* and stock of foreign assets F_0. If the central bank purchase of foreign exchange occurred immediately at time 0, domestic currency would depreciate to s_3'. Thereafter, the market would return back to equilibrium along the TT schedule. If, in contrast, the intervention is expected to occur at some future date T, domestic currency depreciates immediately to s_0'. Thereafter it continues to depreciate while the current account is in surplus. When the interven-

PRICE OF
FOREIGN CURRENCY

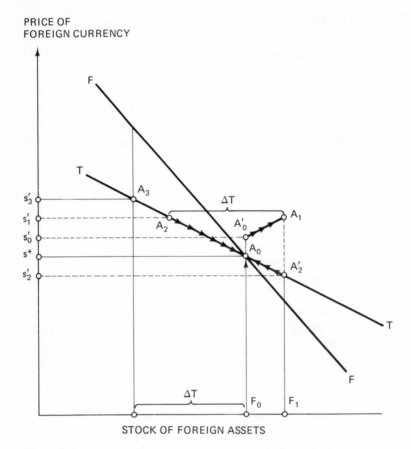

Figure 4.13
Effect of an anticipated cental bank purchase of foreign exchange.

tion actually occurs at time T, there is no effect on the exchange rate, and after the intervention domestic currency gradually appreciates back to its normal value s^*. If the intervention, although anticipated, does not occur, domestic currency appreciates discretely to s_2' and thereafter depreciates gradually back to equilibrium at A_0. In summary, only new information, whether in the form of current unanticipated events, anticipated future events, or mistakes in past expectations, gives rise to discrete and noticeable movements in the exchange rate.

To conclude the analysis, figure 4.14 illustrates market response to an anticipated permanent increase in import demand at some future date T from an initial situation of equilibrium at A_0. Domestic currency depreciates immediately to s_0' and thereafter continues to depreciate while the

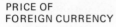

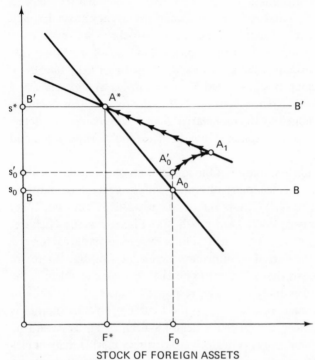

Figure 4.14
Effect of an anticipated increase in import demand.

current account is in surplus in reflection of the expectations induced outflow of capital—an obvious modification to the acceleration hypothesis. When the turnaround in the trade balance occurs at time T there is again no noticeable jump in the exchange, although there is a discrete change in the balance of payments. Adjustment to equilibrium at A_2 now takes a longer time than in the case when the disturbance is not anticipated in advance because the market has to eliminate the "overhang" of speculative holdings of foreign assets.

4.4 Conclusion

This chapter has synthesized the modern theory of exchange rate determination with the older balance of payments approach in the framework of a dynamic partial equilibrium model that is consistent with the nature of the foreign exchange market as an intermediary between the markets for goods and services and assets in two separate currency areas. Explicit analysis of the sources of supply and demand—stocks as well as flows—makes the model a useful tool in empirical analysis of exchange rate behavior. As one example, the model explains the observed tendency of the currencies of countries in current account surplus to appreciate and those of countries in current account deficit to depreciate. This phenomena cannot be explained by the monetarist theory of exchange rate determination, nor can it be explained by the "textbook" supply-demand model.

The partial equilibrium nature of the model is an obvious qualification to the analysis of this chapter, although simple general equilibrium models (Kouri, 1976, 1980; Kouri and de Macedo, 1978; Branson, 1978; Calvo and Rodriguez, 1977; Dornbusch and Fischer, 1980; Niehans, 1978; and Rodgriguez, 1980) yield similar response patterns for the exchange rate. In the partial equilibrium framework, however, there are a number of problems that still need to be analyzed. One problem is the observed slow, and initially perverse, response of the trade balance to changes in the exchange rate, known as the J-curve problem. Another is the distinction between the currency denomination of an asset and its country of origin. This brings in the forward currency market that enables investors to decide separately about currency composition of assets on the one hand and the "nationality" of assets on the other. A third problem, connected with the J-curve problem is the problem of leads and lags in trade payments. In the present chapter, trade credit is treated as any other assets. Finally, models of the foreign exchanges should clearly recognize the existence of more than two currencies and of more than one exchange rate.

Appendix 1   Linear Approximation of the Model[9]

The diagram developed in section 4.2 enables us to study qualitatively the dynamic response of the foreign exchange market to capital account as well as current account disturbances. To get some idea of the quantitative effects of such disturbances, or rather to identify the crucial parameters, we need to consider the approximate solution of the nonlinear model. For this purpose we write the current account equation more explicitly as

$$B(s; x) = E(s; x)/s - M(s; x), \tag{21}$$

where E is the value of exports in domestic currency and M is the value of imports in foreign currency.[10] Substituting this in equation (17) in section 4.2 and linearizing around s^*, we obtain

$$\dot{s} = -\frac{M^*}{f(V/s^*) + gV^*}(\eta_E + \eta_M - 1)(s - s^*) \equiv -\alpha(s - s^*), \qquad (22)$$

where

η_E = elasticity of export earnings in domestic currency with respect to the exchange rate,

η_M = elasticity of imports in foreign currency with respect to the exchange rate,

s^* = long-run equilibrium value of the exchange rate.

Long-run equilibrium value of the exchange rate is determined by

$$B(s^*; x) = 0. \qquad (23)$$

A necessary and sufficient condition for long-run equilibrium s^* to be locally stable is that $\alpha > 0$, or that the "elasticities condition" $\eta_E + \eta_M - 1 > 0$ holds. The solution of the linear differential equation defined by equation (22) is

$$s_t = s^* + (s_0 - s^*)e^{-\alpha t}, \qquad (24)$$

where s_0 is the initial equilibrium value of the exchange rate as determined by equation (4) [or (14)], repeated below for convenience:

$$s_0 = \frac{fV + G_0}{gV^* + F_0}. \qquad (25)$$

Equations (23)–(25) enable us to study the effects of capital account as well as trade account disturbances in the short run as well as in the long run, starting from an initial situation of equilibrium. Equations (23) and (24) seem to suggest that "only capital account disturbances matter in the short run," while "only trade account disturbances matter in the long run." This asymmetry disappears, however, when allowance is made for speculative expectations, as will be shown, and when the analysis applies to any *period* of time. To show this consider the approximate discrete solution of the above model in terms of annual averages. For this purpose we adopt the convention of measuring all flow variables and flow parameters "at annual rates." By integration of equation (24) we can write the average annual exchange rate for the ith year as

$$s_i = (1 - \theta_i)s^* + \theta_i s_0, \qquad (26)$$

where

$$\theta_i = \frac{1}{\alpha} e^{-\alpha(i-1)} (1 - e^{-\alpha}), \qquad i = 1, 2, \ldots.$$

The average exchange rate for any year after time 0 is thus a weighted average of the long-run equilibrium exchange rate s^* on the one hand and the short run equilibrium value of the exchange rate s_0 at time 0 on the other. The weight of the long-run equilibrium exchange rate increases with time. It also increases with an increase in the exchange rate elasticity of the current account $\eta_E + \eta_M - 1$ and with an increase in the level of trade in relation to the level of asset holdings

$$(M^*/[f(V/s^*) + gV^*]), \qquad \text{for } \alpha = (M^*/[f(V/s^*) + gV^*])$$

$$(\eta_E + \eta_M - 1).$$

The cumulative current account surplus associated with the adjustment path is approximately

$$S = \int_0^\infty B_t \, dt = \left(f^* \frac{V}{s^*} - g^* V^* \right) \frac{s_0 - s^*}{s^*}. \tag{27}$$

If foreign residents do not hold domestic assets, the cumulative current account surplus is exactly equal to $F^* - F_0$. Current account surplus in the ith year after the initial moment is a fraction of the cumulative surplus, this fraction decreasing over time:

$$B_i = \psi_i S, \tag{28}$$

where

$$\psi_i = e^{-\alpha(i-1)} (1 - e^{-\alpha}).$$

Finally, there are two possible measures of the speed of adjustment. One is the time it takes the market to eliminate x percent of the initial exchange rate discrepancy $s_0 - s^*$, or x percent of the cumulative current account surplus S; that is,

$$T_1(x) = -\frac{1}{\alpha} \ln(1 - x), \tag{29}$$

where $s_T - s_0 = x(s^* - s_0)$ and $S_T = xS$. This measure is independent of the size of the disturbance. An alternative measure is the time it takes the exchange rate to get to within x percent of its long-run equilibrium value; that is,

Table 4.1
Speeds of adjustment for different values of α

α	0	0.10	0.25	0.50	0.75	1.0	2.0	2.5	5.0	10.0
$e^{-\alpha}$	1	0.90	0.78	0.61	0.47	0.37	0.14	0.08	0.01	0.00
ψ_1	0	0.10	0.22	0.39	0.53	0.63	0.86	0.92	0.99	1.00
ψ_2	0	0.09	0.17	0.24	0.25	0.23	0.12	0.08	0.01	0.00
$1 - \theta_1$	0	0.00	0.12	0.21	0.30	0.37	0.57	0.63	0.80	0.90
$1 - \theta_2$	0	0.10	0.31	0.52	0.67	0.77	0.94	0.97	1.00	1.00
$T_1(0.90)$ (years)	∞	23.0	9.2	4.6	3.1	2.3	1.2	0.9	0.5	0.2

$$T_2(x) = -\frac{1}{\alpha}\ln\left(\frac{x_0}{x}\right), \tag{30}$$

where $x_0 = |(s_0 - s^*)/s^*|$ is the initial deviation of the exchange rate from its long-run equilibrium value. See table 4.1.

Appendix 2 Linear Approximation of the Model

To get an idea of the quantitative effects of disturbances we again consider a linear approximation of the dynamic model defined by equations (19) and (20) in section 4.3. The linear differential equation corresponding to equation (22) in appendix 1 is

$$\frac{\dot{s}}{s^*} = \frac{1}{\beta}\left(\frac{s - s^*}{s^*}\right) + \frac{1}{\beta}\left(\frac{F - F^*}{F^*}\right), \tag{31}$$

where

$\beta = (\partial f/\partial \pi)/f =$ the elasticity of demand for foreign assets with respect to the expected rate of depreciation of domestic currency, evaluated at long-run equilibrium.

The linear approximation of differential equation (30) around long-run equilibrium is

$$\frac{\dot{F}}{F^*} = \alpha\frac{s - s^*}{s^*}, \tag{32}$$

where

$\alpha = (M^*/F^*)(\eta_E + \eta_M - 1)$ as before, except for the assumption that $gV^* = 0$.

The characteristic roots of this system of two linear differential equations are $\frac{1}{2}(1/\beta) \pm \sqrt{(1/\beta)^2 + 4\alpha/\beta}$. If the "elasticities condition" holds, α is positive and therefore the characteristic roots are real and of opposite sign, which means that the rest point of the system is a saddlepoint.[11] There is therefore only one initial value of the free variable, in this case the exchange rate, such that starting from that value the system converges to equilibrium. To determine the stable solution of the above system consider the solution

$$\frac{s_t - s^*}{s^*} = \mu_1 A_1 e^{-\lambda_1 t} + \mu_2 A_2 e^{\lambda_2 t}, \tag{33}$$

$$\frac{F_t - F^*}{F^*} = A_1 e^{-\lambda_1 t} + A_2 e^{\lambda_2 t}, \tag{34}$$

where λ_1 and λ_2 are the absolute values of the negative and positive characteristic roots, respectively; $(\mu_1, 1)$ and $(\mu_2, 1)$ are the associated characteristic vectors; and A_1 and A_2 are constants to be determined by initial and terminal conditions. The terminal condition is that the system converges to equilibrium, and it restricts A_2 to equal zero. The initial condition on the stock of foreign assets restricts A_1 to equal $(F_0 - F^*)/F^*$. From equation (33) the "rational expectations" equilibrium value of the exchange rate at the initial moment, denoted by s_0', must then equal $\mu_1(F_0 - F)^*/F^*$. From this we get the linear approximation of the rational expectations equilibrium schedule:

$$\frac{s - s^*}{s^*} = \mu_1 \frac{F - F^*}{F^*}. \tag{35}$$

This is illustrated by the TT schedule in figure 4.15. The linear approximation of the stationary expectations equilibrium schedule, FF in figure 4.15, is simply

$$\frac{s - s^*}{s^*} = -\frac{F - F^*}{F^*}. \tag{36}$$

The BB schedule, also shown in figure 4.15, is defined by

$$s = s^*. \tag{37}$$

The rational expectations equilibrium value of the exchange rate s_0' at time 0 is thus related to the stationary expectations value s_0 by

$$s_0' - s^* = -\mu_1(s_0 - s^*) \qquad \text{(see figure 4.10).} \tag{38}$$

The value of parameter μ_1 is given by

$$\mu_1 = \tfrac{1}{2}\gamma - \tfrac{1}{2}\sqrt{\gamma^2 + 4\gamma}. \tag{39}$$

where $\gamma = 1/\alpha\beta$.

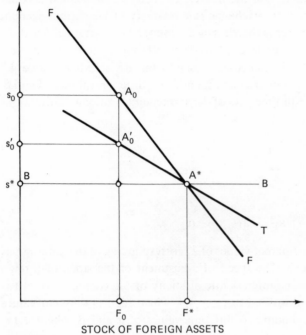

PRICE OF
FOREIGN CURRENCY

STOCK OF FOREIGN ASSETS

Figure 4.15
Linear approximations to the rational expectations equilibrium.

Table 4.2
Different values of $|\mu_1|$[a]

	β								
α	0	0.1	0.25	0.5	1	2	2.5	5	10
10	1	0.62	0.44	0.36	0.27	0.25	0.18	0.13	0.10
5	1	0.73	0.58	0.46	0.36	0.27	0.25	0.18	0.13
2.5	1	0.83	0.61	0.58	0.46	0.36	0.33	0.25	0.18
2	1	0.85	0.73	0.62	0.50	0.37	0.36	0.27	0.25
1	1	0.92	0.83	0.73	0.62	0.50	0.44	0.36	0.27
0.5	1	0.95	0.90	0.83	0.72	0.62	0.58	0.46	0.36
0.25	1	0.98	0.95	0.90	0.83	0.73	0.61	0.58	0.44
0.1	1	0.99	0.98	0.95	0.92	0.85	0.83	0.73	0.62

a. $\mu_1 = \frac{1}{2}\gamma - \frac{1}{2}\sqrt{\gamma^2 + 4\gamma}$, where $\gamma = 1/\alpha\beta$.

The value of μ_1 goes from zero to minus one as γ increases from zero to infinity. The higher are the interest elasticity of the capital account on the one hand and the exchange rate elasticity of the current account on the other, the closer is the TT schedule to the horizontal BB schedule. Also, an increase in the level of trade in relation to the level of asset holdings brings the TT schedule closer to the BB schedule. Table 4.2 shows different values of $|\mu_1|$ corresponding to different values of α and β.

Given s'_0 and F_0, the time path of the market under rational expectations is characterized by

$$s'_t - s^* = (s'_0 - s^*)e^{\lambda_1 t}, \tag{40}$$

$$F_t - F^* = (F_0 - F^*)e^{\lambda_1 t}, \tag{41}$$

where

$$\lambda_1 = \tfrac{1}{2}(1/\beta) - \tfrac{1}{2}\sqrt{(1/\beta)^2 + 4(\alpha/\beta)} < 0.$$

Table 4.3 shows different values of λ_1 corresponding to the same values of α and β as above. The speed of adjustment of the stock of foreign assets decreases as the interest rate elasticity of the capital account (β) increases. This is illustrated in table 4.4, which reports different values of $T_1(0.10)$ corresponding to different values of α and β, where $T_1(x)$ is defined by

$$T_1(x) = -\frac{1}{\lambda_1}\ln(1 - x). \tag{42}$$

The column with β equal to zero is the same as the last row of table 4.1.

$T_1(x)$ does not, however, correctly measure the speed of adjustment of the exchange rate because the exchange rate jumps discretely at the initial moment. An appropriate measure is instead the time it takes to eliminate x percent of deviation $s_0 - s^*$ of which $s_0 - s'_0$ is eliminated immediately. This time is given by

$$T_3(x) = -\frac{1}{\lambda_1}\ln\frac{1 - x}{|\mu_1|}, \tag{43}$$

which is less than $T_1(x)$. Table 4.5 reports different values of $T_3(x)$ for the same range of values of α and β as used in table 4.2.

Finally, the discrete solution of the model is given by

$$s'_i = (1 - |\mu_1|\theta'_i)s^* + |\mu_1|\theta'_i s_0, \tag{44}$$

Table 4.3
Different values of λ_1 [a]

α	β								
	0	0.1	0.25	0.5	1	2	2.5	5	10
10	10	6.20	4.40	3.60	2.70	2.50	1.80	1.30	1
5	5	3.65	2.90	2.30	1.80	1.35	1.25	0.90	0.65
2.5	2.5	2.08	1.53	1.45	1.15	0.90	0.83	0.63	0.45
2	2	1.70	1.46	1.24	1.00	0.78	0.72	0.54	0.50
1	1	0.92	0.83	0.73	0.62	0.50	0.44	0.36	0.27
0.5	0.5	0.48	0.45	0.42	0.37	0.31	0.29	0.23	0.18
0.25	0.25	0.25	0.24	0.23	0.21	0.18	0.15	0.15	0.11
0.1	0.10	0.10	0.10	0.10	0.09	0.08	0.08	0.07	0.06

a. $\lambda_1 = \frac{1}{2}(1/\beta) - \frac{1}{2}\sqrt{(1/\beta)^2 + 4(\alpha/\beta)} = \alpha\mu_1$.

Table 4.4
Different values of T_1 (years) [a]

α	β								
	0	0.1	0.25	0.5	1	2	2.5	5	10
10	0.23	0.37	0.52	0.64	0.85	0.92	1.28	1.77	2.30
5	0.46	0.63	0.79	1.28	1.70	1.84	2.56	3.54	4.60
2.5	0.83	1.11	1.50	1.59	2.00	2.56	2.77	3.65	5.11
2	0.87	1.35	1.58	1.85	2.30	2.95	3.19	4.26	4.60
1	2.30	2.50	2.77	3.15	3.71	4.60	5.23	6.39	8.52
0.5	4.60	4.80	5.12	5.48	6.22	7.42	7.93	10.01	12.79
0.25	9.20	9.20	9.58	10.00	10.25	12.78	15.33	15.33	20.91
0.1	23.0	23.0	23.0	23.0	25.6	28.8	28.8	32.9	38.3

a. $T_1(x) = -(1/\lambda_1)\ln(1 - x)$, $x = 0.90$.

Table 4.5
Different values of T_3 [a]

α	β								
	0	0.1	0.25	0.5	1	2	2.5	5	10
10	0.23	0.29	0.34	0.36	0.37	0.37	0.33	0.20	0
5	0.46	0.55	0.61	0.94	1.13	0.87	1.45	1.64	1.46
2.5	0.83	1.02	1.18	1.22	1.32	1.43	1.43	1.44	1.31
2	0.87	1.26	1.37	1.46	1.61	1.75	1.77	1.80	1.82
1	2.30	2.41	2.55	2.72	2.94	3.22	3.37	3.56	3.68
0.5	4.60	4.70	4.90	4.69	5.38	5.87	6.07	6.62	7.12
0.25	9.20	9.12	9.37	9.57	10.05	11.06	12.06	11.73	13.46
0.1	23.0	22.90	22.80	22.50	24.71	26.80	26.43	28.47	30.47

a. $T_3(x) = -\dfrac{1}{\lambda_1}\ln\dfrac{1 - x}{|\mu_1|} = T_1(x) + \dfrac{1}{\lambda_1}\ln|\mu_1| \leqslant T_1(x)$.

Table 4.6
Different values of $\psi_1'^a$

α	β 0	0.1	0.25	0.5	1	2	2.5	5	10
10	1.00	1.00	0.99	0.97	0.93	0.92	0.83	0.73	0.63
5	0.99	0.97	0.94	0.90	0.83	0.74	0.71	0.59	0.48
2.5	0.92	0.87	0.78	0.76	0.68	0.59	0.56	0.47	0.36
2	0.86	0.82	0.77	0.71	0.63	0.54	0.51	0.42	0.39
1	0.63	0.60	0.56	0.52	0.46	0.39	0.35	0.30	0.24
0.5	0.39	0.38	0.36	0.34	0.31	0.27	0.25	0.21	0.16
0.25	0.22	0.22	0.21	0.20	0.19	0.16	0.14	0.14	0.10
0.1	0.09	0.09	0.09	0.09	0.09	0.08	0.08	0.07	0.06

a. $\psi_1' = 1 - e^{-\lambda_1}$.

Table 4.7
Different values of $1 - |\mu_1|\theta_1'^a$

α	β 0	0.1	0.25	0.5	1	2	2.5	5	10
10	0.90	0.90	0.90	0.90	0.91	0.91	0.92	0.93	0.94
5	0.80	0.81	0.81	0.82	0.83	0.85	0.86	0.88	0.90
2.5	0.63	0.65	0.69	0.70	0.73	0.76	0.78	0.81	0.86
2	0.57	0.59	0.61	0.64	0.68	0.73	0.74	0.79	0.80
1	0.37	0.40	0.44	0.48	0.54	0.61	0.65	0.70	0.76
0.5	0.21	0.25	0.28	0.33	0.39	0.46	0.50	0.58	0.68
0.25	0.12	0.14	0.17	0.22	0.25	0.35	0.43	0.46	0.60
0.1	0.10	0.11	0.12	0.14	0.02	0.15	0.17	0.27	0.38

a. $\theta_1' = (1/\lambda_1)(1 - e^{-\lambda_1})$.

where

$\theta_i' = (1/\lambda_1)e^{-\lambda_1(i-1)}(1 - e^{-\lambda_1})$, $i = 1, 2, \ldots$,

s_i' = average exchange rate for the ith year,

s^* = long-run equilibrium value of the exchange rate,

s_0 = initial exchange rate as determined by (36).

This equation is of the same form as equation (26).

Current account in the ith year is a fraction of the cumulative surplus $F^* - F_0$:

$$B_i = \psi_i' S, \tag{45}$$

where

$$S = F^* - F_0 \quad \text{and} \quad \psi_i' = e^{-\lambda_1(i-1)}(1 - e^{-\lambda_1}).$$

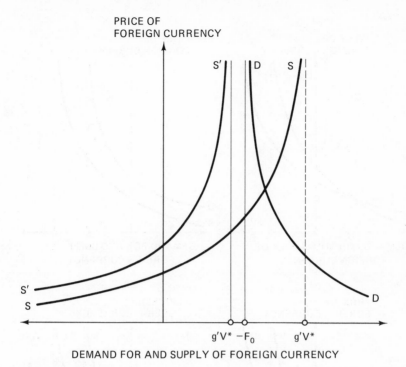

Figure 4.16
The foreign exchange market with foreign currency denominated debt (1).

Because λ_1 is smaller than α, ψ_1' is smaller than ψ_1, while θ_i' is greater than θ_i for sufficiently high values of i. This is, of course, another indication of the fact that, under rational expectations, adjustment to long-run equilibrium is slower, *ceteris paribus*. Tables 4.6 and 4.7 report different values of ψ_1 and $1 - |\mu_1| \theta_1'$ for a range of values of α and β. The columns with β equal to zero are the same as the rows for ψ_1 and $1 - \theta_1$ in table 4.1.

Appendix 3   Implications of Borrowing in Foreign Currency

Residents of most small countries cannot borrow in their own currencies in the international capital market, but instead have to borrow in one of the major currencies. Many of the small countries, furthermore, are net debtors. This introduces problems in the foreign exchange market. To analyze these problems, consider first the case when domestic residents currently are net debtors in foreign currency ($F_0 < 0$) but would like to hold a positive stock of foreign assets ($fV > 0$). If foreign demand

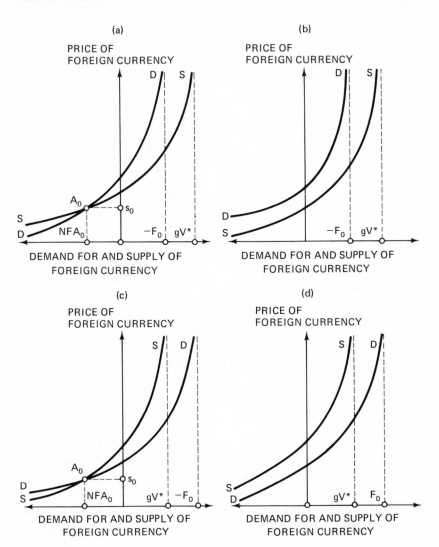

Figure 4.17
The foreign exchange market with foreign currency denominated debt (2):
(a) $G_0 > fV$, $-F_0 < gV^*$; (b) $G_0 < fV$, $-F_0 < gV^*$; (c) $G_0 < fV$, $-F_0 > gV^*$;
(d) $G_0 > fV$, $-F_0 > gV^*$.

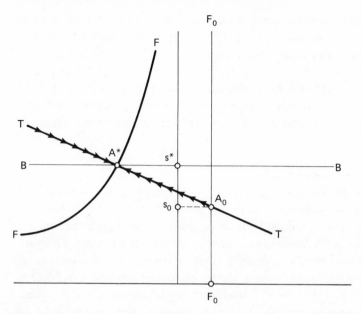

Figure 4.18
The foreign exchange market with foreign currency denominated debt (3).

for other types of domestic assets but bonds is larger (measured in foreign currency) than the foreign debt of domestic residents ($gV^* > F_0$), equilibrium still exists, and is unique and stable as is shown in figure 4.16, where the market reaches equilibrium at A_0 with exchange rate s_0. Suppose, however, that in this situation foreign demand for domestic assets declines so much as to shift the supply schedule to $S'S'$ ($g'V^* < F_0$). Then clearly there does not exist any equilibrium with stationary expectations: Domestic currency would tend to depreciate without limit.

Consider next the case when the desired stock of foreign assets is negative ($fV < 0$). The equilibrium condition is now

$$-f(R, R^* + \pi, z)V/s - F_0 = g(R - \pi, R^*, z)V^* - G_0/s, \qquad (46)$$

where f is replaced by $-f$ to indicate that domestic residents want to borrow foreign currency. $f(R, R^* + \pi, z)V/s$ is the supply schedule of foreign currency denominated domestic loans. It is assumed that foreign demand for these loans is infinitely elastic at interest rate R^*. The equilibrium value of the exchange rate implied by equation (1) is

$$s_0 = \frac{G_0 - fV}{F_0 + gV^*}. \qquad (47)$$

There are four possible constellations in terms of initial asset holdings (F_0, G_0) and desired asset holdings (fV, gV^*), as illustrated in figure 4.17.

Given stationary expectations short run equilibrium exists if and only if $G_0 > fV$ and $-F_0 < gV^*$ or $G_0 < fV$ and $-F_0 > gV^*$ [(a) and (c) in figure 4.17]. However, equilibrium is stable if and only if $G_0 > fV$ and $-F_0 < gV^*$; loosely speaking, it is stable only if actual and desired foreign holdings of domestic currency denominated assets are sufficiently large.

Rational Expectations Equilibrium

Figure 4.18 shows that when expectations are rational the problem of nonexistence of short-run equilibrium does not arise provided that long-run equilibrium is unique.[12] It is assumed in the figure that foreign residents do not hold domestic currency denominated assets. Domestic residents have initially a positive stock of foreign assets, equal to F_0 in the figure while they would like to be net debtors—in other words, they would like to borrow in foreign currency to invest in domestic assets. Clearly, there is no equilibrium under stationary expectations—the FF and the F_0F_0 schedules do not intersect. However, there is a rational expectations equilibrium at A_0 where the TT schedule intersects the vertical F_0F_0 schedule.

Notes

1. For a theory of portfolio diversification between assets of different currency denomination, see Kouri and de Macedo (1978, pp. 118–30).

2. Strictly speaking, domestic marketable wealth cannot be taken as exogenous even in partial equilibrium analysis because of capital gains and losses resulting from exchange rate changes. This is not a real problem, however, because we could equally take the domestic component of wealth as exogenous. This is not done for expositional convenience.

3. J. Williamson (1976, p. 331).

4. Dornbusch (1976, footnote on p. 271).

5. The dimensions of $\dot{s}/s$ and B/F are the same because both $\dot{s}$ and B are flow variables while s and F are stock variables.

6. It is not necessary that the net stock of foreign assets be positive. The analysis applies equally if domestic residents are net debtors abroad. Problems arise only if domestic residents are net debtors in foreign currency, that is, either fV/s, F_0, or both are negative (see appendix 1).

7. Note that along the equilibrium path, after portfolio adjustment at the initial moment, $F^d = F$ and $G^d = G$.

8. From equation (7) in appendix 1 the cumulative current account surplus S is

$$S = \left(f^* \frac{V^*}{s^*} + g^* V^* \right) \frac{s_0 - s^*}{s^*},$$

(i)

where f^* and g^* are the desired portfolio proportions corresponding to the $F'F'$ schedule. From equation (5) in appendix 1, s_0 is given by

$$s_0 = \frac{f^* V + G_0}{g^* V^* + F_0} = \frac{f^* V^* + g V^* s^*}{g^* V^* + f(V/s^*)},$$

(ii)

where f and g correspond to the FF schedule. Substituting this in equation (i) gives

$$S = \frac{f^* V - f V}{s^*} - (g^* V^* - g V) = NFA^* - NFA_0 = A_0 A^*.$$

(iii)

When foreign residents do not hold domestic assets ($g^* V^* = g V = 0$) this approximation is exact: The cumulative surplus equals $F^* - F_0$.

9. The case of multiple long run equilibria is discussed in the next section.

10. Because of the assumption that interest earnings are spent on imports in both countries, the interest service account and the implied net imports cancel out.

11. If the elasticities condition is not met and thus α is negative, there are two possibilities. First, if $4|\alpha| \leqslant 0.25(1/\beta)$, where $|\alpha|$ is the absolute value of α, both characteristic roots are real and positive; second, if $4|\alpha| > 0.25(1/\beta)$, the roots are complex conjugates with a positive real part $(1/\beta)$. In both cases there *does not* therefore *exist* a rational expectations equilibrium.

12. This analysis is not meant to be rigorous, only suggestive.

References

Bickerdicke, C. (1920). "The Instability of Foreign Exchange," *Economic Journal*.

Bilson, J. (1978). "Rational Expectations and the Exchange Rate," in *The Economics of Exchange Rates*, Frenkel and Johnson (eds.). Reading, MA: Addison Wesley.

Branson, W., H. Halttunen, and P. Masson, "Exchange Rates in the Short Run," *European Economic Review*, No. 10.

Calvo, G., and C. Rodriguez (1977). "A Model of Exchange Rate Determination under Currency Substitution and Rational Expectations," *Journal of Political Economy*.

Dornbusch, R. (1976). "The Theory of Flexible Exchange Rate Regimes and Macroeconomic Policy," *Scandinavian Journal of Economics*, No. 2.

Dornbusch, R., and S. Fischer (1980). "Exchange Rates and the Current Account," *American Economic Review*.

Frenkel, J. (1976). "A Monetary Approach to the Exchange Rate: Doctrinal Aspects and Empirical Evidence," *Scandinavian Journal of Economics*, No. 2.

Kouri, P. (1976). "The Exchange Rate and the Balance of Payments in the Short Run and in the Long Run: A Monetary Approach," *Scandinavian Journal of Economics*, No. 2.

Kouri, P. (1980). "Monetary Policy, the Balance of Payments, and the Exchange Rate," in *The Functioning of Floating Exchange Rates: Theory, Evidence and Policy Implications*, D. Bigman and T. Taya (eds.). Cambridge, MA: Ballinger.

Kouri, P., and J. de Macedo (1978) "Exchange Rates and the International Adjustment Process," *Brookings Papers on Economic Activity*, No. 1.

Machlup, F. (1939, 1940). "The Theory of Foreign Exchanges," *Economica*.

Mussa, M. (1976). "The Exchange Rate, the Balance of Payments and Monetary and Fiscal Policy under a Regime of Controlled Floating," *Scandinavian Journal of Economics*, No. 2.

Niehans, J. (1977). "Exchange Rate Dynamics with Stock/Flow Interaction," *Journal of Political Economics*.

Robinson, J. (1937). "The Foreign Exchanges," *Essays in the Theory of Employment*. Oxford: Basil Blackwell.

Rodriguez, C. (1980). "The Role of Trade Flows in Exchange Rate Determination: A Rational Expectations Approach," *Journal of Political Economy*, Vol. 88, No. 6.

Williamson, J. (1976). "Exchange Rate Flexibility and Reserve Use," *Scandinavian Journal of Economics*, No. 2.

5

Exchange Rates in a Global Monetary Model with Currency Substitution and Rational Expectations

Victor A. Canto and Marc A. Miles

As the fixed exchange rate period of the 1960s evolved into the floating rate period of the 1970s, the monetary approach to the balance of payments was transformed into the monetary approach to the exchange rate. Emphasis on the growth of money and income in two countries as determinants of the bilateral balance of payments was switched to an emphasis on these variables as determinants in the bilateral value of money. However, recent developments in macroeconomic theory have made this simple transformation questionable. The incorporation of "efficient markets" and "rational expectations" concepts into the behavior of international money, for example, has raised serious doubts about the reliance on lagged variables for explaining exchange rate behavior. The efficient markets approach emphasizes the efficiency of markets reacting to information, rather than market structure. The rational expectations approach, in contrast, emphasizes the structure of the model that explains fundamental market reactions. But both approaches agree that any known event from previous periods is already incorporated into prevailing prices.

In addition, the theoretical and empirical literature on exchange rates has largely neglected the substitutability of currencies across countries. The emphasis on the growth of money and income in two countries for explaining bilateral exchange rates implicitly assumes that domestic residents hold only domestic currency. Yet a growing body of empirical evidence suggests that, under floating rates, currency portfolio substitution or diversification does in fact take place (Miles [1978, 1981], Evans and Laffer [1977], Putnam and Wilford [1979]). Money demand, money supply, and exchange rates should therefore be analyzed from a global rather than a country-specific perspective.

We are indebted to Rudiger Dornbush and Douglas Joines for their valuable comments.

These additional theoretical economic developments raise some interesting questions. Is a floating rate system likely to work as originally thought? Are floating rates likely to be more volatile than simple monetary models predict, thus creating more uncertainty than initially hoped?

These questions are the subject of this chapter. Starting from a simple closed economy monetary model with rational expectations, a second currency is introduced. The two monies are assumed to be substitutes in demand, and an exchange rate exists between them. The resulting model permits the description of the behavior of the exchange rate in terms of anticipated and unanticipated changes in money supplies, money demands and income. While the model is not complete in the sense of a model of two distinct countries with independent income growth rates and distinct trade and balance of payments accounts, it does approximate the global nature of money demand and exchange rate determination. This model therefore represents an important first step in developing a truly general model of exchange rate determination.

5.1 Model

In order to isolate the effects of currency substitution on exchange rates and inflation, a simple monetary model with rational expectations is developed. The model consists of n markets. While no transaction costs exist, meaningful barriers to the flow of information exist which create separate markets for a single commodity and necessarily preclude the availability of current price information across markets. Individuals are assumed, however, to possess both current price information in a given market and information on past prices across markets. In other words, information is imperfect. Although current prices may differ, the expectation at time t of next period price EP_{t+1} is the same across markets. Alternatively, one could argue, as Cukierman and Wachtel [1979] do, that price differences across markets reflect the possession of heterogeneous information sets by individuals, where the amount of information in a set depends directly on the frequency of transactions by market participants. An index z is used to denote the different markets.

The focus of the model is on monetary policy. In order to isolate the effect of monetary policy, it is assumed that the government (issuer of currency) does not transact in the commodity markets. Instead, the two fiat currencies issued by the monetary authority enter the economy in the form of transfer payments. These transfers, made at the start of each period, are distributed without regard to the recipients' money holdings in prior periods. Individuals are assumed to hold the same proportions of the money stock in each period.[1]

The framework in shich two currencies circulate hand in hand with one economy may, at first, appear unrealistic. However, historic instances, such as the greenback era in the United States and bimetalism during the nineteenth century, show that the assumption of a two-currency country is not as unrealistic as it may first appear.[2] In addition, the framework permits the analysis of the implications of two simultaneously circulating monies without the further complications of two separate economies, two sets of foreign accounts, and so forth.

5.1.1 The Demand for Real Balances

The theoretical basis for the analysis within the model is classical money demand theory. The classical model is not reviewed in great detail here, since good summaries of both theory and empirical evidence are available in the literature (see, for example, Laidler [1977]). One assumption of the classical demand for money theory (Fisher [1911]) worth noting, however, is that real activity is viewed as largely exogenous to the monetary sector. This presumption is implicit in most of the empirical literature on money demand and exchange rate determination since real activity measures are generally used as explanatory variables. There is, however, literature which argues for feedback from the monetary sector to real activity, through unexpected monetary shocks which have an effect on real activity. (see, for example, Friedman [1968], or the rational expectations literature, Lucas [1973], Barro [1976, 1977, 1978] for theoretical developments and empirical findings.)

Explicit considerations of the feedback effects are neglected in this paper. One justification for this neglect is that our goal is to compare the present theoretical model with other models which treat real economic activity as an exogenous variable. Another justification is that the assumption of no feedback simplifies significantly the structure of the model since the assumption of no feedback implies strict money neutrality (both in the short and long runs). Thus, the economy can be dichotomized into real and monetary sectors.

Other issues not treated in this paper include the structure of the financial system and interventions by the monetary authorities in the foreign exchange markets. As a result, throughout the paper the money supply is assumed completely exogenous.[3]

The demand function for total real balances in the economy is expressed in loglinear form as

$$L_t(z) = aY_t(z) - bi(z) \tag{1}$$

where $L_t(z)$ denotes the log of real balances; a, the income elasticity of demand for real balances; b, the interest rate semielasticity of demand for real balances; $i(z)$ is one plus the opportunity cost of holding money; and $Y_t(z)$, the log of a measure of real economic activity. Economic activity is assumed to be a function of a constant growth rate (which is assumed to be zero for simplicity) and a random component; that is,

$$Y_t(z) = U_t, \tag{2}$$

where U_t is assumed to be generated by a random walk process

$$U_t = U_{t-1} + V_t. \tag{3}$$

V_t is assumed to be normally distributed with zero mean and constant variance σ_V^2. Since the random component is common to all markets, fluctuations in real income lead to aggregate disturbances in the money markets.

The model assumes that real balances can be held in the form of either of the two currencies. The allocation of real balances among the two commodities is characterized by a linear homogeneous CES production function. Thus, the log of share of real balances held in each of the two currencies can be expressed as:

$$\alpha_1 = \gamma_1 - (1 - \sigma)(1 - \alpha)(i_{1t}(z) - i_{2t}(z)), \tag{4}$$

$$\alpha_2 = \gamma_2 + (1 - \sigma)\alpha(i_{1t}(z) - i_{2t}(z)), \tag{5}$$

where γ_i is a parameter of the production function. For simplicity, in what follows it is assumed that $\gamma_1 = \gamma_2$. σ denotes the elasticity of substitution between the two monies and $i_{Jt}(z)$ the nominal interest rate in the Jth currency.

The derived demand for real balances held in the form of the different currencies can therefore be expressed:

$$L_{1t}(z) = L_t(z) + \gamma - (1 - \alpha)(1 - \sigma)[i_{1t}(z) - i_{2t}(z)] + \varepsilon_{1t}(z), \tag{6}$$

$$L_{2t}(z) = L_t(z) + \gamma + \alpha(1 - \sigma)[i_{1t}(z) - i_{2t}(z)] + \varepsilon_{2t}(z), \tag{7}$$

where $\varepsilon_{Jt}(z)$ represents a stochastic demand component specific to market (z). It is also assumed to be a white noise process with constant variance $\sigma_{J\varepsilon}^2$.

5.1.2 The Market Clearing Prices

The nominal interest rate of a specific currency can be expressed as the difference between the current and expected future log price level denominated in that currency,

$$i_{Jt}(z) = -P_{Jt}(z) + E[P_{Jt+1}|I_t(z)], \tag{8}$$

where E denotes the expectations operator; and $I_t(z)$, the information at time t.[4]

The difference in the log of the current price levels defines the log of the spot exchange rate:

$$e_t(z) = P_{1t}(z) - P_{2t}(z); \tag{9}$$

and the difference of the expected future prices defines the log of the expected future exchange rate:

$$E[e_{t+1}|I_t(z)] = E[P_{1t}|I_t(z)] - E[P_{2t}|I_t(z)]. \tag{10}$$

Subtracting equation (7) from equation (6) and substituting equations (8)–(10), one obtains the following relation between the spot and expected future exchange rate:

$$M_{1t} - M_{2t} - [\varepsilon_{1t}(z) - \varepsilon_{2t}(z)] - e_t = (1 - \sigma)\{e_t - E[e_{t+1}|I_t(z)]\}. \tag{11'}$$

This equation, in turn, yields the following equation for the spot rate:

$$e_t(z) = \frac{(M_{1t} - M_{2t}) - [\varepsilon_{1t}(z) - \varepsilon_{2t}(z)] + E[e_{t+1}|I_t(z)](1 - \sigma)}{(2 - \sigma)}, \tag{11}$$

where M_J represents the logarithm of the nominal stock of currency J.

Prior to considering how expectations are formed, it is first necessary to specify the process generating the rate of growth of money M_{Jt}. It is posited that M_{Jt} is a function of a constant growth rate (assumed to be zero for simplicity) and a random term m_{Jt}. Thus,

$$\nabla M_{Jt} = m_{jt}, \tag{12}$$

where m_{Jt} is a normally distributed white noise process with zero mean and a constant variance $\sigma_{J,m}^2$. It is also assumed that the error terms $m_{J\varepsilon}$, $\varepsilon_{Jt}(z)$ (for any z), and V_t are all uncorrelated with each other.

Examination of equations (11) and (11') indicates that a geometric index, across the different markets z of any of the prices, is independent of the market specific disturbances $[\varepsilon_{Jt}(z)]$. This result follows from the assumptions that $\varepsilon_{Jt}(z)$ is white noise and the number of markets (z) is sufficiently large.

5.1.3 Solution to the Market Clearing Prices

The formulation of expectations is assumed to be rational in the sense of Muth [1961]. Given current available information, participants in each market use the structure of the economy, which is known to everyone, to form rational operational forecasts of the general price level. Furthermore, actions based on these forecasts generate the assumed economic structure. The equilibrium values of prices and output can therefore be expressed as functions of m_t, U_t, ε_t, and other exogenous variables.

The method of solution employed in this paper has been previously used by Lucas [1972, 1973] and Barro [1976]. Initially, the form of the solution for $e_t(z)$ is expressed in terms of the vector of unknown coefficients on the set of relevant independent variables. Then the market clearing conditions, (11) and (12), are used to determine the coefficients.

The functional form for $e_t(z)$ is expressed in the log-linear form:

$$e_t(z) = \Pi_1 M_{1t-1} + \Pi_2 M_{2t-1} + \Pi_3 m_{1t} \\ + \Pi_4 m_{2t} + \Pi_5 \varepsilon_{1t}(z) + \Pi_6 \varepsilon_{2t}(z), \tag{13}$$

where the Π_i represent the unknown coefficients, and all other variables are defined as before. If individuals know that prices in each period are determined by equation (13), then the expected prices for the next period is

$$E[e_{t+1}|I_t(z)] = \Pi_1 E[M_{1t-1} + m_{1t} + \varepsilon_{1t}(z)|I_t(z)] \\ + \Pi_2 E[M_{2t-1} + m_{2t} + \varepsilon_{2t}(z)|I_t(z)] \tag{14}$$

since the expected values of m_{1t}, m_{2t}, V_t, and $\varepsilon_t(z)$, conditioned on $I_t(z)$, are all zero. The information set $I_t(z)$ is assumed to include observations of M_{1t-1}, M_{2t-1}, Y_{t-1}, and U_{t-1}. The additional information contributed by an observation of $e_t(z)$ amounts, from equation (14), to an observation of the sum of $\Pi_1[m_{1t} + \varepsilon_{1t}(z)] + \Pi_2[m_{2t} + \varepsilon_{2t}(z)]$.

It is apparent from the analysis of the above equations that the expected prices are equal to the current prices. This follows from the assumption that there is no growth component for the money stocks and real economic activity and from the fact that the expectations of m_{Jt}, V_t, and $\varepsilon_{Jt}(z)$ are all equal to zero. The observed values at time $t + 1$ differ from those observed at time t by only the nonzero values of the stochastic terms and their weights in equation (13). Since uncertainty about future prices, then, is only a reflection of uncertainty about the realized values of the stochastic terms, attention centers on the formation of expectations for m_{Jt} and V_t.

It is important to point out that the assumption of an equal income elasticity of demand for the different currencies implies that changes in real variables have no impact on the exchange rate. Therefore, an observation of the exchange rate $e_t(z)$ which is contained in the information set $I_t(z)$ amounts to an observation of the combined disturbances of the monetary variables.

Estimates of the expectations of m_{Jt}, conditioned on the information set $I_t(z)$, which contains $e_t(z)$, can be obtained by regressing Em_{Jt} on their unweighted sum mentioned above:

$$Em_{1t} = \frac{\theta_1}{\Pi_3}[\Pi_3 m_{1t} + \Pi_4 m_{2t} + \Pi_5 \varepsilon_{1t}(z) + \Pi_6 \varepsilon_{2t}(z)], \tag{15}$$

where

$$\theta_1 = \frac{\Pi_3^2 \sigma_{m1}^2}{\Pi_3^2 \sigma_{m1}^2 + \Pi_4^2 \sigma_{m2}^2 + \Pi_5^2 \sigma_{\varepsilon1}^2 + \Pi_6^2 \sigma_{\varepsilon2}^2};$$

$$Em_{2t} = \frac{\theta_2}{\Pi_4}[\Pi_3 m_{1t} + \Pi_4 m_{2t} + \Pi_5 \varepsilon_{1t}(z) + \Pi_6 \varepsilon_{2t}(z)], \tag{16}$$

where

$$\theta_2 = \frac{\Pi_4^2 \sigma_{m2}^2}{\Pi_3^2 \sigma_{m1}^2 + \Pi_4^2 \sigma_{m2}^2 + \Pi_5^2 \sigma_{\varepsilon1}^3 + \Pi_6^2 \sigma_{\varepsilon2}^2}.$$

As stated, the uncertainty about the future exchange rate $e_{t+1}(z)$ can be decomposed into uncertainty about each of the monetary variables. The coefficients θ_J measure the relative contribution of m_{Jt} to the overall variance of the exchange rate $\sigma_{e_{t+1}}^2$. The remaining fraction is attributable to the relative real variance of each market.

Substituting the estimates of $E[m_{Jt}I_t(z)]$ into equations (14) yields

$$E[e_{t+1}I_t(z)] = \Pi_1 M_{1t-1} + \Pi_2 M_{2t-1}$$

$$+ \left(\frac{\theta_1}{\Pi_3} + \frac{\theta_2}{\Pi_4}\right)[\Pi_3 m_{1t} + \Pi_4 m_{2t} + \Pi_5 \varepsilon_{1t}(z)$$

$$+ \Pi_6 \varepsilon_{2t}(z)]. \tag{17}$$

The coefficients must be such that the market clearing conditions equations (11) hold as an identity given equations (13) and (17). The solution to the coefficients is

$$\Pi_1 = -\Pi_2 = 1,$$

$$\Pi_3 = \Pi_6 = -\Pi_4 = -\Pi_5 = \frac{1 + (\theta_1 - \theta_2)(1 - \sigma)}{2 - \sigma}.$$

Given the equilibrium values of the coefficients, the exchange rate implications of our analysis can now be analyzed.

5.2 Determination of Exchange Rates

Substituting the coefficients of the last section into equation (13) yields the solution for the spot exchange rate in each of the markets:

$$e_t(z) = M_{1t-1} - M_{2t-1}$$

$$+ [m_{1t} - m_{2t} - \varepsilon_{1t}(z) + \varepsilon_{2t}(z)] \frac{[1 + (\theta_1 - \theta_2)(1 - \sigma)]}{2 - \sigma} \quad (18)$$

In turn, an aggregate spot rate index e_t can be calculated as a (geometric, unweighted) average of the spot price determined in equation (18), where the relative disturbance terms $\varepsilon_{Jt}(z)$ are averaged out in determining e_t:

$$e_t = M_{1t-1} - M_{2t-1} + (m_{1t} - m_{2t}) \frac{[1 - (\theta_1 - \theta_2)(1 - \sigma)]}{2 - \sigma}. \quad (19)$$

One result for $e_t(z)$ in equation (18) is that, since any real disturbance leads to an equiproportionate change in the demand for the two currencies (given the assumption of a strict money neutrality), real disturbances have no effect on the determination of the exchange rate. In this model, the exchange rate is truly a monetary phenomenon. In addition, M_{1t-1} and M_{2t-1}, which are contained in the information set $I_t(z)$, have a proportional effect on the exchange rate. Past information has an implied coefficient of one ($\Pi_1 = -\Pi_2 = 1$), just as in the standard noncurrency substitution models. The exchange rate in the present model, however, is also affected by concurrent events which the market has not anticipated. But, since market participants do not have separate observations of $e_t(z)$ and the aggregate index e_t, they cannot separate the impact of an increase in the money supply m_{it} from the impact of other excess demand shifts, $\varepsilon_{it}(z)$. Hence, m_{it} and $\varepsilon_{it}(z)$ enter with an equal magnitude opposite sign coefficient in equation (18). Whether this coefficient is less than one depends on whether the contribution of monetary uncertainty of currency 1, $\sigma_{m_1}^2$, to the exchange rate uncertainty σ_e^2 is larger than that of currency 2, $\sigma_{m_2}^2$. In other words, whether the unanticipated components enter with a larger or smaller coefficient than the anticipated components depends on

Table 5.1
The impact of the unanticipated coefficients under three alternative elasticities of substitution

Case	σ	Equation for exchange rate	Effect of unanticipated component
Perfect substitution	∞	$e_t = M_{1t-1} - M_{2t-1} + (m_{2t} - m_{2t})(\theta_1 - \theta_2)$ (20)	Depends on $\theta_1 - \theta_2 \lessgtr 0$
Unitary elasticity	1	$e_t = M_{1t-1} - M_{2t-1} + (m_{1t} - m_{2t}) = M_{1t} - M_{2t}$ (21)	Same as anticipated component
	2	Undefined	Indeterminate

whether $\theta_1 - \theta_2 \gtrless 0$. The magnitude of the coefficient also depends on the value of the elasticity of substitution σ.

The ability of the unanticipated component to have a significantly different effect on the exchange rate than the anticipated component, therefore, represents a major source of difference between models which consider the effect of currency substitution and those which consider currencies to be perfect nonsubstitutes. The implication for the unanticipated components are shown in table 5.1 for three special cases of currency substitution: perfect substitution, unitary elasticity of substitution, and an elasticity of substitution equal to two.

The first case considered is perfect substitutability among currencies. There are two possible ways through which perfect substitution can be achieved. One is perfect substitution in supply, which is nothing more than the fixed exchange rate case.[5] The other possibility is that currencies are perfect substitutes in demand ($\sigma = \infty$), which is considered in table 5.1. As σ approaches ∞, equation (19) reduces to equation (20) in table 5.1, and the coefficient on the unanticipated component of the money supplies reduces to $\theta_1 - \theta_2$. Since each θ_i has a value between zero and one, $\theta_1 - \theta_2$ must unambiguously have a value less than unity. The unanticipated component must have a different effect on the exchange rate than the anticipated component.

In the second possible case, analyzed here, the elasticity of substitution is unity ($\sigma = 1$). As σ approaches zero, the index of the exchange rate across the different markets reduces from equation (19) to equation (21) in table 5.1. In that case, both the anticipated and unanticipated components have implied coefficients of unity. Hence, both components have equal, proportional effects on the exchange rate.

In between these two extreme cases, the value of the coefficient on the unanticipated components varies, depending upon the values of the elasticity of substitution and the θ's However, since $\theta_1 - \theta_2 < 1$, the coefficient always differs from one.

One special case between the two extremes is elasticity of substitution equal to two ($\sigma = 2$). From equation (19) it is apparent that, with $\sigma = 2$, the unanticipated component of monetary policy has an indeterminate effect on the exchange rate. As noted in table 5.1, one cannot determine whether the exchange rate or the price level changes to eliminate the monetary disturbance. This result is at odds with other analyses of currency substitution, such as Evans and Laffer [1977], Laffer and Miles [1981], and Girton and Roper [1981], which argue that the exchange rate is indeterminate in the case of perfect substitutability.[6]

Perhaps more intuitively, an elasticity of substitution equal to two implies that the relative shares or proportions of M_1 and M_2 are unit elastic in the exchange rate; that is,

$$\frac{P_1 M_1}{e P_2 M_2} = \text{constant.}$$

Obviously, given any values of M_1 and M_2, there are an infinite number of combinations of (P_1, P_2) and e which satisfy this condition. Hence, no unique equilibrium e exists.

Equation (21) (the unitary elasticity case) does not exactly represent the model tested in most of the literature on the monetary approach to exchange rates. It is well beyond the scope of this paper to specify a structural model which will enjoy a consensus among the advocates of the monetary approach. However, the model developed allows a presentation of some of the salient features which some of the recent models incorporate, and allows us to focus attention on the forecasting equation for exchange rate changes and the relative money supply changes. References to the monetary approach to exchange rate determination can be found in Frenkel and Johnson [1978], and recent surveys are provided by Bilson [1978].

The equation commonly tested by advocates of the monetary approach is some variant of equation (21). One major difference between equation (21) and the model in this paper is the way real income in different countries has a differential impact on exchange rates. However, as previously mentioned, in the current model aggregate disturbances have no effect on the exchange rate.[7]

5.3 Potential Dangers of Excluding Currency Substitution

Keeping in mind the assumption previously made about the role of real income on the exchange rates, it is interesting to compare the differences between the unitary elasticity of substitution case ($\sigma = 1$), represented by equation (21), and the one that allows for a nonunitary elasticity of substitution. The comparison allows one to gain insights into the effects of currency substitution on exchange rates.

Recent empirical evidence by Miles [1978, 1981] and Laffer and Evans [1977] suggests the existence of a high elasticity of substitution. Thus, the possibility arises that the unitary elasticity of substitution model may be biased. This possibility is illustrated by subtracting equation (19) from (21):

$$d_t = -\frac{(1-\sigma)(\theta_1 - \theta_1 - 1)}{2-\sigma}(m_{1t} - m_{2t}).\tag{22}$$

This equation theoretically represents the residuals of equation (21) on the assumption that the elasticity of substitution is nonzero. It is apparent that the residuals are correlated with the explanatory variables, and, as a result, the estimated coefficient for the unanticipated components are biased. If the exchange rate equation is expressed in terms of the money supply differential, the bias on the unanticipated components can be shown to be (see Johnston [1972, chapter 9])

$$\mu_t = \left(\frac{1-\sigma}{2-\sigma}\right)[1 - (\theta_1 - \theta_2)]\frac{(m_{1t} - m_{2t})}{(M_{1t} - M_{1t})}.\tag{23}$$

Equation (21) implicitly embodies the interest rate parity theory associated with efficient markets. Another variant of this currency nonsubstitutability model commonly used is to assume a stock adjustment behavior in which the expected rate of depreciation of the foreign exchange rate is a function of the gap between the current spot rate and of the expected long-run inflation differential. In this case, the exchange rate equation becomes

$$e_t = (M_{1t} - M_{2t}) + \lambda(\rho_{1t} - \rho_{2t}),\tag{21}$$

where ρ_J represents the current rate of expected long-run inflation in currency J.

From equation (11) it is apparent that the expected long-run differential inflation can be written

$$\rho_{1t} - \rho_{2t} = (m_{1t} - m_{2t})\frac{\{(1-\sigma)[1 - (\theta_1 - \theta_2)]\}}{(2-\sigma)}$$

$$= \mu_t.\tag{24}$$

From an empirical perspective, a single equation estimate of the model described by equation (21) leads to weak estimates because one of the right-hand explanatory variables is an endogenous variable, and the model suffers from simultaneous equation bias. This shortcoming is easily corrected by the use of instrumental variables (see Johnston [1972, chapter 9]), and the empirical results should improve. It is interesting to point out that the inflation differential, equation (24), is a multiple of the residuals of the misspecified model. [Remember that the model by equation (21) is misspecified in the presence of currency substitution.] Thus, the instrumental variables approach is a way of handling the

Table 5.2
Variances of the spot Exchange rate under differing degrees of currency substitution

Case	σ	Variance
(a) Imperfect substitution	$\sigma > 0,\ \sigma \neq 2$	$\sigma_e^2 = \left(1 + \dfrac{(\theta_1 - \theta_2)(1 - \sigma)}{2 - \sigma}\right)^2 (\sigma_{m_1}^2 + \sigma_{m_2}^2)\ (25)$
(b) Perfect substitution	$\sigma = \infty$	$\sigma_e^2 = (\theta_1 - \theta_2)^2(\sigma_{m_1}^2 + \sigma_{m_2}^2)\ (26)$
(c) Unitary elasticity	$\sigma = 1$	$\sigma_e^2 = (\sigma_{m_1}^2 + \sigma_{m_2}^2)\ (27)$
(d)	$\sigma = 2$	Indeterminate

currency substitutability problem. To our knowledge, the only empirical study of exchange rate handled in this manner is that of Frankel [1979]. An interesting point is that our interpretation of Frankel's findings differ from his. Instead of presenting a testable hypothesis to distinguish between the so-called Keynesian and Chicago models, Frankel simply presents a testable hypothesis which allows one to distinguish between the unitary elasticity of substitution models and the nonunitary elasticity of substitution models. If taken at face value, the high coefficient for $p_{1t} - p_{2t}$ in Frankel's study would be interpreted by us to indicate an elasticity of substitution in excess of unity.

5.4 The Volatility of Exchange Rates

The model developed in this paper can also provide some insight into a practical problem that concerns policymakers whether there have been "excessive" fluctuations of the exchange rates. The differing degrees of fluctuation can be examined by comparing the variances of the log of the spot exchange rates under varying degrees of currency substitution. The variances are presented in table 5.2.

In all three cases where the variances are determinate $[\sigma > 0 \, (\sigma \neq 2),$ $\sigma = \infty, \sigma = 0]$ the variance involves the term $\sigma_{m_1}^2 + \sigma_{m_2}^2$, the sum of the variances of the unanticipated monetary policies. In the perfect non-substitution case, the variance is equal precisely to that sum. In the perfect substitution case, the variance equals the sum times $(\theta_1 - \theta_2)^2$. Since $\theta_1 - \theta_2 < 1$, the variance in this case is clearly less than when the currencies' elasticity of substitution is unitary.

In the general case of imperfect substitution, the sum of variances is multiplied by

$$\left(\frac{1 + (1 - \sigma)(\theta_1 - \theta_2)}{1 - \sigma} \right)^2 .$$

There are a number of plausible cases in which the variance of the exchange rate under imperfect substitution should exceed the variance when currencies substitutability is unity, or that of the perfect substitutability cases.

In order to investigate the policy concern of excessive volatility of the exchange rates, however, a reference point is necessary. Often linked with the study of volatility of exchange rates is the distinction between stabilizing and destabilizing speculation. However, as has been pointed out by Bilson [1979], before it is possible to determine whether speculation has

been destabilizing, the assumption of the underlying model that determines the exchange rate is necessary.[8]

If the underlying model of exchange rate determination is assumed to be
the unitary elasticity of substitution [equation (21)], the exchange rate
variance implied by the model will differ from that of the variance implied
by the currency substitution model [equation (19)]. In this analysis, the
unitary case is used as the reference point to determine whether the
presence of currency substitution increases the volatility of exchange rates.
The difference between the two variances is

$$\hat{\sigma}_e^2 = \text{var}(d_t)$$

$$= \left[\left(\frac{1 + (1 - \sigma)(\theta_1 - \theta_2)}{2 - \sigma} \right)^2 - 1 \right] (\sigma_{m_1}^2 + \sigma_{m_2}^2). \tag{28}$$

It is apparent that the variance implied by the currency substitution
model can be larger or smaller than that implied by equation (21), and it
will depend critically on the magnitude of the elasticity of substitution and
$\theta_1 - \theta_2$.

The empirical evidence on the volatility of exchange rates is somewhat
limited. Recently, Huang [1980], using the nonzero elasticity of substitution case as reference points, constructed tests of implied variance
bounds for exchange rates built along the lines suggested by Schiller
[1979]. He concludes that the volatility of exchange rates cannot be
accounted for by changes in rational forecasts of future exchange rates.
This leads him to conclude that the evidence is not consistent with an
efficient market model. As shown in equation (28), however, the higher
observed variance of the exchange rate can be easily explained if one
allows for currency substitution. Since Huang's tests are a joint test of the
model and the market hypothesis, it is possible that the tests reject the
model and not the market efficiency hypothesis. Thus, if one retains the
market efficiency hypothesis, Huang's tests can be interpreted as evidence
of a nonzero elasticity of substitution, which leads to a higher exchange
rate variance than the one implied·by the standard exchange rate models
without currency substitutions.

5.5 Summary and Conclusions

This chapter has investigated the impact of considering the existence of
currency substitution within a rational expectations model of the exchange
rate. Within the rational expectations model, current values of the

exchange rate and prices already incorporate all anticipated components of the disturbance terms.

The inclusion of currency substitution also suggests why the standard monetary model of the exchange rate is misspecified and leads to biased empirical results. Recent empirical evidence seems to support the existence of this bias. Currency substitution also shows how the variance of the exchange rate is a function of σ, the elasticity of substitution across currencies, and provides a theoretic rationale for the increased exchange rate volatility in recent years. It also shows how attempts to discourage trade in money could lead to a breakdown or explosion of the financial system. In all, once currency substitution is considered, it is not at all clear that flexible rates are preferable to a fixed rate system.

While the conclusions of this chapter are interesting and informative, they are somewhat limited by the simplicity of the model. Amplifying the model, however, remains a topic of future research. Among the changes contemplated are accounting explicitly for a domestic financial system, considering two separate currencies in two separate countries, permitting explicit government intervention in the foreign exchange market, and differentiating more explicitly between shocks in money demand and money supply. These changes should produce a more "realistic" model of a country's exchange rate behavior, and also permit an analysis of the relative desirability of a "quantity" versus a "price" rule for conducting an optimal monetary policy.

Notes

1. If people have the same expectations about prices, and current prices are the same across markets, then the only difference in money demand will be the levels of real income (which for simplicity can be assumed constant), and the income elasticity of demand for money (which is assumed to be the same across individuals).

2. The model developed in this paper does not exactly correspond to that of the bimetallic standards. Our model assumes fiat monies for which the quantity of the different monies is exogenously determined, and in the case of bimetallic (commodity standards) a strong argument can be made in favor of endogenous money supplies.

3. Explicit considerations of financial intermediaries, or foreign exchange interactions, will introduce an endogenous component into the money supply. The foreign exchange intervention will also imply that the exchange rate changes will "cause" money supply changes, as well as money supply changes "causing" exchange rate changes. In a future paper, we plan to explicitly consider these extensions; however, at this point, the major objective is to contrast and compare the implications of currency substitution with those that assume perfect nonsubstitutability under flexible exchange rates with no government intervention. We also rule out by

assumption any "cooperation" by the different monetary authorities. This can be easily incorporated into the analysis by explicitly allowing for a nonzero correlation between the increases in the two money supplies.

4. Equation (8) is not strictly correct. The real interest rate r should also be added to the equation. However, since real income and all other real variables are assumed exogenous to the model, for simplicity the real interest rate is assumed equal to zero.

5. Theoretical and empirical analysis for fixed exchange rates can be found elsewhere: Mundell [1968], Laffer [1969], Johnson [1973], and Frenkel and Johnson [1976].

6. The source of this confusion can be traced to the way the hypothesis is tested. The model (Evans and Laffer [1977]) is derived from the following three equations:

(a)   purchasing power party relation

$e_t = P_i - P_J;$

(b)   a quantity theory equation

$M_i + V_i = P_i + Y_i,$

where V_i is the log of the velocity of money, substituting (b) into (a) reduces to

(c) $e_t = (V_i - V_J) + (M_i - M_J) + (Y_J - Y_i).$

The model is then tested in first differences. The authors argue that if currencies are perfect nonsubstitutes, the exchange rate should be proportionately affected by a change in any of the right-hand variables. Conversely, if currencies are perfect substitutes, the right-hand variables should have zero coefficients. However, if one assumes, as in this paper, that the demand for different currencies is a derived demand, and one accounts explicitly for the responsiveness of the velocity of money, the change in exchange rate equations becomes

(d) $e_t - e_{t-1} = \dfrac{1}{2 - \sigma}[(M_{1t} - M_{1t-1}) - (M_{2t} - M_{2t-1})]$

$+ a[(\beta_{11} - \beta_{12})(Y_{1t} - Y_{2t+1})$

$- (\beta_{22} - \beta_{21})(Y_{2t} - Y_{2t+1})],$

where β_{Ji} represents the proportion of the world money supply of currency i held by country J.

Upon inspection of equation (d), it is apparent that it is the case of $\sigma = 2$ for which the exchange rate is underdetermined. Conversely, with perfect substitutability, the exchange rate remains constant. This result explains the paradox presented in Girton and Roper [1981] that, while their theory predicted indeterminate exchange rates with perfect currency substitution, the cases of perfect substitution of which they were aware (such as Federal Reserve notes of different districts) exhibit *constant* exchange rates. They were correct to conclude that "the indeterminancy conclusion is an interesting issue that deserves further attention in a more detailed model" (Girton and Roper [1981, p. 10]).

7. An important aspect of the recent development in money is the dominant role that expectations play in the determination of the equilibrium level of endogenous variables. The formulation of expectations and endogenizing both interest rates and price levels lead to a modification of equation (26). Well-known theoretical papers on this subject include Barro [1978] and Mussa [1976]. The formulation in this model is closer in spirit to that of the models developed by the two authors previously men-

tioned, which fully account for the role of expectations and the endogenous nature of interest rates.

8. However, since stability is defined with respect to an equilibrium condition, by definition an efficient market is one in which speculation is stabilizing with respect to the equilibrium rate.

References

Barro, R. (1976). "Rational Expectations and the Role of Monetary Policy," *Journal of Monetary Economics*, Vol. 2:1–32.

Barro, R. (1977). "Unanticipated Money Growth and Unemployment in the United States," *American Economic Review*, Vol. 67, No. 7:101–15.

Barro, R. (1978). "A Stochastic Equilibrium Model of an Open Economy under Flexible Exchange Rates," *Quarterly Journal of Economics*, Vol. 92:149–64.

Barro, R. (1978). "Unanticipated Money, Output, and the Price Level in the United States," *Journal of Political Economy*, Vol. 86, No. 4: 549–80.

Bilson, J. (1978). "The Current Experience with Floating Exchange Rates: An Appraisal of the Monetary Approach," *American Economic Review*, Vol. 68, No. 2:392–97.

Bilson, J. (1979). "Recent Developments in Monetary Models of Exchange Rate Determination," *International Monetary Funds Staff Papers*, Vol. 426, No. 2:201–23.

Cukierman, A., and P. Watchtel (1979). "Differential Inflationary Expectations and the Variability of the Rate of Inflation," *American Economic Review*, Vol. 69, No. 4:595–609.

Evans, P., and A. Laffer (1977). "Demand Substitutability Across Currencies" (unpublished manuscript).

Fisher, I. (1911). *"The Purchasing Power of Money*, New York, Macmillan.

Frankel, J. (1969). "On the Mark: A Theory of Floating Exchange Rates Based on Real Interest Rate Differentials," *American Economic Review*, Vol. 69, No. 4:610–22.

Frenkel, J., and H. Johnson (eds.) (1976). *The Monetary Approach to Balance of Payments*, Toronto, University of Toronto Press.

Frenkel, J., and A. Johnson (eds.) (1978). *The Economics of Exchange Rates: Selected Studies*, Reading, MA, Addison-Wesley.

Friedman, M. (1968). "The Role of Monetary Policy," *American Economic Review*, Vol. 58, No. 1:7–17.

Girton, L., and D. Roper (1981). "Theory and Implications of Currency Substitution," *Journal of Money, Credit and Banking* 13(1):12–30.

Huang, R. (1981). "Monetary Approach to Exchange Rate Determination, Market Efficiency, and the Volatility of the Exchange Rate" (unpublished manuscript), University of Pennsylvania.

Johnson, H. (1973). "The Monetary Approach to Balance-of-Payments Theory," *International Trade and Money*, M. Connolly and A. Swoboda (eds.), London, Goerge Allen & Unwin.

Johnston, J. (1972). *Econometric Methods*, 2nd ed., New York, McGraw-Hill.

Laffer, A. (1969). "An Anti-traditional Theory of the Balance of Payments Under Fixed Exchange Rates" (manuscript), University of Chicago.

Laffer, A., and M. Miles (1981). *International Economics in an Integrated World*, Glenview, IL: Scott, Forman.

Laidler, D. (1977). *The Demand for Money: Theories and Evidence*, 2nd ed., New York, Harper & Row.

Lucas, R. (1973). "Some International Evidence on Output-Inflation Trade-offs," *American Economic Review*, Vol. 63:326–34.

Lucas, R. (1973). "Expectations and the Neutrality of Money," *Journal of Economic Theory* 80C4):103–24.

✓Miles, M. (1978). "Currency Substitution, Flexible Exchange Rate and Monetary Independence," *American Economic Review*, Vol. 68, No. 3:428–36.

✓Miles, M. (1981). "Currency Substitution: Some Further Results and Conclusions," *Southern Economic Journal* 48(1):78–86.

Mundell, R. (1968). *International Economics*, New York, Macmillan.

Mundell, R. (1971). *Monetary Theory*, Pacific Palisades, Goodyear.

Mussa, M. (1976). "The Exchange Rate, the Balance of Payments and Monetary and Financial Policy under a Regime of Controlled Floating," *Scandinavian Journal of Economics*, Vol. 78, No. 2:229–48.

Muth, J. (1961). "Rational Expectations and the Theory of Price Movements," *Econometrica*, Vol. 29:315–35.

Putman, B., and D. Wilford (1979). *The Monetary Approach to International Adjustment*, Praeger.

Schiller, R. (1979). "The Volatility of Long-term Interest Rate Expectations Models of the Term Structure," *Journal of Political Economy*, Vol. 87, No. 6:1190–1219.

II
ENERGY AND INTERNATIONAL ADJUSTMENT

6
Oil and the Dollar   Paul Krugman

Probably the two most watched prices in the last decade have been the value of the dollar and the price of oil. A natural question is how they are related: How does an increase in the price of oil affect the follar's exchange rate? This chapter sets out a model which can be used to analyze this question.

There are several reasons besides its practical importance why this is an interesting subject for study. First, the interaction between oil prices and exchange rates is inherently a problem of multilateral economic relations, since we are concerned with the dollar rate against other industrial countries' currencies rather than against OPEC currencies. Even a minimal model in this area must invlove at least three countries, in contrast to the one- and two-country models prevalent in the literature on exchange rates.

Second, the problem of analyzing an oil price increase is one in which some commonly used simplifications made in much recent analysis can be shown to be misleading. Recent papers by Findlay and Rodriguez (1977), Buiter (1978), and Obstfeld (1980) have treated an increase in oil prices as an increase in a single country's import bill, invoking "small country" considerations in neglecting the consideration of the effects of the oil price increase on other countries or of how OPEC disposes of its income. In this chapter we shall see that such neglect is never justified, regardless of the size of the country concerned.

Finally, the case of an oil price increase offers an interesting example of possible conflict between an asset market and a goods market view of the exchange rate. Suppose that one were, in practice, to attempt to assess the effects of an oil price increase on the dollar. One approach would be to forus on "real" factors: How does US oil import dependence compare with that of other countries? How much of its increased income with OPEC spend on US goods? Another approach would be to look at financial factors: How will OPEC invest its surplus? As I shall argue, these approaches can easily yield conflicting answers, and in the case of the dollar appear to conflict in fact. The model developed in the chapter suggests a reconciliation: In the short run, before OPEC spending has risen to absorb its higher income, the financial question is the right one, while in the long run, when OPEC is spending its income, the real questions become appropriate.

6.1 Assumptions of the Model

Consider a world consisting of three countries: America, Germany, and OPEC. American and Germany sell manufactured goods to OPEC and each others; OPEC has a single export, oil, the price of which is assumed exogenously fixed in dollars.[1]

Germany's trade balance with respect to the United States, measured in dollars, will be assumed to depend on the exchange rate:

$$T = T(V), \tag{1}$$

where V is the mark price of the dollar. In writing this partial equilibrium relation we are implicitly taking industrial countries' real incomes and price levels as given.

Oil imports will be assumed to be exogenously fixed in volume terms:

$$O_A = \bar{O}_A,$$
$$O_G = \bar{O}_G. \tag{2}$$

Thus we assume away—until section 6.4—the complications introduced by the possibility that countries will be differentially successful in reducing oil consumption.

OPEC import behavior involves spending a share γ of its expenditure on German products, $1 - \gamma$ on American products, where γ in general depends on the dollar-mark exchange rate:

$$X_G = \gamma(V)X,$$
$$X_A = [1 - \gamma(V)]X, \tag{3}$$

where X_G, X_A are OPEC dollar expenditures on German and US goods, and X is total OPEC dollar expenditure.

What determines OPEC expenditure? The crucial aspect of actual OPEC spending behavior that we will want to capture in this paper is the lag in the adjustment of OPEC imports to export earnings. I shall assume that OPEC dollar spending adjusts gradually to the level of dollar export earnings:

$$\dot{X} = \lambda(P_O\bar{O} - X), \tag{4}$$

where $\bar{O} = \bar{O}_G + \bar{O}_A$ is total oil exports.[2]

Notice that there is an asymmetry in the treatment of OPEC imports and the imports of America and Germany. Industrial country imports are assumed to depend only on prices, whereas OPEC's imports are allowed to depend directly on income. The basic reason for assuming this is, of course, that the lag of OPEC spending behind income is central to our story, while income changes in the industrial countries are not. One can, however, offer an empirical justification. The redistribution of world income caused by oil price change involves much larger percentage changes in OPEC real income than in the income of, say, the OECD countries, for the simple reason that oil imports constitute only a few percent of OECD GNP but most of OPEC's GNP. Thus in considering the impact of an oil price increase it may not be too unreasonable to take income changes into account in analyzing OPEC's behavior, while ignoring them in industrial countries.

Let us turn next to the asset markets. There will be assumed to be only two assets, dollars and marks, each held by all three countries. Following Kouri (1981), we shall assume that America holds a fixed dollar value of marks in its portfolio, and that Germany holds a fixed mark value of dollars in its portfolio:[3]

$$M_A/V = H_A,$$
$$D_G V = H_G, \tag{5}$$

where M_A is American mark holdings, and H_A and H_G are constant terms.

OPEC will be assumed to allocate its wealth between dollars and marks. Let W_O be OPEC wealth measured in dollars, that is,

$$W_O \equiv D_O + M_O/V, \tag{6}$$

where D_O and M_O and OPEC dollar and mark holdings. When we will assume that a fraction α of this wealth is held in mark, $1 - \alpha$ in dollars:

$$M_O/V = \alpha W_O, \tag{7}$$

$$D_O = (1 - \alpha)W_O. \tag{8}$$

We have now specified a complete dynamic model. The next step is to analyze its behavior, before applying it to the central question of the paper.

6.2 Dynamic Behavior

To understand the model's dynamic behavior, it is useful to begin by deriving several balance of payments measures. First, let us derive the German current account measured in dollars. This is German net exports to America, plus exports to OPEC, less oil imports:

$$B_G = T(V) + \gamma(V)X - P_O \bar{O}_G. \tag{9}$$

Similarly, the American current account may be written

$$B_A = -T(V) + [1 - \gamma(V)]X - P_O \bar{O}_A. \tag{10}$$

We will assume that the appropriate Marshall-Lerner conditions hold, that is,

$$\partial B_G / \partial V > 0 \quad \text{and} \quad \partial B_A / \partial V < 0.$$

OPEC's current account is simply the difference between exports and imports:

$$B_O = P_O \bar{O} - X. \tag{11}$$

The equation for the rate of change in OPEC's wealth, however, must also take into account capital gains and losses on its German currency holdings; thus we have

$$\dot{W}_O = B_O - \alpha W_O(\dot{V}/V). \tag{12}$$

Next we can write down captial account balances. For continuous exchange rate changes, we can derive a net flow of capital into Germany which equals purchases of marks by America and OPEC, less purchases of dollars by Germany:

$$
\begin{aligned}
K_G &= \dot{M}_A/V + \dot{M}_O/V - \dot{D}_G \\
&= (M_A/V)(\dot{V}/V) + (M_O/V)(\dot{V}/V) + D_G(\dot{V}/V) + \alpha \dot{W}_O \\
&= [M_A/V + \alpha(1 - \alpha)W_O + D_G](\dot{V}/V) + \alpha B_O. \tag{13}
\end{aligned}
$$

Now consider the condition of overall balance of payments equilibrium for Germany (we could equivalently use a condition of equilibrium for America). We must have $B_G + K_G = 0$; that is,

$$[M_A/V + \alpha(1 - \alpha)W_O + D_G](\dot{V}/V) + \alpha B_O + B_G = 0, \tag{14}$$

or

$$\dot{V}/V = \frac{-[B_G + \alpha B_O]}{M_A/V + \alpha(1 - \alpha)W_O + D_G}.$$

This is a variant of the "acceleration equation" derived by Kouri. In Kouri's two-country model, the rate of change of the exchange rate depended on the ratio of the current account to gross international investment. Here we have to extend the equation owing to the presence of a third country, but the principle remains the same. In the special case where OPEC holds no marks, that is, $\alpha = 0$, (14) reduces to Kouri's acceleration equation where the rate of change of the exchange rate depends only on the German current account:

$$\dot{V}/V = \frac{-B_G}{M_A/V + D_G}. \tag{14'}$$

Similarly, if OPEC holds no dollars, that is, $\alpha = 1$, the rate of change of the exchange rate depends only on America's current account:

$$\dot{V}/V = \frac{B_A}{M_A/V + D_G}. \tag{14''}$$

Except in these special cases, however, there is no one-for-one relation between a country's current account and its exchange rate. Figure 6.1 illustrates the dynamic system defined by equations (4) and (14). OPEC expenditure adjusts toward its income, and this behavior is indicated by the vertical schedule $\dot{X} = 0$. For reference I also indicate those combinations of X and V for which the current account of each industrial country is in balance. An increase in OPEC expenditure improves each country's current account, and to restore balance, this must be offset by an appreciation of the dollar in the case of America, a depreciation in the case of Germany. The slopes of these schedules can be derived from (9) and (10):

$$\left.\frac{dV}{dX}\right|_{B_A=0} = \frac{1 - \gamma}{(\partial T/\partial V) + X(\partial \gamma/\partial V)},$$

$$\left.\frac{dV}{dX}\right|_{B_G=0} = \frac{-\gamma}{(\partial T/\partial V) + X(\partial \gamma/\partial V)}. \tag{15}$$

Finally, we have the combinations of X and V for which the exchange rate is stationary: $\dot{V}/V = 0$. In the figure, this is shown as downward sloping, but in fact it can be sloped either way. From (14), the slope is

$$\left.\frac{dV}{dX}\right|_{\dot{V}/V=0} = \frac{\alpha - \gamma}{(\partial T/\partial V) + X(\partial \alpha/\partial V)}. \tag{16}$$

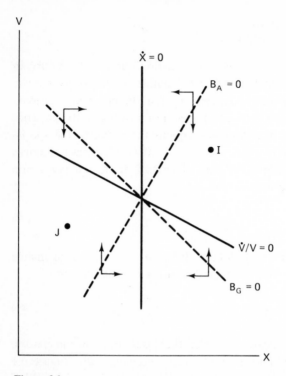

Figure 6.1

Whether the schedule slopes up or down depends on whether α—the share of marks in OPEC's portfolio—is greater of less than γ, the share of German goods in OPEC imports. Clearly, also, the slope of $\dot{V}/V = 0$ lies between those of the current-account balance schedules (15). If OPEC holds only dollars $\alpha = 0$ and the schedule coincides with $B_G = 0$; if OPEC holds only marks, $\alpha = 1$ and the schedule coincides with $B_A = 0$.

The intuition behind these results is straightforward. Suppose OPEC expenditure were to rise from its long-run level. This would have two direct effects on Germany's balance of payments. First, it would improve the current account because part of the expenditure would fall on German goods. On the other hand, it would worsen the German capital account because OPEC would now be running a current account deficit which it would in part finance by liquidating its holdings of marks. Only if OPEC holds no marks can this second effect be neglected.

As long as OPEC holds both currencies, neither country's current account provides an accurate guide to the direction of movement of the exchange rate. At point I in the figure, America is running a current account surplus, yet the dollar is depreciating; at J America is running a deficit, yet the dollar is appreciating. Nor does the bilateral trade balance between America and Germany provide a guide, since given this balance each country's overall balance still depends on OPEC expenditure.

Finally, note that assuming that either Germany or America is "small" does not remove these ambiguities. Suppose we wanted to assume that Germany is "small" and wanted to argue that this would allow us to focus solely on the German current account. Consider the slope of $\dot{V}/V = 0$ relative to that of $B_G = 0$; only if these converge can we use the German current account alone. But the relative slope is $1 - \alpha/\gamma$. If Germany is small, both α and γ will be small numbers, but their ratio need not be. The only justification for an exclusive focus on an individual country's current account is the assumption that it is "smaller" in OPEC's asset holdings than in its import bill.

6.3 Effects of an Oil Price Increase

The effects of an oil price increase on the exchange rate depend primarily on three parameters: α, the share of marks in OPEC's portfolio: γ, the share of German goods in OPEC's imports; and $\sigma = O_G/\bar{O}$, the German share in world oil imports. The short-run impact depends whether α is greater or less than σ; the long-run impact depends on whether γ is more or less than σ.

The intutition behind this is simple. Since OPEC spending lags behind income, an oil price increase initially increases industrial country import bills without a corresponding increase in exports. While American and German current accounts are thus worsened, however, there is an improvement in capital accounts as OPEC invests its trade surplus in dollars and marks. Whether the net effect is favorable or unfavorable for the dollar depends on whether OPEC investment in dollars is more or less than America's share of the industrial world's current account deficit.

Over time, however, OPEC's spending rises to match its income, and it reduces the rate at which it acquires foreign assets. Thus the balance of payments effects of higher oil prices depend to a diminishing extent on OPEC's asset preferences and increasingly upon its preferences for goods. In the long run, OPEC ceases investing abroad, and only a comparison of import and export shares matters.

Formally, we can determine the impact effect of an oil price increase by differentiating (14) with respect to P_O:

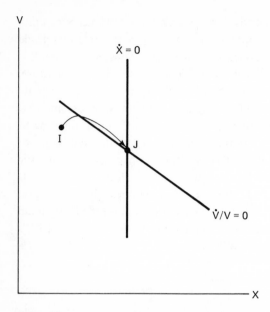

Figure 6.2

$$\frac{d(\dot{V}/V)}{dP_O} = \frac{\overline{O}(\sigma - \alpha)}{M_A/V + \alpha(1 - \alpha)W_O + D_G}. \tag{17}$$

The long-run effect can be determined by setting $X = P_O\overline{O}$ and requiring that $B_O = B_A = 0$, which implies

$$\frac{dV}{dP_O} = \frac{\overline{O}(\sigma - \gamma)}{(\partial T/\partial V) + X(\partial \gamma/\partial V)}. \tag{18}$$

Interestingly, the initial movement of the exchange rate and its long-run change may be in different directions. If $\gamma > \sigma > \alpha$, for instance—that is, speaking loosely, if OPEC prefers American investments and German products—the dollar will appreciate in the short run yet depreciate in the long run. The process is illustrated in figure 6.2. Initially, long-run equilibrium is at I. An increase in the price of oil shifts $\dot{V}/V = 0$ upward and $\dot{X} = 0$ right, so that the new equilibrium is at J. By referring back to figure 6.1, we can see that America remains in current account deficit throughout this process, whereas Germany, after initially running a dificit, may later move into surplus; but the mark will appreciate whether or not this happens, and will begin appreciating before Germany's trade moves into balance if it does.

What makes this case interesting is that it seems to bear some resemblance to the facts. If we view "Germany" as the OECD except for the United States, the relation $\gamma > \sigma > \alpha$ appears to hold. The US share of OECD oil imports is comparable to its share of OECD GNP, while its share of OPEC imports is comparable to its much smaller share of OECD exports. Except for the complicating factors to be discussed in the final section of the paper, this suggests that an oil price increase ought to lead first to dollar appreciation, and later to an even greater dollar depreciation.

6.4 Some Complications

The model presented in this paper contains enough structure so that qualitative behavior depends on only a handful of easily quantifiable parameters. In this section I shall somewhat mar this simplicity by showing that two other factors can matter. The first of these is the effect of oil prices on oil consumption; the second of these is the effect of market anticipation of exchange rate changes.

Suppose that instead of being exogenously fixed, oil imports depend on the price of oil in domestic currency. We would then have to rewrite (2) as

$$O_A = O_A(P_O),$$
$$O_G = O_G(P_O \cdot V),$$
(19)

where $O_A(\ )$ and $O_G(\ )$ are demand curves which may have different elasticities, although in both cases we may safely assume the elasticity to be less than one. The introduction of demand elasticity will modify both the short-run and long-run effects of increasing P_O, since Germany's share of the marginal burden of an oil price increase will no longer equal its share of current oil imports. The appropriate share variable now becomes

$$\tilde{\sigma} = \frac{O_G \cdot (1 - \varepsilon_G)}{O_G(1 - \varepsilon_G) + O_A(1 - \varepsilon_A)},$$

where ε_G, ε_A are the price elasticities of oil demand in Germany and America—numbers much less accessible to casual, or even careful, empiricism than O_A and O_G.

A more difficult analytical problem is posed by market expectations of exchange rate changes. I have been assuming that OPEC holds a fixed share α of its wealth in marks, America holds a fixed dollar value of marks, and Germany holds a fixed mark value of dollars. Realistically, all of these should depend on the expected rate of dollar appreciation:

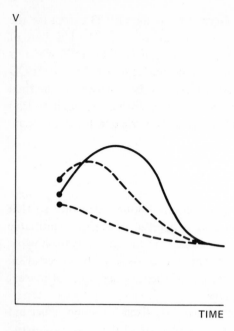

V

TIME

Figure 6.3

$\alpha = \alpha(\pi),$

$H_A = H_A(\pi),$ (20)

$H_G = H_G(\pi),$

where $\pi = E[\dot{V}/V]$.

The effect of introducing these expectations, particularly if we adopt the popular hypothesis of "rational" expectations, is to blur the distinction between short run and long run. As many authors have emphasized, long-run factors, even if they have no effect on the current distribution of asset holdings, can still have an immediate effect on the exchange rate through their effect on expectations. Thus the real factors can dominate the financial ones even from the start.

A complete analysis of the effect of speculation is a difficult task, since it involves three differential equations and hence defies graphical analysis. A heuristic approach, however, suggests the kind of results which ought to emerge. Suppose we distinguish between the "non speculative" value of the dollar—the value it would have if investors expected its value to remain unchanged—and its actual value. If expectations were static, the "nonspeculative" and actual exchange rates would always coincide. What we showed in section 6.3 was that if $\gamma > \sigma > \alpha$, the path of the rate would then look like the solid line in figure 6.3. Now suppose that expectations are rational. This will change the actual path of V; it will also change the path of the "nonspeculative" exchange rate because both trade balances and capital gains will be different from what they would have been under static expectations.

If these effects are not too strong, the *qualitative* features of the "nonspeculative" rate's path will not change: It will first rise, then fall. If this is the case—and I have assumed it, not proved it—then the actual path of the exchange rate can be analyzed using the "nonspeculative" path as a reference. For V will be above its nonspeculative value if $\dot{V}/V$ is positive, below it if $\dot{V}/V$ is negative.

The possibilities are indicated by the broken lines in figure 6.3. Either V is initially expected to rise or it is expected to fall. In the first case there must be an initial jump in the value of the dollar and continuing appreciation for a time before $\dot{V}/V$ turns negative and the dollar falls below its nonspeculative value. (This must happen while the nonspeculative rate is still rising.) In the second case there is an initial discrete devaluation of the dollar, followed by continuing gradual depreciation. Thus in this case the long-run fundamental considerations of current account balance dominate even in the short run. This case is presumably more likely, the faster the adjustment of OPEC spending and the more sensitive portfolio holdings are to expected exchange rate changes.

In this chapter I have developed a simple model which allows us to consider some of the channels through which changes in the price of oil affect exchange rates. Although the model is necessarily a highly oversimplified representation of reality, it does bring out two basic considerations. First, the effect of the price of oil depends on whether the burden to a country's balance of payments created by higher oil imports is greater or less than the improvement due to OPEC imports and investment. Second, the relative importance of OPEC investment preferences falls over time, so that in the long run it is OPEC's import preferences that matter.

Notes

1. Alternatively, we might suppose that OPEC attempts to fix the real price of oil by pegging the price to a basket of dollars and marks. This would not alter the qualitative results.

2. Strictly speaking, it might be more reasonable to assume that real as opposed to

dollar spending adjusts with a lag. Again the qualitative results, though more difficult to derive, remain unchanged.

3. This amounts to assuming that each country has a zero marginal propensity to hold wealth in the other's currency. As Kouri and de Macedo (1978) have shown, what is crucial for explaining the effect of current accounts on exchange rates is the "wealth transfer effect": Each country has a marginal propensity to hold wealth in its own currency, which is larger than that of foreigners. The assumption made here can be viewed as a shorthand way of capturing this effect, one which will be a reasonable approximation if foreign assets are a small fraction of each country's portfolio.

References

Buiter, W., (1978). "Short-Run and Long-Run Effects of External Disturbances under a Floating Exchange Rate," *Economica* 45, 251–72.

Findlay, R., and Rodriguez, C. (1977). "Intermediate Imports and Macroeconomic Policy under Flexible Exchange Rates," *Canadian Journal of Economics* 10, 208–17.

Kouri, P. (1981). "Balance of Payments and the Foreign Exchange Market: A Dynamic Partial Equilibrium Model," in J. Bhandari and B. Putnam, eds., *Economic Interdependence and Flexible Exchange Rates*, MIT Press.

Kouri, P., and J. de Macedo (1978). "Exchange Rates and the International Adjustment Process," *Brookings Papers on Economic Activity* 1.

Obstfeld, M. (1980). "Intermediate Imports, the Terms of Trade, and the Dynamics of the Exchange Rate and Current Account," *Journal of International Economics*, November.

7

Energy and Growth under Flexible Exchange Rates: A Simulation Study

Jeffrey Sachs

The macroeconomic events of recent years have placed a very heavy strain on existing models of the macroeconomy. The dramatic rise in real energy prices, in particular, requires rethinking of current models along a number of lines. First, higher energy prices raise new issues for aggregate supply in the short and long runs. Energy price increases induce a short-run production decline for given capital stock, as well as a decline in net capital accumulation and long-run capital intensity. Second, the energy price increases raise a host of international economic issues. Worldwide interest rates and global production shift when increases in energy prices transfer income to the high-saving OPEC region. The repercussions of the global shifts must be studied in a global context. Finally, energy price increases interact with asset market prices in important ways. Increased attention must be paid to the effect of flexible exchange rates in reacting, and facilitating adjustment, to higher energy prices.

Existing theoretical and econometric models are deficient in addressing these important effects. Progress has been made in each area, but an adequate synthesis of results is wanting. An important reason for this limitation is that theoretical models that adequately treat the supply side, capital accumulation, international repercussion effects, and asset markets are too complex to solve analytically. The strategy in this chapter is to present a theoretically sound model of an oil price increase under flexible exchange rates and to solve the model by taking refuge in computer simulation. The goal of this paper is methodological—to demonstrate the feasibility of an integrated approach to growth and energy—rather

I would like to thank David Lipton for extensive discussions and assistance. This work is part of ongoing research with Michael Bruno of Hebrew University into macroeconomic adjustment with intermediate inputs. Support from the National Science Foundation is gratefully acknowledged.

than empirical. No attempt is made here to calibrate precisely the simulation model, though such an attempt is now under way.

Let us consider each of the three problem areas. Economists have increasingly recognized the need to integrate the production technology into models of aggregate output [Findlay and Rodriguez (1977), Hudson and Jorgenson (1978), and Mork and Hall (1979)] and to explore the effects of alternative technological assumptions on adjustment. There is still, however, an inadequate integration of short-run adjustment and long-run growth in most applied macroeconomic analyses, and with respect to energy the deficiency is particularly acute. While demand or monetary disturbances may influence short-run output with little effect on the growth path, energy prices by nature affect both short-run and long-run outputs, the latter through the effects on capital accumulation and savings. As higher energy prices reduce the profitability of investment, the long-term effect of higher energy prices is a reduction in capital intensity of production. The long-run decline is reflected immediately in the short-run investment rate.

Equity markets provide the link between the long-run capital intensity of production and the short-run investment decisions of firms. In the simulation model, the investment function is built upon Tobin's insight (1969) that a value-maximizing firm will increase its investment rate when the valuation of equity claims to its capital rises relative to the replacement cost of capital. The ratio of these two prices is widely known as Tobin's q; the link between investment and q will be formally justfied. Because q is itself a function of the expected stream of future capital earnings, a decline in anticipated earnings causes a fall in current q and current investment. We shall see that an increase in energy prices depresses q and causes a sharp fall in capital accumulation. The extent of the fall depends on the nature of technology.

The second concern for sound modeling of OPEC disturbances is that worldwide variables will change with a worldwide shock. A "small economy" analysis that takes world interest rates and income as given following a price shock is partial at best, and probably misleading. Similarly, we cannot very well study the postshock exchange rate between two oil-importing economies by studying a model of only one economy. Yet various authors have argued that the exchange rate of a non-OPEC economy vis-a-vis other such economies will move in a particular direction after an OPEC price shock, even though the conclusion cannot be true for all such economies. In our simulation study, we include two growing, industrialized economies in addition to OPEC, so that we may explicitly analyze movements of their bilateral exchange rate.

The multilateral aspect of the model also permits us to address the important issues of policy coordination and repercussion effects between large, open economies. We reach some surprising conclusions about the transmission of policies across national boundaries. In particular, a fiscal expansion may well be begger-thy-neighbor if real wages are sufficiently rigid in the industrial economies.

Our third concern is the proper treatment of asset market prices in a study of the OPEC shocks. The recent advances in "efficient market theory" of exchange rates, equity prices, and the commodity price level demonstrate that asset prices aggregate market expectations of future economic developments. I have mentioned q in this context. Similarly, the current bilateral exchange rate can be written as a discounted stream of the relative money stocks in the two economies [see Mussa (1979)], and the price level is tied to the discounted stream of expected nominal money services in a single economy [see Brock (1974)]. Because asset prices translate expected future economic developments into current decisions, it is now well appreciated that a sound model of expectations is crucial. Therefore, I adopt the perfect foresight assumption throughout the simulation model. This approach has several advantages: (1) It avoids the "Lucas critique" by making explicit how agents' behavior will change with shifts in policy regime; (2) It rules out the possibility of systematically profitable arbitrage given known market conditions; and (3) It is the appropriate base case for optimizing agents in a nonstochastic environment.

As I shall indicate, the perfect foresight assumption raises interesting methodological issues for simulation. Because equity prices, the exchange rate, and the consumption price level are valued according to the entire future path of various endogenous and exogenous variables, it is difficult to find the initial conditions for these prices. Technically, the models pose two-point boundary-value problems, for which final but not initial asset prices are known. Elsewhere, I have helped to implement the method of "multiple shooting," common in certain physical sciences, for the solution of economic simulations [Lipton et al. (1980)]. This method, I shall show, is very powerful in solving the large two-country growth model in this chapter.

A complete description of a related two-country growth model, but without energy inputs or money balances, may be found in Lipton and Sachs (1980). At various points, I shall refer to that study for detailed discussion. A similar two-country model of trade, with perfect foresight but without energy and growth is Obstfeld (1980). In this chapter, the general equilibrium model is set forth in section 7.1; some analytical comparative static results are described in section 7.2. In section 7.3, the full dynamic effects of an OPEC shock on output and growth are studied through simulation under a variety of labor market assumptions. We shall reconfirm in a general equilibrium setting the results of an earlier study by this author on the importance of the labor market setting for adjustments to the oil shock. Furthermore, we shall illustrate how alternative technological assumptions alter the growth paths of the economies. It is important to note that we shall analyze the transmission of macroeconomic policies across national borders. Conclusions and extensions to the model are discussed in section 7.4.

7.1 A Model of Energy, Flexible Exchange Rates, and Two-Country Growth

We consider two growing industrial economies, linked through international commodity and financial markets. Each economy produces a single output, which it consumes, sells abroad for consumption, and uses for domestic capital formuation. The domestic and foreign goods are imperfect consumption substitutes, with each household's consumption bundle depending on the relative price of the two goods. Each country uses only its own output for capital formation.

Households save in the form of home money balances and domestic and foreign equity claims to capital. We assume that each country's money balances yield transaction services to the country's agents. These services are represented by the inclusion of real money balances in the household utility function. Foreign money balances yield no utility. Implicitly international transactions are mediated in equity rather than money [see Obstfeld (1980) for a similar approach]. Equity claims are valued for the stream of real income attached to their ownership. With no transactions costs in international financial markets and perfect foresight, instantaneous holding yields of home and foreign equity are always equalized. We abstract from outside interest-bearing nominal securities, such as government bonds.

Current production uses labor inputs, energy, and the existing stock of reproducible capital. Households supply labor inelastically to the labor market, and competitive firms hire labor to the point where the marginal product of labor equals the wage. Short-run rigidities in nominal or real wages may induce labor market disequilibrium and temporary, involuntary unemployment. [In Lipton and Sachs (1980) we reinterpret the employment fluctuations as movements along the household's (intertemporal) labor-leisure trade-off.] Firms similarly purchase energy inputs according to profit-maximizing criteria. Investment over time in reproducible capital proceeds according to the value-maximizing program of the firm.

Energy requirements are satisfied through imports from OPEC. OPEC in turn uses its oil revenues to consume the output of the two developed economies and to accumulate equity claims in the two economies for later consumption. We abstract from OPEC's own development strategy, and indeed from the nature of OPEC's pricing decision itself. The real price of oil, in terms of OPEC's consumption bundle, is exogenous.

Equilibrium requires that output supply and demand balance, that the *ex ante* yields of home and foreign equities be the same, and that the home and foreign demands for outside money balances equal their respective supplies. Loosely speaking, the world real rate of return adjusts to balance global demand and supply, while the terms of trade (or real exchange rate) shifts demand between the two economies to balance each country's output market. Home and foreign equity prices adjust to equate yields on equity claims today and in the future. Finally, the foreign and home price levels adjust to equate money supplies and demands. The model as written solves for home (P) and foreign prices levels (P^*), and the terms of trade ($\Pi = P/EP^*$), (where E is the exchange rate, in units of home currency per unit of foreign currency, and * indicates "foreign"). The nominal exchange rate is given simply at $E = (P^*/P) \cdot (1/\Pi)$. Obviously, the model can be re-written to solve for E, one price level, and the terms of trade, with the other price level determined residually.

It is important to remember that equilibrium in this model is a full, intertemporal Nash equilibrium as characterized in Brock (1974). Agents make current decisions based upon their anticipations of the entire future paths of prices, which they take as given. By the perfect foresight assumption, all agents' anticipations must be the same and must be equal to the prices that actually unfold over time (barring future, unanticipated shifts in exogenous variables). Thus, to solve for q_0, q_0^*, E_0, P_0, and P_0^* at the initial time, we must solve for sequences $\{q_i\}$, $\{q_i^*\}$, $\{E_i\}$, $\{P_i\}$ and $\{P_i^*\}$, $i = 0, 1, \ldots, \infty$. By examining the intertemporal maximization problems of households and firms, the dependence of today's action on all future prices can be made clear.

In setting forth the model, I shall present the home country equations only, with the understanding that comparable equations exist for the foreign economy. The entire model, for both countries and OPEC, is presented in table 7.1. Aside from the wage equation and the OPEC consumption equation, the model is written in continuous time. All equations are discretized for the simulations.

7.1.1 The Household

On the household side, we postulate Sidrauski-Brock infinitely lived and growing household, which maximizes an additively separable intertemporal utility function in goods and real money balances:

$$\int_0^\infty e^{-\delta t} L_F U(C, C^M, M/P)\, dt.$$

δ is the rate of pure time discount, and L_F is the number of household members at any time (with $\dot{L}_F/L_F = n$). C is per capita domestic consumption of the home final good, and C^M is per capita domestic consumption of the foreign final good. (*All* quantity variables will be written in intensive form, per unit of L_F, unless otherwise noted.) There is no utility to leisure, so that notional labor supply is L_F. Since labor markets do not necessarily clear instantaneously, however, we may have total man-hours $MH < L_F$. We define $L = MH/L_F$ as the employment rate, and $U = 1 - L$ as the unemployment rate. Households have full knowledge of the rationing in the labor market, and they optimize according to their labor market constraints. For simplicity, we assume that rationing is uniform across agent and appears in the form of reduced hours. Since L does not directly enter $U(\cdot)$, there are no goods-market spillover effects of labor rationing, aside from the direct effects caused by a reduction in human wealth.

Let A^M represent the households' *per capita* stock of equity wealth in units of the home good, and let r be the instantaneous yield on equity claims. The familiar intertemporal budget constraint is

$$\dot{A}^M = rA^M + (1 - \tau)\frac{W}{P}L - C - C^M/\Pi - nA^M, \tag{1}$$

where τ is the rate of labor taxation. (There are no other taxes.) We assume that per capita government expenditure on final consumption always adjust to keep $G = \tau(W/P)L$. In addition to direct expenditure, the government makes lump-sum transfer payments to households, financed by money creation: $T = (\dot{M} + nM)/P$. The discounted value of all future transfers W^T may be written

$$\int_0^\infty \exp[-\textstyle\int_0^t (r - n)\, ds]\,[(\dot{M} + nM)/P]\, dt.$$

Integration by parts reveals in the Cobb-Douglas case that W^T is given simply by $(i/(\delta - n) - 1)(M/P)$.[1]

Now, let A be total per capita wealth, with

$$A = A^M + (M/P) + H + W^T \tag{2}$$

with

$$H = \int_0^\infty \exp[-\int_0^t (r - n)\, ds](1 - \tau)\, \frac{W}{P}\, L\, dt \quad \text{(human wealth)},$$

$$W^T = \int_0^\infty \exp[-\int_0^t (r - n)\, ds]\, T\, dt \quad \text{(present value of transfers)}.$$

Using (1) and (2), and the definitions of H and W^T, we can rewrite the budget constraint as

$$\dot{A} = (r - n)A - [C + C^M/\Pi + (r + \dot{P}/P)M/P]. \tag{3}$$

We now see that "full" consumption C_F in any period is equal to goods consumption *plus* the opportunity cost of real balances. The shadow price of real balances is the nominal interest rate $i = r + \dot{P}/P$, which represents the income foregone in holding wealth in the form of money balances.

We may specialize further, by writing $U(\cdot)$ as a constant-relative-risk aversion function of a linear homogeneous function Ψ of C, C^M, and M/P:

$$U(\cdot) = \begin{cases} \dfrac{[\Psi(C, C^M, M/P)]^{1-\sigma}}{1 - \sigma} & \sigma \neq 1 \\[2ex] \log[\Psi(C, C^M, M/P] & \sigma = 1 \end{cases} \tag{4}$$

(for details see [13]; for a similar approach, see [19]). Now, it is easy to show that intertemporal optimization makes

$$\sigma(\dot{\Psi}/\Psi) = (r - \delta - \dot{P}_\psi/P_\psi), \tag{5}$$

where P_ψ is a true price index for Ψ.[2] Note that $C_F = P_\psi \Psi$. In this study, we proceed with the Cobb-Douglas case for Ψ and $U(\cdot)$:

$$\Psi = C^{\alpha(1-s)}(C^M)^{(1-\alpha)(1-s)}(M/P)^s \quad \text{and} \quad \sigma = 1.$$

In this case, consumption expenditures on the three goods in each period is a fixed proportion of C_F, and full consumption C_F is linear in wealth:

(a) $C_F = (\delta - n)A$;
(b) $C = \alpha(1 - s)C_F$;
(c) $C^M = (1 - \alpha)(1 - s)C_{F/\Pi}$;
(d) $i(M/P) = sC_F$.

$$(6)$$

It is very inportant to note that (6d) is the utility-maximizing money demand schedule. Note finally that by the value of W^T shown above, total wealth is

$$A = [i/(\delta - n)] \cdot (M/P) + A^M + H. \tag{7}$$

7.1.2 The Firm

Under certainty and perfect competition, the strategy of value maximization for the firm is unanimously agreed upon by shareholders. We follow Hayashi's argument (1982) that such a strategy, under technical conditions now described, leads to the investment rule

$$J = J(q) \cdot K, \tag{8}$$

where J is gross (per capita) capital formation and K is the preexisting capital stock (per capita). q is, again, the price of equity relative to the price of physical capital, and the latter in this model is just equal to the price of output. The investment schedule arises from an assumed cost of adjustment to new investment which makes the marginal cost of investment rise with the investment rate J/K.

To be specific, suppose that total investment expenditure I equals $J \cdot [1 + \phi(J/K)]$, where $\phi(\cdot)$ is the per unit adjustment cost, $\phi' > 0$. Since the market values new capital according to the real equity price q, the firm's instantaneous change in value due to capital formation J is simply

$$dV = qJ - J \cdot [1 + \phi(J/K)]. \tag{9}$$

If (9) is maximized with respect to J, we see that the firm equates q with $1 + d/dJ[(J \cdot \phi)]$, the marginal adjustment cost. Equation (8) is then simply derived. In the specific and useful case of $\phi(J/K) = (\phi_0/2) \cdot (J/K)$, that is, linear adjustment costs with constant ϕ_0, J and I are given by

(a) $J = (q - 1) \cdot K/\phi_0$,
(b) $I = (q - 1)^2 \cdot K/(2\phi_0)$.

$$(10)$$

For a given K, the firms should behave as a simple short-run profit maximizer, equating marginal products and factor costs of all variable factors. (This assumes that these factors are strictly variable, that is, instantaneously and costlessly adjustable.) In this study we assume that there are two variable factors, labor and energy, and that total output is produced according to the CRS, neoclassical production function $Q = F[L, N, K]$. (Note that the function is written in intensive form, per unit L_F.) A number of recent studies have investigated empirically the form of this three-factor production function to determine the degree of substitutability of energy with the other factors [see Bernadt and Wood (1979), Ford and Halvorsen (1978), Griffen and Gregory (1976), and Mark (1978)]. Some authors have suggested that K and L are weakly separable from E, writing Q as a function of value-added $V(K, L)$ and $N: Q = F[V(K, L)N]$. Others argue that the appropriate assumption is $Q = F[K^+(K, N), L]$. In this form, effective capital K^+ is composed of physical capital with a particular energy rating. The K^+ function may be putty-putty, putty-clay, or strictly fixed proportion. In the simulations, we shall investigate a variety of putty-putty models; I take up the far more complicated perfect foresight putty-clay model in Sachs (1980a).

For the general case, we require

$$Q_L = \frac{\partial F}{\partial L} = \frac{W}{P},$$

$$Q_N = \frac{\partial F}{\partial N} = \frac{P_N}{P}. \tag{11}$$

In the important special case of $Q = \min[V(K, L), N]$, Q_N does not exist; (11) becomes $\partial F/\partial L = W/(P - P_N) = W/P_v$, where P_v is the value-added deflator.

7.1.3 Asset Market Equilibrium

Domestic and foreign equity claims to capital are perfect substitutes in portfolios. Their *ex ante* instantaneous yields must be equated throughout time. Unexpected shocks may induce differing extraordinary capital gains and losses on the assets only at the instant of the disturbance, as equity prices readjust to equalize all future rates of return. The real instantaneous yield on domestic equity is the sum of the dividend yield and capital gains:

$$r = \dot{q}/q + Div/qK. \tag{12}$$

Similarly,

$$r^* = \dot{q}^*/q^* + Div^*/q^*K^*. \tag{13}$$

Now, r and r^* are the pure yields in home and foreign good units, respectively. The foreign yield in *home* good units is $r^* - \dot{\Pi}/\Pi$ ($\Pi = P/EP^*$). World asset market equilibrium requires

$$r = r^* - \dot{\Pi}/\Pi. \tag{14}$$

Note that with $i \equiv r + \dot{P}/P$ and $i^* \equiv r^* + \dot{P}^*/P^*$, (14) implies the standard uncovered interest arbitrage condition of perfect foresight and perfect capital mobility:

$$i = i^* + \dot{E}/E. \tag{15}$$

It remains to specify Div and Div^*. For convenience (and without loss of generality in the absence of interest and corporate income taxes) I assume that all investment is equity financed. For gross capital formation J and geometric depreciation $d \cdot K$, new equity issues raise $q(J - dK)$. Total dividends in domestic goods units are

$$Div = q(J - dK) + Q - \left(\frac{W}{P}\right)L - \left(\frac{P_N}{P}\right)N - I. \tag{16}$$

One of the central relations of the model emerges from (12) and (16). If we assume that the real price of equity does not explode at $t \to \infty$ (i.e., if we rule out speculative bubbles), Tobin's q may be written as the discounted value of future cash flow per unit of today's capital:[3]

$$q \cdot K = \int_0^\infty \exp\left[-\int_0^t (r(s) - n)\,ds\right][Q - (W/P)L - (P_N/P)N - I]\,dt. \tag{17}$$

7.1.4 Output Market Equilibrium

Households in all countries grow at rate n. (With different growth rates, one economy would asymptotically dominate the world economy.) Thus, the ratio of potential labor in all economies is a constant, and without confusion we may normalize all per capita variables in all countries in terms of home potential labor L_F. Consider for example foreign imports of the home good. C^{M^*} will represent foreign imports per L^F. With $\Theta \equiv (L_F^*/L_F)$, C^{M^*}/Θ is foreign per capita imports per unit of foreign potential labor.

Now we may write the equilibrium conditions. Let OPEC consumption per L_F of the domestic good equal OPEC^D, and of the foreign good equal OPEC^*. Total demand for the home good is then $C^D + I + G + C^{M^*} + \text{OPEC}^D$, which must equal Q. Similarly, $Q^* = C^{D^*} + I^* + G^* + C^M + \text{OPEC}^*$. The nature of OPEC demand is described next.

7.1.5 Balance of Payments

At any moment, world financial claims on the domestic economy change because of current account imbalances and capital gains and losses on existing assets. Let W^F represent foreign claims on the domestic income stream. (The precise composition of W^F is described below.) Then along the transition path, the change in W^F equals domestic income $[Q - rW^F - (P_N/P)N]$ less domestic expenditure $(C + C^M/\Pi + G + I)$. Suppose now that W^F is held in the form of domestic equity: $W^F = q \cdot Z$. Thus Z/K of the home capital stock is foreign owned. Then $\dot{W}^F = q\dot{Z} + \dot{q}Z$, and

$$\dot{W}^F = [C^M/ - C^{M*} - \text{OPEC}^D - (P_N/P)N] + Div(Z/K) + \dot{q}Z, \qquad (18)$$

or

$$\dot{W}^F = \text{trade deficit} + \text{service account deficit} + \text{capital gains}.$$

Because of the assumption of perfect capital mobility there is no guide as to how the various economies will hold their financial wealth. With all rates of return equalized, there is no motive for one asset preference over another; along any perfect foresight adjustment path all portfolios earn rate r. The portfolio composition only matters at the time of *unexpected* shocks, when assets experience differing, extraordinary capital gains and losses. Both to simplify bookkeeping and to mimic in a stylized way the underdiversification of international portfolios, I assume that OPEC holds Z and Z^* claims on domestic and foreign capital, while domestic and foreign portfolios contain only equity claims on the own economy. Since OPEC owns Z, the equity wealth of the home economy is $q(K - Z)$, and of the foreign economy $q^*(K^* - Z^*)$.

7.1.6 OPEC Demand

The only matter of concern here is OPEC's savings and consumption decision. Models of OPEC pricing, cartel behavior, and oil depletion are crucial adjuncts to this study, if we are to accurately forecast long-run trends. Unfortunately, these issues are beyond the scope of this paper, and beyond the expertise of the author [for a sophisticated recent discussion, see Nordhaus (1980)]. The principal fact to be noted here is that OPEC consumption appears to lag significantly behind increases in OPEC revenue, following a rise in oil prices. There are a number of reasons for this, including costs of adjustment of rapid changes in consumption level, and perhaps more important, OPEC members' awareness that current high oil revenues are transitory because oil is a depleting resource. Both factors induce short-run wealth accumulation, in order to smooth future consumption.

OPEC's per capita real oil wealth W^N in home good units may be written as the discounted value of future revenues:

$$W^N = \int_0^\infty \exp\left[-\int_0^t (r - n)\,ds\right](P_N/P)(N + N^*)\,dt. \tag{19}$$

OPEC equity wealth is $qZ + q^*Z^*/\Pi$, and total OPEC wealth W^{OPEC} is $W^N + qZ + q^*Z^*/\Pi$. To capture lags in OPEC short-run consumptions, while allowing long-run consumption to match that of the developed economies, we write a stock adjustment equation of the form

$$\text{OPEC} = \lambda(\text{OPEC})_{-1} + (1 - \lambda)(\delta - n)W^{\text{OPEC}}. \tag{20}$$

As λ approaches 1, OPEC has more prolonged trade surpluses following a rise in oil prices. When $\lambda = 0$, the equation matches (6a) exactly.

The division of OPEC spending between home and foreign goods is given according to

(a) $\text{OPEC}^D = \varepsilon(\Pi)\cdot\text{OPEC}$,

(b) $\text{OPEC}^* = (\text{OPEC} - \text{OPEC}^D)\Pi$. $\tag{21}$

7.1.7 Labor Market Equilibrium

The short-run macroeconomic adjustment to an oil price increase depends crucially on wage behavior. To the extent that workers attempt to preserve real consumption wages, firms' profit margins are squeezed and unemployment results. If nominal wages are highly indexed, any attempts by the monetary authority to reduce real wages through inflation will be vitiated. On the other hand, if nomial wage growth is sticky, an inflationary policy will successfully moderate unemployment, while a contractionary response to the price hike will exacerbate the employment shortfall. These points have been extensively discussed in Bruno and Sachs (1979b) and Sachs (1979, 1980a).

These results may be interpreted in terms of exchange rate policy. To the extent that wages are indexed to the consumer price level, an exchange rate depreciation through monetary expansion will simply raise home wages and prices in equiproportion; there will be no expansionary gain in real output. If, contrariwise, the rate of real wage growth can be slowed through exchange rate depreciation, output will expand, with increases in investments and exports.

At most, nominal and real wage rigidity are temporary phenomena, as shifts in the employment rate will drive wages towards full-employment levels. The empirical evidence on OPEC wages during 1973–1979 strongly suggests that real wage growth moderated after the first OPEC price hike, but only after years of high inflation and sustained unemployment in most countries [see Sachs (1979) for evidence]. To model short-run rigidities and long-run labor market clearing, I propose the following expression:

$$W_t/W_{t-1} = (P_t^c/P_{t-1}^c)^\rho (P_{t-1}^c/P_{t-2}^c)^{(1-\rho)} L_t^\gamma. \tag{22}$$

Nominal wages are indexed to consumer prices P^c, but with a partial lag; 100ρ percent indexation is on current inflation, and $100(1 - \rho)$ percent on lagged inflation. The overall rate of wage change is also responsive to the employment rate, with elasticity γ. Consider a few special cases. With $\gamma = 0$ and $\rho = 1$ the real wage is fixed, for $W_t/P_t^c = W_{t-1}/P_{t-1}^c$. With $\gamma > 0$ and $\rho = 1$, the real wage responds to employment, but not to a change in inflation: $W_t/P_t^c = (W_{t-1}/P_{t-1}^c)L_t^\gamma$. In general, real wage change is a negative function of *accelerating* inflation as well as unemployment. Equation (22) can be rewritten

$$(W_t/P_t^c) = (W_{t-1}/P_{t-1}^c) \cdot [(P_{t-1}^c/P_{t-2}^c)/(P_t^c/P_{t-1}^c)]^{(1-\rho)} L_t^\gamma. \tag{23}$$

Each percentage point acceleration in inflation, for given L, reduces real wages by $(1 - \rho)$ percent. Finally, note that as $\gamma \to \infty$, we will have $L \to 1$, with full employment guaranteed.

The true consumer price level for each economy can be written according to the underlying household $U(\cdot)$ function. In the specific Cobb-Douglas case treated here, we write $P_c = P^\alpha(P^*E)^{(1-\alpha)}$, with α the share of domestic consumption on the domestic good.[4]

7.1.8 The Entire Model

The full model is presented in table 7.1. A list of variable definitions appears at the end of the table.

The model is written in a special form in table 7.1, to anticipate the simulations. Consider a variable such as human wealth H, described in (2) in the text, and equations (5) and (7) in the table. H may be defined directly as the present value of the future stream of labor income, as in the text. Alternatively, it may be defined by *two* equations, in time derivative form, as in the table. Differentiating (2), we fine $\dot{H} = (r - n)H - (W/P)(1 - \tau)L$. This equation and the transversality condition $\lim_{t\to\infty} He^{-rt} = 0$ are equivalent to the original equation for H. In effect, the transversality condition imposes the initial condition on the differential

Table 7.1
The complete model[a]

A. The household

(1) $C = (\delta - n)A$

(2) $C^* = (\delta - n)A^*$

(3) $A = q(K - Z) + (M/P)(i/(\delta - n)) + H$

(4) $A^* = q^*(K^* - Z^*) + (M^*/P^*)(i^*/(\delta - n)) + H^*$

(5) $\dot{H} = (r - n)H - (W/P)(1 - \tau)L$

(6) $\dot{H}^* = (r - n)H^* - (W^*/P^*)(1 - \tau^*)L^*$

(7) $\lim_{t \to \infty} e^{-(r-n)t} H = 0$

(8) $\lim_{t \to \infty} e^{-(r^*-n)t} H^* = 0$

(9) $C^D = C^D(\Pi, i) \cdot C$

(10) $(M/P) = m(\Pi, i) \cdot C$

(11) $C^m = (C - C^D - iM/P)\Pi$

(12) $C^{D^*} = C^{D^*}(\Pi, i^*) \cdot C^*$

(13) $(M^*/P^*) = m^*(\Pi, i^*) \cdot C^*$

(14) $C^{m^*} = (C^* - C^{D^*} - i^* M^*/P^*)/\Pi$

B. The firm

(15) $Q = F[K, L, N]$

(16) $Q^* = F^*[K^*, L^*, N^*]$

(17) $Q_L = W/P$

(18) $Q_N = P_N/P$

(19) $Q^*_{L^*} = W^*/P^*$

(20) $Q_{N^*} = P_N/P^*E$

(21) $I = J(1 + \phi(J/K))$

(22) $I^* = J^*(1 + \phi^*(J^*/K^*))$

(23) $J = J(q) \cdot K$

(24) $J^* = J^*(q^*) \cdot K^*$

(25) $\dot{K} = J - \delta K - nK$

(26) $\dot{K}^* = J^* - \delta K^* - nK^*$

C. Asset market equilibrium

(27) $r = \dot{q}/q + Div/qK$

(28) $r^* = \dot{q}^*/q^* + Div^*/q^* K^*$

(29) $E = (P/P^*) \cdot (1/\Pi)$

(30) $r = r^* - \dot{\Pi}/\Pi$

(31) $i = r + (\dot{P}/P)$

(32) $i^* = r^* + P^*/P^*$

Table 7.1 (*continued*)

(33) $\lim_{t \to \infty} e^{-rt}(M/P) = 0$

(34) $\lim_{t \to \infty} e^{-r^*t}(M^*/P^*) = 0$

(35) $Div = q(J - dK) + Q - (W/P)L - (P_N/P)N - I$

(36) $Div^* = q^*(J^* - dK^*) + Q^* - (W^*/P^*)L^* - (P_{N^*}/P^*)N^* - I^*$

(37) $\lim_{t \to \infty} e^{-rt}q = 0$

(38) $\lim_{t^* \to \infty} e^{-r^*t}q^* = 0$

D. Output market equilibrium

(39) $Q = C^D + I + G + C^{M^*} + \text{OPEC}^D$

(40) $Q^* = C^{D^*} + I^* + G^* + C^M + \text{OPEC}$

E. Balance of payments equations

(41) $q\dot{Z} = [C^M/\Pi - C^{M^*} - \text{OPEC}^D - (P_N/P)N] + Div(Z/K)$

(42) $q^*\dot{Z}^* = [C^{M^*}\Pi - C^M - \text{OPEC}^* - (P_{N^*}/P^*)N^*] + Div^*(Z^*/K^*)$

F. OPEC savings and consumption

(43) $\text{OPEC}_t = (1 - \lambda)(\delta - n)W^{\text{OPEC}} + \lambda\text{OPEC}_{t-1}$

(44) $\text{OPEC} = \text{OPEC}^D + \text{OPEC}^*/\Pi$

(45) $\text{OPEC}^D = \text{OPEC}^D(\Pi) \cdot \text{OPEC}$

(46) $W^{\text{OPEC}} = qZ + q^*Z^*/\Pi + W^N$

(47) $\dot{W}^N = (r - n)W^N - (P_N/P)(N + N^*)$

(48) $\lim_{t \to \infty} e^{-(r-n)t}W^N = 0$

(49) $P_N = S \cdot P^\beta(P^*E)^{(1-\beta)}$

G. Labor market equilibrium

(50) $W_t/W_{t-1} = (P_t^c/P_{t-1}^c)^\rho(P_{t-1}^c/P_{t-2}^c)^{(1-\rho)}L^\gamma$

(51) $(W_t^*/W_{t-1}^*) = (P_t^{c^*}/P_{t-1}^{c^*})^{\rho^*}(P_{t-1}^{c^*}/P_{t-2}^{c^*})^{(1-\rho^*)}L^{*\gamma^*}$

(52) $P_c = P^\alpha(P^*E)^{(1-\alpha)}$

(53) $P_c^* = P^{*\alpha}(P/E)^{(1-\alpha)}$

H. Government spending

(54) $G = \tau(W/P)L$

(55) $G^* = \tau^*(W^*/P^*)L^*$

a. Definitions of variables (measured per potential labor): A, wealth; C, consumption; C^D, home consumption of home goods; C^M, home consumption of foreign goods; Div, total dividend payments; E, energy; G, government spending; H, human wealth; I, gross investment expenditures; J, gross capital formation; K, capital; L, employment; N, energy input; OPEC, OPEC consumption; OPEC^D, OPEC consumption of home goods; Q, output; W^N, OPEC oil wealth; W^{OPEC}, OPEC oil wealth; Z, OPEC holdings of home equity.

Other variables: E, exchange rate; i, nominal interest rate; P, home good price; P_c, consumer price; P_N, home price of energy; q, equity price; r, real interest rate; W, wage; Π, final good terms of trade (P/EP^*); τ, labor tax rate.

Parameters: n, labor force growth rate; δ, rate of time discount; d, depreciation; ϕ_0, investment adjustment cost; α, share of home goods in consumption basket; σ, coefficient of relative risk aversion.

equation to insure that the solution for H is equal to its value in integral form.

In this model, the "asset variables" q, q^*, H, H^*, P, P^*, and W^N all may be written in integral form, or in differential form *plus* a transversality condition. In almost all cases, it is easier to simulate the model using the latter representation. As I describe in section 7.3, the model in time derivative form poses a standard two-point boundary-value problem, for which solution techniques are known.

The model has 55 equations, but in fact only 54 are independent. This can be demonstrated by reducing the system to its minimal state-space representation. Let X be the vector of exogenous variables, and S be the vector $\langle Z, Z^*, K, K^*, P, P^*, q, W^N, H, H^* \rangle$. After discretizing the dynamic equations, it may be shown that the model reduces to a nonlinear system of the form.[5]

$$S_{t+1} = F(S_t, X_t, X_{t+1}). \tag{24}$$

All remaining variables of the model are implicit functions of S_t, X_t, and X_{t+1}, and, in particular, q_t^* can be written as such a function. Thus, the transversality condition on q_t^* automatically holds when the transversality conditions on the other asset prices in S_t are satisfied.

The transversality conditions are not needed to reduce the system to the form in (24). In table 7.1, equations (7), (8), (33), (34), (37), and (48) impose *additional* constraints on the dynamics. The six contraints impose implicit initial conditions on P, P^*, q, W^N, H, and H^*. These asset variables always adjust in any period to guarantee that (24) will satisfy the transversality conditions as the system integrates forward. It is readily seen that the initial conditions are functions of the current values of Z, Z^*, K, and K^*, and the entire future path of X_t. Note that the initial conditions of Z, Z^*, K, and K^* are given from past history. Since they are stock variables rather than asset prices, they cannot jump discretely at any instant.

In practice, the method of multiple shooting is used to solve the simulation model. Multiple shooting is a numerical technique for finding the saddlepoint stable trajectory of a differential equation system, and is fully described in Lipton et al. (1980).

7.2 Comparative Statics

The steady-state growth path of the model depends on the equilibrium distribution of wealth. Higher domestic per capita holdings of equity claims raise home wealth and the home terms of trade (Π) in the long run. Because the steady-state distribution of wealth depends upon the entire adjustment path, it can be found only in simulation. Fortunately, important aspects of the steady state, such as the long-run capital stock, rate of return, and product wage, do not depend on wealth or Π. To discuss comparative statics, I proceed in two steps, first asking how a parameter change alters the key variables that are not functions of the wealth distribution, and then how a shift in wealth affects the steady state. The discussion here is brief; a more detailed analysis of many of these points may be found in Lipton and Sachs (1980).

The most important anchor in equilibrium lies in the savings behavior of the Sidrauski-Brock infinitely lived household. From (4) and (5) we note that per capita consumption is in steady-state equilibrium ($\dot{\Psi} = 0$) only when $r = r^* = \delta$, which is the modified golden rule in this economy. Since the rate of return on equity equals the rate of time discount, we may readily determine the long-run capital-labor ratio in each economy. To do so, note that $\dot{K} = 0$ requires $J/K = n + d$. From (10a), we have $\bar{q} = 1 + \phi(n + d)$. (A bar over any variable signifies its steady-state value.) Since $r = \delta$, and $Div/\bar{q}K = r$ in steady state, K adjusts until the dividend yield equals the required rate of return.

What is that level of K? From the dividend expression (16), we may show that steady-state

$$Div/qK = [Q - (W/P)L - P_N/P)]/\bar{q}K + \xi(\bar{q}),$$

where the latter term is a function in $\bar{q}$. Using Euler's equation, the first part of this expression is simply $F_K/\bar{q}$. Since $F_K/\bar{q} + \xi(\bar{q}) = \delta$, F_K is *constant* across steady states. We may proceed further. Full employment is a condition of steady state; the product wage adjusts to force $L = 1$, and $Q = F[L, K, N]$. Since $\partial Q/\partial N = P_N/P$, it is straightforward to use the output equation and this first-order condition to derive the dual expression $F_K = G(P_N/P, K)$, with $G_1 \gtrless 0$, $G_2 < 2$. For $F_{KE} > 0$, G_1 is less than zero. Thus, $dK/d(P_N/P) = -G_1/G_2 \lessgtr 0$. In the simulation, I assume the particular functional form $Q = \min[V(K, L), N]$, with $V(K, L)$ a Cobb-Douglas function. The long-run effects on K of a doubling of P_N/P for this technology and others are shown in table 7.2. Observe that the long-run decline in K is greatest in the case of capital-energy complementarity [see Berndt and Wood (1979) and Hudson and Jorgenson (1979)].

We assume in the simulations that OPEC sets the relative oil price S in terms of a bundle of home and foreign goods. Since $P_N = S \cdot P^\beta (P^*E)^{1-\beta}$,

Table 7.2
Long-run decline in capital intensity following doubling of input price: alternative technologies

Technology $(Q = F[K, L, N])$	F_K at full employment[a] $(L = 1)$	Percent decline in K after oil price shock[b]
1. $Q = \min[V(K, L), N]$ $V(K, L) = K^{1-\alpha}L^\alpha$	$(1 - \alpha)(1 - P_N/P)K^{-\alpha}$	8.9
2. $Q = (K^+)^{1-\alpha}L^\alpha$ $K^+ = \min[K, E]$	$(1 - \alpha)K^{-\alpha} - (P_N/P)$	17.5
3. $Q = K^{1-\alpha}(L^+)^\alpha$ $L^+ = \min[L, E]$	$(1 - \alpha)K^{-\alpha}$	0.0
4. $Q = [\mu_1 L^\rho + \mu_2 K^\rho + (1 - \mu_1 - \mu_2)N^\rho]^{1/\rho}$ (general CES with $\sigma = 1/1 - \rho$	$\Delta\mu_2[\mu_1 K^{-\rho} + \mu_2]^{(1-\rho)/\rho}$ where $\Delta = [1 - (P_N/P)^{-\sigma\rho}(1 - \mu_1 - \mu_2)^{\sigma\rho}]^{1/\rho}$	

a. $F_K = [Q - (W/P)L - (P_N/P)N]/K$, where W/P adjusts to guarantee $\partial Q/\partial L = W/P$ at $L = 1$, and where $\partial Q/\partial N = P_N/P$.
b. Assuming initial shares for labor (0.57), capital (0.38), energy (0.05), $L = 1$, and $F_K = 0.11$.

we see that $P_N/P = S \cdot \Pi^{(1-\beta)}$. For given S, an improvement in the terms of trade reduces the real cost of energy inputs. Thus, a rise in long-run Π can moderate the decline K following an oil price hike.

Let us turn to the long-run effects of money growth in this model. Since $\bar{K}$ is determined by the long-run required rate of return, higher μ $(= \dot{M}/M)$ and higher inflation have no effect on the long-run capital intensity of production. Steady-state changes in μ cause equal increases in i $(d\mu = di)$, with real money balances M/P adjusting to keep iM/P constant. The result can be made much stronger. As long as nominal wages are fully indexed, and utility is Cobb-Douglas in money and goods, the path of money growth has *no* effect on any real variables besides M/P and the inflation rate itself! This means that changes in inflation cannot affect the path of the real exchange rate. A one-shot unanticipated increase in the rate of money growth causes an initial jump in P and E of equal proportion, and subsequent higher inflation and exchange rate depreciation. The decline in real balances does not lead to increased hoarding, as in some models of the open economy.[6]

Finally, we come to the determination of the long-run terms of trade. Here the crucial determinants are the distribution of world equity claims and the division between public and private spending. Since we assume that government consumption falls exclusively on home goods while private consumption falls on home goods and imports, an increase in G that crowds out equal C causes an excess demand for home goods at the initial Π; a labor-tax-financed fiscal expansion raises Π. Starting in a steady state, with fully flexible real wages, a fiscal expansion raises Π with *no* consequences over time for the capital stock or international wealth flows.[7]

The second determinant of Π is the world distribution of wealth, which determines the world distribution of spending (as different countries have differing marginal propensities to spend on home and foreign goods). Home country wealth is given in (7) as

$$q(K - Z) + H + [i/(\delta - n)](M/P).$$

In steady state, $\bar{H}$ is the capitalized value of after-tax wage payments: $\bar{H} = (\bar{W}/\bar{P})(1 - \tau)/(\delta - n)$, and the product wage W/P is a function of P_N/P and $\bar{K}$. Since $\bar{K}$ is itself a function of P_N/P, the main determinants of home wealth are Z and P_N/P. In general, a drop in Z relative to Z^* induces a fall in Π. A rise in P_N/P shifts wealth to OPEC, and the effect on Π depends on OPEC consumption preferences.

Table 7.3
Key parameter values at initial steady-state equilibrium

Labor share in gross output (WL/PQ)	0.57
Energy share in gross output ($P_N N/PQ$)	0.05
Capital share in gross output	0.38
$GDP = Q - P_N N = C^D + I + G + C^{M*} + \text{OPEC}^D - P_N N$	
$\quad C^D/GDP$	0.36
$\quad I/GDP$	0.17
$\quad G/GDP$	0.20
$\quad C^{M*}/GDP$	0.24
$\quad \text{OPEC}^D/GDP$	0.08
$\quad P_N N/GDP$	0.05
n	0.02
δ	0.11
d	0.05
τ_W	0.33
σ_{KL} in value added	1.0

7.3 Simulation Results

A variety of simulations have been undertaken, aiming at (1) an understanding of the general equilibrium effects of an OPEC price increase and (2) an analysis of policy responses to an input price increase. Three simulations are treated in detail, though a number of further studies have been made. In the first, the price hike is studied assuming identical developed economies and fully flexible wages and prices. In the following simulation, I point out the implications of significant domestic oil production in one of the two developed economies. Finally, the mirror-image assumption for the two economies is reintroduced, but the assumption of sluggish real wage adjustment is added. Other simulations have assumed short-run wage rigidity and considered the possibility of expansionary monetary and fiscal policies to combat the unemployment following an input price rise. These are not reported here due to space limitations, but are available in Sachs (1980c).

The baseline steady-state conditions for the simulations are given in table 7.3. In all cases, we assume that the technology for gross output Q is given by $\min[V(K, L), N]$, with $\sigma_{KL} = 1$ in value added. I have devoted a separate note to analyzing the dynamic implications of alternative technologies [see Sachs (1980b)]. The long-run effects of a price rise with this technology were shown in section 7.1. $\overline{K/L}$ falls approximately 0.09 percent for a 1 percent rise in P_N/P, starting from $P_N/P = 0.05$.

In the flexible wage and price case, W/P adjusts at all points to keep $W/P = F_L(K, L)$ at $L = 1$. Under this condition, the marginal product of capital may be written as a function of K (or K/L, since $L = 1$) and the real price of energy P_N/P: $F_K = F_K(K, P_N/P)$. In the case at hand,

$$W/P = \alpha K^{1-\alpha} \cdot (1 - P_N/P),$$

where α is the share of labor in value added. Since

$$F_K = [Q - (W/P)L - (P_N/P)N]/K,$$

we have

$$F_K = (1 - \alpha - (1 - \alpha)P_N/P)K^{-\alpha}.$$

Thus, even with fully flexible real wages, F_K is a negative function of P_N/P at any level of K. It is clear that both W/P and F_K absorb some of the oil shock. This is to be contrasted with cases of capital-energy or labor-energy perfect complementarity in which only one factor price is affected by P_N/P. Indeed with the assumptions here, the percentage changes in F_K and W/P following a rise in P_N/P are equal (assuming $L = 1$).

If OPEC savings behavior is identical to that of the developed economies, the oil price increase causes a fall in capital accumulation at the time of the shock. This seems intuitive, since the fall in F_K and F_{K*} should push down q and q^* and reduce the rate of capital formation. But to nail down the argument, we must understand why savings falls and consumption rises on a global scale, as is implied by the fall in global capital accumulation. The higher oil price per se does not reduce global savings, since the increase in OPEC consumption is matched, at a constant r, by a decline in household consumption in the developed economies. But r does not remain constant. With an investment decline, constant total world consumption, and output fixed in the short run, there is an excess supply of goods; r falls, pushing up consumption and moderating the decline in q, until output markets clear. Remember that a fall in r raises both q and human wealth, since each is a discounted flow of future income streams. In the initial period, q and q^* fall, household consumption declines, and OPEC consumption rises by more than the household decline.

If OPEC has a higher short-run propensity to save out of wealth than do the developed economies, the rise in OPEC consumption does not match the fall in household consumption at constant r. The real interest rate must fall even more in the initial period to clear output markets. If OPEC spends very little of its new wealth initially, r may fall enough actually to *raise* q and q^* in the short run. Even though K and K^* must be lower in the new steady state, they rise temporarily in response to OPEC's high saving propensity. Once OPEC consumption catches up with the revaluation of its oil wealth, the short-term real interest rate is pushed up, q and q^* fall, and the rise in capital accumulation is reversed.

Thus, the short-run investment response to OPEC under flexible wages and prices depends crucially on OPEC savings behavior. Remember from section 7.1 that the parameter λ describes the lag in OPEC spending. $\lambda = 0$ implies identical OPEC and non-OPEC saving behavior, and $\lambda = 1$ implies *fixed* real OPEC expenditure independent of oil prices, (i.e., a zero marginal propensity to consume out of new wealth). In general, a high λ implies a long lag in adjustment of OPEC consumption to higher wealth. Table 7.4 presents simulation results for a doubling of energy prices under two cases of OPEC savings behavior. The developed economies are taken to be identical, so the terms of trade between them are fixed at 1.0, with the two countries' variables adjusting identically to the OPEC shock. The table therefore lists only the home variable values.

Since real wages are fully flexible, full employment is continuously maintained. Real wages in each country fall 5.4 percent at the time of the shock, and decline even more over time as K and K^* fall. Given our assumption of no technical substitution between V and N in production, gross output is wholly unaffected by the higher energy prices at the initial point. There is, however, a major switch in composition of uses of the final output. In the $\lambda = 0.1$ case, q and q^* fall sharply, as does household consumption, while OPEC consumption rises steeply. The fall in home consumption reduces real money demand, and with given nominal stock, the price level jumps sharply, by 5.3 percent. Over time, K and K^* fall, household consumption falls more, and the price level creeps upward. As we have seen, the long-run decline in capital intensity is governed by the return of $(1 - \alpha)(1 - P_N/P)K^{-\alpha}$ to its preshock level. $\overline{K}$ falls 8.9 percent, and $\overline{Q}$ therefore falls $(1 - \alpha) \times 8.9$ percent, or 3.6 percent. Of course, the higher energy price has no persistent effect on $\dot{P}$, but only on the price level itself. With $\lambda = 0.1$, long-run C falls 12.0 percent, and P rises in equiproportion.

A higher λ has no long-run effect on K or Q, but does affect short-run investment and long-run C and P. For a higher λ, the initial interest rate falls more, and the short-run investment decline is moderated or *reversed*.

Table 7.4
Dynamic adjustment with alternative OPEC savings behavior[a]

	$\lambda = 0.1$	$\lambda = 0.75$
Period 1		
Q	0.0	0.0
I	−10.7	0.8
W/P_c	−5.4	−5.4
$\dot{P}$	5.3	2.6
Period 5		
Q	−1.1	−0.3
I	−11.6	−7.0
W/P_c	−6.5	−5.7
$\dot{P}$	0.5	0.8
Period 10		
Q	−2.0	−1.2
I	−10.5	−9.9
W/P_c	−7.5	−6.6
$\dot{P}$	0.3	0.5
Steady state		
Q	−3.6	−3.6
I[b]	−8.9	−8.9
W/P_c	−9.0	−9.0
$\dot{P}$	0.0	0.0

a. All variables except $\dot{P}$ are measured as percentage deviations from the preshock steady-state growth path, specifically, $\log(x/\bar{x}) \cdot 100$. $\dot{P}$ is $[P_t - P_{t-1}] \cdot 100$.
b. Note that the long-run proportional decline in I equals the proportional decline in $\bar{K}$, since $\bar{J} = (n + d)\bar{K}$ and $\bar{I} = \bar{J} \cdot (1 + \phi/2 \cdot (n + d))$.

Also, as r falls more upon the shock, households dissave to a greater extent, driving down their stock of assets. $\bar{C}$ is therefore lower for higher λ, making long-run $\bar{P}$ higher for given M. With $\lambda = 0.75$, long-run C falls 14.1 percent.

Suppose now that the home economy satisfies a portion of its oil inputs through domestic production of energy. To simplify, we assume an exogenous, permanent, constant flow of domestic oil equal to one half of initial energy inputs. Furthermore, we abstract from all domestic costs of production, assuming a costlessly producible stream of resources. The oil price hike now induces a windfall in domestic energy wealth (i.e., the discounted value of future energy production) that in part compensates for the fall in human wealth and physical wealth occasioned by the rise in P_N/P. The consumption demand in the oil-producing home economy falls less than in the foreign economy, and given that output is fixed in the short run, its real exchange rate appreciates 1.1 percent. Also, the

Table 7.5
Dynamic adjustment with home production of oil[a]

	Period 1	Period 5
Q	0.0	−0.5
I	−2.7	−8.0
W/P_c	−4.8	−5.4
$\dot{P}$	−1.3	0.8
CA/GDP	−3.5	−1.7
Q^*	0.0	−0.5
I^*	−2.9	−8.4
$(W/P_c)^*$	−5.9	−6.4
$\dot{P}*$	3.6	0.7
CA^*/GDP^*	−3.3	−1.5
$\dot{E}$	−6.8	0.0
Π	1.1	0.9

	Period 10	Steady state
Q	−1.4	−3.6
I	−10.0	−8.8
W/P_c	−6.3	−8.5
$\dot{P}$	0.5	0.0
CA/GDP	−0.9	−0.8
Q^*	−1.5	−3.6
I^*	−10.3	−9.0
$(W/P_c)^*$	−7.3	−9.4
$\dot{P}*$	0.4	0.0
CA^*/GDP^*	−0.8	−0.8
$\dot{E}$	0.0	0.0
Π	0.9	0.9

a. See note a, table 7.4. $\dot{E}$ is $\left[(E_t - E_{t-1})/E_{t-1}\right] \cdot 100$.

Table 7.6
Dynamic adjustment with real wage rigidity

	Rigid wages[b]	Flexible wages
Period 1		
Q	−2.0	0.0
I	−7.3	0.1
W/P_c	−4.1	−5.4
$\dot{P}$	3.9	2.7
Period 5		
Q	−0.6	−0.3
I	−6.9	−7.0
W/P_c	−5.9	−5.7
$\dot{P}$	0.8	0.8
Period 10		
Q	−1.4	−1.2
I	−10.1	−9.9
W/P_c	−6.7	−6.6
$\dot{P}$	0.5	0.5
Steady-state		
Q	−3.6	−3.6
I	−8.9	−8.9
W/P_c	−9.0	−9.0
$\dot{P}$	0.0	0.0

a. See note a, table 7.4.
b. Wage "rigidity" is specified as $\gamma = \gamma^* = 1.2$ in wage equation, with $\rho = \rho^* = 1.0$.

nominal exchange rate appreciates by 6.8 percent since demand for real money balances falls less in the oil-rich than in the oil-poor economy. The results are given in table 7.5.

The smaller energy holdings of the foreign economy do *not* lead to larger current account deficits in that economy, even though it is more "dependent" on OPEC. Simply, its larger oil imports more fully crowd out other forms of consumption, so that the income/absorption balance is no different for the two economies.[8] In principle, the higher terms of trade for the oil-rich economy slightly reduces its real cost of imported oil, so its long-run capital stock should be marginally higher. This is the *opposite* of the "Dutch disease" conclusion that higher domestic energy holdings reduce an economy's capital stock. The effect on the capital stock, however, turns out to be wholly unimportant in the simulations, given the mere 0.9 percent long-run terms-of-trade improvement.

So far I have assumed that the labor market is continuously in balance. However, I have argued at great length elsewhere [see Sachs (1979), for example] that after the OPEC price increase of 1973/74, real wages in most developed economies did *not* fall sufficiently in the short run to keep labor fully employed. If real wages respond sluggishly to unemployment, a major initial effect of oil price hike is a reduction in employment and output. In the simulation reported in table 7.6, I assume that each 1.0 percent decline in employment reduces real wages from the previous period by 1.2 percent. Now, a doubling of oil prices causes an initial drop in output of 2.0 percent, and investment falls by 7.3 percent. This compares with a zero initial output drop and a 0.1 percent rise in investment in the case of fully flexible real wages. The steeper investment decline derives from two factors. Higher W/P reduces F_K, and thus pushes down q. Also, the decline in aggregate supply reduces or reverses the fall in short-term interest rates, also driving q down. Finally, note that prices jump by more than in the flexible real wage case since the demand for real money balances drops.

What is the scope for policy in moderating the short- and long-run output declines following an oil price shock? To maintain steady-state per capita output levels, the profitability of capital at the initial K/L ratio must be restored. Demand management policies will in general be useless for this purpose, though tax and subsidy policies might play a role (of course the desirability of such policies is another matter). In the short run there is far more scope for maintaining output close to potential through monetary and fiscal policies. Bruno and I [Bruno (1979b) and Sachs (1980a)] have emphasized the following aspects of short-run policy. If nominal wages are fully indexed and real wages adjust sluggishly to unemployment, a monetary expansion or exchange rate depreciation will have *no* effect on output, but will have a significant inflationary effect on prices. Fiscal policy *can* raise output with real wage rigidity, by favorably shifting the terms of trade and reducing the product wage W/P for given levels of the real wages W/P_c. The conclusions are reversed for monetary policy if nominal wages are sluggish, with low levels of wage indexation. Now a monetary expansion induces an exchange rate depreciation, drives down the real wage, and causes output to rise. Depending on the nature of indexation, the beneficial effect on output may be very short-lived or highly persistent. Fiscal policy remains effective at low levels of wage indexation. All of these effects are illustrated in simulations reported in Sachs (1980c).

7.4 Conclusions and Extensions

The simulations in this chapter demonstrate the feasibility of studying applied problems in macroeconomic adjustment in large models with efficient asset markets and intertemporal optimization by economic agents. The assumption of efficient asset markets imposes a great computational burden in theoretical models because of the difficulty of solving the two-point boundary-value problems that result. Thus, studies of flexible exchange rates, energy prices, or capital accumulation in open economies typically simplify greatly the structure of the economy in all aspects but the one under study. At the beginning of this chapter I suggested that the analysis of the OPEC price hikes demands an integrated approach, with a specification of all major aspects of the macroeconomy. Leaving out capital accumulation, or OPEC savings behavior, for example, would change the patterns of adjustment of all other macroeconomic variables.

The model in this chapter illustrates many key facets of adjustment to an energy price rise. First, higher energy prices almost surely require a long-run decline in capital intensity (relative to trend) in the developed economies, in order that preshock profitability may be partially or wholly restored. Second, the short-run movement in capital accumulation results from the interplay of many factors, including the short-run profitability decline, differential savings behavior in OPEC and the developed economies, and real wage behavior in the developed economies. The first factor tends to reduce I at time zero and to encourage consumption. The second, OPEC's higher short-run propensity to save, reduces world interest rates and counterbalances the first effect. Finally, short-run real wage rigidity reduces output at the time of an oil shock, forces up world interest rates, and lowers investment.

The view of macropolicy set forth in section 7.3 ties expansion to a reduction in real factor costs, whether through inflation (with monetary and exchange rate policy) or a terms-of-trade improvement (with fiscal policy). With specific parameters assumed for simulation, we may quantify the effects of alternative policies.

Obviously the most important next task for this research strategy is a more realistic calibration of the model. Michael Bruno and this author are now undertaking this project with data for the OECD economies. We are using original econometric work as well as published estimates to set the parameters of the model. The plan is to expand the model to include three importing regions (Europe, Japan, the United States) as well as OPEC.

The theoretical framework warrants refinement as well. The assumption of continuous output-market clearing can be relaxed for the very short run, allowing households to make intertemporal decisions with rational expectations of market constraints. Blanchard and Sachs (1982) introduce such a model for a closed economy. In another aspect of the model, more work remains in the specification of aggregate technology. It will be useful to distinguish traded and nontraded goods in the developed economies, as well as to extend the technology to the case of putty-clay capital. Further discussion of alternative technological assumptions is offered in Sachs (1980b). Finally, the treatment of OPEC can be deepened in a number of ways. OPEC holdings of oil can be treated within a dynamic portfolio model, which stresses the real return to oil and alternative assets. The nonrenewable nature of oil should be explicitly modeled, as well as the presence of backstop energy technologies in the developed economies.

Notes

1. See Sachs (1980c, footnote 1) for a derivation.
2. See Sachs (1980c, footnote 2) for a derivation.
3. To derive (17), we rewrite (12) using the condition that $V - qK$, so $\dot{V}/V = \dot{q}/q = \dot{K}/K$:

$$r - \dot{V}/V = Div/V - \dot{K}/K. \tag{35}$$

Also, $\dot{K}/K - J/K - d - n$. Using (16) and (35), direct substitution gives

$$r - n + \dot{V}/V + [Q - (W/P)L - (P_N/P)N - I]/V. \tag{36}$$

This is a simple first-order differential equation, with the solution

$$V = \exp\left[\int_0^t (r - n)\,ds\right] V_0 - V_0 \exp\left[\int_0^t (r - n)\,ds\right]$$
$$\cdot \int_0^t \exp\left[-\int_0^s (r - n)\,dz\right] [Q - (W/P)L - (P_N/P)N - I]\,ds. \tag{37}$$

Now, if we impose the condition that

$$\lim_{t\to\infty} \exp\left[\int_0^t (r - n)\right] V = 0,$$

we have

$$V_0 = \int_0^t \exp\left[-\int_0^s (r - n)\,dz\right] [Q - (W/P)L - (P_N/P)N - I]\,ds, \tag{38}$$

which was to be proved.

4. The price index is written here in terms of commodities, as is conventional, though the price index for full instantaneous consumption would include the price of money balances i.

5. Actually, the specific vector of state variables depends on certain key parameters in the model. The vector shown above (24) is correct for $\gamma = \gamma^* = \infty$. For γ and γ^* finite, lagged real wages $(W/P_c)_{-1}$ and $(W^*/P_{c^*})_{-1}$ and lagged inflation are state variables.

6. See, for example, Frenkel and Rodriguez (1982, p. 18). The difference in result may depend upon the more limited menu of assets available in the economy in

8

Oil, Disinflation, and Export Competitiveness: A Model of the "Dutch Disease"

Willem H. Buiter
and
Douglas D. Purvis

The 1970s were a decade of major economic upheaval and turbulence, leaving many unresolved issues competing for the attention of economists. Although consensus on the appropriate analysis of, and policy response to, these events is no doubt still a long way off, there is considerable agreement as to what the major issues are. Two phenomena which share honors in this regard are the advent and questionable performance of flexible exchange rates, and the developments associated with the price and availability of oil. Both of these are important elements of the "great stagflation" experienced during the seventies; as both are well documented elsewhere,[1] in the remainder of this introduction we outline only briefly the aspects that we wish to focus on. Our main objective is to provide a framework which can be used to disentangle the effects on the real exchange rate of increases in the world price of oil, discoveries of domestic oil reserves, and monetary disinflation. While the main part of the chapter involves a small analytical model that we hope to be of fairly general interest, much of what follows is motivated by our observations of recent developments in the United Kingdom.

With respect to the "oil shocks" of the 1970s, the major developments ensued from the formation of the OPEC cartel leading to the quadrupling of oil prices in 1974 and a doubling in 1979. One of the paradoxical features of the 1970s was that industrial economies which were net exporters of oil (and other energy-related products whose prices also rose) experienced considerable problems adjusting to a price increase

An earlier version of this chapter was presented to the Annual Meetings of the American Economics Association in Denver, September 1980. We would like to thank Slobodan Djajic, Robert Dunn, Marcus Miller, and Peter Neary for their helpful comments. The research reported here is part of the NBER's research in International Studies. Any opinions expressed as those of the authors and not those of the National Bureau of Economic Research.

which, on standard microeconomic grounds, should have made them better off. More generally, the burden of adjustment to the oil price shocks does not appear to have been inversely related to a country's net export position in oil. These adjustment problems often took the form of a decline in the level of activity in the export oriented and import-competing manufacturing sector. This experience is now commonly referred to as the "Dutch disease," whereby a booming resource sector is presumed to lead to a contraction of the manufacturing sector via the loss of "competitiveness" due to appreciation of the domestic currency.

In this chapter we critically examine the implicit analysis leading to this diagnosis; while a detailed description is postponed until the model is set out, there are a number of comments concerning "oil shocks" that we wish to make at the outset.

First, the nature of an oil price shock is obviously such that a country does not face it in isolation; it is a disturbance which also influences its major trading partners simultaneously. One possible explanation of the paradox noted above is then that the nonoil export sectors of the oil-rich manufacturing nations experienced a decline in foreign demand simultaneously with the oil price shock, due to recession set off in major oil importers such as the United States. However, this possibility is not explored further in this chapter.

Second, it is obviously desirable to distinguish between price and quantity shocks, that is, between the impact of an exogenous increase in the world price of oil and that of an exogenous "discovery" of new domestic reserves of oil.[2] To the extent that the returns from a new discovery are captured by agents who consume the domestic manufactured goods, the discovery of a new reserve is essentially an income, or "demand" shock. An oil price shock in principle involves elements of both a supply and a demand shock. In this chapter we focus on the (positive or negative) income- or wealth-motivated demand effects; in the conclusions we offer some comments on extending the model to incorporate supply effects arising from oil's role as an intermediate input and possible domestic factor market responses.

A third issue is that the long-run effects of an oil shock on the trading sector are usually couched in terms of the condition of current account balance. (Occasionally this analysis is also applied to the short run.) Abstracting from service account developments indicates that a resource boom then implies that *net* nonoil exports must fall. The first point to note is that this does not automatically imply a shrinking of gross manufacturing exports or output. For example, in a small economy that takes the world price of manufactures as given, manufacturing output could be maintained with the increased domestic absorption associated with the resource boom accounting for the required decline in net exports. If the domestic nonoil good is an imperfect substitute for the imported manufactured good and if the home country is large in the world market for domestically produced good, as we shall henceforth assume, then an "oil shock" will in most cases raise the relative price of the home good, thus reducing net exports. The response of output of the home good depends upon the nature of the shock and on details of the model. However, oil discoveries are not likely to be a source of unemployment, nor is there any presumption that oil price increases will be more harmful to countries with large oil reserves.

The model used in our paper differs from others in the literature in a number of important ways. First, we abstract from oil's role as an intermediate good, a feature emphasized, for example, by Findlay and Rodriguez [1977], Bruno and Sachs [1979], and Djajic [1980]. One result of this specification is that there are no long-run negative implications for the manufacturing sector of an increase in oil prices. This allows us to focus on short-run macroeconomic adjustment problems. Our short-run dynamics arise from sluggish adjustment of domestic prices; that is, we have a nominal rigidity rather than a real rigidity as analyzed, for example, by Bruno and Sachs [1979], Branson and Rothenberg [1980], and Purvis [1979]. Our specification is more in conformity with that of Dornbusch [1976], a point we return to below.

Our model also abstracts from the role of nontraded goods, a feature that has been emphasized in other theoretical and applied discussions. For example, in the Dutch case the Slochteren gas discoveries led in the 1960s and 1970s to a substantial public sector revenue increase, a large part of which was allocated to an expansion of the labor-intensive public service sector. This put upward pressure on wages in the manufacturing sector which exacerbated the unfavourable exchange rate effects on competitiveness resulting from the gas discovery. Corden and Neary [1980], for example, focus on this aspect of the issue. They examine a specific factor model in which the resource boom can create an excess demand for labor and drive up manufacturing wages. One problem with this result is that the "demise" of the manufacturing sector is seen as the mirror image of a boom in prosperity for labor. This does not seem to accurately reflect the experience of countries currently experiencing the Dutch disease, particularly the United Kingdom. Nevertheless, the role of the nontraded goods sector is likely an important

Table 8.1
List of symbols[a]

m	logarithm of the nominal money stock
p	logarithm of the domestic general price level (c.p.i.)
p_H	logarithm of the price of domestic non oil goods
e	logarithm of the nominal exchange rate (domestic currency price of foreign exchange)
p_b^f	logarithm of the world price of oil (exogenous)
r	domestic nominal interest rate
r^f	world nominal interest rate (exogenous)
y^p	permanent real income (logarithm)
y	actual real income (logarithm)
q_H	actual production of domestic non oil goods (logarithm)
q_b	actual production of oil (logarithm)
q_H^p	permanent production of domestic nonoil goods (logarithm)
q_b^p	permanent production of oil (logarithm)
μ	$\dot{m}$, rate of growth of the nominal money stock (exogenous)
v	share of non oil production in domestic value added
l	logarithm of real liquidity in terms of the non oil domestic good
c	logarithm of the real exchange rate

a. A dot over a variable indicates a time derivative.

part of the Dutch disease story, but one we shall not address in this chapter; we do return briefly to this issue in our conclusions.

Given nominal inertia in domestic prices and costs, our model can generate transitional deindustrialization and unemployment in response to an oil price (or indeed an oil discovery) shock. We wish to argue, however, that this is not a complete explanation of the real appreciation, deindustrialization, and unemployment experienced by many industrial countries in the late 1970s. There is no necessary reason to associate all or even most of the "deindustrialization" with the oil shocks; due consideration must also be given to the role of domestic stabilization policies. In particular, we wish to suggest as an additional explanation the tight monetary policies implemented in some countries in response to the acceleration of inflation set off by the initial 1974 increase in oil prices. Under flexible exchange rates, with international capital mobility, monetary contraction will lead to a large and rapid fall of the nominal exchange rate. As Dornbusch [1976] has emphasized, if in addition inflation inertia is strong, so that domestic prices are sluggish to adjust, then there will also be a real appreciation in the short run with adverse consequences for the competitiveness of the domestic manufacturing sector.[3]

8.1 A Macroeconomic Model with Oil as Income and Wealth

In this section we consider the effects of an unanticipated discovery of oil, an unanticipated increase in the world price of oil, and an unanticipated reduction in the rate of monetary growth using a model that abstracts from the use of oil as an intermediate input. Oil is produced and consumed domestically and can be imported or exported at an exogenous world price in terms of the foreign currency. The flow of domestic oil production is treated as exogenous; the relation between current oil production and the permanent income derived therefrom is treated in detail below. There is also a nonoil domestic good which is produced at home but consumed at home and abroad; foreign demand is less than perfectly elastic. The home country also imports a nonoil good available in infinitely elastic supply; by appropriate choice of units the foreign price of the nonoil import is unity so its domestic price equals the nominal exchange rate. The model is given in equations (1)–(9); the variables are as defined in table 8.1:

$$p = \beta_1 p_H + \beta_2(e + p_b^f) + (1 - \beta_1 - \beta_2)e, \tag{1}$$
$$0 \leqslant \beta_1, \beta_2, 1 - \beta_1 - \beta_2 \leqslant 1;$$

$$q_H = -\gamma_1(r - \dot{p}) + \gamma_2(e - p_H) + \gamma_3 y^p + \gamma_4(e + p_b^f - p_H), \tag{2}$$
$$\gamma_1, \gamma_2, \gamma_3 > 0, \quad \gamma_4 \gtrless 0;$$

$$\dot{p}_H = \phi q_H + \mu, \quad \phi \geqslant 0; \tag{3}$$

$$m - p = k y^p + (1 - k)y - \lambda^{-1}r, \quad k, \lambda > 0; \tag{4}$$

$$r = r^f + \dot{e}; \tag{5}$$

$$y = v q_H + (1 - v)q_b + (1 - v - \beta_2)p_b^f + (\beta_1 - v)(e - p_H), \tag{6}$$
$$0 \leqslant v \leqslant 1;$$

$$y^p = v q_H^p + (1 - v)q_b^p + (1 - v - \beta_2)p_b^f + (\beta_1 - v)(e - p_H); \tag{7}$$

$$c = e - p_H; \tag{8}$$

$$l = m - p_H. \tag{9}$$

The domestic cost of living is a weighted average of the price of domestic nonoil goods, the price of oil, and the price of nonoil imports [equation (1)]. Output of nonoil goods is demand determined and depends on the real interest rate, the relative prices of foreign and domestic goods, and permanent income [equation (2)]. The rate of change of the price of domestic nonoil goods in excess of the underlying trend rate of inflation depends on the excess demand for them [equation (3)];[4] the underlying rate of inflation is proxied by the rate of growth of the nominal money supply, a specification also adopted by Liviatan [1979] and Dornbusch [1980b]. The demand for real money balances depends on permanent income (wealth), actual income (transactions demand), and the nominal interest rate [equation (4)]. The domestic rate of interest equals the world rate plus the expected rate of exchange rate depreciation [equation (5)]. Perfect foresight is assumed throughout.

Equations (6) and (7) contain the definitions of actual and permanent income; they are log-linear approximations to real income.[5] Note that $v \equiv P_H Q_H / PY$ is the share of nonoil production in total value added. We use the ratio of the price of nonoil imports to the price of the domestic nonoil manufactured goods as a measure of competitiveness; this ratio, denoted by $c \equiv e - p_H$, is also referred to as the real exchange rate [equation (8)]. The predetermined state variable is real balances in terms of the home good [equation (9)].

Oil prices and output enter this model through their influence on income; changes in either influence demand via their implications for permanent income. While exogenous oil price increases might well be viewed as being permanent, new discoveries of oil resources are necessarily finite, so that the flow of current income they generate is of limited duration. Nevertheless we argue that either will change the steady-state terms of trade. For the latter case, the relevant concept for determining demand patterns is the permanent income change thus elicited; increased demand for the home good will thus be spread out over time, so that an oil discovery leading to an oil flow of *finite* duration will alter the steady-state terms of trade.

Permanent production of nonoil goods is identified with its steady-state value; we choose units so that $q_H^p = 0$. We abstract from the possibility that steady-state changes in relative prices alter q_H^p.

Actual oil production evolves according to

$$q_b(t) = \begin{cases} \bar{q}_b, & t < 0 \text{ and } t > T, T > 0 \\ \bar{\bar{q}}_b > \bar{q}_b, & 0 \leqslant t \leqslant T. \end{cases} \tag{10}$$

Output is small prior to $t = 0$, rises unexpectedly to a new constant level for a period of length T, and then returns to its previous low level. We do not model output decisions in the oil-producing sector; the new discovery is of known size and the flow of production from it occurs at a given, known rate. In addition, oil production is assumed not to require labor, so that the short-run dynamics in (4) are not affected by changes in the volume of oil production. The increase in output is unanticipated as at $t = 0$. But, at $t = 0$, the return of oil production to its original low level at $t = T$ is anticipated. To formalize this, let $\hat{q}_b^A(t, s)$ be the volume of actual oil production at time t, anticipated at time s. We assume

$$\hat{q}_b(t, s) = \begin{cases} \bar{q}_b & \text{for all } t, s \leqslant 0 \\ q_b(t) & \text{for all } t, s > 0. \end{cases} \tag{11}$$

Permanent income accruing from oil production[6] is given by

$$q_b^p(t) = \begin{cases} \bar{q}_b, & t < 0 \\ \alpha\bar{q}_b + (1 - \alpha)\bar{\bar{q}}_b, & t > 0; \quad \alpha = \alpha(T); \quad \alpha' < 0, \\ & \quad \alpha(0) = 1, \quad \alpha(\infty) = 0. \end{cases} \tag{12}$$

Figure 8.1 illustrates the behavior of q_b and q_b^p.

Using equations (2) and (7), we define for future use the following "gross price elasticities" of demand:

$$\eta_b \equiv \partial q_H/\partial p_b^f = \gamma_4 + \gamma_3(1 - v - \beta_2); \tag{13}$$

$$\eta_c \equiv \partial q_H/\partial(e - p_H) = (\gamma_2 + \gamma_4) + \gamma_3(\beta_1 - v). \tag{14}$$

In principle, either elasticity could be of either sign. Consider first η_b: The pure substitution term γ_4 could be positive or negative;[7] the income effect could also be positive or negative depending upon whether the share of oil in domestic output $1 - v$ is greater than or smaller than its share in domestic consumption. In what follows we shall consider both positive and negative values for η_b. For η_c we assume that foreign and domestic manufactured goods are sufficiently close substitutes that γ_2 is sufficiently large to ensure that the direct substitution effect $(\gamma_2 + \gamma_4)$ is positive. Note that if β_1 (the share of the home good in consumption) were small relative to v (its share in domestic value added)—a not im-probable situation for countries which are significant oil exporters—then the income effect of an increase in p_H would work in the opposite direction to the substitution effect. We assume that γ_2 would still be sufficiently large to ensure also $\eta_c > 0$.

It is also useful at this stage to note the differential effects of a given percentage change in the price and quantity of oil. It is easily seen that $\partial q_H/\partial q_b^p = \gamma_3(1 - v) = \eta_b + \gamma_3\beta_2 - \gamma_4$, which may be greater than or

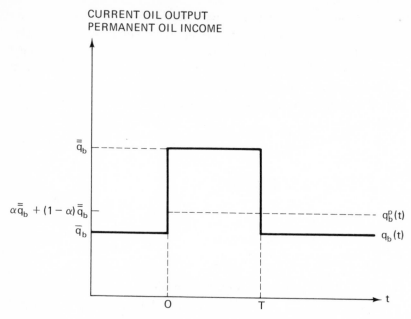

CURRENT OIL OUTPUT
PERMANENT OIL INCOME

Figure 8.1
Exogenous paths of actual oil output and permanent oil income.

smaller than η_b, depending upon whether the weighted income elasticity $\beta_2 \gamma_3$ is greater than or smaller than the price elasticity γ_4.

Using the definitions of p, y^p, and c, we can rewrite the demand for the home good in a semi-reduced form as[8]

$$q_H = \eta_c c + \eta_b p_b^f + \gamma_3 (1 - v) q_b^p - \gamma_1 r^f - \gamma_1 \beta_1 \dot{c}. \qquad (2')$$

This is only a semireduced form since c (and $\dot{c}$ outside of long-run equilibrium) are endogenous variables. However, this particular expression will be useful later in evaluating the impact effects of the various shocks under consideration on q_H. Recognizing from equations (4) and (9) that l just equals $-\phi q_H$, we see that the model can be expressed as a system of two dynamic equations in real money balances in terms of the home good l and the real exchange rate c. Except at those instants when the level of the nominal money supply is altered, l is predetermined because p_H is sticky and m evolves according to $\dot{m} = \mu$. However, c is not predetermined because e can take discrete jumps in response to current and anticipated future changes in the values of the parameters or the exogenous variables. The dynamic system is given by equation (15):

$$
\begin{bmatrix} \dot{c} \\ \\ \dot{l} \end{bmatrix} = \begin{bmatrix} a_{11} & a_{12} \\ \\ a_{21} & a_{22} \end{bmatrix} \begin{bmatrix} c \\ \\ l \end{bmatrix} + \begin{bmatrix} b_{11} & b_{12} & b_{13} & b_{14} & b_{15} \\ \\ b_{21} & b_{22} & b_{23} & b_{24} & b_{25} \end{bmatrix} \begin{bmatrix} p_b^f \\ q_b^p \\ q_b \\ \mu \\ r^f \end{bmatrix}, \tag{15}
$$

where the elements of the state transition and forcing matrices are given in the appendix.

8.2 Long-Run Comparative Statics

Before examining the dynamics in detail, it is useful to examine the long-run or steady-state equilibrium conditions, characterized by

$$
\dot{p}_H = \dot{p} = \dot{e} = \mu; \quad r = r^f + \mu; \quad q_H = q_H^p = 0. \tag{16}
$$

The last equation ensures that there are no long-run output effects.

The long-run goods market equilibrium locus (LIS curve) and money-market or portfolio balance locus (LLM) can be written as

$$
\eta_c c = \gamma_1 r^f - \eta_b p_b^f - \gamma_3 (1 - v) q_b^p, \tag{17}
$$

$$
l = \lambda(1 - v)(c + p_b^f + k q_b^p + (1 - k)q_b) - (\mu + r^f). \tag{18}
$$

The LIS and LLM equations can be solved to yield the following reduced form expressions for steady-state competitiveness and liquidity:

$$
c^* = \eta_c^{-1} \{\gamma_1 r^f - \gamma_3 (1 - v) q_b^p - \eta_b p_b^f\}; \tag{19}
$$

$$
l^* = \eta_c^{-1}(1 - v)\{(\gamma_1 - \delta)r^f - \delta\mu + (\eta_c - \eta_b)p_b^f
$$

$$
+ (k\eta_c - (1 - v)\gamma_3)q_b^p + (1 - k)\eta_c q_b\}. \tag{20}
$$

These are depicted as the intersections of the LIS and LIM curves in figures 8.2–8.4. Note that the LIS curve is independent of l due to the absence of a real balance effect in our specification of the expenditure function. If a real balance effect were included, the LIS curve would be downward sloping since a higher relative domestic price would be required to offset the effect of larger real balances. The LLM curve is positively sloped, indicating that a fall in the relative price of home goods increases the long-run desired value of money holdings in terms of home goods.[9]

We can use the LIS and LLM curves to analyze the long-run steady-state effects of a change in the exogenous variables μ, p_b^f, and q_b^p.[10] In what follows we continue to assume η_c to be greater than zero; this is

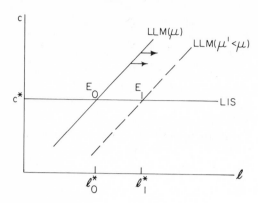

Figure 8.2
Long-run effects of monetary disinflation.

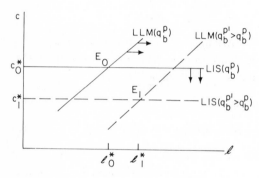

Figure 8.3
Long-run effects of a domestic oil discovery.

simply the condition that an increase in p_H reduce the demand for the home good. As noted in the appendix, we also assume that η_c is sufficiently large to ensure that $a_{21} \equiv \partial i/\partial c$ is negative.

8.2.1 Monetary Disinflation

The simplest case is that of the long-run effects of a reduction in the rate of monetary growth μ. This has no effect on the real exchange rate in the long run: The LIS does not shift. The lower steady-state nominal interest rate creates an increased demand for real money balances and hence a larger l; this is reflected in the fact that the LLM curve shifts to the right, as shown in figure 8.2. While μ thus exerts no long-run effect on c, we shall see below that it does exert important short-run effects.

8.2.2 Discovery of Domestic Oil Reserves

Consider next the long-run effects of a domestic oil discovery. Given our assumption that $\eta_c > 0$, it is easily seen from equation (19) that an increase in q_b^p will cause a fall in competitiveness as measured by c; thus a real appreciation arises since as shown in figure 8.3 the LIS curve shifts down. An increase in the relative price of home goods is required to counter the larger demand arising from the increase in permanent income. As can be seen directly from equation (20), the effect on long-run liquidity is ambiguous. The real income effect causes $m - p$ to rise, but since $p_H - p$ also rises due to the fall in c, $m - p_H$ can go either way. In figure 8.3 we illustrate the case in which the increase in permanent oil income increases real liquidity. In what follows, for simplicity we treat only this case; note that it arises when the gross price elasticity η_c is relatively large.

8.2.3 Increase in the World Price of Oil

Finally, consider the long-run effects of an increase in the world price of oil p_b^f. Here there are three possibilities to consider, depending upon the sign of η_b, and then on the sign of $(\eta_c - \eta_b)$ if the latter is positive. If η_b is negative, a case that arises if the country is a sufficiently large net user of oil that the negative income effect dominates the substitution effect, then it follows that an increase in p_b^f will reduce long-run demand for the home good; to equate demand with the fixed long-run supply there must ensue a real depreciation. This is illustrated in figure 8.4A, where the LIS curve has shifted up. The LLM curve shifts right, indicating that due to the rise in p_b^f, steady-state liquidity, for a given value of c, must rise. Hence l also rises and the new equilibrium is at E_1.

If the country is a net producer of oil, or at least only a "small" net user, so that η_b is positive, then the LIS curve shifts down and the increase in p_b^f causes a fall in competitiveness as in figure 8.4B. In this case there is an increased demand for the home good which must be offset by a real appreciation. The LLM curve still shifts to the right, so that the effect on l^* is ambiguous; while the real income effects captured by the change in c will have an unambiguous effect on $m - p$, the changes in relative prices render the change in $l = m - p_H$ ambiguous. As can be seen from equation (20), the direction l changes depends upon the sign of $\eta_c - \eta_b$.[11] In figure 8.4B we illustrate the case where $\eta_c - \eta_b > 0$, so l rises and the new equilibrium E_1 lies to the southeast of E_0.[12] However, the case where l falls, so that E_1 is southwest of E_0, is a possibility that will be of interest in the next section.[13]

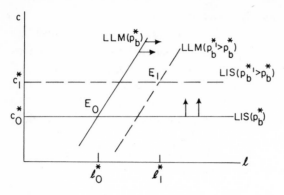

Figure 8.4A
Long-run effects of an increase in p_b^f: real depreciation ($\eta_b < 0$); l must rise.

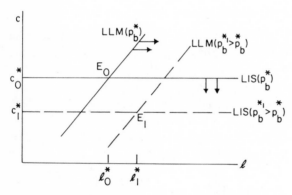

Figure 8.4B
Long-run effects of an increase in p_b^f: real appreciation ($\eta_b > 0$) and l rises $[(\eta_c - \eta_b) > 0]$.

Table 8.2
Long-run comparative statics results

Disturbance		Case	Response of c	l	
Monetary disinflation	$(u\downarrow)$	1	0	+	
Foreign oil		2	+	+	if $\eta_b < 0$
price	$(p_b^f\uparrow)$	3	−	−	if $\eta_b > 0$ and $\eta_c - \eta_b < 0$
increase		4	−	+	if $\eta_b > 0$ and $\eta_c - \eta_b > 0$
Domestic oil		5	−	+	if $k\eta_c - (1 - v)\gamma_3 > 0$
discovery	$(q_b^p\uparrow)$	6	−	−	if $k\eta_c - (1 - v)\gamma_3 < 0$

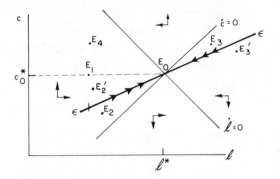

Figure 8.5
Adjustment dynamics—saddle path given by $\varepsilon\varepsilon$.

The six possible results are summarized in table 8.2; the cases are numbered to facilitate reference in the next section.

8.3 Dynamic Adjustment

A variety of different dynamic adjustment paths are consistent with our specifications; however, we shall only analyze what we consider to be the "standard" case arising with the sign patterns given in the appendix. Given the sign pattern of the state transition matrix A,

$$A = \begin{bmatrix} + & - \\ - & - \end{bmatrix} \tag{21}$$

(where we have used the assumption of η_c large to ensure $a_{21} < 0$), there is one stable and one unstable root. The phase diagram is given in figure 8.5. The $\dot{l} = 0$ locus is negatively sloped and the $\dot{c} = 0$ locus is positively sloped. The unique saddle path leading to long-run equilibrium e is the upward-sloping line $\varepsilon\varepsilon$; stability requires that, for any predetermined value of l, the nominal exchange rate "jump" so that c takes on the value required to put the economy on a convergent solution path. In the case of an unanticipated, contemporaneous, permanent shock that changes the long-run equilibrium to E_0 from initial positions like E_1 or E_2, c will have to jump to a point on the saddle path $\varepsilon\varepsilon$.[14]

Before turning to the specific case, it is useful now to return to the quasi-reduced form for q_H, rewritten here for convenience as (2″):

$$(q_H^P - q_H) = \eta_c(c^* - c) + \gamma_1\beta_1\dot{c}. \tag{2''}$$

From (2″) it is clear that if the economy moves toward the long-run equilibrium from below and to the left, then during the entire period of adjustment c is below c^* and $\dot{c}$ is positive; hence from equation (2″) output of the domestic good is below its long-run value. Similarly, if adjustment toward E_0 is from the northeast, q_H exceeds q_H^P.

8.3.1 Monetary Disinflation

The simplest case concerns the dynamic adjustment to an unanticipated but, once announced, immediately implemented and fully perceived permanent reduction in the rate of monetary expansion. As our long-run analysis showed, the $\dot{c} = 0$ and the $\dot{l} = 0$ loci shift to the right by an equal amount, so that in the new long-run equilibrium, c is unchanged and l rises. This is illustrated in figure 8.5, where only the $\dot{c} = 0$ and $\dot{l} = 0$ loci for the new, lower value of μ are drawn. With the new long-run equilibrium at E_0 we know from the long-run analysis above that the initial equilibrium would have been at a point like E_1. Initially, since l is predetermined, the reduction in μ causes the real exchange rate to fall so as to place the economy on the saddle path; the dynamics then involve monotonically improving competitiveness and increasing real liquidity until E_0 is achieved. The time path of the real exchange rate is shown in figure 8.6.

These results, similar to those presented by Dornbusch [1976, 1980b] and Liviatan [1979], illustrate one of the central problems posed for stabilization policy in an open economy. The exchange rate is an asset price and as such adjusts quickly. As a result, policies such as monetary contractions, which are essentially neutral in the long run, can generate systematic responses in relative prices and output in the short run. In figure 8.6 the time path of the real exchange rate also depicts the qualitative response of manufacturing output and exports. The initial appreciation results in a sharp fall in activity in the manufacturing sector, while the ensuing real depreciation signals a recovery.[15]

The dynamics underlying this short-run real appreciation warrant further explanation. Suppose instead that c were in fact to stay at its long-run value. If $\dot{c}$ were also to remain at its long-run value (zero), so that (by 2′) q_H remained at q_H^P, then $\dot{e}$ and $\dot{p}_H$ would adjust to the new value of μ. But from (5) this implies a fall in the domestic interest rate and hence an excess demand for money from (1). Hence if c remains at its long-run value, monetary equilibrium requires that q_H fall and $\dot{c}$ rise. But $\dot{c} > 0$ implies that at the next instant c is higher, and hence on this count q_H will be higher. For monetary equilibrium then, an even higher value of $\dot{c}$ is required; this further increase in $\dot{c}$ of course means that the

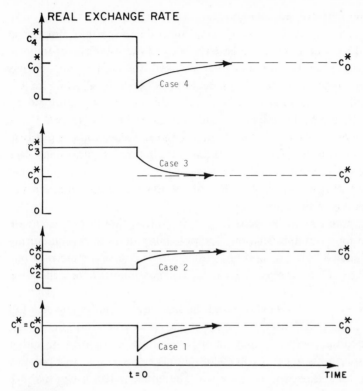

Figure 8.6
Time path of real exchange rate: case 1—monetary disinflation; case 2—oil price shock, net importer; case 3—oil price shock, net exporter (inflationary); case 4—oil price shock, net exporter (Dutch disease).

process is unstable since the long-run value of $\dot{c}$ is zero. The conditions of monetary equilibrium and perfect foresight require that the dynamic path through the initial equilibrium E_1 be positively sloped and that it increase in slope as l increases; hence it is an unstable path. For stability, c *must* fall initially, causing an initial fall in q_H, so that the adjustment elicited by positive $\dot{c}$ is consistent with stability; $\dot{c}$ approaches 0 as c approaches c^* and q_H approaches q_H^p.

8.3.2 Increase in the World Price of Oil

As noted above, there are three cases to consider here, depending on the signs of η_b and $\eta_c - \eta_b$. Although this case involves a taxonomy, the dynamics in each subcase are simpler than those for the oil discovery case; hence we treat the oil price increase case first.

Consider first the "net oil importer" case from table 8.2, where $\eta_b < 0$, so that an increase in p_b^f leads to a long-run real depreciation. But l^* also rises, so the old equilibrium must have been to the southeast of the new one. Since the saddle path is positively sloped, the impact effect on c is ambiguous; the initial equilibrium could be either E_2 or E_2' in figure 8.5, and the initial jump in c could be positive or negative. In figure 8.6 we show the time path for c from an initial position like E_2. In either case the impact effect leaves c below its new long-run value, and $\dot{c}$ is positive. Manufacturing output falls at $t = 0$, and the dynamic adjustment involves continuous depreciation and output recovery. A country which is a net oil consumer suffers a transitory loss of manufacturing output as a result of the increase in the price of oil.

Consider now what happens if $\eta_b > 0$, so that the oil price increase leads to a long-run appreciation. The possibility that the manufacturing sector of such a "net oil exporter" declines is of course the focus of one aspect of the "Dutch disease." There are two possibilities here, depending on the sign of $\eta_c - \eta_b$.

In case 3, $\eta_c - \eta_b$ is negative and the new equilibrium involves a fall in both c and l. The initial position could be either E_3 or E_3' in figure 8.5; again the initial jump in c may be either positive or negative. In either case dynamic adjustment involves continuous appreciation; one possible time-path for c is shown in figure 8.6. The impact effect leaves c above its new equilibrium value, $\dot{c}$ is negative, and output is above its steady-state level but falling throughout the adjustment process. This case does not give rise to the "Dutch disease."

In case 4, where $\eta_c - \eta_b$ is positive, the long-run fall in c is accompanied by a rise in l. Hence the new equilibrium must lie to the southeast of the old one; in terms of the phase diagram, figure 8.5, the initial equilibrium must be one like E_4. Again the impact effect is a discrete fall in c to the saddle path $\varepsilon\varepsilon$. Since the saddle path is positively sloped, this initial "jump" appreciation is followed by a continuous real depreciation until E_0 is achieved; that is, the real exchange rate overshoots its long-run value. The time path of the real exchange rate is illustrated in figure 8.6; it is similar to that generated by monetary disinflation except that now the long-run real exchange rate falls. Although the direct effect of the increase in p_b^f on the demand for the home good is positive with $\eta_b > 0$, the fact that c overshoots means on balance there is a decline in the demand for the home good; from equation (2') we see that this decline is reinforced by the fact that $\dot{c}$ is positive. Hence the increase in p_b^f results in a drop in manufacturing output even for the case in which $\eta_b > 0$. A prescription that commodities are gross substitutes amounts to a prescription in favor of case 4 over case 3; see note 11.

Case 4 corresponds to the Dutch disease which is a direct result of real exchange rate overshooting; if c fell only to its new long-run value, $\dot{c}$ would be zero and there would be no short-run effects on output. However, that possibility is ruled out since monetary equilibrium and perfect foresight combine to place that point on an unstable path. For stability, the real exchange rate must overshoot its long-run value. Although the increase in oil prices has a positive direct effect on the demand for the home good ($\eta_b > 0$), this is offset by the indirect reduction in demand due to the real appreciation, and the economy suffers "Dutch disease"-style deindustrialization.

In this model, nonoil output eventually returns to its exogenously given full employment level; that is, in this model there is no long-run run Dutch disease.[16] However, a "transitional" Dutch disease arises in response to an oil price shock if the real exchange rate overshoots its new equilibrium value, that is, if $\eta_c - \eta_b > 0$. The impact of this variable can be seen by considering what would happen if c and $\dot{c}$ were to attain their new equilibrium values (c^* and 0, respectively) immediately. Nonoil output would be at q_H^p and r would be unchanged; from (1) we see that the impact in the money market depends on whether c falls proportionately more or less than the initial change in p_b^f.[17] But from (21), the relative change in c^* depends upon the ratio η_b/η_c. If $\eta_b < \eta_c$, then the fall in c^* is less than the initial rise in p_b^f; an instantaneous movement to c^* with $\dot{c} = 0$ would then imply an excess demand for money. The above discussion of the monetary disinflation case would now apply here; monetary equilibrium requires a further real appreciation, which, of course, in this case implies overshooting of the real exchange rate. If, on the other hand, $\eta_b > \eta_c$, c^* changes more than p_b^f and at c^* with the initial value of p_H there would be an excess *supply* of money. Monetary equilibrium and stability would then require a depreciation relative to c^*, and there would be no overshooting or Dutch disease.

8.3.3 Discovery of Domestic Oil Reserves

Last, consider the implications of a domestic oil discovery. Although the long-run equilibrium is relatively easy to access (the increased demand for the home good necessitating a real appreciation), the dynamics are complicated by the fact that the oil production disturbance is known to be of finite duration. We treat the unanticipated but fully perceived discovery of oil at $t = 0$ as the combination of two disturbances: a

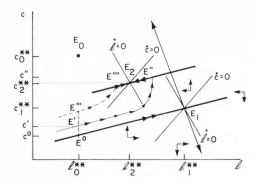

Figure 8.7
The response to a domestic oil discovery.

permanent unanticipated increase in oil output effective immediately and the perception and therefore anticipation of an equal permanent fall in oil output occurring at some known future time T.[18] In what follows we treat only case 5, in which l^* rises, abstracting from the possibility discussed earlier that l^* might fall; the time path of c appears qualitatively the same in either case.

The adjustment paths of c and l in case 5 are illustrated in figure 8.7. E_0 is the original long-run equilibrium. E_1 is the long-run equilibrium if the unanticipated increase in oil production is permanent; E_2 is the long-run equilibrium when there is a temporary increase in oil production.

If the unanticipated increase in oil production were permanent, the real exchange rate would immediately jump to c^0, putting the economy at E^0 on the saddle path converging to E_1. The unanticipated increase in real income (actual and permanent) increases the demand for money; with both m and p_H predetermined, monetary equilibrium is restored by a fall in q_H and a rise in r. This in turn is brought about by a jump in the real exchange rate. Afterward c rises steadily toward E_1.

If the increase in oil production is temporary, the rise in permanent income is correspondingly smaller. c still jumps downward, but to a position above E^0 such as E' with c equal to c'. This position is defined by the requirement that E' be on the unstable solution path (drawn with reference to the eigenvectors of E_1) that crosses the unique stable path through E_2 at the moment that oil production falls back to its lower level, that is, at $t = T$. One such "unstable" solution path is given in figure 8.7 by $E'E''$. It crosses the saddle path through E_2 at E''. At time T (i.e., at E''), the real depreciation is reversed and there is then continuous real appreciation along the new saddle path to E_2. The time path of c for this

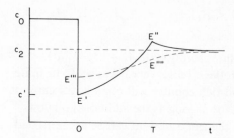

Figure 8.8
Possible paths of real exchange rate.

case is graphed in figure 8.8 as the solid line; for the afficionado, there is "double" overshooting! Alternatively, the initial jump in c could be toward a point like E''' in figure 8.7, with continuous real depreciation from E''' to E_2. At $t = T$ the economy arrives at E'''', on the stable saddle path through E_2, after which c continues to depreciate. This solution is shown in figure 8.8 as the dashed line, where there is only initial overshooting. The reader can confirm that if l^* falls, there might not be any overshooting. The reader can also readily see that there is a rich variety of possible time paths for real output, with a possibility of as many as two "turning points" and with output rising, falling, or both during the adjustment process.

8.4 The Exchange Rate and the Current Account

As noted in the introduction, the literature dealing with the Dutch disease often couches the analysis in terms of a balanced trade condition. As the foregoing analysis has, it is hoped, made clear, this is inappropriate. If current account balance is imposed as a long-run condition, any implication for net manufactured exports does not also apply to manufactured output. If, as we have assumed, the oil flow is finite, then the long run or steady state after an oil discovery will be characterized by a trade account deficit. However, that deficit does not mean reduced demand for home goods; rather, it reflects increased *total* demand due to the permanent income effect of the oil discovery; part of that demand is for imports and results in a larger volume of imports; part of that demand is for home goods and results in a higher relative price of home goods.

The trade account deficit D is given by

$$D = A(Y, Y^p, r - \dot{p}) - Y; \qquad 0 < A_1, A_2, \quad A_1 + A_2 < 1, \quad A_3 \leqslant 0,$$
$$(22)$$

where A denotes private plus public absorption. If $A_1 + A_2 \partial Y^p/\partial Y < 1$, as is ensured in our case, in which the oil discovery is known to be finite so $\partial Y^p/\partial Y < 1$, then the newly oil-rich country will run a larger current account surplus or smaller deficit for as long as the additional oil flows.

Note that this improvement in the trade account can be accompanied by a wide variety of exchange rate dynamics; in this model there is no necessary relation between the trade account and the exchange rate as arises in recent models (see, e.g., Dornbusch and Fischer [1980] or Rodriguez [1980]) which focus on net-wealth accumulation aspects of trade account imbalances.

8.5 Conclusion

We have analyzed the response of a small open economy, with some market power in the world market for its nonoil good, to two kinds of oil shocks and to a monetary policy shock. Both oil shocks—the unanticipated change in the world price of oil and the unanticipated discovery of domestic oil—require an adjustment in the long-run relative price of nonoil tradables. The typical long-run response to an oil discovery is a worsening of the competitive position of the nonoil good. The long-run response to an oil price increase will be a rise in the relative price of nonoil goods if the country is a net exporter of oil, a fall if it is a significant net importer. A reduction in the rate of growth of the nominal money stock does not alter long-run competitiveness, but will raise the steady-state level of real money balances.

A perhaps surprising result is that even in the context of our model, which fixes steady-state nonoil output, increases in the price of oil or in known domestic oil reserves can have a transitional negative effect on manufacturing output, even for a net oil exporter. This negative output response was seen to be intrinsically linked to the possibility that the real exchange rate overshoots its long-run value. This overshooting results from our assumption that the price of nonoil goods is predetermined and responds only sluggishly to excess demand or supply, while the nominal exchange rate (and hence the domestic price of the imported manufactured good) adjusts immediately to maintain equilibrium in the asset markets.

The model focused on the role of oil prices and oil production in influencing income. In particular, we argued that the relevant concept was the permanent income accruing from current oil production. One implication of modeling demand in terms of permanent income is that in the period during which there is the increased oil production, actual income will be above permanent income. An implication of this is that the full employment current account can be expected to be in surplus because current income is high relative to current consumption, not simply because oil exports are larger. More precisely, the excess of current over permanent income means that the sum $I + X - M$ will increase, where I stands for total private and public capital formation. The economy must allocate this increase in domestic saving between domestic capital formation and net foreign investment. When the oil runs out, consumption is maintained via the returns from past domestic and foreign investment. Current account balance and a trade account deficit are reconciled via increased interest and dividends from abroad.

There are a number of extensions to the model that suggest themselves, including elaboration on the production side to incorporate the role of oil as an intermediate good and thus allow a distinction between domestic costs and prices. To the extent that oil is an intermediate input into the production process, and to the extent that oil is consumed directly by workers, so that changes in its price can alter workers' real supply price of labor, then from the point of view of the manufacturing sector an increase in the price of oil entails a significant supply shock. In terms of our model, one consequence of having oil as an intermediate input is that a negative real income effect of an oil price increase is more likely. Adverse supply effects and substitution of nonoil inputs for oil also become important—for an early analysis of this see Bruno and Sachs [1979].

We referred throughout to the domestically produced nonoil good as "manufactures." This can be taken as shorthand for all domestically produced goods, including (nontraded) services. Our aggregation of domestic nonoil tradables and services yields the commodity structure of part (a) table 8.3. Our conclusions about the effects of an oil discovery on domestic production of, and employment in, nonoil goods applies to this aggregate of traded and nontraded goods. There may be shifts in the composition of domestic nonoil production that our model cannot handle. Such shifts are likely to be out of manufacturing into nontraded services, because both the price of nonoil tradables may be effectively given in the world market (contrary to our model) and the income elasticity of demand for services may be higher. Such a shift of resources

Table 8.3

(a) Commodity structure of the present model

(1) Oil	Fixed world price	Uses no labor
(2) Domestic nonoil (manufacturers and services or traded and nontraded)	Endogenous world price	Labor intensive Uses oil as input[a]
(3) Imported nonoil	Fixed world price	

(b) Commodity structure of the alternative model

(1) Oil	Fixed world price	Uses no labor
(2) Domestic nonoil traded (manufacturers)	Fixed world price	Fairly labor intensive, uses oil as input
(3) Domestic nonoil nontraded (services)	Endogenous price	Very labor intensive
(4) Imported nonoil	Fixed world price	

a. Not considered in the formal model.

from manufacturing into services may be described by the term "de-industrialization," but it certainly should not be a source of concern. Also, except for problems of short-run intersectoral labor mobility, the employment implications should be favorable, since services are more labor intensive than manufactures. This scenario would follow in an alternative model sketched in part (b) of table 8.3. There is assumed to be a fixed world price for the country's nonoil exports and a nontraded good ("services"). The income and wealth increasing effects of an oil discovery raise the price of services relative to all other goods whose world prices are given. Resources flow from manufacturing into services. As in our model, there is no reason for believing that total employment and the value of total nonoil production would fall.

We assumed in our model that oil production does not compete for resources with nonoil production. This is clearly realistic as regards labor, but is less appropriate as regards capital. In the long run, however, a small country facing a perfect world capital market can accumulate its oil sector capital stock without diminishing the capital stocks of the nonoil sectors.

The model as it stands does permit some insights into the policy problems created by the divergent speeds of adjustment in goods and asset markets in an open economy. Our model focuses on the responses of aggregate demand to various shocks, and it would be straightforward to devise fiscal policies which mitigate those effects. Responding to a rise in the world price of oil with a reduction in the rate of monetary growth will, in the context of the model, intensify the loss of competitiveness and decline in output. The overshooting of the real exchange rate

Table 8.4
Reduced form and dynamic coefficients

$a_{11} = V[\lambda(1 - v) + z\eta_c]$	$(+)?$	$a_{21} = \psi a_{11} - \phi\eta_c$ $(-)?$
$a_{12} = -V\lambda$	$(-)$	$a_{22} = \psi a_{12}$ $(-)$
$b_{11} = V[\lambda(1 - v) + z\eta_b]$	$(+)?$	$b_{21} = \psi b_{11} - \phi\eta_b$ $(+)?$
$b_{12} = V(1 - v)[\lambda k + z\gamma_3]$	$(+)$	$b_{22} = \psi b_{12} - \phi\gamma_3(1 - v)$ $(+)?$
$b_{13} = V\lambda(1 - k)(1 - v)$	$(+)$	$b_{23} = \psi b_{13}$ $(+)$
$b_{14} = -V$	$(-)$	$b_{24} = \psi b_{14}$ $(-)$
$b_{15} = -V(1 + z\gamma_1)$	$(-)$	$b_{25} = \psi b_{15} + \phi\gamma_1$ $(+)$

where $V = (1 + \gamma_1\beta_1 z)^{-1}$ $(>0$ if $z > -(\gamma_1\beta_1)^{-1} < 0$; assumed throughout$)$

$z = (1 - k)v\lambda - \phi$ $(\equiv \partial\dot{c}/\partial q_H; >0$ in Dornbusch case$)$

$\psi = \phi\gamma_1\beta_1 > 0$

Note also: $a_{21} = V[\psi\lambda(1 - v) - \phi\eta_c]$

$b_{21} = V[\psi\lambda(1 - v) - \phi\eta_b]$

$b_{22} = V(1 - v)[\psi\lambda k - \phi\gamma_3]$

$b_{25} = Vv\phi(1 - \beta_1) > 0$

since $(\psi V z - \phi) = -\phi V$

a. Caution: Rows in equation (15) appear as columns here.

results from the stickiness of the real money supply. Even if the stickiness of the price of domestic output or domestic wages is taken as an unalterable institutional constraint, the real money supply can be made flexible by permitting finite responses in the *level* of the nominal money stock. This would remove the need for the sticky domestic price to do any adjusting. If the parameters of the model were known with certainty, the level of the nominal money stock could be adjusted in such a way as to achieve immediately the new long-run equilibrium, without any need for over-shooting. For example, in the case of an oil discovery shock, the increase in the nominal money stock that permits the immediate achievement of the new steady-state values of c and l can be calculated directly from equation (20). It can therefore be argued that it is sticky nominal money as much as sticky domestic costs that is responsible for the short-run overshooting of the real exchange rate.

Appendix

Table 8.4 gives the elements of the statetransition and the forcing matrices of equation (15) in the text. In table 8.4 we also indicate the likely sign pattern of the coefficients; a question mark indicates that the sign is a priori ambiguous, while the sign in the brackets indicates the case we treat as the standard one. We assume throughout that the parameter V, the coefficient of $\dot{c}$ that arises when (2′) is substituted into (4), is positive. From table 8.4 it can be seen that a sufficient condition for V to be positive is that z be positive, where z is defined to be the influence of a change in output of home goods q_H on the rate of change of competitiveness $\dot{c}$. From table 8.4, $z \equiv \partial \dot{c} / \partial q_H = (1 - k)v\lambda - \phi$. The first term indicates the influence of q_H on the rate of change of the nominal exchange rate operating through the money market, while the second indicates the influence on the rate of change of p_H operating through the home goods market; assuming z to be positive would be following Dornbusch in assuming the short-run adjustment in asset markets dominates that in goods markets. In fact we assume only that $z > -(\gamma_1 \beta_1)^{-1}$, which is less than zero; this is necessary and sufficient to ensure $V > 0$. The ambiguities indicated in table 8.4 remain after $V > 0$ has been imposed; for example, with z negative a_{11} could also be negative.

Note that the coefficients of $\dot{l}$ can be represented as simple linear functions of the coefficients of $\dot{c}$; all are adjusted by the multiplicative factor $\psi = \phi\gamma_1\beta_1 > 0$, and four (corresponding to c, p^f, q_b^p, and r^f) also have an additive adjustment of $-\phi$ times the relevant elasticity. We shall usually assume that ϕ is small, so that this adjustment does not alter the sign of the relevant coefficient; the one exception is a_{21}, for which case we assume that η_c is sufficiently large to render a_{21} negative even though a_{11} is positive.

Notes

1. See, for example, Dornbusch [1980] and Blinder [1980].

2. A third shock, not considered in this paper, is a change in the relation between the domestic and world prices of oil measured in terms of a common currency, say because of taxes, subsidies, or tariffs on oil.

3. Indeed, as Dornbusch showed, the sluggishness of prices may in fact cause the *nominal* exchange rate to overshoot its long-run equilibrium path in addition to the real exchange rate overshooting its long-run equilibrium value.

4. Capacity output of domestic nonoil goods is exogenous and, through choice of units, its logarithm is set equal to zero. Fixing capacity output, of course, precludes any possibility of long-run deindustrialization.

5. The *levels* of current and permanent real income are defined, respectively, by

$$Y = (P_H Q_H + E P_b^f Q_b)/P, \tag{6'}$$

$$Y^p = (P_H Q_H^p + E P_b^f Q_b^p)/P, \tag{7'}$$

where uppercase symbols are the antilogarithms of the corresponding lowercase ones. In what follows we abstract from changes in v occurring as a result of the oil discovery and so treat v as the same in actual and permanent income and as constant through time. For convenience, we define permanent income in terms of actual rather than permanent prices.

6. Permanent oil production for $t \geqslant 0$ is derived as follows. The real interest rate used in these calculations is the steady-state real interest rate r^f:

$$\int_0^\infty Q_b^p e^{-r^f t}\, dt = \int_0^T \bar{\bar{Q}}_b e^{-r^f t}\, dt + \int_T^\infty \bar{Q}_b e^{-r^f t}\, dt.$$

This yields

$$Q_b^p(t) = \bar{\bar{Q}}_b + e^{-r^f T}[\bar{Q}_b - \bar{Q}_s].$$

The log-linear approximation is thus $\alpha \bar{q}_b + (1 - \alpha)\bar{\bar{q}}_b$.

7. A negative γ_4 would indicate that either the domestic good is complementary to oil or an increase in p_b^f leads to recession in the country's trading partners, thus reducing export demand.

8. Note that the real interest rate, $r - \dot{p}$, can be written as $r - \beta_1 \dot{c}$ using (1) and (9).

9. In (20), δ is defined as $\eta_c / \lambda (1 - v)$, so that in the l^* equation the coefficient of μ is λ^{-1}. The term $\eta_c - \eta_b = \gamma_2 - \gamma_3(1 - \beta_1 - \beta_2)$ takes on significance below.

10. Recall that permanent oil income q_b^p equals $\alpha \bar{q}_b + (1 - \alpha)\bar{\bar{q}}_b$, where $\bar{q}_b$ is "normal" oil output, $\bar{q}_b = q_b$. When we consider the effect of an increase in q_b^p, holding q_b constant, this is equivalent to examining the effect of a "larger" oil discovery, that is, to examining the effect of an increase in $\bar{\bar{q}}_b$.

11. As $m - p$ increases, $m - p_H$ will only fall if $p_H - p$ increases more than $m - p$. Therefore, $m - p_H$ will fall only if $c = e - p_H$ falls considerably when p_b^f increases. A large fall in c is required to re-equilibrate the goods market at full employment if (a) the effect of the real exchange rate on q_H is weak (η_c is small) and (b) the effect of an oil price increase on the demand for domestic nonoil goods is positive and large (η_b is positive and large). The increase in $m - p$ is achieved by a fall in the path of p relative to that of m. Now $p = \beta_1 p_H + (1 - \beta_1)e + \beta_2 p_b^f$. If $\eta_c - \eta_b < 0$, the lower path of p is achieved entirely by appreciation of e; p_b^f is higher and the path of p_H has risen relative to that of m.

As Peter Neary has pointed out to us in correspondence, the difference $(\eta_c - \eta_b)$, equal to $\gamma_2 - \gamma_3(1 - \beta_1 - \beta_2)$, can be interpreted as the gross cross-price elasticity of the demand for home goods with respect to the price of nonoil imports. A presumption that goods are gross substitutes is therefore a presumption that $(\eta_c - \eta_b) > 0$.

12. Note that for a "small" country ($\gamma_2 = \infty$), $dc/dp^f = 0$ and $dl/dp_b^f = (1 - v)$, $0 < 1 - v < 1$.

13. The reason there are long-run effects of an increase in the foreign currency price of oil is that this increase in a nominal price also represents an increase in the relative price of oil in terms of nonoil imports whose price remains fixed at

$p^f = 0$. If nonoil imports are omitted from the model ($\beta_2 = 1 - \beta_1$ and $\gamma_2 = 0$), there will be no long-run effects of an increase in the nominal foreign price of oil on l or $e + p_b^f$. If oil price increases were indexed on the price of domestic nonoil goods, long-run real effects of an increase in the price of oil would be present even if $\beta_2 = 1 - \beta_1$ and $\gamma_2 = 0$ (see Buiter [1978]).

14. If z were negative, then a_{11} could be negative and the $\dot{c} = 0$ locus would be negatively sloped. As long as it still cuts the $\dot{l} = 0$ locus from above, the analysis in the text holds; in particular, the saddle path would still be positively sloped. Necessary and sufficient for the equilibrium to be a saddle point is that $|A|$ be negative. For anticipated or "preannounced" disturbances the analysis is a little more complicated. This is treated in the context of the oil discovery case below.

15. Note that while our model has a sticky price *level*, the inflation rate is a jump variable. In fact, by equation (3) the initial fall in q_H means that the inflation rate falls immediately by more than the reduction in μ. The model could be extended to allow for inertia in the inflation rate.

16. In a more complete model incorporating oil as an intermediate input, long-run real output might be altered. In that case the drop in real output on impact would be relative to that new value of q_H^p.

17. From (4), a unit fall in c creates an excess supply of money of $1 - v$ while a unit rise in p_b^f creates an equivalent excess demand.

18. See Wilson [1979] for an early analysis of the dynamics of anticipated future disturbances.

References

Blinder, A. (1980). *Government Policy and the Great Stagflation* (Academic Press).

Branson, W. H., and J. Rothenberg (1980). "International Adjustments with Wage Rigidity," *European Economic Journal* 13, 309–42.

Bruno, M., and J. Sachs (1979). "Macroeconomic Adjustment with Import Price Shocks: Real and Monetary Aspects," mimeo.

Buiter, W. (1978). "Short-Run and Long-Run Effects of External Disturbances Under a Floating Exchange Rate," *Economica* 45, 251–72.

Corden, M., and P. Neary (1980). "Booming Sector and De-Industrialization in a Small Open Economy," unpublished.

Djajic, S. (1980). "Intermediate Inputs and International Trade: An Analysis of Real and Monetary Effects of an Oil Price Shock," unpublished.

Dornbusch, R. (1976). "Expectations and Exchange Rate Dynamics," *Journal of Political Economy* 84, 1161–76.

Dornbusch, R. (1980a). "Exchange Rate Economics: Where Do We Stand?," *Brookings Papers on Economic Activity*, 143–86.

Dornbusch, R. (1980b). "Monetary Stabilization, Intervention and Real Appreciation," National Bureau of Economic Research Working Paper No. 472, April.

Dornbusch, R., and Stanley Fischer (1980). "Exchange Rates and the Current Account," *American Economics Review* 70, 960–71.

Findlay, R., and C. Rodriguez (1977). "Intermediate Imports and Macroeconomic Policy Under Flexible Exchange Rates," *Canadian Journal of Economics* 10, 208–17.

Liviatan, N. (1979). "Neutral Monetary Policy and the Capital Import Tax," unpublished.

Purvis, D. (1979). "Wage Responsiveness and the Insulation Properties of a Flexible Exchange Rate," in A. Lindbeck (ed.), *Inflation and Employment in Open Economies* (North-Holland).

Rodriguez, Carlos (1980). "The Role of Trade Flows in Exchange Determination: A Rational Expectations Approach," *Journal of Political Economy* 88, 1148–58.

Wilson, C. (1979). "Anticipated Shocks and Exchange Rate Dynamics," *Journal of Political Economy* 87, 639–47.

III
POLICY
INTERDEPENDENCE

9

Monetary and Fiscal Policy with Flexible Exchange Rates

William H. Branson
and
Willem H. Buiter

The implications of "perfect" capital mobility for the effectiveness of monetary and fiscal policy and the transmission of disturbances under floating or fixed exchange rates were drawn in the classic paper by Mundell (1963). With fixed rates, fiscal policy moves output but monetary policy does not, and vice versa under flexible rates. These results are among the most enduring and best known in international economics.

The ineffectiveness of monetary policy under fixed rates depends on perfect capital mobility and the inability of the monetary authorities to sterilize balance of payments surpluses or deficits. By now, it is well known that during the fixed rate period many countries did indeed sterilize to a large extent. Earlier evidence on this is cited in Whitman (1975); more recent empirical work confirming this proposition has been reported by Obstfeld (1980). Thus the sharpness of Mundell's result for monetary policy with fixed rates does not hold up in light of the empirical evidence on sterilization.

However, the flexible-rate result for fiscal policy has fared better. The model was dynamized by Dornbusch (1976). In his paper, a change in fiscal policy (for example, an increase in government purchases), gives rise to a change in the real exchange rate that yields an exactly offsetting change in the trade balance, transmitting the entire disturbance abroad. A crucial feature of both the Mundell and Dornbusch analyses, though, is the exclusion of the exchange rate from the money-market equilibrium condition. This is a focal point of this chapter.

If the domestic price level is sensitive to changes in the exchange rate, then a movement in the rate changes real balances. Thus fiscal policy influences real balances through the exchange rate, opening the way for effects on home output in the Mundell model or the price level in the Dornbusch version. This reduces the effect transmitted abroad.

In addition to excluding the exchange rate from money-market equilibrium, Mundell and Dornbusch do not consider constraints of long-run portfolio balance. In a stationary economy, these would require balance on the current account in the long-run equilibrium, while the Mundell-Dornbusch model permits current account imbalance indefinitely. This is a point noted earlier by both of the present authors [see Branson (1972), Buiter (1978)].

In this chapter we revisit the Mundell-Dornbusch model to study its behavior with the price level dependent on the exchange rate, and with long-run portfolio balance constraints. We find that the flexible-rate fiscal policy result is a special case, dependent on the assumption of insensitivity of the price level to movement in the exchange rate.

9.1 The Mundell-Dornbusch Model

With "perfect" capital mobility and a freely floating exchange rate, the exchange rate is the transmission belt by which monetary policy affects real output q, while movement in the exchange rate makes output invariant to fiscal policy. These are the results of Mundell's classic paper (1963, 1968). With the price level fixed and the interest rate determined by the world market (and static exchange-rate expectations), an increase in the money stock increases the level of real income consistent with money-market equilibrium. The increase comes through depreciation of the currency (a rise in the exchange rate e) until the increase in the real current account balance gives the requisite increase in income. However, an increase in government spending does not move the money-market equilibrium q; the currency appreciates until the trade balance deteriorates exactly to offset the fiscal expansion.

Dornbusch (1976) updated and extended Mundell's model. He added exchange-rate dynamics with "perfect foresight" expectations about movement in the long-run equilibrium exchange rate $\bar{e}$. In the basic model of Dornbusch's paper, the level of output is exogenous, and the rate of inflation $\dot{p}$ responds to the excess demand for goods. Here movements in p (or short-run effects on $\dot{p}$) are the analogue to changes in output q in Mundell. Briefly, in section V of his 1976 paper, Dornbusch treats a case with short-run variability in output. Here the analogy to Mundell is clearer.

In both models, monetary policy moves the domestic price level in the long run, and the rate of inflation in the short run. This is the analogue to Mundell's effectiveness of monetary policy. However, in Dornbusch as well as in Mundell, a change in government spending moves the exchange rate to create an exactly offsetting effect on the current account balance. Fiscal policy is "ineffective" in both cases; it has no effect on q in Mundell's version, and no effect on p or $\dot{p}$ in Dornbusch.

9.1.1 Fiscal Policy Effects

The ineffectiveness of fiscal policy in the Mundell model can be illustrated simply. Money-market equilibrium is given by an "LM" curve,

$$\frac{M}{p} = l(i, q), \tag{1}$$

where q is domestic output. The interest rate is fixed at the world rate i^* by "perfect" capital mobility:

$$i = i^*. \tag{2}$$

If a forward discount on the domestic currency ε were included, (2) would be

$$i = i^* + \varepsilon. \tag{2'}$$

The IS curve describing goods market equilibrium is

$$q = a(q - T, i) + g + x\left(\frac{p}{e}, a\right). \tag{3}$$

Here a is private absorption, T is real tax revenue, g is government purchases, and x is net exports.

With i fixed by (2) and p given exogenously, or, alternatively, by a supply curve $p = p(q)$ with $p_q > 0$, equation (1) determines q. There is no room for fiscal effects here. Given T, i, g, and q, the exchange rate is determined by the goods-market equation (3) at the value which sets $x = q - a - g$. An increase in g will require a decrease in e to maintain goods-market equilibrium. Thus in the Mundell model, the exchange rate is determined by requirements of goods-market equilibrium, and fiscal policy changes generate offsetting changes in e.

The Dornbusch model is more complicated, being dynamic, but the result is the same. Dornbusch writes his model as linear in the logs of quantities and prices and the level of the interest rate. His "LM" curve, analogous to the combination of (1), (2'), and $\varepsilon = \theta(\bar{e} - e)$, is

$$p - m = -\phi q + \lambda i^* + \lambda\theta(\bar{e} - e), \tag{4}$$

where $\bar{e}$ is the long-run equilibrium exchange rate. [This is Dornbusch's equation (3), in our notation.] His "IS" curve (in the basic model with q exogenous) is given by

$$\dot{p} = \pi \ln(D/Y) = \pi[u + \delta(e - p) + (\gamma - 1)q - \sigma i]. \tag{5}$$

This is Dornbusch's equation (8); his u is "exogenous" expenditure, our g. D is real demand, and Y is exogenous real output.

In long-run equilibrium $e = \bar{e}$, so (4) determines p independently of u (our g), just as in Mundell, money-market equilibrium determines q. An increase in u requires a change in e given by $de/du = -1/\delta$ to hold $\dot{p} = 0$ in (5). With perfect foresight, $d\bar{e} = de$, causing no disturbance in the money market. Thus again, the effect of a change in g (u here) is to generate an offsetting change in e.

9.1.2 The Role of Capital Mobility

The Mundell-Dornbusch assumption of "perfect" capital mobility combines two assumptions. This first is freedom of capital movement—absence of impediments to capital flows in the forms of capital controls, taxes, and so forth. The second is perfect substitutability of assets denominated in home currency and foreign exchange. The Mundell financial "sector" of equations (1) and (2) can be obtained by simplifying a more general structure with imperfect substitutability as follows. Assume three assets—money M, bonds B, and net claims on foreigners F. Then a plausible financial-market structure [see Branson (1977), Katseli-Marion (1980)] could be written

$$\frac{M}{P} = m(i, q), \tag{6}$$

$$\frac{B}{P} = b\left(i, i^*, q, \frac{W - M}{P}\right), \tag{7}$$

$$\frac{eF}{P} = f\left(i, i^*, \frac{W - M}{P}\right), \tag{8}$$

$$W \equiv M + B + eF. \tag{9}$$

If we assume that the foreign interest rate i^* is fixed by world-market conditions (small-country assumption) *and* that b_{i^*} and $f_i \to \infty$, then the B and F equations (7) and (8) collapse to the perfect capital mobility condition $i = i^*$. [In Branson (1977, p. 73) the FF and BB curves become vertical at $r = r^*$.]

In the more general case of less-than-perfect substitutability, i can move relative to i^* and the extreme form of the Mundell-Dornbusch fiscal policy result disappears. An increase in g will raise i relative to i^*. This will yield an appreciation of the currency and a decrease in x, partially offsetting the g increase. But the offset is only partial, because the increase in i raises velocity, permitting an increase in q, given M. Thus it is clear that the result of literally *zero* effect of fiscal policy on q (or $\dot{p}$ in the Dornbusch model) is an extreme case with assets being perfect substitutes; it is not a general result with "high" substitutability. This is already a familiar result in the literature.

For example, in his earlier paper on "Flexible Exchange Rates and Employment Policy," Mundell (1961) showed that with *zero* capital mobility, flexible exchange rates increase the closed-economy effectiveness of fiscal policy. A fiscal expansion leads to a trade deficit and depreciation of the currency in that paper.[1] This effect is also seen clearly in Branson (1976). In intermediate cases between zero and perfect capital mobility, the exchange rate may appreciate or depreciate, depending on the relative size of current-account and capital-account effects, thus partially offsetting or supplementing the effect of the fiscal expansion. [See Branson (1976) and the discussion of Dornbusch (1980) for a fuller discussion of the empirical evidence on the capital-mobility question.] In the discussion below we shall follow the now traditional literature in assuming perfect substitutability and the "arbitrage" condition with risk-neutral speculation, so that

$$i = i^* + \left(\frac{\hat{e}}{e}\right).$$

This will permit us to focus on the importance of exclusion of the exchange rate from the money-market equilibrium condition.

9.1.3 Stock versus Flow Equilibrium
In the conventional model with perfect capital mobility, movements in the current account balance offset the effects of fiscal policy on equilbrium output. In equation (3), the real exchange rate p/e adjusts to provide offsetting variation in x to movements in g. This implies that in momentary equilibrium the current account balance is in general nonzero. If in an initial equilibrium the current account is balanced, then the change in x that offsets a change in g must unbalance the current account. In the model of equations (1)–(3), net foreign investment (= the current account) is nonzero indefinitely. This implies that the rest of the world is willing to accumulate claims on or liabilities to the home country in indefinite amounts and that the home country is willing to issue them. There is no requirement of portfolio balance in this model. The current account imbalance in the Mundell-Dornbusch model will upset portfo-

lio balance in both the home country and the rest of the world and, by altering wealth, change saving behavior. The *IS* and *LM* schedules will not settle to a full equilibrium as long as net foreign investment is non-zero. The implication is that in long-run equilibrium, the current account balance must be zero. (This assumes no real growth in long-run equilibrium.) The simplest form of this model was developed in Branson (1976), where it was apparent that the Mundell (1963) results can be obtained with any source of endogenous adjustment of the money stock; they are not unique to the international setting.

In sections 9.3 and 9.4 we shall analyze monetary and fiscal policy in a framework that includes explicit consideration of stock versus flow equilibrium. In the instantaneous short run, with historically given values of the stocks in the system, and with static expectations, flow equilibrium conditions determine the level of output and employment, the vector of prices and interest rates, including the exchange rate, and the rates of accumulation of the stocks. These provide the dynamics that move the system from one equilibrium to the next, and toward a steady state in which the relevant stocks are constant. This characterization of instantaneous and long-run equilibrium is developed, for example, in Branson (1972, 1976) and Buiter (1975, 1978). Long-run equilibrium in section 9.3 will include the requirement that the current account be in balance, so that the national rate of accumulation of net claims (or liabilities) on foreigners be zero. With rational expectations or perfect foresight even the current momentary equilibrium depends on the entire future path of the economy.

9.2 The Exchange Rate and Money-Market Equilibrium

The importance of the exclusion of the exchange rate from the money-market equilibrium condition (1) in the conventional model can be seen if we write $p = p(e)$ with $0 < p_e < 1$ there and in the *IS* curve (3). In this case, a change in government spending g moves the price level. This changes the real money stock, shifting the *LM* curve. The result is a change in the equilibrium level of output q, in either the Mundell or the Dornbusch version of the model. By writing $p = p(e)$, we convert equations (1)–(3) into a simultaneous system in e and q.

Consider the revision of equations (1) and (3) to include $p = p(e)$:

$$\frac{M}{p(e)} = l(i, q); \tag{1'}$$

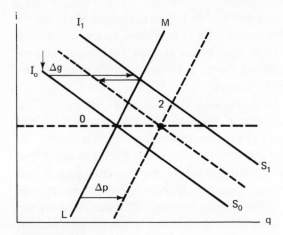

Figure 9.1
Effect of fiscal policy.

$$q = a(q - T, i) + g + x\left(\frac{p(e)}{e}, a\right). \tag{3'}$$

If we substitute $i = i^*$ from (2), this is a two-equation system in q and e. Initialize $p = e = 1$ and take the total differential of (1') and (3') with $di^* = 0$ to obtain

$$\underset{A}{\begin{bmatrix} l_q & Mp_e \\ 1 - a_q(1 + x_a) & (1 - p_e)x_s \end{bmatrix}} \begin{pmatrix} dq \\ de \end{pmatrix} = \underset{B}{\begin{bmatrix} 1 & 0 & 0 \\ 0 & -a_q(1 + x_a) & 1 \end{bmatrix}} \begin{pmatrix} dM \\ dT \\ dg \end{pmatrix}. \tag{10}$$

Here $x_s = \partial x/\partial(p/e)$. The determinant of the coefficient matrix $\text{Det}(A) < 0$. The solutions for a change in g, with $dM = dT = 0$, are given by

$$\frac{dq}{dg} = \frac{1}{\text{Det}(A)}(-Mp_e) > 0; \qquad \frac{de}{dg} = \frac{1}{\text{Det}(A)}l_q < 0.$$

An increase in g causes an appreciation of the currency ($de/dg < 0$) but not enough to eliminate the effect on q. For comparison to section 9.3 it is useful to note that a balanced-budget expansion with $dT = dg$ would multiply each of these multipliers by the quantity $1 > [1 - a_q(1 + x_a)] > 0$. This would preserve the signs of the fiscal-policy results, simply reducing their magnitudes. As long as the exchange rate enters the excess demand for money with a positive sign, $dq/dg > 0$ in the short run.

These results are illustrated in figure 9.1. The g increase initially takes the IS curve to $I_1 S_1$. The result is upward pressure on the interest rate and appreciation of the currency (e falls). The rise of p/e shifts the IS curve back to the left. But as e falls, p falls, increasing the real money stock. LM shifts right to a new equilibrium at point 2. There e, p and p/e have fallen and q has increased. Fiscal policy has an effect through the exchange rate changing real balances.

Clearly this result can be generalized. Any argument for inclusion of the exchange rate in the demand function for nominal balances will eliminate the extreme result of the conventional model that $dq/dg = 0$. We chose to include $p(e)$ both because it provides a clear example and because there is good econometric evidence for this link. [See Bruno (1978)]. However, the same result would be obtained if we include wealth as an argument in the money demand function. Then as the exchange rate falls, if the country is a net creditor in foreign denominated assets, the home-currency value of wealth falls, reducing the demand for M. Similarly, the inclusion of exchange-rate expectations in the demand for money would make the effect of fiscal policy nonzero.

Thus it is apparent that the usual result depends on a very strong assumption—that the exchange rate can be excluded from the money-market equilibrium condition. Since there is ample evidence that it must be included at least through its effect on the price level, it seems clear that the conventional wisdom is too extreme. The basic model of monetary and fiscal policy with floating exchange rates needs modification to include the exchange rate properly in specification of the LM curve, or of the financial sector generally. We next turn to a full specification of the basic model with perfect capital mobility.

9.3 A Model of Monetary and Fiscal Policy with Floating Exchange Rates: Mundell Revisited with Stock Adjustments and Rational Expectations

When domestic and foreign bonds are perfect substitutes in private portfolios, the full model can be represented as in equations (11)–(24):

$$\frac{M}{p} = l\left(i, q, \frac{W}{p}\right), \qquad l_i < 0, \qquad l_q > 0, \qquad 0 \leqslant l_w \leqslant 1; \tag{11}$$

$$a\left(y_d, i - \left(\frac{\hat{p}}{p}\right), \frac{W}{p}\right) + g + x(s, a) = q, \tag{12}$$

$$0 \leqslant a_y \leqslant 1, \qquad a_i \leqslant 0, \qquad a_w > 0,$$

$$x_s < 0, \qquad -1 \leqslant x_a \leqslant 0;$$

$$i = i^* + \left(\frac{\hat{e}}{e}\right); \tag{13}$$

$$W \equiv M + B + eF; \tag{14}$$

$$p \equiv V^{\alpha}e^{(1-\alpha)}, \qquad 0 \leqslant \alpha \leqslant 1; \tag{15}$$

$$y_d \equiv y + \frac{iB}{p} - T - \frac{ei^*R}{p}; \tag{16}$$

$$y \equiv \frac{V}{p}q + \frac{i^*e(F + R)}{p}; \tag{17}$$

$$s \equiv \frac{V}{e}; \tag{18}$$

$$\dot{M} + \dot{B} - e\dot{R} \equiv Vg + iB - ei^*R - pT; \tag{19}$$

$$e\dot{R} \equiv Vx + ei^*(F + R) - e\dot{F}; \tag{20}$$

$$\delta M + \delta B - e\,\delta R \equiv 0; \tag{21}$$

$$\delta M + \delta B + e\,\delta F \equiv 0; \tag{22}$$

$$\left(\frac{\hat{e}}{e}\right) = \begin{cases} 0 & \text{(23a)} \\ \dot{e}/e; & \text{(23b)} \end{cases}$$

$$\left(\frac{\hat{p}}{p}\right) = \begin{cases} 0 & \text{(24a)} \\ \dot{p}/p. & \text{(24b)} \end{cases}$$

Table 9.1 gives a list of definitions of symbols.

Equation (11) is the *LM* equation, equating the supply of real balances to the demand. Money demand depends negatively on the nominal interest rate, positively on a transactions variable, proxied by domestic value added, and (in principle) positively on real financial wealth. The price index used to deflate nominal money balances is the consumer price index, which is a function both of the price of domestically produced goods and of the price of imports ep_f^*. (p_f^*, the foreign currency price of imports, is set equal to unity for simplicity.) A depreciation of the exchange rate will therefore, *ceteris paribus*, reduce the real stock of money. Equation (12) is the *IS* equation. Domestic private absorption (expressed in terms of domestic goods) plus government spending on goods and services plus the trade balance surplus (expressed in terms of domestic output) equals domestic production. Private absorption depends on real disposable income, the real interest rate, and real private financial wealth. Net exports decline when the terms of trade improve

Table 9.1

List of symbols

A. Notation

M nominal stock of domestic money

B nominal stock of domestic government bonds

F stock of net private sector claims on the rest of the world, denominated in foreign currency

R stock of official foreign exchange reserves, denominated in foreign currency

q domestic output

y real national income

y_d real disposable private income

a private absorption

g government spending on goods and services

x net exports (trade balance surplus)

T real taxes net of transfers

i domestic nominal interest rate

i^* world nominal interest rate (exogenous)

p domestic general price level (c.p.i.)

V price of domestic value added

e foreign exchange rate (number of dollars ($) per unit of foreign currency)

s terms of trade

$\dot{z}$ $\equiv (d/dt)z$

δ stock shift (differential) operator

$\hat{z}$ the expected value of z

B. Parameter combinations

$$\Omega_1 = (1 - \alpha)\frac{M}{pe} - \frac{l_w(M + B - \alpha W)}{ep} > 0$$

$$\Omega_2 = (1 + x_a)\left\{a_y\left[(q - g)(1 - \alpha)\frac{s^{1-\alpha}}{e} - \frac{\alpha i^* F}{p}\right] + \frac{a_w}{ep}[M + B - \alpha W]\right\} + \frac{s}{e}x_s < 0$$

$$\Omega_3 = 1 - (1 + x_a)a_y s^{1-\alpha} > 0$$

$$\Omega_4 \equiv x_s s^2 - i^* F + Vx_a\left\{a_y\left[(q - g)(1 - \alpha)\frac{s^{1-\alpha}}{e} - \frac{\alpha i^* F}{p}\right] + \frac{a_w}{ep}(M + B - \alpha W)\right\} < 0$$

$$\Omega_5 \equiv e\left[Vx_a\frac{(a_y i^* + a_w)}{p} + i^*\right] < 0$$

$$\Omega_6 \equiv a_y\left[(q - g)(1 - \alpha)\frac{s^{1-\alpha}}{e} - \frac{\alpha i^* F}{p}\right] + \frac{a_w}{ep}[M + B - \alpha W] > 0$$

$$\Omega_7 \equiv \left[\Omega_3\frac{l_i}{e} + \frac{a_i}{e}\alpha l_q\right]^{-1} < 0$$

$$\Omega_8 = \frac{\alpha s^{\alpha-1}}{p^2}[M - l_w W] > 0$$

$$\Omega_9 = (1 + x_a)\left\{a_y\left[(q - g)(1 - \alpha)\frac{s^{-\alpha}}{e} - \frac{\alpha i^* Fs^{-\alpha}}{V}\right] - \frac{a_w \alpha W s^{\alpha-1}}{p^2}\right\} + \frac{1}{e}x_s < 0$$

$$\Omega_{10} = x + sx_s + Vx_a\left\{a_y\left[(q - g)(1 - \alpha)\frac{s^{-\alpha}}{e} - \frac{\alpha i^* Fs^{-\alpha}}{V}\right] - \frac{a_w W\alpha s^{\alpha-1}}{p^2}\right\} < 0$$

$$\Omega_{11} = -\left(\frac{l_i\Omega_9}{e} - \frac{a_i\alpha}{e}\Omega_8\right)^{-1} < 0$$

and when private domestic absorption expands. The marginal propensity to import is less than unity. For simplicity we assume that all government spending is on domestic output. Private capital formation and real capital stock adjustment are omitted.

Equation (13) reflects the assumption of risk-neutral speculation in the foreign exchange market: The domestic interest rate equals the exogenous world interest rate plus the expected proportional rate of depreciation of the home currency. Private financial wealth equals the sum of private holdings of domestic money, domestic government bonds, and foreign bonds [equation (14)]. It is assumed that only domestic residents hold domestic government bonds. All foreign lending or borrowing is done in foreign currency-denominated bonds. The general price level used to deflate nominal assets and nominal income is defined in (15). The Mundell-Dornbusch analysis represents the special case where α, the weight of home goods prices in the c.p.i., is unity. Equation (16) defines real private disposable income. Real national income is defined in (17). Note that changes in the terms of trade can alter the real income corresponding to a given volume of domestic output. The open-economy government budget constraint is given in (19). It is assumed that a competitive interest rate is paid on official foreign exchange reserves. The balance of payments identity is given in (20). Complementing these flow constraints are the stock-shift constraints for the public sector (21) and the private sector (22). These constrain the instantaneous portfolio reallocations that public and private agents can engage in. Expectations are either static [(23a) and (24a)] or rational [(23b) and (24b)].

We shall make two further simplifying assumptions about government financing behavior. The first is that the government always balances its budget by endogenous changes in taxes. Thus, when we consider fiscal policy, we shall be deriving short-run and long-run balanced budget multipliers. This is represented by (25):

$$Vg + iB - ei^*R - pT \equiv 0. \tag{25}$$

The second assumption is that the government does not engage in "flow" open market operation and does not sterilize balance of payments deficits or surpluses. This means that

$$\dot{B} = 0. \tag{26a}$$

We shall assume that there is a preexisting stock of government debt; that is,

$$B > 0. \tag{26b}$$

The implication of (25) and (26a) is, from (19), that

$$\dot{M} = e\dot{R}. \tag{27}$$

Our model is the standard neo-Keynesian open-economy model. The country is small in the market for its imports and in the world capital market but large in the market for its exportable. The terms of trade are therefore endogenous.

Under a freely floating exchange rate, $\dot{R} = \delta R = R = 0$, and therefore, given our assumptions of a balanced budget and of no continuous open market operations, $\dot{M} = 0$. The model can be summarized as in equations (28)–(30):

$$\frac{M}{V^\alpha e^{1-\alpha}} = l\left(i^* + \left(\frac{\hat{e}}{e}\right), q, \frac{M + B + eF}{V^\alpha e^{1-\alpha}}\right); \tag{28}$$

$$a\left(\left(\frac{V}{e}\right)^{1-\alpha}(q - g) + \frac{i^*eF}{V^\alpha e^{1-\alpha}}, i^* + \alpha\left[\left(\frac{\hat{e}}{e}\right) - \left(\frac{\hat{V}}{V}\right)\right], \frac{M + B + eF}{V^\alpha e^{1-\alpha}}\right)$$

$$+ g + x\left(\frac{V}{e}, a(\cdot, \cdot, \cdot)\right) = q. \tag{29}$$

$$e\dot{F} = Vx\left(\frac{V}{e}, a(\cdot, \cdot, \cdot)\right) + ei^*F. \tag{30}$$

9.4 Adjustment with a Fixed Price of Domestic Output V

In this section we study the behavior of the model of section 9.3 with a fixed price of domestic output V. This is the version of the model that is closest in spirit to the original Mundell model. The price rigidity permits us to observe output effects of policy experiments. In subsection 9.4.1 we study the model with static expectations; in subsection 9.4.2 we consider rational expectations.

9.4.1 Static Expectations
If exchange rate expectations are static, $\hat{e} = 0$. The impact multipliers are derived from the matrix equation (31):

$$\begin{bmatrix} -(1-\alpha)\dfrac{M}{pe} + \dfrac{l_w(M + B - \alpha W)}{pe} & -l_q \\[2ex] -(1 + x_a)\left\{a_y\left[(q - g)(1-\alpha)\dfrac{s^{1-\alpha}}{e} - \dfrac{\alpha i^*F}{p}\right] + \dfrac{a_w}{ep}[M + B - \alpha W]\right\} - \dfrac{s}{e}x_s & (1 + x_a)a_y s^{1-\alpha} - 1 \end{bmatrix}\begin{bmatrix} de \\ dq \end{bmatrix}$$

$$= \begin{bmatrix} \dfrac{l_w - 1}{p} & \dfrac{l_w}{p} & \dfrac{l_w e}{p} & 0 \\[2ex] -(1 + x_a)\dfrac{a_w}{p} & -(1 + x_a)\dfrac{a_w}{p} & -(1 + x_a)\dfrac{e}{p}[a_y i^* + a_w] & -(1 - (1 + x_a)a_y s^{1-\alpha}) \end{bmatrix}\begin{bmatrix} dM \\ dB \\ dF \\ dg \end{bmatrix} \tag{31}\cdot$$

For future reference we define

$$\Omega_1 \equiv (1 - \alpha)\frac{M}{pe} - l_w\frac{(M + B - \alpha W)}{pe} > 0, \tag{32a}$$

$$\Omega_2 \equiv (1 + x_a)\left\{a_y\left[(q - g)(1 - \alpha)\frac{s^{1-\alpha}}{e} - \frac{\alpha i^* F}{p}\right]\right.$$

$$\left. + \frac{a_w}{ep}[M + B - \alpha W]\right\} + \frac{s}{e}x_s < 0, \tag{32b}$$

$$\Omega_3 \equiv 1 - (1 + x_a)a_y s^{1-\alpha} > 0. \tag{32c}$$

Ω_1 is assumed to be positive. This will be the case if depreciation of the exchange rate, by raising the general price level, reduces the real supply of money balances by more than it reduces the demand for real money balances. This is more likely the larger the effect of import prices on the c.p.i. (the smaller α). If the country is a net external debtor ($F > 0$), exchange depreciation will increase the real value of debts to the rest of the world. This will reduce the demand for money if l_w is positive. We assume that l_w is sufficiently small for this demand effect to be dominated by the effect of changes in e on the real money supply. There probably is little loss of generality in assuming $l_w = 0$: Money is dominated by short bonds as a share of value and wealth-related demand for money is likely to be small at the margin. See Ando-Shell (1975) for a case in which it is literally zero. Ω_2 is assumed to be negative. This will be so if a depreciation of the exchange rate boosts total (domestic and foreign) spending on home goods. This is the traditional assumption of the elasticities approach: Exchange rate depreciation shifts the *IS* curve to the right. This effect, captured by $(s/e)x_s$, is present, but it is countered by two absorption-reducing effects of exchange rate depreciation. Subject to the qualification of net ownership claims on the rest of the world, exchange rate depreciation, by raising the general price level, reduces real wealth. This reduces absorption and is captured by $(a_w/ep)(M + B - \alpha W)$. Exchange rate depreciation, by turning the terms of trade against the depreciating country, reduces the real income corresponding to a given value of domestic output. This is reflected in $a_y(q - g)(1 - \alpha)(s^{1-\alpha}/e)$. Against this goes the positive effect on real income represented by the increased real value of net property and interest income from abroad (if F is positive). This is captured by $-a_y(\alpha i^* F/p)$. We assume that the elasticity effects dominate the absorption reducing effects. Ω_3 is positive if an increase in output raises demand for output by less than the increase in output. We assume this to be the case.

Let the determinant of the matrix on the left-hand side of (31) be denoted by Δ_1:

$$\Delta_1 = \Omega_1\Omega_3 - l_q\Omega_2 > 0. \tag{33}$$

The impact effect of an open market purchase of bonds, a balanced budget increase in public spending and an increase in net claims on the rest of the world on the two short-run endogenous variables e and q, are given below. The initial equilibrium is always assumed to be a full stationary equilibrium:

$$e = h^e(F; M, B, g); \tag{34}$$

$$h^e_M - h^e_B = \frac{1}{p}\Omega_3\Delta_1^{-1} > 0; \tag{35a}$$

$$h^e_g = -\Omega_3 l_q\Delta_1^{-1} < 0; \tag{35b}$$

$$h^e_F = -\left[l_w\frac{e}{p}\Omega_3 + (1 + x_a)\frac{e}{p}(a_w + a_y i^*)l_q\right]\Delta_1^{-1} < 0; \tag{35c}$$

$$q = h^q(F; M, B, g); \tag{36}$$

$$h^q_M - h^q_B = -\frac{1}{p}\Omega_2\Delta_1^{-1} > 0; \tag{37a}$$

$$h^q_g = \Omega_1\Omega_3\Delta_1^{-1} > 0; \tag{37b}$$

$$h^q_F = \left[\Omega_1(1 + x_a)\frac{e}{p}[a_y i^* + a_w] + \frac{l_w e}{p}\Omega_2\right]\Delta_1^{-1} > 0 \qquad \text{if } l_w \text{ is small.} \tag{37c}$$

In the *IS-LM* space of figure 9.2, an open market purchase of bonds shifts the *LM* curve to the right, at a given exchange rate. The resulting incipient demand for foreign bonds (capital outflow) causes the exchange rate to depreciate (35a). This depreciation shifts the *IS* curve to the right and, by raising the general price level, shifts the *LM* curve back to the left, although not all the way to its original position. In the Mundell-Dornbusch analysis the effect of the exchange rate on the *LM* curve is ignored. In that model the new short-run equilibrium would be at E_1' rather than at E_1 as in our model. The current account, which was balanced at E_0 is in surplus at E_1. Output increases.

An increase in public spending raises output, causes the exchange rate to appreciate, and turns the current account into deficit. This case is essentially the same as shown in figure 9.1. The *IS* curve shifts to the

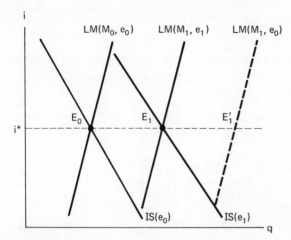

Figure 9.2
Static expectations, short-run effect of open-market purchase: $e_1 > e_0$; $M_1 > M_0$; original equilibrium, E_0; new equilibrium, E_1.

right at a given exchange rate. The incipient stock-shift inflow of capital causes the exchange rate to appreciate. In the Mundell model the appreciation proceeds until net exports have fallen by the same amount as the increase in public spending. In our model, the appreciation of the exchange rate shifts the *LM* curve to the right, preserving effectiveness of fiscal policy under a floating exchange rate and perfect capital mobility.

An increase in net claims on the rest of the world shifts the *IS* curve to the right through the wealth effect on private absorption. Output expands and the exchange rate appreciates. Any wealth effect on the demand for money is assumed to be sufficiently small not to reverse this result.

Long-run stock equilibrium Long-run equilibrium is defined by the *IS-LM* equilibrium plus current account balance: $\dot{F} = 0$ in (30). The long-run equilibrium conditions determining the steady-state values of e, q, and F are

$$\frac{M}{V^\alpha e^{1-\alpha}} = l\left(i^*, q, \frac{M + B + eF}{V^\alpha e^{1-\alpha}}\right),$$

$$a\left(\left(\frac{V}{e}\right)^{1-\alpha}(q - g) + \frac{i^*eF}{V^\alpha e^{1-\alpha}}, i^*, \frac{M + B + eF}{V^\alpha e^{1-\alpha}}\right) + g$$

$$+ x\left(\frac{V}{e}, a(\cdot, \cdot, \cdot)\right) = q,$$

$$0 = Vx\left(\frac{V}{e}, a(\cdot, \cdot, \cdot)\right) + ei^*F.$$

Note that these steady-state conditions and consequently the steady-state multipliers are the same for both static and rational expectations. These multipliers are obtained from (38):

$$
\begin{bmatrix}
-\Omega_1 & -l_q & -l_w\dfrac{e}{p} \\[2ex]
-\Omega_2 & -\Omega_3 & (1 + x_a)\dfrac{e}{p}(a_y i^* + a_w) \\[2ex]
\Omega_4 & -Vx_a a_y s^{1-\alpha} & -\Omega_5
\end{bmatrix}
\begin{bmatrix}
de \\[2ex] dq \\[2ex] dF
\end{bmatrix}
$$

$$
=
\begin{bmatrix}
\dfrac{l_w - 1}{p} & \dfrac{l_w}{p} & 0 \\[2ex]
-(1 + x_a)\dfrac{a_w}{p} & -(1 + x_a)\dfrac{a_w}{p} & -\Omega_3 \\[2ex]
\dfrac{V}{p}x_a a_w & \dfrac{V}{p}x_a a_w & -Vx_a a_y s^{1-\alpha}
\end{bmatrix}
\begin{bmatrix}
dM \\[2ex] dB \\[2ex] dg
\end{bmatrix},
\tag{38}
$$

where

$$\Omega_4 \equiv x_s s^2 - i^*F + Vx_a\left\{a_y\left[(q - g)(1 - \alpha)\frac{s^{1-\alpha}}{e} - \frac{\alpha i^*F}{p}\right]\right.$$

$$\left. + \frac{a_w}{ep}(M + B - \alpha W)\right\} < 0, \tag{39a}$$

$$\Omega_5 \equiv e\left[Vx_a\frac{(a_y i^* + a_w)}{p} + i^*\right] < 0. \tag{39b}$$

Ω_4 is negative if exchange-rate depreciation improves the current account. The elasticities effect is reinforced by the increase in the domestic currency value of service account income denominated in foreign exchange (assuming F is positive). It is also bolstered by an adverse terms-of-trade effect which reduces absorption and by the reduction in real financial wealth associated with the rise in the general prive level resulting from the depreciation. Ω_5 is negative if an increase in F worsens the current account. This will only be true if the current-account-improving effect of increased foreign interest income is more than offset by the boost to absorption caused by an increase in F via the wealth effect.

Given these assumptions, (38) has the following sign pattern:

$$
\begin{bmatrix}
- & - & -(0) \\
\hline
+ & - & \vdots\ + \\
- & + & \vdots\ +
\end{bmatrix}
\begin{bmatrix}
de \\
dq \\
dF
\end{bmatrix}
=
\begin{bmatrix}
-\dfrac{1}{p} & 0 & 0 \\
- & - & - \\
- & - & +
\end{bmatrix}
\begin{bmatrix}
dM \\
dB \\
dg
\end{bmatrix}. \tag{38'}
$$

Let Δ_2 be the determinant of the matrix on the left-hand side of (38):

$$
\Delta_2 \equiv -\Omega_1\left[\Omega_3\Omega_5 + Vx_a a_y s^{1-\alpha}(1 + x_a)\frac{e}{p}(a_y i^* + a_w)\right]
$$

$$
+ l_q\left[\Omega_2\Omega_5 - \Omega_4(1 + x_a)\frac{e}{p}(a_y i^* + a_w)\right]
$$

$$
- l_w\frac{e}{p}[\Omega_2 Vx_a a_y s^{1-\alpha} + \Omega_3\Omega_4] > 0. \tag{39c}
$$

Note that the 2×2 submatrix indicated in (38') has a negative determinant. It simplifies the long-run comparative statics to assume that the marginal wealth effect on the demand for money is zero: $l_w = 0$. This is assumed in the derivation of the long-run multipliers below. The steady-state multipliers can now be derived easily:

$$
\frac{de}{dg} = \frac{\begin{vmatrix} 0 & - & 0 \\ - & - & + \\ + & + & + \end{vmatrix}}{\Delta_2} = \frac{-}{+} < 0; \tag{40a}
$$

$$
\frac{de}{dM} - \frac{de}{dB} = \frac{\begin{vmatrix} -\dfrac{1}{p} & - & 0 \\ 0 & - & + \\ 0 & + & + \end{vmatrix}}{\Delta_2} = \frac{+}{+} > 0; \tag{40b}
$$

$$
\frac{dq}{dg} = \frac{\begin{vmatrix} - & 0 & 0 \\ + & - & + \\ - & + & + \end{vmatrix}}{\Delta_2} = \frac{+}{+} > 0; \tag{40c}
$$

$$
\frac{dq}{dM} - \frac{dq}{dB} = \frac{\begin{vmatrix} - & -\dfrac{1}{p} & 0 \\ + & 0 & + \\ - & 0 & + \end{vmatrix}}{\Delta_2} = \frac{+}{+} > 0; \tag{40d}
$$

$$\frac{dF}{dg} = \frac{l_q[s^2 x_s[1 - a_y s^{1-\alpha}] - i^* F\Omega_3 + Vx_a\Omega_6]}{\Delta_2} = \frac{-}{+} < 0; \qquad (40e)$$

$$\frac{dF}{dM} - \frac{dF}{dB} = \frac{\begin{vmatrix} - & - & -\dfrac{1}{p} \\ + & - & 0 \\ - & + & 0 \end{vmatrix}}{\Delta_2}$$

$$= -\frac{1}{p} \frac{[s^2 x_s[1 - a_y s^{1-\alpha}] - i^* F\Omega_3 + Vx_a\Omega_6]}{\Delta_2} = \frac{+}{+} > 0, \qquad (40f)$$

where

$$\Omega_6 \equiv a_y\left[(q - g)(1 - \alpha)\frac{s^{1-\alpha}}{e} - \frac{\alpha i^* F}{p}\right] + \frac{a_w}{ep}[M + B - \alpha W] > 0. \qquad (41)$$

The signs of these long-run multipliers are as expected. Expansionary fiscal policy creates a current account deficit in the short run and a lower stock of claims on the rest of the world in the long run (40e). Expansionary monetary policy has the opposite effect on $\dot{F}$ in the short run and on F in the long run (40f).

Assuming $l_w = 0$, the only direct consequence of the lower long-run stock of external net worth associated with an increase in g is on the IS curve. It shifts to the left relative to the new short-run equilibrium. The result is a depreciation of the exchange rate and a decline in output relative to the new short-run equilibrium. Relative to the initial equilibrium, however, the exchange rate appreciates and output expands.

The long-run effect of an open market purchase is to further increase output above its new short-run equilibrium level. The exchange rate appreciates relative to the new short-run equilibrium level, but not enough to bring it below the initial equilibrium value—there remains a long-run depreciation of the currency.

Stability   The stability of the model under static expectations can be studied by substituting the short-run equilibrium solutions for e and q ((34) and (36)) into the dynamic equation for $\dot{F}$ given in (30). Linearizing the resulting expression at the long-run equilibrium yields

$$\dot{F} = \left[sx_a \left\{ a_y \left(s^{1-\alpha} h_F^q - \left[(q - g)(1 - \alpha) \frac{s^{1-\alpha}}{e} - \frac{i^* F \alpha s^{-\alpha}}{e} \right] h_F^e + i^* s^{-\alpha} \right) \right. \right.$$

$$\left. \left. - a_w \frac{(M + B - \alpha W)}{ep} h_F^e - \frac{e}{p} - \frac{s}{e} (x + sx_s) h_F^e + i^* \right] F. \tag{42}$$

This is the full version of the simpler "super Marshall-Lerner" condition in Branson (1977).

A clear destabilizing influence is exercised by the effect of larger external net worth on the service account ($i^* > 0$). Foreign asset accumulation causes exchange rate appreciation ($h_F^e < 0$), and provided the Marshall-Lerner conditions are satisfied this will cause the trade balance to deteriorate:

$$\frac{-s}{e}(x + sx_s) h_F^e < 0.$$

Increased service account income raises absorption and this causes the trade balance to deteriorate:

$$sx_a a_y i^* s^{-\alpha} < 0.$$

Larger F boosts output which will also increase absorption and reduce net exports:

$$sx_a a_y s^{1-\alpha} h_F^q < 0.$$

The exchange rate appreciation resulting from the larger stock of foreign assets has two further effects on private income. It improves the terms of trade, raising real income and absorption and reducing net exports:

$$-sx_a a_y (q - g)(1 - \alpha) \frac{s^{1-\alpha}}{e} h_F^e < 0.$$

It also reduces the real value of foreign interest income which works in the opposite direction:

$$sx_a a_y \frac{i^* F \alpha s^{-\alpha}}{e} h_F^e > 0.$$

Larger F, by increasing wealth, raises absorption and worsens the trade balance:

$$sx_a a_w \frac{e}{p} < 0.$$

The exchange rate appreciation further raises wealth by lowering the general price level. (This assumes the country is not a very large net foreign creditor in which case exchange rate appreciation would cause a large capital loss on external holdings.) This again worsens the trade balance:

$$-sx_a a_w \frac{(M + B - \alpha W)}{ep} h_F^e < 0.$$

Whether the stability condition that an increase in net claims on the rest of the world worsens the trade balance by more than it improves the service account is satisfied is an empirical issue.

9.4.2 Rational Expectations

With rational expectations or perfect foresight, the model of equations (28)–(30) becomes

$$\frac{M}{V^\alpha e^{1-\alpha}} = l\left(i^* + \frac{\dot{e}}{e}, q, \frac{M + B + eF}{V^\alpha e^{1-\alpha}}\right), \tag{43}$$

$$a\left(\left(\frac{V}{e}\right)^{1-\alpha}(q - g) + \frac{i^* eF}{V^\alpha e^{1-\alpha}}, i^* + \alpha\frac{\dot{e}}{e}, \frac{M + B + eF}{V^\alpha e^{1-\alpha}}\right)$$

$$+ g + x\left(\frac{V}{e}, a(\cdot, \cdot, \cdot)\right) = q, \tag{44}$$

$$\dot{F} = \frac{V}{e}x\left(\frac{V}{e}, a(\cdot, \cdot, \cdot)\right) + i^*F. \tag{45}$$

Linearizing this system at the long-run equilibrium where $\dot{e} = \dot{F} = 0$, we obtain

$$
\begin{bmatrix} \dot{e} \\ \dot{F} \end{bmatrix} =
\begin{bmatrix}
(-\Omega_3\Omega_1 + l_q\Omega_2)\Omega_7 & -\left(\Omega_3 l_w\frac{e}{p} + l_q(1 + x_a)(a_w + a_y i^*)\frac{e}{p}\right)\Omega_7 \\[2mm]
\hline
-(1 - x_a a_y s^{1-\alpha})\frac{sx_a a_i\alpha}{e}\Omega_1\Omega_7 & -(1 - x_a a_y s^{1-\alpha})\frac{sx_a a_i\alpha}{e}\frac{l_w e}{p}\Omega_7 \\[2mm]
+\left(-\frac{l_i}{e}x_a a_y s^{-\alpha} + \frac{sx_a a_i\alpha}{e}\right)\Omega_2\Omega_7 - \frac{\Omega_4}{e} & -\left(\frac{l_i}{e}x_a a_y s^{-\alpha} + \frac{sx_a a_i\alpha}{e}\right)(1 + x_a)(a_w + a_y i^*)\frac{e}{p}\Omega_7 + \frac{\Omega_5}{e}
\end{bmatrix}
\begin{bmatrix} e \\ F \end{bmatrix} \tag{46}
$$

in $\dot{e}$, $\dot{F}$, plus

$$q = \left[-\frac{a_i\alpha}{e}\Omega_1 - \frac{l_i}{e}\Omega_2 \quad \Omega_7 e\right]$$

$$+ \left[-\frac{a_i}{e}\alpha l_w\frac{e}{p} + \frac{l_i}{e}(1 + x_a)[a_w + a_y i^*]\frac{e}{p}\right]\Omega_7 F \tag{47}$$

for q, where

$$\Omega_7 \equiv \left[\Omega_3 \frac{l_i}{e} + \frac{a_i}{e} \alpha l_q \right]^{-1} < 0. \tag{48}$$

The sign pattern of the matrix in (46) is

$$\begin{bmatrix} \dot{e} \\ \dot{F} \end{bmatrix} = \begin{bmatrix} + & + \\ ? & - \end{bmatrix} \begin{bmatrix} e \\ F \end{bmatrix}. \tag{46'}$$

$\partial\dot{F}/\partial F$ is negative if the effect of an increase in F improving the service account is more than balanced by a deterioration in the trade account.

For this system to have a unique "saddle path" converging to the steady state, the determinant of the matrix in (46) must be negative. This will always be the case if $\partial\dot{F}/\partial e$ is positive. In e-F space, the $\dot{e} = 0$ locus is downward sloping. If the $\dot{F} = 0$ is upward sloping, a unique downward sloping saddle path exists. This is shown in figure 9.3, where the saddle path is labeled SS'. If $\partial\dot{F}/\partial e$ is negative, the $\dot{F} = 0$ locus too is downward sloping. A unique convergent solution then exists only if the $\dot{F} = 0$ locus is steeper than the $\dot{e} = 0$ locus.

F is predetermined at any given moment, but e is free to make discrete jumps in response to "news." Unanticipated current or future (announced) policy changes or other parameter changes cause e to jump onto the unique convergent solution path. This is the implication of the assumptions of complete (short-run and long-run) perfect foresight and an efficient foreign exchange market. For simplicity, we only consider the case where the policy changes are both unanticipated and implemented as soon as they are announced.

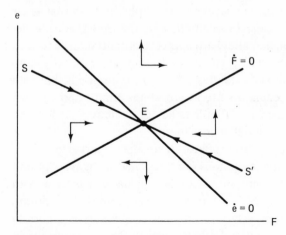

Figure 9.3
Equilibrium with rational expectations.

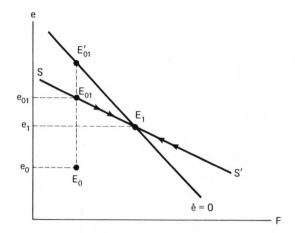

Figure 9.4
Rational expectations, open-market purchase.

To obtain the complete solution under rational expectations, we combine the information of figure 9.3 with the long-run comparative statics of equations (40a)–(40f).

The long-run effect of an open market purchase is for both F and e to rise. In figure 9.4 the initial long-run equilibrium is at E_0, the new one at E_1. In response to the unanticipated open market purchase, the exchange rate depreciates at once to e_{01}. With F predetermined, this is the only way the economy can move onto the convergent solution path through E_1. The exchange rate overshoots its long-run equilibrium, and after the initial jump depreciation appreciates smoothly toward e_1. Along the adjustment path, the current account is in surplus and external assets are accumulated. With static expectation, too, the exchange rate depreciates in jump fashion and afterward appreciates continuously toward the new long-run equilibrium.[2] It can be shown, however, that the jump will be smaller under rational extations. The intuitive reason is that with rational expectations speculators are aware of the future appreciation of the currency. This increases the demand for domestic money and reduces the amount of the initial depreciation.[3]

The comparison of the impact effects of an open market purchase under static and rational expectations is represented in figures 9.4 and 9.5. In figure 9.4 the economy moves to E'_{01} on the $\dot{e} = 0$ locus with static expectations, above E_{01}, the rational expectations equilibrium. In figure 9.5, with static expectations, the new momentary equilibrium is at E_1, say. The domestic interest rate is equal to the exogenous world

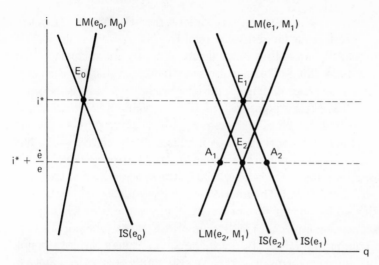

Figure 9.5
Open-market purchase, comparisons of impact effects under static and rational expectations: initial equilibrium, E_0; short-run equilibrium under static expectations, E_1; short-run equilibrium under rational expectations, E_2; $M_1 > M_0$; $e_1 > e_2 > e_0$.

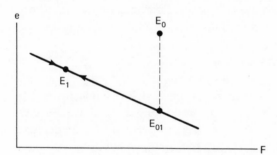

Figure 9.6
Rational expectations, public spending increase.

interest rate at i^*. With rational expectations, the new IS and LM curves have to interest at an interest rate equal to $i^* + \dot{e}/e$. From figure 9.4 we know that $\dot{e}/e$ is negative immediately after the unanticipated open market purchase. Since we know also from figure 9.4 that the exchange rate sharply depreciates on impact, the new equilibrium must lie between A_1 and A_2, that is, at a point such as E_2. e is higher at E_2 than at E_0, but lower than at E_1. Thus, relative to E_1, the IS curve shifts to the left and the LM curve to the right. q has increased at E_2 relative to E_0, but it can be either below or above the value of output associated with E_1.

The long-run effect of a balanced budget increase in public spending is for both e and F to fall. The solution in e-F space is shown in figure 9.6. The original long-run equilibrium is at E_0, the new one at E_1. On impact, the exchange rate appreciates with a jump to E_{01}. It overshoots its new long-run equilibrium value. Afterward, the country runs a current account deficit and the exchange rate depreciates smoothly toward E_1. Since $\dot{e}$ is positive along the adjustment path, the currency is at a forward discount throughout. The jump appreciation of the exchange rate is less under rational expectations than under static expectations because the forward discount reduces the demand for domestic money. The reasoning is identical to the case of an open market purchase. The impact effect on output under rational expectations is positive but many either fall short or exceed that under static expectations.

9.5 Adjustment with a Flexible Price of Domestic Output

We now consider the case in which output is always equal to its full employment level and the price of domestic output V adjusts flexibly to clear the domestic goods market. This is the version of the model that is closest in spirit to Dornbusch (1976). Full employment output is taken to be constant. Changes in labour supply due to changes in the terms of trade are not considered. See Branson-Rotemberg (1980) for these complications. The recent paper by Dornbusch and Fischer (1980) treats a version of the model, simplified by the elimination of domestic bonds and the service account in the balance of payments. Our results can be considered an extension of theirs to include these aspects of portfolio choice and dynamic behavior.

9.5.1 Static Expectations
With static expectations, $\hat{\dot{e}} = \hat{\dot{V}} = 0$. Since q is exogenous, the two short-run endogenous variables determined by the LM and IS curves are V and e.

The impact multipliers relating the instantaneous change in e and V to the changes in the predetermined or exogenous variables M, B, F, and g are obtained by totally differentiating (28) and (29):

$$
\begin{bmatrix} -\Omega_1 & -\Omega_8 \\ -\Omega_2 & \Omega_9 \end{bmatrix} \begin{bmatrix} de \\ dV \end{bmatrix}
$$

$$
= \begin{bmatrix} \dfrac{l_w - 1}{p} & \dfrac{l_w}{p} & l_w\dfrac{e}{p} & 0 \\[2ex] -(1 + x_a)\dfrac{a_w}{p} & -(1 + x_a)\dfrac{a_w}{p} & -(1 + x_a)\dfrac{e}{p}[a_w + a_y i^*] & -\Omega_3 \end{bmatrix} \begin{bmatrix} dM \\ dB \\ dF \\ dg \end{bmatrix},
$$

$$\tag{49}$$

where

$$
\Omega_8 = \frac{\alpha s^{\alpha-1}}{p^2}[M - l_w W] > 0, \tag{50a}
$$

$$
\Omega_9 = (1 + x_a)\left\{ a_y\left[(q - g)(1 - \alpha)\frac{s^{-\alpha}}{e} - \frac{\alpha i^* F s^{-\alpha}}{V} \right] - \frac{a_w \alpha W s^{\alpha-1}}{p^2} \right\}
$$

$$
+ \frac{1}{e}x_s < 0. \tag{50b}
$$

The effect of a change in V on money market equilibrium is given by Ω_8. If an increase in the price of domestic output reduces the real supply of money balances by more than it lowers the demand for real money balances, as we shall assume, Ω_8 is positive. Ω_9 measures the effect of V on domestic goods market equilibrium. An increase in V *Ceteris paribus* worsens competitiveness and lowers net exports:

$$
\frac{1}{e}x_s < 0.
$$

By raising the general price level, it also reduces absorption via the wealth effect:

$$
-(1 + x_a)a_w\frac{\alpha W s^{\alpha-1}}{p^2} < 0.
$$

An increase in V also represents an improvement in the terms of trade. This raises real income and boosts absorption:

$$
(1 + x_a)a_y(q - g)(1 - \alpha)\frac{s^{-\alpha}}{e} > 0.
$$

Finally, the real value of any net interest income from abroad is reduced by a higher value of V:

$$-(1 + x_a)a_y\alpha i^* \frac{Fs^{-\alpha}}{V} \lessgtr 0 \qquad \text{as } F \lessgtr 0.$$

We assume that, on balance, an increase in V will tend to create an excess supply of domestic output, that is, that $\Omega_9 < 0$. Given these conditions, Δ_3, the determinant of the matrix on the left-hand side of (49), is positive:

$$\Delta_3 = -[\Omega_1\Omega_9 + \Omega_2\Omega_8] > 0. \tag{51}$$

From (49) we obtain the reduced form expressions for e and V:

$$e = h^e(F; M, B, g); \tag{52}$$

with

$$h_M^e - h_B^e = -\frac{1}{p}\Omega_9\Delta_3^{-1} > 0; \tag{53a}$$

$$h_g^e = -\Omega_3\Omega_8\Delta_3^{-1} < 0; \tag{53b}$$

$$h_F^e = \left[l_w\frac{e}{p}\Omega_9 - (1 + x_a)\frac{e}{p}(a_w + a_y i^*)\Omega_8 \right]\Delta_3^{-1} < 0; \tag{53c}$$

$$V = h^V(F; M, B, g); \tag{54}$$

with

$$h_M^V - h_B^V = -\frac{1}{p}\Omega_2\Delta_3^{-1} > 0; \tag{55a}$$

$$h_g^V = \Omega_1\Omega_3\Delta_3^{-1} > 0; \tag{55b}$$

$$h_F^V = \left[\Omega_1(1 + x_a)\frac{e}{p}(a_y i^* + a_w) + \frac{l_w e}{p}\Omega_2 \right]\Delta_3^{-1} > 0 \quad \text{if } l_w \text{ is small.} \tag{55c}$$

Qualitatively, these results are similar to those derived for the fixed domestic price level case [reported in (34)–(37)], with the role of q as the short-run endogenous variable taken over by V. An open-market purchase causes exchange rate depreciation (53a) and a rise in the general price level (55a). Note that an increase in the money supply will only be neutral (that is, will only lead to a depreciation of e and a rise in V by the same percentage as the rise in M) if nominally denominated public sector debt (bonds) is absent from the model. This will be the case either if bonds are not neutral but B happens to be zero or if bonds are neutral, in which case they cease to be part of private sector net worth. With B omitted from the model, it is immediately apparent from (28) and (29) that money is neutral in the short-run.[4]

With a positive value of B entering into private sector wealth, a percentage rise in V and e equal to the percentage rise in M (brought about either by a helicopter drop or by an open market purchase) would not leave the real equilibrium unaltered—the real value of the stock of interest-bearing public debt would be reduced. With output given exogenously, there would be downward pressure on the interest rate. With perfect capital mobility and static expectations, this would be translated into further depreciation of the exchange rate. After an initial open market purchase, the original i, q equilibrium is regained via further depreciation of e and an increase in the price level.

A balanced budget increase in public spending raises V and causes the exchange rate to appreciate [(53b) and (55b)]. In i-q space, the IS curve shifts to the right at given e and V, creating excess demand for home goods and, by raising i above i^*, threatening a stock-shift gain in reserves. The original i, q equilibrium is restored by a rise in V and a fall in e that shifts the IS curve back to its original position. The increase in V and the reduction in e exactly cancel each other out as regards their combined effects on money market equilibrium.

A larger value of net claims on the rest of the world will be associated with an appreciation of the currency (53c) and an increase in the price of domestic output (55c).

An increase in public spending will lead to a current account deficit (assuming the initial equilibrium to be a stationary state). An open market purchase will not affect the current account (or any other real variable), if money is neutral which in turn requires bonds to be neutral. If bonds are nonneutral, then e increases more (in percentage terms) than V. This improvement in competitive position should lead to a current account surplus.

Long-run effects of monetary and fiscal policy   The long-run comparative static results again apply to both the static and the rational expectations cases. The long-run multipliers are derived from (56) which is obtained by totally differentiating (28)–(30) with $\dot{F} = 0$:

$$
\begin{bmatrix}
-\Omega_1 & -\dfrac{(M - l_w W)\alpha}{pV} & -l_w \dfrac{e}{p} \\[2mm]
-\Omega_2 & \Omega_9 & (1 + x_a)\dfrac{e}{p}(a_y i^* + a_w) \\[2mm]
\Omega_4 & -\Omega_{10} & -\Omega_5
\end{bmatrix}
\begin{bmatrix}
de \\[2mm]
dV \\[2mm]
dF
\end{bmatrix}
$$

$$
=
\begin{bmatrix}
\dfrac{l_w - 1}{p} & \dfrac{l_w}{p} & 0 \\[2mm]
-(1 + x_a)\dfrac{a_w}{p} & -(1 + x_a)\dfrac{a_w}{p} & -\Omega_3 \\[2mm]
-\dfrac{V}{p}x_a a_w & \dfrac{V}{p}x_a a_w & -Vx_a a_y s^{1-\alpha}
\end{bmatrix}
\begin{bmatrix}
dM \\[2mm]
dB \\[2mm]
dg
\end{bmatrix}
,
\tag{56}
$$

where

$$
\Omega_{10} = x + sx_s + Vx_a\left\{a_y\left[(q - g)(1 - \alpha)\dfrac{s^{-\alpha}}{e} - \dfrac{\alpha i^* F s^{-\alpha}}{V}\right]\right.
$$

$$
\left. - a_w\dfrac{W}{p^2}\alpha s^{\alpha-1}\right\} < 0.
\tag{57}
$$

Ω_{10} is negative if an increase in the price of domestic output tends to worsen the current account. The elasticities approach suggests that this will be so, provided the Warshall-Lerner conditions are satisfied:

$$
x + sx_s < 0.
$$

Against this, the monetary approach focuses on the effect of changes in the general price level on the real value of given stocks of nominal assets and thus in private spending. A higher value of V would tend to improve the current account through this channel:

$$
- Vx_a a_w \dfrac{W}{p^2}\alpha s^{\alpha-1} > 0.
$$

Similarly, if F is positive, a higher value of V reduces the real value of income from foreign ownership:

$$
- Vx_a a_y \alpha i^* \dfrac{F s^{-\alpha}}{V} \gtreqless 0 \qquad \text{as } F \gtreqless 0.
$$

The improvement in the terms of trade associated with an increase in V increases the real income corresponding to any given amount of domestic output. This will boost spending and worsens the current account:

$$Vx_a a_y (q - g)(1 - \alpha)\frac{s^{-\alpha}}{e} < 0.$$

On balance, we assume that an increase in V will cause the current account to deteriorate.

A sufficiently small value of l_w is again sufficient (although not necessary) to ensure that Δ_4, the determinant of the matrix on the left-hand side of (56), is positive:

$$\Delta_4 = \Omega_1 \left[\Omega_9 \Omega_5 - \Omega_{10}(1 + x_a)\frac{e}{p}(a_y i^* + a_w) \right]$$

$$+ \left(\frac{M - l_w W}{pV} \right) \alpha \left[\Omega_2 \Omega_5 - \Omega_4 (1 + x_a)\frac{e}{p}(a_y i^* + a_w) \right]$$

$$- l_w \frac{e}{p} [\Omega_2 \Omega_{10} - \Omega_4 \Omega_9] > 0. \tag{58}$$

The long-run monetary and fiscal policy multipliers (assuming that $l_w = 0$) are given by

$$\frac{de}{dg} = \frac{\begin{vmatrix} 0 & - & 0 \\ - & - & + \\ + & + & + \end{vmatrix}}{\Delta_4} = \frac{-}{+} < 0, \tag{59a}$$

$$\frac{de}{dM} - \frac{de}{dB} = \frac{\begin{vmatrix} -\dfrac{1}{p} & - & 0 \\ 0 & - & + \\ 0 & + & + \end{vmatrix}}{\Delta_4} = \frac{+}{+} > 0, \tag{59b}$$

$$\frac{dV}{dg} = \frac{\begin{vmatrix} - & 0 & 0 \\ + & - & + \\ - & + & + \end{vmatrix}}{\Delta_4} = \frac{+}{+} > 0, \tag{59c}$$

$$\frac{dV}{dM} - \frac{dV}{dB} = \frac{\begin{vmatrix} - & -\dfrac{1}{p} & 0 \\ + & 0 & + \\ - & 0 & + \end{vmatrix}}{\Delta_4} = \frac{+}{+} > 0, \tag{59d}$$

$$\frac{dF}{dg} = \left[\frac{M - l_w(M + B)}{ep} \right]$$

$$\times \left\{ \frac{(x + sx_s)(1 - a_y s^{1-\alpha})}{\Delta_4} \right.$$

$$+ \frac{Vx_a \left[a_y \left((g - q)(1 - \alpha)\frac{s^{-\alpha}}{e} - \frac{\alpha i^* F s^{-\alpha}}{V} \right) - \frac{a_w W a s^{\alpha-1}}{p^2} \right]}{\Delta_4} \right\}$$

$$+ \frac{\alpha[M - l_w W]}{pV}$$

$$\times \frac{\left\{ x_a a_y s^{1-\alpha} i^* F + Vx_a(1 + x_a)\frac{a_w}{ep}(M + B) \right\}}{\Delta_4} < 0 \, (?), \qquad (59e)$$

$$\frac{dF}{dM} - \frac{dF}{dB} = \frac{-(1/p)(\Omega_2 \Omega_{10} - \Omega_4 \Omega_9)}{\Delta_4}$$

$$= \frac{-(1/p)[(a_w/ep)(M + B)(1 + x_a)x + sx_s]}{\Delta_4} > 0. \qquad (59f)$$

The long-run effect of an expansionary open-market operation is to raise the price of domestic output (59d), depreciate the exchange rate (59b), and increase the stock of private claims on the rest of the world (59f), with no effect on i and q. The impact effect with flexible prices is to create a current account surplus, which increases the long-run stock of external wealth. If there are no domestic bonds or if domestic government debt is neutral, an increase in M causes e, V, and p to rise in the same proportion as the increase in M with no effect on F. In that case, the impact effect and steady state effect are identical.

A balanced-budget increase in public spending leads to long-run exchange rate appreciation (59a), an increase in the price of domestic output (59c), and (probably) a net loss of external wealth (59e). The impact effect of a balanced budget increase in g is to create a current account deficit. This is matched by a decline in the long-run stock of external wealth.

Note that with e falling and V increasing, there is a magnified long-run appreciation of the real exchange rate (or loss of competitiveness) as a result of an increase in g. To maintain current account equilibrium, private absorption has to fall. This fall in absorption is brought about by a reduction in external wealth. (We must assume that the loss of service account income when F falls is not too strong.) For both fiscal and monetary policy, the long-run endogeneity of F reduces the magnitudes of the effects on e and V but does not reverse them.

Stability   To analyze the stability of the system under static expectations, we substitute (52) and (54) into (20). This yields

$$\dot{F} = \frac{h^V(V; \cdot)}{h^e(F; \cdot)} \times \left[\frac{h^V(F; \cdot)}{h^e(F; \cdot)}, a\left(\left(\frac{h^V(F; \cdot)}{h^e(F; \cdot)}\right)^{1-\alpha} (q-g) \right.\right.$$

$$\left.\left. + \frac{i^*F}{h^V(F; \cdot)^\alpha h^e(F; \cdot)^{-\alpha}}, i^*, \frac{M + Bh^e(F; \cdot)F}{h^V(F; \cdot)^\alpha h^e(F; \cdot)^{1-\alpha}}\right)\right] + i^*F. \qquad (60)$$

This external wealth adjustment equation will be stable if an increase in F causes the trade balance to deteriorate by enough to offset the increased service income from the rest of the world. Since a higher value of F raises V and lowers e, a significant deterioration in the trade balance due to loss of competitiveness is certainly possible. The precise stability condition (for local stability) is $\partial \dot{F}/\partial F < 0$.

9.5.2 Rational Expectations
With rational expectations and a flexible domestic price level, the dynamic model of (28)–(30) becomes

$$\frac{M}{V^\alpha e^{1-\alpha}} = l\left(i^* + \frac{\dot{e}}{e}, q, \frac{M + B + eF}{V^\alpha e^{1-\alpha}}\right),$$

$$a\left(\left(\frac{V}{e}\right)^{(1-\alpha)} (q-g) + \frac{i^*eF}{V^\alpha e^{1-\alpha}}, i^* + \alpha\left(\frac{\dot{e}}{e} - \frac{\dot{V}}{V}\right), \frac{M + B + eF}{V^\alpha e^{1-\alpha}}\right)$$

$$+ g + x\left(\frac{V}{e}, a(\cdot, \cdot, \cdot)\right) = q,$$

$$\dot{F} = \frac{V}{e} x\left(\frac{V}{e}, a(\cdot, \cdot, \cdot)\right) + i^*F.$$

Satisfactory treatment of this model would involve dealing with a system of three simultaneous differential equations, in e, V, and F. To be able to continue our convenient diagrammatic analysis, it is necessary to remove $\dot{V}$ from the model. This can be done provided one of the following three conditions is satisfied:

1. Absorption is interest inelastic ($a_i = 0$).

2. It is the nominal rather than the real interest rate that affects absorption, in which case $i^* + (\dot{e}/e)$ is the appropriate argument in the a function.

3. While exchange rate expectations are rational, expectations about the price of domestic output are static. In this case, $i^* + \alpha(\dot{e}/e)$ is the appropriate argument in the a function.

We shall include $i^* + \alpha(\dot{e}/e)$ as the interest rate argument in the absorption function to stay as close as possible to the analysis of the fixed domestic price level case.

Linearizing the system at the long-run equilibrium, where $\dot{e} = \dot{F} = 0$, we obtain

$$\begin{bmatrix} \dot{e} \\ \dot{F} \end{bmatrix} = \begin{bmatrix} (\Omega_9\Omega_1 + \Omega_8\Omega_2)\Omega_{11} & \left(\frac{\Omega_9 l_w e}{p} - \Omega_8(1 + x_a)(a_w + a_y i^*)\frac{e}{p}\right)\Omega_{11} \\ \left(\frac{-a_i\alpha}{e}\Omega_{10} + \frac{s x_a a_i\alpha}{e}\Omega_9\right)\Omega_2\Omega_{11} & \left(-\frac{a_i\alpha}{e}\Omega_{10} + \frac{s x_a a_i\alpha}{e}\Omega_9\right)\frac{l_w e}{p}\Omega_{11} \\ + \left(-\frac{l_i\Omega_{10}}{e} + \frac{s x_a a_i\alpha}{e}\right)\Omega_2\Omega_{11} - \frac{\Omega_4}{e} & -\left(\frac{-l_i\Omega_{10}}{e} + \frac{s x_a a_i\alpha}{e}\right)(1 + x_a)(a_w + a_y i^*)\frac{e}{p}\Omega_{11} + \frac{\Omega_5}{e} \end{bmatrix} \begin{bmatrix} e \\ F \end{bmatrix} \quad (61)$$

for $\dot{e}$ and $\dot{F}$, plus

$$V = -\left(\frac{a_i\alpha}{e}\Omega_1 + \frac{l_i}{e}\Omega_2\right)\Omega_{11}e + \left[-\frac{a_i\alpha}{e}l_w\frac{e}{p}\right.$$

$$\left. + \frac{l_i}{e}(1 + x_a)(a_w + a_y i^*)\frac{e}{p}\right]\Omega_{11}F \quad (62)$$

for V, where

$$\Omega_{11} = -\left(\frac{l_i\Omega_9}{e} - \frac{a_i\alpha}{e}\Omega_8\right)^{-1} < 0. \quad (63)$$

The sign pattern of the matrix in (62) (assuming l_w to be small) is

$$\begin{bmatrix} \dot{e} \\ \dot{F} \end{bmatrix} = \begin{bmatrix} + & + \\ +(?) & -(?) \end{bmatrix} \begin{bmatrix} e \\ F \end{bmatrix}. \quad (61')$$

For reasons of space, we shall ignore the possible ambiguities, indicated in (61'), attached to the signs of $\partial\dot{F}/\partial e$ and $\partial\dot{F}/\partial F$.

We therefore have a saddlepoint equilibrium with the same general properties as the one drawn in figure 9.3. Combining the downward slope of the convergent saddle path with our long-run comparative static results, the complete dynamic adjustment paths after an unanticipated open market purchase and an unanticipated balanced budget increase in public spending can be derived. The diagrams drawn from the fixed domestic price level case can also serve for the flexible price level case. Thus in figure 9.4, after an unanticipated open market purchase, the currency jump depreciates from E_0 to E_{01}, overshooting its long-run equilibrium. The current account goes into surplus. After the initial jump, the currency gradually appreciates to E_1 with F rising along the way. (We assume that bonds are net worth and that money therefore is not neutral.) The absence of long-run neutrality may seem surprising even if bonds are net worth, as domestic and foreign bonds are perfect substitutes. The reason that a restoration of the original value of private bond holdings (domestic and foreign) does not take place in the long run is the following. Let the open-market purchase increase M by a fraction λ. $M + B$ is constant. If this operation were to be neutral in the long run, e and V would have to increase by the same fraction λ. To maintain real net worth at its original level with $M + B$ constant, F will have to increase by a fraction δ, defined by

$$(1 + \lambda)(M + B + eF) = M + B + (1 + \lambda)e(1 + \delta)F.$$

However, any change in F will affect the current account equilibrium through its effect on the term i^*F. (It will also affect disposable income.) Therefore, unless there is debt neutrality, changes in portfolio composition effected through current account deficits or surpluses will not make open market purchases neutral, even in the long run.

The dynamics of a government spending increase under rational expectations are shown in figure 9.6. The impact effect of an unanticipated increase in g is a jump appreciation of the exchange rate from E_0 to E_{01} which overshoots its long-run equilibrium. The economy runs a current account deficit. After the initial shock, the exchange rate depreciates smoothly toward E_1 with the economy reducing its stock of claims on the rest of the world.

As with a fixed V, rational expectations reduce the magnitude of the initial jump in e relative to what it would be under static expectations. Under static expectations, the impact effect on e exceeds the long-run effect. For example, with an open market purchase, the initial jump depreciation overshoots the long-run equilibrium depreciation. After the jump, the currency appreciates steadily. Speculators and arbitrators endowed with rational expectations are aware of this steady future rate of appreciation. They immediately increase their demand for the domestic currency, thus reducing but not eliminating the magnitude of the initial jump and the extent to which the exchange rate overshoots its long-run equilibrium.

Notes

1. In his 1968 adaptation of this paper, Mundell added a footnote calling attention to the difference between the zero and perfect capital mobility cases. See Mundell (1968, p. 247, footnote 9).

2. With static expectations, it is irrelevant whether the policy changes are anticipated or unanticipated.

3. With static expectations the economy always moves along the $\dot{e} = 0$ locus in figure 9.3. This can be seen by noting that (35c) gives the same relation between e and F under static expectations as does $\dot{e} = 0$ under rational expectations (46).

4. With $B = 0$, the effect of a change in M on e and V is given by h_M^e and h_M^V.

5. Note that to obtain the result that money is neutral, it is not sufficient to set $B = 0$ in (59f). One also has to replace (59f) by

$$\frac{dF}{dM} = \begin{vmatrix} -\Omega_1 & -\dfrac{(M - l_w W)\alpha}{pV} & \dfrac{l_w - 1}{p} \\[2ex] -\Omega_2 & \Omega_9 & (1 + x_a)\dfrac{a_w}{p} \\[2ex] \Omega_4 & -\Omega_{10} & \dfrac{V}{p}x_a a_w \end{vmatrix} \Delta_4^{-1}.$$

The neutrality results is more easily established through inspection of the long-run equilibrium conditions (28)–(30).

References

Ando, Albert, and Karl Shell (1975). "Demand for Money in a General Portfolio Model in the Presence of an Asset That Dominates Money," appendix to "Some Reflections on Describing Structures of Financial Sectors," in Gary Fromm and Lawrence R. Klein, eds., *The Brookings Model: Perspectives and Recent Developments*, Amsterdam, North-Holland.

Branson, William H. (1972). "Macroeconomic Equilibrium with Portfolio Balance in Open Economies," Seminar Paper No. 22, Stockholm, Institute for International Economic Studies.

Branson, William H. (1976). "The Dual Roles of the Government Budget and the Balance of Payments in the Movement from Short-Run to Long-Run Equilibrium," *Quarterly Journal of Economics*, Vol. 90, No. 3, August.

Branson, William H. (1977). "Asset Markets and Relative Prices in Exchange Rate Determination," *Sozialwissenschaftliche Annalen*. Reprint in International Finance No. 20, Princeton, NJ, Princeton University, International Finance Section, 1980.

Branson, William H., and Julio Rotemberg (1980). "International Adjustment With Wage Rigidity," *European Economic Review*, May.

Bruno, Michael (1978). "Exchange Rates, Import Costs and Wage-Price Dynamics," *Journal of Political Economy*, Vol. 86, No. 3, June.

Buiter, Willem H. (1975). Temporary and Long-Run Equilibrium, New York, Garland Publishing, Inc.

Buiter, Willem H. (1978). "Short-Run and Long-Run Effects of External Disturbances under a Floating Exchange Rate," *Economica*, Vol. 45, No. 179, August.

Dornbusch, Rudiger (1976). "Expectations and Exchange Rate Dynamics," *Journal of Political Economy*, Vol. 84, No. 6, December.

Dornbusch, Rudiger (1980). "Exchange Rate Economics: Where Do We Stand?," *Brookings Papers on Edonomic Activity*, No. 1.

Dornbusch, Rudiger, and Stanley Fischer (1980). "Exchange Rates and the Current Account," *American Economic Review*, Vol. 70, No. 5, December.

Katseli-Papaefstratiou, Louka T., and Nancy Peregrim Marion (1980). "Adjustment to Variations in Imported Input Prices: The Role of Economic Structure," National Bureau of Economic Research Working Paper No. 501, July.

Mundell, Robert A. (1961). "Flexible Exchange Rates and Employment Policy," *Canadian Journal of Economics and Political Science*, Vol. 27, No. 4, November.

Mundell, Robert A. (1963). "Capital Mobility and Stabilization Policy under Fixed and Flexible Exchange Rates," *Canadian Journal of Economics and Political Science*, Vol. 29, No. 4, November.

Mundell, Robert A. (1968). *International Economics*, New York, Macmillan.

Obstfeld, Maurice (1980). "Imperfect Asset Substitutability and Monetary Policy under Fixed Exchange Rates," *Journal of International Economics*, Vol. 10, No. 2, May.

Whitman, Marina v. N. (1975). "Global Monetarism and the Monetary Approach to the Balance of Payments," *Brookings Papers in Economic Activity*, No. 3.

10

Exchange Market Intervention Policies in a Small Open Economy

Stephen J. Turnovsky

Traditionally, the international macroeconomic literature has been concerned almost exclusively with analyzing perfectly fixed or perfectly flexible exchange rate systems. Yet both of these regimes represent polar forms of intervention policy. In the former, the domestic monetary authorities continually intervene in the foreign exchange market so as to maintain the exchange rate at some given target level. In the latter case, the domestic monetary authorities abstain from any active intervention, allowing the exchange rate to fluctuate freely in response to market forces. Intermediate between these two extremes is that of a "managed float" in which the monetary authorities intervene partly to offset movements in the exchange rate, so that the adjustment to changes in market pressure are met by a combination of both movements in the exchange rate and the accumulation or decumulation of foreign reserves. The intensity with which the domestic monetary authorities intervene in the foreign exchange market can be treated as a policy parameter, subject to their choice. Accordingly, it is natural to address the question of the optimal degree of intervention. This issue is the topic of the present chapter.

The question of optimal exchange market intervention has begun to receive attention in the literature. Boyer (1979) and Roper and Turnovsky (1980) analyze the problem by extending the framework developed by Poole (1970) in his well-known analysis of the monetary instrument problem. These analyses are based on the assumption that the price of domestic output remains fixed. While this assumption may be convenient for pedagogic purposes, it obviously needs to be relaxed if the analysis is to be at all relevant for current conditions in which the price mechanism is one key channel through which the international transmission of distur-

I wish to thank Bill Branson, Don Hanson, and Don Roper for helpful comments on a previous version of this chapter.

bances takes place. Another recent paper, by Buiter (1979), analyzes intervention policy in terms of discrete time control theory. Casting the intervention rule in the form of a feedback control law is restrictive, however, because current intervention is related only to past rather than present market data.[1] Some market data, such as the exchange rate and the quantity of central bank liabilities outstanding, are observable on a fairly current basis. As Kareken, Muench, and Wallace (1973) have shown in their work on optimal monetary strategy for a closed economy, currently observable data provides information about the sources of random shocks to the economy, the exploitation of which allows a greater degree of stability to be achieved in the economy.[2]

The present chapter analyzes optimal intervention policy in a small open economy in which the domestic price level, as well as domestic real output, is endogenously determined, with the policymaker's objective being to stabilize a function involving both these variables. Particular attention is devoted to exchange rate expectations and price expectations, both of which are assumed to be formed rationally. Also, the analysis in this chapter follows the Kareken, Muench, and Wallace strategy in considering an intervention policy designed to exploit the information contained in observable market data.

10.1 A Small Open Economy

In order to keep the technical details to a minimum, we shall base our analysis on the simplest model. Specifically we shall assume that there is one traded commodity whose price in terms of foreign currency is given. Also, there is a single traded bond, with the domestic bond market perfectly integrated with that in the rest of the world. Thus purchasing power parity and interest rate parity hold throughout.

The model can be summarized as follows:[3]

$$P_t = Q_t + E_t, \tag{1a}$$

$$M_t - P_t = \alpha_1 Y_t - \alpha_2 r_t + u_{1t}, \tag{1b}$$

$$r_t = \Omega_t + E_{t+1,t}^* - E_t, \tag{1c}$$

$$M_t = \overline{M} - \mu(E_t - \overline{E}), \tag{1d}$$

$$Y_t - \hat{Y} = \gamma(P_t - P_{t,t-1}^*) + u_{2t}, \tag{1e}$$

while for any variable, X say,

$$X_{s,t}^* = \mathscr{E}_t(X_s), \tag{1f}$$

where

$\mathscr{E}_t$ = conditional expectations operator, conditional on information at time t,

P_t = domestic price of the traded good at time t, expressed in logarithms,

Q_t = world price of the traded good at time t, expressed in logarithms,

E_t = current exchange rate (measured in units of the domestic currency per unit of foreign currency), expressed in logarithms,

$\overline{E}$ = equilibrium (steady-state) level of E, endogenously determined,

M_t = domestic nominal money supply, expressed in logarithms,

Y_t = real domestic output at time t, expressed in logarithms,

$\hat{Y}$ = full employment level of Y,

r_t = domestic nominal interest rate at time t,

Ω_t = foreign nominal interest rate at time t,

$\overline{M}$ = fixed exogenous component of the domestic nominal supply,

$E^*_{t+s,t}$ = expectation of E for time $t + s$, held at time $t, s = 1, 2, \ldots$, all t,

$P^*_{t+s,t}$ = expectation of P for time $t + s$, held at time $t, s = 1, 2, \ldots$, all t,

u_{1t} = stochastic distrubance in demand for domestic money,

u_{2t} = stochastic disturbance in domestic output supply,

The equations of the model are in the main fairly standard. Given purchasing power parity, the domestic price of a freely traded commodity equals the price abroad multiplied by the exchange rate. Equation (1a) is just the logarthmic version of this relation. The domestic monetary sector is summarized by equations (1b)–(1d). The first of these equations describes the domestic *LM* curve, making the usual assumption that all domestic money is held by domestic residents, who also hold no foreign currency.[4] The assumption of perfect capital market integration is embodied in the interest rate parity condition (1c). The intervention policy is specified by (1d), which describes the degree of intervention by the authority as a function of the observed deviation of the exchange rate from its long-run equilibrium level and which the authorities are assumed to know. The limiting cases $\mu = \infty$, $\mu = 0$ correspond to fixed and flexible regimes, respectively, while any finite, nonzero value of μ describes a managed float. A policy of setting $\mu > 0$ implies that if the current exchange rate is above its long-run level, the monetary authorities should introduce a monetary contraction (set M below $\overline{M}$), thereby reducing the pressure on the exchange rate. Differentiating (1d) with respect to t implies $\dot{M} = -\mu \dot{E}$; that is, the domestic money supply is decreased at a rate which is proportional to the rate of exchange depreciation. Such a policy is often described as "leaning against the wind." If $\mu < 0$, the monetary authorities react to a devaluating exchange rate by adopting an expansionary policy, thereby adding to the pressure on the exchange rate. This may be referred to as "leaning with the wind." The optimal intervention policy is to choose μ to optimize an objective, yet to be specified, and as we shall demonstrate, an optimal policy may involve either $\mu > 0$ or $\mu < 0$, depending upon the primary source of the stochastic disturbances. Note that the reaction function (1d) is expressed in terms of current values of M and E, which are therefore assumed to be instantly observable.[5]

The supply of domestic output is specified by (1e). This relation postulates the deviation in output from its full employment level to depend upon the unanticipated component of the current domestic price of output. This formulation resembles a Lucas (1973) supply function, although as Flood (1979) has argued with both international and intranational trading, this rationale is inappropriate. Rather, it may be justified in terms of the wage determination model of Gray (1976) and Fischer (1977a). Finally, equation (1f) describes the rationality of expectations.

The two domestic stochastic disturbances u_{1t}, u_{2t} are assumed to have zero means, and finite second moments satisfying

$$\mathscr{E}(u_{1t}) = \mathscr{E}(u_{2t}) = 0, \tag{2a}$$

$$\mathscr{E}(u_{1t}^2) = \sigma_1^2, \qquad \mathscr{E}(u_{2t}^2) = \sigma_2^2, \qquad \mathscr{E}(u_{1t}u_{2t}) = \sigma_1\sigma_2\rho, \tag{2b}$$

where ρ is the correlation coefficient between the two variables. While we have written u_{1t} as reflecting a stochastic disturbance in demand, it can equally well be interpreted (with sign change) as being a stochastic disturbance in supply. The two foreign variables in the system Ω_t, Q_t are also assumed to be random, being described by

$$Q_t = \bar{Q} + q_t, \tag{3a}$$

$$\Omega_t = \bar{\Omega} + \omega_t, \tag{3b}$$

where $\bar{Q}, \bar{\Omega}$ are constant (see appendix) and

$$\mathscr{E}(q_t) = \mathscr{E}(\omega_t) = 0, \tag{4a}$$

$$\mathscr{E}(q_t^2) = \sigma_q^2, \qquad \mathscr{E}(\omega_t^2) = \sigma_\omega^2, \qquad \mathscr{E}(q_t\omega_t) = \sigma_q\sigma_\omega\eta, \tag{4b}$$

while η denotes the corresponding correlation coefficient. In addition, all random variables are assumed to be independently distributed over time and for simplicity we assume that domestic and foreign variables are uncorrelated. This enables us to distinguish quite clearly between domestic and foreign stochastic influences.

But whereas q_t, ω_t are exogenous to the small country, they are themselves endogenously determined in the rest of the world, reflecting the various disturbances occurring there. It is important to recognize this endogeneity when it comes to determining the optimal degree of intervention. This is because the sign of the correlation coefficient, η, which appears in the expression for the optimal degree of intervention depends crucially upon the origin of the random fluctuations in the foreign price level and interest rate.

To determine q_t and ω_t, it is reasonable, given the small-country assumption of the domestic economy, to treat the rest of the world as effectively a closed economy. As such, we shall assume that its structure is described by

$$Z_t = d_1' Z_t - d_2'[\Omega_t - (Q_{t+1,t}^* - Q_t)] + v_{0t}, \tag{5a}$$

$$\overline{M}' - Q_t = \alpha_1' Z_t - \alpha_2' \Omega_t + v_{1t}, \tag{5b}$$

$$Z_t - \hat{Z} = \gamma'(Q_t - Q_{t,t-1}^*) + v_{2t}, \tag{5c}$$

where Z_t denotes output in the rest of the world, with $\hat{Z}$ its full employment level; $\overline{M}'$ denotes the nominal money supply in the rest of the world, taken to be fixed exogenously. These three equations describe output market equilibrium, money market equilibrium, and output supply function, respectively, in the rest of the world, with v_{0t}, v_{1t}, v_{2t} denoting the corresponding random disturbances assumed to have zero means and finite variances $\sigma_0'^2$, $\sigma_1'^2$, $\sigma_2'^2$, respectively. While v_{1t} has been introduced in the form of a random disturbance in the foreign demand for money, it may equally well (with sign change) be interpreted as being a random disturbance in the foreign supply of money. We shall refer to v_{1t} quite neutrally as being a disturbance in the monetary sector. As shown in the appendix, the solutions for the two foreign variables, q_t, ω_t which impinge on the domestic economy are

$$q_t = \frac{\alpha_2' v_{0t} - d_2' v_{1t} - [(1 - d_1')\alpha_2' + \alpha_1' d_2']v_{2t}}{\gamma'[\alpha_2'(1 - d_1') + \alpha_1' d_2'] + d_2'(1 + \alpha_2')}, \tag{6a}$$

$$\omega_t = \frac{(1 + \alpha_1'\gamma')v_{0t} + [\gamma'(1 - d_1') + d_2']v_{1t} + [d_2'\alpha_1' - (1 - d_1')]v_{2t}}{\gamma'[\alpha_2'(1 - d_1') + \alpha_1' d_2'] + d_2'(1 + \alpha_2')}. \tag{6b}$$

From (6a) and (6b) it is immediately apparent that the sign of the correlation between q_t and ω_t depends critically upon the source of the random disturbances abroad.[6] For example, if the only foreign random disturbances are in output demand, then an increase in v_{0t} will raise both q_t and

ω_t proportionately, so that $\eta = 1$. On the other hand, for random fluctuations in the monetary sector, $\eta = -1$, while for disturbances originating on the supply side $\eta = 1$ or -1, depending upon whether $d_2'\alpha_1' - (1 - d_1') \gtrless 0$.

The steady-state or stationary equilibrium of the small open economy being considered is defined by setting all disturbances in (1a)–(1e) to zero and assuming that expectations are realized. Denote the steady state by bars; then this can be summarized by

$$\bar{P} = \bar{Q} + \bar{E}, \tag{7a}$$

$$\bar{M} - \bar{P} = \alpha_1 \bar{Y} - \alpha_2 \bar{r}, \tag{7b}$$

$$\bar{r} = \bar{\Omega}, \tag{7c}$$

$$\bar{Y} = \hat{Y}. \tag{7d}$$

These four equations determine the steady-state equilibrium values of the four endogenous variables $\bar{r}$, $\bar{Y}$, $\bar{E}$, $\bar{P}$. It should be noted that these equilibrium values relate to the means of the long-run distributions of the random variables r_t, Y_t, E_t, P_t, not conditional on any knowledge of disturbances.

Differentiating these equations with respect to $\bar{M}$, $\bar{Q}$, we deduce the following familiar neutrality properties:

$$\frac{d\bar{P}}{d\bar{M}} = \frac{d\bar{E}}{d\bar{M}} = 1, \qquad \frac{d\bar{Y}}{d\bar{M}} = \frac{d\bar{r}}{d\bar{M}} = 0; \tag{8}$$

$$\frac{d\bar{E}}{d\bar{Q}} = -1, \qquad \frac{d\bar{Y}}{d\bar{Q}} = \frac{d\bar{r}}{d\bar{Q}} = \frac{d\bar{P}}{d\bar{Q}} = 0. \tag{9}$$

A 1% increase in the exogenous component of the domestic money supply will raise the domestic level and exchange rate by 1%. It will have no effect on domestic output or interest rate, which are determined by real phenomena. A 1% increase in the equilibrium foreign price level will lead to a 1% revaluation of the domestic exchange rate, insulating the remaining domestic variables fully from this disturbance.

Substracting (7) from (1), the behavior of the system can be expressed in the following deviation form:

$$p_t = q_t + e_t, \tag{10a}$$

$$-\mu e_t - p_t = \alpha_1 y_t - \alpha_2 [e_{t+1,t}^* - e_t] + u_{1t} - \alpha_2 \omega_t, \tag{10b}$$

$$y_t = \gamma(p_t - p_{t,t-1}^*) + u_{2t}, \tag{10c}$$

where lowercase letters denote deviations, that is, $p_t \equiv p_t - \bar{P}$, and so forth, and for convenience r_t and m_t have been eliminated. Equations (10a)–(10c) yield three stochastic difference equations in domestic output y_t, the domestic price of output p_t and its expectations, together with the exchange rate e_t and its expectation.

10.2 Solution of System

There are various procedures for solving the system (10). The most convenient in the present context is the original method proposed by Muth (1961). The reason is that this highlights certain nonuniqueness problems which may characterize rational expectations systems (see Taylor, 1977).

We begin by writing (10a)–(10c) in the following matrix form:

$$
\begin{bmatrix} 0 & 1 & -1 \\ \alpha_1 & 1 & \mu + \alpha_2 \\ 1 & -\gamma & 0 \end{bmatrix} \begin{bmatrix} y_t \\ p_t \\ e_t \end{bmatrix} = \begin{bmatrix} q_t \\ \alpha_2 e^*_{t+1,t} - u_{1t} + \alpha_2 \omega_t \\ -\gamma p^*_{t,t-1} + u_{2t} \end{bmatrix}. \tag{11}
$$

Taking conditional expectations of (10a) at time $t - 1$ and noting that q_t is assumed to be independently distributed over time, we have

$$
p^*_{t,t-1} = e^*_{t,t-1}. \tag{12}
$$

Solving (11) for e_t and using (12), we derive the following equation involving e_t and its conditional expectations:

$$
(1 + \alpha_2 + \mu + \alpha_1 \gamma)e_t = \alpha_2 e^*_{t+1,t} + \alpha_1 \gamma e^*_{t,t-1} + \xi_t, \tag{13}
$$

where

$$
\xi_t \equiv -u_{1t} - \alpha_1 u_{2t} + \alpha_2 \omega_t - (1 + \alpha_1 \gamma)q_t. \tag{14}
$$

We now propose a solution for e_t of the form

$$
e_t = \delta_0 \xi_t + \delta_1 \xi_{t-1} + \delta^2 \xi_{t-2} + \cdots, \tag{15}
$$

where δ_i are parameters to be determined and ξ_{t-i} are defined by (14). Taking conditional expectations of (15) at time $t - 1$, we have

$$
e^*_{t,t-1} = \delta_1 \xi_{t-1} + \delta_2 \xi_{t-2} + \cdots. \tag{16}
$$

Calculating $e^*_{t+1,t}$ from (16) and substituting this expression with $e^*_{t,t-1}$, e_t back into (13) yields

$$
(1 + \alpha_2 + \mu + \alpha_1 \gamma)[\delta_0 \xi_t + \delta_1 \xi_{t-1} + \delta_2 \xi_{t-2} \cdots]
$$
$$
= \alpha_2 [\delta_1 \xi_t + \delta_2 \xi_{t-1} + \cdots] + \alpha_1 \gamma [\delta_1 \xi_{t-1} + \delta_2 \xi_{t-2} + \cdots] + \xi_t, \tag{17}
$$

which is a set of identities in the parameters δ_i. Equating coefficients of ξ_{t-i} we obtain the following relations:

$$\delta_0 = \frac{1 + \alpha_2\delta_1}{1 + \alpha_2 + \mu + \alpha_1\gamma}, \tag{18a}$$

$$\delta_{i+1} = \left(\frac{1 + \alpha_2 + \mu}{\alpha_2}\right)^i \delta_1, \tag{18b}$$

where δ_1 is a constant yet to be determined.

Substitute from (18a) and (18b) into (15); then the solution for e_t is

$$e_t = \left(\frac{1 + \alpha_2\delta_1}{1 + \alpha_2 + \mu + \alpha_1\gamma}\right)\xi_t + \delta_1[\xi_{t-1} + \theta\xi_{t-2} + \theta^2\xi_{t-3}\cdots], \tag{19a}$$

where

$$\theta \equiv \frac{1 + \alpha_2 + \mu}{\alpha_2}. \tag{20}$$

Moreover, taking conditional expectations of (19a), which yields $e^*_{t,t-1}$, and using (12), we may substitute for e_t, $p^*_{t,t-1}$ back into (10a), (10c) to obtain the following solutions for p_t and y_t:

$$y_t = \gamma\left(\frac{1 + \alpha_2\delta_1}{1 + \alpha_2 + \mu + \alpha_1\gamma}\right)\xi_t + \gamma q_t + u_{2t}, \tag{19b}$$

$$p_t = \left(\frac{1 + \alpha_2\delta_1}{1 + \alpha_2 + \mu + \alpha_1\gamma}\right)\xi_t + \delta_1[\xi_{t-1} + \theta\xi_{t-2} + \theta^2\xi_{t-3}\cdots] + q_t. \tag{19c}$$

It is evident from (19a) and (19c) that whether the asymptotic variances of e_t and p_t, σ_e^2 and σ_p^2, respectively, are infinite or finite depends critically upon whether θ lies outside or inside the unit circle. This in turn depends upon the intervention parameter μ, and the two cases $|\theta| > 1, |\theta| < 1$ need to be treated separately. We shall refer to these two cases as characterizing unstable intervention and stable intervention, respectively.

10.2.1 Unstable Intervention

A necessary and sufficient condition for θ to lie outside the unit circle and for the intervention to imply instability is that[7]

$$\text{either } \mu > -1 \quad \text{ or } \mu < -(1 + 2\alpha_2). \tag{21a}$$

In this case, as long as $\delta_1 \neq 0$, the asymptotic variances σ_e^2, σ_p^2 will both be infinite. Let us impose the requirement that these asymptotic variances remain finite. It then follows that $\delta_1 = 0$, and the solutions for domestic output and the associated price level are

$$
y_t = \frac{\gamma(\alpha_2 + \mu)q_t + (1 + \alpha_2 + \mu)u_{2t} + \gamma(\alpha_2\omega_t - u_{1t})}{1 + \alpha_2 + \mu + \alpha_1\gamma}, \tag{22a}
$$

$$
p_t = \frac{(\alpha_2 + \mu)q_t - \alpha_1 u_{2t} + \alpha_2\omega_t - u_{1t}}{1 + \alpha_2 + \mu + \alpha_1\gamma}. \tag{22b}
$$

That is, both y_t and p_t fluctuate in response to the domestic random variables (u_{1t}, u_{2t}) as well as the foreign random variables (q_t, ω_t), which themselves are generated by (6a), (6b). Note that the intervention parameter affects how both variables respond to all the random variables.

The notion that an intervention rule satisfying (21a) will lead to infinite asymptotic variances σ_e^2, σ_p^2 unless the exchange rate fluctuates independently over time (i.e., $\delta_1 = 0$) is not as surprising as may at first appear. Consider, for example, the case of a perfectly flexible exchange rate (no intervention, $\mu = 0$), which is consistent with this condition. It is known that under rational expectations such a system is inherently unstable in the sense that unless initial conditions are chosen appropriately, expectations of future exchange rates will diverge. Moreover, a policy of leaning against the wind ($\mu > 0$) will increase the tendency to diverge. This is because for given exchange rate expectations $e^*_{t,t-1}$, such a policy reduces the expected money supply, thereby forcing up the expected rate of interest, and hence the expected rate of exchange for the next period $e^*_{t+1,t-1}$, thereby accentuating the instability.

Indeed, the requirement that σ_e^2 remain finite is equivalent to the requirement that the time path of the conditional exchange rate expectations $e^*_{t+i,t-1}$ be stable as the forecast horizon $i \to \infty$. To see this consider the difference equation (13). Taking conditional expectations at time $t - 1$ for time $t + i$ yields

$$
(1 + \alpha_2 + \mu)e^*_{t+i,t-1} = \alpha_2 e^*_{t+i+1,t-1}, \tag{13}
$$

the solution to which is

$$
e^*_{t+i,t-1} = A\theta^i, \qquad i = 1, 2, \ldots,
$$

where A is an arbitrary constant and θ is as defined above. If θ lies outside the unit circle, $e^*_{t+i,t-1}$ will diverge unless the arbitrary constant A is set to zero. Indeed, setting $A = 0$ is precisely equivalent to setting $\delta_1 = 0$ in (19a). The rationale for this former procedure is usually given by appealing to transversality conditions for corresponding models based on optimizing behavior, which under appropriate conditions impose boundedness on expectations. Thus setting $A = 0$ and using (12), we have $e^*_{t,t-1} = p^*_{t,t-1} = 0$; that is, exchange rate expectations and price expectations must be static. The same conclusions can be obtained by setting $\delta_1 = 0$ in (19a) and taking conditional expectations at time $t - 1$.

Thus while we refer to the present case as being one of "unstable intervention," this term is something of a convenient shorthand. The system is more appropriately characterized as being "inherently" unstable in the sense that if it were to start from some arbitrary initial condition, it would diverge. However, by appropriate choice of initial condition the instability is eliminated, so that *in fact* the system remains stable.

10.2.2 Stable Intervention
Suppose now that

$$-(1 + 2\alpha_2) < \mu < -1, \tag{21b}$$

implying that $|\theta| < 1$. In this case, the requirement that the asymptotic variances σ_e^2, σ_p^2 remain finite imposes no restrictions on δ_1. For any arbitrary value δ_1, we can calculate the finite asymptotic variance

$$\sigma_e^2 = \left\{ \left(\frac{1 + \alpha_2\delta_1}{1 + \alpha_2 + \mu + \alpha_1\gamma} \right)^2 + \frac{\delta_1^2}{1 - \theta^2} \right\} \sigma_\xi^2, \tag{23}$$

and a corresponding expression can be determined for σ_p^2. The rational expectations solution to the system is accordingly nonunique.

One procedure for determining all the weights δ_1 uniquely is to appeal to the stronger requirement that the asymptotic variance, σ_e^2 say, be minimized. The value of δ_1 can thus be obtained by differentiating (23) with respect to δ_1 and setting $\partial\sigma_e^2/\partial\delta_1 = 0$. This procedure, however, is essentially arbitrary. There is no obvious market mechanism which ensures that σ_e^2 will be minimized in this way. Furthermore, the value of δ_1 which minimizes σ_e^2 is *not* the same as that which minimizes σ_p^2, and the question of what variances (if any) rational expectations do actually minimize is not at all clear. Indeed, the same objection might be raised with respect to the requirement adopted in section 10.2.1 that relevant asymptotic variances be finite, although as we have noted, in this case some justification may be provided by appealing to appropriate transversality conditions. In fact, in the present instance, choosing δ_1 to minimize σ_e^2 (or σ_p^2) turns out to be extremely cumbersome. It yields a complicated solution for y_t and p_t, rendering the subsequent determination of the optimal intervention policy too complicated to be of much interest.

However, in the absence of any fully developed theory of rational expectations in disequilibrium, some arbitrary procedure such as the above must be followed in order to determine the weights uniquely. Accordingly, we shall choose a modification of the Taylor procedure, which at least is analytically simple yet able to illustrate the main issues involved. Specifically, we shall assume that δ_1 is chosen to minimize the conditional variance of e_t, $\mathcal{E}_{t-1}[e_t - \mathcal{E}_{t-1}(e_t)]^2$. From (19a) we obtain

$$\mathcal{E}_{t-1}[e_t - \mathcal{E}_{t-1}(e_t)]^2 = \left(\frac{1 + \alpha_2\delta_1}{1 + \alpha_2 + \mu + \alpha_1\gamma}\right)^2 \sigma_\xi^2, \tag{24}$$

which is minimized by setting

$$\delta_1 = -1/\alpha_2. \tag{25}$$

Substituting (25) into (19b) and (19c) gives these solutions for y_t and p_t:

$$y_t = \gamma q_t + u_{2t}, \tag{26a}$$

$$p_t = \frac{-1}{\alpha_2}[\xi_{t-1} + \theta\xi_{t-2} + \theta^2\xi_{t-3} + \cdots] + q_t. \tag{26b}$$

From (26a) it is seen that in this case y_t is independent of u_{1t} and ω_t and, more significantly, is *invariant* with respect to the intervention parameter μ. The time path of prices is now generated by a distributed lag of all the past disturbances, the coefficient of which depends critically upon the intervention parameter.

The invariance of y_t with respect to μ is not a robust proposition. It depends critically upon the fact that we have chosen δ_1 to minimize (24) rather than (23).[8] While we readily acknowledge the arbitrariness of this choice, the interim justification for the whole approach provided by Taylor would seem to be at least as applicable to minimizing (25) as it is to minimizing (23). Taylor suggests that in the absence of a theory of transitional expectations, the procedure may be justified by appealing to the notion that since people have a preference for price stability, "collective rationality" will lead them to choose their expectations to generate the most stable system for the exchange rate. But since the expectations in the model pertain to a single period forecast horizon, it seems reasonable for the associated stability to relate to the single-period variances as well.

10.3 Determination of Optimal Intervention: General Analysis

We now turn to the question of the optimal degree of intervention. In choosing the optimal μ, we shall assume that the policymaker's objective is to minimize the asymptotic variance[9]

$$C(\mu) \equiv \lambda\sigma_y^2 + (1 - \lambda)\sigma_p^2, \qquad 0 \leq \lambda \leq 1. \tag{27}$$

That is, the objective is assumed to be to stabilize a weighted average of domestic real income and the domestic price level, with λ denoting the relative weight assigned to each of these objectives in the overall objective function. A value of $\lambda = 1$ means that the objective involves only income stability; if $\lambda = 0$, the sole concern is with price stability.

To determine the optimal μ, both the cases of unstable intervention and stable intervention must be considered. Furthermore, the optimal μ which emerges from the optimization must be consistent with the initial restriction imposed on μ by the stability consideration. The eventual choice of the optimal μ is obtained by comparing the asymptotic variance (27) in the two cases.

10.3.1 Unstable Intervention

As demonstrated in section 10.2, the solutions for y_t and p_t in this case are given by (22a) and (22b), respectively, with the intervention parameter μ satisfying

$$\text{either} \quad \mu > -1 \quad \text{or} \quad \mu < -(1 + 2\alpha_2). \tag{21a}$$

To calculate the objective function (27) prior to optimization, we introduce the following notation:

$$a_t \equiv \gamma q_t + u_{2t}, \tag{28a}$$

$$b_t \equiv u_{2t} + \gamma(\alpha_2\omega_t - u_{1t}), \tag{28b}$$

$$c_t \equiv q_t, \tag{28c}$$

$$d_t \equiv -\alpha_1 u_{2t} + \alpha_2\omega_t - u_{1t}. \tag{28d}$$

We then have

$$y_t = \frac{(\alpha_2 + \mu)a_t + b_t}{1 + \alpha_2 + \mu + \alpha_1\gamma}, \tag{29a}$$

$$p_t = \frac{(\alpha_2 + \mu)c_t + d_t}{1 + \alpha_2 + \mu + \alpha_1\gamma}, \tag{29b}$$

so that the objective function (27) becomes

$$C(\mu) = \frac{(\alpha_2 + \mu)^2[\lambda\sigma_a^2 + (1 - \lambda)\sigma_c^2] + [\lambda\sigma_b^2 + (1 - \lambda)\sigma_d^2]}{(1 + \alpha_2 + \mu + \alpha_1\gamma)^2}$$
$$+ \frac{2(\alpha_2 + \mu)[\lambda\sigma_{ab} + (1 - \lambda)\sigma_{cd}]}{(1 + \alpha_2 + \mu + \alpha_1\gamma)^2}, \tag{30}$$

where σ_a^2, etc. are the variances of the composite disturbances defined in (28), and σ_{ab} and σ_{cd} are the corresponding covariances. Using the definitions (28), these parameters can be expressed in terms of the variances and covariances of the underlying random variables in the system.

The optimal intervention policy is obtained by differentiating (30) with respect to μ and setting $\partial C/\partial \mu = 0$, yielding[10]

$$\mu = \hat{\mu}_1$$

$$= -\alpha_2 + \frac{[\lambda\sigma_b^2 + (1 - \lambda)\sigma_d^2]}{(1 + \alpha_1\gamma)[\lambda\sigma_a^2 + (1 - \lambda)\sigma_c^2] - [\lambda\sigma_{ab} + (1 - \lambda)\sigma_{cd}]}$$

$$- \frac{(1 + \alpha_1\gamma)[\lambda\sigma_{ab} + (1 - \lambda)\sigma_{cd}]}{(1 + \alpha_1\gamma)[\lambda\sigma_a^2 + (1 - \lambda)\sigma_c^2] - [\lambda\sigma_{ab} + (1 - \lambda)\sigma_{cd}]}. \tag{31}$$

However, the value $\hat{\mu}_1$ given by (31) must be consistent with unstable intervention, since that is the assumption underlying the solutions (22a), (22b), from which the objective function (30) is derived. In other words, $\hat{\mu}_1$ implied by (31) must satisfy either $\hat{\mu}_1 > -1$ or $\hat{\mu}_1 < -1 - 2\alpha_2$. If $\hat{\mu}_1$ as given by (31) lies in the range $-(1 + 2\alpha_2) < \hat{\mu}_1 < -1$, then one must set $\mu = -1$ or $\mu = -1 - 2\alpha_2$ (strictly letting μ tend to these values from above and below, respectively) and choose that value which yields the lower variance.[11]

10.3.2 Stable Intervention
The optimization in this case is much more straightforward. Output and the domestic price level are now given by (26a), (26b), with y_t being independent of the intervention parameter μ. Accordingly, the optimization of (27) simply reduces to minimizing σ_p^2. With p_t being generated by (26b), the asymptotic variances of p_t is

$$\sigma_p^2 = \sigma_q^2 + \frac{\sigma_\xi^2}{\alpha_2^2 - (1 + \alpha_2 + \mu)^2},$$

where σ_ξ^2 denotes the variance of ξ_t. This is minimized by setting

$$\mu = \hat{\mu}_2 \equiv -(1 + \alpha_2), \tag{32}$$

which obviously lies within the stable region and is therefore consistent with those values of μ for which p_t is generated by (26b). Hence, if μ is to be chosen in the range $(-1 - 2\alpha_2, -1)$, then the solution is always (32). This expression is much simpler than the policy in the unstable case, (31), and in contrast to it, is independent of the variances and covariances of the underlying random disturbances. The corresponding minimized value of the objective function in this case is

$$\lambda[\sigma_2^2 + \gamma^2\sigma_q^2] + (1 - \lambda)[\sigma_q^2 + \sigma_\xi^2/\alpha_2^2]. \tag{33}$$

The overall optimal degree of intervention, μ°, can now be obtained by considering the various cases in turn. First, the asymptotic variance (30) corresponding to $\hat{\mu}_1$ is calculated; second, if $\hat{\mu}_1$ lies within the range $-(1 + 2\alpha_2) < \hat{\mu}_1 < -1$, the variances corresponding to the limiting values $\mu = -1$, $\mu = -1 - 2\alpha_2$, are also calculated; third, the variance (33) corresponding to stable intervention is calculated. The optimal policy is then determined as being the one which yields the lowest variance.

In general, the properties of the optimal intervention policy, insofar as it is given by (31), are complex. Thus, in order to obtain more insight, it is important to focus on the separate stochastic disturbances in turn. This shall be undertaken in section 10.4. In concluding the present discussion, we wish to make two observations. First, since μ does not in general equal ∞ or 0, fixed or flexible rates that correspond to these extreme values are not generally optimal. Second the optimal policy may involve either leaning against the wind ($\mu > 0$) or leaning with the wind ($\mu < 0$).

10.4 Optimal Intervention Policy: Specific Cases

Because of the intractability of the general expression (31), we now focus on the optimal intervention policy corresponding to the separate individual random disturbances, taken one at a time. We shall deal with the domestic and foreign disturbances in turn. In most cases it is convenient to focus on the solutions (22), (24) for y_t, p_t directly.

10.4.1 Domestic Disturbances

Domestic monetary disturbance μ_{1t} If the only stochastic disturbance in the economy occurs in the domestic monetary sector (i.e., $u_{2t} \equiv q_t \equiv \omega_t \equiv 0$), the optimal intervention policy (31) is $\hat{\mu}_1 = \infty$. Setting $\hat{\mu} = \infty$ in the solutions for y_t, p_t corresponding to unstable intervention (22a), (22b), we see that this implies

$$y_t \equiv p_t \equiv 0,$$

and hence

$$\sigma_y^2 = \sigma_p^2 = 0.$$

The optimal policy corresponding to stable intervention $\hat{\mu}_2 = -(1 + \alpha_2)$ yields

$$\sigma_y^2 = 0, \qquad \sigma_p^2 = \sigma_1^2/\alpha_2^2.$$

Thus setting $\mu^\circ = \infty$, so that the exchange rate is fixed, is the global optimum, stabilizing both prices and income perfectly.

The economic reasoning behind this result is straightforward. Given that the domestic price level is determined by the purchasing power parity condition (10a), it follows that if e is fixed, and there are no disturbances in q_t, then p_t must be fixed as well. It then follows from the domestic output supply function (10c) that if p_t is fixed, and if in addition (i) price expectations are static, as the stability condition requires, and (ii) there are no disturbances in domestic supply, then domestic output itself must also remain fixed.

The perfect stability of y_t and p_t can also be viewed as an example of the following general characteristic. As noted in the introduction, the current observability of certain market variables implies information on the sources of the random shocks in the economy. More specifically, the observability of m_t and e_t can be shown to be equivalent to the observability of a known linear combination of the random variables in the system.[12] With only *one* random variable present, it follows that its actual value can be inferred and be appropriately offset, thereby maintaining perfect stability of the system.

Domestic output supply disturbance u_{2t}. In this case, the optimal policy (31) corresponding to unstable intervention is

$$\hat{\mu}_1 = \frac{(1 - \lambda)\alpha_1 - \gamma\lambda(1 + \alpha_2)}{\gamma\lambda},$$

provided $\hat{\mu}_1 > -1$ or $\hat{\mu}_1 < -1 - 2\alpha_2$. It can also be shown that the value of the asymptotic variance corresponding to the two limiting values $C(\mu = -1)$, $C(\mu = -1 - 2\alpha_2)$ satisfies $C(\mu = -1) < C(\mu = -1 - 2\alpha_2)$, so that if $\hat{\mu}_1$ lies in the range $-1 - 2\alpha_2 < \mu_1 < -1$, the policy $\hat{\mu}_1 = -1$ will be superior. The optimal policy corresponding to stable intervention is as before, $\hat{\mu}_2 = -(1 + \alpha_2)$. A comparison of (30) for $\mu = -1$ with (33) shows that the stable intervention policy yields a larger asymptotic variance. Hence, the optimal intervention policy is[13]

$$\frac{\alpha_1}{\gamma\alpha_2} \begin{cases} > \dfrac{\lambda}{1 - \lambda}, & \text{then } \mu^\circ = \dfrac{\alpha_1(1 - \lambda)}{\gamma\lambda} - (1 + \alpha_2) \qquad (34a) \\[2mm] < \dfrac{\lambda}{1 - \lambda}, & \text{then } \mu^\circ = -1. \qquad (34b) \end{cases}$$

The optimal policy in this case depends critically upon the relative weight λ given to the two components of the overall objective function, and through this the targets of price stability and output stability involve a conflict of policy. If $\lambda = 0$, so that the policy maker is concerned entirely with price stability, the optimal intervention policy is one of a perfectly fixed exchange rate ($\mu = \infty$). If λ is small, that is, the objective function is weighted primarily toward price stability, then the optimal policy will be one of leaning against the wind. But for the very specific relative weight $\lambda = \alpha_1/(\alpha_1 + \gamma(1 + \alpha_2)) < 1$, a perfectly flexible rate will be optimal, while as the objective function becomes more heavily weighted toward output stability, the optimal policy will move toward being one of leaning with the wind.

Most discussions of intervention policy limit their attention to parameters which characterize leaning against the wind. The intuitive idea is that such a policy will alleviate fluctuations in the exchange rate, thereby increasing the stability within the economy. The fact that an optimal policy may involve exacerbating swings in the exchange rate is therefore of interest and merits further comment. Suppose (34a) holds, so that intervention is unstable. It follows from (12), (19a), together with the requirement that $\delta_1 = 0$, that $e_{t+1,t}^* = p_{t.t-1}^* = 0$. With the only stochastic disturbance being in u_{2t}, the system (10a)–(10c) reduces to[14]

$$-\mu e_t = (1 + \alpha_2)e_t + \alpha_1 y_t, \tag{10b'}$$

$$y_t = \gamma e_t + u_{2t}. \tag{10c'}$$

It is evident from (10b') that a policy of leaning with the wind ($\mu < 0$) will tend to provide greater insulation for y_t from the random disturbance u_{2t}, forcing it to be absorbed more fully by the exchange rate. Thus if, for instance, the exchange rate tends to appreciate, the domestic interest rate must take on higher values and m_t must be contracted to keep y_t from rising. If the objective function puts most of the weight on the stabilization of output, this strategy is clearly appropriate.

10.4.2 Foreign Disturbances

We now consider the various foreign disturbances. While these impinge on the domestic economy through the foreign variables q_t and ω_t, as discussed in section 10.1, these variables are themselves endogenous, reflecting more fundamental random disturbances abroad. These sources are indicated in equations (6a), (6b), and shall be considered in turn.

Foreign output demand disturbance v_{0t} In this case, the solution for y_t and p_t corresponding to unstable expectations, expressed in terms of the basic foreign random variable v_{0t}, is

$$y_t = \frac{\gamma[(\alpha_2 + \mu)\alpha_2' + \alpha_2(1 + \alpha_1'\gamma')]v_{0t}}{(1 + \alpha_2 + \mu + \alpha_1\gamma)\Delta'}, \tag{35a}$$

$$p_t = \frac{[(\alpha_2 + \mu)\alpha_2' + \alpha_2(1 + \alpha_1'\gamma')]v_{0t}}{(1 + \alpha_2 + \mu + \alpha_1\gamma)\Delta'}, \tag{35b}$$

where

$$\Delta' \equiv \gamma'[\alpha_2'(1 - d_1') + \alpha_1'd_2'] + d_2'(1 + \alpha_2) > 0.$$

The optimal policy (23) is

$$\hat{\mu}_1 = -\frac{\alpha_2}{\alpha_2'}(1 + \alpha_1'\gamma') - \alpha_2 < 0, \tag{36}$$

which when implemented yields $y_t \equiv p_t \equiv 0$. The policy (36) is consistent with instability as long as

$$\frac{\alpha_2}{\alpha_2'}(1 + \alpha_1'\gamma') < 1 - \alpha_2 \quad \text{or} \quad \frac{\alpha_2}{\alpha_2'}(1 + \alpha_1'\gamma') > 1 + \alpha_2. \tag{37a}$$

If, on the other hand, $\hat{\mu}_1$ lies in the stable range, so that

$$1 - \alpha_2 < \frac{\alpha_2}{\alpha_2'}(1 + \alpha_1'\gamma') < 1 + \alpha_2, \tag{37b}$$

we must also consider the limiting cases $\mu = -1$, $\mu = -(1 + 2\alpha_2)$, as well as the policy corresponding to stable expectations $\hat{\mu}_2 = -(1 + \alpha_2)$. It can be shown that of the two polar cases $C(\mu = -1) < C(\mu = -1 - 2\alpha_2)$, so that $\mu = -(1 + 2\alpha_2)$ is never optimal. However, whether $C(\mu = -1) \gtrless (33)$ depends in a rather complicated way upon the various parameter values, and either $\mu = -1$ or $\hat{\mu}_2 = -(1 + \alpha_2)$ may be optimal. The precise conditions favoring one or the other turn out to be cumbersome and not worth reporting. Suffice it to note that whether (37a) or (37b) holds, the optimal policy will always be one of leaning with th wind.

Foreign monetary disturbance v_{1t} While the foreign monetary disturbances have been introduced as occurring in demand, they may equally well be interpreted (with appropriate sign change) as representing stochastic disturbances in foreign money supply.[15] Whatever the interpretation one chooses to give, the solution for y_t and p_t, corresponding to unstable expectations, is

$$y_t = \frac{\gamma[-\mu d_2' + \alpha_2\gamma'(1 - d_1')]v_{1t}}{(1 + \alpha_2 + \mu + \alpha_1\gamma)\Delta'}, \tag{38a}$$

$$p_t = \frac{[-\mu d_2' + \alpha_2 \gamma'(1 - d_1')]v_{1t}}{(1 + \alpha_2 + \mu + \alpha_1 \gamma)\Delta'}. \tag{38b}$$

It is clear that the optimal policy is

$$\hat{\mu}_1 = \frac{\alpha_2 \gamma'(1 - d_1')}{d_2'} > 0. \tag{39}$$

This policy, which is one of leaning against the wind (and therefore consistent with $\mu > -1$ as required for instability of expectations), ensures that $y_t \equiv p_t \equiv 0$, and hence $\sigma_y^2 = \sigma_p^2 = 0$. It is therefore clearly the overall optimum.

Foreign output supply disturbance v_{2t} This case is similar to the case involving v_{0t}. The solutions for y_t and p_t corresponding to unstable expectations are

$$y_t = \frac{-\gamma[\mu[(1 - d_1')\alpha_2' + \alpha_1' d_2'] + \alpha_2(1 - d_1')(1 + \alpha_2')]v_{2t}}{(1 + \alpha_2 + \mu + \alpha_1 \gamma)\Delta'}, \tag{40a}$$

$$p_t = \frac{-[\mu[(1 - d_1')\alpha_2' + \alpha_1' d_2'] + \alpha_2(1 - d_1')(1 + \alpha_2')]v_{2t}}{(1 + \alpha_2 + \mu + \alpha_1 \gamma)\Delta'}. \tag{40b}$$

The optimal policy corresponding to (31) is

$$\hat{\mu}_1 = \frac{-\alpha_2(1 - d_1')(1 + \alpha_2')}{(1 - d_1')\alpha_2' + \alpha_1' d_2'}, \tag{41}$$

which when implemented yields perfect stabilization $y_t \equiv p_t \equiv 0$. For the solution to be consistent, we require that (41) satisfy (21a). If, instead it satisfies (21b), we must consider the limiting cases $\mu = -1$, $\mu = -(1 + 2\alpha_2)$, as well as the optimal policy for stable expectations $\hat{\mu}_2 = (1 + \alpha_2)$. As for the case involving v_{0t}, it can be shown that $\mu = -(1 + 2\alpha_2)$ is never optimal and that the choice between $\mu = -1$ and $\hat{\mu}_2 = -(1 + \alpha_2)$ depends in a rather complicated way upon the parameters of both the domestic and foreign economies. In any event, however, the optimal policy is one of leaning with the wind.

Taken together, these expressions for optimal intervention policies in the face of foreign random disturbances yield interesting conclusions. First, provided the random fluctuations in the foreign price level and foreign nominal interest rate originate in a *single* sector abroad, it may be possible to achieve perfect insulation of the domestic output and price level (in the sense $\sigma_y^2 = \sigma_p^2 = 0$) against such random fluctuations. This will generally require the domestic monetary authorities to engage in some form of active intervention policy, and except for very special cases a perfectly flexible rate will never be optimal. Perfect insulation can never be achieved by the simple intervention rule we are considering if the random fluctuations in q_t and ω_t reflect more than a single foreign disturbance.[16] In this case, however, the nonoptimality of perfectly flexible rates remains true.

Second, a comparison of the optimal policies for the three cases shows that the appropriate policy can vary quite dramatically, depending upon what factors the random fluctuations in the foreign price level and nominal interest rate are reflecting. In the cases involving v_{0t} and v_{2t} the appropriate policy is to lean with the wind, whereas in the case involving v_{1t} it is to lean against the wind. The reason for the difference involves the covariances between q_t and ω_t, which varies depending upon the source of the foreign random disturbances. In all cases, the critical expression determining y_t and p_t (for unstable intervention) is

$$\alpha_2(q_t + \omega_t) + \mu q_t$$

and in all three cases μ must be chosen to ensure that this expression is zero, thereby ensuring $y_t = p_t = 0$. In the cases involving v_{0t} and v_{2t} the covariance between q_t and ω_t is such as to make $\text{cov}(q_t + \omega_t, q_t) > 0$, while in the case involving v_{1t} we have $\text{cov}(q_t + \omega_t, q_t) < 0$. It is this change in the sign of the covariance which is the essential feature giving rise to the qualitative difference in the optimal policies.

10.5 Fixed versus Flexible Exchange Rates

One of the most extensively debated topics in international macroeconomics, going back to Friedman (1953) and Meade (1955), concerns the relative advantage of fixed versus flexible exchange rates. While these early discussions were conducted at a fairly general level, recently the issue has been reconsidered by a number of authors at a more formal level, but from the narrower perspective of the relative stability of the two regimes (see Turnovsky, 1976; Fischer, 1977b; Flood, 1979). Within the present context, the debate can be viewed as comparing the relative stability properties (in the sense of appropriate variances) of the two specific intervention policies corresponding to $\mu = 0$ (flexible rates) and $\mu = \infty$ (fixed rates). Just as in the earlier models, a general comparison in which all random variables appear simultaneously is quite impractical, and we shall focus on the separate random variables individually, in turn. We consider their effects on the variances of prices and income under the two regimes and summarize the results in table 10.1.[17]

Table 10.1
Fixed versus flexible exchange rates

	σ_y^2	σ_p^2

A. Domestic disturbances
(i) domestic monetary sector

$$\mu = 0 \qquad \left[\frac{\gamma}{1 + \alpha_2 + \alpha_1\gamma}\right]^2 \sigma_1^2 \qquad\qquad \frac{\sigma_1^2}{(1 + \alpha_2 + \alpha_1\gamma)^2}$$

$$\mu = \infty \qquad 0 \qquad\qquad\qquad\qquad\qquad 0$$

fixed rate is superior (optimal)

(ii) domestic supply of output

$$\mu = 0 \qquad \left[\frac{1 + \alpha_2}{1 + \alpha_2 + \alpha_1\gamma}\right]^2 \sigma_2^2 \qquad\qquad \left[\frac{\alpha_1}{1 + \alpha_2 + \alpha_2\gamma}\right] \sigma_2^2$$

$$\mu = \infty \qquad \sigma_2^2 \qquad\qquad\qquad\qquad\qquad 0$$

get a conflict: flexible rates favor income stability
                  fixed rates favor price stability

	σ_y^2	σ_p^2

B. Foreign disturbances
(i) foreign output demand

$$\mu = 0 \qquad \left[\frac{\gamma\alpha_2(1 + \alpha_2' + \alpha_1'\gamma')}{(1 + \alpha_2 + \alpha_1\gamma)\Delta'}\right]^2 \sigma_0'^2 \qquad \left[\frac{\alpha_2(1 + \alpha_2' + \alpha_1'\gamma')}{(1 + \alpha_2 + \alpha_1\gamma)\Delta'}\right]^2 \sigma_0'^2$$

$$\mu = \infty \qquad \left[\frac{\gamma\alpha_2'}{\Delta'}\right]^2 \sigma_0'^2 \qquad\qquad\qquad \left[\frac{\alpha_2'}{\Delta'}\right]^2 \sigma_0'^2$$

fixed rate is superior if $\alpha_2(1 + \alpha_1'\gamma') - \alpha_2'(1 + \alpha_1\gamma) > 0$
flexible rate is superior if $\alpha_2(1 + \alpha_1'\gamma') - \alpha_2'(1 + \alpha_1\gamma) < 0$

(ii) foreign monetary sector

$$\mu = 0 \qquad \left[\frac{\gamma\gamma'\alpha_2(1 - d_1')}{(1 + \alpha_2 + \alpha_1\gamma)\Delta'}\right]^2 \sigma_1'^2 \qquad \left[\frac{\gamma'\alpha_2(1 - d_1')}{(1 + \alpha_2 + \alpha_1\gamma)\Delta'}\right]^2 \sigma_1'^2$$

$$\mu = \infty \qquad \left[\frac{\gamma d_2'}{\Delta'}\right]^2 \sigma_1'^2 \qquad\qquad\qquad \left[\frac{d_2'}{\Delta'}\right]^2 \sigma_1'^2$$

fixed rate is superior if $\gamma'\alpha_2(1 - d_1') - d_2'(1 + \alpha_2 + \alpha_1\gamma) > 0$
flexible rate is superior if $\gamma'\alpha_2(1 - d_1') - d_2'(1 + \alpha_2 + \alpha_1\gamma) < 0$

(iii) foreign output supply

$$\mu = 0 \qquad \left[\frac{\gamma\alpha_2(1 - d_1')(1 + \alpha_2')}{(1 + \alpha_2 + \alpha_1\gamma)\Delta'}\right]^2 \sigma_2'^2 \qquad \left[\frac{\alpha_2(1 - d_1')(1 + \alpha_2')}{(1 + \alpha_2 + \alpha_1\gamma)\Delta'}\right]^2 \sigma_2'^2$$

$$\mu = \infty \qquad \left[\frac{\gamma[(1 - d_1')\alpha_2' + \alpha_1'd_2']}{\Delta'}\right]^2 \sigma_2'^2 \qquad \left[\frac{(1 - d_1')\alpha_2' + \alpha_1'd_2'}{\Delta'}\right]^2 \sigma_2'^2$$

fixed rate is superior if $\alpha_2[(1 - d_1') - \alpha_1'd_2'] - [(1 - d_1')\alpha_2' + \alpha_1'd_2'](1 + \alpha_1\gamma) > 0$
flexible rate is superior if $\alpha_2[(1 - d_1') - \alpha_1'd_2'] - [(1 - d_1')\alpha_2' + \alpha_1'd_2'](1 + \alpha_1\gamma) < 0$

Since the topic has been discussed at length elsewhere in the literature, our discussion can be brief. The superiority of a fixed exchange rate in the face of domestic monetary disturbances follows immediately from the result obtained previously that the fixed rate is in fact optimal. The choice of regime when the disturbances originate on the domestic supply side gives rise to a conflict. A fixed exchange rate provides a greater degree of price stability, but a lesser degree of income stability than does a flexible rate. The choice therefore depends critically upon how these two goals are weighted in the overall objective function. The reason for the conflict can be easily explained as follows. Under a fixed rate regime and with no foreign disturbances, given purchasing power parity, the domestic price level remains fixed [see (10a)]. With the expected price $p_{t,t-1}^{*} = 0$ [obtained by taking conditional expectations of (22b)] and the actual price level fixed, it follows from the domestic supply function (10c) that any random fluctuation u_{2t} is fully met by a corresponding fluctuation in output. On the other hand, under a flexible rate, the domestic price level is no longer fixed. Accordingly, any random disturbance in u_{2t} is shared between fluctuations in domestic output and fluctuations in the domestic price level. The amount of random fluctuation in output therefore declines, while the variation in the domestic price level is increased.

The choice between the two regimes in the face of foregin disturbances is in all cases ambiguous, depending upon the various parameters at home and abroad. No definitive conclusions can be drawn, and either regime may prove to provide greater stability. One case worth noting arises when the domestic economy is "similar" to the rest of the world in the sense that corresponding parameters are equal, that is, $\alpha_1 = \alpha_1'$, and so forth. Under this assumption, fixed and flexible rates yield equal stability in the case involving v_{0t}, while the flexible rate will be superior in the case involving v_{2t}. The relative stability where the disturbances originate in the foreign monetary sector remains indeterminate.

10.6 Concluding Comments

This chapter has investigated the question of the optimal degree of exchange market intervention. To illustrate the procedure, the model has been kept as simple as possible. However, even for such a simple model, no strong conclusions emerge. In general, it is seen that the optimal policy may require the monetary authorities to lean with or against the wind, depending upon the source of the random disturbances impinging on the domestic economy. Most policy discussions of intervention policy have been expressed in terms of the monetary authorities responding to downward market pressure by adopting a contractionary policy. The fact that quite the opposite may in fact be appropriate for maximizing domestic stability is quite significant.

The second general conclusion to be drawn is that the case for a perfectly flexible exchange rate is not very great, at least not from the viewpoint of domestic stability. Whereas, under appropriate circumstances—for example, when the disturbances originate in the domestic monetary sector—a fixed rate may be optimal, this is not the case for flexible rates, unless appropriate coefficients take on extreme values.[18] Furthermore, a fixed rate may provide greater stability in circumstances in which a traditionally flexible rate may be thought to be superior. For example, abstracting from capital gains resulting from the effects of exchange rate changes on the components of wealth denominated in different currencies—an issue not addressed in the present analysis—it is sometimes argued that flexible exchange rates will provide perfect insulation in the face of foreign monetary disturbances. The present analysis shows that this is not so. On the contrary, a conclusion of the comparison in section 10.5 is that a fixed rate may be superior, even in this case. This will be so if, for example, the domestic interest elasticity of the demand for money is sufficiently large.

Obviously it is difficult to extrapolate the implications of a simple model such as this to provide reliable guidance to real world intervention policies. But the conclusions of our analysis do suggest that the appropriate choice of policy is an extremely difficult one, being highly sensitive to relevant parameters in the domestic economy and the rest of the world, as well as the relative importance of the various sources of the random disturbances impinging on the economy. Clearly, reliable information on these empirical issues is a necessary ingredient for the implementation of appropriate intervention policies.

Appendix   Determination of Short-Run Solution in the Rest of the World

This appendix derives the expressions given in (6a) and (6b) in the text for q_t and ω_t in terms of the stochastic disturbances in the rest of the world.

We begin by recalling the specification of the behavioral relations in the rest of the world, (5a)–(5c):

$$Z_t = d_1' Z_t - d_2' [\Omega_t - (Q_{t+1,t}^* - Q_t)] + v_{0t}, \tag{A.1a}$$

$$\overline{M}' - Q_t = \alpha_1' Z_t - \alpha_2' \Omega_t + v_{1t}, \tag{A.1b}$$

$$Z_t - \hat{Z}_t = \gamma'(Q_t - Q_{t,t-1}^*) + v_{2t}, \tag{A.1c}$$

where all variables are as defined in the text. The deterministic steady-state equilibrium solution to this system, obtained by setting all stochastic disturbances to zero and assuming that expectations are realized, is

$$(1 - d_1')\overline{Z} = -d_2'\overline{\Omega}, \tag{A.2a}$$

$$\overline{M}' - \overline{Q} = \alpha_1'\overline{Z} - \alpha_2'\overline{\Omega}, \tag{A.2b}$$

$$\overline{Z} = \hat{Z}. \tag{A.2c}$$

Subtracting (A.1) from (A.2) and noting (3a), (3b), the system may be expressed in deviation form as

$$z_t = d_1' z_t - d_2'[\omega_t - (q_{t+1,t}^* - q_t)] + v_{0t}, \tag{A.3a}$$

$$-q_t = \alpha_1' z_t - \alpha_2' \omega_t - v_{1t}, \tag{A.3b}$$

$$z_t = \gamma'(q_t - q_{t,t-1}^*) + v_{2t}. \tag{A.3c}$$

Solving (A.3) for q_t yields the equation

$$[H + \gamma' d_2'(1 + \alpha_2')]q_t - Hq_{t,t-1}^* - \gamma' \alpha_2' d_2' q_{t+1,t}^*$$

$$= \gamma' \alpha_2' v_{0t} - \gamma' d_2' v_{1t} + Hv_{2t}, \tag{A.4}$$

where

$$H \equiv \alpha_2'(1 - d_1') + \alpha_1' d_2' > 0,$$

and taking expectations of (A.4) at time $t - 1$ for time $t + i$, we obtain the following difference equation in $q_{t+i,t-1}^*$:

$$(1 + \alpha_2')q_{t+i,t-1}^* - \alpha_2' q_{t+i+1,t-1}^* = 0, \qquad i = 0, 1, \ldots . \tag{A.5}$$

In order for this solution to be stable, we require

$$q_{t+i,t-1}^* = 0, \qquad i = 0, 1, \ldots, \quad \text{all } t. \tag{A.6}$$

Substituting (A.6) into (A.3), the three endogenous variables satisfy the matrix equation

$$\begin{bmatrix} 1 - d_1' & d_2' & d_2' \\ \alpha_1' & -\alpha_2' & 1 \\ 1 & 0 & -\gamma' \end{bmatrix} \begin{bmatrix} z_t \\ \omega_t \\ q_t \end{bmatrix} = \begin{bmatrix} v_{0t} \\ -v_{1t} \\ v_{2t} \end{bmatrix} . \tag{A.7}$$

The solution to this equation is

$$q_t = \frac{1}{\Delta'}[\alpha_2' v_{0t} - d_2' v_{1t} - [(1 - d_1')\alpha_2' + \alpha_1' d_2']v_{2t}], \tag{A.8a}$$

$$\omega_t = \frac{1}{\Delta'}[(1 + \alpha_1' \gamma')v_{0t} + [\gamma'(1 - d_1') + d_2']v_{1t}$$

$$+ [d_2' \alpha_1' - (1 - d_1')]v_{2t}], \tag{A.8b}$$

where Δ' is defined in section 10.4.2, thus yielding (6a), (6b) of the text, together with

$$z_t = \frac{1}{\Delta'}[\gamma' \alpha_2' v_{0t} - \gamma' d_2' v_{1t} + d_2'(1 + \alpha_2')v_{2t}], \tag{A.8c}$$

which is not required.

Notes

1. It is, of course, possible to formulate control laws in terms of current data, as well as past data, provided that the current data are immediately observable. Indeed, this is what is proposed here.

2. Other recent contributions to intervention policy that should be mentioned include Henderson (1979) and Cox (1980).

3. For simplicity we abstract from all issues pertaining to wealth accumulation.

4. We therefore abstract from the possibility of "currency substitution," an issue, which is receiving increasing attention in the international monetary literature.

5. In deriving the optimal intervention policy, it is important to distinguish between those variables which the authority can in effect currently observe and those that are, at least in the short run, unobservable. Given that data on exchange rates and the money supply are available with much greater frequency than income figures, we shall assume that E_t and M_t are observable and that Y_t is unobservable (at time t). This is one of the reasons why in general policymakers cannot stabilize income perfectly. The period of time for which this assumption is most applicable would be something like a month since income is usually observed only quarterly and weekly money figures have considerable noise.

6. The foreign stochastic demand disturbances satisfy the "adding up condition"
$$v_{0t} + v_{1t} + v_{3t} = 0,$$
where v_{3t} is the random disturbance in the foreign bond market, which has been eliminated by virtue of the overall foreign budget constraint. Thus the disturbances to v_{0t}, v_{1t} discussed in the text, are in both cases offset by corresponding changes in v_{3t}.

7. It is interesting to note that if $\alpha_2 = 0$, so that the LM curve is vertical, that only the unstable case exists.

8. When δ_1 is chosen to minimize (25), the resulting expression for y_t is a rather complicated function of μ. On the other hand, it is possible for the value of δ_1 which provides a *finite* asymptotic variance in the unstable case to be identical to that which yields the *minimized* variance in the stable case. If this is so, the solutions for y_t and p_t in the two cases will be given by the same expression. This phenomenon occurs if (following Flood, for example) we were to modify the interest rate parity condition (1c) to

$$r_t = \Omega_t + E^*_{t+1,t-1} - E^*_{t,t-1}$$

conditioning the expectations at time $t-1$. This specification, however, has the disadvantage of rendering the domestic interest rate as predetermined at time t.

9. The specification of the objective function in terms of the asymptotic variance is the standard approach in stabilization problems of this type. However, in the present context one might consider whether some shorter-run variance conditional on current information is more appropriate. This issue only arises in the stable case; in the case of unstable intervention, the system is always fluctuating around steady state, and so the conditional variances and the steady-state variance coincide.

10. The equation $\partial C / \partial \mu = 0$ has multiple roots, namely, (31) and $\mu = -(1 + \alpha_2 + \alpha_1 \gamma)$. Of these, (31) is consistent with the second-order condition $\partial^2 C / \partial \mu^2 > 0$. The second root yields a maximum rather than a minimum; indeed, when this value of μ is inserted into (30), the asymptotic variance becomes infinite.

11. In other words, we should consider $\mu = -1 + \varepsilon$, $\mu = -1 - 2\alpha_2 - \varepsilon$, where $\varepsilon > 0$ tends to zero. In the limit we have $\mu = -1+$, $\mu = -1 - 2\alpha_2 -$.

12. For example, setting $e^*_{t+1,t} = p^*_{t,t-1} = 0$ (as instability of the intervention rule implies) in (10a)–(10c), writing $m_t = -\mu e_t$, and eliminating y_t reduces these three equations to the single relation between m_t and e_t

$$m_t = (1 + \alpha_2 + \alpha_1 \gamma)e_t + u_{1t} + \alpha_1 u_{2t} + (1 + \alpha_1 \gamma)q_t - \alpha_2 \omega_t.$$

The observability of m_t, e_t, together with the fact that the coefficients are assumed to be known, implies that the composite disturbance $u_{1t} + \alpha_1 u_{2t} + (1 + \alpha_1 \gamma)q_t - \alpha_2 \omega_t$ is in effect observed. Roper and Turnovsky (1980) describe the above relation between m_t and e_t as measuring exchange market pressure.

13. Strictly speaking, the optimum in (34b) should be $\mu = -1 + \varepsilon$, where $\varepsilon > 0$ is infinitesimally small.

14. Perfect insulation of y_t would require $\mu = -(1 + \alpha_2)$. However, this is not feasible, as it is inconsistent with the requirement that intervention be unstable.

15. This is the form of foreign stochastic disturbance considered by Cox (1980).

16. This is because the correlation between q_t and ω_t is less than perfect, making it impossible to offset the disturbance exactly.

17. It is worth noting that the choice of exchange rate system under perfect capital mobility is equivalent to the familiar monetary instrument problem. The fixed exchange rate is equivalent to pegging the interest rate; the flexible rate corresponds to pegging the money supply.

18. For example, a flexible rate will be optimal in the face of foreign disturbances (from all sources) if $\alpha_2 = 0$.

References

Boyer, R. (1978). "Optimal Foreign Exchange Market Intervention," *Journal of Political Economy* 86, 1045–56.

Buiter, W. (1979). "Optimal Foreign Exchange Market Intervention with Rational Expectations," in J. Martin and A. Smith eds., *Trade and Payments Adjustment under Flexible Exchange Rates*, Macmillan, London.

Cox, W. M. (1980). "Unanticipated Money, Output, and Prices in the Small Economy," *Journal of Monetary Economics* 6.

Fischer, S. (1977a). "Wage Indexation and Macroeconomic Stability," in K. Bruner and A. Meltzer, eds., *Stabilization of the Domestic and International Economy*, North-Holland, Amsterdam.

Fischer, S. (1977b). "Stability and Exchange Rate Systems in a Monetarist Model of the Balance of Payments," in R. Aliber, ed., *The Political Economy of Monetary Reform*, Allanheld, Osmun and Co., Montclair, NJ.

Flood, R. (1979). "Capital Mobility and the Choice of Exchange Rate System," *International Economic Review* 20, 405–16.

Friedman, M. (1953). "The Case for Flexible Exchange Rates," in M. Friedman, ed., *Essays in Positive Economics*, University of Chicago Press, Chicago.

Gray, J. (1976). "Wage Indexation: A Macroeconomic Approach," *Journal of Monetary Economics* 2, 221–35.

Henderson, D. W. (1979). "Financial Policies in Open Economics," *American Economic Review, Papers and Proceedings*, 69, 232–39.

Lucas, R. E., Jr. (1973). "Some International Evidence on Output-Inflation Trade-offs," *American Economic Review* 63, 326–34.

Kareken, J. H., Muench, T., and N. Wallace, (1973). "Optimal Open Market Strategy: The Use of Information Variables," *American Economic Review* 63, 156–72.

Meade, J. (1955). "The Case for Variable Exchange Rates," *Three Banks Review* 3–27.

Muth, J. F. (1961). "Rational Expectations and the Theory of Price Movements," *Econometrica* 29, 315–35.

Poole, W. (1970). "Optimal Choice of Monetary Policy Instruments in a Simple Stochastic Macro Model," *Quarterly Journal of Economics* 84, 197–216.

Roper, D. E., and S. J. Turnovsky (1980). "Optimal Exchange Market Intervention in a Simple Stochastic Macro Model," *Canadian Journal of Economics* 13.

Taylor, J. (1977). "Conditions for Unique Solutions in Stochastic Macroeconomic Models with Rational Expectations," *Econometrica* 45, 1377–85.

Turnovsky, S. J. (1976). "The Relative Stability of Alternative Exchange Rate Systems in the Presence of Random Disturbances," *Journal of Money, Credit, and Banking* 8, 29–50.

11

Policy Interdependence under Flexible Exchange Rates: A Dynamic Analysis of Price Interactions

Willard E. Witte

During the 1960s economists and policymakers increasingly came to realize that the then existing system of fixed exchange rates implied definite restrictions on the extent to which individual countries could pursue independent economic policies. In a world which was increasingly characterized by integrated goods markets, interdependence seemed particularly strong with respect to domestic inflation rates. Theoretical underpinnings for the international transmission of inflation under fixed rates were easily worked out. Further, these theoretical models generally suggested that a flexible exchange rate system could completely insulate a country from unwanted changes in the overall level of foreign prices with appreciation of the domestic currency offsetting a rise in foreign relative to domestic prices. As a result, many (most?) economists hailed the adoption of flexible rates in the early 1970s as a means of shielding domestic economies from the effects of foreign inflation (and other external disturbances).

The period since, however, suggests that international interdependence has not been eliminated by the flexible rate system.[1] To be sure, the recent experience is not a faultless test. Exogenous events like the OPEC price shocks are bound to give an appearance of interdependence. Central bank intervention in foreign exchange markets has been frequent and often very heavy. Even so, it seems clear that the insulating properties of flexible rates are considerably less than perfect, particularly in the relatively short-run time frame which often seems most relevant to policymakers. Our purpose in this chapter is to investigate the dynamics of price and exchange rate adjustment as a partial explanation of such short-run imperfection.

I would like to thank Jeffrey Frankel and the editors for helpful comments on earlier drafts of this chapter.

In the next section we develop a two-country model characterized by noninstantaneous adjustment of the price level in each country. The exchange rate, by contrast, responds immediately to asset market conditions. In equilibrium, the model does exhibit independence of domestic inflation rates; price movements in each country will follow the expansion of its domestic money supply, and the exchange rate will move to maintain the appropriate relation between domestic and foreign prices. But in the short run, following a policy change or other shock to the system, non-insulation is possible. Monetary policy shifts in one country, for example, will have an immediate impact on the exchange rate and may produce a divergence between national price levels. If so, there will be a price movement response in *both* countries.

Section 11.2 examines the reaction of the system to a change in domestic monetary policy. A crucial element in the outcome is the adjustment of expectations following the change. This adjustment is handled on an admittedly somewhat ad hoc basis, and advocates of rational expectations may, as a consequence, consider the analysis seriously flawed. Our own feeling, spelled out below, is that the imposition of rationality in the context of short-run disequilibrium analysis is at least equally suspect. Nonrationality (implying continuous systemic error in expectations) is much harder to justify in an equilibrium setting, but long-run expectational accuracy is permitted by our analysis.

The analysis in section 11.2 concludes that domestic policy adjustments will have an unavoidable and perverse impact on the foreign inflation rate. In section 11.3 we examine the implications of a foreign response to this spillover. Such response has often in the past been viewed as a theoretical possibility of little empirical importance. Recent experience, especially during early 1980 when central banks seemed clearly to be reacting to each other, suggests it may now be more relevant. In our model the result of a foreign reaction, somewhat paradoxically, is to reduce the immediate effectiveness of the domestic policy in spite of the fact that foreign policy will move in the same direction as domestic policy. Section 11.4 summarizes our results and contains a few concluding comments.

11.1 Model

The model we develop in this section consists of two essentially identical countries. Each country is described by three equations, two relating to the domestic goods market and one to the money market. A seventh equation establishes a link between asset market conditions in the two countries. Goods markets are influenced by relative international prices, establishing a second link between the two economies. In what follows we shall concentrate initially on the domestic side of the model. The following notational conventions have been used, with exceptions as noted:

1. All variables are interpreted as logarithms except interest rates. Thus, $P = \ln(\text{price level})$, but $R = \text{interest rate}$.

2. Uppercase variable symbols represent the level of a variable. Lowercase variable symbols represent rates of change. That is, $p = dP/dt$. Dot notation is used for acceleration of variables. Thus, $\dot{p} = dp/dt$.

3. Foreign variables are indicated by an asterisk. For example, $P^* = \ln(\text{foreign price level})$.

4. Exogenous (or policy determined) variables are indicated by a bar, $\bar{Y}$.

5. A tilde over a variable is used to represent its current steady-state level.

6. Parameters are represented by lowercase letters with numerical subscripts. To avoid some clutter, different letters are used for corresponding domestic and foreign parameters. *All parameters are defined positively.*

The central elements of the model are the pair of equations describing the adjustment of domestic and foreign prices. These relate price movements to the terms of trade, the gap between output and capacity, and the expected inflation rate. For the domestic economy

$$p = a_1 T + a_2(Y - \bar{Y}) + \pi. \tag{1}$$

p is the rate of increase in domestic prices; T is the relative price of foreign to domestic good ($= P^* + E - P$); Y is domestic output; π is the expected inflation rate. Equation (1) and its foreign counterpart (in which T enters negatively) are essentially expectations-augmented Phillips curve equations for an open economy. They can be rationalized in several ways. Our personal preference is for an explanation in terms of firms who adjust prices in line with their expectations concerning the domestic inflation rate adjusted for movements in their costs relative to this trend. An elegant formulation along these lines has been worked out by Bilson (1979, especially footnote 16).[2] In this model the terms of trade enter as a result of the use of imported inputs as well as through an impact of foreign goods prices on domestic nominal wages. The output term reflects adjustment of prices to achieve the profit-maximizing level of production $\bar{Y}$. If aggregate demand Y exceeds this level, the firm will increase production in the short run, to meet the demand, and begin to raise its price more rapidly in order to reestablish its desired operating level.

Alternatively, equation (1) can be viewed as a Lucas-type aggregate

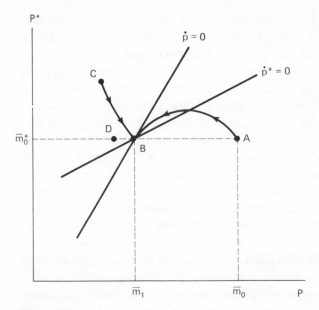

Figure 11.2

shown in figure 11.2. The system is initially in equilibrium at point A. The policy change relocates the equilibrium to point B. Throughout the adjustment, which will follow a trajectory like that shown between A and B, the inflation rate in the foreign economy is elevated above its original level. The domestic rate, by contrast, falls monotonically toward $\bar{m}_1$. Furthermore, as we shall see, this worsening in the foreign situation enhances the effectiveness of the domestic policy.

The adjustment is more complex if there is an immediate expectational response to the policy shift. As π drops, $\tilde{P}$ is reduced [reference equation (10b)]. This results from the fact that in the steady state, inflationary expectations are fully reflected in nominal interest rates. The decline in π is accompanied by an equal decline in $\tilde{R}$, which in turn implies an increased demand for cash balances. Given steady-state income (which is determined by $\tilde{T}$ and by $\tilde{R} - \pi$ and is consequently independent of monetary conditions), and the current level of $\overline{M}$, the price level (that is $\tilde{P}$) must be lower if the money market is to clear. As can be seen in equation (11), this decline in $\tilde{P}$ tends to lower the domestic inflation rate beyond the one-for-one adjustment resulting from the change in π itself. Moreover, there is again a perverse foreign impact; the decline in $\tilde{P}$ implies a rise in p^* as can be seen from equation (12). In figure 11.2, the system makes a discrete jump from point A to a location similar to point C. It then adjusts in continuous fashion toward its steady-state equilibrium at point B with the domestic inflation rate rising and the foreign rate falling.

In reality neither extreme case of expectations adjustment is particularly credible. The full adjustment case seems to us to be particularly non-credible. It is superficially in the spirit of some of the rational expectations literature in that the long-run implications of policy are immediately perceived and acted upon. But such a response is nonrational in the short run and in fact leads to the divergence of actual and anticipated inflation rates. It should perhaps be noted that monetary policymakers could prevent this effect by a once-and-for-all increase in $\overline{M}$ accompanying the shift to a lower $\overline{m}$. If this is done, and if expectations full reflect the lower $\overline{m}$, the systems will hop neatly from A to B in figure 11.2, moving from one steady state to another. This is very hard to swallow. It requires that the public (everyone whose expectations affect pricing decisions) completely believe the central bank when it announces that it will henceforth follow a policy of reduced monetary growth, but will allow a one-time money supply expansion to smooth the transition. Even central bankers (especially central bankers?) do not have this level of credibility.

The stationary expectations case is also, beyond a certain point at least, unacceptable. Initially, however, it is in fact "rational." For as was seen, if expectations do not change, neither do inflation rates, instantaneously, that is. But an evolution does begin. The completely rational response would require the policy change produce an immediate reaction involving $\dot{\pi} < 0$ and $\dot{\pi}^* > 0$ (but $\Delta\pi = \Delta\pi^* = 0$). Our own feeling is that the system might have to get rather well into trajectory AB, allowing actual demonstrations that $\overline{m}$ has been lowered, before there will be much impact on expectations. When this impact does come, moreover, it will tend to exaggerate the system response. In particular, when π does begin to fall, it will speed the decline in p and raise p^*. If the higher p^* along AB produces a temporary rise in π^*, it will enhance these effects. The perverse foreign price impact of the domestic policy will still be present.

It would probably be in order at this point to say a few words about movements of other variables in the system during the adjustment period. We will concentrate our discussion on the stationary expectations case, and begin with the domestic real money supply, which falls during the adjustment, as does its foreign counterpart. Initially the former effect is larger (reflecting the discrete drop in $\overline{m}$), and consequently the domestic interest rate will rise relative to that abroad. This produces an appreciation of the domestic currency (a decline in E and, as a result, in T). Both the rise in interest rates and the decline in the terms of trade tend to lower demand in the domestic goods market, leading to a drop in output. Also, both the lower terms of trade and the lower output contribute to the deceleration of domestic inflation. Abroad the changes in interest rates and in the terms of trade impinge in opposite fashions on the goods market, but a rise in output seems likely. In any case, the lower terms of trade lead to a rise in foreign inflation. In the next section we shall look at the implications of a foreign response to the inflation spillover.

11.3 Foreign Reactions

In this section we examine the implications of a systematic reaction by foreign monetary authorities to the contractionary shift of the domestic policy. Although it may overstate the perspicacity of some central bankers, we shall assume that this reaction takes the form of a manipulation of $\bar{m}^*$, the growth rate of the foreign money supply, as required to keep their inflation rate constant at its initial level.

In the stationary expectations case, in which the inflation rates are not subject to discontinuous change, this is equivalent to holding $\dot{p}^* = 0$. With $\tilde{p} = \bar{m}$ and $\tilde{p}^* = \bar{m}^*$, equation (14) then implies that the foreign money supply must be manipulated according to

$$\bar{m}^* = p^* + (v_1/v_2)(\bar{m} - p). \tag{15}$$

When the domestic central bank shifts to a lower growth rate policy, the expression $\bar{m} - p$ will become negative (assuming the initial situation is one of steady-state equilibrium). The foreign central bank from equation (15) will respond by lowering the growth rate of its money supply.

Substitute equation (15) into equation (13); then the domestic price level follows a path described by

$$\dot{p} = [u_1 - u_2(v_1/v_2)](\bar{m} - p). \tag{16}$$

The expression in brackets is positive, so the system's stability is not impaired. However, the deceleration of domestic prices is slower than in section 11.2. This can be seen by considering the immediate effect of the domestic policy change (that is, of $\Delta\bar{m} < 0$) in equation (16) as compared to equation (13). In the latter, with no foreign reaction, we have

$$\Delta\dot{p} = u_1 \Delta\bar{m}.$$

In the former

$$\Delta\dot{p} = [u_1 - u_2(v_1/v_2)]\Delta\bar{m}.$$

Clearly, the change in $\dot{p}$ is reduced by the foreign monetary adjustment, and (initially) the domestic inflation rate will decline more slowly. In fact, this reduced response will persist well into the adjustment period. Substituring for $\tilde{p}^* - p^*$ from equation (14) into equation (13) gives

$$\dot{p} = [u_1 - u_2(v_1/v_2)](\bar{m} - p) - (u_2/v_2)\dot{p}^*. \tag{17}$$

As long as $\dot{p}^*$ is positive (that is, over the rising part of trajectory AB in figure 11.2), it exerts downward pressure on domestic inflation. In the latter part of the adjustment, of course, the situation is reversed. Thus, a foreign reaction may not cause the adjustment period to lengthen overall, but it will tend to reduce early gains, which politically may be just as troublesome.

If there is an immediate, discrete expectations reaction to the domestic policy change, the required foreign central bank maneuvering to forestall fluctuation in the foreign inflation rate is more complex. The discrete change in expectation ($\Delta\pi < 0$) will cause a jump in foreign inflation unless offset by a discrete change in $\bar{M}^*$. From equation (12)

$$\Delta p^* = -v_1(\Delta\tilde{P} - \Delta P) + v_2(\Delta\tilde{P}^* - \Delta P^*) + \Delta\pi^*. \tag{18}$$

If the foreign central bank is following a policy of holding Δp^* equal to zero, there should be no changes in π^*; and, of course, P and P^* are not subject to discrete changes. Equation (10b) implies that $\Delta\tilde{P} = l_2\,\Delta\pi$ (assuming $\Delta\bar{M} = 0$), while (10c) yields $\Delta\tilde{P}^* = \Delta\bar{M}^*$. Substituting these conditions into (18) and solving for $\Delta\bar{M}^*$ gives the monetary adjustment required by the foreign central bank to hold p^* constant in response to a discrete change in domestic inflation expectations:

$$\Delta\bar{M}^* = l_2(v_1/v_2)\Delta\pi. \tag{19}$$

If the domestic tightening causes an immediate change in expectations, the foreign central bank must react with a once-and-for-all reduction in its money supply if it wants to prevent an inflationary spillover into its own economy.

As in the stationary expectations case, this contractionary foreign reaction lessens the initial impact of the domestic contraction. With no foreign reaction (so that $\Delta\tilde{P}^* = 0$) the domestic counterpart of (18) gives

$$\Delta p = (u_1 l_2 + 1)\,\Delta\pi.$$

With the reaction of equation (19), on the other hand, the result is

$$\Delta p = [u_1 l_2 - u_2 l_2(v_1/v_2) + 1]\,\Delta\pi.$$

A discontinuous drop in π has a smaller favorable impact on domestic inflation without the foreign reaction. The expression in brackets is greater than unity, however, so there is still a change in domestic inflation which exceeds the expectational shift. If $\Delta\pi = \Delta\bar{m}$, as in section 11.2, the result will be movement from point A to point D rather than point C. Consideration of equation (17) shows, however, that the subsequent deterioration of the domestic situation will be muted compared with the no foreign reaction case. The domestic inflation rate p is lower at point C than at D, while $\dot{p}^*$ is negative at C and zero at D due to the foreign central bank policy. Both of these factors tend to lower $\dot{p}$, implying that the reacceleration of domestic inflation toward its new equilibrium rate of $\bar{m}_1$ is less quick (but from a higher starting point).

11.4 Concluding Remarks

The past decade has seen a profusion of theoretical work in the international finance literature which has been slowly chipping away at the rather naive view of the prefloat era that flexible exchange rates would provide considerable insulation between national economies. In this chapter we have continued this chipping specifically in the area of price level independence. We have done so with a two-country model which in equilibrium is consistent with full insulation between the domestic and foreign price levels. But in the short run, following a policy change or exogenous shock, international transmission of price changes is possible.

The basic underlying source of this transmission lies in the different adjustment characteristics of prices and the exchange rate. The former adjust slowly while the latter adjusts instantaneously in response to asset market conditions. As a result a shock to the system can cause (temporarily, at least) change in the terms of trade. This in turn, produces price level adjustment in both countries, both directly and also through an impact on aggregate demand.[6]

In Sections 11.2 and 11.3 we examined the behavior of the system following a change (decline) in the rate of monetary expansion by the domestic monetary authorities. Summarizing briefly, our findings are

1. The system is dynamically stable and will converge to a steady state characterized by price level independence, with each country's inflation rate mirroring its rate of money supply growth.

2. The domestic policy shift will immediately begin to bring down the domestic inflation rate, but the precise path of the adjustment depends on the evolution of expectations with regard to the inflation rate. If these drop

discretely, there will be a quick improvement (a discrete decline) in domestic inflation. If they change in continuous fashion, domestic inflation will subside gradually.

3. In either case there will be a *rise* in the foreign inflation rate—either a discrete jump or a gradual rise. Eventually these changes will be reversed, returning foreign inflation to its original level.

4. Theoretically, foreign monetary authorities can neutralize such spillover by manipulating their money supply and its rate of growth. If expectations evolve continuously, changes in money growth rates alone will suffice. The required manipulations will be of a contractionary nature, causing the foreign money supply to be lower than if no neutralization were undertaken.

5. Neutralization of spillover by foreign monetary authorities has generally negative implications for the short-run efficacy of the domestic anti-inflation effort. If expectations move continuously, the immediate deceleration of inflation domestically is reduced. If expectations decline in a discontinuous manner, the immediate drop in domestic inflation will be less dramatic.

The analysis which leads to these conclusions is not without its weaknesses. For one thing, it is short run in character, even in its steady-state configuration. In particular, the effects of wealth on real and asset demand and the accumulation of wealth through trade imbalances are neglected. For another, our treatment of expectations is not entirely satisfactory. Exchange rate expectations, which are modelled explicitly, will not be consistent with "rationality" (that is, perfect foresight in disequilibrium situations). Rather, they are what Mathieson (1977) has dubbed "semi-rational," reflecting knowledge of the steady-state nature of the model, but not its exact dynamic characteristics. Price expectations are treated as exogenous in our analysis. But considerable attention is given to their possible evolution, and it is clear that even if they exhibit perfect foresight, our basic conclusions will remain. In the context of policy changes like those we are considering, however, we do not believe that explicit full rationality is a prerequisite for analytic acceptability. Rather, we tend to agree with Buiter (1980) that rational expectations are most reasonable as a representation of behavior in situations of steady-state equilibrium. Our analysis is consistent with this view.

Our model and analysis can be extended in a variety of directions. An obvious possibility is to consider other (nonmonetary) sources of disturbance. An exogenous element could easily be added on the demand side of the domestic and foreign goods markets to represent fiscal policy. Changes in the capacity output levels (a supply side shock) could be examined. An exogenous OPEC-style element could be added to the price determination mechanism. This latter possibility, aside from its current relevance, raises some interesting theoretical issues. If the OPEC price is denominated in the domestic currency, the symmetry of the above model breaks down. Additional asymmetry can be introduced if the "oil" price is allowed to exert an influence on aggregate demand in the two countries (reflecting its impact on the domestic and foreign current accounts). Other forms of central bank behavior could also be analyzed. In this regard, policies of interest rate stabilization or partial exchange rate stabilization would seem to be of particular relevance.

Returning, by way of conclusion, to the analysis of *this* chapter, we are not entirely sure whether it should incline one to be optimistic or pessimistic about the operation of a flexible exchange rate regime. On the optimistic side, the international transmission of inflation we have examined is a short-run phenomenon. Moreover, even its short-run effects can be neutralized by foreign policymakers. On the other hand, there is a beggar-thy-neighbor aspect to the short-run behavior of this model—domestic success in combatting inflation is enhanced by a worsening of the foreign siutation. We were careful to describe foreign policy behavior in this predicament with the words "response" and "reaction," but several times "retaliation" seemed more appropriate. In a floating rate world which is subject to price-increasing exogenous shocks (e.g., OPEC), we find this suggestion of "competitive appreciation" to be a troubling possibility.

Appendix

This appendix provides details of the derivation of equations in the text.

1. Full basic model:

$$p = a_1 T + a_2 (Y - \bar{Y}) + \pi, \tag{1}$$

$$p^* = -b_1 T + b_2 (Y^* - \bar{Y}^*) + \pi^*, \tag{1*}$$

$$Y = d_1 T - d_2 (R - \pi), \tag{2}$$

$$Y^* = -f_1 T - f_2 (R^* - \pi^*), \tag{2*}$$

$$\bar{M} - P = l_1 Y - l_2 R, \tag{3}$$

$$\bar{M}^* - P^* = k_1 Y^* - k_2 R^*, \tag{3*}$$

$$R = R^* + g_1 (\tilde{E} - E) + (\pi - \pi^*). \tag{4/5}$$

2. Condensed model: Substitution using (2), (2*), (4/5) to eliminate Y, Y^*, and R^* gives equations (6)–(9) in the text.

3. Condensed steady-state model: Setting $p = \pi$, $p^* = \pi^*$, $Y = \tilde{Y}$, $Y^* = \tilde{Y}^*$, $R = \tilde{R}$, and $T = \tilde{T}$ in (6)–(9) gives

$$\overline{M} - \tilde{P} = l_1 d_1 \tilde{T} - (l_1 d_2 + l_2)\tilde{R} + l_1 d_1 \pi, \tag{6'}$$

$$0 = (a_1 + a_2 d_1)\tilde{T} - a_2 d_2(\tilde{R} - \pi) + a_2 \overline{Y}, \tag{7'}$$

$$\overline{M}^* - \tilde{P}^* = -k_1 f_1 \tilde{T} - (k_1 d_2 + k_2)(\tilde{R} - \pi) - k_2 \pi^*, \tag{8'}$$

$$0 = -(b_1 + b_2 f_1)\tilde{T} - b_2 f_2(\tilde{R} - \pi) - b_2 \overline{Y}^*. \tag{9'}$$

Solving (7') and (9') simultaneously gives expressions for $\tilde{R}$ and $\tilde{T}$:

$$\tilde{R} = \pi - \gamma_1 \overline{Y} - \gamma_2 \overline{Y}^*, \tag{10a}$$

where

$$\gamma_1 \equiv a_2 BC, \qquad \gamma_2 \equiv b_2 AC,$$

$$A \equiv (a_1 + a_2 d_1), \qquad B \equiv (b_1 + b_2 f_1),$$

$$C \equiv (b_2 f_2 A + a_2 d_2 B)^{-1},$$

$$\tilde{T} = \gamma_7 \overline{Y} - \gamma_8 \overline{Y}^*, \tag{10d}$$

where

$$\gamma_7 \equiv a_2 b_2 f_2 C, \qquad \gamma_8 \equiv a_2 b_2 d_2 C.$$

Substituting in (6') and (8') then gives expression for $\tilde{P}$ and $\tilde{P}^*$:

$$\tilde{P} = \overline{M} + l_2 \pi - \gamma_3 \overline{Y} - \gamma_4 \overline{Y}^* \tag{10b}$$

where

$$\gamma_3 \equiv a_2 C[l_1 d_1 b_2 f_2 + (l_1 d_2 + l_2)B],$$

$$\gamma_4 \equiv b_2 C[a_1(l_1 d_2 + l_2) + a_2 l_2 d_1],$$

$$\tilde{P}^* = \overline{M}^* + k_2 \pi^* - \gamma_5 \overline{Y} - \gamma_6 \overline{Y}^*, \tag{10c}$$

where

$$\gamma_5 \equiv a_2 C[b_1(k_1 d_2 + k_2) + b_2 k_2 f_1],$$

$$\gamma_6 \equiv b_2 C[k_1 f_1 a_2 d_2 + (k_1 f_2 + k_2)A].$$

4. Reduced form price adjustment model: The two sets of equations (6)–(9) and (6')–(9') can be used to derive equations (11) and (12) in the

text. One approach is to subtract one set from the other giving four equations which are functions of $\tilde{P} - P$, $\tilde{P}^* - P^*$, $\tilde{R} - R$, $\tilde{T} - T$, and $\tilde{E} - E$. These four and the fact that $(\tilde{E} - E) = (\tilde{T} - T) + (\tilde{P} - P) - (\tilde{P}^* - P)$ can then be reduced to (11) and (12). The result is

$$p = u_1(\tilde{P} - P) - u_2(\tilde{P} - P^*) + \pi, \tag{11}$$

where

$$u_1 \equiv \{[a_1(l_1d_2 + l_2) + a_2l_2d_1][(k_1f_2 + k_2)(1 + l_1d_2g_1$$
$$+ l_2g_1)] + a_2d_2D\},$$

$$u_2 \equiv \{[a_1(l_1d_2 + l_2) + a_2l_2d_1][(l_1d_2 + l_2)(1 + k_1f_2g_1 + k_2g_1)]\},$$

$$D \equiv [(k_1f_2 + k_2)(l_1d_2 + l_2)g_1 + (l_1d_2 + l_2)k_1f_1 + (k_1f_2 + k_2)l_1d_1].$$

$$p^* = -v_1(\tilde{P} - P) + v_2(\tilde{P}^* - P^*) + \pi^*, \tag{12}$$

where

$$v_1 \equiv \{[b_1(k_1f_2 + k_2) + b_2k_2f_1][(k_1f_2 + k_2)(1 + l_1d_2g_1 + l_2g_1)]\},$$

$$v_2 \equiv \{[b_1(k_1f_2 + k_2) + b_2k_2f_1][(l_1d_2 + l_2)(1 + k_1f_2g_1$$
$$+ k_2g_1)] + b_2f_2D\}.$$

It is easy to show from the above that $(u_1/u_2) > (v_1/v_2)$, as asserted in the text.

Notes

1. As Morris Goldstein (1980, p. 54) has recently observed, "It is abundantly clear from the experience of the last six years, however, that we must abandon the old textbook views of flexible rates as insulators *par excellence* against a wide variety of foreign disturbances." The old textbook view has also been theoretically obsolete for some time. See, for instance, Mundell (1968, especially the appendix to chapter 18); Argy and Porter (1972); Dornbusch (1976); Mussa (1979).

2. Bilson's model contains wage as well as price dynamics. Equation (1) can be derived from Bilson's framework by assuming equilibrium in his labor market.

3. In Liederman's model, expectational errors with respect to foreign prices also affect domestic output. His rationale for this effect is not fully explained, however.

4. Our formulation also assumes that exchange rate expectations held by domestic and foreign residents are the same. This is, it seems to us, consistent with perfect substitution between domestic and foreign securities. On the other hand, if domestic and foreign wealth holders are sufficiently different to have divergent exchange rate expectations, it seems likely that these differences also render domestic and foreign securities less than perfect substitutes.

5. Full derivations and definitions of parameters are given in the appendix.

6. Bhandari (1980) uses a similar model and comes to conclusions consistent with our own. But since his model does not contain direct effects of the terms of trade on price adjustment, his results are more ambiguous than ours.

References

Argy, V., and M. Porter (1972). "The Forward Exchange Market and the Effects of Domestic and External Disturbances under Alternative Exchange Rate Regimes," *IMF Staff Papers* 19, 503–32.

Bhandari J. S. (1981). "A Simple Transnational Model of Large Open Economies," *Southern Economic Journal* 47:990–1006.

Bilson, J. F. P. (1979). "The 'Vicious Circle' Hypothesis," *IMF Staff Papers* 26, 1–37.

Buiter W. H. (1980). "The Macroeconomics of Dr. Pangloss: A Critical Survey of the New Classical Macroeconomics," *Economic Journal* 90, 34–50.

Dornbusch, R. (1976). "The Theory of Flexible Exchange Rate Regimes and Macroeconomic Policy," *Scandanavian Journal of Economics* No. 2, 78, 255–75.

Frankel J. A. (1979). "On the Mark: A Theory of Floating Exchange Rates Based on Real Interest Differentials," *American Economic Review* 69, 610–22.

Goldstein, M. (1980). "Have Flexible Exchange Rates Handicapped Macroeconomic Policy?" Special Papers in International Economics No. 14, Princeton University, International Finance Section.

Leiderman, L. (1979). "Expectations and Output-Inflation Tradeoffs in a Fixed-Exchange-Rate Economy," *Journal of Political Economy* 87, 1285–306.

Mathieson, D. J. (1977). "The Impact of Monetary and Fiscal Policy under Flexible Exchange Rates and Alternative Expectations Structures." *IMF Staff Papers* 24, 535–68.

Mundell, R. (1968). *International Economics*, New York.

Mussa, M. (1979). "Macroeconomic Interdependence and the Exchange Rate Regime," in R. Dornbusch and J. Frenkel, eds., *International Economic Policy*, Baltimore, pp. 160–204.

12

A Model of Stabilization Policy in a Jointly Floating Currency Area

Jay H. Levin

This chapter develops a model to analyze stabilization policy and the transmission of disturbances in a currency area when the exchange rate of the area is floating against the rest of the world.[1] On the assumption that the currency area is small and that the securities issued in its countries are regarded as perfect substitutes for those issued elsewhere, equilibrium interest rates within the area are tied to the exogenous interest rates on foreign securities. The model is thus an extension of the classic Fleming (1962) and Mundell (1963) analyses of stabilization policy in a small country under conditions of perfect capital mobility and exchange rate flexibility. Furthermore, since the countries within the currency area have fixed exchange rates with each other, the model also extends Mundell's seminal two-country fixed exchange rate analysis (1964). It turns out, however, that the joint float produces results for the individual countries within the currency area and for the area as a whole that in some cases differ sharply from those in the Fleming and Mundell papers.

The paper is organized as follows. The structural model, consisting of a two-country currency area and the outside world, is developed in section 12.1 and represented by a simple diagram showing goods market and financial sector equilibrium within the currency area. Section 12.2 then derives the comparative static effects on domestic and partner country income resulting from monetary and fiscal policy actions undertaken by one of the countries in the currency area. In section 12.3 the model subsequently is used to derive the comparative static effects of demand switches within the currency area, a realignment of exchange rates within the currency area, and disturbances originating in the out-

I wish to thank Jagdeep Bhandari, Paul De Grauwe, Walter Enders, Harvey Lapan, Robert M. Stern, and especially W. M. Corden and Alan Deardorff for their valuable comments. I am also grateful to the referee for his suggestions. Any remaining errors are solely my responsibility.

. side world. Concluding observations are presented in section 12.4. Perhaps the most surprising finding to emerge is that fiscal expansion by one of the countries in the currency area produces a contraction in economic activity in the other country. In fact, this beggar-my-neighbor transmission effect can be so strong as to cause a decline in economic activity within the area as a whole! (Indeed, as shown in note 19, the latter event necessarily happens if the central bank of the country undertaking the fiscal expansion engages in sterilization operations. The beggar-my-neighbor effect then constitutes the *entire* change in economic activity in the currency area.)

12.1 The Structural Model

The following structural model describes the steady state of a small two-country currency area with equilibrium interest rates equal to exogenous interest rates in the rest of the world and the exchange rate floating against the outside world's currency:

$$S_1(\overset{+}{Y_1}) = I_1(\overset{-}{\bar{r}}) + G_1 + B_1(\overset{-}{Y_1}, \overset{+}{Y_2}, \overset{+}{\bar{Y}_w}, \overset{+}{\Pi}) \tag{1}$$

$$S_2(\overset{+}{Y_2}) = I_2(\overset{-}{\bar{r}}) + G_2 + B_2(\overset{+}{Y_1}, \overset{-}{Y_2}, \overset{+}{\bar{Y}_w}, \overset{+}{\Pi}), \tag{2}$$

$$H_1 + H_2 + Z = L_1(\overset{-}{\bar{r}}, \overset{+}{Y_1}) + L_2(\overset{-}{\bar{r}}, \overset{+}{Y_2}), \tag{3}$$

$$H_1 + R = L_1(\bar{r}, Y_1), \tag{3a}$$

$$H_2 + Z - R = L_2(\bar{r}, Y_2), \tag{3b}$$

where subscripts 1, 2, and w refer to countries 1 and 2 and the outside world respectively; Y = gross national product; S = saving; I = investment; G = government spending; B = trade balance, measured in units of the country's goods; $\bar{r}$ = equilibrium interest rate; Π = foreign exchange rate (units of each currency area currency/unit of outside world currency); [2] H = central bank's holdings of domestic securities; Z = total international reserves held by the central banks of the currency area; L = demand for the monetary base; R = international reserves of country 1's central bank; and parameter signs are shown above the arguments. Equations (1) and (2) describe goods market equilibrium in the two countries of the currency area, respectively. In order to focus on movements in economic activity produced by various disturbances, the domestic price of each country's domestically produced good is taken to be constant and normalized at unity on the assumptions of fixed money wages and constant returns in production. In addition, government spending is included in aggregate demand in order to analyze fiscal policy by a currency area country. Finally, only trade in consumption goods is considered in the specification of each country's trade balance, and the foreign currency price of the outside world good is exogenous and also normalized at unity. The model is completed with equation (3), which describes financial sector equilibrium in the currency area. This equation is derived by adding together the two countries' money market equilibrium conditions (3a) and (3b), respectively, and equation (3) thus indicates equality between the supply of and demand for the monetary base within the currency area.[3] Furthermore, H_1 and H_2 are treated as exogenous variables in this equation on the assumption that neither central bank undertakes sterilization operations.[4] The endogenous variables of system (1)–(3) are Y_1, Y_2, and Π. G_1, G_2, H_1, H_2, Z, $\bar{r}$ and $\bar{Y}_w$ are exogenous.[5] Also, observe that the signs of the structural parameters are as follows:

$$s_1 \left(= \frac{\partial S_1}{\partial Y_1} \right), \qquad s_2 \left(= \frac{\partial S_2}{\partial Y_2} \right),$$

$$m_1 \left(= -\frac{\partial B_1}{\partial Y_1} \right), \qquad m_2 \left(= -\frac{\partial B_2}{\partial Y_2} \right),$$

$$m_{12} \left(= \frac{\partial B_2}{\partial Y_1} \right), \qquad m_{21} \left(= \frac{\partial B_1}{\partial Y_2} \right),$$

$$m_{w_1} \left(= \frac{\partial B_1}{\partial \bar{Y}_w} \right), \qquad m_{w_2} \left(= \frac{\partial B_2}{\partial \bar{Y}_w} \right)$$

$B_{1\Pi}, B_{2\Pi}, L_{1Y_1},$ and $L_{2Y_2} > 0$;

and

$I_{1\bar{r}}, I_{2\bar{r}}, L_{1\bar{r}},$ and $L_{2\bar{r}} < 0$.

Notice in particular that a devaluation of the area's currencies against the rest of the world is assumed to expand not only the currency area's trade balance (i.e., $B_{1\Pi} + B_{2\Pi} > 0$), as the Marshall-Lerner condition requires in the steady state, but also the trade balance of each country in the currency area. Although it is conceivable that one of the countries' trade balances might decline as the result, say, of a highly inelastic demand for outside world goods, this possibility seems unlikely and certainly much less plausible than the assumption of gross substitutability among currencies.[6] Finally, the reader should keep in mind that exchange rate

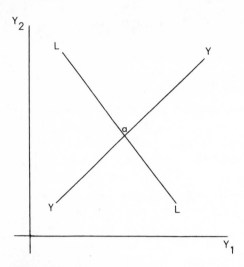

Figure 12.1
Equilibrium in the currency area.

expectations must be fulfilled in the steady-state equilibrium. Consequently, these expectations do not appear as an additional variable in the model.

Figure 12.1 represents the model graphically. The schedule labeled YY is a reduced form relation obtained from equations (1) and (2), with Π varied parametrically, that indicates combinations of Y_1 and Y_2 consistent with goods market equilibrium in the currency area for each possible exchange rate. Starting from an initial position of goods market equilibrium, a devaluation of the area's currencies will increase aggregate demand in each currency area country. Each country's income will expand and through the usual trade linkage mechanism produce further expansion in the currency area.[7] Thus, the YY schedule is upward sloping, and each point on the schedule corresponds to a specific exchange rate. Similarly, the LL schedule shows combinations of Y_1 and Y_2 consistent with financial sector equilibrium in the currency area. Since equilibrium interest rates within the currency area must coincide with those in the outside world, an increase in one currency area country's income, which increases the demand for money and puts upward pressure on currency area interest rates, requires a simultaneous reduction in the other country's income to maintain financial sector equilibrium in the steady state.[8] Consequently, the LL schedule is downward sloping, and the steady-state equilibrium of the system occurs at point a.[9] The remainder of this chapter analyzes the effects of various disturbances to this system.

12.2 Stabilization Policy in the Currency Area

In order to determine the comparative static effects of stabilization policy in the currency area, it will prove convenient for expositional purposes to make two assumptions about the system when it is not in full equilibrium. First, output is taken to adjust instantaneously to preserve continuous goods market equilibrium in the currency area; and second, interest rates continuously remain at the outside world level, but the exchange rate adjusts whenever the financial sector is not in equilibrium. In particular, an excess demand for money in the currency area, which would put upward pressure on currency area interest rates, induces an incipient net capital inflow from the outside world, producing an appreciation of the area's currencies at a speed proportionate to the excess demand for money. These assumptions serve to simplify the dynamics of the system as it moves toward a new steady state and consequently help to establish readily the ultimate comparative static results. However, the reader should keep in mind that the asset view of exchange rate adjustment suggests a quite different set of dynamics, in which the speeds of adjustment in the goods and asset markets would be reversed, and movements in currency area interest rates would serve, along with the exchange rate, to preserve asset market equilibrium. Consequently, the true dynamic paths of the system will differ considerably from those obtained below, but the comparative static results, which are the real objective here, of course are unaffected.[10]

With the aid of the above two assumptions, consider first a fiscal expansion in the currency area, represented by a rise in government spending on domestic goods in country 1 with unchanged central bank domestic security holdings.[11] This action is depicted in figure 12.2 as a rightward shift of the YY schedule since, at a given level of Y_2, economic activity would rise in country 1 in response to the higher level of aggregate demand. However, in the face of the resulting higher demand by country 1 for country 2's exports, maintenance of the original level of economic activity in country 2 would require a simultaneous revaluation of the area's currencies. Thus, at point b on the new YY schedule, the foreign exchange rate is lower than at point a.[12] However, since the exchange rate actually does not move at first in response to the fiscal shock, the system in fact jumps to a point like c on the new YY schedule, where the exchange rate coincides with its initial level. At this point, however, the system is not in full equilibrium since the higher levels of income produce an excess demand for money in the currency area. Consequently, the foreign exchange rate begins to depreciate, lowering economic activity within

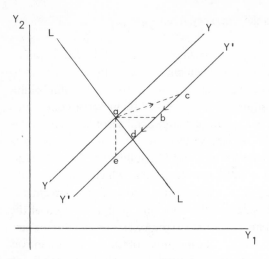

Figure 12.2
Effects of fiscal expansion in country 1.

the currency area, as represented by a southwesterly movement of the system along the new *YY* schedule. This deflationary process continues until the excess demand for money is eliminated at point *d*, where the system reaches its new equilibrium. Although this description of the system's dynamics is purely hypothetical, as indicated above, it does suggest the remarkable result that the fiscal expansion in country 1 eventually will produce a decline in economic activity in country 2 despite the trade linkage between the two countries. As far as country 2 is concerned, the overriding factor is the contractionary effect of the appreciation of the area's currencies, which restores financial sector equilibrium in the currency area. In order words, financial sector equilibrium requires that the expansion in country 1 be accompanied by a contraction in country 2, as the construction of the *LL* schedule has already indicated, and the exchange rate movement, with its deflationary impact on currency area incomes, is the mechanism that produces the required crowing-out effect in country 2.[13] In contrast, Mundell (1964, p. 265) found that in a two-country fixed exchange rate world with perfect capital mobility, fiscal expansion in one country might raise economic activity in the other because of the trade linkage effect.[14] In that event, despite the higher level of income in both countries, financial sector equilibrium would be preserved by a higher level of world interest rates induced by the world income expansion. In the small currency area, however, there is no scope in the steady state for currency area interest rates to serve as an equilibrating variable in the financial sector when capital is perfectly mobile vis à vis the outside world. Consequently, income must eventually fall in the second country if financial sector equilibrium is to be maintained.[15]

Further insight into the effects of fiscal expansion can be gained by examining the following fiscal policy multipliers of the system:

$$\frac{dY_1}{dG_1} = \frac{B_{2\Pi}L_{2Y_2}}{\Delta}, \tag{4a}$$

$$\frac{dY_2}{dG_1} = -\frac{B_{2\Pi}L_{1Y_1}}{\Delta}, \tag{4b}$$

and

$$\frac{d\Pi}{dG_1} = \frac{-m_{12}L_{2Y_2} - (s_2 + m_2)L_{1Y_1}}{\Delta}, \tag{4c}$$

where

$$\Delta = B_{1\Pi}[m_{12}L_{2Y_2} + (s_2 + m_2)L_{1Y_1}]$$
$$+ B_{2\Pi}[m_{21}L_{1Y_1} + (s_1 + m_1)L_{2Y_2}].$$

Notice first that the income multipliers both rise in absolute value as $B_{2\Pi}$ increases, that is, as country 2's trade balance becomes more sensitive to a movement in the foreign exchange rate. The reason is quite straightforward. Since an appreciation of the area's currencies is required to restore financial sector equilibrium in the currency area, the deflationary effect on country 2 clearly will be larger with higher values of $B_{2\Pi}$. However, the greater is the contraction in country 2, the greater is the scope for expansion in country 1, since financial sector equilibrium must be restored in the currency area. In essence, as (4c) shows, an increase in $B_{2\Pi}$ cuts down the required appreciation, and in turn the retarding exchange rate effect on country 1. Conversely, the larger is $B_{1\Pi}$, the greater will be the retarding effect of the appreciation on country 1; but the smaller is the ultimate expansion in country 1, the less must be the contraction in country 2 if financial sector equilibrium is to be preserved.[16] In other words, an increase in $B_{1\Pi}$ also reduces the required appreciation, as (4c) indicates, and hence the contractionary effect on country 2. Second, the *relative* effect of the fiscal expansion on the two countries, $(dY_1/dG_1)/|dY_2/dG_1|$, coincides exactly with the relative income sensitiv-

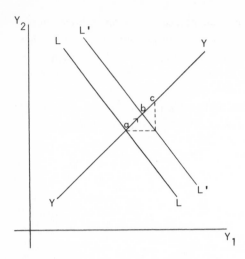

Figure 12.3
Effects of monetary expansion in the currency area.

ities of their demands for money, L_{2Y_2}/L_{1Y_1}. The reason is that financial sector equilibrium in the currency area, for a given monetary base and world interest rate level, requires that the increased demand for money due to income expansion in country 1, $L_{1Y_1}(dY_1/dG_1)$, be exactly offset by the reduction in the demand for money due to income contraction in country 2, $L_{2Y_2}(dY_2/dG_1)$. Furthermore, it follows that total economic activity within the currency area will rise or fall as the income sensitivity of money demand in country 2 exceeds or falls short of the income sensitivity of money demand in country 1. Thus, if the country that undertakes fiscal expansion has the larger income sensitivity of money demand, the beggar-my-neighbor effect on the other country will be so strong as to cause a decline in total currency area income![17] This result for the small currency area can be compared with the Fleming-Mundell result for the single small country, according to which fiscal expansion under floating exchange rates has *no* ultimate effect on income since the demand for money in the country must be restored exactly to its original level at the world interest rate. In contrast, if a small currency area is properly disaggregated into its component countries, it becomes evident that currency area income will change to the extent that the countries differ in their income sensitivities of money demand.[18,19]

Now consider a monetary expansion in the currency area, represented by an open market purchase by country 1's central bank. In figure 12.3

this action shifts the LL schedule to the right since it increases the monetary base of the currency area and, at a given level of Y_2, requires a higher level of Y_1 to restore financial sector equilibrium in the currency area. Thus, at the initial point a, there is now an excess supply of money in the currency area, and the area's currencies consequently begin to depreciate, raising economic activity in the currency area. This expansionary process is represented by a northeasterly movement of the system along the YY schedule until the excess supply of money eventually is eliminated at point b. Thus, the exchange rate movement, with its effect on currency area incomes, is again the mechanism that restores financial sector equilibrium in the currency area.[20] Furthermore, since the same excess supply of money would be caused by an identical open market purchase in country 2, the income expansion in each country is independent of which central bank undertakes the open market operation.[21,22]

Consider next the following monetary policy multipliers of the system:

$$\frac{dY_1}{dH_1} = \frac{(s_2 + m_2)B_{1\Pi} + m_{21}B_{2\Pi}}{\Delta}, \tag{5a}$$

$$\frac{dY_2}{dH_1} = \frac{(s_1 + m_1)B_{2\Pi} + m_{12}B_{1\Pi}}{\Delta}, \tag{5b}$$

and

$$\frac{d\Pi}{dH_1} = \frac{(s_1 + m_1)(s_2 + m_2) - m_{12}m_{21}}{\Delta}. \tag{5c}$$

One can easily show that as $B_{1\Pi}$ increases, the expansionary effect on country 1 increases and that on country 2 declines.[23] Clearly, since a depreciation of the area's currencies is required to restore financial sector equilibrium in the currency area, the expansionary effect on country 1 will be larger with higher values of $B_{1\Pi}$. However, the greater is the expansion in country 1, the less is the scope for expansion in country 2 due to the financial sector equilibrium constraint. Essentially, as $B_{1\Pi}$ increases, the required depreciation declines, as (5c) indicates, reducing the expansionary effect in country 2. Conversely, as $B_{2\Pi}$ increases, the expansionary effect on country 2 increases and that on country 1 declines. It follows that the relative effects of the monetary expansion on the two countries, $(dY_1/dH_1)/(dY_2/dH_1)$, depend directly on their relative trade balance sensitivities to the exchange rate, $B_{1\Pi}/B_{2\Pi}$, which in turn depends on their relative size, given their degree of openness. In fact, if country 1 were of negligible size in comparison with country 2, the predominant (although still hardly noticeable) effect of the exchange rate depreciation would be felt in country 2. Monetary policy would be essentially powerless to affect income in country 1, just as Mundell (1963) found for the small country in a fixed exchange rate world, because open market operations in the small country would have a negligible percentage effect on the currency area's monetary base.[24] Conversely, the large country can use monetary policy successfully, at the same time having a noticeable percentage effect on economic activity in the small country.

12.3 Other Disturbances Affecting the Currency Area

Consider now the comparative static effects of changes in tastes for the goods produced in the currency area. First, an increase in outside world demand for the exports of *one* of the countries in the currency area works exactly like a fiscal expansion within that country since it directly increases aggregate demand there. Consequently, that country's income will rise, income in the other currency area country eventually will fall, and overall economic activity in the currency area will rise (fall) if the first country's income sensitivity of money demand is less (greater) than the second country's. Second, an increase in one country's demand for the other country's exports in place of expenditures on outside world goods has the same effect in the currency area as the first taste switch. Even though the first country's demand for its own goods has not changed, the appre- ciation of the common currency necessary to restore financial sector equilibrium in the currency area eventually will produce a decline in its level of economic activity. Third, a taste switch toward one currency area country's exports and away from the exports of the other country, originating from either within or outside the currency area, acts like a fiscal expansion in the first country and an equal fiscal contraction in the second. It is clear that economic activity will rise in the first country and fall in the second since a fiscal expansion (contraction) in one country raises (lowers) domestic income and lowers (raises) income in the other currency area country. In addition, recall again that a fiscal expansion (contraction) in one currency area country raises (lowers) total currency area income if its income sensitivity of money demand is less than that of the second country's. Applying this result to both countries produces the conclusion that the intracurrency area taste switch raises (lowers) total economic activity in the currency area if the first country's income sensitivity of money demand is less (greater) than that of the second country's. Finally, a realignment of the currencies within the currency area that improves the competitiveness of the first country's exports vis à vis the second's normally has the same effect as the intracurrency area taste switch just discussed.[25]

Consider next the ultimate effect of a rise in income in the outside world, which increases the demand for the exports of *both* currency area countries and consequently acts like a fiscal expansion in both countries. Each country is now subject to the expansionary effect of a rise in domestic aggregate demand and the contractionary effect of a rise in aggregate demand in the partner country. The overall effect on economic activity in each country is therefore uncertain, although the financial sector equilibrium constraint again requires that an ultimate rise in income in one country be accompanied by an ultimate decline in income in the other. To obtain the precise effects on economic activity in each country, system (1)–(3) can be differentiated with respect to $\bar{Y}_w$, yielding

$$\frac{dY_1}{d\bar{Y}_w} = \frac{L_{2Y_2}(m_{w1}B_{2\Pi} - m_{w2}B_{1\Pi})}{\Delta}, \tag{6a}$$

and

$$\frac{dY_2}{d\bar{Y}_w} = \frac{-L_{1Y_1}(m_{w1}B_{2\Pi} - m_{w2}B_{1\Pi})}{\Delta}. \tag{6b}$$

Thus, income rises in country 1 and falls in country 2 if and only if the following condition holds:

$$\frac{m_{w1}}{m_{w2}} > \frac{B_{1\Pi}}{B_{2\Pi}}, \tag{7}$$

that is, if and only if the rest of the world's relative marginal import propensity for country 1's goods exceeds country 1's relative trade balance sensitivity to the exchange rate. This condition is intuitively sensible since the relative direct expansionary effects in the two countries depend on the relative marginal import propensities, whereas the relative contractionary effects in the two countries due to the appreciation of the area's currencies depend on the relative trade balance sensitivities to the exchange rate.[26] Finally, the effect on total economic activity in the currency area will depend on the direction in which income changes in the two countries and their income sensitivities of money demand. For example, if condition (7) is fulfilled, so that income rises in country 1 and falls in country 2, then, as in the case of a pure fiscal expansion in country 1, total income in the currency area will rise (fall) if country 1's income sensitivity of money demand is less (greater) than country 2's.

Finally, consider the ultimate effect of a rise in world interest rates, which affects each country through two channels. At the initial level of economic activity in each currency area country, this disturbance creates an excess supply of money in the currency area. As shown above in the discussion of monetary policy, such an excess supply of money would lead to a depreciation of the area's currencies and an expansion of income in both countries. However, the higher interest rate has the additional effect of directly reducing aggregate demand in each country and through this second channel operates in a manner similar to a reduction in outside world income. Thus, the second channel ultimately has an expansionary effect on one country and a contractionary effect on the other, so that at least one of the countries will experience an overall rise in economic activity. This conclusion in consistent with the condition of financial sector equilibrium in the currency area, which requires an income expansion in at least one of the countries to remove the excess supply of money produced by the higher world interest rate. However, it is possible for economic activity actually to decline in one of the countries, for the first channel would be unimportant if the interest sensitivities of money demand in the two countries were relatively low. In that event, the country with the relatively higher interest sensitivity of investment spending would experience a contractionary effect through the second channel that would dominate the expansionary effect of the first channel.[27] This possibility

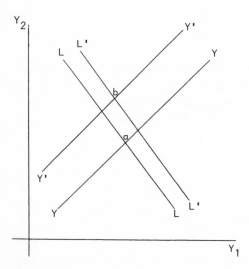

Figure 12.4
Possible effects of a rise in world interest rates.

is shown in figure 12.4, where the first channel is represented by a rightward shift in the LL schedule, and the second channel by a leftward shift of the YY schedule on the assumption that investment spending is relatively more interest sensitive in country 1. Furthermore, if country 1's income sensitivity of money demand were lower than country 2's, the second channel would produce a reduction in total economic activity in the currency area, as in the case of a pure fiscal contraction in country 1. It is conceivable, then, that total income in the currency area would decline, but this would require a sufficiently low interest sensitivity of money demand in the two countries, as well as a lower income sensitivity of money demand in the country with the relatively higher interest sensitivity of investment spending.[28] In contrast, this possibility is completely ruled out in the Fleming-Mundell small-country case, where an increase in the world interest rate must cause economic activity to rise through a domestic currency depreciation to maintain equilibrium in the financial sector.

12.4 Conclusions

Rather than summarizing the results obtained in sections 12.2 and 12.3, I shall conclude this chapter with several observations. First, since the comparative static cross effects of fiscal expansion in one currency area country may well be negative because of the joint float, it is crucial for econometric model builders concerned with linkages within a currency area to incorporate the induced exchange rate movements into their models. At the moment, the cross effects that have been reported for the current participants in the European Monetary System—Belgium-Luxembourg, Denmark, France, Germany, Ireland, Italy, and the Netherlands—are all positive, but the simulations all hold exchange rates vis à vis the outside world constant.[29] Second, the work of Fleming and Mundell long ago demonstrated that flexible exchange rates do not insulate countries from each other when capital is mobile. Any disturbance that alters interest rates in one country or group of countries eventually will affect economic activity in other countries through induced movements in exchange rates.[30] By the same token, any foreign disturbance that does *not* alter foreign interest rates has no *lasting* transmission effect on the domestic country. The model developed in this paper, however, indicates that this last proposition does not apply to the individual countries within a currency area or to the currency area as a whole. In particular, a currency area is not insulated from a shift in outside world preferences or a movement in foreign economic activity at given world interest rates. Third, the model developed here assumes fixed wages and prices in order to predict the short-run employment effects of stabilization policy and other disturbances in a currency area. Clearly, an important extension would be to incorporate wage and price dynamics arising from disequilibrium in the labor market in order to obtain an accurate picture of the path of these employment effects. Fourth, the results obtained here are directly applicable to a monetary union, in which the exchange rates are permanently fixed between the national currencies, or in which the national currencies are replaced with a single union currency. In the latter case, the financial sector constraint is

$$Q = L_1(\bar{r}, Y_1) + L_2(\bar{r}, Y_2), \tag{8}$$

where Q denotes the union's monetary base, but this equation is equivalent to (3). In a monetary union, in fact, the permanent fixity of exchange rates serves to increase the degree of capital mobility between the member countries, and consequently it is this monetary arrangement which is most likely to correspond to the assumption in the model of a single interest rate within the currency area.[31] Fifth, the possibility of labor movements between the member countries has been ignored in this short-run analysis, but if the countries in the model constitute an optimum currency area, such movements eventually will occur. A long-run analysis clearly would have to take them into account. Finally, the case of imperfect capital mobility within a currency area, allowing all of its countries to undertake sterilization policies, ought to be explored. Even here, however, one country's fiscal expansion might still produce an appreciation of the area's currencies, and negative fiscal policy transmission therefore remains a possibility.

Notes

1. Mundell (1961, p. 177) has defined a currency area as "a domain within which exchange rates are fixed." On this definition, a currency area may consist of two or more countries each issuing its own national currency and maintaining a separate monetary policy, an arrangement which Corden (1972, pp. 3–5) calls a "pseudo-exchange rate union." It is this type, exemplified by the present European Monetary System, which is analyzed explicitly in this paper.

2. The exchange rate between the currencies within the currency area is held constant by central bank intervention in the foreign exchange market involving these currencies. For convenience, this exchange rate is normalized at unity.

3. Since residents in each country can hold either money or securities, equilibrium

in money holdings in each country implies that residents there are holding an optimal amount of securities by virtue of the wealth constraint. Consequently, equation (3) indicates financial sector equilibrium in the currency area as a whole. Notice also that the demand for money, which is assumed to be a transactions demand, is taken to be independent of the exchange rate, as in the Fleming and Mundell models. Firms' money holdings are likely to depend on the nominal value of production, and household money holdings are presumably related to nominal household income.

4. An alternative assumption, that one country's central bank undertakes sterilization operations, is discussed in later notes. It is not possible for both central banks to sterilize, however, since that would enable the governments to maintain separate interest rate levels, which are not consistent with perfect asset substitutability and fixed exchange rates between the two countries. Massive capital outflows would force the central bank in the lower interest rate country to cease sterilizing.

5. $\bar{Y}_w$ is treated as exogenous in order to ensure that economic changes in the currency area have no noticeable repercussion effects on the demand for the currency area's exports. One could instead set the parameters m_{w1} and m_{w2} below to zero. However, the procedure used here permits an examination in section 12.3 of the effects of large exogenous changes in outside world income when m_{w1} and m_{w2} are very small but nonzero.

6. See Mundell (1960, pp. 52–53). A devaluation of country 1's currency alone would expand country 1's trade balance, and a devaluation of country 2's currency alone would normally reduce country 1's trade balance. On the plausible assumption that the positive effect of the former devaluation is greater than the negative effect of an equal latter devaluation, it follows that a common devaluation of the area's currencies increases country 1's trade surplus. A similar argument applies to country 2.

7. If equations (1) and (2) are differentiated with respect to Π, one obtains
$$\frac{dY_1}{d\Pi} = \frac{B_{1\Pi}(s_2 + m_2) + B_{2\Pi}m_{21}}{(s_1 + m_1)(s_2 + m_2) - m_{12}m_{21}},$$
which is positive. After dividing through by $s_2 + m_2$, the numerator reduces to the expression
$$\left(B_{1\Pi} + \frac{B_{2\Pi}m_{21}}{s_2 + m_2}\right).$$
The first term represents the direct aggregate demand effect of the devaluation on country 1, and the second term denotes the trade linkage effect associated with the direct expansion in country 2. Interchanging subscripts 1 and 2 produces the analogous multiplier for counry 2.

8. When the system is not in steady-state equilibrium, interest rates within the currency area can diverage from the outside world interest rates by the expected percentage depreciation of the exchange rate. This follows from Dornbusch's result (1976b, p. 1168) for the small-country case.

9. Since the effects of growing wealth on aggregate demand in each country are neglected, the steady state is a conventional Keynesian equilibrium one, as in the Fleming and Mundell models cited earlier. Consequently, the system differs fundamentally from the class of open economy models in which the steady state pertains

to a stationary economy with zero saving and investment, examples of which are Dornbusch (1976a), Kenen (1976), and McKinnon and Oates (1966). Notice, however, that "portfolio balance" or financial sector equilibrium is a property shared by both types of models. In addition, each country's balance of payments also is in equilibrium in the steady state.

10. Under conditions of perfect capital mobility, the fixed interest rate assumption implies that, throughout the dynamic adjustment process, the exchange rate is expected to remain at its current level. This assumption of static expectations would be clearly inadequate in a full-fledged dynamic model, but here it is extremely useful for the purpose of obtaining comparative steady-state results, which are insensitive to the specification of exchange rate expectations.

11. The possibility that increased government spending in country 1 includes purchases of country 2's goods is discussed in note 26. A third possibility, that the increased government spending falls on the rest of the world's goods, involves no effects on Y_1, Y_2, or Π since it does not alter aggregate demand for goods produced within the currency area. The incipient depreciation of the area's currencies would have an incipient expansionary effect on currency area income, putting upward pressure on currency area interest rates. However, the slightest increase in the latter would produce capital inflows sufficient to prevent any noticeable depreciation of the exchange rate.

12. If equations (1) and (2) are differentiated with respect to G_1, allowing Π to vary but holding Y_2 constant, one obtains

$$\frac{dY_1}{dG_1} = \frac{1}{(s_1 + m_1) + (m_{12}/B_{2\Pi})B_{1\Pi}}.$$

The first expression in the denominator denotes the standard single-country open economy multiplier effect. However, this is diluted by the deflationary effect of the hypothetical revaluation, indicated by the second term.

13. As the monetary approach suggests, the income expansion in country 1 would be accompanied by a cumulative balance of payments surplus in order to satisfy the increased demand for money there. International reserves simultaneously would be redistributed away from country 2 since the demand for money declines there.

14. It is also possible for income to fall in the second country because the higher level level of interest rates produced by the fiscal expansion in turn retards investment spending there.

15. However, if the currency area were a significant part of the world economy, income *might* rise in the second country since the fiscal expansion would raise world interest rates, thus reducing the currency appreciation required to restore financial sector equilibrium in the currency area. Alternatively, if capital were not perfectly mobile with the outside world, the fiscal expansion would raise interest rates within the currency area, directly helping to restore financial sector equilibrium, and again leading to the possibility of a rise in economic activity in the second country. These possibilities are elaborated in an appendix, which is available from the author on request.

16. In the limit, if country 2 is of negligible size in comparison with country 1, so

that $B_{2n}/B_{1n} \to 0$, the YY schedule becomes horizontal, and fiscal expansion in country 1 has no effect on either country. Since the currency area is of negligible size in the world economy, country 1 essentially assumes the role of the Fleming-Mundell small floating exchange rate country, for which fiscal policy is powerless to affect economic activity. On the other hand, fiscal expansion in country 2 does raise economic activity there, and lowers it in country 1, since the appreciation of the area's currencies required to restore financial sector equilibrium has a negligible deflationary effect on country 2 in comparison with its effect on country 1. *In general then, the small country in the currency area can use fiscal policy successfully, but the large country cannot.*

17. If there are economies of scale in the demand for money, as suggested by the Baumol-Tobin model of transactions demand, for example, smaller countries *ceteris paribus* would have larger income sensitivities of money demand. It would follow that fiscal expansion by a small country would produce a contraction in currency area income. Also, in less economically advanced countries, the transactions costs in asset conversions would be higher, again raising the income sensitivity of money demand in the Baumol-Tobin framework.

18. However, if the currency area is a significant part of the world economy, currency area income is more likely to rise since the fiscal expansion will raise world interest rates and therefore increase the velocity of money in the currency area countries.

19. The results for fiscal expansion in country 1 differ dramatically if one of the central banks undertakes sterilization operations. In the case of sterilization by country 1's central bank, the insulation of country 1's money supply implies that economic activity in country 1 ultimately must recede to its original level as a condition of financial sector equilibrium there. This would be achieved by a sufficient appreciation of the area's currencies to move the system all the way to point e in figure 12.2 since the LL schedule now becomes vertical. Consequently, economic activity would fall even more in country 2, and currency area economic activity would decline. In this case, fiscal expansion is necessarily deflationary! On the other hand, in the case of sterilization by country 2's central bank, economic activity in country 2 will remain unchanged as a condition for financial sector equilibrium there. This is achieved by a currency appreciation that moves the system from c to b, the intersection with the now horizontal LL schedule. In this case, currency area economic activity will necessarily rise. Finally, in the case of *partial* sterilization by both central banks, one can easily show that currency area income will rise or fall as L_{1Y_1}/L_{2Y_2} is less or greater than $(1 - \alpha_1)/(1 - \alpha_2)$, where the α_i are the central banks' sterilization coefficients.

20. This result is consistent with Allen's suggestion (1976, p. 49) that "expansive monetary policy [in a monetary union] works through the exchange rate when securities markets are highly intergrated."

21. When the open market purchase is undertaken by country 1's central bank, the income expansion in country 2 would be accompanied by a cumulative balance of payments surplus there in order to satisfy country 2's increased demand for money. Thus, international reserves are redistributed away from country 1, but this redistribution must be less than the original open market purchase since country 1's monetary base must expand to satisfy country 1's increased demand for money.

22. The results for an open market purchase in country 1 also differ dramatically if one of the central banks undertakes sterilization operations. In the case of sterilization by country 1's central bank, the monetary base in country 1 expands by the full amount of the open market operation, and income in country 1 thus expands by the maximum amount, namely, the increase in the monetary base times the reciprocal of the income sensitivity of the demand for money. Thus, the area's currencies must depreciate by an even larger amount, producing an even larger expansion in country 2's income. In terms of figure 12.3, the LL schedule now becomes vertical, and although it shifts to the right by the same amount as the original LL schedule, its intersection with the YY schedule now occurs farther out at point c. On the other hand, if country 2's central bank undertakes sterilization, the insulation of its money supply requires an unchange level of economic activity there as a condition for financial sector equilibrium. Furthermore, any attempt by country 1's central bank to expand the money supply will be defeated by capital outflows to country 2, preventing an excess supply of money from arising in the currency area and thus avoiding any need for a depreciation of the currencies. Monetary policy consequently remains powerless to affect economic activity in country 1 and simply produces a redistribution of international reserves to country 2. In terms of figure 12.3, the LL schedule now becomes horizontal and remains unaffected by the open market operation in country 1.

23. The slope of the YY schedule is $(dY_2/dH_1)/(dY_1/dH_1)$, or, from (5a) and (5b),

$$\frac{(s_1 + m_1)B_{2\Pi} + m_{12}B_{1\Pi}}{(s_2 + m_2)B_{1\Pi} + m_{21}B_{2\Pi}}.$$

Differentiating this expression with respect to $B_{1\Pi}$ yields

$$\frac{B_{2\Pi}[m_{12}m_{21} - (s_1 + m_1)(s_2 + m_2)]}{[(s_2 + m_2)B_{1\Pi} + m_{21}B_{2\Pi}]^2},$$

which is negative. Thus, the YY schedule becomes flatter as $B_{1\Pi}$ increases, implying a larger expansion in country 1 and a smaller expansion in country 2.

24. Notice that country 1's monetary policy multiplier can be written

$$\frac{(s_2 + m_2)(B_{1\Pi}/B_{2\Pi}) + m_{21}}{[m_{12}L_{2Y_2} + (s_2 + m_2)L_{1Y_1}](B_{1\Pi}/B_{2\Pi}) + [m_{21}L_{1Y_1} + (s_1 + m_1)L_{2Y_2}]},$$

and as $B_{1\Pi}/B_{2\Pi} \to 0$, the multiplier reduces to

$$\frac{m_{21}}{m_{21}L_{1Y_1} + (s_1 + m_1)L_{2Y_2}}.$$

Furthermore, as country 1 becomes negligibly small in comparison with country 2, $m_{21} \to 0$, and the multiplier vanishes.

25. Call country 1's currency the mark, country 2's currency the franc, and the outside world currency the dollar. In equations (1) and (2) let Π denote the mark/dollar exchange rate, and now introduce separately the franc/mark exchange rate into the trade balance functions B_1 and B_2, in equations (1) and (2), respectively. For a given mark/dollar exchange rate, a reduction in the franc/mark exchange rate is equivalent to a revaluation of the franc, which reduces B_2 and normally increases B_1, and thus acts like a fiscal expansion in country 1 and fiscal contraction in country 2. Of course, the reader should keep in mind that this discussion assumes initial balance of pay-

ments equilibrium within the currency area, whereas currency realignments normally are undertaken to *restore* balance of payments equilibrium.

26. By the same line of argument, an increase in government spending in country 1 that would fall partly on country 2's goods would raise income in country 1 and lower income in country 2 if and only if $\theta_1/(1 - \theta_1)$ exceeds $B_{1\Pi}/B_{2\Pi}$, where θ_1 is the fraction of the increased government spending that falls on country 1's goods.

27. Differentiating system (1)–(3) with respect to $\bar{r}$ leads to the following multiplier for country 1:

$$\frac{dY_1}{d\bar{r}} = \frac{-(L_{1r} + L_{2r})[(s_2 + m_2)B_{1\Pi} + m_{21}B_{2\Pi}] + L_{2Y_2}(B_{2\Pi}I_{1r} - B_{1\Pi}I_{2r})}{\Delta}.$$

The two terms in the numerator represent the positive "monetary effect" and the uncertain "direct aggregate demand effect" in country 1. The second effect is contractionary in country 1 if and only if I_{1r}/I_{2r} exceeds $B_{1\Pi}/B_{2\Pi}$, a result which is analogous to condition (7).

28. After obtaining the multiplier for country 2 by interchanging subscripts 1 and 2 in note 27, one can derive the following effect on total income in the currency area Y^*:

$$\frac{dY^*}{d\bar{r}} = \frac{-(L_{1r} + L_{2r})[B_{1\pi}(s_2 + m_2 + m_{12}) + B_{2\pi}(s_1 + m_1 + m_{21})]}{\Delta}$$

$$+ \frac{(B_{2\pi}I_{1r} - B_{1\pi}I_{2r})(L_{2Y_2} - L_{1Y_1})}{\Delta}.$$

The two terms in the numerator now represent the positive "monetary effect" and the uncertain "direct aggregate demand effect" in the currency area.

29. See Barten et al (1976, p. 100), Centraal Planbureau (1975, p. 33) cited in Deardorff and Stern (1977), Hickman (1974, pp. 211–13), OECD (1980, p. 12), and Waelbroeck and Dramais (1974, p. 315). The Centraal Planbureau has now replaced the mini-METEOR model with the METEOR model, which has been merged with the COMET model constructed by the Center for Operations Research and Econometrics in Louvain, Belgium. However, this model does not yet incorporate floating exchange rates.

30. This statement abstracts, of course, from movements in foreign interest rates produced by changes in the (expected) rate of foreign inflation. The latter eventually would lead to an offsetting movement in the rate of exchange depreciation and leave the terms of trade unchanged.

31. This consideration suggests that one might want to relax the assumption of perfect capital mobility when analyzing stabilization policy in a currency area in which the exchange rates between the national currencies are subject to revision. Strangely enough, however, the well-known paper by Kouri and Porter (1974) contains at least one "offset coefficient" for Germany, Italy, and the Netherlands that is not significantly different from unity and hence is consistent with the hypothesis of perfect capital mobility.

References

Allen, Polly R. (1976). "Organization and Administration of a Monetary Union," Princeton Studies in International Finance No. 38 (June).

Barten, A. P., G. d'Alcantara, and G. J. Carrin (1976). "COMET: A Medium-term Macroeconomic Model for the European Economic Community," *European Economic Review* (January).

Centraal Planbureau (1975), "Mini-Meteor: A Simple Multi-Country Simulation Model," processed, The Hague (June).

Corden, W. M. (1972). "Monetary Integration," *Princeton Essays in International Finance* No. 93 (April).

Deardorff, Alan V., and Robert M. Stern (1977). "International Economic Interdependence: Evidence from Econometric Models," University of Michigan, Seminar Discussion Paper No. 71 (January).

Dornbusch, Rudiger, (1976a). "Capital Mobility, Flexible Exchange Rates, and Macroeconomic Equilibrium," in E. Claassen and P. Salin, eds., *Recent Issues in International Monetary Economics* (North-Holland).

Dornbusch, Rudiger (1976b). "Expectations and Exchange Rate Dynamics," *Journal of Political Economy* (December).

Fleming, J. Marcus (1962). "Domestic Financial Policies under Fixed and under Floating Exchange Rates," I.M.F. *Staff Papers* (November), reprinted in Richard N. Cooper, ed., *International Finance* (Penguin Books, 1969).

Hickman, Bert G. (1974). "International Transmission of Economic Fluctuations and Inflation," in Albert Ando, Richard Herring, and Richard Marston, eds., *International Aspects of Stabilization Policies*, Conference Series No. 12, Federal Reserve Bank of Boston.

Kenen, Peter B. (1976). "Capital Mobility and Financial Integration: A Survey," *Princeton Studies in International Finance* No. 39 (December).

Kouri, Pentti J. K., and Michael G. Porter (1974). "International Capital Flows and Portfolio Equilibrium," *Journal of Political Economy* (May/June).

McKinnon, Ronald I., and Wallace E. Oates (1966). "The Implications of International Economic Integration for Monetary, Fiscal, and Exchange-Rate Policy," *Princeton Studies in International Finance* No. 16 (March).

Mundell, Robert A. (1960). "Generalization of the Classical Model," *American Economic Review* (March), reprinted as chapter 13 in Robert A. Mundell, *International Economics* (Macmillan, 1968).

Mundell, Robert A. (1961). "A Theory of Optimum Currency Areas," *American Economic Review* (September), reprinted as chapter 12 in Robert A. Mundell, *International Economics* (Macmillan, 1968).

Mundell, Robert A. (1963). "Capital Mobility and Stabilization Policy under Fixed and Flexible Exchange Rates," *Canadian Journal of Economics and Political Science*

(November), reprinted as chapter 18 in Robert A. Mundell, *International Economics* (Macmillan, 1968).

Mundell, Robert A. (1964). "A Reply: Capital Mobility and Size," *Canandian Journal of Economics and Political Science* (August), reprinted as appendix to chapter 18 in Robert A. Mundell, *International Economics* (Macmillan, 1968).

Organization for Economic Cooperation and Development (1980). *Economic Outlook. Occasional Studies*, "Fiscal Policy Simulations with the OECD International Linkage Model" (OECD, July).

Waelbroeck, Jean, and A. Dramais (1974). "Desmos: A Model for the Coordination of Economic Policies in the EEC Countries," in Albert Ando, Richard Herring, and Richard Marston, *eds.*, *International Aspects of Stabilization Policies*, Conference Series No. 12, Federal Reserve Bank of Boston.

13

Reserve Requirements on Eurocurrency Deposits: Implications for the Stabilization of Real Outputs

Dale W. Henderson
and
Douglas G. Waldo

The development of closer links between domestic financial markets and the Eurocurrency markets has provided an incentive for further investigation of the implications of placing reserve requirements on Eurocurrency deposits.[1] In this chapter a rational expectations model of a two-country world economy, to be described in section 13.1, is employed to analyze the implications of placing a reserve requirement on Eurodollar deposits for the stabilization of real outputs.[2] The approach is similar to that of other recent contributions to the analysis of monetary policy. Suggested changes in financial regulations are evaluated under various assumptions about the relative magnitudes of different unanticipated and contemporaneously unobservable shocks to the world economy.[3] Specifically, it is assumed that the monetary authorities in each of the two countries, the United States and Germany, set their policy instrument in an attempt to achieve a desired value for their country's real output, which is their ultimate target.[4] Two policy regimes are considered. Under the fixed exchange rate regime studied in section 13.2 the policy instrument of the US authorities is the US monetary base, and the policy instrument of the German authorities is the exchange rate. Under the flexible exchange rate regime studied in section 13.3 the policy instrument of each set of authorities is its country's monetary base, and the exchange rate is allowed to vary. Under both exchange rate regimes, deviations between the actual

The authors have benefited greatly from discussions of many of the issues considered in this chapter with Stephen Axilrod, Ralph Bryant, Michael Dooley, Richard Froyen, Lance Girton, Don Roper, Jeffrey Shafer, and Roger Waud. Helpful suggestions were received from Peter Clark, Walter Enders, Robert Flood, James Healy, Robert Hodrick, Pentti Kouri, Paul Krugman, Harvey Lapan, and Maurice Obstfeld. This chapter represents the views of the authors and should not be interpreted as reflecting the views of the Board of Governors of the Federal Reserve System or other members of its staff.

values and desired values of real outputs arise because the authorities have incomplete current information about the shocks which buffet the world economy. Changes in the level of the reserve requirement on Eurodollar deposits affect the variances of these deviations because they affect the responsivenesses of the demand for US high-powered money to changes in the endogenous variables and the impact effects of some exogenous shocks. Some conclusions are contained in section 13.4.

13.1 The Model

The model is a description of economic interactions among agents in the United States and Germany, denominated in two currencies, the dollar and the Deutsche Mark (DM). The nine groups of agents whose behavior is portrayed are US nonbanks, German nonbanks, US banks' home country offices (US banks), German banks' home country offices (German banks), US and German banks' foreign affiliates (Eurobanks), the US central bank (Federal Reserve), the German central bank (Bundesbank), the US Treasury, and the German Treasury.

First, attention is focused on the financial sector of the model. Eight financial instruments are mentioned below, but simplifying assumptions and balance sheet constraints imply that attention can be focused on the markets for only two instruments: US high-powered money and German high-powered money.

The composition of the portfolio of each group of agents is described below and is summarized in table 13.1. Table 13.1 also contains a list of all financial instruments included in the model and a summary of the market clearing conditions for these financial instruments. So that holdings of financial instruments can be aggregated, all DM denominated magnitudes are converted to dollars using the exchange rate (E), which is defined as the dollar price of a DM. The sum of the entries in any row of table 13.1 is the balance sheet constraint for the associated group of agents and, therefore, must be identically equal to zero. Also, the sum of entries in any column except the last is the excess demand for the associated financial instrument and, therefore, must be equal to zero in equilibrium.

United States banks' holdings and German banks' holdings (rows 1 and 2) are designated with the superscript B, and the latter are differentiated with an asterisk, as are all German holdings. The banks in each country have as liabilities, home currency demand deposits; and as assets, home currency high-powered money, home currency claims on both nonbanks and the home treasury, and foreign currency claims on both nonbanks and the foreign treasury.[5]

Table 13.1
Composition of agents' portfolios and market clearing conditions for the financial instruments[a]

Instruments	H	EA	L	ES	D	EG	V	EX	W
Agents									
US banks	H^B		L^B	ES^B	$-D^B$				$-W^B$
German banks		$E\overset{\ast}{A}{}^{B}$	$\overset{\ast}{L}{}^{B}$	$E\overset{\ast}{S}{}^{B}$		$-E\overset{\ast}{G}{}^{B}$			$-\overset{\ast}{W}{}^{B}$
Eurobanks	H^A		L^A	ES^A			$-V^A$	$-EX^A$	$-W^A$
US nonbanks			$-L^N$	$-ES^N$	D^N		V^N	EX^N	$-W^N$
German nonbanks			$-\overset{\ast}{L}{}^{N}$	$-E\overset{\ast}{S}{}^{N}$		$E\overset{\ast}{G}{}^{N}$	$\overset{\ast}{V}{}^{N}$	$E\overset{\ast}{X}{}^{N}$	$-\overset{\ast}{W}{}^{N}$
Federal Reserve	$-H^C$		L^C						
Bundesbank		$-E\overset{\ast}{A}{}^{C}$		$E\overset{\ast}{S}{}^{C}$					
US Treasury			$-\overline{L}$						W^T
German Treasury				$-\overline{ES}$					$\overset{\ast}{W}{}^{T}$

a. Key: H, US high-powered money; A, German high-powered money; L, dollar claims on nonbanks and US Treasury; S, DM claims on nonbanks and German Treasury; D, US banks' dollar demand deposits; G, German banks' DM demand deposits; V, Eurodollar deposits; X, Euro-DM deposits; W, net worth in dollars.

The Eurobanks (row 3), whose holdings are designated with the superscript A, have as liabilities, Eurodollar deposits and Euro-DM deposits; and as assets, US high-powered money, dollar claims on both nonbanks and the US Treasury, and DM claims on both nonbanks and the German Treasury.

United States nonbanks' holdings and German nonbanks' holdings (rows 4 and 5) are designated with the superscript N, and the latter are differentiated by an asterisk. Nonbanks in each country hold all the financial instruments except for home and foreign currency high-powered moneys and foreign currency demand deposits.[6]

United States central bank holdings and German central bank holdings are designated with the superscript C, and the latter are differentiated by an asterisk. The central bank in each country holds home currency claims against both nonbanks and the home treasury and issues home currency high-powered money. In addition, the US (German) Treasury issues a stock of dollar (DM) denominated liabilities denoted by $\overline{L}$ $(\overline{S})$.

Certain assumptions about commerical banks and central banks guarantee that there are only two nominal interest rates in this model and that these nominal interest rates satisfy the uncovered interest parity condition. First, it is assumed that the interest rates on demand deposits at commercial banks in both countries are fixed at zero. Second, it is assumed that all commercial banks are risk neutral price takers that have zero intermediation costs. Third, it is assumed that the Federal Reserve (Bundesbank) pays interest on dollar (DM) bank reserves at a rate equal to the rate on dollar (DM) claims on nonbanks and the US Treasury (German Treasury). Under these assumptions all variable-rate instruments denominated in a given currency pay the same rate of interest. Furthermore, the representative dollar interest rate (i) must equal the representative DM interest rate $(\overset{*}{i})$ plus the expected rate of depreciation of the dollar:

$$i = \overset{*}{i} + \bar{e} - e, \tag{1}$$

where e is the (logarithm of the) exchange rate (E) and $\bar{e}$ is the constant expected value of e. Only when these conditions are met will Eurobanks expect neither profits nor losses from accepting deposits denominated in either currency and holding claims denominated in either currency.[7]

Now consider the demands by US and German nonbanks for the various financial instruments. Three asset demand functions are specified explicitly: US nonbanks' demands for demand deposits and Eurodollar deposits and German nonbanks' demand for demand deposits:

$$\frac{D^N}{Q} = \underline{d}\left(\frac{PY}{Q}, i\right) - \alpha - \gamma, \tag{2a}$$

$$\frac{V^N}{Q} = \underline{v}\left(\frac{PY}{Q}, i\right) + \alpha - \beta, \tag{2b}$$

$$\frac{\overset{*}{G}{}^N}{\overset{*}{Q}} = \underline{\overset{*}{g}}\left(\frac{\overset{*}{P}\overset{*}{Y}}{\overset{*}{Q}}, \overset{*}{i}\right). \tag{2c}$$

D^N, V^N, and $\overset{*}{G}{}^N$ are the nominal values of the desired holdings. Q $(\overset{*}{Q})$ is the price deflator for US (German) nonbanks measured in dollars (DM). Each country produces only one good, and the two goods are different. P $(\overset{*}{P})$ is the price of a unit of US (German) output measured in dollars (DM). Y $(\overset{*}{Y})$ is the output of the single good produced in the United States (Germany) measured in physical units. α, β, and γ are stochastic disturbance terms associated, respectively, with shifts by US residents out of demand deposits into Eurodollar deposits, out of Eurodollar deposits into nonreservable instruments, and out of demand deposits into nonreservable instruments. It is assumed that these disturbance terms and those introduced below have zero means and constant variances and that they are mutually and serially uncorrelated.

The following partly linear, partly log-linear approximations of equations (2) will be employed:

$$D^N = d_0 + d_1 q + d_2 p + d_3 Y - d_4 i - \alpha - \gamma, \tag{3a}$$

$$d_1 = \bar{D}^N - \underline{d}_1 \bar{Y}, \qquad d_2 = \underline{d}_1 \bar{Y}, \qquad d_3 = \underline{d}_1, \qquad d_4 = -\underline{d}_2,$$

$$V^N = v_0 + v_1 q + v_2 p + v_3 Y + v_4 i + \alpha - \beta, \tag{3b}$$

$$v_1 = \bar{V}^N - \underline{v}_1 \bar{Y}, \qquad v_2 = \underline{v}_1 \bar{Y}, \qquad v_3 = \underline{v}_1, \qquad v_4 = \underline{v}_2,$$

$$\overset{*}{G}{}^N = \overset{*}{g}_0 + \overset{*}{g}_1 \overset{*}{q} + \overset{*}{g}_2 \overset{*}{p} + \overset{*}{g}_3 \overset{*}{Y} - \overset{*}{g}_4 \overset{*}{i}, \tag{3c}$$

$$\overset{*}{g}_1 = \overset{*}{\bar{G}}{}^N - \underline{\overset{*}{g}}_1 \overset{*}{\bar{Y}}, \qquad \overset{*}{g}_2 = \underline{\overset{*}{g}}_1 \overset{*}{\bar{Y}}, \qquad \overset{*}{g}_3 = \underline{\overset{*}{g}}_1, \qquad \overset{*}{g}_4 = -\underline{\overset{*}{g}}_2.$$

p, q, $\overset{*}{p}$, and $\overset{*}{q}$ are the logarithms of P, Q, $\overset{*}{P}$, and $\overset{*}{Q}$. A bar over a variable denotes its zero-disturbance value, the value that variable would assume if all disturbance terms in the markets for financial instruments and goods were zero. In deriving equations (3) it has been assumed that units are chosen so that $\bar{P} = \bar{Q} = \overset{*}{\bar{P}} = \overset{*}{\bar{Q}} = 1$. d_0, v_0, and $\overset{*}{g}_0$ are constants. $\underline{d}_j$, $\underline{v}_j$, and $\underline{\overset{*}{g}}_j$, $j = 1, 2$, are the derivatives of $\underline{d}$, $\underline{v}$, and $\underline{g}$ with respect to their jth arguments evaluated at the zero-disturbance values of the relevant variables.

Demand deposits can be used directly in making transactions. In this paper US residents' Eurodollar deposits are viewed as short-term deposits that can be converted into demand deposits without much delay. It is assumed that as real incomes rise, nonbanks' portfolio preferences shift toward assets that are relatively more useful in making transactions; thus d_j, v_j, and $\overset{*}{g}_j$, $j = 2, 3$, are positive. Furthermore, it is assumed that the real income elasticities of the real demands given by equations (2) are less than or equal to one ($\underline{d}_1 \bar{Y}/\bar{D}^N$, $\underline{v}_1 \bar{Y}/\bar{V}^N$, $\underline{\overset{*}{g}}_1 \overset{*}{\bar{Y}}/\overset{*}{\bar{G}}{}^N \leqslant 1$), so d_1, v_1, and $\overset{*}{g}_1$ are positive or zero.[8]

Assumptions made earlier along with one additional assumption that is stated below imply that US (German) nonbanks' demand for any financial instrument can be expressed as a function of one rate of return, the nominal interest rate on variable-rate dollar (DM) instruments. First, the assumptions made above about banking institutions imply that variable-rate instruments denominated in the same currency pay the same rate of interest. Hence nonbanks face at most four different real rates of return: real returns on fixed-rate and variable-rate instruments denominated in each currency. Second, it has been assumed that nonbanks of a given country do not hold fixed-rate instruments denominated in the currency of the other country; thus at most three real rates of return are relevant to nonbanks of a given country. Third, banks guarantee that variable nominal interest rates satisfy uncovered interest parity. Thus, the variable-rate financial instruments considered by nonbanks of a given country offer the same real rate of return. The difference between this real rate of return and the real rate of return on home currency fixed-rate assets is the nomial yield on home currency variable-rate instruments. Finally, it is assumed that for each group of nonbanks only this difference affects the allocation of its net worth between all variable-rate instruments and the home currency fixed-rate instrument.

It is assumed that all nonbanks regard all the instruments in their portfolios as *strict gross substitutes.*[9] This assumption implies that whenever the interest rate on a given asset (liability) rises, the desired holding of that asset (liability) rises (falls) and the desired holdings of all other assets (liabilities) fall (rise) while the desired holdings of all liabilities (assets) rise (fall). It is also assumed that for each financial instrument *the own rate effect exceeds the sum of cross rate effects.* This assumption implies that if all variable interest rates rise by the same amount, as they must if the expected rate of depreciation of the dollar remains unchanged, then the desired holdings of each interest-bearing asset must rise, the desired holding of each interest-bearing liability must fall, and the desired holdings of demand deposits must fall. Thus $\underline{d}_2$ and $\overset{*}{\underline{g}}_2$ are negative and $\underline{v}_2$ is positive, so d_4, $\overset{*}{g}_4$, and v_4 are all positive.

Two conditions guarantee equilibrium in financial markets.[10] The demands for both kinds of high-powered money must equal the supplies:

$$H^C = H^B + H^A, \tag{4}$$

$$\overset{*}{A}{}^C = \overset{*}{A}{}^B. \tag{5}$$

It is assumed that US banks hold the high-powered money implied by the required reserve ratio on their demand deposits (k_D), that German banks hold the German high-powered money implied by the required reserve ratio on their demand deposits ($\overset{*}{k}_G$), and that Eurobanks hold the US high-powered money implied by the required reserve ratio on Eurodollar deposits accepted from US residents (k_V).[11] Furthermore, it is assumed that the reserve ratio for dollar demand deposits is greater than the reserve ratio for Eurodollar deposits of US residents ($k_D > k_V$). Thus equilibrium conditions for the two high-powered money markets can be written

$$H^C = h_0 + h_1 q + h_2 p + h_3 Y - h_4 i - (k_D - k_V)\alpha - k_V \beta - k_D \gamma, \tag{6}$$

$$h_j = k_D d_j + k_V v_j, \quad j = 0, 1, 2, 3, \quad h_4 = k_D d_4 - k_V v_4,$$

$$\overset{*}{A}{}^C = \overset{*}{a}_0 + \overset{*}{a}_1 \overset{*}{q} + \overset{*}{a}_2 \overset{*}{p} + \overset{*}{a}_3 \overset{*}{Y} - \overset{*}{a}_4 \overset{*}{i}, \tag{7}$$

$$\overset{*}{a}_j = \overset{*}{k}_G \overset{*}{g}_j, \quad j = 0, 1, 2, 3, 4.$$

It follows from assumptions made above that the demand for US
(German) high-powered money depends positively on the (logarithms of
the) US (German) price deflator and price of US (German) output as
well as on US (German) output and that the demand for German high-
powered money depends negatively on $\overset{*}{i}$. However, it must be established
that the demand for US high-powered money depends negatively on i.
Given the assumptions made above about nonbanks' demands for financial instruments, it is an implication of the balance sheet constraint for
US residents that

$$\overset{(-)}{D_i^N} + \overset{(+)}{V_i^N} \equiv \overset{(-)}{L_i^N} + E(\overset{(-)}{S_i^N} - \overset{(+)}{X_i^N}) < 0, \tag{8}$$

where $D_i^N = -d_4$ and $V_i^N = v_4$. $-h_4 = -(k_D d_4 - k_V v_4)$ is more negative than k_D times the left-hand side of (8) because $k_D > k_V$, so US
high-powered money demand must respond negatively to i.

Now attention is turned to the real sector of the model. Equilibrium
output in the United States (Y) and Germany $(\overset{*}{Y})$ must be equal to
aggregate demand for that output:

$$Y = y_0 + y_1 Y + y_2 \overset{*}{Y} - y_3 r - y_4 \overset{*}{r} + y_5 t + \lambda + \mu, \tag{9}$$

$$\overset{*}{Y} = \overset{*}{y}_0 + \overset{*}{y}_1 \overset{*}{Y} + \overset{*}{y}_2 Y - \overset{*}{y}_3 \overset{*}{r} - \overset{*}{y}_4 r - y_5 t - \mu. \tag{10}$$

The demands for both US and German output respond positively to both
countries' incomes (outputs), and the sums of the marginal propensities
to consume the two goods is less than one in both countries ($y_1 + \overset{*}{y}_2 < 1$,
$\overset{*}{y}_1 + y_2 < 1$). The demands for both outputs respond negatively to both
the expected real return to saving for US residents (r), which is given by

$$r = i - (\bar{q} - q), \tag{11}$$

and the expected real return to saving for German residents $(\overset{*}{r})$, which is
given by

$$\overset{*}{r} = \overset{*}{i} - (\overset{*}{\bar{q}} - \overset{*}{q}), \tag{12}$$

where $\bar{q}$ and $\overset{*}{\bar{q}}$ are the zero-disturbance values of the (logarithms of the)
US and German price deflators. The (logarithm of the) price deflator for
residents of each country is a weighted average of the (logarithms of the)
prices of the two goods expressed in that country's currency:

$$q = \delta p + (1 - \delta)(e + \overset{*}{p}), \tag{13}$$

$$\overset{*}{q} = (1 - \overset{*}{\delta})(p - e) + \overset{*}{\delta} \overset{*}{p}, \tag{14}$$

where δ and $\overset{*}{\delta}$ represent the ratio of spending on home output to total spending in the United States and Germany, respectively. Demand for the US (German) good responds positively (negatively) to the (logarithm of the) relative price of the German good (t), which is given by

$$t = e + \overset{*}{p} - p. \tag{15}$$

It is assumed that trade is initially balanced and that units are defined so that one unit of the German good would trade for one unit of the US good if all disturbances were zero. Under these assumptions the responsivenesses of the demands for US and German goods to the relative price of the German good are equal in absolute value. λ and μ are stochastic terms which represent respectively shifts up in the demand for the US good alone and shifts up in the demand for the US good at the expense of the German good.

Equilibrium output in the United States and Germany must also be equal to aggregate supply:

$$Y = \bar{Y} + (1/f)(p - \bar{p}), \tag{16}$$

$$\overset{*}{Y} = \overset{\bar{*}}{Y} + (1/\overset{*}{f})(\overset{*}{p} - \overset{\bar{*}}{p}). \tag{17}$$

The deviations of actual outputs (Y, $\overset{*}{Y}$) from their zero-disturbance values ($\bar{Y}$, $\overset{\bar{*}}{Y}$) depend positively on the deviations of the (logarithms of) actual prices (p, $\overset{*}{p}$) from their zero-disturbance values ($\bar{p}$, $\overset{\bar{*}}{p}$).[12]

The description of the model is now complete. It is convenient to obtain equilibrium conditions for the markets for the US good, the German good, US high-powered money, and German high-powered money as functions of US output, German output, the representative dollar nominal interest rate, the exchange rate, and the German high-powered money supply:[13]

$$-y_Y \hat{Y} + y_{\overset{*}{Y}} \overset{*}{\hat{Y}} - y_i \hat{\imath} + y_e \hat{e} = -\lambda - \mu, \tag{18a}$$

$$\overset{*}{y}_Y \hat{Y} - \overset{*}{y}_{\overset{*}{Y}} \overset{*}{\hat{Y}} - \overset{*}{y}_i \hat{\imath} - \overset{*}{y}_e \hat{e} = \mu, \tag{18b}$$

$$h_Y \hat{Y} - h_i \hat{\imath} = (k_D - k_V)\alpha + k_V \beta + k_D \gamma, \tag{18c}$$

$$\overset{*}{a}_{\overset{*}{Y}} \overset{*}{\hat{Y}} - \overset{*}{a}_i \hat{\imath} - \overset{*}{a}_e \hat{e} - \overset{*}{A}^c = 0, \tag{18d}$$

where

$$y_Y = 1 - y_1 + f[\delta y_3 + (1 - \overset{*}{\delta})y_4 + y_5], \qquad h_Y = h_2 f + h_3,$$

$$y_{\overset{*}{Y}} = y_2 + \overset{*}{f}[-(1 - \delta)y_3 - \overset{*}{\delta}y_4 + y_5],$$

$$y_i = y_3 + y_4, \qquad\qquad\qquad h_i = h_4,$$

$$y_e = y_5 - (1 - \delta)y_3 - \mathring{\delta}y_4,$$

$$\mathring{y}_Y = \mathring{y}_2 + f[-(1 - \mathring{\delta})\mathring{y}_3 - \delta\mathring{y}_4 + y_5],$$

$$\mathring{y}_{\mathring{Y}} = 1 - \mathring{y}_1 + \mathring{f}[\mathring{\delta}\mathring{y}_3 + (1 - \delta)\mathring{y}_4 + y_5], \qquad \mathring{a}_{\mathring{Y}} = \mathring{a}_2\mathring{f} + \mathring{a}_3,$$

$$\mathring{y}_i = \mathring{y}_3 + \mathring{y}_4, \qquad\qquad\qquad \mathring{a}_i = \mathring{a}_4,$$

$$\mathring{y}_e = y_5 + \mathring{\delta}\mathring{y}_3 + (1 - \delta)\mathring{y}_4, \qquad \mathring{a}_e = \mathring{a}_4.$$

In equations (18) a hat over a variable represents the deviation of that variable from its zero disturbance value. Furthermore, in order to simplify the analysis we have assumed that the income elasticities of the three deposit demands given by equations (3) are equal to one, so that $d_1 = v_1 = \mathring{g}_1 = h_1 = \mathring{a}_1 = 0$.[14] An increase in US (German) output has a negative direct effect on excess demand for US (German) output and a negative indirect effect which occurs because the associated increase in the US (German) price level implies higher real interest rates and a lower (higher) relative price for the German good. An increase in German (US) output has a positive direct effect on excess demand for US (German) output and indirect effects through associated changes in the relative price and real interest rates. The positive relative price effect is assumed to dominate the negative real interest rate effects. An increase in US (German) output increases excess demand for US (German) high-powered money directly and indirectly through the associated rise in the price of the US (German) good. The representative dollar nominal interest rate is positively associated with the real interest rates and negatively associated with excess demand in all four markets. The exchange rate is positively associated with the German nominal interest rate, both real interest rates, and the relative price of the foreign good. It follows that a depreciation of the dollar ($\hat{e} > 0$) definitely reduces excess demand in the German high-powered money and German output markets. It is assumed that the positive relative price effect dominates the negative real interest rate effects, so that a depreciation raises excess demand for US output. Thus, under the assumptions laid out above all of the coefficients in equations (18) are positive. The four equations (18) determine $\hat{Y}$, $\mathring{\hat{Y}}$, $\hat{\imath}$, and either (under fixed exchange rates) $\mathring{A}^c$ or (under flexible exchange rates) $\hat{e}$ given an unchanging value of the exogenous US high-powered money supply and the disturbances α, β, γ, λ, and μ.

The policy change considered in this paper is the imposition of a reserve requirement on the Eurodollar deposits of US residents at both

US- and German-owned Eurobanks with the payment of interest on required reserves. If the cooperation of the German monetary authorities were not obtained, only the subset of those deposits consisting of deposits at US-owned Eurobanks could be reserved. However, since interest would be paid on required reserves, US-owned Eurobanks would incur no opportunity cost when they held reserves, would not be placed at a competitive disadvantage, and would not lose the reserved deposits to German owned Eurobanks. Thus, reserving only the subset of deposits at US-owned Eurobanks would have qualitative effects similar to those of reserving all the deposits. Of course, the cooperation of the German monetary authorities would be more likely if the reserve requirement helped them achieve their macroeconomic goal.

In order to determine the circumstances under which monetary authorities might find it desirable to place a reserve requirement on the Eurodollar deposits of US residents, it is necessary to specify the goals and operating strategies of the monetary authorities. The goal of the authorities in each country is to minimize deviations of output from a desired level. Since it is assumed that the monetary authorities do not observe Y, $\overset{*}{Y}$, or the five disturbances, the operating strategy for each monetary authority involves setting its policy instrument so that the expected value of its country's output equals the desired value. The policy instrument of the US authorities is always the US high-powered money supply. Under fixed exchange rates the policy instrument of the German authorities is the exchange rate, while under flexible exchange rates it is the German high-powered money supply. Since policy instruments are set before the values of current disturbances are known, there are generally deviations between the actual values of outputs and their desired (and their expected) values. However, the size of these deviations can be influenced by the exchange rate regime and reserve requirements.

The purpose of the remainder of this paper is to determine how deviations of US and German outputs from their desired values are affected when the reserve ratio for Eurodollar deposits held by US residents is increased. It is assumed that k_V can be varied within a range which has a lower limit of zero and an upper limit of the exogenous reserve requirement on demand deposits. Given the earlier assumption that the disturbance terms are mutually uncorrelated, it is possible to consider the effect of an increase in k_V when each of the stochastic shifts is the only source of uncertainty. These effects can then be combined to obtain the overall effect of an increase in k_V.

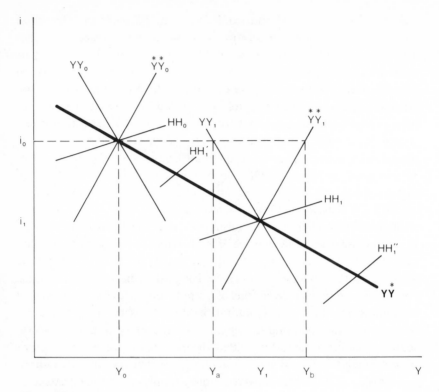

Figure 13.1
Shifts in asset demands, fixed exchange rates.

13.2 Fixed Exchange Rates

In this section it is assumed that the Bundesbank keeps the exchange rate fixed ($\hat{e} = 0$) by varying the supply of German high-powered money with exchanges of German high-powered money for DM claims on nonbanks and the German Treasury.[15] Under this assumption the change in the German high-powered money supply is determined recursively by the change in German high-powered money demand, so equation (18d) can be ignored.

Figure 13.1 is useful in illustrating the workings of the model under fixed exchange rates. Given a value of $\overset{*}{Y}$ the YY, $\overset{*}{Y}\overset{*}{Y}$, and HH schedules represent the pairs of i and Y which clear the markets for US output, German output, and US high-powered money. The signs of the slopes of these schedules are implications of the previously made assumptions about the coefficients in equations (18). However, these earlier assumptions do not determine the relative slopes of the $\overset{*}{Y}\overset{*}{Y}$ and HH schedules. The implications of alternative assumptions about the relative slopes of these schedules will be pointed out at later stages in the analysis. As $\overset{*}{Y}$ rises, the YY and $\overset{*}{Y}\overset{*}{Y}$ schedules in figure 13.1 shift. The $\overset{*}{Y}\overset{*}{Y}$ schedule shifts southeast, for instance from $\overset{*}{Y}\overset{*}{Y}_0$ to $\overset{*}{Y}\overset{*}{Y}_1$, reflecting the negative influence of $\overset{*}{Y}$ on the excess demand for German output. The YY schedule shifts northeast, for instance from YY_0 to YY_1, reflecting the positive influence of $\overset{*}{Y}$ on the demand for US goods. The remaining schedule, $Y\overset{*}{Y}$, is the locus of combinations of i, Y, and (implicitly) $\overset{*}{Y}$ that clear the US and German goods markets. The $Y\overset{*}{Y}$ schedule has a negative slope and is flatter than the YY schedule. Consider a rise in $\overset{*}{Y}$ at a fixed i. The increase in Y required to clear the German goods market ($Y_b - Y_0$) is larger than the increase in Y required to clear the US goods market ($Y_a - Y_0$); thus the $\overset{*}{Y}\overset{*}{Y}$ schedule shifts farther to the right than the YY schedule. Since the YY and $\overset{*}{Y}\overset{*}{Y}$ schedules always intersect along the $Y\overset{*}{Y}$ schedule, the $Y\overset{*}{Y}$ schedule has a negative slope and is flatter than the YY schedule.

The familiar analysis of the implications of fixing the money supply in a closed economy provides some initial intuition about the circumstances under which an increase in k_V would be desirable, at least from the US point of view.[16] If the money supply in a closed economy is fixed and there are no disturbances in the goods market so that the IS curve is stable, the variance of output is lower the smaller are disturbances in the money market, that is, the more stable the LM curve.[17] Furthermore, if there are disturbances in the goods market, fixing the money supply is more successful at dampening these disturbances when the income responsiveness of the demand for money is high and the interest rate responsiveness of the demand for money is low in absolute value, that is, when the LM curve is steep.

In our framework under fixed exchange rates the US authorities have adopted a policy of fixing the monetary base, but the Eurodollar reserve requirement can be set so as to complement that policy. Specificially, the analogue of the closed economy IS schedule is the $Y\overset{*}{Y}$ schedule, and the analogue of the closed economy LM schedule is the HH schedule. By varying the Eurodollar reserve requirement k_V, the policy maker changes both the magnitude of the exogenous shifts in the HH schedule and the slope of that schedule.

Consider the consequences of an increase in k_V for the impact effects of the exogenous disturbances on the market for US high-powered money. First, given $k_V < k_D$, an increase in k_V decreases the absolute value of the impact effects resulting from shifts between demand deposits and Eurodollar deposits (α). Second, an increase in k_V increases the absolute value of the impact effects resulting from shifts between Eurodollar deposits and nonreservable instruments (β).

Now consider the consequences of an increase in k_V for the slope of the HH schedule. First, an increase in k_V raises the responsiveness of the demand for US high-powered money to changes in US output (h_Y):

$$\frac{\partial h_Y}{\partial k_V} = v_2 f + v_3 > 0. \tag{19}$$

h_Y rises because increasing k_V raises the weight on US residents' demand for Eurodollars in the demand for H. The demand for Eurodollars responds positively to an increase in Y because of the direct effect of the increase in Y (v_3) and because of the indirect effect of the associated increase in p ($v_2 f$). Second, an increase in k_V reduces the absolute value of the responsiveness of the demand for US high-powered money to changes in the representative dollar interest rate (h_i):

$$\frac{\partial h_i}{\partial k_V} = -v_4 < 0. \tag{20}$$

h_i is equal to the negative of the weighted sum of the interest rate responsivenesses of the nominal demands for demand deposits and Eurodollar deposits where the weights are the appropriate reserve requirements. Since the interest responsiveness of Eurodollars is positive, h_i falls when k_V rises. As a result of the rise in h_Y and the fall in h_i, the slope of the HH schedule increases.

The various consequences of an increase in k_V for the market for US high-powered money often have conflicting implications for the dampening influence of this increase. We suggest an approach which can sometimes be used to resolve these conflicts.

It is useful to explain this approach in the course of analyzing a particular disturbance, a shift from demand deposits to Eurodeposits. The impact effect of this disturbance is an excess supply of H, which implies a shift of HH from HH_0 to HH_1. This excess supply puts downward pressure on the interest rate which induces excess demand in both goods markets and results in increases in both types of output. The increase in $\overset{*}{Y}$ shifts the $\overset{*}{Y}\overset{*}{Y}$ schedule to the southeast and the YY schedule to the northeast. At the new equilibrium represented by the point (Y_1, i_1), Y and $\overset{*}{Y}$ are higher and i is lower.

It is not immediately clear whether an increase in k_V dampens or amplifies the increases in Y and $\overset{*}{Y}$. It is definitely true that the impact effect of the disturbance on the excess supply of US high-powered money is smaller and that the HH schedule is steeper. However, it is not clear whether the net result of these changes is to produce a shift in the HH schedule along the $Y\overset{*}{Y}$ schedule which is smaller (HH_1') or larger (HH_1''). Although the smaller impact effect and the increased income responsiveness imply a smaller shift, the decreased absolute interest rate responsiveness implies a larger shift.

Our approach to resolving this ambiguity is based on the observation that if there is an excess demand for (supply of) H given the initial equilibrating responses of i and Y (i_1 and Y_1), then the HH_1' (HH_1'') schedule is relevant, so that an increase in k_V dampens (amplifies) the increase in Y, the decrease in i, and the increase in $\overset{*}{Y}$. Our approach consists of holding the initial equilibrating responses of the endogenous variables constant, raising the reserve requirement on Eurodollar deposits, and determining whether there is an excess demand for or supply of H.[18]

To apply this approach to the shift from demand deposits to Eurodeposits note that the change in the excess demand for US high-powered money ($E\hat{X}DH/\alpha$) resulting from the initial equilibrating responses of Y and i to a positive α ($\hat{Y}/\alpha$ and $\hat{i}/\alpha$) must be zero:[19]

$$0 = \frac{E\hat{X}DH}{\alpha} = h_Y \frac{\hat{Y}}{\alpha} - h_i \frac{\hat{i}}{\alpha} - (k_D - k_V). \tag{21}$$

Holding the initial equilibrating responses of Y and i the same, the effect of an increase in k_V on the change in excess demand resulting from a positive α is given by

$$\frac{\partial(E\hat{X}DH/\alpha)}{\partial k_V} = \overset{(+)}{\frac{\partial h_Y}{\partial k_V}} \overset{(\pm)}{\frac{\hat{Y}}{\alpha}} - \overset{(-)}{\frac{\partial h_i}{\partial k_V}} \overset{(-)}{\frac{\hat{i}}{\alpha}} + 1. \tag{22}$$

The disturbance has a smaller impact on excess supply, and the initial equilibrating increase in Y creates more excess demand, but the initial equilibrating decline in i creates more excess supply. To see that the former effects outweigh the latter effect divide (21) by $k_D - k_V$ and add the result to (22) to obtain

$$\frac{\partial(E\hat{X}DH/\alpha)}{\partial k_V} = \left(\overset{(+)}{\frac{\partial h_Y}{\partial k_V}} + \frac{h_Y}{(k_D - k_V)}\right) \overset{(\pm)}{\frac{\hat{Y}}{\alpha}} - \left(\overset{(+)}{\frac{\partial h_i}{\partial k_V}} + \frac{h_i}{k_D - k_V}\right) \overset{(-)}{\frac{\hat{i}}{\alpha}} > 0. \tag{23}$$

Equation (23) is positive because the term in the last set of parentheses on the right-hand side has the same sign as

$$(k_D - k_V)\frac{\partial h_i}{\partial k_V} + h_i = k_D(d_4 - v_4) > 0, \tag{24}$$

which is positive by the earlier proof that $h_i = k_D d_4 - k_V v_4 > 0$ for all $k_D \geqslant k_V$. Thus, an increase in k_V creates an excess demand for H, holding the equilibrating responses of the endogenous variables constant; the HH_1' schedule is relevant, and raising k_V dampens the equilibrating responses of Y and $\overset{*}{Y}$ to a shift from demand deposits to Eurodeposits.[20]

The remaining two shifts in asset demands are also defined so that their impact effects are increases in the excess supply of H that shift the HH schedule from HH_0 to HH_1 in figure 13.1. Thus, they both have the same qualitative effects on the endogenous variables as a shift from demand deposits to Eurodeposits. However, the implications of raising k_V are not the same for all the asset shifts.

Consider a shift from Eurodeposits to a nonreservable instrument. For this shift an increase in k_V implies that the impact effect on the excess supply of H is larger rather than smaller. Once again it is not immediately apparent whether HH_1' or HH_1'' is relevant. Although the increased income responsiveness implies a smaller shift, the larger impact effect and decreased absolute interest responsiveness imply a larger shift. It is now demonstrated that the latter two effects dominate. The initial equilibrating responses of Y and i must clear the market for US high-powered money:

$$0 = \frac{E\hat{X}DH}{\beta} = h_Y\frac{\hat{Y}}{\beta} - h_i\frac{\hat{i}}{\beta} - k_V. \tag{25}$$

Differentiating with respect to k_V holding the initial equilibrating responses of the endogenous variables constant yields

$$\frac{\partial(E\hat{X}DH/\beta)}{\partial k_V} = \overset{(+)}{\frac{\partial h_Y}{\partial k_V}}\overset{(\pm)}{\frac{\hat{Y}}{\beta}} - \overset{(-)}{\frac{\partial h_i}{\partial k_V}}\overset{(-)}{\frac{\hat{i}}{\beta}} - 1. \tag{26}$$

Dividing (25) by k_V and subtracting the result from (26) implies

$$\frac{\partial(E\hat{X}DH/\beta)}{\partial k_V} = \overset{(-)}{\left(\frac{\partial h_Y}{\partial k_V} - \frac{h_Y}{k_V}\right)}\overset{(\pm)}{\frac{\hat{Y}}{\beta}} - \overset{(-)}{\left(\frac{\partial h_i}{\partial k_V} - \frac{h_i}{k_V}\right)}\overset{(-)}{\frac{\hat{i}}{\beta}} < 0, \tag{27}$$

since the term in the first set of parentheses has the same sign as

$$k_V\frac{\partial h_Y}{\partial k_V} - h_Y = -k_D(d_2 f + d_3) < 0. \tag{28}$$

Thus, an increase in k_V creates an excess supply of H; the H_1'' schedule is relevant, and increasing k_V amplifies the equilibrating responses of Y and $\overset{*}{Y}$ to a shift from Eurodeposits to nonreservable assets.[21]

As the final shifts in asset demands, consider a shift from demand deposits to a nonreservable instrument. In contrast to both of the previous two shifts, the impact effect of the shift on excess supply is not changed by an increase in k_V. Once again it is not immediately apparent whether HH'_1 or H''_1 is relevant since the increased income responsiveness and decreased absolute interest responsiveness work in opposing directions. However, in this case the ambiguity cannot be resolved without further restrictions on asset demands. The initial equilibrating responses of Y and i must clear the market for US high-powered money:

$$0 = \frac{E\hat{X}DH}{\gamma} = h_Y \frac{\hat{Y}}{\gamma} - h_i \frac{\hat{i}}{\gamma} - k_D. \tag{29}$$

Differentiating with respect to k_V yields

$$\frac{\partial(E\hat{X}DH/\gamma)}{\partial k_V} = \overset{(+)}{\frac{\partial h_Y}{\partial k_V}} \overset{(\pm)}{\frac{\hat{Y}}{\gamma}} - \overset{(-)}{\frac{\partial h_i}{\partial k_V}} \overset{(-)}{\frac{\hat{i}}{\gamma}} \gtreqless 0. \tag{30}$$

The stronger the output and price responsivenesses of the demand for Eurodeposits (that is, the larger $\partial h_Y/\partial k_V$) and the weaker the interest rate responsiveness of the demand for Eurodeposits (that is, the smaller $-\partial h_i/\partial k_V$) the more likely it is that an increase in k_V will create excess demand and, therefore, reduce the change in Y induced by shifts between demand deposits and nonreservable instruments.[22]

The first shift in the demand for goods to be considered is a shift up in the demand for the US good alone. In terms of figure 13.2, the increase in demand for the US good shifts the YY schedule to the right, say to YY_1. Consider the changes in Y and i that clear the US and German goods markets at a constant $\overset{*}{Y}$. The increased demand for the US good causes US output to increase. The rise in Y implies an excess demand for the German good which can only be offset by a rise in i. The higher values of Y and i that clear the two goods markets are represented by the point (i_1, Y_1). Note that (i_1, Y_1) is a point on the new $Y\overset{*}{Y}$ schedule $Y\overset{*}{Y}_1$.

In the new equilibrium i and Y are definitely higher than their pre-disturbance values as indicated by the intersection of $Y\overset{*}{Y}_1$ and HH_0 at the point (i_2, Y_2). To determine whether $\overset{*}{Y}$ will rise or fall consider the point (i_1, Y_1). If HH is flatter than $\overset{*}{Y}\overset{*}{Y}$, so that this point implies an excess supply of H as in figure 13.2, then $\overset{*}{Y}$ must be higher in the new equilibrium. The increase in $\overset{*}{Y}$ shifts the YY and $Y\overset{*}{Y}$ schedules southeast along YY_1 from (i_1, Y_1) to (i_2, Y_2). If HH were steeper than $\overset{*}{Y}\overset{*}{Y}$, so that the point (i_1, Y_1) implied an excess demand for H, then $\overset{*}{Y}$ would be lower in the new equilibrium.

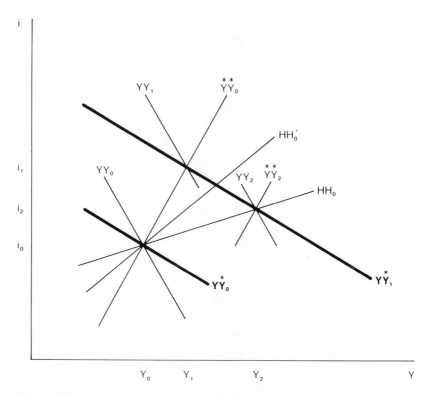

Figure 13.2
Shift up in demand for US good alone, fixed exchange rates.

When k_Y is increased, the slope of the HH schedule becomes steeper (HH rotates from HH_0 to HH'_0), unambiguously dampening the increase in Y and amplifying the increase in i. The smaller increase in Y and the larger increase in i both work to decrease the final value of $\overset{*}{Y}$. Therefore, if $\overset{*}{Y}$ rises (falls) with a shift up in demand for the US good alone, then an increase in k_Y dampens (amplifies) the response of $\overset{*}{Y}$.[23]

Now consider a shift in demand from the German good to the US good. In terms of figure 13.3 this disturbance shifts YY_0, $\overset{*}{Y}\overset{*}{Y}_0$, and $Y\overset{*}{Y}_0$ to YY_1, $\overset{*}{Y}\overset{*}{Y}_1$, and $Y\overset{*}{Y}_1$. At a fixed i and $\overset{*}{Y}$ the increase in Y which clears the German goods market ($Y_b - Y_0$) must be larger than the increase in Y which clears the US goods market ($Y_a - Y_0$). Hence $\overset{*}{Y}\overset{*}{Y}$ shifts further to the right than YY, and at their new intersection (i_1, Y_1) the interest rate is lower.

At (i_1, Y_1) there is an excess demand for H; hence $\overset{*}{Y}$ and Y fall, and i rises, shifting the goods market schedules back along $Y\overset{*}{Y}_1$. As for the final equilibrium values, Y and i definitely rise, and $\overset{*}{Y}$ definitely falls.

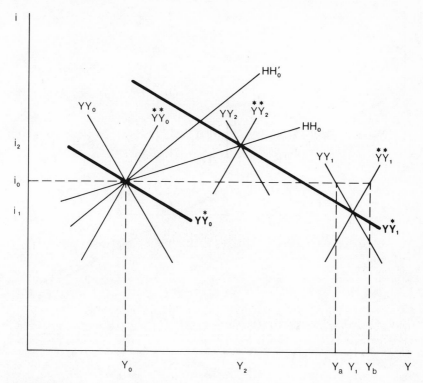

Figure 13.3
Shift from German good to US good, fixed exchange rates.

Once again, when k_V is increased, the HH schedule becomes steeper (rotates from HH_0 to HH_0'), dampening the increase in Y and amplifying the increase in i. As before, the smaller increase in Y and the larger increase in i work to decrease the final value of $\overset{*}{Y}$. Since $\overset{*}{Y}$ unambiguously falls with a demand shift from German to US goods, this decrease in the final value amplifies the response of $\overset{*}{Y}$.[24]

13.3 Flexible Exchange Rates

In this section it is assumed that the Bundesbank sets the supply of German high-powered money ($\hat{\overset{c}{A}}{}^{c} = 0$) and allows the exchange rate to vary. Under this assumption all four of equations (18) are employed in determining $\hat{Y}$, $\hat{\overset{*}{Y}}$, and $\hat{i}$ as well as $\hat{e}$.

Figure 13.4 is useful in illustrating the workings of the model under flexible exchange rates. Given values of $\overset{*}{Y}$ and e, the YY, $\overset{*}{Y}\overset{*}{Y}$, HH, and

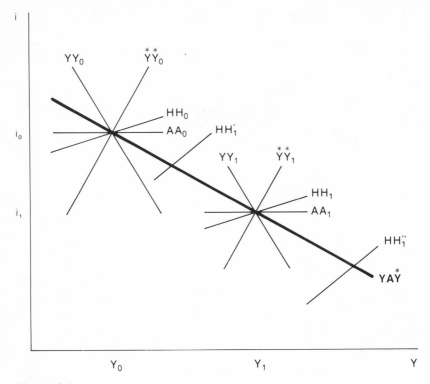

Figure 13.4
Shifts in asset demands, flexible exchange rates.

AA schedules represent the pairs of i and Y which clear the markets for US output, German output, US high-powered money, and German high-powered money. The signs of the slopes of these schedules are implications of the previously made assumptions about the coefficients in equations (18). As noted, these earlier assumptions do not determine the relative slopes of the $\overset{*}{Y}\overset{*}{Y}$ and HH schedules. The implications of alternative assumptions about the relative slopes of these schedules will be pointed out at later stages in the analysis.

Under flexible exchange rates the analogue of the closed economy IS curve is the $YA\overset{*}{Y}$ schedule in figure 13.4. This schedule is the locus of combinations of i, Y, and (implicitly) $\overset{*}{Y}$ and e that clear both goods markets and the German high-powered money market.

Figure 13.5 is useful in establishing the important properties of the $YA\overset{*}{Y}$ schedule. Given values of i and e, the $\tilde{Y}\tilde{Y}$, $\overset{\approx}{Y}\overset{\approx}{Y}$, and $\tilde{A}\tilde{A}$ schedules represent the pairs of Y and $\overset{*}{Y}$ which clear the markets for US output,

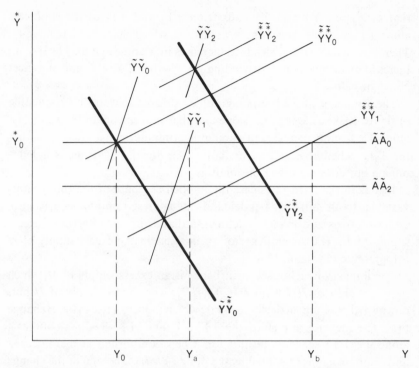

Figure 13.5
Derivation of $YA\overset{*}{Y}$ schedule, flexible exchange rates.

German output, and German high-powered money. The signs of the slopes of these schedules and their relative slopes are implications of previously made assumptions about the coefficients in equations (18). The $\tilde{Y}\overset{\approx}{Y}$ schedule represents the combinations of Y, $\overset{*}{Y}$, and (implicitly) e which clear both the markets for US and German output. To determine the slope of the $\tilde{Y}\overset{\approx}{Y}$ schedule, consider a rise in e at a fixed $\overset{*}{Y}$ and i. The increase in Y required to clear the German goods market ($Y_b - Y_0$) is larger than the increase in Y required to clear the US goods market ($Y_a - Y_0$), so the $\tilde{Y}\overset{\approx}{Y}$ schedule shifts farther to the right than the $\tilde{Y}\tilde{Y}$ schedule. Since the $\tilde{Y}\tilde{Y}$ and $\overset{\approx}{Y}\overset{*}{Y}$ schedule always intersect along the $\tilde{Y}\overset{\approx}{Y}$ schedule, the $\tilde{Y}\overset{\approx}{Y}$ schedule has a negative slope.

Now the properties of the $YA\overset{*}{Y}$ schedule can be established using figure 13.5. First, note that a decrease in i with e constant creates excess demand in all three markets. Thus it shifts the $\tilde{A}\tilde{A}$ schedule to the south, the $\tilde{Y}\tilde{Y}$ schedule to the southeast, and the $\overset{\approx}{Y}\overset{*}{Y}$ schedule to the northwest, for example to $\tilde{A}\tilde{A}_2$, $\tilde{Y}\tilde{Y}_2$, and $\overset{\approx}{Y}\overset{*}{Y}_2$. Second, note that the new $\tilde{Y}\overset{\approx}{Y}$ schedule ($\tilde{Y}\overset{\approx}{Y}_2$) passes through the intersection of $\tilde{Y}\tilde{Y}_2$ and $\overset{\approx}{Y}\overset{*}{Y}_2$. Third, note that as e rises, $\tilde{Y}\tilde{Y}$ and $\overset{\approx}{Y}\overset{\approx}{Y}$ shift from $\tilde{Y}\tilde{Y}_2$ and $\overset{\approx}{Y}\overset{\approx}{Y}_2$ to the southeast along $\tilde{Y}\tilde{Y}_2$ until they reach the $\tilde{A}\tilde{A}$ schedule, which shifts north from $\tilde{A}\tilde{A}_2$. Therefore, a decrease in i leads to increases in Y and e and may lead to an increase or decrease in $\overset{*}{Y}$ depending on whether $\tilde{Y}\tilde{Y}$, $\overset{\approx}{Y}\overset{\approx}{Y}$, and $\tilde{A}\tilde{A}$ meet above or below $\overset{*}{Y}_0$.[25]

The argument of the last paragraph establishes that the $YA\overset{*}{Y}$ schedule of figure 13.4 has a negative slope and that movements to the southeast along $YA\overset{*}{Y}$ imply increases in e and indeterminate changes in $\overset{*}{Y}$. Whether the $YA\overset{*}{Y}$ schedule is steeper or flatter than the YY schedule is indeterminate but does not affect the analysis.

Just as in the fixed rates case the implied response of the endogenous variables to all shifts in asset demands are analyzed simultaneously since each shift in asset demands is defined so that its impact effect is an excess supply of H. The general case of an increase in the excess supply of H is represented in figure 13.4.

The impact of each asset disturbance is an excess supply of H, which implies a shift of HH from HH_0 to HH_1. The excess supply of H puts downward pressure on the interest rate which induces a rise in the exchange rate. The increase in e shifts the YY, $\overset{*}{Y}\overset{*}{Y}$, and AA schedules southeast along the $YA\overset{*}{Y}$ schedule resulting in a new equilibrium at the higher Y and e and lower i represented by the point (Y_1, i_1). The sign of the change in $\overset{*}{Y}$ is ambiguous.

The next step in the analysis is to determine whether an increase in k_V dampens or amplifies the equilibrating responses of Y and $\overset{*}{Y}$. For each shift in asset demands an increase in k_V has exactly the same effect on the HH schedule under flexible exchange rates as it did under fixed exchange rates. As before, for each shift it is not clear from a graphical analysis whether an increase in k_V dampens or amplifies the equilibrating responses of Y and $\overset{*}{Y}$, that is, whether HH_1' or HH_1'' is relevant. For two of the three cases the ambiguity can be resolved by applying our approach of holding the initial equilibrating responses of the endogenous variables constant, raising k_V and determining whether there is an excess demand for or supply of US high-powered money. An increase in k_V dampens the increase in Y and the ambiguous equilibrating response of $\overset{*}{Y}$ if it increases the excess demand for H at the old postdisturbance equilibrium.

For each shift in asset demands the same steps are followed under flexible exchange rates as under fixed exchange rates, and the final results are once again given by equations (23), (27), and (30). Under flexible exchange rates as under fixed exchange rates $\hat{Y}/\alpha$, $\hat{Y}/\beta$, $\hat{Y}/\gamma > 0$ and $\hat{i}/\alpha$, $\hat{i}/\beta$, $\hat{i}/\gamma < 0$. Thus, the conclusions regarding whether an increase in k_V creates excess demand for or excess supply of H, whether HH_1' or

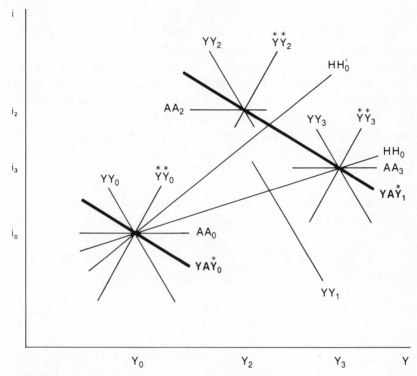

Figure 13.6
Shift up in demand for US good alone, flexible exchange rates.

HH_1'' is relevant, and whether an increase in k_Y dampens or amplifies the equilibrating responses of Y and $\overset{*}{Y}$ are the same under both exchange rate regimes.

The first shift in the demand for goods to be considered is a shift up in the demand for the US good alone, and the analysis of this shift is illustrated in figure 13.6. Consider the changes in i, Y, and (implicitly) $\overset{*}{Y}$ required to clear the US and German goods markets and the German high-powered money market at a fixed e. The increased demand for the US good shifts YY to the northeast, for instance from YY_0 to YY_1, and causes US output to increase. The rise in Y implies an excess demand for the German good inducing an increase in $\overset{*}{Y}$. The rise in $\overset{*}{Y}$ implies an excess demand for German high-powered money inducing an increase in i. Thus, in order to clear these three markets, Y, $\overset{*}{Y}$, and i must rise. The increase in $\overset{*}{Y}$ shifts the AA schedule to the north, for instance from AA_0 to AA_2; shifts the $\overset{*}{Y}\overset{*}{Y}$ schedule to the southeast, for instance from $\overset{*}{Y}\overset{*}{Y}_0$ to $\overset{*}{Y}\overset{*}{Y}_2$; and results in an additional northeasterly shift in the YY schedule, for instance from YY_1 to YY_2. The higher values of Y, i, and (implicitly) $\overset{*}{Y}$ that clear the three markets are represented by the point (i_2, Y_2). Note that (i_2, Y_2) is a point on the new $YA\overset{*}{Y}$ schedule $YA\overset{*}{Y_1}$.

In the new final equilibrium i and Y are definitely higher, as indicated by the intersection of $YA\overset{*}{Y_1}$ and HH_0 at the point (i_3, Y_3). Variations in e shift the YY, $\overset{*}{Y}\overset{*}{Y}$, and AA schedules along $YA\overset{*}{Y_1}$ from (i_2, Y_2) to (i_3, Y_3). If (i_2, Y_2) implies an excess supply of H as in figure 13.6, then e must rise shifting the three schedules to the southeast along $YA\overset{*}{Y_1}$. If (i_2, Y_2) implied an excess demand for H, then e would fall. It can be shown that a sufficient, but not necessary, condition for the point (i_2, Y_2) to imply an excess demand for H is that HH be steeper than $\overset{*}{Y}\overset{*}{Y}$.[26] Whatever happens to e, the final equilibrium value of $\overset{*}{Y}$ may be higher or lower than the predisturbance value. It can be shown that a sufficient, but not necessary, condition for $\overset{*}{Y}$ to rise is that HH be flatter than $\overset{*}{Y}\overset{*}{Y}$.

When k_V is increased, the slope of the HH schedule becomes steeper

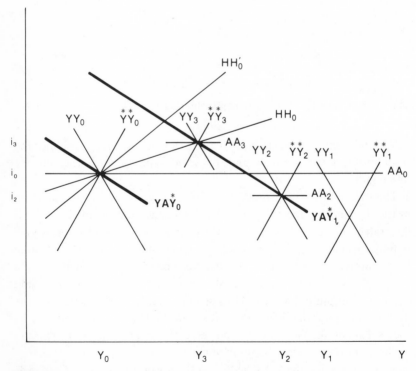

Figure 13.7
Shift from German good to US good, flexible exchange rates.

(HH rotates from HH_0 to HH_0'), unambiguously dampening the increase in Y. Whether the ambiguous equilibrating response in $\overset{*}{Y}$ is dampened or amplified cannot be determined without further information about the relative magnitudes of some of the parameters. Given the increase in k_V, there is definitely an excess demand for H at the old postdisturbance equilibrium values of the endogenous variables represented by the point (i_3, Y_3). Unfortunately, as has been shown, an excess demand for H has an ambiguous effect on $\overset{*}{Y}$. Thus, for example, even if the HH schedule is flatter than the $\overset{*}{Y}\overset{*}{Y}$ schedule, so that a shift up in the demand for the US good definitely raises $\overset{*}{Y}$, an increase in k_V might dampen or amplify this increase.

Now consider a shift in demand from the German good to the US good. The analysis of this shift is illustrated in figure 13.7. Consider the Y, i, and (implicitly) $\overset{*}{Y}$ that clear the US and German goods markets and the German high-powered money market at a fixed e. First suppose both e and $\overset{*}{Y}$ are fixed. The increased demand for the US good shifts YY to the northeast, for instance from YY_0 to YY_1, and the reduced demand for the German good shifts $\overset{*}{Y}\overset{*}{Y}$ to the southeast, for instance from $\overset{*}{Y}\overset{*}{Y}_0$ to $\overset{*}{Y}\overset{*}{Y}_1$. $\overset{*}{Y}\overset{*}{Y}$ shifts farther to the east than YY because a larger increase in Y is required to clear the market for the German good at a fixed i. Now allow $\overset{*}{Y}$ to vary. The Y and i which clear the markets for the US good and German high-powered money (i_0 and Y_1) imply an excess supply of the German good; hence $\overset{*}{Y}$ must fall. The fall in $\overset{*}{Y}$ shifts YY to the southwest, for instance from YY_1 to YY_2; $\overset{*}{Y}\overset{*}{Y}$ to the northwest, for instance from $\overset{*}{Y}\overset{*}{Y}_1$ to $\overset{*}{Y}\overset{*}{Y}_2$; and AA to the south, for instance from AA_0 to AA_2. Note that the point of intersection of the three shifted schedules (i_2, Y_2) lies on the new $YA\overset{*}{Y}$ schedule $YA\overset{*}{Y}_1$.

In the final equilibrium i and Y are definitely higher, as indicated by the intersection of $YA\overset{*}{Y}_1$ and HH_0 at the point (i_3, Y_3). The point (i_2, Y_2) definitely implies excess demand for US high-powered money. Hence e must fall shifting the YY, $\overset{*}{Y}\overset{*}{Y}$, and AA schedules to the northwest along $YA\overset{*}{Y}_1$. Although movements along $YA\overset{*}{Y}$ may imply increases or decreases in $\overset{*}{Y}$, it can be shown that the decrease in $\overset{*}{Y}$ required to reach (i_2, Y_2) dominates any possible rise associated with the movement from (i_2, Y_2) to (i_3, Y_3).[27] Thus, the final equilibrium value of $\overset{*}{Y}$ must be lower than its predisturbance value.

As before, when k_V is increased, the slope of the HH schedule becomes steeper (HH rotates from HH_0 to HH_0'), unambiguously dampening the increase in Y. Whether the decrease in $\overset{*}{Y}$ is dampened or amplified cannot be determined without further information about the relative magnitudes of some parameters. Given the increase in k_V, there is definitely an excess demand for H at the old postdisturbance equilibrium values of the endogenous variables represented by the point (i_3, Y_3). However, an excess demand for H has an ambiguous effect on $\overset{*}{Y}$.

13.4 Conclusions

We have considered the implications of imposing (increasing) a reserve requirement on US residents' Eurodollar deposits (k_V) for the stabilization of US output (Y) and German output $(\overset{*}{Y})$ given three types of asset demand shifts and two types of goods demand shifts. In this section we restate our general approach, briefly summarize our results, and draw some general conclusions.

A single general approach underlies all the specific results in the chapter. Suppose an initial set of equilibrating responses in the endogenous variables clears all markets following a particular shift at an initial value of the Eurodollar reserve requirement. Depending on the shift under consideration, an increase in k_V may create an excess demand for or an excess supply of US high-powered money (H) given the initial equilibrating responses in the endogenous variables. Demand for H varies directly with Y, inversely with the US interest rate (i), and inversely with each of the asset demand disturbance terms as we have defined them. An increase in k_V alters the responsivenesses to changes in both endogenous variables and the impact effects of two of the asset demand disturbances. The initial set of equilibrating responses no longer clears the markets, and there must be further equilibrating responses. These further equilibrating responses are exactly the ones associated with an increase in the excess demand for or supply of H. Thus, while a small change in k_V does not change the qualitative effects of a particular shock on the endogenous variables, it does modify the quantitative effects in the same way that they would be modified by a small decrease or increase in the supply of H.

The specific results for asset demand shifts under the two exchange rate regimes are quite similar. Y and i are the only endogenous variables that affect the demand for H. Since all asset demand shifts are defined so that they lead to an excess supply of H, they all imply a rise in Y and a fall in i. Furthermore, an increase in k_V always increases the income responsiveness of the demand for H and reduces the absolute value of the interest rate responsiveness. However, depending on the type of asset demand disturbance, an increase in k_V may decrease, increase, or leave unchanged the impact effect on the demand for H.

For a shift out of demand deposits into Eurodollar deposits, an increase in k_v reduces the impact effect on the demand for H. It has been shown that the effects of the increase in the Y responsiveness and the smaller impact effect dominate the effect of the decrease in the absolute value of the i responsiveness, so that an increase in k_v creates an excess demand for H given the initial set of equilibrating responses. The effects of this excess demand partially offset the effects of the excess supply created by the disturbance, thereby dampening the responses of all the endogenous variables including Y and $\overset{*}{Y}$.

For a shift out of Eurodollar deposits into nonreserved instruments, an increase in k_v increases the impact effect on the demand for H. It has been shown that the effects of the decrease in the absolute value of the i responsiveness and the larger impact effect dominate the effect of the increase in the Y responsiveness, so that an increase in k_v creates an excess supply of H given the initial set of equilibrating responses. The effects of this excess supply add to the effects of the excess supply created by the disturbance, thereby amplifying the responses of all the endogenous variables including Y and $\overset{*}{Y}$.

For the two shifts just discussed between reserved Eurodollars and other instruments, the results confirm the wisdom of a strategy of minimizing the difference between reserve requirements on the instruments involved. Specifically, when the Eurodollar reserve requirement is between the reserve requirement on demand deposits and zero, an increase in the Eurodollar reserve requirement dampens the response of both real outputs to shifts between Eurodollar deposits and demand deposits and amplifies the response of real outputs to shifts between Eurodollar deposits and nonreserved instruments (instruments with zero reserve requirements).

A shift in asset demands between demand deposits and nonreserved instruments is an example of a shift between a reserved and a nonreserved instrument in which neither instrument is a Eurodollar deposit. For this type of shift an increase in k_v does not affect the impact of the disturbance on the excess demand for H. It has been shown that the net effect of the increase in the Y responsiveness of the demand for H and the decrease in the absolute value of the i responsiveness may be to create either an excess demand for, or an excess supply of, H given the initial equilibrating responses. Thus, the implications of an increase in k_v for the stabilization of both outputs are ambiguous.

Now we turn to the results for shifts in goods demands. Both a shift up in the demand for the US good alone and a shift in demand from the German good to the US good imply initial equilibrating responses which include rises in both Y and i. Since an increase in k_v increases the Y

responsiveness of the demand for H and decreases the absolute value of the i responsiveness, it always creates an excess demand for H for the initial set of equilibrating responses. Thus, for both kinds of shifts in goods demands under both exchange rate regimes, an increase in the Eurodollar reserve requirement is unambiguously helpful in stabilizing US output.

This result provides the basis for a more general conclusion. Suppose that stabilization of home output is the objective of the monetary authorities, shifts in goods demands of the type studied here are the only disturbances to the economy, and fixed-rate demand deposits have already been reserved. In these circumstances it is helpful to reserve deposits for which demand varies directly with home output and with the interest rate. Of course, in our chapter, US residents' Eurodollar deposits are an example of this type of deposits. Another might be relatively short-maturity, variable-rate time deposits at home banks that are not subject to an interest rate ceiling. What matters for the desirability of reserving a particular type of deposit is how the demand for that deposit responds to home output and the interest rate and not that the deposit is "checkable" or is a "transactions deposit" except in so far as these attributes are associated with desirable properties of the demand for the deposit.

The implications of an increase in k_V for the stabilization of German output in the cases of shifts in goods demand are usually ambiguous. First consider the fixed exchange rate regime. An increase in k_V creates an excess demand for H given the initial equilibrating responses of Y and i, and an excess demand for H definitely leads to a decline in $\overset{*}{Y}$. While this decline in $\overset{*}{Y}$ unambiguously amplifies the initial equilibrating decline in $\overset{*}{Y}$ in the case of a shift from the German good to the US good, it may dampen or amplify the ambiguous initial response of $\overset{*}{Y}$ in the case of a shift up in the demand for the US good alone. Now consider the flexible exchange rate regime. As before, an increase in k_V creates an excess demand for H given the initial equilibrating responses. However, it has been shown that an increase in the excess demand for H has an ambiguous effect on $\overset{*}{Y}$. Thus, even if the sign of the initial equilibrating response of $\overset{*}{Y}$ is unambiguous, as it is in the case of a shift in demand from the German good to the US good, whether an increase in k_V dampens or amplifies the response of $\overset{*}{Y}$ cannot be determined without further information about some of the parameters.

For asset demand shifts a Eurodollar reserve requirement is helpful in stabilizing $\overset{*}{Y}$ if and only if it is helpful in stabilizing Y, so there is no potential policy conflict. For shifts in goods demands a Eurodollar reserve requirement is always helpful in Y stabilization, but often has ambiguous implications for $\overset{*}{Y}$ stabilization and sometimes definitely destabilizes $\overset{*}{Y}$. These effects are not unique to a Eurodollar reserve requirement. As suggested above they would also be associated with a reserve requirement on a variable-rate time deposit at a US bank the demand for which varied directly with US output. Changes in financial regulations that affect the demand for US high-powered money have implications for foreigners whether or not they directly affect the Eurodollar market. However, the implications for foreigners of regulations affecting the Eurodollar market have a larger impact on the likelihood of the adoption of such regulations because of the obvious claim of the authorities in several countries to a voice in deciding on them.

Appendix

This appendix contains proofs of three assertions made in the text and a brief discussion of the implications of assuming that the income elasticities of the deposit demands given by equations (2) are less than, rather than equal to, one.

Under flexible exchange rates the equilibrium conditions are obtained by setting $\overset{*}{A}{}^C$ equal to zero in equations (18). Let Δ represent the determinant of the resulting system and Δ_{ij} represent the ijth minor of that system. Then

$$\Delta = h_Y \Delta_{31} - h_i \Delta_{33} > 0, \tag{A1}$$

$$\Delta_{31} = \overset{*}{a}_{\overset{*}{Y}}(y_i \overset{*}{y}_e + \overset{*}{y}_i y_e) + (1 - \overset{*}{y}_1 - y_2)\overset{*}{a}_4(y_i + y_e)$$
$$+ y_2 \overset{*}{a}_4(y_i + y_e + \overset{*}{y}_i - \overset{*}{y}_e) > 0, \tag{A2}$$

$$\Delta_{33} = \overset{*}{a}_e(\overset{*}{y}_Y y_{\overset{*}{Y}} - y_Y \overset{*}{y}_{\overset{*}{Y}}) + \overset{*}{a}_{\overset{*}{Y}}(\overset{*}{y}_Y y_e - y_Y \overset{*}{y}_e) < 0, \tag{A3}$$

since the assumptions made in the text imply that

$$y_i + y_e + \overset{*}{y}_i - \overset{*}{y}_e > 0,$$

$$\overset{*}{y}_Y y_{\overset{*}{Y}} - y_Y \overset{*}{y}_{\overset{*}{Y}} < 0,$$

and

$$\overset{*}{y}_Y y_e - y_Y \overset{*}{y}_e < 0.$$

Consider the effects of an increase in the demand for the US good alone ($\lambda > 0$) on e and $\overset{*}{Y}$:

$$\hat{e}/\lambda = (1/\Delta)[\mathring{a}_{\mathring{Y}}(\mathring{y}_Y h_i - h_Y \mathring{y}_i) - \mathring{a}_4 h_Y \mathring{y}_i] \gtrless 0, \tag{A4}$$

$$\hat{\mathring{Y}}/\lambda = (1/\Delta)[\mathring{a}_4(\mathring{y}_Y h_i - h_Y \mathring{y}_i) + \mathring{a}_4 h_Y \mathring{y}_e] \gtrless 0. \tag{A5}$$

HH is steeper (flatter) than $\mathring{Y}\mathring{Y}$ if and only if $\mathring{y}_Y h_i - h_Y \mathring{y}_i$ is negative (positive). If HH is steeper than $\mathring{Y}\mathring{Y}$, then e definitely falls. If HH is flatter than $\mathring{Y}\mathring{Y}$, then $\mathring{Y}$ definitely rises.

Consider the effect of a shift from the German good to the US good ($\mu > 0$) on $\mathring{Y}$:

$$\hat{\mathring{Y}}/\mu = -(\mathring{a}_e/\Delta)[h_i(y_Y - \mathring{y}_Y) + h_Y(y_i + y_e + \mathring{y}_i - \mathring{y}_e)] < 0, \tag{A6}$$

since $y_Y - \mathring{y}_Y > 0$ and $y_i + y_e + \mathring{y}_i - \mathring{y}_e > 0$.

If the income elasticities of the deposit demands given by equations (2) are less than rather than equal to one, then equations (18c) and (18d) become

$$\tilde{h}_Y \hat{Y} + \tilde{h}_{\mathring{Y}} \hat{\mathring{Y}} - \tilde{h}_i \hat{\imath} + \tilde{h}_e \hat{e} = (k_D - k_V)\alpha + k_V \beta + k_D \gamma, \tag{A7}$$

$$\tilde{a}_Y \hat{Y} + \tilde{a}_{\mathring{Y}} \hat{\mathring{Y}} - \tilde{a}_i \hat{\imath} - \tilde{a}_e \hat{e} - \hat{\mathring{A}}^C = 0, \tag{A8}$$

where

$$\tilde{h}_Y = (h_1\delta + h_2)f + h_3, \quad \tilde{h}_{\mathring{Y}} = (1 - \delta)\mathring{f}h_1, \quad \tilde{h}_i = h_4, \quad \tilde{h}_e = (1 - \delta)h_1,$$

$$\tilde{a}_Y = (1 - \mathring{\delta})f\mathring{a}_1, \quad \tilde{a}_{\mathring{Y}} = (\mathring{a}_1\delta + \mathring{a}_2)\mathring{f} + \mathring{a}_3, \quad \tilde{a}_i = \mathring{a}_4, \quad \tilde{a}_e = (1 - \mathring{\delta})\mathring{a}_1 + \mathring{a}_4.$$

Note that under each exchange rate regime US high-powered money demand can be expressed as a function of Y, i, and one additional variable. Under fixed exchange rates that variable is $\mathring{Y}$ since $\hat{e} = 0$ in (A7); under flexible exchange rates it is t since $\hat{e}$ can be set equal to $\hat{\imath} - \mathring{f}\hat{Y} + f\hat{\mathring{Y}}$ in (A7).

The approach of the text can be used to obtain some results for this case. Proofs of these results are available from the authors on request. For shifts in asset demands the qualitative results are similar to those in the text. Under both exchange rate regimes an increase in k_V dampens the effects on Y and $\mathring{Y}$ of variations in α, amplifies the effects of variations in β, and has an ambiguous impact on the effects of variations in γ.

For shifts in goods demands the results are less clear cut. If $\delta \to 1$ with $\mathring{\delta}$ anywhere in the permissible range between zero and one, the additional variable drops out of US high-powered money demand, and the qualitative results for both shifts in goods demands under both exchange rate regimes are similar to those in the text.[28] Otherwise, the qualitative results may or may not be similar.

Consider a shift up in the demand for the US good alone under both exchange rate regimes. The initial equilibrating responses of Y and i are increases, and an increase in k_V raises the Y responsiveness of the demand for H, lowers the absolute value of the i responsiveness, and increases the responsiveness to changes in the additional variable. Thus, if the initial equilibrating response of the additional variable is an increase, as it may be under either exchange rate regime, an increase in k_V definitely creates an excess demand for H given the initial equilibrating responses of the endogenous variables. Furthermore, even when the equilibrating response of the third variable is a decrease, an increase in k_V definitely creates excess demand for H if the income responsiveness of Eurodollar deposits exceeds the income responsiveness of demand deposits for then the effect of the increased responsiveness of the demand for H to changes in Y dominates the effect of the increased responsiveness to changes in the additional variable.

Now consider a shift in demand from the German good to the US good under both exchange rate regimes. The initial equilibrating response of Y and the effects of an increase in k_V on all the responsivenesses of the demand for H to changes in the endogenous variables are the same as those described in the preceding paragraph. However, the initial equilibrating response of i may be either an increase or a decrease, and the initial equilibrating response of the additional variable is definitely a decrease. A set of sufficient conditions under which an increase in k_V creates excess demand for H given the initial equilibrating responses is made up of the condition that the initial equilibrating response of i be an increase and the condition that the effect of the increased responsiveness of the demand for H to changes in Y dominate the effect of the increased responsiveness to changes in the additional variable.

Notes

1. Among the studies which consider important questions raised by the existence and rapid growth of the Eurocurrency markets are Freedman (1977), Hewson and Sakakibara (1975), Masera (1973), and Niehans and Hewson (1976).

2. This model is a flexible price, rational expectations version of the model in the appendix to chapter 18 of Mundell (1968).

3. This approach to the evaluation of alternative monetary policy regimes originated with Poole (1970) and has subsequently been developed and applied by many analysts. It has been applied in the open economy context by Bryant (1980). It has been used in analyzing the implications of alternative reserve requirement systems for money stock stabilization by Froyen and Kopecky (1979), Kaminow (1977), Kopecky (1978), Laufenberg (1979), and Sherman, Sprenkle, and Stanhouse (1979)

and for real output stabilization by Baltensperger (1982), Rolnick (1976), Santomero and Siegel (1981), and Sprenkle and Stanhouse (1981) and in a related study of the implications of alternative definitions of a monetary aggregate for real output stabilization by Roper and Turnovsky (1980).

4. Henderson and Waldo (1982) investigate the implications of Eurocurrency reserve requirements for the control of a monetary aggregate, which is the intermediate target of the monetary authorities.

5. It is assumed that there is no interbank lending. If the deposits of a bank exceed the sum of required reserves and dollar and DM claims, then it purchases dollar or DM claims from another bank.

6. It could be assumed that US (German) nonbanks hold US (German) currency which, of course, is high-powered money without affecting the analysis. However, if it were assumed that US (German) nonbanks held German (US) demand deposits and currency, some of the results below could not be obtained unless additional assumptions were made about the relative magnitudes of parameters. For example, it could not be proved that the interest rate responsiveness of the demand for US high-powered money is definitely negative.

7. The profits and losses of banks do not affect the wealth of nonbanks participating in the market for traded financial assets because it is assumed that the risk neutral owners of banks do not sell shares to risk averse holders of traded financial assets and do not hold traded financial assets.

8. The best available data suggest that about half of US nonbanks' Eurodollar deposits have original maturities of less than thirty days. If US residents' Eurodollar deposits were viewed as long-term deposits that could only be converted into demand deposits with a significant delay, then v_2 and v_3 would be negative, and while some of our results would be unaffected, others might be changed. See notes 20–24.

9. The assumption that dollar demand deposits at US banks and Eurodollar deposits are imperfect substitutes is crucial for the analysis to follow. This assumption is plausible and empirically supportable. The two types of deposits have somewhat different payment provisions and are subject to different political risk factors. Furthermore, legal restrictions have some effect on depositors' decisions about where to place their funds. Factors such as these may explain (1) why some nonbanks actually hold dollar certificates of deposit issued by US banks instead of Eurodollar deposits despite an opportunity cost which usually exactly reflects US reserve requirements and (2) why there is substitution in favor of Eurodollar deposits when rising nominal interest rates lead to an increase in this opportunity cost.

10. In Henderson and Waldo (1982) it is demonstrated that these two conditions guarantee equilibrium in financial markets in a model with more financial instruments. There, as here, banks are assumed to be risk neutral.

11. It could be assumed that both US and German banks hold excess reserves on which no interest is paid. Under this assumption the qualitative effects of interest rate changes on the desired holdings of excess reserves would be the same as those on desired holdings of demand deposits, and none of the results of the paper would be affected. It could also be assumed that all Eurodollar deposits were reservable, but unless additional assumptions were made about the relative magnitudes of

parameter values, some of the results derived below could not be obtained. For example, it could not be proved that the interest rate responsiveness of the demand for US high-powered money is definitely negative.

12. Theories of supply under which deviations of actual aggregate supply from a "natural" level depend on price forecast errors have been developed by Lucas (1973), Sargent (1973), and Fischer (1977).

13. Equation (18a) is derived using equations (1), (9), and (11)–(17). Equation (18b) is derived using equations (1) and (10)–(17). Equation (18c) is derived using equations (6), (13), (16), and (17). Equation (18d) is derived using equations (1), (7), (14), (16), and (17).

14. A brief discussion of how our results are affected by relaxing this assumption is contained in the appendix.

15. It makes no difference whether the German authorities exchange German high-powered money for dollar claims on nonbanks and the US Treasury or for DM claims on nonbanks and the German Treasury since banks regard these two types of claims as perfect substitutes.

16. This analysis originated with Poole (1970).

17. This conclusion also definitely holds when there are disturbances in the goods market that are uncorrelated with disturbances in the money market.

18. It is assumed that H^C is increased when k_V is increased so that when all the disturbances are zero, the values of all the other nominal variables are the same at both the original and the new higher values of k_V.

19. The equilibrating responses could also be expressed as partial derivatives; for example, $\hat{Y}/\alpha = \partial Y/\partial \alpha$.

20. It can be shown that if $v_2, v_3 < 0$, then the equilibrating responses of Y and $\overset{*}{Y}$ are dampened under both fixed and flexible exchange rates.

21. It can be shown that if $v_2, v_3 < 0$, then the equilibrating responses of Y and $\overset{*}{Y}$ are amplified under both fixed and flexible exchange rates.

22. If $v_2, v_3 < 0$, then the equilibrating responses of Y and $\overset{*}{Y}$ are unambiguously amplified under both fixed and flexible exchange rates.

23. If $v_2, v_3 < 0$, then HH becomes steeper if and only if $d_4(v_2 f + v_3) + v_4(d_2 f + d_3) > 0$. Otherwise HH becomes flatter, and the results under both fixed and flexible exchange rates must be modified accordingly.

24. See note 23.

25. If expectations were static, so that $i = \overset{*}{i}$, then $\overset{*}{Y}$ would definitely fall, as in Mundell's model, since $\overset{*}{i}$ and $\overset{*}{Y}$ would have to move in the same direction to keep the demand for A constant.

26. For proof of this assertion and the one made later in this paragraph, see the appendix. If expectations were static, then $\overset{*}{Y}$ would definitely rise, as in Mundell's model, in accordance with the reasoning of note 25.

27. For proof of this assertion, see the appendix.

28. The assumption that US nonbanks' average propensity to import $(1 - \delta)$ approaches zero does not imply that their marginal propensity to import $(\mathring{y}_2)$ approaches zero.

References

Baltensperger, Ernst (1982). "Reserve Requirements and Economic Stability," *Journal of Money, Credit and Banking*, Vol. 14, No. 2, May.

Bryant, Ralph (1980). *Money and Monetary Policy in Interdependent Nations*, Brookings Institution, Washington.

Fischer, Stanley (1977). "Long-Term Contracts, Rational Expectations, and the Optimal Money Supply Rule," *Journal of Political Economy*, Vol. 83, No. 2, April.

Freedman, Charles (1977). "A Model of the Eurodollar Market," *Journal of Monetary Economics*, Vol. 3, No. 2, April.

Froyen, Richard, and Kenneth J. Kopecky (1979). "Reserve Requirements and Money Stock Control with a Flexible Deposit Rate," unpublished paper, University of North Carolina.

Henderson, Dale W., and Douglas G. Waldo (1982). "Reserve Requirements on Eurocurrency Deposits: Implications for Eurodeposit Multipliers, Control of a Monetary Aggregate, and Avoidance of Redenomination Incentives," in Jacob S. Dreyer, Gottfried Haberler, and Thomas D. Willett, eds., *The International Monetary System Under Stress*, American Enterprise Institute for Public Policy Research, Washington.

Hewson, John, and Eisuke Sakakibara (1975). *The Eurocurrency Markets and Their Implications*, Lexington Books, Lexington.

Kaminow, Ira (1977). "Required Reserve Ratios, Policy Instruments, and Money Stock Control," *Journal of Monetary Economics*, Vol. 3, No. 4, October.

Kopecky, Kenneth (1978). "The Relationship between Reserve Ratios and the Monetary Aggregates under Reserves and Federal Funds Operating Targets," Staff Economic Studies No. 100, Board of Governors of the Federal Reserve System, Washington, DC.

Laufenberg, Daniel E. (1979). "Optimal Reserve Requirement Ratios against Bank Deposits for Short-Run Monetary Control," *Journal of Money, Credit and Banking*, Vol. 11, No. 1, February.

Lucas, Robert E. (1973). "Some International Evidence on Output-Inflation Trade-offs," *American Economic Review*, Vol. 63, No. 3, June.

Masera, Rainer (1973). "Deposit Creation, Multiplication and the Euro-dollar Market," in *A Debate on the Eurodollar Market*, Quaderni di Ricerche, No. 11, Ente per gli Studi Monetari, Bancari e Finanziari Luigi Einaudi, Rome.

Mundell, Robert (1968). *International Economics*, Macmillan, New York.

Niehans, Jürg, and John Hewson (1976). "The Eurodollar Market and Monetary Theory," *Journal of Money, Credit and Banking*, Vol. 8, No. 1, February.

Poole, William (1970). "Optimal Choice of Monetary Policy Instruments in a Simple Stochastic Macro Model," *Quarterly Journal of Economics*, Vol. 84, No. 2, May.

Rolnick, Arthur J. (1976). "Evaluating the Effectiveness of Monetary Reforms," *Journal of Monetary Economics*, Vol. 2, No. 3, July.

Roper, Don E., and Stephen J. Turnovsky (1980). "The Optimal Monetary Aggregate for Stabilization Policy," *Quarterly Journal of Economics*, Vol. 95, No. 2, September.

Santomero, Anthony M., and Jeremy J. Siegel (1981). "Bank Regulation and Macroeconomic Stability," *American Economic Review*, Vol. 71, No. 1, March.

Sargent, Thomas J. (1973). "Rational Expectations, the Real Rate of Interest and the Natural Rate of Unemployment," *Brookings Papers on Economic Activity*, No. 2.

Sherman, Lawrence F., Case M. Sprenkle, and Bryan E. Stanhouse (1979). "Reserve Requirements and Control of the Money Supply," *Journal of Money, Credit and Banking*, Vol. 11, No. 4, November.

Sprenkle, Case M., and Bryan E. Stanhouse (1981). "A Theoretical Framework for Evaluating the Impact of Universal Reserve Requirements," *Journal of Finance*, Vol. 36, No. 4, September.

14

The Choice of an Invoice Currency in International Transactions

John F. O. Bilson

From the numerous studies of invoicing practices in international trade, a number of interesting empirical generalizations have emerged. A short list would include the following:

1. Trade between developed countries in manufactured products is likely to be invoiced in the exporter's currency. This regularity is now known as Grassman's rule (Grassman, 1973a,b).

2. Although Grassman's rule imposes the foreign exchange exposure on the importer, it is generally true that importers have not hedged this exposure in forward or currency futures markets. There has been some increase, however, in the use of forward markets associated with the greater flexibility of exchange rates in the 1970s.

3. Trade in primary products and capital assets is typically denominated in major vehicle currencies, particularly the US dollar.

4. Trade between developed and less developed countries tends to be denominated in the currency of the developed country.

5. If one country has a larger and more unstable inflation rate than its trading partners, there is a tendency not to use the country's currency for international trade invoices.

Of these generalizations, the first two have been very important in understanding the relation between the exchange rate and the current account. Magee (1973) demonstrated that the J curve dynamics of the current account in response to a discrete change in the exchange rate could be explained by Grassman's rule invoicing practices. For example,

This chapter originated from joint work with Stephen Magee, whose assistance is gratefully acknowledged. The research is part of the NBER Program in International Studies, and has been partially funded by the National Science Foundation through Grant No. SES-8009458. The opinions expressed are solely the responsibility of the author and are not necessarily shared by the sponsoring institutions.

almost all US exports to Japan are invoiced in dollars, whereas a significant fraction of Japanese imports to the United States are invoiced in yen. If the dollar depreciates, the dollar value of export earnings is not influenced, whereas the number of dollars required to pay for the imports increases. Hence even though the real value of trade is fixed by previous contracts, the current account will deteriorate in the short term. Seen in this light, the traditional separation of the capital account and the current account is shown to be misleading. Within the current account is hidden a set of implicit futures contracts written between exporters and importers. When the exchange rate changes, speculative profits and losses are distributed across countries through the invoicing conventions. Since these flows are the result of an asset decision by the corporation—they are equivalent to the purchase or sale of a forward exchange contract, or borrowing in one currency to lend in another—they should properly be included as a capital account item rather than as a current account item.

This point is of particular importance in the interpretation of the correlation between unanticipated exchange rates and unanticipated current account movements during the current floating rate period. After the initial infatuation with the asset market approach, a number of economists have adopted a position which attributes a causal role to the current account in the determination of the exchange rate. Since exchange rates are asset prices, these economists recognize that generally only unanticipated changes in the current account will have an influence on the exchange rate. In particular, Dornbusch (1980) tests the theory by regressing the market forecast error of the exchange rate on the current account forecast error of the OECD. For a number of countries, he finds that an unanticipated current account deficit is significantly correlated with an unanticipated depreciation of the exchange rate. On the basis of this evidence, he concludes that the current account does have an influence on the exchange rate.

It is clear, however, that the significant correlations observed by Dornbusch are also consistent with Grassman's law of invoicing practices. Further, since international trade contracts are often subject to significant time delays, it is unlikely that the real trade balance is difficult to predict, particularly for the government economists of the OECD. Hence the major source of uncertainty in the OECD forecasts is likely to be the valuation effect of changes in the exchange rate. If this is the case, Dornbusch is actually regressing the unanticipated change in the exchange rate on a function of the unanticipated change in the exchange rate. Under these conditions, statistically significant coefficients are not surprising.

Some evidence on these issues has recently been presented by Golub (1981). Golub makes use of the fact that the OECD breaks down its forecasts of the trade balance into forecasts of the volume of trade and the terms of trade. He demonstrates that in 1978, most of the observed forecast errors were in the terms of trade forecast errors rather than the volume forecast errors and that, in some cases, there was a tendency for the volume and terms of trade forecasts to move in opposite directions. All in all, the failure to consider the invoicing issue, and the resulting J curve effects, has resulted in a misinterpretation of the true relation between the current account and the exchange rate.

As far as the theory is concerned, the invoicing approach suggests that much of the unanticipated change in the exchange rate is the result of implicit forward contracts which have been written between importers and exporters. Under Grassman's law, an unanticipated increase in the domestic price of foreign currency results in an immediate transfer from the domestic to the foreign country. Conceptually, these transfers are capital account items since they are structurally the same as a forward exchange contract, or uncovered interest arbitrage. If included in the capital account, it is likely that they would be offset by other capital account items, so that the "true" current would be both stable and unrelated to unanticipated changes in the exchange rate. The major part of true international commodity trade is contractual, as Magee (1973) has demonstrated, and the average contract length is around six months. Unless there is a great deal of flexibility in international trade negotiations, it is difficult to see how the real current account can transmit information to the economy about current changes in its competitive position.

All of this is not meant to imply that current account news does not influence the exchange rate. At any point in time, an existing stock of contracts to import and export will exist. Unanticipated changes in the real value of these contractual stocks may trigger revisions in public information about competitiveness and savings behavior, and these revisions may have an influence on the exchange rate. The difficulty with the Dornbusch approach is that the link between unanticipated changes in the actual current account and unanticipated changes in the contracted stock of imports and exports is very weak.

Although it is clear that the invoicing practices are an important determinant of cross-country flows of foreign currency gains and losses, the existing theoretical attempts to explain the empirical regularities have not been notably successful. Early writers on the topic attributed Grassman's law to convenience (the exporter writes the invoice), market power (exporters are bigger than importers), or tradition. Although these explanations have some power, they fail to explain why invoicing practices are different for different commodities and why invoicing practices have changed in response to changes in macroeconomic conditions. Page (1977) reports that invoicing in the exporter's currency is more prevalent for goods with long contractual lags (machinery is a good example) and that there has been a tendency for the percent of exports contracted in the exporter's currency to be negatively related to the inflation rate in the exporter's country.

There have also been a number of attempts to develop an optimizing model of the invoicing decision. In an interesting contribution, Baron (1976) developed a model of an exporter who must choose between fixing a price in its own or its customer's currency. The importer is assumed to be able to purchase and sell simultaneously so that the importer does not face risk. If the exporter invoices in its own currency, the price faced by the importer will vary with the exchange rate and so will the desired purchases by the importer, so that the exporter faces quantity risk. If the exporter invoices in the importer's currency, the quantity demanded is known but the domestic currency value of the sales is uncertain. It is clear, then, that the relative risk of the two pricing strategies depends upon the elasticity of the importer's demand curve. If demand is inelastic, as the evidence appears to suggest, invoicing in the exporter's currency will reduce risk. Baron's model suggests, however, that the importer only contracts to purchase the goods when they are delivered to the home market. If this is not the case, the importer faces risk during the period between when the contract is signed and when the goods are finally delivered and paid for. If the importer does wait for the goods to be delivered, it is likely that his demand will be very elastic and that, consequently, invoicing in the home currency will be the preferred strategy. In any case, it is difficult to see how the exporter can both deliver a quantity of goods to a country and also fix their price. Once the selling price is allowed to be flexible, the exchange rate issue becomes unimportant. Hence while Baron's contribution is valuable, it does not appear to be capable of accounting for the empirical generalizations listed in the beginning of the paper.

In a very general setting, Baron and Forsythe (1979) argue for the existence of a separation theorem in which management attempts to maximize profit whereas shareholders manage risk. The basic argument here is that one man's foreign exchange exposure is another man's international portfolio diversification and that management should not attempt to manage the risk for its shareholders. Magee (1980), Magee and Rao (1980), and Cornell (1980) put forth a similar case b ised upon integrated commodity markets. Magee and Rao conclude that the invoicing decision should be a random variable so that the average over a large number of contracts will be 50 percent. Cornell extends the argument by allowing for inflation rates to be more variable for different currencies. He concludes that trade will tend to be invoiced in stable currencies. As with Baron's paper, the excellent quality of the analysis in these papers should not hide the fact that they do not provide a convincing explanation of the empirical facts from the invoicing survey literature.

As far as the structure of international markets is concerned, a number of points need to be accounted for. First, international financial markets are generally considered to be efficient. Second, international trade contracts are generally negotiated between an importer and an exporter at a time three to six months before the goods are delivered and nine to twelve months before the invoice is paid. The situation envisaged by Baron may apply to certain standardized commodities, but it is not generally true. Third, although forward markets exist for currency, they generally do not exist for nonstandardized manufactured goods. These three facts form the basis for the theory of invoicing described in this chapter.

The elements of the theory are as follows. Since international financial markets are efficient, the foreign exchange risk is itself unimportant. Either the exporter or the importer can sell of foreign exchange exposure in the forward market at a price which is likely to be a close approximation to the expected future spot price. Previous writers have been mesmerized by the foreign exchange risk elements of the problem and have neglected the fact that the main risk from the transaction is the risk faced by the importer when it attempts to sell the goods in the domestic market. To a lesser extent, the exporter also faces the risk of unanticipated changes in costs during the period between when the contract was written and when the goods were signed. The most important element in the negotiations between the exporter and the importer is that the importer's price risk is likely to be both larger and more highly correlated with the exchange rate than the exporter's cost risks. Hence by accepting the foreign exchange risk, the importer obtains an important hedge against the price risk of the transaction. In contrast, the exporter will not generally be able to hedge its costs with an open position in foreign currency since the production lag is short and costs are unlikely to respond rapidly to the exchange rate.

An example may help to clarify the theory. Consider an American firm importing Volkswagens from Germany and assume that there is a six-month lag between the time when the contract was signed and the sale of the automobile in the American market. If the contract is invoiced in Deutsche Marks (DM), the importer will be uncertain about both the dollar value of its revenues and the dollar value of its costs. If the dollar should depreciate against the DM, the importer will have to pay a larger number of dollars to close his account. However, the depreciation will also increase the expected price at which future German imports will sell in the United States and hence, to some extent, the importer will be able to offset the higher costs with higher prices. In accounting terms, the point is that there will tend to be a covariance between accounts payable and inventory valuation that will induce the importer to invoice in the exporter's currency.

In the extreme case in which purchasing power parity holds and all macroeconomic shocks occur in the importer's country, the importer can avoid all risk by invoicing in the exporter's currency. This extreme case is most likely to occur in a small country with an unstable inflation rate and in which imports constitute a significant fraction of the total supply of the commodity in question. In less extreme cases, it will still be true that the importer will have a greater preference for foreign exchange risk relative to the exporter. More generally, we can consider a case similar to that studied by Baron in which the desired level of foreign exchange risk depends upon the elasticity of the demand curve for the product. Clearly if all automobiles are imported, invoicing in the exporter's currency is preferable, whereas if a large domestic industry exists, the foreign currency risk does not provide much of a hedge against foreign exchange exposure.

It is possible for the importer to buy foreign exchange exposure in the forward exchange market. However, since these markets are often thinner than spot markets, and since they are characterized by larger bid ask spreads, both partners in the negotiation have a natural incentive to limit their activity in the forward market. If the exporter's preference is to fully cover anticipated receivables, whereas the importer's preference is to hedge only 20 percent of payables, then invoicing in the exporter's currency is a natural outcome.

This simple hypothesis does appear appear to be consistent with most of the observed regularities concerning invoicing practices in manufactured goods between developed country trading partners. Most important, it explains Grassman's law and the "failure" of importers to utilize forward markets. In addition, it is also consistent with the observation that Grassman's law applies more strongly when a large domestic import-competing industry does not exist. Hence small countries are likely to use large country currencies for trade. More generally, the hypothesis suggests that the key to the invoicing question is the covariance between costs and exchange rates, on the one hand, and receipts and exchange rates, on the other. These covariances will depend upon the inflationary environment in the two countries. If one country has a stable inflation rate, while another country has a variable inflation rate, the latter country will have greater covariance between prices and exchange rates, and this will encourage invoicing in the stable currency.

14.1 A Formal Analysis of the Choice of an Invoice Currency

In Baron's model, the exporter is assumed to sell to a large group of importers at a fixed price. Because of the assumption that both trading partners are influenced by the contractual lag, the analysis presented here will view the trade negotiation as a two-parameter game between the exporter and the importer. The negotiation is assumed to be carried out in terms of unit costs, so that the actual quantity traded is not subject to negotiation.

Although most invoicing decisions are decided either in terms of complete export currency or complete import currency invoicing, it is easier to consider the game in which a proportion of the contract is invoiced in one currency. In general, we consider the total dollar price p to be the sum of p^d units of the importer's currency and p^f units of the exporter's currency. For expositional purposes, we consider the dollar to be the importer's currency and the pound to be the exporter's currency. Under these conditions, the actual dollar price is

$$\tilde{p} = p^d + \tilde{e}p^f, \tag{1}$$

where $e =$ the exchange rate, which is expressed in terms of the number of dollars required to purchase 1 pound and is assumed to have, and is assigned, an expected value of unity. (This assignment is also for purposes of exposition and should not be considered as a forecast.) Random variables are signified by a tilde and expected values by an overbar, and we assume that the conditional distribution of all random variables is multivariate normal.

The actual price in equation (1) is a random variable because the exchange rate is not known at the time that the contract is signed. By varying p^d and p^f over the range between zero and p, the exchange risk is distributed between the importer and the exporter. If p is equal to p^d, the contract is invoiced in the importer's currency; if p is equal to p^f, the contract is invoiced in the exporter's currency. In the negotiation, the trading partners must decide a total price and an invoicing practice. This decision may be restated as a choice of both p^d and p^f.

We begin by considering the importer's strategy. The importer's unit profit is

$$\tilde{\Pi} = \tilde{q} - p^d - \tilde{e}p^f, \tag{2}$$

where q is the price received by the importer in the US market. It is important to note that this equation abstracts from other influences on the firm's profits. In particular, the expression does not consider sales from domestic production, domestic costs, or the possibility of purchasing or selling foreign exchange on the forward market. The domestic costs and sales may be important if these values are also related to the exchange rate. However, these factors may be introduced into the analysis with some increase in complexity but with little change in the results.

The neglect of hedging is an important omission. Hedging and invoicing may be considered as alternative ways of purchasing and selling foreign exchange risk. In the absence of transactions costs, the importer should be indifferent between the two alternatives and no determinant solution to the invoicing problem is possible. It is likely, however, that the costs of purchasing foreign exchange exposure through the forward market are larger than through invoicing. As was mentioned, forward markets are thinner than spot markets and bid ask spreads are larger. The firm may find that the purchase or sale of a large quantity of forward foreign exchange is more expensive than simply invoicing in the exporter's currency. There is also a tendency for upper management to view forward exchange transactions as more speculative than an equal amount of exposure through invoicing. There are many corporations with unhedged foreign exchange revenues of over a billion dollars; it is almost inconceivable that these corporations would directly set up departments to directly purchase this quantity of exposure in the forward market, even if the argument was made that this exposure hedges a domestic price risk.

For these reasons, it apears plausible to assume that the trading partners have a preference for avoiding forward exchange contracts and that the contract is initially negotiated without explicit consideration of the possibility of forward hedging. If hedging is required, then the gain from the invoicing negotiations should be viewed as a reduction in the transactions costs that would otherwise have to be incurred in the forward foreign exchange market. For the most part, however, the model presented here suggests that the observed failure of corporations to hedge in the forward market may well reflect a general recognition of the effect of exchange rates on prices and costs.

In the absence of risk aversion, the parties to the negotiation would be reduced to haggling over the price. Risk aversion is introduced through the assumption that the firm desires to maximize the level of profit for some given level of risk, where risk is measured by the variance of profit. The specific function is

$$U(\Pi) = \Pi - (\lambda/2)\sigma_\pi^2. \tag{3}$$

The parameter λ is a constant reflecting the corporations degree of risk aversion. Equation (3) assumes that that the firm derives utility from the expected level of profit and disutility from the variance of profit. This contrasts with the general principle that the corporation should attempt to maximize its market value, a value that depends upon nondiversifiable rather than total risk. This is a very important point in the international financial context since the practice of hedging foreign exchange exposure often implies that portfolio managers must purchase foreign stocks in order to diversify their portfolios internationally. It may well be the case that foreign exchange risk is a desirable characteristic which will enhance the value of the firm.

Despite the logic of this position, it is fair to say that it has not had a major impact on hedging or invoicing practices at the present time. In the United States, the FASB-8 requirement that current foreign exchange gains and losses must be reported on the quarterly earnings statement have led many corporations to ensure that their exposure to changes in exchange rates is limited. The present model assumes that corporations do recognize that exchange rates can have predictable effects on prices, but it assumes that the wider aspects of diversification strategy are ignored. In addition, many importers are small corporations engaged in trade with a limited number of countries. If such a corporation faces a significant risk of bankruptcy, or if the capital tied up in the corporation is a significant fraction of the manager's wealth, the profit-based utility function may be an adequate description of the corporation's objective function.

In order to derive the importer's indifference map, we totally differentiate the utility function with respect to the two choice variables p^d and p^f. Setting the total derivative equal to zero, the slope of the indifference curve is given by

$$dp^d/dp^f = -1 - \lambda\sigma^2(p^f - \beta), \tag{4}$$

where σ^2 is the variance of the exchange rate and β is the covariance between the retail price q and the exchange rate divided by the variance of the exchange rate. If the exporter was risk neutral, the importer would prefer to have the foreign currency price p^f set equal to β since this would minimize the variance of profit. After this value was set, all further negotiation over the total price would be in terms of domestic prices. Since we have chosen units so that the expected value of the exchange rate is unity, the indifference curve has a unit slope at the profit variance minimizing point. As the exporter chooses values of p^f that are different from β, the importer would require an increasingly lower overall price in order to maintain the same level of utility.

Equation (4) is of particular importance for explaining the relation between inflation and invoicing. The β coefficient may be estimated from a regression of domestic prices on the exchange rate. If all disturbances are monetary and domestic, the regression coefficient is approximately equal to p^f, so that the importer's risk-minimizing position is to cover the expected selling price totally by invoicing this amount in the exporter's currency. With this strategy, any unanticipated decrease in the domestic inflation rate, which will create an unanticipated loss in revenue, will also result in an appreciation of the domestic currency, thereby lowering the domestic currency cost. This negative covariance between revenue and costs should constitute a powerful incentive for invoicing in strong currencies when the variability of the domestic inflation rate is high. More generally, it is likely to be the case that some of the source of change in the exchange rate is domestic, so that a partial invoice in foreign currency is called for.

The importer's indifference curve is displayed in figure 14.1 as the downward sloping curve MM. The negative slope reflects the natural tendency for the importer to dislike any increase in price, and the slope of the indifference curve is minus unity (remember that the expected exchange rate is set at unity) at the point of optimal risk diversification. At points on either side of this optimal point, the importer will require a more favorable price, expressed in terms of either currency, in order to accept the greater exchange risk. Indifference curves that are closer to the origin reflect a higher degree of utility for the importer.

It is useful to begin with the case in which the exporter is risk neutral. Under this condition, the importer is free to choose any composition between foreign and domestic currencies, since the exporter is only interested in the total revenue from the transaction. The previous analysis has demonstrated that the importer would set the foreign currency price

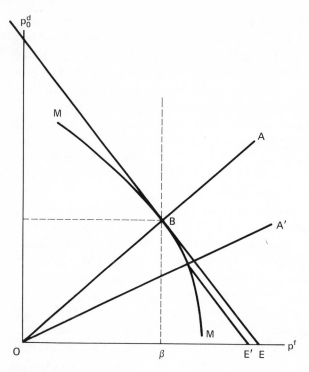

Figure 14.1
The importer's indifference curve. The curve MM represents the combinations of domestic and foreign currency payments that yield the same level of utility to the importer. At point B, the contract specifies payment of Op_0^d units of domestic currency and $O\beta$ units of foreign currency. This contract has a total foreign currency value of OE.

equal to β in figure 14.1 and would then negotiate the amount of domestic currency. If, for example, the domestic currency price was set at p_0^d, the currency composition of the transaction would be defined by the ray OA, and the exporter would receive OE units of foreign currency, as measured along the horizontal axis. Of this amount, $O\beta$ would be independent of the value of the exchange rate and βE would represent a long position in the domestic currency. The contract curve in the risk neutral exporter case is a verticle line erected at β on the horizontal axis. Hence increases in the exporter's market power will actually result in a greater proportion of the contract being denominated in the importer's currency. This prediction conflicts with the widely held view that exporters use their market power to demand invoicing in their own currency. This prediction typically ignores the fact that market power can be used to increase prices or influence the invoicing decision.

Now consider the case in which the exporter would prefer the invoicing composition OA' rather than OA. The importer would be willing to accomodate this demand if the exporter was willing to reduce the total price, expressed in erms of foreign currency, from OE to OE'. For the given value of β, the primary determinant of the trade-off between total price and currency composition is the importer's degree of risk aversion and the variance of the exchange rate. An increase in either of these factors will make the indifference curve more steeply sloped to the right of β and less steeply sloped to the left of β in figure 14.1.

We now turn to the exporter's strategy. At the time that the contract is negotiated, the exporter will be uncertain about the costs of producing and delivering the goods to the importer. At the same time, if the contract is denominated in the importer's currency, the exporter will also be uncertain about the local currency value of the receipts. As in the importer's case, there are consequently two sources of risk to be considered. Expressed in terms of its own currency, the exporter's profit may be written as

$$\tilde{\Pi} = p^d/\tilde{e} + p^f - \tilde{w}, \tag{5}$$

where w represents the uncertain level of unit costs. In order to avoid the problems associated with Jensen's inequality, the first term in the definition of profit is approximated by the Taylor series expansion around the expected value:

$$p^d/\tilde{e} = p^d - p^d(\tilde{e} - e). \tag{6}$$

In equation (6), units have again been chosen so that the expected value of the exchange rate is unity.

As in the importer's case, the exporter is assumed to maximize the expected level of profit for a given level of the variance of profit. The utility function is

$$U = \Pi - (\gamma/2)\sigma_\pi^2, \tag{7}$$

where γ is a measure of the exporter's degree of risk aversion. Total differentiation of (7) with respect to the two choice variables yields the exporter's indifference curve. The slope of the indifference curve may be shown to be

$$dp^d/dp^f = -1/(1 - \gamma\sigma^2(p^d + \delta)) \tag{8}$$

where δ is the covariance between domestic costs and the exchange rate divided by the variance of the exchange rate. For the exporter, setting the domestic price component (the component denominated in the importer's currency) equal to $-\delta$ results in the minimum possible level of profit risk. If there is a variable inflation rate in the exporter's country, and a stable inflation rate in the importer's country, it is likely that the value of δ will be negative: An unanticipated inflation in Britain, for example, will both increase production costs w and lower the price of the pound in the foreign currency market. Hence a tendency will exist for exporters to invoice in the importer's currency if the exporter's inflation rate is very uncertain. Another important case occurs when many of the inputs into the production process are invoiced in the importer's currency: In Japan, for example, where cars are produced with imported raw materials and energy that are invoiced in dollars and where wage negotiations include profit sharing provisions, invoices are often in dollars rather than yen.

As far as trade in semimanufactures between developed countries is concerned, however, it is likely that the value of δ will be small. When the exporter is negotiating the contract, it will be considering a number of acts which must be completed before the revenue is finally received: The goods must be produced; they must be shipped to the importer; the importer has to sell them; and, finally, the invoice has to be paid. At any point in this process, a major change in the exchange rate can occur, but even if it occurs soon after the contract is signed, it is unlikely to have much of an effect on the costs of producing the good unless a substantial amount of the raw materials are imported. If the covariance is close to zero, then the exporter will have a clear preference for invoicing in its own currency. There is a clear difference here between the two partners in the trade negotiation: The uncertain revenues of the importer are realized at the end of the contractual process, and the importer typically has a greater degree of flexibility in both adjusting the sale price and the timing of the payments to the exporter; the exporter incurs its costs at the beginning of the process, and these costs are unlikely to be influenced by subsequent fluctuations in the exchange rate. It is this difference in the timing of risk which forms the basis for the practice of invoicing in the exporter's currency.

The final equilibrium is derived by finding the points of tangency between the importer's and the exporter's indifference curve. At any point off the contract curve, it would be possible to negotiate a new contract that would make one party better off without making the other

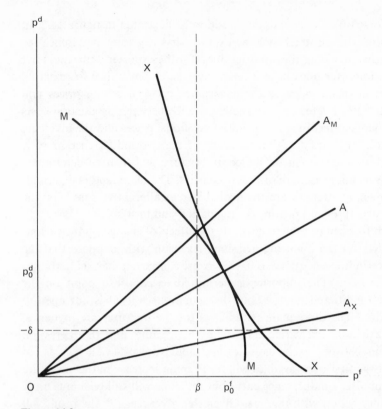

Figure 14.2
The contractual equilibrium. The importer's preference is to pay $O\beta$ in foreign currency, while the exporter's preference is to only receive $-\delta$ in domestic currency. The equilibrium illustrates a case in which both have compromised: p_0^f is greater than β, but p_0^d is greater than $-\delta$. At the currency composition represented by the ray OA, the importer is paying less in total than it would have at its preferred point OA_M, and the exporter is receiving more than it would have if the currency composition had been at its preferred point OA_X.

party worse off. The negotiating position is illustrated in figure 14.2. In the figure, it is assumed that the exporter has a greater preference for its own currency than the importer does (for the exporter's currency) but that the importer does have a relatively greater preference for external currency invoicing because the covariance between selling prices and exchange rates is greater than the covariance between production costs and exchange rates. From their initial positions, prices and the invoicing proportion are varied until a tangency of the two indifference maps is found. The actual point on the contract curve will then be determined by the bargaining strength of the two parties. The main factors determining bargaining strength are the availability of alternative suppliers, the market structure, and factors like regulation and tariffs.

Figure 14.2 can be used to illustrate the effects of changes in the various parameters on the invoicing decision. To begin with, suppose that the exporter's indifference curve is fixed because a large number of alternative importers exist. The importer is permitted to choose a point on the exporter's indifference curve, but the actual curve itself is not open to negotiation. The three main parameters for the importer are its degree of risk aversion, the variance of the exchange rate, and the regression coefficient between exchange rates and domestic costs. An increase in either of the first two variables will result in an increase in the curvature of the importer's indifference curve but the slope will still be minus unity at the intersection with the line. Given that p^f exceeds β, the result will be a greater tendency toward own-currency invoicing. An increase in the β coefficient will horizontally displace the importer's indifference curve, and the new tangency will imply a greater amount of foreign currency invoicing. The reduction in risk associated with the higher β will also allow the importer to purchase at a lower total price.

Similar results hold for an exporter facing a given importer indifference curve: Greater risk aversion, or more exchange rate variance, will lead to greater invoicing in the exporter's currency, but a higher negative covariance between domestic costs and the exchange rate will encourage invoicing in the importer's currency. Since the exchange risk pushes the two parties in opposite directions, each toward its own currency, it is clearly not possible to predict the influence of exchange rate variability on invoicing.

The final issue to be addressed concerns the relation between market power and invoicing. It is obvious that greater market power for the exporter will push the equilibrium up the contract curve and that the total price paid by the importer will generally be higher as a result, but it is not obvious that the exporter will respond to its greater market power by demanding invoicing in its own currency. In order to answer this question, we need to investigate the slope of the contract curve. Setting (4) equal to (8) defines the points of tangency of the two indifference maps. This leads to the following expression for the contract curve:

$$(1 + \lambda\sigma^2(p^f - \beta))(1 - \gamma\sigma^2(p^d + \delta)) = 1. \tag{9}$$

Total differentiation of (9) with respect to p^d and p^f yields the slope of the contract curve:

$$dp^d/dp^f = (\lambda/\gamma)/(1 + \lambda\sigma^2(p^f - \beta))^2. \tag{10}$$

The first part of this expression yields the obvious conclusion that the slope of the contract curve will reflect the relative risk aversion of the two trading partners. If the importer is more risk averse, there will be a greater tendency for the exporter's market strength to be taken out in the form of higher total prices, rather than in imposing the exporter's invoicing preferences. For a given degree of relative risk aversion, higher total prices, as represented by higher values of p^f, will flatten the contract curve, so that there will be a tendency for greater exporter market strength to be used to increase the proportion of the contract that is invoiced in the exporter's currency. Although these results do offer some support for the theory that invoicing reflects market strength, this support must be seen within the context that a small importer facing a large exporter is likely to be more risk averse with respect to a single trade contract. For this reason, it is more likely that the tendency for trade to be invoiced in the exporter's currency reflects other factors.

14.2 Conclusion

The difficulty with the invoicing literature is its inability to make a firm case for having a strong preference for a particular currency, since, in a world with well-developed and efficient financial markets, foreign exchange exposure may be purchased or sold with relative ease. The object of this chapter has been to demonstrate that importer and exporter may have a common preference for invoicing in the exporter currency since the importer revenues may be partially hedged by accepting the foreign exchange exposure, while the exporter's costs are more likely to be independent of the exchange rate. Particularly in trade in manufactured goods, in which direct commodity price hedging is not available and competition from new imports is likely to be the major source of revenue variance, Grassman's law offers an indirect way of reducing profit risk. The observed lack of direct foreign currency hedging by importers is also consistent with this interpretation.

Although the invoicing decision is a minor one for each corporation, the tendency for the majority of corporations to adopt the same invoicing practices is of great importance in the interpretation of the relation between the exchange rate and the current account. To see this, consider the following ballpark figures for the United States. In 1980 US exports were valued at $220 billion and imports at $253 billion. Based on statistics from the early 1970s, Magee (1978) has estimated that the outstanding value of international trade contracts is equal to approximately half of the value of trade. Using Grassman's estimate that one third of exports are denominated in foreign currency while three quarters of imports are denominated in foreign currency, these estimates suggest that the total long position of US exporters is $36.6 billion, while the total short position of US importers is $132.3 billion. Thus the net short position, under the assumption of no hedging, is around $100 billion. During the floating rate period, the standard deviation of the International Monetary Fund's MERM exchange rate for the US dollar has been about 5 percent on an annual basis. Consequently, a decline of 1 standard deviation in the trade-weighted exchange rate could result in a $5-billion transfer from the United States to its trading partners. Invoicing is consequently a major source of change in the current account and an extremely important determinant of international short-term capital flows.

References

Baron, David P. (1976). "Fluctuating Exchange Rates and the Pricing of Exports," *Economic Enquiry* 14:425–38.

Baron, David P., and R. Forsythe (1979). "Models of the Firm and International Trade under Uncertainty," *American Economic Review* 69:565–75.

Cornell, Bradford (1980). "The Denomination of Foreign Trade Contracts Once Again," Working Paper, Graduate School of Management, UCLA.

Dornbusch, Rudiger (1980). "Exchange Rates and the Capital Mobility Problem," *Brookings Papers on Economic Activity* 1:143–85.

Golub, Stephen S. (1981). "Testing for the Effect of Current Account 'News' on Exchange Rates: A Critique," Manuscript, Yale University.

Grassman, Sven (1973a). *Exchange Reserves and the Financial Structure of Foreign Trade* (Westmead: Saxon House).

Grassman, Sven (1973b). "A Fundamental Symmetry in International Payment Patterns," *Journal of International Economics* 3:105–16.

Magee, Stephen P. (1973). "Currency Contracts, Pass-Through and Devaluation," *Brookings Papers on Economic Activity* 1:303–23.

Magee, Stephen P. (1978). "Contracting and Spurious Deviations from Purchasing Power Parity," in Jacob A. Frenkel and Harry G. Johnson, *Studies in the Economics of Exchange Rates* (Addison-Wesley).

Magee, Stephen P. (1980). "The Currency of Denomination of International Trade Contracts," in Richard M. Levich and Class Whilbourg (eds.), *Exchange Risk and Exposure: Current Developments in International Financial Management* (Lexington, MA: D. C. Heath).

Magee, Stephen P., and Ramesh K. S. Rao (1980). "Vehicle and Non-Vehicle Currencies in International Trade," *American Economic Review: Papers and Proceedings* 70 (May).

Page, S. A. B. (1977). "The Currency of Invoicing in International Trade," *National Institute Economic Review* 81:77–81.

15

International Trade, Indebtedness, and Welfare Repercussions among Supply-Constrained Economies under Floating Exchange Rates

Bryce Hool
and
J. David Richardson

The analytical foundation of traditional international macroeconomics has been as shaken by recent events as that of closed economy macroeconomics. Its usefulness has been clouded by enduring stagflation, globally parallel declines in capital formation and productivity trends, synchronous cyclical movements even under floating exchange rates, and puzzling volatility and unpredictability of exchange rates.

One of several problems with traditional international macroeconomics is that it often supposes stylized equilibrium states of the world, with thoroughgoing market clearing. Yet its concerns have much more the flavor of "disequilibrium" states of the world, especially during the past fifteen years, with measures of excess capacity, unemployment, inflationary gaps, labor shortages, and current account flux suggesting enduring excess supply or demand.

A disequilibrium characterization seems especially appropriate to the recurrent global overheating in the 1970s, coupled with widespread recourse to wage-price guidelines and incomes policies. To the extent that such policies were successful (President Carter's were enforced by federal purchasing threats, for example), output markets have been frequently supply constrained (with transactions rationed or deferred), and input markets have featured unemployment or shortages depending on whether incomes policies over- or undervalued factors of production.

During the late 1970s, almost all developed economies seemed supply constrained. Even much of measured excess capacity was arguably

Support for the research reported here has been provided by the National Science Foundation, and the project is part of the National Bureau of Economic Research Program in International Studies. The authors would also like to thank participants in an NBER Summer Institute seminar for many helpful suggestions. None of the institutions or individuals mentioned, however, should be held responsible for the result. Any opinions expressed are those of the authors.

redundant due to energy price shocks, environmental policy, and other structural flux of the 1970s. In the United States, labor markets seemed similarly supply constrained even in the presence of unprecedented unemployment, because of the large number of job seekers who were "structurally unemployed"—possessing skills or preferences that made them a noncompeting group for vacant positions at ruling wages. In European labor markets, by contrast, excess supply seemed more aptly to characterize the 1970s, given the rapid 1972–1974 run-up in real wages that was preserved by inertia and indexation (International Monetary Fund, 1980, chapter 1).

Little analytical work has been carried out on the macroeconomics of open economies under such constraints, despite the intriguing correlation of widespread wage-price guidelines, exchange rate volatility, and the explosion of international trade and investment relative to other economic activity in the early 1970s. This chapter attempts a beginning. Its focus is on transmission of various macroeconomic shocks between output supply-constrained economies and on their implications for the current account, capital account, and exchange rate. For empirical relevance the chapter abandons the small-country and fixed exchange rate assumptions that have characterized antecedent related research.[1] Unlike the latter, the analysis in this chapter treats both the foreign repercussions and the terms-of-trade effects of various shocks.

Section 15.1 describes an analytical model that assigns behavior to each of two regions relating to one nontradable input, one tradable output, and one tradable financial asset. International exchange between the two regions is characterized by sequential "temporary equilibria," each consistent with economically and institutionally constrained optimization, yet each simultaneously consistent with failure of some markets to clear. International transactions take place through a foreign exchange market that does clear continuously through flexible exchange rates.

Section 15.2 and the appendixes describe the reduced form of the model and apply it empirically, using parameters and initial values that incorporate data and consensus beliefs about the United States and the rest of the world in the late 1970s. The most important conclusions of the exercise are

1. Floating exchange rates fail to insulate either supply-constrained economy from unanticipated shocks in the other. Their international transmission is direct—the impacts of any shock on the two regions are qualitatively similar. Cross-region spillover effects, however, are quantitatively small relative to the own-region effects.

2. Exchange rates and the terms of trade between the supply-constrained economies are moderately sensitive to incomes policies and changes in technology/productivity trends (elasticities of 0.5 to 1.5 in absolute value). They are relatively insensitive to fiscal policy and to distributionally neutral wage-price guidelines (elasticities of 0.0 to 0.2 except that the terms of trade are moderately sensitive to the wage-price guidelines). Wage-favoring incomes policies, liquidity-financed fiscal expansion, tighter wage-price guidelines, and slackening of technology/productivity growth all cause depreciation of the domestic currency and deterioration of the terms of trade.

3. One-percent changes in incomes policies and technology/productivity trends in the supply-constrained economies have quantitative impacts on *all* variables that are generally three to five times the impact of 1-percent changes in government spending or in distributionally neutral wage-price guidelines.

4. Wage-favoring incomes policies, liquidity-based fiscal expansion, tighter wage-price guidelines, and slackening of technology/productivity growth all promote "internationalization" of commodity and financial markets. Export volume, import volume, claims on foreigners, and indebtedness to them can grow significantly in response to each (elasticities up to 1.5), and especially so in response to several taken together.

15.1 An Abstract Model

The abstract model that we work with is a structurally symmetric generalization of Malinvaud (1977). Malinvaud explores a closed economy with one input (labor), one output (goods), and one asset (money, also the numeraire). His focus is on the temporary equilibrium attained when economic agents optimize subject to quantity constraints consistent with sluggish prices and the absence of barter.

Our model posits for each economy one input (with others, entrepreneurship and fixed physical capital, implied), one output, and one asset (liquid wealth or money), each unique to that economy. Input markets are bounded by national borders; output markets and asset holding span them. All international transactions are financed through a foreign exchange market with a potentially flexible exchange rate. The model pushes beyond other "internationalizations" of Malinvaud's model by Dixit (1978) and Neary (1979): (1) by eschewing their small-country assumption (which allows them to ignore the terms of trade and foreign repercussions that are an important focus of our work, and to lump exportables and importables into one aggregate "commodity"); and (2) by analyzing floating in the foreign exchange market in addition to their fixed exchange rate regimes.

Each of the two trading economies is subject to potential price sluggishness or government policies that cause output and input markets to clear only slowly compared to foreign-exchange and financial capital "markets." When this happens, the short side of the input or output market rules, in the sense that the volume of transactions carried out matches the smaller of supply and demand. Frustrated sellers or buyers on the long side of such markets are induced by their rationing there to alter their demands for and supplies of different goods elsewhere, alterations that are referred to as spillover effects.

Each economy is populated by three groups of agents: households, firms, and government. Households and firms act as price takers, although the economy as a whole (being large) influences the world price for the unique commodity it produces. The foreign currency price of each country's output is flexible to the extent that the exchange rate is.[2] Governments have the capacity to alter prices and wages by legislative decree. Expectations of future prices and wages are formed taking this into account, but only unanticipated shocks will be examined below.

Households are buyers in two markets, for the outputs of firms in both countries. They are sellers in one market, for inputs to domestic firms. The only such input is labor services, the supply of which is fixed exogenously. Households may be constrained in any of these markets in principle, as buyers of either good or as sellers of labor. If rationed as buyers in a product market, households will tend to increase demands in other markets. If rationed as sellers in the labor market, that is, if unemployed, households will tend to reduce demands in other markets. These are spillover effects of rationing. Households hold liquid financial claims denominated in both domestic and foreign currencies. If such claims pay interest, the interest rate is taken to be invariant given the assumptions of stable wage-price trajectories and a fixed physical capital stock mentioned. These claims are the means of transferring purchasing power to the future. Households are never rationed in their acquisition of liquid assets, making them and whatever deferred purchases they represent a sink for current spillover effects.

Firms are sellers in one market, selling their (domestic) output to households in both countries and to the domestic government, and buyers in one market, purchasing only domestic labor services. Firms may be rationed as buyers of labor, in which case their output will be less than they would like, or as sellers of output, in which case the spill-over effect is a reduction in their demand for labor services. Firms hold domestic financial claims in an amount equal to current profits (the reward to the implied factors, entrepreneurship and fixed capital), which are then fully distributed to household/shareholders in the subsequent period (see below).

Governments purchase domestic output only (government imports are neglected) and are never rationed. They finance their purchases by creating new domestic money or other liquid assets. Taxes and transfers (including any interest payments on liquid debt) are assumed to balance.

The optimizing behavior of the three groups of agents is expressed in algebraic detail as follows:

Households   Households maximize utility that is defined over current and future[3] consumption of commodities:

$$\max_{X_{ii}, X_{ji}, M_{ii}, M_{ji}} V_i(X_{ii}, X_{ji}, M_{ii}, M_{ji}),$$

where $i = 1, 2$ as $j = 2, 1$ and

V_i = an index of household welfare,

X_{ii} = domestic consumption of domestic output,

X_{ji} = domestic consumption of imports,

M_{ii} = household stocks of domestic liquid assets,

M_{ji} = household stocks of foreign liquid assets, net (i.e., net foreign currency claims).

Household stocks of domestic liquid assets at the beginning of each period are equal to the amount then in existence less the sum of holdings by foreign households and holdings by domestic firms for subsequent distribution to domestic households (see below):

$$M_{ii}^0 = L_i^0 - (M_{ij}^0 + \pi_i^0), \tag{1}$$

where zero superscripts denote beginning-of-period values and

L_i = country i's stock of financial assets outstanding,

π_i = profits of firms, distributed to household/shareholders the period after firms earn them.

When households are not rationed in any market, the maximization is carried out subject only to the budget constraint:

$$p_1 X_{11} + rp_2 X_{21} + M_{11} + rM_{21} = w_1 \bar{N}_1 + \pi_1^0 + M_{11}^0 + rM_{21}^0, \tag{2.1}$$

$$(p_1/r)X_{12} + p_2 X_{22} + M_{12}/r + M_{22} = w_2 \bar{N}_2 + \pi_2^0 + M_{12}^0/r + M_{22}^0, \tag{2.2}$$

where

p_i = the nominal domestic price of the commodity produced in country i,

r = the exchange rate, the price of country 2's financial assets in units of country 1's financial assets,

w_i = country i's wage rate,

$\bar{N}_i$ = country i's labor force (exogenous), implicitly aggregating across identical households.

When households are rationed as sellers of labor services, excess supply and unemployment characterize labor markets, and $w_i\bar{N}_i$ is replaced in (2) by $w_i\bar{N}_i(1 - u_i)$, where

$u_i = 1 - N_i/\bar{N}_i$ = country i's unemployment rate,

N_i = employment in country i, again implicitly aggregating across identical households.

Households may be rationed in principle as buyers of country 1's commodity, or of country 2's commodity, or of both. Excess demand then exists in commodity markets. In these cases, household maximization is further constrained in that consumption cannot exceed available supplies:[4]

$$C_{11} + C_{12} \leqq Y_1 - G_1, \tag{3.1}$$

$$C_{21} + C_{22} \leqq Y_2 - G_2, \tag{3.2}$$

where

C_{ij} = rationed (constrained) consumption of country i's output by country j's residents,

Y_i = domestic output,

G_i = government purchases of domestic output.

Firms Firms maximize current profits π as in

$$\max_{N_i, Y_i} \pi_i(N_i, Y_i), \tag{4}$$

implicitly aggregating across identical firms. When firms are not rationed in any market, the maximization in (4) is carried out subject only to the (aggregate) production function:

$$Y_i = Y_i(N_i). \tag{5}$$

When firms are rationed as buyers of labor services, excess demand and labor shortages characterize labor markets, and $\bar{N}_i$ (the labor force) replaces N_i (employment) in (5). When firms are rationed as sellers of commodities, incipient excess supply characterizes output markets. Optimizing firms will produce only what they can sell ($X_{ii} + X_{ij} + G_i$, which is predetermined from their point of view), and will employ the minimal amount of labor necessary to do so:

$$N_i = Y_i^{-1}(X_{ii} + X_{ij} + G_i); \tag{6}$$

where $Y_i^{-1}(\ )$ is the inverse of the production function in (5), and X_{ii}, X_{ij} take into account any rationing of good j.

Government Governments do not optimize, but are responsible in their fiscal, monetary, price, and incomes policies for the values of four important exogenous variables: G_i, L_i, p_i, w_i. Fiscal, monetary, and price control policies are necessarily interdependent. Choice of any two implies the third, as revealed in the government's budget constraint:

$$p_i G_i = L_i - L_i^0. \tag{7}$$

The foreign exchange market The foreign exchange market is a financial market that is the locus for trade between the two countries' financial assets and that establishes their relative price r. This price, the exchange rate, is never sluggish, and therefore the foreign exchange market always clears.[5] These observations are reflected in the familiar requirement that variation in the exchange rate brings about budget constraint consistency such that a nation's aggregate current account and capital account sum to zero:

$$0 = [p_1 X_{12} - r p_2 X_{21}] + [(M_{12} - M_{12}^0) - r(M_{21} - M_{21}^0)], \tag{8}$$

where X_{12} should be replaced by C_{12}, and X_{21} by C_{21}, if households are rationed in the corresponding commodities markets, and

$M_{ij} - M_{ij}^0 = $ trade in financial assets during the period.

It is this market clearing condition that confirms the link between firms' financial asset stocks and current profits, mentioned above.[6]

15.2 An Application to a US/Rest-of-World Regime of Binding Output Supply Constraints

As outlined in the introduction, the model of section 15.1 can be usefully applied to global settings of recent vintage (the 1970s) that may also characterize the near future. "Supply-constrained" economies are those with measured and "repressed" inflation (Malinvaud, 1977) in markets for their output, where the elements repressing inflation, that is, rationing or deferring demand, might include contractual sluggishness and any price guidelines or incomes policies of a central government. These same elements plus explicit wage guidelines might lead labor markets to be similarly supply constrained, but can conceivably cause excess supply as well, for which case the label "classical unemployment" is usually applied (Malinvaud, 1977) and Europe in the 1970s cited as an example.

In this setting both commodity and factor markets will fail to clear, the first being characterized by excess demand, and the second by either excess supply or demand. All these excesses will spill over into markets that are not subject to rationing. These will include financial and foreign exchange markets that seem realistically to clear continuously. Spillovers into financial markets are more accurately thought of as spillovers into future purchases, one counterpart to deferred purchases in current periods.

Since price controls and guidelines are not traditionally applied to exports and imports, excess commodity demand domestically will also spill over into current imports, a spillover that will be accommodated readily by foreign suppliers who are not constrained in export sales and pricing. Thus although domestic buyers may find themselves rationed, foreign buyers (importers) will not. This last phenomenon has the potential to create infinitely profitable arbitrage, since the prices that suppliers receive on foreign sales can rise relative to those they are allowed on domestic sales. But since export markets for most suppliers are usually smaller than domestic markets, modest reallocations of sales toward exports will generally be sufficient to reduce the export price to its traditional relation to domestic price,[7] and the arbitrage opportunity will be eliminated. This elimination of infinite arbitrage profits should be immediate and continuous, even when overall markets do not clear. (Suppliers will, of course, make profits on inframarginal sales adjustments due to arbitrage, thus justifying the arbitrage.)

There is more than a suggestion in this discussion that supply-constrained regimes may be afflicted with volatile responses of exports, imports, capital movements, and exchange rates to wage-price guidelines and other familiar policies. And indeed the potential for volatile international transactions and exchange rates can be confirmed in the abstract using the appropriate version of the model of section 15.1. But any such demonstration is worthless if these spillovers could not even in principle be quantitatively important determinants of observed volatility. Empirically sensible measures of their impact are not immediately clear.

To address both the empirical and the abstract concerns, we shall describe the results from investigating a "central value version" of section 15.1's model. Parameter values were chosen "centrally" in the sense that they reflect well-established empirical regularities: approximate medium-term invariance of budget and factor shares to most changes and the tendency of estimated own-price and income elasticities of demand to center (in absolute value) around one. Log-linear utility and production functions yield precisely these properties, and, as side benefits, both empirical measurability (shares) and analytical tractability:[8]

$$V_1(X_{11}, X_{21}, M_{11}, M_{21}) = v_1 + \alpha_1 \log X_{11} + \beta_1 \log X_{21}$$
$$+ \gamma_{11} \log M_{11} + \gamma_{21} \log M_{21}, \tag{9.1}$$

$$V_2(X_{12}, X_{22}, M_{12}, M_{22}) = v_2 + \alpha_2 \log X_{12} + \beta_2 \log X_{22}$$
$$+ \gamma_{12} \log M_{12} + \gamma_{22} \log M_{22}, \tag{9.2}$$

as the specific forms of $V_i(\ )$ to be considered, where α_i, β_i, and γ_{ij} denote budget shares, and v_i denotes a constant, and

$$\log Y_i = \log a_i + \delta_i \log N_i \tag{10}$$

as the specific form of (5), where δ_i denotes a factor share and a_i denotes a constant.

Maximization subject to the constraints that characterize the supply-constrained economies described, in which all consumers are rationed, yet only in their respective domestic markets, yields the following system of equations. For country 1's commodity exports and imports (2's imports and exports, respectively), effective demands are

$$p_1 X_{12} = \left(\frac{\alpha_2}{1 - \beta_2}\right)(r)(w_2 N_2 + \pi_2^0 + M_{12}^0/r + M_{22}^0 - p_2 C_{22}), \tag{11.1}$$

$$p_2 X_{21} = \left(\frac{\beta_1}{1 - \alpha_1}\right)(1/r)(w_1 N_1 + \pi_1^0 + M_{11}^0 + r M_{21}^0 - p_1 C_{11}). \tag{11.2}$$

Spillover effects on trade as a result of domestic rationing are reflected in the first and last terms on the right-hand side of (11). If wages and prices could vary to clear markets, then the denominators $1 - \beta_2$ and $1 - \alpha_1$ would be replaced by 1, and the $p_i C_{ii}$ terms would vanish. Unrationed international commodity trade in turn feeds back on domestic output rationing, as reflected in the last term of the domestic demand equations, given the assumed constraints:

$$C_{ii} = Y_i - G_i - X_{ij}. \tag{12}$$

This sets commodity trade apart from international capital movements, which are subject to spillover influences from domestic output rationing, but do not feed back on it. Net international claims (stocks) are given by

$$M_{12} = \left(\frac{\gamma_{12}}{1 - \beta_2}\right)(r)(w_2 N_2 + \pi_2^0 + M_{12}^0/r + M_{22}^0 - p_2 C_{22}), \qquad (13.1)$$

$$M_{21} = \left(\frac{\gamma_{21}}{1 - \alpha_1}\right)(1/r)(w_1 N_1 + \pi_1^0 + M_{11}^0 + rM_{21}^0 - p_1 C_{11}). \qquad (13.2)$$

The exchange rate is sensitive to the spillover effects of domestic rationing on trade and capital movements, as well as reflecting its standard role in valuing relative asset stocks (implicit in the M_{21}^0 and M_{12}^0 influences below):[9]

$$r = \frac{[(\beta_1 + \gamma_{21})/(1 - \alpha_1)](w_1 N_1 + \pi_1^0 + M_{11}^0 + rM_{21}^0 - p_1 C_{11}) - rM_{21}^0}{[(\alpha_2 + \gamma_{12})/(1 - \beta_2)](w_2 N_2 + \pi_2^0 + M_{12}^0/r + M_{22}^0 - p_2 C_{22}) - M_{12}^0/r}. \qquad (14)$$

In the absence of rationing and spillovers, the exchange rate would reflect only the relative nominal output trends and valuation of national financial asset stocks, in a manner familiar from the monetary/portfolio approach to floating exchange rates.[10]

Wages w_i, prices p_i, government spending $p_i G_i$, and beginning-of-period values (superscript zero) are exogenously fixed by assumption. When firms are rationed in the labor market (repressed inflation), then employment N_i and output supply Y_i are fixed by the exogenous labor force $\bar{N}_i$ and by the rule that quantities are dictated by the short side of the market. When households are rationed in the labor market (classical unemploy-

Table 15.1
Stylized empirical correspondents to the parameters and representative values of equations (11)–(14)

Stylized United States	Stylized rest of world
Shares	
$\alpha_1 = 0.49$	$\alpha_2 = 0.03$
$\beta_1 = 0.06$	$\beta_2 = 0.57$
$\gamma_{11} = 0.42$	$\gamma_{12} = 0.02$
$\gamma_{21} = 0.03$	$\gamma_{22} = 0.38$
Trillions of US Dollars	
$p_1 Y_1 = 2.369$	$r^0 p_2 Y_2 = 4.738$
$p_1 G_1 = 0.476$	$r^0 p_2 G_2 = 0.953$
$w_1 N_1 = 1.796$	$r^0 w_2 N_2 = 3.591$
$\pi_1^0 = 0.517$	$r^0 \pi_2^0 = 1.034$
$M_{11}^0 = 1.238$	$M_{12}^0 = 0.174$
$r^0 M_{21}^0 = 0.138$	$r^0 M_{22}^0 = 1.966$

Source: appendix B.

Table 15.2
Policy and output elasticities in supply-constrained open economies: percentage effects on endogenous variables (row headings) of a 1-percent change in exogenous variables (column headings)[a]

	Stylized United States				Stylized rest of world			
	$-w_1, p_1^b$	w_1^c	a_1	g_1	$-w_2, p_2^b$	w_2^c	a_2	g_2
Dollar price of foreign currency (r)	0.04	0.69	−0.91	0.18	−0.05	−0.92	1.21	−0.24
US terms of trade (p_1/rp_2)	−1.04	−0.69	0.91	−0.18	1.05	0.92	−1.21	0.24
US real welfare (p_1Y_1 deflated by price index of p_1, rp_2)	−0.10	−0.07	0.09	−0.02	0.10	0.09	−0.12	0.02
Foreign real welfare (p_2Y_2 deflated by price index of $p_2, p_1/r$)	0.05	0.03	−0.05	0.01	−0.05	−0.05	0.06	−0.01
Real US commodity exports (X_{12})	1.03	0.68	−0.89	0.18	0.02	0.31	−0.42	0.08
Real US commodity imports (X_{21})	0.02	0.32	−0.42	0.08	1.05	0.89	−1.18	0.24
Dollar value of US exports (p_1X_{12})	0.03	0.68	−0.89	0.18	0.02	0.31	−0.42	0.08
Dollar value of US imports (rp_2X_{21})	0.06	1.01	−1.33	0.26	−0.00	−0.03	0.03	−0.00
Foreign currency value of US exports (p_1X_{12}/r)	−0.01	−0.01	0.02	−0.00	0.07	1.23	−1.63	0.32
Foreign currency value of US imports (p_2X_{21})	0.02	0.32	−0.42	0.08	0.05	0.89	−1.18	0.24
US liabilities to foreigners (M_{12})	0.03	0.61	−0.79	0.16	0.02	0.28	−0.37	0.07
US real claims on foreigners (M_{21})	0.02	0.27	−0.35	0.07	0.04	0.74	−0.98	0.20
Foreign currency value of liabilities to foreigners (M_{12}/r)	−0.01	−0.08	0.12	−0.02	0.07	1.20	−1.58	0.31
Dollar value of real claims on foreigners (rM_{21})	0.06	0.96	−1.26	0.25	−0.01	−0.18	0.23	−0.04
Real domestic purchases in United States (C_{11})	−0.14	−0.10[d]	1.55	−0.31	−0.00	−0.04	0.06	−0.01
Real domestic purchases in rest of world (C_{22})	−0.00	−0.02	0.03	−0.01	−0.06	−0.06[d]	1.41	−0.28

a. Column-heads: $-w_i, p_i = $ 1-percent tighter wage/price guidelines in region i with distributional neutrality ($dw_i/w_i = dp_i/p_i = -0.01$); $w_i = $ 1-percent looser wage guideline for given price guideline ($dw_i/w_i = 0.01$); $a_i = $ 1-percent technological improvement, measured by total factor productivity ($da_i/a_i = 0.01$); $g_i = $ 1-percent increase in government spending ($dg_i/g_i = 0.01$).

b. The impact of 1-percent looser price guidelines, with no change in wage guidelines ($dp_i/p_i = 0.01$), can be obtained by adding the entries in the $-w_i, p_i$ column to those in the w_i column, then reversing the sign. These results would represent the impacts from an unanticipated incomes policy within wage-price guidelines that favored "capital" instead of labor. For the parameters underlying the table (specifically $\delta_i = 0.757$), a 1-percent increase in price with no change in wage represents an increase in returns to "capital" of 4.12 percent.

c. For every experiment except those in the w_i columns, there are no employment (N_i) or output (Y_i) effects even when households are rationed in labor markets, so that firms are on their labor demand curves, and employment is negatively responsive to the real wage w_i/p_i. This is because neither equiproportional wage-price guidelines $-w_i, p_i$; technological improvement a_i; nor fiscal policy g_i alters the real wage w_i/p_i. w_i policy, by contrast, does, and hence causes N_i and Y_i to fall when there is excess supply in labor markets (not otherwise). One percent looser wage guidelines in either region, for given price guidelines ($dw_i/w_i = 0.01$) causes employment to fall (and unemployment to rise) 4.12 percent, and causes output to fall 3.12 percent. Such employment-output adjustments do not alter the elasticities recorded in the w_i columns, except in the case of C_{ii}, for reasons outlined in appendix B.

d. These entries are appropriate only to the case of supply constraint (excess demand) in the labor market. When, by contrast, households are rationed in the labor market and firms are on their labor demand curves, the appropriate entries are for C_{11}, -4.55; for C_{22}, -4.22.

ment), then employment and output vary as determined by the production function and the labor demand curve implied by profit maximization.[11] In any event, other variables that are determined endogenously and simultaneously by the system include commodity trade X_{12}, X_{21}; rationed domestic purchases C_{11}, C_{22}; international financial claims M_{12}, M_{21}; and the exchange rate r.[12]

Reduced form equivalents of (11)–(14) are derived in appendix A. Empirical approximations to the reduced form of (11)–(14) are calculated in appendix B. Parameters and initial values were chosen to create a stylized but "central value" representation of the United States and the rest of the world in the late 1970s. The following discussion is based on this empirically stylized reduced form, the elements of which are summarized in table 15.1.

The multipliers of exogenous variables on endogenous are displayed in elasticity form in table 15.2. The table is divided, the left-hand side recording the impact of shocks in country 1, the "stylized United States," and the right-hand side recording those in country 2, the "stylized rest of the world."[13] Each column on each side represents a different experiment:

Columns labeled $-w_i$, p_i display the impacts of an unanticipated 1-percent tightening of wage-price guidelines in some overall price controls program.

Columns labeled w_i display the impact of an unanticipated incomes policy that favors labor by 1 percent (specifically a policy that allows wages to rise one percent faster than prices).[14] Without intending to prejudice we shall occasionally refer to such policies below as "progressive" incomes policies.

Columns labeled a_i display the impact of an unanticipated 1 percent increase in growth due to disembodied technological progress.[15]

Columns labeled g_i display the impact of unanticipated 1-percent fiscal expansion, financed either by monetization or by borrowing in liquid financial instruments [see equation (7)].

It is an interesting property of the log-linear utility and production functions employed to establish central values that the results of table 15.2 are, with two exceptions, invariant to whether the labor market features excess demand or excess supply. In the former case, employment N_i and output Y_i are unaffected by any of the shocks [being fixed at $\bar{N}_i$ and $Y_i(\bar{N}_i)$]; in the latter, both respond negatively to an increased wage (w_i), but in a quantitatively offsetting way.[16]

Table 15.2 reveals the following conclusions:

1. Cleanly floating exchange rates do not insulate either supply-

constrained region from shocks in the other. They would have done so only if financial claims on foreigners and indebtedness to them had been zero. With positive international claims and indebtedness, each exogenous change causes exchange rate-related capital gains and losses on national portfolios that alter real demands for goods and assets.

2. The international transmission of shocks between supply-constrained regimes under floating exchange rates is direct. Each policy, and productivity-based growth as well, generates an effect abroad that is qualitatively similar to that at home. Additional rationing at home causes increased spillover purchases of unconstrained imports from foreign producers (at flexible prices) and these ration out additional foreign buyers. In symmetric fashion, relief from domestic rationing creates repercussions abroad that relieve foreign rationing as well. Such "rationing repercussions" increase the sensitivity of domestic shortages to any given domestic policy or change.

3. The quantitative size of this international transmission is important only for real welfare (national purchasing power). Otherwise, own-country influences are generally 3–40 times larger than cross-country influences.[17] The results provide little practical support for international policy coordination that is rooted in avoiding the import of foreign vice (e.g., imported rationing and inflationary pressure) or in encouraging the import of foreign virtue (e.g., locomotive or convoy approaches).

4. The quantitative impact of what might be loosely called "supply side" policies—toward factor shares (w_i columns) and growth (a_i columns)— are, with a few exceptions, from 3–5 times larger than the quantitative impacts of more traditional wage-price controls $-w_i$, p_i and fiscal initiatives g_i.

5. Distributionally neutral wage-price guidelines, "progressive" (in the sense of favoring wages) incomes policies, and liquidity-based fiscal expansion all have qualitatively similar effects. All such policies weaken a nation's currency in the foreign exchange market, with consequent terms-of-trade deterioration and a decline in its standard of living (as measured by national purchasing power). (The impacts on real national welfare, however, are quantitatively small.) Technology-based output growth, by contrast, strengthens a nation's currency, improves its terms of trade and standard of living, and loosens up the ration that constrains domestic purchasers, thereby reducing shortages and order backlogs.[18]

6. Tighter wage-price controls, more "progressive" incomes policies, and fiscal expansion all ration domestic consumers more tightly (reduce C_{ii}), as one would expect. And . . .

7. Frustrated purchasing power spills over toward unconstrained imports of commodities ($rp_2 X_{21}$ for 1; $p_1 X_{12}/r$ for 2) and toward claims on future commodities (M_{11} and rM_{21} for 1; M_{22} and M_{12}/r for 2); ...

8. Such international spillovers of purchasing power cause exchange-rate depreciation that, in turn, causes. . .

9. Real exports of both commodities and ownership of domestic assets (X_{ij} and M_{ij} stocks for country i) to vary *positively* with wage-price controls, "progressive" incomes policies, and fiscal expansion, counter to casual intuition, but consistent with the remarkable burgeoning of export volume and international liabilities during the inflation-prone early 1970s in which each of these policies enjoyed some unanticipated prominence.

10. Finally, because these policies cause spillover increases in imports and claims on foreigners, as well as exports and liabilities to them,[19] they could all be characterized as increasing the "internationalization" of commodity and financial capital markets, in a way that again seems consistent with observation in the 1970s.

11–15. Conversely to (6)–(10), technological progress, productivity growth, and supply expansion shrink supply constraints and rationing dramatically, leading to currency appreciation, larger imports and exports, symmetric changes in international asset positions, and declining internationalization of world commodity and asset markets.

Appendix A Reduced Form of Model under Cleanly Floating Exchange Rates

When exchange rates are allowed to float cleanly between the two supply-constrained economies described by the model, the exchange rate r that appears in equations (11)–(13) of the text is endogenous. Its value is determined from equation (14) of the text, rearranged to express r as a function of C_{11} and C_{22}, then solved simultaneously with (11) and (12) for r, X_{12}, X_{21}, C_{11}, and C_{22}. The resulting expressions can be used to solve (13) recursively for M_{12} and M_{21}:

$$p_1 X_{12} = Z_1 \cdot \frac{\left(\dfrac{\beta_1}{1-\alpha_1}\right)\left(1+\dfrac{\gamma_{21}}{\beta_1}\right) - \dfrac{M_{12}^0}{Z_1} - \left(\dfrac{\beta_1}{1-\alpha_1}\right)\dfrac{M_{21}^0}{Z_2} + \left(1-\dfrac{\gamma_{21}}{1-\alpha_1}\right)\dfrac{M_{12}^0}{Z_1}\dfrac{M_{21}^0}{Z_2}}{\varepsilon_1 - \left(\dfrac{1-\beta_2}{\alpha_2}\right)\left(\varepsilon_1 - \dfrac{\gamma_{12}}{\alpha_2}\Delta\right)\dfrac{M_{21}^0}{Z_2}},$$

$$\text{(11.1A)}$$

$$p_2 X_{21} = Z_2 \cdot \frac{\left(\dfrac{\alpha_2}{1 - \beta_2}\right)\left(1 + \dfrac{\gamma_{12}}{\alpha_2}\right) - \left(\dfrac{\alpha_2}{1 - \beta_2}\right)\dfrac{M_{12}^0}{Z_1} - \dfrac{M_{21}^0}{Z_2} + \left(1 - \dfrac{\gamma_{12}}{1 - \beta_2}\right)\dfrac{M_{12}^0}{Z_1}\dfrac{M_{21}^0}{Z_2}}{\varepsilon_2 - \left(\dfrac{1 - \alpha_1}{\beta_1}\right)\left(\varepsilon_2 - \dfrac{\gamma_{21}}{\beta_1}\Delta\right)\dfrac{M_{12}^0}{Z_1}},$$

$$(11.2A)$$

where

$$\Delta = \left(\frac{\beta_1}{1 - \alpha_1}\right)\left(\frac{\alpha_2}{1 - \beta_2}\right) - 1, \text{ negative in sign,}$$

$$\varepsilon_1 = \left(\frac{\beta_1}{1 - \alpha_1}\right)\left(1 + \frac{\gamma_{21}}{\beta_1}\right) - \left(1 + \frac{\gamma_{12}}{\alpha_2}\right), \text{ negative in sign,}$$

$$\varepsilon_2 = \left(\frac{\alpha_2}{1 - \beta_2}\right)\left(1 + \frac{\gamma_{12}}{\alpha_2}\right) - \left(1 + \frac{\gamma_{21}}{\beta_1}\right), \text{ negative in sign,}$$

$$Z_1 = p_1 Y_1 - p_1 G_1 - w_1 N_1 - \pi_1^0 - M_{11}^0, \text{ negative in sign,}$$

$$Z_2 = p_2 Y_2 - p_2 G_2 - w_2 N_2 - \pi_2^0 - M_{22}^0, \text{ negative in sign;}$$

$$p_1 C_{11} = p_1 Y_1 - p_1 G_1 - p_1 X_{12} \quad \text{from (11.1B);} \tag{12.1A}$$

$$p_2 C_2 = p_2 Y_2 - p_2 G_2 - p_2 X_{21} \quad \text{from (11.2B);} \tag{12.2A}$$

$$M_{12} = \left(\frac{\gamma_{12}}{\alpha_2}\right) p_1 X_{12} \quad \text{from (11.1B);} \tag{13.1A}$$

$$M_{21} = \left(\frac{\gamma_{21}}{\beta_1}\right) p_2 X_{21} \quad \text{from (11.2B);} \tag{13.2A}$$

$$r = \frac{Z_1 \cdot \left\{\left(\dfrac{\beta_1}{1 - \alpha_1}\right)\varepsilon_2 + \left[\left(\dfrac{\alpha_2}{1 - \beta_2}\right)\varepsilon_1 - \Delta\right]\dfrac{M_{12}^0}{Z_1}\right\}}{Z_2 \cdot \left\{\left(\dfrac{\alpha_2}{1 - \beta_2}\right)\varepsilon_1 + \left[\left(\dfrac{\beta_1}{1 - \alpha_1}\right)\varepsilon_2 - \Delta\right]\dfrac{M_{21}^0}{Z_2}\right\}}. \tag{14.A}$$

Table 15.2 and the accompanying discussion are based on the central value version of the reduced form system (11A)–(14A). The presence of the terms M_{12}^0/Z_1 and M_{21}^0/Z_2 is quite striking because it is solely their influence that undermines the insulation properties of cleanly floating exchange rates. In the absence of any international financial claims or liabilities ($M_{12}^0 = M_{21}^0 = 0$), floating exchange rates would guarantee insulation: X_{12}, C_{11}, and M_{12} would depend on the country 1 variables in Z_1 alone, and not on Z_2; X_{21}, C_{22}, and M_{21} would depend on Z_2 alone, and not on Z_1. A peculiarity of such insulation would be that each supply-constrained region could independently influence its real exports and the domestic currency value of its liabilities to foreigners, but would have *no* ability to influence its real imports or the foreign currency value of its claims on foreigners.

Appendix B Data Sources and Notes for Central-Value Version of Model

Sources for Data in Table 15.1[20]

$p_1 Y_1$: US gross national product in 1979 ($2.369 trillion).

$p_1 G_1$: US government spending on goods and services in 1979 ($0.476 trillion).

$w_1 N_1$: US share of national income represented by employee compensation in 1979 applied to $p_1 Y_1$ (1.459/1.925 times $2.369 trillion).

$\pi_1^0 + M_{11}^0$: US liquid[21] wealth at the end of 1978 (measured by L) $-$ M_{12}^0 (see below) ($1.930 trillion $-$ $0.174 trillion).

$r^0 M_{21}^0$: US-owned foreign currency and foreign short-term[21] assets at the end of 1978, from US Department of Commerce, *Survey of Current Business*, August 1979, p. 56, lines 12, 20, and 22 and 23 ($0.138 trillion).

$r^0 p_2 Y_2$, $r^0 p_2 G_2$, $r^0 w_2 N_2$: twice the value of their US counterparts.

M_{12}^0: foreign-owned US currency and short-term[21] assets at the end of 1978, from US Department of Commerce, *Survey of Current Business*, August 1979, p. 56, lines 39, 41, and 43 ($0.174 trillion).

$r^0 \pi_2^0 + r^0 M_{22}^0$: arbitrary value of rest-of-world liquid[21] wealth chosen to be somewhat less than $p_2 Y_2 / p_1 Y_1$, in order to reflect maintained hypothesis (see note 13) that rest of world is less wealthy relative to income than the United States; dollar value of foreign L less $r^0 M_{21}^0$ set equal to $3.000 trillion.

$\alpha_1, \beta_1, \gamma_{11}, \gamma_{21}$: established from simultaneous solution of the budget share equations consistent with constrained maximization of the log-linear utility function (9.1) from the text—

$$\frac{\gamma_{11} + \gamma_{21}}{\alpha_1 + \beta_1} = \frac{\pi_1^0 + M_{11}^0 + r^0 M_{21}^0}{p_1 Y_1 - p_1 X_{12} + r p_2 X_{21}} = \frac{1.756 + 0.138}{2.373},$$

$$\frac{\gamma_{11}}{\gamma_{21}} = \frac{\pi_1^0 + M_{11}^0}{r^0 M_{21}^0} = \frac{1.756}{0.138},$$

using data above;

$\dfrac{\alpha_1}{\beta_1}$ = ratio of US budget share for domestic purchases to US budget share for imports ≈ 8;

$\alpha_1 + \beta_1 + \gamma_{11} + \gamma_{21} = 1$.

$\alpha_2, \beta_2, \gamma_{12}, \gamma_{22}$: established from simultaneous solution of the budget share equations consistent with constrained maximization of the log-linear ultility function (9.2) from the text—

$$\frac{\gamma_{12} + \gamma_{22}}{\alpha_2 + \beta_2} = \frac{M_{12}^0 + r^0\pi_2^0 + r^0 M_{22}^0}{r^0 p_2 Y_2 - r^0 p_2 X_{21} + p_1 X_{12}} = \frac{0.174 + 3.000}{4.733},$$

$$\frac{\gamma_{22}}{\gamma_{12}} = \frac{r^0\pi_2^0 + r^0 M_{22}^0}{M_{12}^0} = \frac{3.000}{0.174},$$

using data above;

$\dfrac{\beta_2}{\alpha_2}$ = ratio of rest-of-world budget share for domestic purchases to rest-of-world budget share for imports from the United States ≈ 17;

$\alpha_2 + \beta_2 + \gamma_{12} + \gamma_{22} = 1$.

D_1, D_2 [implied values of inflationary gaps (shortages or deferred purchases) from data above]: \$0.151, \$0.297, each approximately 6 percent of $p_1 Y_1$ or $r^0 p_2 Y_2$, respectively (see note 12).[22]

Excess Supply or Demand in the Labor Market: Invariance of the International Trade Results to the Issue

It will be shown that Z_i, on which all but two of the reduced form results rest in appendix A, has the same elasticity with respect to w_i regardless of the type or size of nonmarket clearing in the labor market.

Z_i are defined by

$$Z_1 = p_1 Y_1 - p_1 G_1 - w_1 N_1 - \pi_1^0 - M_{11}^0,$$

$$Z_2 = p_2 Y_2 - p_2 G_2 - w_2 N_2 - \pi_2^0 - M_{22}^0.$$

When firms are rationed in labor markets, so that employment N_i is fixed at $\bar{N}_i$ by supply and output at $Y_i(\bar{N}_i)$, the elasticity of Z_i with respect to w_i (say E_{Z_i, w_i}) is given by

$$E_{Z_i, w_i} \equiv \frac{\partial Z_i}{\partial w_i} \cdot \frac{w_i}{Z_i} = -\frac{w_i N_i}{Z_i}.$$

When households are rationed in labor markets, employment N_i is determined by firms' labor demand curves, which have a real-wage elasticity of $1/(\delta_i - 1)$ for log-linear production functions such as (10).[23] Output Y_i is determined by employment, with an employment elasticity of δ_i for log-linear production functions such as (10), making output indirectly elastic to real wages to a degree given by the product of the last two elasticities: $\delta_i/(1 - \delta_i)$. Making use of simple rules for elasticity operators $[E_{AB} = E_A + E_B; \; E_{A+B} = AE_A/(A + B) + BE_B/(A + B)]$ readily shows that the elasticity of Z_i with respect to w_i is the same as above:

$$E_{Z_i, w_i} = p_i Y_i E_{Y_i, w_i}/Z_i - w_i N_i (E_{w_i, w_i} + E_{N_i, w_i})/Z_i$$

$$= \frac{p_i Y_i}{Z_i} \frac{\delta_i}{\delta_i - 1} - \frac{w_i N_i}{Z_i} \left(1 + \frac{1}{\delta_i - 1}\right)$$

$$= -\frac{\delta_i}{1 - \delta_i} \left(\frac{p_i Y_i - w_i N_i}{Z_i}\right),$$

which, remembering that δ_i is labor's share of $p_i Y_i$ given log-linear production functions,

$$= -\frac{w_i N_i}{p_i Y_i - w_i N_i} \left(\frac{p_i Y_i - w_i N_i}{Z_i}\right)$$

$$= -\frac{w_i N_i}{Z_i},$$

as above.

Notes

1. Related efforts that apply temporary equilibrium or 'disequilibrium' insights to international macroeconomics include Brito and Richardson (1975, 1977), Cuddington (1979, 1980), Dixit (1978), Gordon (1977), Grossman, Hanson, and Lucas (1977), Owen (1979), Neary (1979), and Steigum (1979).

2. On the usefulness of the assumptions of price-taking agents and "price-setting" large open economies, see Muellbauer and Portes (1978, pp. 817–18).

3. Financial assets are the means by which consumption can be transferred between the present and the future. Current household stocks of assets thus vary directly, *ceteris paribus*, with intended future consumption, and can be taken to represent it. That is one reason why they appear in the household utility function. Another is any intrinsic "utility value" that they may have. Expectations are, as mentioned, assumed to be stable because of our principal focus in this paper on shocks that are difficult or impossible to anticipate.

4. When both countries' households are rationed in either goods market, then rationing rules must be defined to allocate available supplies $(Y_i - G_i)$ between domestic and foreign buyers. Such rationing rules further constrain the household maximization process. For examples: (1) ration according to historical shares— $C_{ii}/C_{ij} = (C_{ii}/C_{ij})^0$; (2) ration the larger purchaser only—$C_{ii} = \min[X_{ii}, 0.5$ times $(Y_i - G_i)]$, $C_{ij} = Y_i - G_i - C_{ii}$; (3) discriminate against foreign buyers—$C_{ii} = \min(X_{ii}, Y_i - G_i)$, $C_{ij} = Y_i - G_i - C_{ii}$.

5. Instantaneous clearing in the foreign exchange market remains characteristic even under "fixed" exchange rates and managed floating, once account is taken of both private (firm and household) and official (government) supplies and demands. Excess *private* supply of or demand for foreign exchange still exist in this case, however, and hence a "balance of payments" can be defined. But the exchange rate is nevertheless flexible, and responsive to both government intervention and private action.

6. This can be seen by summing the household and government budget constraints [(2) and (7)], adding and subtracting exports of goods ($p_1 X_{12}$ if unconstrained) and rearranging the result in order to apply the substitution of $M_{12} - M_{12}^0 - r(M_{21} - M_{21}^0)$ for $-p_1 X_{12} + r p_2 X_{21}$ from (8):

$$\pi_i - \pi_i^0 = (L_i - L_i^0) - (M_{ii} - M_{ii}^0) - (M_{ij} - M_{ij}^0),$$

from which, using (1),

$$\pi_i = L_i - (M_{ij} + M_{ii}).$$

7. There are many reasons why export prices will differ in equilibrium from domestic prices, including taxes, transport costs, and price discrimination (Kravis and Lipsey, 1971, 1977). The text describes how price controls and extraordinary sluggishness can cause the actual wedge between export and domestic prices to diverge temporarily from the equilibrium wedge, creating supplier arbitrage that restores the equilibrium wedge. Note that this would imply that uncontrolled export prices would change at the same rate as domestic prices subject to control. In the United States, between 1971 and mid-1980, the ratio of US export unit values to wholesale prices rose at an average annual rate of only 0.7 percent per year (International Monetary Fund, *International Financial Statistics*).

8. The use of specific and empirically plausible functions in this way has illustrative precedent as a means of easing computational burdens and alleviating indeterminacy in both the disequilibrium-macroeconomics literature (Malinvaud, 1977; Muellbauer and Portes, 1978, appendix; Ito, 1978) and in the exchange rate-dynamics literature (Dornbusch, 1976; Flood, 1979).

9. Equation (14) is obtained by substituting (11) and (13) into (8) and partially solving for r—"partially solving" in the sense that r remains on the right-hand side of (14) as well, in both numerator and denominator.

10. This can be seen in (14) by observing that the $p_i C_{ii}$ would vanish without rationing, and the $w_i N_i$ could be rewritten as nominal output $p_i Y_i$ less current profits, where current profits are exactly equal to firms' stocks of financial assets. See equation (1) and note 6.

11. We do not highlight these for reasons cited in note 12. But they are easily calculated—see footnote c to table 15.2.

12. We have ignored certain other endogenous variables, such as domestic asset stocks M_{11}, M_{22}, and measures of the "inflationary gap" because of the international focus of our chapter. They are easily examined, however, using the results from table 15.2 because they are recursively determined with respect to the impact recorded there. They, too, are influenced fundamentally by spillovers, even with respect to their functional determinants, making conclusions that rely on "stable"

behavior (e.g., the demand for cash balances or the Phillips curve) doubtful at best. Each country's aggregate "inflationary gap" or "shortage" D_1, D_2 would be best measured by the excess of notional demand facing its domestic producers over available supply:

$$D_1 = \alpha_1(w_1 N_1 + \pi_1^0 + M_{11}^0 + r M_{21}^0) + X_{12} + G_1 - Y_1,$$
$$D_2 = \beta_2(w_2 N_2 + \pi_2^0 + M_{12}^0/r + M_{22}^0) + X_{21} + G_2 - Y_2.$$

It is worth noting the implicit international interdependence of inflationary gaps in these equations. The unconstrained X_{12} and X_{21} should be obtained from equations (11), and will reflect spillovers. Hence D_1 will depend through X_{12} on rationing in country 2 (C_{22}, which will be reflected in D_2), and D_2 will depend likewise on rationing in country 1 (C_{11}, which will be reflected in D_1). International transmission of rationing, gaps, and shortages in discussed below.

13. Comparisons of the left-hand-side results to their counterparts on the right-hand side provide an elementary sensitivity analysis for the calculations. All of the results are quantitatively robust to the one change in parameters implicit in focusing on one region compared to the other. The two stylized regions are asymmetric in that (1) the United States is wealthier relative to its income than the rest of the world (about 20 percent better endowed with liquid wealth relative to income); (2) the United States is more "open" than the rest of the world taken together (trade is about 10 percent of output, rather than 5 percent; liquid liabilities to foreigners are around 9 percent of liquid wealth, rather than 4 percent); and (3) the United States is a net debtor on liquidity account (net international indebtedness equal to roughly 2 percent of liquid wealth), whereas the rest of the world is a net creditor (net claims on the United States equal to roughly 1 percent of rest-of-world liquid wealth).

14. Footnote b to table 15.2 describes the way to determine the impact of an incomes policy that favors profits.

15. The impact of a guidelines program that allowed permissible wage increases to exceed permissible price increases by the amount that productivity increases exceeded a critical value (maybe zero) can be calculated by adding the entries in the w_i column to those in the a_i column. It will be observed that this kind of productivity-conditioned incomes policy has qualitatively opposite effects to unconditional incomes policies that favor wages.

16. See appendix B and footnote c to table 15.2.

17. This conclusion has nothing to do with "small-country effects." The two regions are in ratio roughly 1 : 2 in size. See note 13.

18. The effect of a region's output growth on its inflationary gap (D_i from note 12) is negative and substantial—revealed in elasticities of 15 or so in absolute value.

19. Note that table 15.2's entries also suggest that wage-price guidelines, "progressive" incomes policies, fiscal expansion, and technological sluggishness will "weaken" a nation's current account. Under floating exchange rates, there would be a concomitant "improvement" in the capital account $[(M_{12} - M_{12}^0) - r(M_{21} - M_{21}^0)$ for country 1; $(M_{21} - M_{21}^0) - (M_{12} - M_{12}^0)/r$ for country 2)] that is not directly revealed in table 15.2 because of its focus on asset *stocks* rather than asset

flows. It is worth noting that all shocks cause real commodity exports (X_{ij} for country i) to move parallel with commodity imports (X_{ji} for country i), and also to move parallel with stocks of liabilities to foreigners (M_{12}), which themselves move parallel with the stock of claims on foreigners (M_{21}). This seems to suggest the possibility of simultaneous surpluses (or deficits) on both "real" current account and capital account. Such "real" changes are of course consistent with cleanly floating exchange rates, and are actually accommodated by them to bring about market clearing in the foreign exchange market through revaluation of commodity trade and through capital gains or losses on existing portfolio positions (M_{12}^0 and M_{21}^0).

20. Except where noted, data was taken from Board of Governors of the Federal Reserve System, *Federal Reserve Bulletin*, May 1980.

21. Measures of liquid wealth were chosen because of the belief that it, rather than illiquid wealth, would be the sink for spillover effects due to temporary nonmarket clearing. For the same reason, only it appears explicitly in household budget constraints [equations (2)] and as an influence on the exchange rate [equation (8)].

22. This proportion may seem unduly large, since given log-linear utility functions (unit price-elastic demand functions), and given repressed inflation and the fixed output supply $\overline{Y}_i$ that would accompany excess demand in the labor market, 6-percent gaps would correspond to sluggish or controlled prices that were roughly 6 percent below market-clearing levels. Given classical unemployment, however, with excess supply in the labor market and output supply elasticities of roughly 3 ($\delta_i/(1 - \delta_i)$, as shown below) with respect to price, 6 percent gaps would correspond to holding prices only 1.5 percent below market-clearing levels. And in any event, (1) outright shortages represent only a fraction of inflationary gaps, the remainder being accounted for by delivery delays; (2) shortfalls of current production over "normal" demand may be considerably smaller than 6 percent, which is a proportion that is mushroomed by previous periods' accumulated shortages, deferred purchases, and spillover effects.

23. Employment is determined by setting labor's marginal product equal to its real wage, which for (10) implies

$$\frac{\partial Y_i}{\partial N_i} = \delta_i a_i N_i^{\delta_i - 1} = \frac{w_i}{p_i},$$

so that

$$N_i = \left[\left(\frac{1}{\delta_i a_i}\right)\left(\frac{w_i}{p_i}\right)\right]^{1/(\delta_i - 1)},$$

for which the elasticity of N_i with respect to w_i/p_i is $1/(\delta_i - 1)$.

References

Brito, D. L., and J. David Richardson (1975). "Some Disequilibrium Dynamics of Exchange-Rate Changes," *Journal of International Economics* 5: (February), 1–13.

Brito, D. L., and J. David Richardson (1977). "Some Disequilibrium Dynamics of Exchange-Rate Change: A German Application," manuscript, October.

Cuddington, John T. (1979). "Import Quotas and Non-Price Rationing: A Two-Sector, Fix-Price Model," manuscript.

Cuddington, John T. (1980). "Fiscal and Exchange Rate Policies in a Fix-Price Trade Model with Export Rationing," *Journal of International Economics* 10 (August), 319–340.

Dixit, Avinash (1978). "The Balance of Trade in a Model of Temporary Equilibrium with Rationing," *Review of Economic Studies* 45 (October), 393–404.

Dornbusch, Rudiger (1976). "Expectations and Exchange-Rate Dynamics," *Journal of Political Economy* 84 (December), 1161–76.

Flood, Robert P. (1979). "An Example of Exchange-Rate Overshooting," *Southern Economic Journal* 46 (July), 168–78.

Gordon, Robert J. (1977). "Interrelations between Domestic and International Theories of Inflation," in Robert Z. Aliber, ed., *The Political Economy of Monetary Reform*, Montclair, New Jersey: Allanheld, Osmun, and Co.

Grossman, Herschel L., James A. Hanson, and Robert Lucas (1977). "The Effects of Demand Disturbances under Alternative Exchange-Rate Regimes," manuscript, May.

International Monetary Fund (1980). *Annual Report 1980*, Washington.

Ito, Takatoshi (1978). "A Note on Disequilibrium Growth Theory," *Economic Letters* 1, 45–9.

Kravis, Irving B., and Robert E. Lipsey (1971). *Price Competitiveness in World Trade*, New York: National Bureau of Economic Research and Columbia University Press.

Kravis, Irving B., and Robert E. Lipsey (1977). "Export Prices and the Transmission of Inflation," *American Economic Review* 67 (February), 155–63.

Malinvaud, Edmond (1977). *The Theory of Unemployment Reconsidered*, New York: John Wiley.

Muellbauer, John, and Richard Portes (1978). "Macroeconomic Models With Quantity Rationing." *Economic Journal* 88 (December), 788–821.

Neary, J. Peter (1980). "Non-Traded Goods and the Balance of Trade in a Neo-Keynesian Temporary Equilibrium," *Quarterly Journal of Economics* 95 (November), 403–429.

Owen, Robert F. (1979). "Domestic Disequilibrium and Balance of Trade Adjustment in Open Economies," Institut Nationale de la Statistique et des Etudes Economiques, Working Paper No. 7910, manuscript, November.

Steigum, Erling, Jr. (1979). "Keynesian and Classical Unemployment in an Open Economy," manuscript, August.

IV
SIMULATIONS

16

International Transmission under Pegged and Floating Exchange Rates: An Empirical Comparison

Michael R. Darby

The Mark III international transmission model was constructed to test and measure the importance of alternative channels of international transmission including the effects of capital and trade flows on the money supply of export shocks on aggregate demand, asset substitution on money demand, and variations in the real price of oil. This quarterly econometric model was estimated using data for 1957–1976 for the United States, the United Kingdom, Canada, France, Germany, Italy, Japan, and the Netherlands. The results, reported in Darby and Stockman (1980), indicated surprisingly slow and weak transmission from country to country. The startling implication that substantial sterilization policies were successful in achieving short-run monetary control under pegged exchange rates was confirmed by simple reduced-form tests in Darby (1980a). This chapter continues the investigation of these findings by presenting the results of experiments with a simulation version of the Mark III international transmission model.

The results here generally support the earlier findings of weak transmission under pegged exchange rates. Monetary linkages with the United States appear strongest for Germany, moderate for the Netherlands, and

The good counsel of Arthur Gandolfi, Dan Lee, James Lothian, and Michael Melvin made this chapter possible, but they are not to be implicated in the results. Other valuable comments were received from Anthony Cassese, Robert P. Flood, Jr., and especially Anna J. Schwartz and participants in the UCLA Money Workshop and the NBER Summer Institute. The calculations were performed by Michael Melvin and Andrew Vogel on the TROLL System at MIT. The author acknowledges the generous support of the National Science Foundation (Grant Nos. APR78-13072 and DAR-7922874), the Relm Foundation, the Scaife Family Trusts, and the Alex C. Walker Foundation. The research reported here is part of the NBER's research Program in International Studies, but this chapter has not been submitted to the Board of Directors and therefore is not an official statement of the National Bureau of Economic Research.

practically nonexistent for the United Kingdom and Canada although absorption-type channels are operative for the latter two countries. While monetary shocks in nonreserve countries have sensible domestic effects, international transmission is trivial. Similarly the domestic effects of real government spending shocks are too small to have an appreciable foreign impact in any case examined. These results force us to question the standard assumptions which imply strong channels for international transmission since those channels are not obvious in the data.

Unlike the pegged case, the floating simulations display dynamic instabilities. This difference is attributable to the relatively short sample period. The simulations do indicate how a J-curve phenomenon due to short-run inelasticity of import demand can affect the adjustment process.

16.1 The Simulation Model

The Mark III model was designed to test a number of popular hypotheses about the transmission of inflation while allowing for a variety of lag patterns across countries. Unfortunately the large number of insignificant coefficients and collinear endogenous variables makes the model unusable for simulation purposes. A special simulation version of the model (the Mark IV) has been created by dropping insignificant variables and combining terms[1] except where variables are left in to permit transmission or for strong a priori reasons (such as the interest-rate terms in the money-demand or price-level equation). The resulting model thus includes the significant relations of the Mark III model but is sufficiently simplified for the reasonable calculation of simulation results. Given the way in which the model was derived, classical statistical statements cannot be made with respect to the Mark IV. Its purpose instead is to illustrate the implications of the relation found significant in the Mark III model.

The Mark IV model exists in two versions. The pegged-exchange-rate version (Mark IV-PEG) combines the reserve-country (US) submodel with the pegged-rate submodels for the seven nonreserve countries. Floating-rate nonreserve submodels are used instead in the floating-exchange-rate version (Mark IV-FLT). A detailed presentation of the basic structure is available in the description of the Mark III model.[2] A complete statement of both the Mark III and Mark IV models is available from the author on request.

The Mark III model was formulated to test and measure the empirical importance of alternative channels of international transmission including the effects of capital and trade flows on the money supply, export shocks on aggregate demand, asset substitution on money demand, and varia-

Table 16.1
Summary of Mark IV structure: normalization of equations[a]

Mnemonic	Left-hand-side variables		
	Reserve submodel	Nonreserve pegged submodels	Nonreserve floating submodels
Behavioral equations			
Real income	$\log y_1$	$\log y_j$	$\log y_j$
Price level	$\log P_1$	$\log P_j$	$\log P_j$
Unemployment rate[b]	u_1	u_j	u_j
Nominal money	$\log M_1$	$\log M_j$	$\log M_j$
Interest rate	R_1	R_j	R_j
Exports	$(X/Y)_1$	$(X/Y)_j$	$(X/Y)_j$
Import demand	$(I/Y)_1$	$(I/Y)_j$	$\log(P_j^I/P_j)$
Import supply[c]	$\log P_1^I$	$\log P_j^I$	$\log E_j$
Capital flows	$(C/Y)_1$	$(C/Y)_j$	$(C/Y)_j$
Exchange intervention[d]	–	–	$(B/Y)_j$
Identities			
Permanent income	$\log y_1^P$	$\log y_j^P$	$\log y_j^P$
Transitory income	$\log(y_1/y_1^P)$	$\log(y_j/y_j^P)$	$\log(y_j/y_j^P)$
Balance of payments	$(B/Y)_1$	$(B/Y)_j$	$(I/Y)_j$
Expected money	$\log M_1^*$	$\log M_j^*$	$\log M_j^*$
Money shock	$\hat{M}_1$	$\hat{M}_j$	$\hat{M}_j$
Expected exports	$(X/Y)_1^*$	$(X/Y)_j^*$	$(X/Y)_j^*$
Export shock	$\hat{x}_1$	$\hat{x}_j$	$\hat{x}_j$
Import relative price[c]	$\log(P_1^I/P_1)$	$\log(P_j^I/P_j)$	$\log P_j^I$
Expected inflation	$(4\Delta\log P_{1,t+1})^*$	$(4\Delta\log P_{j,t+1})^*$	$(4\Delta\log P_{j,t+1})^*$
Expected depreciation	–	$(4\Delta\log E_{j,t+1})^*$	$(4\Delta\log E_{j,t+1})^*$
Foreign income	$\log y_1^R$	$\log y_j^R$	$\log y_j^R$
Foreign prices	$\log P_1^R$	$\log P_j^R$	$\log P_j^R$

a. Asterisk denotes expectation based on prior quarter's information set. Exogenous variables for Mark IV-PEG: $\hat{g}_1$, $\hat{g}_2$, $\hat{g}_3$, $\hat{g}_4$, $\hat{g}_5$, $\hat{g}_6$, $\hat{g}_7$, $\hat{g}_8$, $\log E_2$, $\log E_3$, $\log E_4$, $\log E_5$, $\log E_6$, $\log E_7$, $\log E_8$, $\log P^{RO}$, t. Exogenous variables for Mark IV-FLT: $\hat{g}_1$, $\hat{g}_2$, $\hat{g}_3$, $\hat{g}_4$, $\hat{g}_5$, $\hat{g}_6$, $\hat{g}_7$, $\hat{g}_8$, $\log P^{RO}$, t. Notation: 1, United States (US); 2, United Kingdom (UK); 3, Canada (CA); 4, France (FR); 5, Germany (GE); 6, Italy (IT); 7, Japan (JA); 8, Netherlands (NE); B_j, balance of payments; C_j, net capital outflows; E_j, exchange rate (per US dollar); $\hat{g}_j$, real government-spending shock (the innovation in an ARIMA process fitted to $\log g$); I_j, value of imports; M_j, nominal money; $\hat{M}_j$, money shock ($\log M_j - \log M_j^*$); P_j, price level (deflator); P_j^I, import price index; P_j^R, index of foreign prices (in US dollars); P^{RO}, index of real price of oil; R_j, short-term interest rate; u_j, unemployment rate; X_j, value of exports; $\hat{x}_j$, export shock $[(X/Y)_j - (X/Y)_j^*]$; y_j, real gross output; Y_j, nominal gross output $(y_j \cdot P_j)$; y_j^P, permanent income; y_j^R, index of foreign real income.
b. The unemployment equation occurs only in the American, British, and French submodels.
c. The import-supply equation and import-relative-price identity are deleted as redundant for the German pegged submodel.
d. The exchange-intervention equation occurs only in the seven nonreserve floating submodels.

tions in the real price of oil. The Mark IV model incorporates these channels to the extent that they were supported by the data.

The basic structure of the model is outlined in table 16.1. This table lists the dependent variable of each behavioral equation and identity together with the exogenous variables and notation used in the model. Lagged values of both endogenous and exogenous variables also appear as explanatory variables in the model. The reserve-country submodel of the Mark IV consists of nine behavioral equations and 13 identities.[3] The behavioral equations determine a skeletal macroeconometric model (real income, price level, unemployment rate, nominal money, and interest rate) together with a bit more detailed international sector (exports, imports, import prices, and capital flows). The pegged-exchange-rate nonreserve submodels are basically the same as the reserve submodel with the important exception that the balance of payments enters the nonreserve (but not the reserve) countries' money-supply reaction functions.[4] The floating nonreserve submodels differ only in their international sectors: To make the seven domestic-currency-per-dollar exchange rates endogenous, an exchange-intervention reaction function is added to determine the balance of payments previously determined by an identity. The sector is then renormalized to solve for the exchange rate.[5]

Let us first examine the skeletal macroeconometric model included in each of the submodels. Real income and the (nominal) interest rate are determined by shocks (innovations) in the money supply, real government spending, and real exports, and for the interest-rate equation only, the expected inflation rate.[6] Thus real income and the *real* interest rate are affected by the factors which unexpectedly shift aggregate demand relative to aggregate supply. The price-level equations simply equate short-run money demand to money supply.[7] Nominal money supply is determined by a reaction function in response to lagged inflation and unemployment rates, current and lagged government spending shocks, and, for nonreserve countries, current and lagged balances of payments. The unemployment rate is determined by a dynamic version of Okun's law for the United States, the United Kingdom, and France. Changes in measured unemployment and real income were uncorrelated for the other countries; so for them the unemployment equation is deleted and logarithmic transitory income used instead in the money-supply reaction function.

The channels by which international shocks can be transmitted to these basic macroeconomic variables are three in number: (1) For the nonreserve countries, the current and lagged balances of payments affect the nominal money supply. The estimates indicated very substantial if not total sterilization of the *current* balance of payments in every case, however. This is consistent with the central banks' pursuing money-growth or interest-rate goals set in response, among other things, to past data on the balance of payments. (2) Export shocks affect both real income and the interest rate along standard Keynesian absorption lines. (3) An asset substitution channel exists by which foreign interest rates adjusted by expected depreciation can affect money demand and the price level in the United Kingdom, France, and Japan. The real oil price does not enter in this sector but in the international sector and influences the domestic economy through these three channels. Tests of direct real influences are reported at length in Darby (1982).

The reserve and pegged-nonreserve international sectors will be discussed next. The export equation depends on foreign real income, the real price of oil, the domestic and foreign price levels, and the exchange rate. Imports are explained by a demand equation including domestic real income and current and lagged import prices relative to the price level. Import prices in turn depend on import supply variables such as the size of imports, foreign price levels, and the exchange rate. The capital-flows equations allow for interest-rate and expected-depreciation effects, foreign and domestic real-income effects, and trade-deficit financing. In the floating-nonreserve models the import demand and supply equations are renormalized to relative-import-price and exchange-rate equations, respectively. The added balance-of-payments or intervention equation relates the balance to changes in exchange rates relative to lagged changes and lagged changes in relative purchasing power.

One check of model adequacy which might uncover omitted channels of transmission was suggested by Bob Flood. Omitted channels will show up as correlations of the residuals of the model's equations. These correlations were checked for the Mark III model both within each country and for US nominal money, real income, and price level versus all foreign variables. Little more than the expected number of correlations were significant at the 5 percent level for either the pegged or floating period, and no pair of correlations was significant in more than two cases. Therefore it was concluded that the model adequately represented the channels apparent in the data.

The international sector thus incorporates a variety of potential channels of transmission. For example, as suggested by the monetary approach, either trade or capital flows might cause huge movements in the balance of payments (and hence money) if domestic prices or interest rates were to begin to differ from international parity values. This did not appear

Table 16.2
Standard errors of estimate compared with base simulation root-mean-square errors: Mark IV-PEG and Mark IV-FLT

Variables	Statistics[a]	Countries							
		United States	United Kingdom	Canada	France	Germany	Italy	Japan	Netherlands
Logarithm of real output: $\log y_j$	Mark IV-PEG								
	S.E.E.	0.0089	0.0136	0.0118	0.0177	0.0129	0.0132	0.0152	0.0130
	4 qtr. RMSE	0.0063	0.0116	0.0059	0.0153	0.0230	0.0076	0.0118	0.0148
	31 qtr. RMSE	0.0321	0.0241	0.0399	0.0372	0.0246	0.0206	0.0902	0.0316
	Mark IV-FLT								
	S.E.E.	0.0089	0.0136	0.0118	0.0177	0.0129	0.0132	0.0152	0.0130
	4 qtr. RMSE	0.0084	0.0078	0.0176	0.0080	0.0339	0.0131	0.0148	0.0102
	7 qtr. RMSE	0.0256	0.0199	0.0233	0.0068	0.0448	0.0187	0.0129	0.0124
Logarithm of price level: $\log P_j$	Mark IV-PEG								
	S.E.E.	0.0035	0.0148	0.0115	0.0103	0.0062	0.0115	0.0121	0.0109
	4 qtr. RMSE	0.0025	0.0213	0.0062	0.0183	0.0047	0.0191	0.0167	0.0143
	31 qtr. RMSE	0.0110	0.1115	0.0388	0.0960	0.0311	0.0496	0.0998	0.0168
	Mark IV-FLT								
	S.E.E.	0.0035	0.0148	0.0115	0.0103	0.0062	0.0115	0.0121	0.0109
	4 qtr. RMSE	0.0135	0.0224	0.0070	0.0215	0.0078	0.0241	0.0103	0.0212
	7 qtr. RMSE	0.0207	0.0310	0.0170	0.0192	0.0093	0.0437	0.0242	0.0262
Unemployment rate: u_j	Mark IV-PEG								
	S.E.E.	0.0018	0.0015	NA	0.0009	NA	NA	NA	NA
	4 qtr. RMSE	0.0028	0.0012		0.0004				
	31 qtr. RMSE	0.0067	0.0057		0.0036				

Mark IV-FLT								
S.E.E.	0.0018	0.0015		0.0009				
4 qtr. RMSE	0.0017	0.0023		0.0010				
7 qtr. RMSE	0.0071	0.0033		0.0009				
Logarithm of nominal money: log M_j								
Mark IV-PEG								
S.E.E.	0.0045	0.0160	0.0156	0.0118	0.0126	0.0188	0.0148	0.0153
4 qtr. RMSE	0.0074	0.0438	0.0321	0.0339	0.0118	0.0584	0.0728	0.0132
31 qtr. RMSE	0.0082	0.1253	0.0556	0.1088	0.0313	0.0574	0.1219	0.0217
Mark IV-FLT								
S.E.E.	0.0045	0.0160	0.0156	0.0118	0.0126	0.0188	0.0148	0.0153
4 qtr. RMSE	0.0057	0.0240	0.0112	0.0065	0.0356	0.0207	0.0171	0.0163
7 qtr. RMSE	0.0166	0.0259	0.0200	0.0200	0.0454	0.0163	0.0269	0.0220
Short-term interest rate: R_j								
Mark IV-PEG								
S.E.E.	0.0043	0.0074	0.0063	0.0090	0.0109	0.0038	0.0011	0.0090
4 qtr. RMSE	0.0008	0.0060	0.0053	0.0081	0.0042	0.0051	0.0013	0.0075
31 qtr. RMSE	0.0095	0.0106	0.0131	0.0173	0.0166	0.0076	0.0067	0.0111
Mark IV-FLT								
S.E.E.	0.0043	0.0074	0.0063	0.0090	0.0109	0.0038	0.0011	0.0090
4 qtr. RMSE	0.0162	0.0239	0.0053	0.0130	0.0182	0.0078	0.0023	0.0194
7 qtr. RMSE	0.0137	0.0218	0.0094	0.0273	0.0166	0.0137	0.0056	0.0323

Table 16.2 (*continued*)

Variables	Statistics[a]	Countries							
		United States	United Kingdom	Canada	France	Germany	Italy	Japan	Netherlands
Ratio of nominal exports to nominal output: $(X/Y)_j$	**Mark IV-PEG**								
	S.E.E.	0.0022	0.0069	0.0062	0.0049	0.0056	0.0067	0.0022	0.0141
	4 qtr. RMSE	0.0018	0.0056	0.0016	0.0053	0.0042	0.0045	0.0017	0.0074
	31 qtr. RMSE	0.0054	0.0255	0.0198	0.0202	0.0107	0.0091	0.0030	0.0180
	Mark IV-FLT								
	S.E.E.	0.0022	0.0069	0.0062	0.0049	0.0056	0.0067	0.0022	0.0141
	4 qtr. RMSE	0.0046	0.0330	0.0059	0.0154	0.0140	0.0031	0.0014	0.0394
	7 qtr. RMSE	0.0040	0.0521	0.0095	0.0384	0.0295	0.0129	0.0022	0.0560
Ratio of nominal imports to nominal output: $(I/Y)_j$	**Mark IV-PEG**								
	S.E.E.	0.0027	0.0069	0.0044	0.0033	0.0048	0.0074	0.0017	0.0146
	4 qtr. RMSE	0.0026	0.0059	0.0061	0.0053	0.0023	0.0125	0.0017	0.0166
	31 qtr. RMSE	0.0049	0.0344	0.0060	0.0060	0.0066	0.0123	0.0111	0.0295
Logarithm of relative price of imports[b]: $\log(P^I_j/P_j)$	**Mark IV-FLT**								
	S.E.E.	0.0027	0.0179	0.0178	0.0221	0.0393	0.0477	0.0245	0.0247
	4 qtr. RMSE	0.0063	0.1138	0.0748	0.1700	0.2982	0.0683	0.0784	0.0773
	7 qtr. RMSE	0.0078	0.1700	0.2568	0.2891	0.4776	0.1109	0.0739	0.1695
Logarithm of import price index: $\log P^I_j$	**Mark IV-PEG**								
	S.E.E.	0.0129	0.0157	0.0076	0.0194	NA	0.0165	0.0118	0.0111
	4 qtr. RMSE	0.0187	0.0179	0.0198	0.0150		0.0148	0.0233	0.0067
	31 qtr. RMSE	0.0565	0.0322	0.0224	0.0521		0.0520	0.0871	0.0501

Logarithm of exchange rate[c]: $\log E_j$	Mark IV-FLT							
S.E.E.	0.0129	0.0482	0.0129	0.0340	0.0436	0.0340	0.0285	0.0387
4 qtr. RMSE	0.0300	0.0957	0.0196	0.0781	0.2670	0.0484	0.0276	0.0278
7 qtr. RMSE	0.0436	0.0999	0.0484	0.1400	0.4146	0.0869	0.0613	0.0359
Ratio of nominal net capital outflows to nominal output: $(C/Y)_j$	Mark IV-PEG							
S.E.E.	0.0074	0.0291	0.0103	0.0159	0.0246	0.0138	0.0125	0.0198
4 qtr. RMSE	0.0062	0.0122	0.0383	0.0094	0.0105	0.0077	0.0049	0.0262
31 qtr. RMSE	0.0059	0.0314	0.0235	0.0160	0.0284	0.0124	0.0064	0.0220
	Mark IV-FLT							
S.E.E.	0.0074	0.0291	0.0103	0.0159	0.0246	0.0138	0.0125	0.0198
4 qtr. RMSE	0.0159	0.0409	0.0788	0.0203	0.1586	0.0160	0.0284	0.0166
7 qtr. RMSE	0.0144	0.0327	0.3483	0.0211	0.1891	0.0128	0.0238	0.0359
Ratio of nominal balance of payments to nominal output: $(B/Y)_j$	Mark IV-FLT							
S.E.E.	NA	0.0071	0.0017	0.0044	0.0049	0.0044	0.0038	0.0063
4 qtr. RMSE	0.0109	0.0109	0.0027	0.0061	0.0117	0.0039	0.0064	0.0059
7 qtr. RMSE	0.0084	0.0084	0.0051	0.0049	0.0234	0.0034	0.0054	0.0069

a. The first six equations and the $(C/Y)_j$ equation were estimated for the period 1957:I–1976:IV and so have identical S.E.E.s in both the Mark IV-PEG and Mark IV-FLT. The other equations are estimated over only pegged or floating periods, respectively.

b. For the United States only, this equation is not renormalized and the reported statistics are for $(I/Y)_1$.

c. For the United States only, this equation is not renormalized and the reported statistics are for $\log P_1^l$.

likely from the small estimated coefficients, but only simulations can determine this definitely.

In preparation for such simulation experiments and as a check on the simulation models, we first obtained a base dynamic simulation for each version of the model.[8] For the Mark IV-PEG this base simulation was computed for 1962 : III–1970 : I, which was the entire period during which all nonreserve countries were maintaining firm pegged exchange rates with the dollar. The corresponding period for the Mark IV-FLT would be 1971 : III–1976 : IV, but dynamic instabilities in the model became important after seven quarters (1973:I), so the base simulation covers only this shorter period for which the simulations might be informative. The dynamic instability of the Mark IV-FLT should be sufficient warning that the results of the floating-period simulations must be read with considerable skepticism.[9]

Table 16.2 compares the standard errors of estimate for each behavioral equation with the root-mean-square errors (RMSEs) of the simulated values of the dependent variables both for the first year and for the entire period of the simulation. The standard errors reported here are generally lower than those reported for the corresponding equations in the Mark III international transmission model because of the deletion of insignificant variables and the imposition of constraints discussed above.[10] The first-year RMSEs appear to be generally reasonable, but errors do accumulate over the entire simulation period, especially for the international sectors and especially for the floating model even though the simulation period is much shorter. On this basis, the first-year simulations would appear to be most informative, with longer periods at most suggestive of general tendencies.

16.2 US Money-Shock Experiments

As is well known,[11] a common problem with policy studies based on econometric models is that policy experiments are often inconsistent with the policy regimes for which the models are estimated. As a result, simulated behavior may be irrational under alternative policy regimes. Thus one must choose a policy experiment which is consistent with the estimated model. The consistent policy experiment chosen is a 0.01 increase in the disturbance term of the US nominal-money-supply reaction function for one quarter. Thereafter the money supply develops according to the endogenous structure of the model.

This experiment was performed for both the pegged and floating ver-

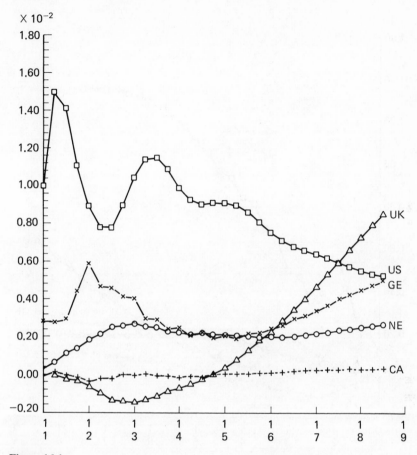

Figure 16.1a

Figure 16.1
Deviations of key variables from base simulation, American money-shock experiment—pegged period: (a) nominal money, $\log M_i$; (b) price level, $\log P_i$; (c) real income, $\log y_i$; (d) short-term interest rate, R_i; (e) scaled exports, $(X/Y)_i$; (f) scaled balance of payments, $(B/Y)_i$. Legend: □, United States (US); △, United Kingdom (UK); +, Canada (CA); ×, Germany (GE); ○, Netherlands (NE).

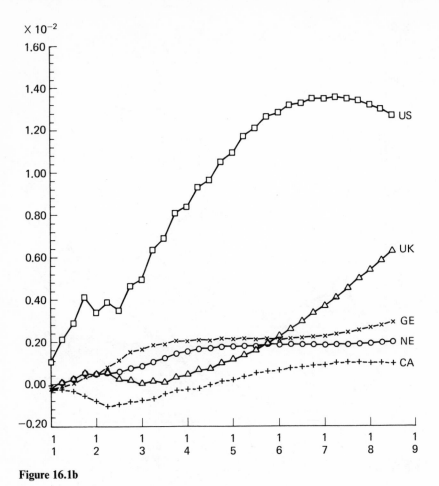

Figure 16.1b

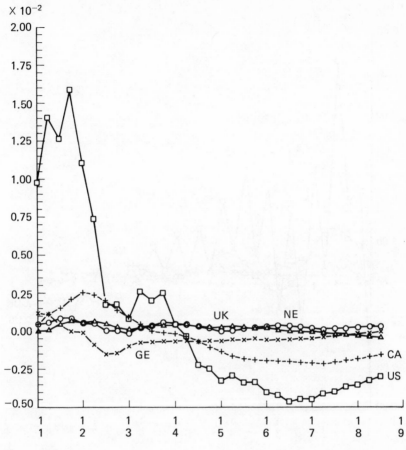

Figure 16.1c

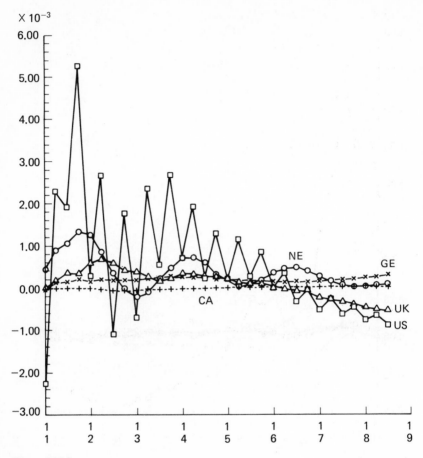

Figure 16.1d

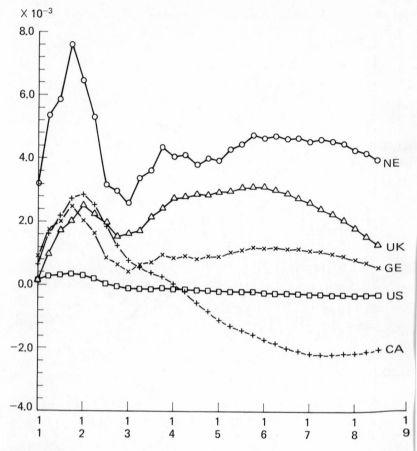

Figure 16.1e

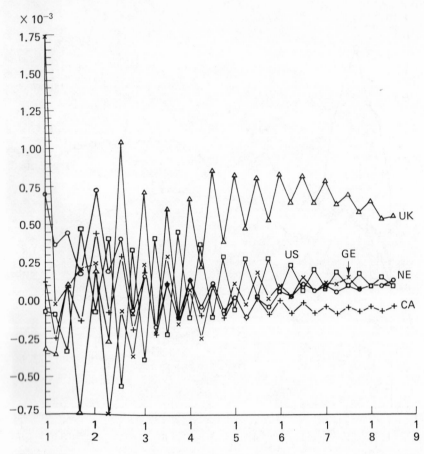

Figure 16.1f

sions of the Mark IV simulation model. The main results for the pegged simulation are summarized in figures 16.1a–16.1f. This figure shows the difference between the simulated values of the major variables given the 1 percent money shock and the values in the corresponding base simulation without the money shock. Note that the vertical scales are adjusted to the simulated variations so that similar appearing movements may be for much different magnitudes. Examining first the results for the United States, we note that nominal money (figure 16.1a) initially increases by 1 percent (100 basis points) and then fluctuates between 150 and 75 basis points for the first 5 years, eventually tailing down to about 50 basis points at the end of the simulation period. The price level effect builds up gradually, reaching 1 percent some 3.5 years after the initial shock and peaking at almost 140 basis points some 3 years after that. There is a transitory increase in real output (peaking at 160 basis points in the fourth quarter) which is all but eliminated after 7 quarters and even turns negative later as money persistently falls.[12] The interest rate displays a small, brief liquidity effect, but this is quickly dominated by income and expectations effects.[13] Imports (not displayed here) do rise slightly initially, but the trivial export variation in figure 16.1e suggests that feedback from foreign effects is negligible for the United States. Aside from oscillations, the balance-of-payments behavior is also consistent with standard lore at least initially when deficits dominate; the small (0–3 basis points) surpluses later can be rationalized by declining nominal money.[14]

Figure 16.1 also displays the results of the same experiment for the United Kingdom, Canada, Germany, and the Netherlands.[15] Looking again at figure 16.1a, only for Germany do we see a large initial increase in nominal money suggested by the classical presentations of the monetary approach to the balance of payments, and this percentage increase is less than a third of that in the reserve country. The Netherlands displays a more gradual adjustment of nominal money, while Canadian money never rises significantly and British money rises only after 5 years.[16] Thus Germany provides the sole example in figure 16.1f of the sharp initial balance-of-payments surplus due to capital flows so much emphasized in the recent literature. Considering the other variables for Germany alone, we see an attenuated version of the US pattern aside from the absence of an initial liquidity effect on the interest rate. In the Netherlands, the induced increase in exports is initially important for both real income and the interest rate, with both money and prices rising more gradually. This pattern seems consistent with a Humean specie-flow process in which monetary transmission is more gradual and there are significant

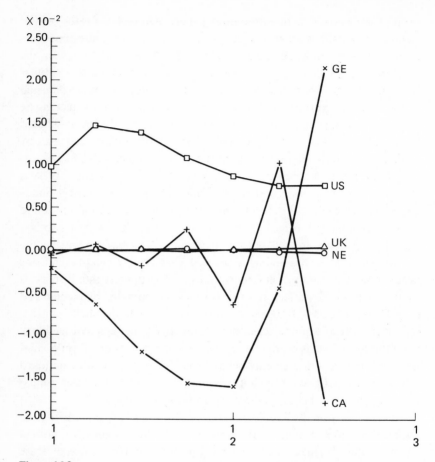

Figure 16.2a

Figure 16.2
Deviations of key variables from base simulation, American money-shock
experiment—floating period: (a) nominal money, $\log M_i$; (b) price level, $\log P_i$;
(c) real income, $\log y_i$; (d) short-term interest rate, R_i; (e) scaled exports, $(X/Y)_i$;
(f) scaled balance of payments, $(B/Y)_i$; (g) exchange rate, $\log E_i$. Legend: same
as for figure 15.1.

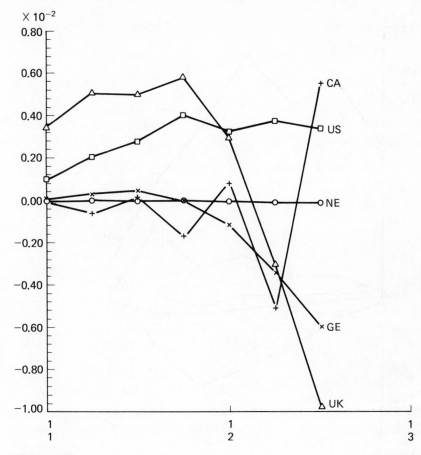

Figure 16.2b

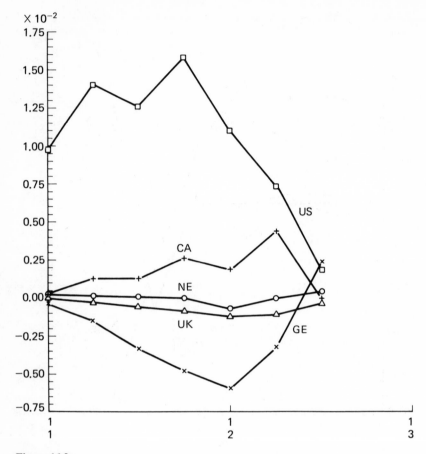

Figure 16.2c

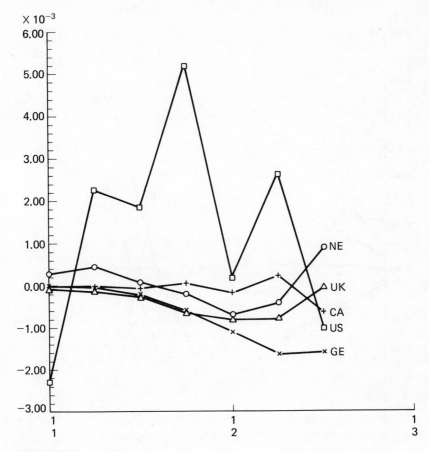

Figure 16.2d

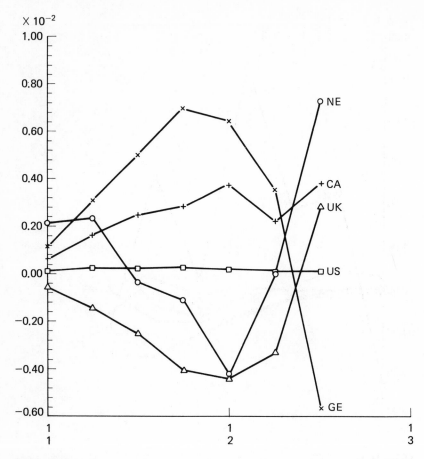

Figure 16.2e

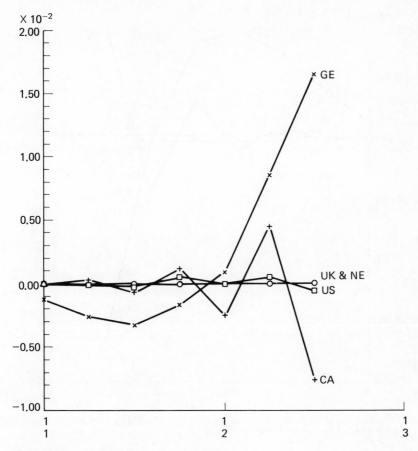

Figure 16.2f. UK, NE both represented by ○.

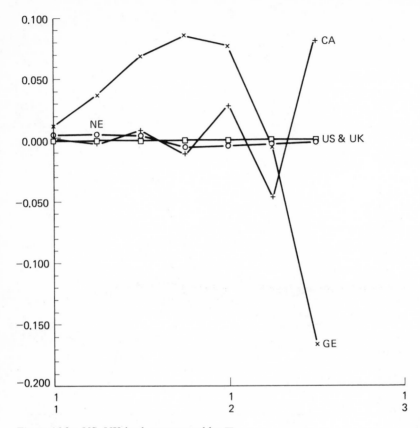

Figure 16.2g. US, UK both represented by □.

short-run effects on trade flows through both absorption (real-income) and relative-price channels. For the United Kingdom and Canada, however, there is no sign of monetary transmission—unless the United Kingdom increase after 4 years is taken seriously. There is evidence of real-income (and for the United Kingdom interest rate) effects, but these seem to derive from absorption-type effects of increases exports. The Canadian price level even falls slightly at first due to income effects increasing the real quantity of money demanded.

Summing up, under pegged exchange rates the simulation results vary from the monetary-approach paradigm (Germany), through the Humean lagged-monetary-adjustment paradigm (the Netherlands), to the simple Keynesian absorption in which prices and interest rates are irrelevant (the United Kingdom and Canada). Clearly the results are partially puzzling whatever view of transmission one might hold. The construction of the Mark III model had attempted to allow the data to choose which transmission patterns are important; at least that attempt appears to have been successful.

The floating-period results summarized in figure 16.2 are problematical in that the initial effect (if any) of the US money supply increase is to depreciate the foreign currencies.[17] To understand this result we must examine the structure of the Mark IV model. Only in the import-supply equation were strong, consistent exchange-rate effects obtained in the pegged period. This equation was solved for the logarithmic change in the exchange rate in the floating period. (An intervention equation was also added to explain the balance of payments.) In initial unconstrained estimates for the floating period, the logarithmic change in import prices entered with a coefficient of between 0.3 and 0.5, while the change in the dollar-denominated rest-of-the-world price index entered with coefficients of $-1.5--3$. In theory, these coefficients should be of equal magnitude and opposite signs; this theory is consistent with the pegged-period estimates. Unfortunately the floating-period estimates appear to be dominated by common movements in exchange rates against the dollar. Simulations using the unconstrained, inconsistent coefficients resulted not only in greater dynamic instability in the base simulations but also in nearly universal initial exchange-rate appreciations of 2 percent which grew much larger over time with no corresponding movements in interest rates or price levels in the experiment at hand. For this reason, the constraint of a single coefficient on the logarithmic change in the ratio of import to rest-of-world prices was imposed. When the constraint is imposed, however, the surprising initial depreciation results. These results are reported since, as will be explained immediately, some sense can be made of them and they do illustrate the potentially perverse effects of a J-curve phenomenon.

First, note that the simulated effects within the United States are nearly identical to those for the first seven quarters of the pegged experiment, so that discussion need not be repeated here. Given an initial exchange-rate depreciation, the German monetary authorities intervene to support the mark and the money supply falls. Prices and income follow the monetary movements. The initial movement in the German exchange rate occurs in the simulation because of an estimated J-curve pattern in the import-demand (relative-price-of-imports) equation. Since exports rise with the rise in US income and capital outflows fall with the fall in the US interest rate, imports plus the balance-of-payments surplus has to

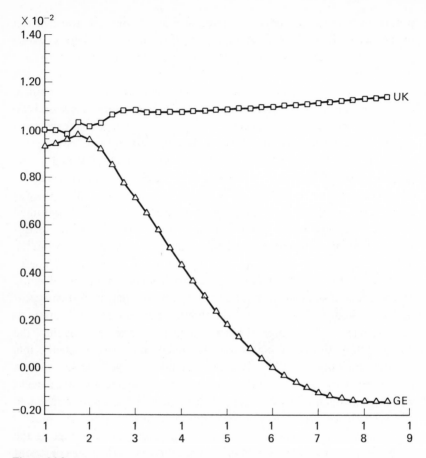

Figure 16.3a

Figure 16.3
Deviations of key domestic variables from base simulation, British and German
money-shock experiments—pegged period: (a) nominal money, $\log M_i$; (b) price
level, $\log P_i$; (c) real income, $\log y_i$; (d) short-term interest rate, R_i; (e) scaled
exports, $(X/Y)_i$; (f) scaled balance of payments, $(B/Y)_i$. Legend: □, United
Kingdom (UK); △, Germany (GE).

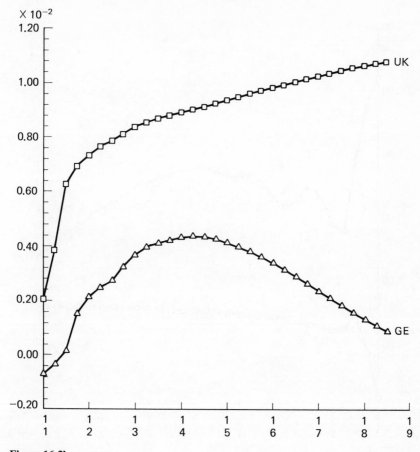

Figure 16.3b

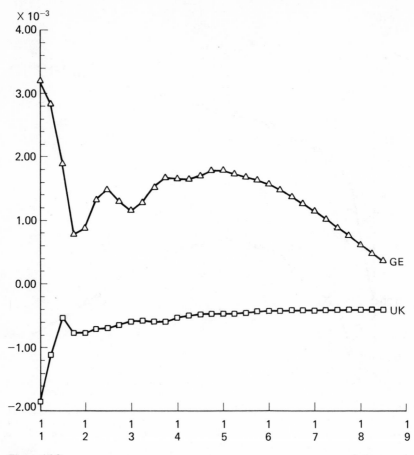

Figure 16.3c

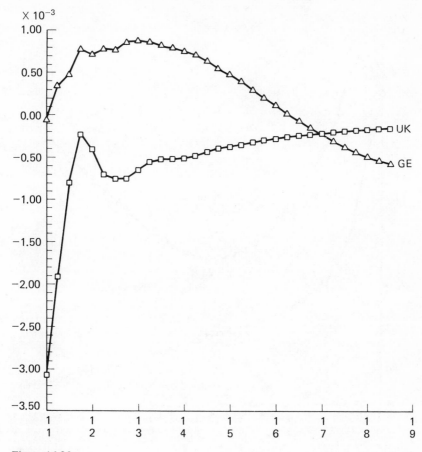

Figure 16.3d

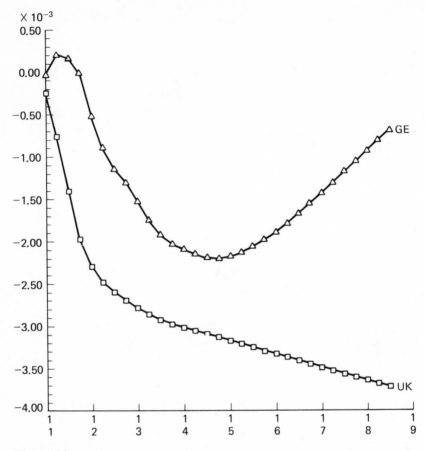

Figure 16.3e

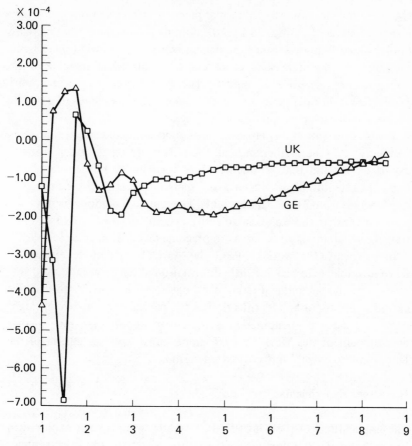

Figure 16.3f

rise given the identity. The balance of payments (intervention) is not very responsive under floating rates, so the dominant movement is an increase in the value of imports. Since the demand curve is somewhat inelastic in the short run, the increase in value requires a substantial increase in the domestic-currency price of imports. The more rapid growth in import prices than dollar-denominated rest-of-the world prices leads to a higher (depreciated) exchange rate.

The other countries display less exaggerated simulated effects than does Germany: For the Netherlands all the effects are trivial except for the export effect, and that is much smaller than in the pegged case. The exchange rate initially depreciates and then appreciates, but the range of movement is from 2 to − 5 basis points. The United Kingdom displays few effects other than those associated with a perverse decrease in exports. For Canada instability is so severe as to preclude any characterization.

In contrast to the Mark IV-PEG, the Mark IV-FLT model appears to be so unstable as to provide little information about international transmission of shocks under floating exchange rates. The main fruit of this exercise appears to be identification of the perverse results which might occur if a J-curve phenomenon is present in import demand. Further development of the Mark IV-FLT model must await extension of the Data Bank to cover a longer floating period.

16.3 Other Experiments

The implications of the Mark IV-PEG model were further explored in five additional experiments. Two of these compare the effects under pegged exchange rates of one-quarter money shocks (such as described in section 16.2) in Germany and the United Kingdom. The other three involve a one-quarter increase of 0.01 (1 percent of government spending) in the government spending shock in the United States, Germany, and the United Kingdom, respectively.

The domestic effects of the German and British money-shock experiments are contrasted in figure 16.3. Examining first the German case we see that nominal money is in fact increased by almost 1 percent throughout the first year. The initial increase is less than the amount of the shock to the money-supply reaction function because of the partially offsetting effects of the induced balance-of-payments deficit (figure 16.3f). Nonetheless, a remarkably high degree of monetary control is exhibited and the deficits are never large: Nominal money does not start falling until after the first year (largely as a result of the induced increases in inflation and real income), and even after 2 years a 75 basis-point increase in nominal money remains; it takes some 4 years for the initial increase in the nominal money supply to drop to 20 basis points. The real-income, price-level, and export effects are predictable given the movements in the nominal money supply. But unlike the United States, no noticeable transmission to any other countries is detected in the simulations (or graphed here): None of these six major variables in any of the other four countries in any quarter deviates from the base simulation by as much as 10 basis points, and *peak* effects on the order of 1 basis point or less are the rule.

The simulated effects of the British money-shock experiment are also plotted in figure 16.3. The one-quarter shock to the British nominal-money growth rate is not only never offset, but indeed British nominal money displays a slight tendency to rise further over time. Domestic prices rise and exports fall as a result, but the simulated balance-of-payments deficits never become unmanageable. The only remarkable result is the (incredible) negative impact of a money shock on British real income.[18] Again there was no noticeable transmission to other countries (on the 10-basis-point-peak criterion) to report.

These two nonreserve money-shock experiments confirm the impression gained from the US money shock experiment: The German monetary authorities displayed the tendencies suggested by the monetary approach, although those tendencies are attenuated in magnitude and here slow in effect. For Britain, in contrast, monetary transmission appears to be essentially nil, with policy conducted as if the United Kingdom were a closed economy.

The next set of experiments involves one-quarter increases of 100 basis points in unexpected real government spending. This sort of government spending shift is consistent with the policy regime for which the model was estimated. However, the implications of this shock for the actual level of real government spending differ according to the actual process observed to govern the evolution of real government spending in each country. Because the logarithm of US real government spending appears to follow a random walk with drift, the 100 basis-point increase in real government spending is implicitly a permanent one. The corresponding German variable follows a first-order moving average process which implies that the level of real government spending is increased by 100 basis points in the initial quarter but by only 25 basis points thereafter. For the United Kingdom the pattern is more complicated due to a second-order autoregressive process, but the effect on the level of real government spending is very nearly approximated by an initial 100 basis-point increase and a 57 basis-point increase thereafter.[19]

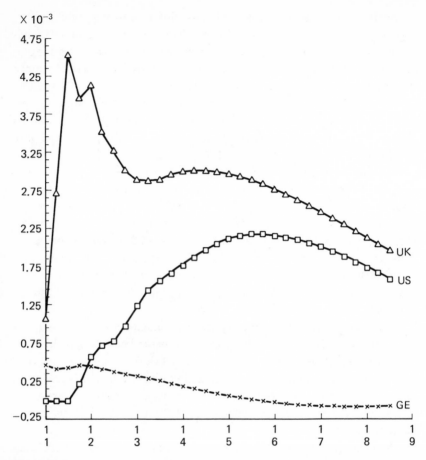

Figure 16.4a

Figure 16.4
Deviations of key domestic variables from base simulation, American, British, and German government-spending-shock experiments—pegged period: (a) nominal money, $\log M_i$; (b) price level, $\log P_i$; (c) real income, $\log y_i$; (d) short-term interest rate, R_i; (e) scaled exports, $(X/Y)_i$; (f) scaled balance of payments, $(B/Y)_i$. Legend: $\square$, United States (US); $\triangle$, United Kingdom (UK); $\times$, Germany (GE).

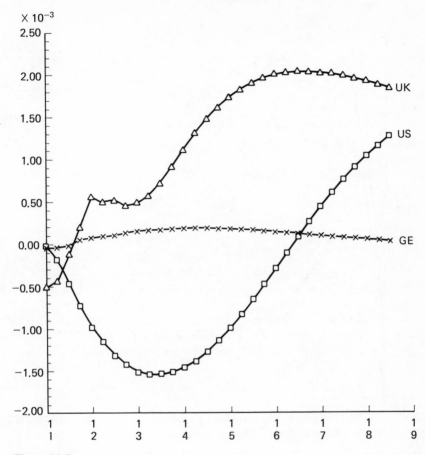

Figure 16.4b

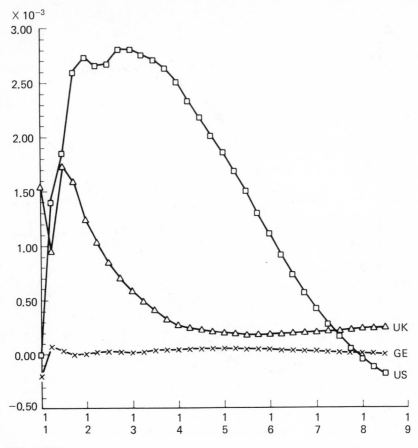

Figure 16.4c

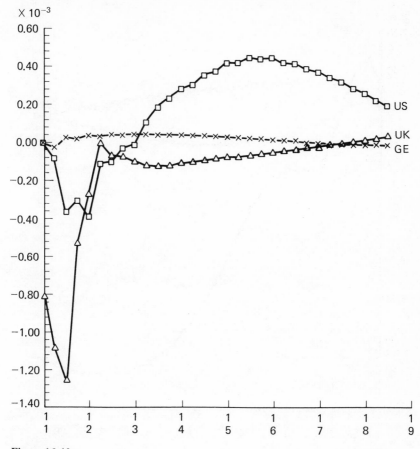

Figure 16.4d

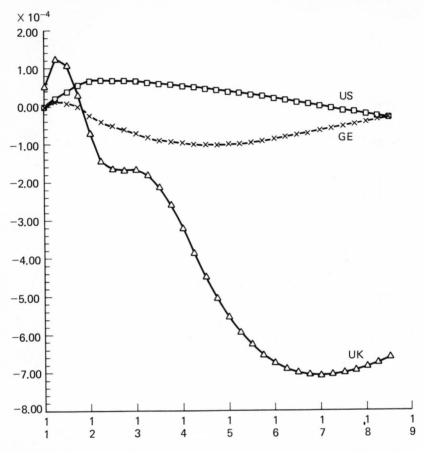

Figure 16.4e

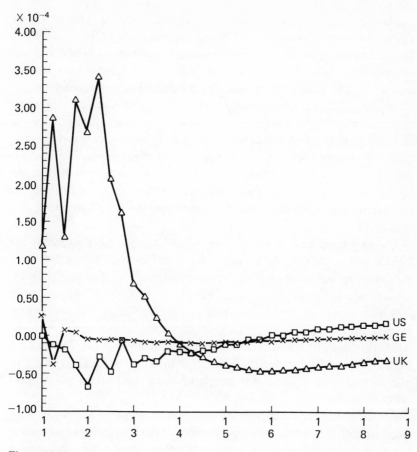

Figure 16.4f

The domestic results of these three experiments are summarized in figure 16.4. The peak effect on US real income is about 27 basis points. Given that real government expenditures average about one sixth of real income, this implies a peak multiplier of about 1.5. Although on the high end of recent estimates of the bond-financed government-spending multiplier, a value of 1.5 is not surprising since it reflects as well reinforcing effects of a small, lagged induced increase in nominal money. Since the simulated effect of real income in increasing money demand initially dominates interest-rate effects and the small nominal money increase, the price level first falls and then rises as the real-income effects die out. As might be supposed from the small size of the home-country effects, simulated transmission to other countries is too small to merit discussion.[20]

The simulated British real-income effects are not as large as for the United States, but both occur and decay more quickly. The relatively fast decay may reflect the implicit partial elimination of the government spending increase in the second quarter. For the British experiment, the peak multiplier is only about 0.75 even based on the smaller permanent increase in government spending.[21] This multiplier may be reconciled with the American value of 1.5 by recalling that the induced increase in money is estimated to reduce rather than reinforce the effect on real income. No international transmission was simulated using the 10 basis-point peak-effect criterion.

For Germany the coefficients of government spending shocks are very small in both the real-income and nominal-money equations and zero in the interest-rate equations. Perhaps this reflects the estimate that only a quarter of such spending shocks remain after the first quarter. In any case, the simulated effects even within Germany are negligible.

In conclusion, neither British nor German money or government spending shocks appeared to have significant international repercussions under pegged exchange rates. An American government spending shock had slightly larger international effects—perhaps due to the induced increase in American nominal money—but the absolute magnitudes were nonetheless very small. The domestic effects of a British money shock were primarily on the price level, with real-income effects negligible; a government spending shock had significant transitory real-income effects as well as price effects. A German money shock, on the other hand, had significant effects on both the domestic price level and real income, while a government spending shock had none. The American government-spending shock affected both the domestic price level and real income.

16.4 Conclusion and Implications for Future Research

Simulation experiments help us to understand the workings of a large model in which the simultaneous and dynamic relation are too complicated to consider analytically. The results of the experiments tell us something about how the world would operate for a given model specification and coefficient values which are not inconsistent with a set of data. The results may tell us something about the way the world works, but they surely tell us more about just which simplifications in our *simple* models may lead to erroneous results.

Consider, for example, standard models in which an increased domestic money supply leads to lower domestic relative to foreign interest rates and a resulting adjustment process. This implicitly assumes that the liquidity effect dominates any inflationary expectations effect on interest rates during the relevant adjustment period. With relatively weak liquidity effects and strong expectations effects as estimated here, the transmission and adjustment process does not follow standard lines.[22]

The simulations confirm the apparent implications of the Mark III estimates: International transmission of inflation through money flows is a weak and slow process even under pegged exchange rates, with non-reserve countries exercising considerable short-run control over their money supplies. Of the four nonreserve countries examined, only Germany appeared to adjust its money supply quickly—if partially—to a US monetary shock, while for the United Kingdom and Canada the only simulated transmission was via absorption effects. Further, when a German monetary supply shock was simulated, overwhelming balance-of-payments flows were not simulated so that substantial money, real-income, and price effects were observed. These simulations certainly do not disprove the usefulness of the monetary approach to the balance of payments in the short run, but they do contribute to a growing body of literature which raises questions about its short-run usefulness.

The floating results, albeit unstable, suggest that the implications of short-run inelasticity of import demand (J curves) should be investigated further. If the world, like the Mark IV model, is characterized by imperfect international substitutability among goods and assets, J curves may play a significant role in the adjustment and transmission process.

The nonreserve money-shock experiments revealed no significant international transmission under either pegged or floating rates. Some monetary-approach writers[23] have argued that an increase in these countries' domestic credit would result in a generalized increase in the world money supply, but this is incorrect for a system such as Bretton Woods tied to a fiat reserve currency with reserves being dollar-denominated bonds.[24] Since monetary transmission is nil under either pegged or floating rates, only the very small increase in world export demand is operative, and this is trivial in magnitude for a money shock in any one of these nonreserve countries.

The government-spending shocks were generally too weak in their domestic effects to have any appreciable impact abroad. The largest simulated effect was in the United States, with a peak government spending multiplier of about 1.5 *inclusive* of the reinforcing effects of an induced nominal money increase. However, the initial 1 percent increase in real government spending is implicitly permanent in the United States, half permanent in the United Kingdom, and one-quarter permanent in Germany.

In conclusion, the simulation results suggest a great deal of national economic independence under pegged and—by direct implication—floating exchange rates. These results, although surprising, are consistent with the results obtained in other recent empirical research. A first order for research in international macroeconomics is to explain why the data fail to disclose the strong transmission channels we customarily assume.

Notes

1. Collinearity is reduced where the coefficients of various lagged levels of a variable indicate that either a sum or first difference is the appropriate variable. Similarly a number of hypotheses implying equality of coefficients permitted combining terms into simple logarithmic sums or differences. In one case (Germany in the Mark IV-PEG), this made the whole equation for the logarithm of import prices and the associated identity for relative import prices redundant; so they were dropped.

2. Darby and Stockman (1980).

3. The thirteenth identity (not listed in table 16.1) defines a lagged prediction error term needed for dynamic simulation. Similar identities were added to all the other submodels to obtain consistent dynamic simulations.

4. As is appropriate for a reserve country, the balance of payments was found to have no influence on the US money supply. See Darby (1980b, 1981).

5. The equations are solved for exports, relative price of imports, exchange rate, net capital outflows, and the balance of payments.

6. Variables such as real income, prices, and money are measured in logarithms. The interest rates and unemployment rates are decimal fractions. Exports, imports, net capital outflows, and the balance of payments are all scaled by dividing by nominal income. Shocks are deviations of actual values from optimal ARIMA predictions of the variables.

7. The short-run money-demand function is adapted from Carr and Darby (1981). It allows for money-supply shocks to effect money demand. In the Mark III model a foreign interest rate adjusted for expected depreciation was included to test for asset substitution, but this was significant only for the United Kingdom and Japan and (at only a 15 percent significance level) France.

8. In a dynamic simulation, the input series are the exogenous variables plus the initial conditions (endogenous variables before the beginning of simulation). The values of endogenous variables within the simulation period are assigned their predicted values. Especially for a large model with few exogenous variables, the cumulative errors in the endogenous variables eventually may take the simulation off track even if the model is dynamically stable.

9. The dynamic instability does not seem to depend on when we begin the simulation. It apparently results from our inability to do much to eliminate simultaneous equation bias with such a short sample. Three pieces of evidence besides experience with other models point to this conclusion: (1) The instability appears to arise in the renormalized international-sector equations which are estimated over the short sample period. (2) The pegged model is estimated over a longer sample period but with the same basic structure and is rather stable. (The instability in the Mark IV-FLT remains even if we artificially constrain the exchange rates to equal their actual values as in the Mark IV-PEG, where they are exogenous.) (3) Only for Canada—which has the short pegged period—is there a hint of instability in the pegged version of the model.

10. These standard errors will thus be on the optimistic side. The few cases of increase apparently reflect deletion of variables which individually appear insignificant but are jointly significant with other deleted variables. The only important increases occur in the exchange-rate equations, where it was necessary to impose a constraint generally rejected by the data for reasons discussed in section 16.2.

11. See Lucas (1976).

12. The negative real income in the latter part of the adjustment is thus a result (artifact?) of basing expected nominal money on a univariate expectations function rather than full rational expectations.

13. The oscillations in the indicated adjustment process would appear to be spurious.

14. These oscillations apparently reflect the interaction of the expected depreciation and capital-flows equations.

15. The simulation results for France, Japan, and Italy were so erratic as to be inexplicable. The peculiar estimated coefficients—which we attribute to severe data problems for these countries—appears to be the problem. See Darby and Stockman (1980) for further discussion.

16. The initial decline in British money is due to the perverse (negative) balance-of-payments coefficients.

17. The exchange rates are measured in domestic-currency units per dollar so an increase is a depreciation of the domestic currency.

18. The negative coefficients on money shocks were not jointly significant in the

Mark III model, but were retained in the reestimation of the Mark IV model, so that this channel was not foreclosed.

19. To be precise, the implied increase in UK real government spending compared to the base run for the first nine quarters is 100, 56, 44, 63, 59, 55, 58, 58 and 57 basis points, respectively.

20. It is not strictly true that there are no effects greater than 10 basis points, however, As would be inferred from the previous money-shock experiment, a sympathetic variation in German nominal money was simulated, peaking at 12 basis points after 2 years. Also, British nominal money drifted down, passing − 10 basis points after 4.5 years and troughing at − 19 basis points during the seventh year. An induced decline in the British price level to − 14 basis points after 7 years completes the list of exceptions to the 10-basis-point criterion.

21. That is, the 100-basis-point increase in government spending is implicitly a 57-basis-point permanent increase. Government spending averages about 40 percent of total income in Britain, so this increase is 0.4 × 57 or 0.228 percent of real income.

22. Dan Lee shows in his dissertation (1980) that Dornbusch's (1976) famous overshooting result for floating exchange rates follows from allowing participants in the financial markets to have rational expectations with respect to exchange rates but not prices: Recall that Dornbusch argued that lower home interest rates after a money-supply increase must be balanced by (rational) expectations of an appreciating currency and that this implies an initial overdepreciation. If the interest rate instead rises with (rational) inflationary expectations, then expectations of depreciation are appropriate and the overshooting argument falls.

23. See, for example, Swoboda (1976), Meiselman and Laffer (1975), and Parkin and Zis (1976a, b).

24. This point is developed at length in Darby (1980a).

References

Carr, Jack, and Darby, Michael R. (1981). "The Role of Money Supply Shocks in the Short-Run Demand for Money," *Journal of Monetary Economics* 8:183–99.

Darby, Michael R. (1980a). "Sterilization and Monetary Control under Pegged Exchange Rates: Theory and Evidence," NBER Working Paper No. 449, February.

Darby, Michael R. (1980b). "The Monetary Approach to the Balance of Payments: Two Specious Assumptions," *Economic Inquiry* 18:321–26.

Darby, Michael R. (1981). "The International Economy as a Source of and Restraint on United States Inflation," in W. A. Gale, ed., *Inflation: Causes, Consequents, and Control*, Cambridge, MA: Oelgeschlager, Gunn, and Hain.

Darby, Michael R. (1982). "The Price of Oil and World Inflation and Recession," *American Economic Review* 72 (in press).

Darby, Michael R., and Stockman, Alan C. (1980). "The Mark III International Transmission Model," NBER Working Paper No. 462, March.

Dornbusch, Rudiger (1976). "Expectations and Exchange Rate Dynamics," *Journal of Political Economy* 84:1161–76.

Lee, Dan (1980). "The Effects of Open Market Operations and Foreign Exchange Market Operations," PhD Dissertation, UCLA, Department of Economics.

Lucas, Robert E., Jr. (1976). "Econometric Policy Evaluation: A Critique," in K. Brumer and A. H. Meltzer, eds., *The Phillips Curve and Labor Markets*, Carnegie-Rochester Conference Series on Public Policy Vol. 1, Amsterdam: North-Holland.

Meiselman, David I., and Laffer, Arthur B. (1975). *The Phenomenon of Worldwide Inflation*, Washington: American Enterprise Institute.

Parkin, Michael, and Zis, George (1976a). *Inflation in the World Economy*, Toronto: University of Toronto Press.

Parkin, Michael, and Zis, George (1976b). *Inflation in Open Economies*, Toronto: University of Toronto Press.

Swoboda, Alexander K. (1976). "Monetary Policy under Fixed Exchange Rates: Effectiveness, the Speed of Adjustment, and Proper Use," in J. A. Frenkel and H. G. Johnson, eds., *The Monetary Approach to the Balance of Payments*, Toronto: University of Toronto Press.

17

Tariff and Exchange Rate Protection under Fixed and Flexible Exchange Rates in the Major Industrialized Countries

Alan V. Deardorff
and
Robert M. Stern

There has been considerable interest in the theory and measurement of effective rates of protection since the mid-1960s. Most of the early theoretical work, and practically all of the actual calculations of effective protection, have been conducted in a partial equilibrium framework. On the theoretical side, these early developments have been followed by more rigorous and complete theoretical examination of the general equilibrium properties of effective protection, and much of the partial equilibrium analysis has been questioned on grounds of ignoring interactions and feedback effects among different sectors in an economy. At the same time, substantial efforts have also been devoted to the construction of computational general equilibrium models for different countries for the purpose of analyzing changes in government policies including tariffs. It is somewhat surprising, therefore, that these more sophisticated computational models have been used comparatively so little in measuring the levels of effective protection arising from the structure of tariffs and changes in exchange rates. In this chapter we use our own computational model for these purposes in order to assess the empirical significance of general equilibrium considerations for the measurement of effective protection.

In the context of this volume, the issue is important since the instruments of protection may affect a country's trading partners as much as itself. Thus, tariffs themselves can become a significant international disturbance or a means of transmitting the effects of a domestic disturbance abroad. For precisely this reason, we shall argue that a proper measure of effective protection should encompass foreign as well as

This study is based upon one section of a report prepared by the authors entitled *A Disaggregated Model of World Production and Trade* under Contract No. 1722-920000, which was funded by the Departments of State and Treasury. Views and conclusions contained in this study should not be interpreted as representing the official opinion or policy of the United States Government.

domestic tariffs, and we shall provide such a measure. In addition, we argue that exchange rate movements—both those which are induced by other protective devices and those which are used deliberately as instruments of protection—should be accounted for in the assessment of protection internationally.

Following Corden (1966 p. 22), the level of effective protection afforded by the structure of tariffs may be defined as "the percentage increase in value added per unit in an economic activity which is made possible by the tariff structure." Our computational model, which we shall describe in section 17.1, is designed specifically to analyze the effects of tariff changes and so can be used to compute the effects of removal or imposition of a particular set of tariffs. In previous applications of the model, we have focused our attention on the employment effects of tariff changes, particularly in Deardorff and Stern (1979, 1981), where the changes negotiated in the Tokyo Round are analyzed. But our model also solves for effects on prices and is therefore well suited to the measurement of value added. Our procedure, later in the chapter, will therefore be to use our model's computation of the change in per unit value added to measure levels of effective protection by the industrial sector for a sampling of the major industrialized countries of the world.

In section 17.2 we discuss some conceptual issues regarding the measurement of effective protection. The simple partial equilibrium formula that has most often been used for this purpose is shown to be inadequate for general equilibrium reasons and in addition because of the only moderate degree of substitution between imports and home-produced goods that appears to characterize behavior in international trade. Our computational model, which incorporates both of these considerations, can therefore give a more realistic indication of the degree to which industries are protected.

Problems of definition remain, however, since one can examine tariff changes under a variety of assumptions about which tariffs are allowed to change and whether exchange rates are allowed to adjust in response. In section 17.3, therefore, we evaluate and compare measures of the effective protection afforded by tariffs under both fixed and flexible exchange rates and for both unilateral and multilateral changes in tariffs. In all cases our experiment consists of assuming complete elimination of 1976 tariffs and using our model to work out the resulting effects on per unit value added by country and industry. Results are then reported with their signs reversed to indicate what would have been the effects of imposing the 1976 tariff structure starting from a zero base. These measures of the 1976 structure of effective protection are compared with both nominal tariffs and a partial equilibrium measure of effective protection for the following selected countries: Canada, West Germany, Japan, the Netherlands, and the United States.

The role of exchange rates in effective protection is partially indicated by the comparison of fixed and flexible rate estimates in section 17.3. In section 17.4 we look at this issue more directly by using our model to compute, for each country, the effects of a 1 percent exogenous devaluation. The solution, again focusing on changes in per unit value added, gives us a measure of the effective protection that would be provided by such an exchange rate change.

17.1 Brief Description of Model

The calculations to be described in the later sections of the chapter are based upon a disaggregated model of world production and trade that we have developed and have been using at the University of Michigan over the last several years to analyze a variety of questions, including the economic effects of the Tokyo Round, exchange rate changes, and changes in aggregate expenditure and wages. A detailed description of the model and references to our earlier work can be found especially in Deardorff and Stern (1981).

The model incorporates supply and demand functions and market-clearing conditions for 22 tradable industries in world markets, plus markets for these and another 7 nontradable industries in individual countries. The model covers explicitly the 18 major industrialized countries plus 16 major developing countries, and there is also an aggregated sector representing the rest of the world. Supply and demand functions from each country and industry interact with one another on both national and world markets to determine equilibrium values of prices and quantities traded and produced. The demand functions also determine amounts of labor demanded, and thus employment, in each industry and country.

The size of the model precludes our obtaining a meaningful and general analytical solution. We have therefore restricted the functional forms to ones whose parameters are either readily observable from available data or which have been estimated by others using econometric techniques. Within these constraints, however, we have tried to select functional forms which permit a rich variety of behavior and which experience suggests provide a reasonable description of economic reality.

The two groups of industrialized and developing countries included in the model are as follows: industrialized countries: Australia, Austria, Belgium-Luxembourg, Canada, Denmark, Finland, France, West Germany, Ireland, Italy, Japan, Netherlands, New Zealand, Norway, Sweden, Switzerland, United Kingdom, United States; developing countries: Argentina, Brazil, Chile, Colombia, Greece, Hong Kong, India, Israel, South Korea, Mexico, Portugal, Singapore, Spain, Taiwan, Turkey, Yugoslavia.

We have already noted that world industry has been categorized into 29 classifications, of which 22 are tradable. These categories, identified by numbers adapted from the International Standard Industrial Classification (ISIC), are given in table 17.1.

In order to specify the supply and demand functions of the model, we needed data on trade, tariff and nontariff barriers, production, and employment for each of these industries and countries. All of these data were available or could be constructed readily for the industrialized countries with the exception of nontariff barriers (NTBs), which for purposes of the present paper were assumed not to exist.[1] For most developing countries, because there is little systematic and accessible information on either tariffs or NTBs, we have been unable to date to represent their commercial policies with any accuracy. But we have made an effort to model the system of import licensing with exchange rate pegging that is followed in several developing countries, so that we do capture important elements of their nontariff controls. In addition to the foregoing, estimates of import-demand elasticities and of elasticities of substitution between capital and labor in each industry were required. Finally, to implement the model we needed input-output tables for each of the countries.[2] Limitations of time and of funds have prevented us so far from collecting such tables for all countries, and we therefore have used only the 1967 input-output table for the US economy and have applied it to describe technology in all countries. This undoubtedly introduces some errors into our analysis, the size and importance of which cannot be assessed until the tables for other countries are available for comparison.

17.2 Conceptual Framework

The value added per unit of an activity which produces a good j may be defined as follows:

$$v_j = p_j^O - \sum_{i=1}^{n} a_{ij} p_i^I, \tag{1}$$

Table 17.1
Categories of world industry

ISIC group	Description
Tradables	
1	Agriculture, hunting, forestry & fishing
310	Food, beverages & tobacco
321	Textiles
322	Wearing apparel, exc. footwear
323	Leather & leather & fur products
324	Footwear
331	Wood products, exc. furniture
332	Furniture & fixtures, exc. metal
341	Paper & paper products
342	Printing & publishing
35A	Industrial chemicals (351); Other chemical products (352)
35B	Petroleum refineries (353); Misc. Products of petroleum & coal (354)
355	Rubber products
36A	Pottery, china & earthenware (361); Other nonmetallic mineral products (369)
362	Glass & glass products
371	Iron & steel basic industries
372	Nonferrous metal basic industries
381	Metal products, exc. machinery, etc.
382	Machinery, exc. electrical
383	Electrical machinery, apparatus, etc.
384	Transport equipment
38A	Plastic products, n.e.c. (356); Professional, photographic goods, etc. (385); Other manufacturing industries (390)
Nontradables	
2	Mining and quarrying
4	Electricity, gas, and water
5	Construction
6	Wholesale & retail trade, restaurants & hotels
7	Transport, storage & communication
8	Finance, insurance, real estate, etc.
9	Community, social & personal services

where v_j is value added per unit in production of good j, p_j^O is the price that producers receive for their output of good j, p_i^I is the price they must pay for intermediate input of good i, and a_{ij} is the number of units of good i used in producing one unit of good j. Effective protection is defined as the percentage change in v_j that will result from the implementation of some measure of protection. From (1), this is

$$\frac{\Delta v_j}{v_j} = \left(\frac{1}{1 - \sum\limits_{i=1}^{n} b_{ij}} \right) \left[\frac{\Delta p_j^O}{p_j^O} - \sum\limits_{i=1}^{n} b_{ij} \frac{\Delta p_i^I}{p_i^I} \right], \tag{2}$$

where

$$b_{ij} = \frac{p_j^I a_{ij}}{p_j^O} \tag{3}$$

is the share of input i in the value of production of a unit of good j. The changes (Δs) in equation (2) can refer to any protective policy one wishes to examine. Most often, they refer to the results of implementing an entire structure of tariffs, starting from a base of free trade. But they could just as easily be used to measure the effects of changing particular tariffs or groups of tariffs, installing or removing a system of nontariff barriers, or, as we shall do in section 17.4, devaluing the country's currency.

Calculation of all of the price changes that appear on the right-hand side of (2) would normally be very difficult, though, of course, that is what our computational model is designed to do. In previous studies of effective protection, however, the problem has been considerably simplified by assuming that all traded goods are infinitely elastically supplied at given world prices p_i^W. It follows, for imported goods, that the domestic prices p_i^D of both outputs and inputs are given by the world price plus the tariff. For *ad valorem* tariffs t_i, this gives us

$$p_i^D = (1 + t_i)p_i^W. \tag{4}$$

The price changes that result when these tariffs are levied, starting from tariffs of zero, are just the tariffs themselves, and (2) simplifies to

$$\frac{\Delta v_j}{v_j} = \frac{t_j - \sum\limits_{i=1}^{n} b_{ij}t_i}{1 - \sum\limits_{i=1}^{n} b_{ij}}. \tag{5}$$

This is the formula used by Corden (1966) and many others to measure the effective protection due to a tariff structure.

As our derivation of (5) indicates, and as Corden himself acknowledges, the validity and usefulness of (5) depend upon a number of assumptions, of which the following three will be of particular interest to us here:[3]

1. Goods are infinitely elastically supplied or demanded on world markets, so that tariff-exclusive prices are independent of the tariffs themselves.

2. Exchange rates are held constant.

3. Foreign tariffs are either constant or irrelevant.

We shall deal with them in order.

17.2.1 Exogeneity of Tariff-Exclusive Prices

For this to be true, two further assumptions are necessary. First, the country must be sufficiently small, as a participant in world markets, so that its changes in supply and demand do not affect world prices. For some countries this may be approximately true, but for the United States it most certainly is not. When the United States levies tariffs and consequently reduces its demand for imports, the world prices in affected sectors will fall and the US domestic price will not rise by the full amount of the tariff. The precise implication of this phenomenon for the effective protection calculation in (2) depends upon how the country's importance to world markets is distributed among outputs and inputs. But we would expect in general that by damping the domestic price changes that occur, country size should tend to reduce somewhat the levels of effective protection.

The second assumption needed for price exogeneity is that domestic and foreign goods are perfect substitutes. If they are not, then even if the price of an import rises by the full amount of the tariff, the price of a corresponding domestic good will not. Thus imperfect substitutability will further dampen the price changes in (2) and reduce levels of effective protection below what would be calculated in (5).

Imperfect substitutability is also what warrants the distinction we made in (1) and (2) between input and output prices. Outputs are, by definition, domestically produced, while inputs will in general come from both imported and domestic sources. If the two are imperfect substitutes, with the prices of domestic goods varying by less than the prices of imports as just suggested, then the prices of outputs will also vary by less than the prices of inputs. When, as we impose a structure of tariffs, all are tending to rise, this means that the positive term in (2) is dampened by more than the negative terms, and the level of effective protection is reduced algebraically compared to (5).

All prices are endogenous in our computational model. World prices are determined simultaneously by the interaction of all countries together, and no country is assumed ex ante to be small. Further, domestic and traded goods are distinct, with finite elasticities of substitution between them based on empirically estimated import elasticities. Thus from what we have said so far, we would expect our calculations of effective protection based on (2) to be both smaller in absolute value and more often negative compared to traditional calculations based on the Corden formula (5).

17.2.2 Exogeneity of Exchange Rates

Writing during the era of Bretton Woods, Corden naturally defined effective protection under the assumption of a fixed exchange rate. He recognized, however, the inevitability of an eventual exchange rate change in response to the imposition or elimination of a complete structure of tariffs and therefore suggested a simple adjustment of all effective rates to take this into account. Such an ad hoc procedure is not necessary for us here, since our computational model can be solved for endogenous exchange rates along with everything else. Nor need the effect of the exchange rate change be quite so trivial as it was for Corden, since different sectors can be affected differently by exchange rates in our model. (These differences will be explored further in section 17.4.)

In general terms, both we and Corden expect exchange rate adjustment to alter the effective protection calculation as follows. When a country imposes tariffs in most industries, its trade balance is expected to improve. If the exchange rate is flexible, its currency will appreciate to restore equilibrium, and this will reduce the domestic prices of both imports and exports, leading to negative effective protection in those sectors which were least protected by the tariffs themselves. Thus exchange rate flexibility should reduce and make more negative our effective protective rates based on (2) as compared to analogous rates based on fixed currency values.

17.2.3 Exogeneity of Foreign Tariffs

There is nothing in the concept of effective protection that limits it to a country's own tariffs, though these are obviously the only policies that can be taken into account in the simplified formula (5). Industries also experience protective and antiprotective effects from the tariffs levied by other countries, and one might want to include them with own-country tariffs in a complete analysis of the structure of protection world wide. Whether to do so is largely a matter of choice, depending less on economic reasoning than on the question one wishes to answer. But given that tariffs today are almost never reduced unilaterally, but only by multilateral negotiation, the world view here does seem the most appropriate.

Presumably a country's own tariffs tend to protect its industries and foreign tariffs tend to play the opposite role. Therefore we expect levels of effective protection to be even smaller and more negative when foreign tariffs are allowed for. Thus all of the modifications of the simple analysis that we have discussed here—endogenizing prices and exchange rates and allowing for foreign tariffs—all tend to reduce, either absolutely or algebraically, the levels of effective protection we should expect.

17.2.4 Traded versus Nontraded Goods

The treatment of nontraded goods has always been a source of difficulty in calculations of effective protection. The problem is that the prices of nontraded goods are not pegged to any world prices as in equation (4). Corden (1966) describes two alternative procedures for handling them, neither of which is wholly satisfactory. One alternative is to include them with the traded inputs in both summations of equation (5), letting their tariffs in the numerator be zero. This would be valid only if the nontraded goods were themselves infinitely elastically supplied, so that their prices would be unaffected by the tariffs on traded goods. Since this is manifestly implausible, especially if the nontraded goods are themselves produced with traded inputs, Corden prefers the second alternative of including nontraded goods with value added, and thus excluding them from both summations in (5). This second alternative—which differs from the first only in the denominator—leaves us with no clear idea of which sectors are actually being protected by the levels of effective protection that we measure.

An important advantage of using our computational model to estimate effective protection via (2) instead of (5) is that none of this difficulty arises. From the model we do have estimates of how all prices are affected by tariffs, and these include the prices of nontraded goods. Thus we can include nontraded with traded goods in calculating (2) and the results refer clearly to the protection of value added actually employed directly in each sector. Protection of value added in nontraded sectors is handled in the same way.

Using the simple formula (5) to estimate effective protection of nontraded sectors, one would of course find their levels of protection to be negative. This results from the rise in the prices of traded inputs that are used in the nontraded sectors. In a general equilibrium context, however, this is likely to be reversed. Tariffs on most tradable goods, especially if levied by all countries at once, tend to act like a consumption tax on tradables, raising their prices relative to nontradables. As demanders substitute toward nontradables, their prices also tend to rise, and since the output price in (2) gets a larger weight than even the combined prices of the inputs, the nontradables in general may be protected positively. This phenomenon, that tariffs may afford positive effective protection to nontradable industries, is an important implication of a general equilibrium model that deserves to be studied further.

17.3 The Structure of Tariff Protection in 1976

In this section we report the results of three experiments, each designed to measure the structure of effective protection due to the tariffs that existed in 1976. Results are reported in columns (3)–(5) of Tables 17.2–17.6 for several representative countries.[4]

All three of these columns contain values calculated from equation (2) for the various industries and countries, with price changes determined by our computational model. The ordinal rankings of the values within columns are also reported. In each case the experiment consisted of reducing tariffs from their 1976 levels to zero and then using the negative of the resulting price changes in equation (2). Since our model distinguishes production for export from production for home use, with different prices for each, our calculation is based on an appropriately weighted average of the two sectors. In order to focus attention exclusively on the structures of tariffs, all three experiments are done assuming that nontariff barriers do not exist in the industrialized countries. Our model calculates results for all 34 of the countries, with interaction among all of them taken into account. However, we have data on tariffs for only the 18 most industrialized countries listed in section 17.1, and it was therefore only for these that we analyzed the tariff structure.

Column (3) for each country reports the effective protection due to own-country tariffs alone with fixed exchange rates for all countries. In column (4), exchange rates of all industrialized countries are allowed to fluctuate, but it is still only the own-country tariffs that are analyzed. Finally, in column (5), tariffs in all 18 industrialized countries are analyzed simultaneously, so that the results indicate the protection provided by the tariff structure of the developed world as a whole—again, like column (4), with flexible exchange rates. These results are compared, in columns (1) and (2), with nominal tariffs and levels of effective protection as

Table 17.2
Protection measures in Canada

	(ISIC)	Nominal tariffs		Effective protection (Corden)		% change value added (fixed-own)		% change value added (flex-own)		% change value added (flex-all)	
		Level	Rank	Level	Rank	Level	Rank	Level	Rank	Level	Rank
Trade goods											
Agr., for., & fish.	(1)	3.4	19	3.6	19	0.07	16	−0.43	20	−3.06	27
Food, bev., & tob.	(310)	6.9	14	12.2	13	−0.19	20	−0.21	18	−0.09	16
Textiles	(321)	18.9	4	33.1	3	1.66	1	1.44	2	1.55	1
Wearing apparel	(322)	25.4	1	39.0	2	1.63	3	1.57	1	1.32	2
Leather products	(323)	8.2	12	13.7	11	−4.01	29	−5.19	29	−3.46	29
Footwear	(324)	24.5	2	43.5	1	0.75	8	0.68	8	0.60	5
Wood products	(331)	5.8	17	7.3	16	−0.81	23	−1.40	23	−1.02	21
Furniture & fixt.	(332)	19.4	3	32.9	4	0.28	11	0.14	11	−0.16	17
Paper & paper prod.	(341)	11.8	8	18.4	7	−1.10	24	−1.63	24	−1.15	24
Printing & publ.	(342)	5.7	18	5.2	18	0.51	9	0.42	9	0.47	6
Chemicals	(35A)	7.9	13	12.7	12	1.17	5	0.69	7	0.20	9
Petrol. & rel. prod.	(35B)	0.2	22	−1.0	25	−0.32	21	−0.63	21	−0.17	18
Rubber products	(355)	12.2	7	17.2	8	1.66	2	1.31	2	1.29	3
Nonmetallic min. prod.	(36A)	9.5	10	15.4	10	0.26	12	−0.12	17	−0.62	20
Glass & glass prod.	(362)	11.3	9	15.5	9	1.06	6	0.78	5	0.42	8
Iron & steel	(371)	6.7	15	10.8	15	−0.07	19	−0.36	19	−0.28	19
Nonferrous metals	(372)	2.0	21	1.2	20	−3.31	28	−4.11	28	−2.86	26
Metal products	(381)	14.1	5	25.5	5	1.35	4	1.13	4	0.80	4
Nonelec. machinery	(382)	6.1	16	6.0	17	−2.08	27	−2.66	26	−2.03	25

Elec. machinery	(383)	12.9	6	18.8	6	0.89	7	0.70	6	0.44	7
Transport equip.	(384)	2.4	20	-2.9	28	-1.91	26	-2.49	25	-3.46	28
Misc. manufact.	(38A)	8.8	11	10.8	14	-0.72	22	-1.20	22	-1.15	23
Average traded		7.7		10.8		-0.22		-0.60		-1.07	
Nontraded goods											
Mining & quarrying	(2)			-1.4	26	-1.36	25	-2.72	27	-1.13	22
Elec., gas, & water	(4)			-0.2	21	0.29	10	0.21	10	0.19	10
Construction	(5)			-7.9	29	-0.07	18	-0.05	16	-0.05	15
Wh. & ret. trade	(6)			-0.8	24	0.08	15	0.07	13	0.07	13
Transp., stor., & comm.	(7)			-0.5	22	0.05	17	-0.01	15	0.01	14
Fin., ins., & real est.	(8)			-1.4	27	0.15	13	0.06	14	0.08	12
Comm., soc., & pers. serv.	(9)			-0.8	23	0.12	14	0.14	12	0.14	11
Average nontraded				-2.2		-0.05		-0.20		-0.06	
Average, all industries				1.8		-0.10		-0.32		-0.37	

Table 17.3
Protection measures in Germany

	(ISIC)	Nominal tariffs		Effective protection (Corden)		% change value added (fixed-own)		% change value added (flex-own)		% change value added (flex-all)	
		Level	Rank	Level	Rank	Level	Rank	Level	Rank	Level	Rank
Traded goods											
Agr., for., & fish.	(1)	7.5	12	9.7	14	0.81	1	0.85	1	−0.54	19
Food, bev., & tob.	(310)	13.4	2	27.4	1	−0.75	22	−0.75	22	−0.44	17
Textiles	(321)	10.3	5	13.8	8	−4.10	29	−4.05	29	−3.11	29
Wearing apparel	(322)	16.8	1	26.8	2	−0.08	13	−0.07	13	−0.82	23
Leather products	(323)	5.1	18	−0.9	25	−2.38	28	−2.33	28	−1.12	25
Footwear	(324)	11.7	3	19.5	4	0.07	9	0.07	9	−0.01	12
Wood products	(331)	3.9	19	3.5	19	−0.00	10	0.03	10	0.30	5
Furniture & fixt.	(332)	8.5	10	12.4	10	−0.40	17	−0.37	17	−1.04	24
Paper & paper prod.	(341)	7.1	13	10.0	13	−0.41	18	−0.38	18	0.08	11
Printing & publ.	(342)	3.3	20	2.6	20	−0.07	12	−0.05	12	−0.02	13
Chemicals	(35A)	11.6	4	20.5	3	−1.12	24	−1.06	24	−1.74	26
Petrol. & rel. prod.	(35B)	1.8	22	4.5	17	−0.09	14	−0.07	14	0.28	6
Rubber products	(355)	5.7	16	3.7	18	−0.53	20	−0.49	20	−0.52	18
Nonmetallic min. prod.	(36A)	5.4	17	8.1	15	0.25	5	0.27	5	0.10	9
Glass & glass prod.	(362)	10.2	6	14.5	7	−0.02	11	0.01	11	−0.29	16
Iron & steel	(371)	6.3	15	10.2	12	−0.48	19	−0.44	19	−0.17	15
Nonferrous metals	(372)	2.3	21	2.1	21	−1.04	23	−0.99	23	−0.10	14
Metal products	(381)	8.0	11	12.0	11	−0.16	15	−0.12	15	−0.73	20
Nonelec. machinery	(382)	6.6	14	8.0	16	−1.51	25	−1.46	25	−0.79	22

Elec. machinery	(383)	10.2	7	14.8	6	-0.31	16	-0.27	16	-0.73	21
Transport equip.	(384)	9.9	8	15.0	5	-1.68	26	-1.62	26	-2.39	28
Misc. manufact.	(38A)	9.1	9	12.9	9	-2.11	27	-2.05	27	-1.88	27
Average traded		8.6		13.3		-0.78		-0.74		-0.87	
Nontraded goods											
Mining & quarrying	(2)			-1.3	27	-0.72	21	-0.61	21	0.66	1
Elec., gas, & water	(4)			-0.2	22	0.43	2	0.44	2	0.41	2
Construction	(5)			-5.3	29	0.09	8	0.09	8	0.09	10
Wh. & ret. trade	(6)			-0.7	24	0.19	6	0.19	6	0.19	7
Transp., stor., & comm.	(7)			-0.6	23	0.12	7	0.13	7	0.14	8
Fin., ins., & real est.	(8)			-1.4	28	0.36	3	0.37	3	0.37	3
Comm., soc., & pers. serv.	(9)			-0.9	26	0.32	4	0.32	4	0.32	4
Average nontraded				-1.9		0.17		0.17		0.23	
Average, all industries		5.7		5.7		-0.31		-0.28		-0.32	

Table 17.4
Protection measures in Japan

	(ISIC)	Nominal tariffs		Effective protection (Corden)		% change value added (fixed-own)		% change value added (flex-own)		% change value added (flex-all)	
		Level	Rank	Level	Rank	Level	Rank	Level	Rank	Level	Rank
Traded goods											
Agr., for., & fish.	(1)	18.4	2	27.9	3	4.30	1	3.86	1	3.35	1
Food, bev., & tob.	(310)	25.4	1	51.0	1	-0.50	28	-0.45	25	-0.36	23
Textiles	(321)	3.3	13	-0.3	18	-0.50	29	-1.05	29	-0.41	26
Wearing apparel	(322)	13.8	4	25.9	4	0.49	4	0.36	3	0.08	9
Leather products	(323)	3.0	15	-15.0	29	-0.10	25	-0.62	26	-0.13	17
Footwear	(324)	16.4	3	33.5	2	0.29	6	0.22	4	0.19	4
Wood products	(331)	0.3	21	-4.7	28	-0.07	23	-0.33	19	-0.19	18
Furniture & fixt.	(332)	7.8	6	14.1	6	0.11	10	0.10	8	0.05	12
Paper & paper prod.	(341)	2.1	17	2.0	15	0.01	19	-0.16	16	-0.05	14
Printing & publ.	(342)	0.2	22	-0.9	23	0.09	13	0.05	11	0.06	11
Chemicals	(35A)	6.2	10	9.9	10	0.39	5	-0.11	14	-0.26	20
Petrol. & rel. prod.	(35B)	2.8	16	8.7	12	0.49	3	0.41	2	0.55	3
Rubber products	(355)	1.5	18	-1.2	25	-0.07	24	-0.37	20	-0.40	24
Nonmetallic min. prod.	(36A)	0.6	20	-0.3	19	0.04	17	-0.11	15	-0.20	19
Glass & glass prod.	(362)	7.5	7	11.4	8	0.01	18	-0.17	17	-0.28	21
Iron & steel	(371)	3.3	14	4.7	14	-0.20	26	-0.68	27	-0.40	25
Nonferrous metals	(372)	1.1	19	0.3	16	0.06	14	-0.39	22	-0.10	16
Metal products	(381)	6.9	9	11.9	7	0.04	16	-0.21	18	-0.43	27
Nonelec. machinery	(382)	9.1	5	14.6	5	-0.06	22	-0.44	23	-0.09	15

Elec. machinery	(383)	7.4	8	10.8	9	0.01	20	−0.38	21	−0.80	28
Transport equip.	(384)	6.0	11	8.1	13	−0.22	27	−0.89	28	−1.48	29
Misc. manufact.	(38A)	6.0	12	8.7	11	0.00	21	−0.44	24	−0.33	22
Average traded		8.4		13.2		0.47		0.11		0.03	
Nontraded goods											
Mining & quarrying	(2)			−1.0	24	1.03	2	0.01	13	0.68	2
Elec., gas, & water	(4)			−0.2	17	0.23	8	0.10	7	0.11	7
Construction	(5)			−3.5	27	0.06	15	0.07	10	0.07	10
Wh. & ret. trade	(6)			−0.6	21	0.10	12	0.08	9	0.08	8
Transp., stor., & comm.	(7)			−0.5	20	0.10	11	0.03	12	0.04	13
Fin., ins., & real est.	(8)			−1.4	26	0.28	7	0.17	5	0.17	5
Comm., soc., & pers. serv.	(9)			−0.9	22	0.13	9	0.14	6	0.14	6
Average nontraded				−1.2		0.14		0.09		0.10	
Average, all industries				5.2		0.28		0.10		0.07	

Table 17.5
Protection measures in the Netherlands

	(ISIC)	Nominal tariffs		Effective protection (Corden)		% change value added (fixed-own)		% change value added (flex-own)		% change value added (flex-all)	
		Level	Rank	Level	Rank	Level	Rank	Level	Rank	Level	Rank
Traded goods											
Arg., for., & fish.	(1)	6.6	14	8.1	14	-3.38	21	-1.44	20	-5.61	27
Food, bev., & tob.	(310)	13.0	2	27.1	1	-2.12	17	-1.64	21	-1.14	19
Textiles	(321)	11.8	4	17.0	5	-15.04	29	-13.55	29	-11.57	29
Wearing apparel	(322)	16.8	1	25.7	2	-5.93	27	-5.07	27	-7.03	28
Leather products	(323)	5.2	17	-0.4	23	-7.95	28	-5.82	28	-3.34	24
Footwear	(324)	11.2	5	18.0	4	-1.30	14	-0.71	15	-1.10	17
Wood products	(331)	3.6	20	3.2	19	-0.34	11	0.47	3	0.93	2
Furniture & fixt.	(332)	8.5	10	12.1	10	-0.86	12	-0.06	13	-0.93	15
Paper & paper prod.	(341)	8.4	11	12.4	9	-2.32	18	-1.25	19	-0.48	14
Printing & publ.	(342)	3.5	21	2.5	20	-0.20	7	0.03	10	0.07	9
Chemicals	(35A)	11.9	3	21.1	3	-5.56	26	-3.96	26	-5.22	26
Petrol. & rel. prod.	(35B)	1.0	22	1.6	21	-0.22	9	0.13	8	0.47	3
Rubber products	(355)	6.1	16	4.1	18	-1.87	15	-1.06	18	-1.13	18
Nonmetallic min. prod.	(36A)	4.4	18	6.0	17	-0.01	4	0.74	1	0.27	5
Glass & glass prod.	(362)	9.3	8	12.9	8	-2.50	20	-1.04	17	-2.27	22
Iron & steel	(371)	7.1	13	11.7	12	-1.25	13	-0.25	14	0.06	10
Nonferrous metals	(372)	4.3	19	6.3	16	-3.83	22	-2.37	22	-0.97	16
Metal products	(381)	7.8	12	10.7	13	-0.34	10	0.52	2	-0.35	13
Nonelec. machinery	(382)	6.4	15	7.3	15	-3.98	23	-2.59	23	-1.62	20

Elec. machinery	(383)	10.0	7	14.1	7	-2.11	16	-1.01	16	-1.89	21
Transport equip.	(384)	10.9	6	16.9	6	-4.68	24	-3.36	25	-4.23	25
Misc. manufact.	(38A)	8.7	9	11.7	11	-4.72	25	-3.12	24	-2.95	23
Average traded		8.2		13.3		-2.72		-1.69		-2.24	
Nontraded goods											
Mining & quarrying	(2)			-1.3	27	-2.32	19	0.42	5	2.45	1
Elec., gas, & water	(4)			-0.2	22	-0.17	5	0.19	6	0.13	7
Construction	(5)			-5.2	29	0.06	3	0.01	11	0.01	12
Wh. & ret. trade	(6)			-0.7	25	0.14	2	0.18	7	0.17	6
Transp., stor., & comm.	(7)			-0.6	24	-0.22	8	-0.01	12	0.03	11
Fin., ins., & real est.	(8)			-1.4	28	-0.19	6	0.12	9	0.11	8
Comm., soc., & pers. serv.	(9)			-0.9	26	0.46	1	0.43	4	0.43	4
Average nontraded				-1.7		-0.03		0.10		0.11	
Average, all industries				4.6		-1.15		-0.65		-0.87	

Table 17.6
Protection measures in the United States

	(ISIC)	Nominal tariffs		Effective protection (Corden)		% change value added (fixed-own)		% change value added (flex-own)		% change value added (flex-all)	
		Level	Rank	Level	Rank	Level	Rank	Level	Rank	Level	Rank
Traded goods											
Agr., for., & fish.	(1)	2.2	18	2.2	18	0.11	17	−0.63	27	−2.31	29
Food. bev., & tob.	(310)	6.3	10	13.9	5	−0.06	28	−0.08	17	−0.01	13
Textiles	(321)	14.4	2	26.4	2	0.76	2	0.29	3	0.70	2
Wearing apparel	(322)	27.8	1	48.0	1	1.22	1	1.11	1	1.08	1
Leather products	(323)	5.6	11	8.8	11	0.22	10	−0.85	29	−0.07	19
Footwear	(324)	8.8	5	12.8	6	0.39	4	0.31	2	0.32	3
Wood products	(331)	3.6	15	4.7	15	0.20	12	−0.20	19	−0.08	20
Furniture & fixt.	(332)	8.1	6	12.1	8	0.13	16	0.06	5	0.02	11
Paper & paper prod.	(341)	0.5	22	−1.2	28	0.02	26	−0.22	21	−0.10	22
Printing & publ.	(342)	1.1	21	1.1	20	0.03	25	−0.03	14	−0.02	14
Chemicals	(35A)	3.8	14	6.0	14	0.28	7	−0.25	23	−0.40	27
Petrol. & rel. prod.	(35B)	1.4	19	4.1	16	0.06	21	−0.04	16	−0.02	15
Rubber products	(355)	3.6	16	2.8	17	0.38	5	0.06	6	0.07	5
Nonmetallic min. prod.	(36A)	9.1	4	16.1	4	0.34	6	0.17	4	0.15	4
Glass & glass prod.	(362)	10.7	3	16.5	3	0.21	11	−0.03	15	−0.09	21
Iron & steel	(371)	4.7	13	7.7	12	0.11	18	−0.14	18	−0.07	18
Nonferrous metals	(372)	1.2	20	0.7	21	0.08	19	−0.35	25	−0.14	24
Metal products	(381)	7.5	8	12.8	7	0.25	8	−0.00	13	−0.06	17
Nonelec. machinery	(382)	5.0	12	6.3	13	−0.17	29	−0.70	28	−0.40	26

Elec. machinery	(383)	6.6	9	9.3	10	0.15	13	−0.24	22	−0.35	25
Transport equip.	(384)	3.3	17	2.1	19	0.05	22	−0.55	26	−0.70	28
Misc. manufact.	(38A)	7.8	7	12.1	9	0.25	9	−0.20	20	−0.05	16
Average traded		5.2		8.2		0.13		−0.23		−0.37	
Nontraded goods											
Mining & quarrying	(2)			−0.9	27	0.42	3	−0.27	24	−0.12	23
Elec., gas, & water	(4)			−0.1	22	0.15	14	0.05	7	0.07	6
Construction	(5)			−5.0	29	−0.01	27	0.00	12	0.00	12
Wh. & ret. trade	(6)			−0.4	24	0.03	23	0.02	10	0.03	9
Transp., stor., & comm.	(7)			−0.4	23	0.06	20	0.01	11	0.02	10
Fin., ins., & real est.	(8)			−0.7	26	0.13	15	0.04	8	0.06	7
Comm., soc., & pers. serv.	(9)			−0.5	25	0.03	24	0.04	9	0.04	8
Average nontraded				−1.0		0.08		0.01		0.03	
Average, all industries				1.8		0.10		−0.06		−0.09	

computed from the simplified formula (5).[5] For the latter, we use the first of Corden's alternatives for handling nontraded goods. That is, they are included in both summations in (5) but with zero tariffs.

The most noticeable feature of these results is that all of our own calculations of effective protection are an order of magnitude smaller than both the nominal tariffs and the effective tariffs calculated from the Corden formula. Also there are a great many more industries with negative protection in our calculations. In section 17.2 we listed a number of reasons why we expect smaller and more negative values for effective protection than have traditionally been calculated, and we see now that our expectations have been borne out with a vengeance.

Of the reasons for low effective protection discussed earlier, the most important—based on our model—appears to be the imperfect substitutability between domestic and foreign goods. The damping of effective protection due to country size does not appear to be significant, and the effects of exchange rate flexibility and foreign tariffs do not appear until columns (4) and (5), while low values appear already in column (3). Since the role of imperfect substitution appears so important, it is worth recapitulating how it works.

When tariffs are increased, they raise the prices of imports. If domestic goods were perfect substitutes for imports, their prices too would rise by the same amount. But if substitution is imperfect, an equal rise in domestic prices would leave demand unchanged while increasing supply. Equilibrium requires instead that domestic prices rise by less than import prices so as to stimulate both supply and demand by equal amounts. This smaller rise in domestic prices means that effective protection, as calculated from equation (2), is reduced from what it would be if substitution were perfect.

Note further that domestic prices are only part of what appears in the numerator of (2). Import prices also enter, but negatively, to the extent that imports are used as inputs. Thus imperfect substitution reduces substantially the protective effect of tariffs on output prices, but does not reduce by nearly as much the antiprotective effect of tariffs on input prices. Together these two mechanisms can account for much of the reduction in effective rates going from columns (2) to (3) in the tables. Note incidentally that a more open economy will experience the antiprotective effect on input prices more severely than will an economy in which most of demand is for domestic goods. This may account for much of the negative protection measured for small countries like the Netherlands.

A related phenomenon, not mentioned so far, is the effect of tariffs on exports. If domestic and foreign goods were perfect substitutes, then a given industry could not both export and import. But with imperfect substitution such two-way trade can and does take place. Now, producers for export enjoy no increase at all in their output price when tariffs are raised and, if anything, suffer a fall in price if world markets weaken. Thus producers for export experience only antiprotective effects of tariffs. When they are averaged in with producers for domestic markets, as they are in the calculations we report, they account still further for the small-ness of effective protection. They may also account for the largely negative rates that we get for Germany in table 17.3, since exports in Germany are so important.

Finally we should note that our other expectations in section 17.2 have been borne out. Looking at average rates of protection, we see that exchange rate flexibility [compare columns (3) and (4)] does indeed reduce protection in all countries but the Netherlands. And allowing for foreign tariffs [compare columns (4) and (5)] reduces protection still further in all five countries. The reason for the anomalous result in the case of the Netherlands is that its currency actually depreciates when it levies tariffs, according to our model. The Netherlands is so small and open that protection mainly raises the prices of inputs to its export sectors, and worsens its balance of trade.

Regarding nontraded goods, we find as expected that they tend to be protected positively rather than negatively in a general equilibrium model.

So far we have looked only at the levels of protection overall and have ignored the comparisons among industries that are provided by the ordinal rankings that are also reported in the tables. Yet it is precisely such comparisons that constitute the major rationale for measurements of effective protection. The concept is intended to indicate how resources are reallocated due to tariffs, with movement being from the lowest to the highest industries in terms of the level of effective protection.

By and large the rankings of industries in the tables are fairly similar regardless of which measure of effective protection is used. Yet there are also particular examples of industries whose rankings change substan-tially as we move across the tables from less to more sophisticated mea-sures of protection. Thus the use of a general equilibrium model, as well as the complications introduced by flexible exchange rates and foreign tariffs, can have significant implications for the position in the tariff structure of particular industries. As one example, the leather products industry (ISIC 323) in Canada enjoys above average protection according

Table 17.7
Protection due to 1% devaluation

	(ISIC)	Canada		West Germany		Japan		Netherlands		United States	
		Level	Rank	Level	Rank	Level	Rank	Level	Rank	Level	Rank
Traded goods											
Agr., for., & fish.	(1)	0.81	8	0.86	9	0.53	9	1.54	3	0.55	2
Food, bev., & tob.	(310)	0.03	26	0.07	26	−0.05	29	0.38	21	0.01	26
Textiles	(321)	0.35	16	0.96	6	0.67	3	1.18	6	0.34	7
Wearing apparel	(322)	0.10	24	0.36	18	0.15	19	0.69	14	0.08	18
Leather products	(323)	1.86	2	1.18	2	0.62	5	1.71	2	0.79	1
Footwear	(324)	0.10	23	0.19	24	0.09	23	0.47	20	0.05	22
Wood products	(331)	0.96	4	0.56	14	0.32	13	0.65	16	0.30	10
Furniture & fixt.	(332)	0.23	19	0.46	17	0.02	25	0.64	18	0.05	23
Paper & paper prod.	(341)	0.89	7	0.55	15	0.21	16	0.85	12	0.19	14
Printing & publ.	(342)	0.15	20	0.21	22	0.04	24	0.19	25	0.04	24
Chemicals	(35A)	0.76	10	1.02	4	0.63	4	1.27	5	0.39	5
Petrol. & rel. prod.	(35B)	0.50	13	0.24	20	0.11	21	0.29	22	0.07	20
Rubber products	(355)	0.55	12	0.70	10	0.37	12	0.64	17	0.24	12
Nonmetallic min. prod.	(36A)	0.60	11	0.35	19	0.19	17	0.59	19	0.13	17
Glass & glass prod.	(362)	0.44	15	0.49	16	0.23	15	1.16	8	0.18	16
Iron & steel	(371)	0.46	14	0.64	11	0.60	6	0.79	13	0.18	15
Nonferrous metals	(372)	1.32	3	0.94	7	0.56	7	1.17	7	0.33	8
Metal products	(381)	0.34	17	0.57	12	0.31	14	0.69	15	0.19	13
Nonelec. machinery	(382)	0.91	6	0.91	8	0.48	11	1.11	9	0.39	6
Elec. machinery	(383)	0.29	18	0.57	13	0.48	10	0.88	11	0.29	11

Industry	Code									
Transport equip.	(384)	0.93	5	0.99	5	0.84	2	1.05	10	0.44	4
Misc. manufact.	(38A)	0.77	9	1.08	3	0.55	8	1.27	4	0.33	9
Average traded		0.60	16	0.67	6	0.44	3	0.82	6	0.27	7
Nontraded goods											
Mining & quarrying	(2)	2.18	1	1.73	1	1.27	1	2.19	1	0.51	3
Elec., gas, & water	(4)	0.13	22	0.21	21	0.16	18	0.28	23	0.07	19
Construction	(5)	-0.03	29	-0.03	29	-0.02	28	-0.04	29	-0.01	29
Wh. & ret. trade	(6)	0.01	27	0.02	27	0.02	26	0.03	27	0.01	27
Transp., stor., & comm.	(7)	0.10	25	0.13	25	0.09	22	0.17	26	0.04	25
Fin., ins., & real est.	(8)	0.14	21	0.19	23	0.14	20	0.25	24	0.07	21
Comm., soc., & pers. serv.	(9)	-0.02	28	-0.02	28	-0.02	27	-0.03	28	-0.01	28
Average nontraded		0.24	28	0.14	28	0.06	27	0.10	28	0.05	28
Average, all industries		0.35	16	0.40	6	0.23	3	0.40	6	0.12	7

to the Corden formula but drops to the bottom of the list in all three of the calculations using our model. In the United States, agriculture (ISIC 1) has average protection both with the Corden formula and with our model under fixed exchange rates. But when exchange rates are flexible, and especially when foreign tariffs are accounted for, protection of US agriculture becomes the most negative of all industries. Many other similar examples can be found in the tables, which indicate the importance of knowing exactly what environment one is dealing with in assessing whether a particular industry is protected.

17.4 The Protective Effects of Exchange-Rate Changes

Our final experiment was to analyze the effects of a 1 percent devaluation for each country, assuming that the exchange rates for all other countries remain unchanged. The devaluation was treated as an exogenous change and the model was then solved for the changes in the endogenous variables. As before, we are interested in the percentage changes in value added by sector, as calculated in equation (2).

The effect of a devaluation will be to increase the domestic prices of exportable and importable goods. This in turn will stimulate both production for exports and for the home market so that value added can be expected to rise. There will be some offset, however, to the extent that the prices of imported intermediates will be increased as the result of the devaluation. The nontradable industries may be affected favorably insofar as they provide inputs into the expanding home and export sectors. The nontradables should also benefit by a shift in demand since they will become relatively cheaper compared to tradable goods due to the devaluation. Finally, depending upon the size of an industry in world markets, the benefits of the devaluation in terms of price changes may be diminished to some extent as world prices fall. We may expect therefore that the effects of a devaluation will be positive depending upon the degree to which an industry expands and its output is used in the expansion of other industries. The effects of a devaluation will be diminished depending upon the degree to which an industry uses imported inputs and the larger the industry is in world markets.

The results of our experiment are summarized in table 17.7. For Canada, the greatest percentage increases in value added are in mining and quarrying, leather products, nonferrous metals, wood products, transport equipment, nonelectrical machinery, and paper products. For Germany, the greatest increases are in mining and quarrying, leather products, miscellaneous manufactures, chemicals, transport equipment, textiles, and nonferrous metals. For Japan, the greatest increases are in mining and quarrying, transport equipment, textiles, chemicals, leather products, iron and steel, and nonferrous metals. For the Netherlands, the greatest increases are in mining and quarrying, leather products, agriculture, miscellaneous manufactures, chemicals, textiles, and nonferrous metals. Finally, for the United States, the greatest increases are in leather products, agriculture, mining and quarrying, transport equipment, chemicals, nonelectrical machinery, and textiles. The effects on the other sectors in each of the countries can of course be gauged from the rankings indicated in the table. By the same token, if we had assumed an appreciation of the exchange rate, the effects would be the opposite of those shown.

If we compare the results in table 17.7 with those for the individual countries in tables 17.2–17.6, there is of course a similarity with our second experiment, in which each country was assumed to impose its tariff structure and permit its exchange rate to adjust to restore the initial trade balance. In the country tables, the industries with the highest numerical rankings had the least protection or the greatest antiprotection. These are the industries generally that are stimulated the most by the assumed devaluations whose effects are summarized in table 17.7. Presumably, if tariff removal were coupled with exchange rate flexibility, the industries with the least protection would expand the most and those with the greatest protection would expand the least. Assuming that there are not other distortions in the economies, these changes would foster an improved allocation of resources among the industries.

17.5 Conclusion

We have attempted in this chapter to analyze the effects of tariffs and exchange rates on the structure of protection in the major industrialized countries. For this purpose, we have used our disaggregated model of world production and trade, with all data inputs referring to 1976. A number of conclusions have emerged from our calculations:

1. The ranking of industries according to nominal and effective tariff rates as conventionally calculated does not provide an accurate indication of the structure of protection because it fails to take into account how the sectors within an industry will respond to changes in prices when there is imperfect substitutability between imports and home goods.

2. The ranking of industries by the degree of protection should take account of any exchange rate changes that would have to accompany changes in tariffs. Exchange rate flexibility tends to moderate the protective effect of a tariff structure, bringing the average level of protection closer to zero.

3. Protection and antiprotection are provided not only by a country's own tariffs, but also by the tariffs of its trading partners. Rankings of protection should take these foreign tariffs into account if the net effect on resource allocation is to be understood. Our rankings based on tariff removal by all countries simultaneously indicate that the presence of foreign tariffs lowers the average level of protection in all countries considered.

4. Changes in exchange rates by themselves can be an effective instrument of protection. A 1 per cent devaluation has effects on per unit value added that are comparable in size to those of existing tariffs. The effects vary among industries, however, depending upon each good's use as an intermediate input, the industry's reliance upon imported inputs, and the size of the industry in world markets.

Notes

1. In the version of our model that we have used to analyze the effects of reductions in tariffs and selected NTB's in the Tokyo Round—see Deardorff and Stern (1979) —NTBs are included in terms of the fraction of trade that is covered by NTBs of all kinds. It would be preferable to measure directly the combined ad valorem effects of tariffs and NTBs, but the available data do not permit this.

2. The sources for all data and parameter estimates used in the model are listed in Deardorff and Stern (1979).

3. It is also common to assume fixed production coefficients, which we shall do throughout the paper. Our model is capable of handling variable coefficients, but we decided not to use this facility for our calculations to be presented.

4. Results for the countries not reported here are available from the authors on request.

5. The nominal tariffs are weighted averages of the pre-Tokyo Round tariff levels based on 1976 own-country imports. The effective rates in column (2) are calculated using the 1967 input-output and value-added relations for the United States, which we have applied across all countries in our model in the absence of separate data for each country. We have not attempted to make adjustments in the coefficients to correct for any biases in using actual rather than free trade conditions.

References

Corden, W. M. (1966). "The Structure of a Tariff System and the Effective Protective Rate," *Journal of Political Economy* 74.

Deardorff, A. V., and R. M. Stern (1979). *An Economic Analysis of the Effects of the Tokyo Round of Multilateral Trade Negotiations on the United States and the Other Major Industrialized Countries*, MTN Studies 5, Committee on Finance, US Senate, 96th Congress, 1st Session. Washington, DC: US Government Printing Office.

Deardorff, A. V., and R. M. Stern (1981). "A Disaggregated Model of World Production and Trade: An Estimate of the Impact of the Tokyo Round," *Journal of Policy Modeling* 3.

18

Economic Change and Policy Response in Canada under Fixed and Flexible Exchange Rates

Malcolm D. Knight
and
Donald J. Mathieson

In this chapter we specify and estimate a small disequilibrium model of the behavior of private transactors and policymakers in Canada under both fixed and flexible exchange rate regimes.[1] In terms of its size, our model is a compromise between large structural models of the Canadian economy[2] and unrestricted reduced forms (see, for example, Dugay 1978). An advantage of our approach is that the model can be estimated by systems methods with overidentifying restrictions imposed both within and across equations, so that not only the behavioral parameters but also the spillover effects which are major components of its dynamic structure can be identified. The model describes the behavior of output and prices, private expenditure, the balance of payments, the domestic interest rate, and the exchange rate. Our model is designed to study the channels by which developments in the rest of the world (ROW) impinge upon the Canadian economy. In addition, simple reaction functions for both the money supply and the stock of official foreign exchange reserves are included so that the motivations for, and effects of, the authorities' money supply and exchange market intervention policies can be examined.

The model consists of *ex ante* supply and demand functions, adjustment functions, and identities. It is specified in continuous time and estimated using a discrete approximation that has the same structural form as the continuous system.[3] While the restrictions on the supply and demand functions are derived from standard macroeconomic theory, the adjustment equations include a number of spillover effects. Since across-equation restrictions are imposed in order to identify the parameters of *ex ante* demands and supplies, it is possible to determine which of these

This chapter represents views of the authors that are not necessarily those of the International Monetary Fund. We are grateful to a number of colleagues, and particularly to Sterie T. Beza, Mohsin Khan, Russell Kincaid, Desmond Lachman and George von Furstenberg for helpful comments and suggestions on a previous draft.

spillover effects are statistically significant, giving insights into the way economic disturbances are transmitted internationally.

18.1 Specification

In the model, both the Canadian economy and the ROW contain markets for domestic and foreign goods, money balances, and securities. Economic variables in the ROW are assumed exogenous.[4] Canadians and ROW residents each produce a stream of output that is used either for export or as a consumption/investment good domestically. We assume that Canadian residents can purchase all the imports they want without significantly affecting their price on world markets. However, since Canada is a major exporter of certain traded goods and it sells manufactured goods in an imperfectly competitive world market, the model assumes that domestic and foreign goods are less-than-perfect substitutes.

Two foreign goods appear in the model: a final consumption/investment good produced by the other industrialized countries with which Canada trades; and energy, which is used both as a consumer good and as an input to domestic production. The relative price of the first good [defined in equation (16)] is $p/\varepsilon p_f$. The variables ε and p_f are taken as weighted indices of exchange rates and prices, respectively, in four countries: Germany, Japan, the United Kingdom, and the United States. The price of energy is represented by the relative price of oil. Since the Canadian authorities have controlled the price paid for oil by domestic consumers in recent years, two separate prices—one domestic and one international—are included in the model. The foreign price q_1 is an index of the world market price in US dollars; the consumer price q_2 is the Canadian industry selling price index for petroleum products. The price relatives for petroleum are $p/\theta q_1$ and p/q_2, respectively.

Financial markets are equilibrated by movements in relative interest rates between Canada and the ROW. Although domestic and foreign securities are close substitutes when covered forward, wealth owners may not adjust their international portfolios immediately in response to change. Thus the model allows domestic yields to deviate temporarily from interest rate parity. International interest parity and (relative) purchasing power parity are long-run (i.e., steady-state) properties of the model, but they need not hold at every instant. The model also assumes, however, that Walras's identity holds: Since the excess demands of the domestic and foreign private sectors must each sum to zero, the excess demand for money is, in each case, equal to the sum of the excess supplies of goods and securities.

Definitions of the variables are:[5]

Endogenous variables:

E	real[6] consumption and investment expenditure by domestic residents,
Y	real domestic output,
I	real imports of goods and services (National Accounts basis),
X	real exports of goods and services (National Accounts basis),
p	implicit price deflator for domestic output,
M	nominal money stock [narrow (M1) definition],
r	domestic interest rate (quarterly yield on Canadian government treasury bills),
R	international reserves of gold and foreign exchange (valued in US dollars),[7]
ε	effective exchange rate index (units of domestic currency per unit of foreign currency, 1970 = 1.0),
θ	US dollar exchange rate (Canadian dollars per US dollar),
DK	capital account of the balance of payments (in domestic currency; inflow = +),
p^*	expected domestic price level,
ε^*	expected level of the effective exchange rate;

Exogenous variables:

G	real domestic government expenditure on current goods and services,
θ_0	par exchange rate (Canadian dollars per US dollar),
a	exchange rate regime variable (equals unity in periods when Canada maintained a par value for its currency; zero otherwise),
t	quarterly time trend (1970:II = 0)
p_f	index of prices in the rest of the world,
r_f	index of ROW interest rates,
M_f	US dollar value of nominal money stock in ROW,
Y_f	US dollar value of real output in ROW,
$E_f + G_f + X_f$	total sales of goods and services in ROW,

r_B Bank of Canada discount rate,

q_1 index of the US dollar price of crude oil on the world market (1970 = 1.0),

q_2 index of the Canadian industry selling price of petroleum products (in Canadian dollars, 1970 = 1.0).

In the model the α are proportions or marginal propensities, the γ are adjustment coefficients, the λ are parameters of policy reaction functions, and the β refer to demand and supply elasticities. Except where noted, all parameters are expected to be positive. Superscript d represents the *ex ante* demand; an asterisk indicates an expected value. All variables are at time t, the letter D is the time differential operator d/dt, and stochastic disturbance terms are omitted.

The model investigates the channels through which disequilibrium in one market spills over into other parts of the economy. This is illustrated by the equation for domestic output, which is assumed to respond both to supply and demand in the goods market and to spillover effects from money markets. Growth in the supply of output relative to the trend ρ in capacity output responds to the relation of current output to full-capacity supply, excess domestic demand for home output, excess foreign demand for Canadian exports, and the excess supplies of domestic and foreign money balances:

$$D \ln Y = \rho + \gamma_1 [\ln(\hat{Y} e^{\rho t}) - \ln Y] + \gamma_2 [\ln Y^d - \ln Y]$$

$$+ \gamma_3 [\ln X_f^d - \ln X] + \gamma_4 \left[\ln\left(\frac{M}{p}\right) - \ln\left(\frac{M}{p}\right)^d \right]$$

$$+ \gamma_5 \left[\ln\left(\frac{M_f}{p_f}\right) - \ln\left(\frac{M_f}{p_f}\right)^d \right], \tag{1}$$

$$\ln \hat{Y} = \ln Y_0 + \beta_1 \ln\left(\frac{p}{\theta q_1}\right), \tag{1a}$$

$$\ln Y^d = \ln \alpha_1 - \beta_2 \ln\left(\frac{p}{\varepsilon p_f}\right) + \ln(E + G + X), \tag{1b}$$

$$\ln X_f^d = \ln \alpha_2 - \beta_3 \ln\left(\frac{p}{\varepsilon p_f}\right) + \ln \theta + \ln(E_f + G_f + X_f), \tag{1c}$$

$$\ln\left(\frac{M}{p}\right)^d = \ln \alpha_3 + \beta_4 \ln Y - \beta_5 r - \beta_6 D \ln p^*, \tag{1d}$$

$$\ln\left(\frac{M_f}{p_f}\right)^d = \ln \alpha_4 + \beta_7 \ln Y_f - \beta_8 r_f - \beta_9 D \ln p_f^*. \tag{1e}$$

$$D \ln p = D \ln p^* + \gamma_8 [\ln Y - \ln(\hat{Y} e^{\rho^t})] + \gamma_9 [\ln(M/p) - \ln(M/p)^d)]$$

$$- \gamma_{10} [\ln p - \ln \alpha_7 - \ln \varepsilon - \ln p_f]. \tag{5}$$

Domestic prices are assumed to be set by firms operating in conditions of monopolistic competition. The first term represents the extent to which producers adjust prices to changes in the expected rate of inflation, while the second implies that each firm tends to raise its price more quickly when sales are above sustainable capacity output. If there is excess aggregate demand in the conomy, all firms will respond more or less simultaneously, so that the aggregate price level rises. The third term reflects the assumption that monetary disequilibrium may spill over into the goods market and affect the domestic inflation rate, while the last term captures the influence of foreign price movements on domestic price formation. Producers are assumed to respond negatively to any rise in domestic prices above the purchasing power parity level and positively to an increase in the rate of foreign inflation or a depreciation of the home currency.

Our specification of the financial sector assumes that there are three broad markets in the economy: goods, money, and securities. Since Walras's identity holds, the excess demands for goods, money, and securities must sum to zero. This means that if we specify the determinants of the excess demands in the goods and money markets, the excess demand for securities is also implicitly specified. Our analysis of the money market assumes that changes in the domestic money supply and the nominal interest rate are the outcome of interaction between the Bank of Canada's monetary policies and private sector portfolio adjustments.

Our model builds on Gordon's (1977) analysis of official money supply processes by specifying simple reaction functions for the Canadian authorities' money supply and exchange market intervention policies. If these policy responses have contained important systematic components during our sample period, then the inclusion of reaction functions in the estimated model allows us to avoid two significant pitfalls of econometric work. First, failure to specify the authorities' monetary reactions might cause us to overlook important feedbacks that could potentially affect the dynamic behavior of the model. Second, provided that there are systematic reactions, the assumption that monetary and intervention policies are endogenous removes a potential source of simultaneous equations bias.

Our analysis has tentatively assumed that official reaction functions contain both systematic and transitory responses. Systematic responses are policy adjustments that have taken place continuously throughout the will rise whenever there is a rise in foreign interest rates; the nominal return on physical capital relative to the money rate of interest;[15] or the Bank of Canada's discount rate.

Under the fixed exchange rate regime, the Canadian authorities used their foreign reserves to keep the spot rate within a set of upper and lower margins around a published parity rate θ_0 (defined in units of Canadian dollars per US dollar). Once the Canadian dollar was allowed to float in May 1970, however, the authorities had more flexibility in their intervention strategy. A specification of the intervention function that is applicable for the full (1964–1977) sample period is:

$$D \ln R = \rho_R + a\lambda_{12}(\ln \theta_0 - \ln \theta)$$
$$+ (1 - a)\lambda_{13}[\ln p - \ln \alpha_8 - \ln p_f - \ln \varepsilon]$$
$$-\lambda_{14} D \ln \varepsilon + \sum_{i=15}^{20} \lambda_i z_{i-10}. \tag{8}$$

In (8) the exchange rate regime variable a has the value unity during the pegged exchange rate system and zero otherwise. Thus the first term is a log-linear approximation to the authorities' intervention policies during the period when there was a fixed par value for the Canadian dollar (Knight and Mathieson, 1979). The second term refers to intervention during periods of managed floating exchange rates. It is, of course, quite possible that no stable reaction function for exchange reserves exists when the Canadian exchange rate is flexible. If the authorities consistently operate a "managed" float, however, it may be possible to write a function which approximates their behavior. One assumption [embodied in the second term of (8)] is that the authorities have some notion of the long-run equilibrium level of domestic prices relative to prices abroad (α_8) and that they intervene more heavily the more the actual exchange rate deviates from this level. The final term reflects a second hypothesis, namely, throughout the sample period the authorities attempted to slow movements in the effective exchange rate by leaning against the wind.

The part of equation (8) that deals with fixed exchange rates is specified in terms of deviations of the country's dollar exchange rate θ from its dollar par value θ_0 but the part that refers to managed floating is specified in terms of the *effective* exchange rate ε. Thus an equation that relates the dollar exchange rate to the effective exchange rate index is needed. This is

$$\ln \theta = \ln \varepsilon - \ln \varepsilon', \tag{9}$$

where $\ln \varepsilon'$ (the effective exchange rate index excluding the dollar component) is derived from the definition of the exchange rate in equation (14).

Since the domestic private sector's excess demand for money equals the sum of its excess supplies of goods and securities, the rate of change in any market price in a three-sector model should be expressed as a function either of the excess supplies of both goods and securities in the domestic and foreign economies, or alternatively as a function of the excess demand for money. In this chapter the rate of change of the exchange rate is expressed as a function of the excess demands for money in both the domestic and foreign economies. This formulation can be modified to allow for government intervention to influence the market price of foreign exchange. Exchange rate movements are also influenced by the fact that economic agents attempt to arbitrage goods and security prices across countries. As we have already noted, long-run equilibrium in the goods market requires that relative purchasing power parity hold between the domestic price index and the foreign price index (multiplied by the exchange rate). Similarly, long-run equilibrium in the asset market requires that the domestic interest rate must equal the foreign interest rate plus the anticipated rate of appreciation in the price of foreign currency (i.e., interest rate parity holds). Any departure from either purchasing power parity or interest rate parity will naturally lead to arbitrage flows and give rise to movements in the exchange rate. Thus, we have chosen the following structural form:

$$D \ln \varepsilon = \rho_\varepsilon + a\gamma_{14}[\ln \theta_0 - \ln \theta] + (1 - a)\gamma_{15}[\ln p - \ln \alpha_7$$
$$- \ln \varepsilon - \ln p_f] - \gamma_{16}[r - \alpha_9(r_f + D \ln \varepsilon^*)]$$
$$+ \gamma_{17}[\ln(M/p) - \ln(M/p)^d] + \gamma_{18}[\ln(M_f/p_f)^d - \ln(M_f/p_f)]$$
$$+ \gamma_{19} D \ln R + \gamma_{20}a, \tag{10}$$

where the domestic and foreign demands for money are as given in (1d) and (1e). An excess supply of domestic money, or a purchase of foreign exchange by the authorities, causes the price of foreign currency to rise, while an excess supply of money on the part of foreign residents will cause it to fall. A domestic interest rate above the corresponding covered foreign yield will stimulate a capital inflow that appreciates the domestic currency, whereas a domestic price level that is above the equivalent foreign price level will lead to a depreciation of the domestic currency. Thus, the exchange rate responds either to differential movements in home and foreign prices and interest rates or to disequilibrium in the goods and securities markets.[16] The international sector of the model is completed by the balance-of-payments identity, which determines the nominal value of capital flows ($DK \geqslant 0 =$ inflow):

$$DK = pI - pX + \theta\,DR. \tag{11}$$

The model (1)–(11) contains the expected inflation rate ($D \ln p^*$) and the anticipated rate of change in the exchange rate ($D \ln \varepsilon^*$), both of which are unobservable. Our model employs a simple adaptive mechanism for price expectations (see Burmeister and Turnovsky, 1976):

$$D^2 \ln p^* = \gamma_{21}[D \ln p - D \ln p^*]. \tag{12}$$

For a given par value, the exchange rate is a continuous function of time. But the possibility of a par value change always exists under a regime of fixed exchange rates, and the *rate* of change of the exchange rate is undefined at the time of a devaluation or revaluation. This discontinuity can be avoided by using a probabilistic interpretation of the expected rate of change in the exchange rate. We assume that the expected value of the rate of acceleration of the exchange rate $D^2 \ln \varepsilon^*$ is the sum of two terms:

$$D^2 \ln \varepsilon^* = E(D^2 \ln \varepsilon | \theta_0 = \bar{\theta}_0) \cdot P(\theta_0 = \bar{\theta}_0) + E(\Delta^2 \ln \varepsilon | \Delta^2 \ln \theta_0)$$
$$\cdot [1 - P(\theta_0 = \bar{\theta}_0)], \tag{13a}$$

where E is the expectation operator and P denotes a probability. The first term in (13a) is the expected value of $D^2 \ln \varepsilon$ given that the par value ($\bar{\theta}_0$) remains unchanged over the next 90 days, multiplied by the probability that no par value change will occur. (In the latter years of the Bretton Woods system, $\ln \varepsilon$ was allowed to move such that changes in the bilateral rate against the US dollar of up to 4 percent could occur). The second term gives the expected change in $\Delta \ln \varepsilon$ if the par value does change, multiplied by the probability that the par value is altered. Provided that the latter probability moves continuously in the range (0, 1), $D^2 \ln \varepsilon^*$ can be treated as a continuous variable. The first term in (13a) can be described by a simple error-learning process, whereas the part of the expected rate of change in the effective exchange rate that is due to par value changes depends on a number of factors. In the present model, the trade balance is used as an indicator of expected par value movements for two reasons. First, during the Bretton Woods era of adjustable par values, exchange rates were typically "defended" until the last moment via large-scale exchange market intervention and/or increased borrowing from abroad. Thus, while the actual nominal exchange rate would remain virtually unchanged, there would be a sharp deterioration in the country's net asset position vis à vis the rest of the world (i.e., the sum of official intervention and the capital account balance), reflected in a worsening current account balance. We have therefore assumed that market participants gauge the likelihood of discrete changes in the exchange rate by the size of the deterioration in the country's net foreign asset position (as proxied by the state of the trade balance). Thus

$$D^2 \ln \varepsilon^* = \gamma_{22}[D\ln \varepsilon - D\ln \varepsilon^*] - \gamma_{23}[\ln \alpha_{10} - D\ln X + D\ln I]. \quad (13)$$

As noted, the influence of economic developments abroad is represented by indices for the effective exchange rate and for real income, prices, interest rates, and nominal money balances in the rest of the world. The ROW price and interest rate variables are weighted indices of the corresponding variables in the four industrial countries that have the strongest trade and financial linkages with Canada, namely, Germany, Japan, the United Kingdom, and the United States. Our specification of the effective exchange rate index for Canada is of the form

$$\ln \varepsilon = \sum_{j=1}^{4} w_j \ln[\theta_j/\bar{\theta}_j], \qquad \sum w_j = 1, \quad (14)$$

where

ε = nominal effective exchange rate for Canada,

θ_j = bilateral exchange rate (Canadian dollars per unit of country j currency),

$\bar{\theta}_j$ = exchange rate between Canada and country j in the base year (1970).

To construct the weights w_i, we first calculated the dollar value of nominal GNP in 1970[17] for each of the countries included in the index, and then derived country j's share of the total GNP of the four industrial countries that represent the ROW:

$$w_j = \frac{1970 \text{ GNP (country } j)}{1970 \text{ GNP (sum of four industrial countries)}}.$$

The index of foreign interest rates must be calculated in the same way as the effective exchange rate in order to allow for the possibility of interest rate parity in the long run. Thus, we have

$$r_f = \sum_{j=1}^{n} w_j r_j, \quad (15)$$

where r_j is the nominal interest rate on short-term government securities in country j and w_j is as defined earlier.

Similarly, the foreign price level is

$$p_f = \exp\left[\sum_{j=1}^{n} w_j \ln p_j\right],$$ (16)

where $p_j = $ GNP deflator in country j.

The indices for the dollar value of foreign expenditures, money supply, and real income do not require a weighting scheme since we only want the sum of expenditures in all the foreign countries. Thus, summing over the j foreign countries gives

$$E_f + G_f + X_f = \sum_{j=1}^{n} (E_j + G_j + X_j),$$ (17)

$$M_f = \sum_{j=1}^{n} M_j,$$ (18)

$$Y_f = \sum_{j=1}^{n} Y_j,$$ (19)

where all magnitudes are expressed in terms of dollars.

18.2 Estimation Work

This section presents parameter estimates for the model based on a sample of 54 quarterly observations for the period 1964:II–1977:III using the full information maximum likelihood method. For estimation, the continuous model of section 18.1 was approximated using a discrete time system described in Wymer (1972).[18] The data were converted into logarithms and deseasonalized using an index of the deviations of the seasonal means about the mean of each variable.[19]

Since the adaptive parameters of equations (12) and (13) cannot be estimated directly, time series for p^* and ε^* were calculated using different values of γ_{21} and γ_{22}, and the model was reestimated with alternative combinations of p^* and ε^* representing a course grid (0.2, 0.5, 0.8, 1.0, 1.4, 1.6, 1.8, 2.0) of values of the adaptive parameters. The value of 2.0 was chosen as the upper limit of the grid because this is the value for which, in the discrete approximation,

$$\Delta \ln p^* = 0.5*(1 - L^2) \ln p.$$

The values of γ_{21} and γ_{22} that yielded a *maximum maximorum* for the

Table 18.1
Parameter estimates

Adjustment parameters			Other		
Parameter	Estimate	t-value	Parameter	Estimate	t-value
Output [equation (1)]					
γ_1	0.477	(4.27)	β_1	0.062	(4.89)
γ_2	0.045	(0.15)	$(\gamma_2\beta_2 + \gamma_3\beta_3)$	−0.081	(0.87)
γ_3	0.142	(3.02)	β_4	0.733	(25.27)
γ_4	0.0*	–	β_5	10.854	(8.91)
γ_5	0.376	(4.23)	β_6	−0.373	(0.70)
			β_7	1.090	(16.54)
			β_8	5.010	(3.12)
			β_9	0.0[a]	–
			Constant	2.176	(4.88)

MSE $= 6.8 \times 10^{-5}$

Private expenditure [equation (2)]					
γ_6	0.899	(3.45)	β_{10}	0.849	(27.86)
			β_{11}	1.682	(1.52)
			β_{12}	0.140	(0.86)
			β_{13}	−0.105	(4.40)
			β_{14}	1.502	(1.25)
			α_5	1.659	(7.48)

MSE $= 2.1 \times 10^{-4}$

Imports [equation (3)]					
γ_7	0.775	(4.51)	$(\beta_{15} + 1)$	0.731	(2.51)
			β_{16}	1.272	(27.64)
			β_{17}	0.903	(2.82)
			$[Z_6]$	0.135	(5.24)
			α_6	0.001	(0.72)

MSE $= 7.49 \times 10^{-4}$

Price level [equation (5)]					
γ_8	0.035	(1.10)	$[Z_{10}]$	−0.010	(2.28)
γ_9	0.005	(0.15)	Constant	−0.153	(1.00)
γ_{10}	0.061	(2.00)			

MSE $= 2.2 \times 10^{-5}$

Money stock [equation (6)]					
λ_1	0.010	(1.20)	λ_6	0.467	(4.48)
λ_2	0.212	(1.65)	λ_7	0.0[a]	–
λ_3	1.020	(0.53)	$\lambda_8[Z_1]$	−0.022	(2.14)
λ_4	0.103	(2.40)	$\lambda_9[Z_2]$	0.020	(3.25)
λ_5	−0.010	(1.46)	$\lambda_{10}[Z_3]$	0.022	(4.62)
			$\lambda_{11}[Z_4]$	0.022	(3.67)
			Constant	−1.331	(2.21)

Table 18.1 (*continued*)

Adjustment parameters			Other		
Parameter	Estimate	t-value	Parameter	Estimate	t-value
MSE $= 5.0 \times 10^{-5}$					
Interest rate [equation (7)]					
γ_{11}	0.066	(3.36)	$[Z_{11}]$	-0.002	(4.31)
γ_{12}	0.007	(1.06)			
γ_{13}	0.505	(4.29)			
MSE $= 1.0 \times 10^{-6}$					
Exchange market intervention [equation (8)]					
λ_{12}	5.607	(3.41)	$\lambda_{15}[Z_1]$	0.102	(5.78)
λ_{13}	0.057	(0.44)	$\lambda_{16}[Z_5]$	-0.041	(4.70)
λ_{14}	1.339	(6.61)	$\lambda_{17}[Z_6]$	-0.136	(8.19)
			$\lambda_{18}[Z_7]$	0.109	(6.44)
			$\lambda_{19}[Z_8]$	0.044	(3.73)
			$\lambda_{20}[Z_9]$	0.045	(2.68)
			ρ_R	0.0036	(1.40)
MSE $= 4.54 \times 10^{-4}$					
Exchange rate [equation (10)]					
γ_{14}	2.516	(4.55)	$[Z_{12}]$	-0.005	(1.57)
γ_{15}	0.270	(8.61)	$[Z_9]$	-0.006	(1.67)
γ_{16}	2.574	(21.17)	Constant $= (\rho_\varepsilon - \gamma_{14} \ln \alpha_3 + \gamma_{15} \ln \alpha_4)$		(1.42)
γ_{17}	0.169	(4.21)	$= 0.046$		
γ_{18}	0.102	(3.89)			
γ_{19}	0.0[a]				
γ_{20}	0.013	(3.92)			
MSE $= 2.0 \times 10^{-6}$					
Price and exchange rate expectations [equations (12) and (13)]					
γ_{21}	2.0	–			
γ_{22}	1.30	–			
γ_{23}	0.021	(3.29)			

a. Value constrained to equal zero during estimation.

likelihood function were chosen. This is the pair of values for which the likelihood ratio test yields the lowest χ^2 value for the estimated model.

The estimation technique allows the model to be nonlinear in parameters, but requires it to be linear in variables. The evolution from fixed par values to managed floating is taken into account by using an exchange regime variable a that alters the equations which determine the exchange rate and the degree of official intervention in the foreign exchange market. The value of a is unity for Canada's fixed par value period and zero otherwise. In order to make the stochastic equations of the model log-linear, the exchange regime variable a has been subsumed into the time series for the par value and the desired exchange rate such that the first term in equations (9) and (11) is nonzero only at times when a par value is in force, and vice versa for the second term.[20] The linear identities (4) and (11) must also be approximated by log-linear relations.[21]

During the sample period, and especially after 1970, there were fundamental changes in the international economic environment that had a strong impact on reserve flows, exchange rates, prices, and so forth. These events included the temporary imposition of wage and price controls in the United States, the collapse of the Bretton Woods system of adjustable par values, the shift to managed floating exchange rates among the major industrialized countries, and the increase in oil prices. In order to reduce the biases in parameter estimates that would result from failure to take account of these exogenous developments, a small number of dummy variables have been included in the estimated equations representing the behavior of the private sector. (For details, see the appendix.)

Estimation results for the model are presented in table 18.1, where the point estimate of each parameter is listed, together with its t-ratio[22] (in parentheses). Parameters marked with an asterisk have been restricted to a given value.

The parameter estimates and dynamic forecasting experiments suggest that our model provides quite a reasonable description of major economic aggregates in Canada during the sample period. In the discussion of the empirical results in table 18.1 the model can be separated into its basic components: parameters representing the dynamic aspects of the private sector's behavior (γ), parameters of partial equilibrium demands and supplies (α and β), and the policy reactions of the authorities (λ). Of the 17 estimated private sector adjustment parameters, 13 are significant with the correct sign at the 5 percent level. For supply and demand functions of the private sector (some of which are estimated from more than one equation) 11 of the 16 parameters[23] are significant. Among the policy response parameters that have been specified for the authorities' desired money supply and intervention functions, 15 of 20 are significant at the 5 percent level.

The estimated adjustment parameters indicate that the rate of growth of output has been influenced by both supply and demand elements during the sample period. The most important factors are the excess foreign demand for Canadian output and deviations of current output from its capacity level. The spillover from an excess foreign demand for money, which has the expected negative effect on output, is also significant. The excess domestic demand for Canadian output does not appear to have been very significant during the sample period, although it does enter the output equation with the correct sign. The adjustment parameters indicate that the mean time lag in the adjustment of current output to a deviation from its capacity level (the time required for 63 percent of this difference to be eliminated) is just over two quarters. The estimates of other adjustment parameters indicate that a 1 percent difference between the foreign demand for Canadian goods and the current level of exports increases the rate of growth of output in Canada by about 0.15 percent per quarter, while a 1 percent difference between foreigners' desired money balances and their current holdings alters it by about 0.4 percent per quarter, implying that the spillover effect of foreign monetary disequilibrium on Canadian output is quite strong.

Both total private spending and imports respond fairly rapidly to the private sector's excess demand. These responses are well determined statistically and imply a mean time lag of about three months (t-value = 3.45) in the case of total private expenditure and four months (t-value = 4.51) for imports.

The main determinants of prices in Canada seem to be the expected rate of change of prices and the level of prices abroad, converted at the current exchange rate. Neither the rate of capacity utilization nor the excess supply of money appears to have had an empirically robust direct effect on domestic price formation during the sample period, though both enter with the expected sign. There is a rather obvious rationale for this finding. In the first place, during the fixed exchange rate period the domestic inflation rate was very closely tied to that prevailing abroad because of the pervasive goods market linkages between Canada and the rest of the world. Second, our estimates of the exchange rate equation indicate that during the period since the floating of the Canadian dollar in May 1970, domestic monetary disequilibrium has affected the exchange rate quite strongly. Thus, while monetary disequilibrium does not have a discernible direct impact on the domestic price level, it has a strong indirect effect via the exchange rate, which enters the fourth term of the price equation.

The model assumes that the interest rate in Canada is sensitive to interest rate rate movements in foreign markets. There is also a significant Fisherian expectations effect in which the nominal interest rate adjusts to changes in the expected rate of inflation, but it appears to have operated with a rather long time lag during the sample period. The liquidity preference effect has the expected sign, though it is not significant. The estimate of γ_{13} implies that the interest rate responds immediately (but less than proportionately), to a change in the Bank of Canada's discount rate.

The exchange rate equation in the model is well determined, despite the complexity of this structural relation. The main reason for this is the extensive use of across-equation restrictions during estimation. The arbitrage terms which operate during the fixed and floating rate periods, respectively, are both highly significant. As might be expected, the response of the exchange rate to deviations from the par value during the fixed exchange rate period (which has a mean time lag of less than five weeks) is much more rapid than the commodity arbitrage process that has operated during the flexible rate period, which has a mean time lag of nearly a year. The interest arbitrage term and the two monetary spillovers (all of which are assumed to have operated continuously throughout the whole sample period) also have strong effects on the foreign exchange market. The effective exchange rate of the Canadian dollar is highly responsive to any deviation from international interest parity. A 1 percent deviation of the Canadian interest rate from its equilibrium relation with covered foreign yields induces, on average, a 2.5 percent movement in the exchange rate in the short run. The exchange rate is also subject to spillover effects arising from monetary disequilibrium either within Canada or abroad. Not surprisingly, the positive impact of an excess demand for domestic money on the value of the Canadian dollar is almost twice as strong as that of an excess supply of money in the rest of the world.

The ex ante demand and supply functions are generally well determined, especially in cases in which the estimated parameters are obtained from more than one equation. In the output equation, $p/\varepsilon p_f$ is assumed to work from the demand side (since it enters both domestic and foreign demands for domestic goods) and $p/\theta q_1$ (which is viewed essentially as the price of an intermediate input) operates from the supply side, while p/q_2 is the price faced by domestic consumers. The estimated elasticity of capacity output Y with respect to the relative price of oil is highly significant. Our estimates indicate that a 1 percent increase in the relative price of oil reduces capacity output by approximately 0.06 percent, despite the fact that Canada is a significant oil producer. The estimate of the elasticity of capacity output with respect to energy prices in Canada is somewhat smaller than similar estimates for the United States, which are in the range of -0.10 (see Tatom, 1979, pp. 7–8). By contrast, we have been unable to isolate any significant effect for the relative price $p/\varepsilon p_f$ in the output equation. This result probably reflects the fact that, as has already been noted, both domestic prices and the exchange rate respond quite quickly to foreign price developments, so that it is difficult to separate this second price effect in the estimates of the output equation.

The income elasticity of private expenditure—which is very well ·determined—is significantly less than unity. This result is consistent with a gradual fall in the ratio of private expenditure to total domestic income and is a reflection of the secular rise in the relative size of the government sector over time. By contrast, the scale elasticity of import demand is significantly greater than unity, a result of the fact that, as in other countries, the degree of openness of the Canadian economy increased during the sample period. Cyclical factors also have a strong effect on imports. The estimate of β_7 indicates that the elasticity of desired imports with respect to a rise in current output relative to capacity is almost unity. The negative estimated elasticity on the price of domestic output relative to that of oil in the expenditure function implies that, on balance, domestic spenders acted as if their real incomes had been increased by the 1974 oil price increase, a result that has been noted elsewhere (Jump and Wilson, 1975).

Because our model assumes that monetary disequilibrium produces significant spillover effects, the domestic and foreign money demands enter a number of equations, and the imposition of the resulting across-equation restrictions greatly assists the estimation of individual parameters in the model. The parameters of the ROW demand for money are obtained from both the output and exchange rate equations, while those of the domestic demand for money come from the money stock, interest rate, price, and exchange rate equations. Using a narrow (M1) definition of the Canadian money stock, we obtain an income elasticity that is significantly less than unity. As regards the opportunity cost of holding money balances, the domestic interest rate is significant with the correct sign at the 1 percent level, and its coefficient implies an interest elasticity of demand for money (calculated at the sample mean level of the interest rate) of approximately 0.12. On the other hand, the elasticity of the anticipated domestic inflation rate is not significant. Perhaps surprisingly, the parameters of the function representing the demand for money in the rest of the world are also well estimated in the model. The income elasticity is slightly greater than unity and the interest elasticity is significant with the correct sign, with a value of 0.06.

Finally, we turn to the estimates of the authorities' reaction functions for the target rate of monetary expansion and the rate of intervention in the foreign exchange market. While the estimated parameters of these functions must be interpreted with caution, they do provide some evidence that changes in the authorities' desired rate of monetary expansion during the sample period were the result of systematic factors. The authorities' estimated reaction to deviations of domestic prices from their equilibrium level has the correct sign and a t-value of 1.5, and the reaction in response to an output gap is significant at the 10 percent level on an asymptotic test. The sign of the latter term implies that monetary policy tended to vary procyclically during the sample period, a phenomenon that has also been observed in the United States (see Poole, 1979). There is little evidence of systematic changes in money supply in response to foreign interest rate movements, but the coefficient of the money supply reaction function with respect to movements in official holdings of international reserves is significant with the correct sign.[24] Finally, there is evidence that monetary policy became significantly more restrictive in Canada in response to the oil shock of 1973–1974.

As regards the terms λ_6 and λ_7, the first-order term, λ_7, never appeared with the correct sign, and its value was therefore set to zero in order to obtain more efficient estimates of the other parameters. By contrast, λ_6, which reflects the influence of changes in the private sector's demand for money on the authorities' reactions, is estimated to be about 0.47 and is significant. The adjustment parameter implies a mean time lag in the response of the money supply of about two quarters, a much shorter lag than has been found in standard demand for money studies. This result may be due to the fact that, unlike the standard empirical studies, our model takes explicit account of the effect of the authorities' reaction function on the actual money stock.

In the intervention function there appears to be strong evidence of substantial reserve use by the Canadian authorities in response to deviations of the Canadian dollar from its par value during the fixed exchange rate period ($\lambda_{12} = 5.61$). There is also strong evidence that the authorities "leaned against the wind" in their exchange market policy throughout the sample period. In addition to systematic elements, several of the transi-

Table 18.2
Canada: mean and root-mean-square errors of in-sample forecasts:
1964:II–1977:IV (percent)

Variables	Root-mean-square error of single-period forecasts (1)	Dynamic forecasts	
		Mean error (2)	Root-mean-square error (3)
Y	0.83	0.0	1.07
E	1.45	−0.0	1.70
I	2.74	0.0	3.51
X	3.53	−0.0	3.71
P	0.47	0.0	0.56
M	0.70	0.0	1.57
r	0.07[a]	0.0	0.14[a]
$D\ln R$	1.05	−0.0	2.91
θ	0.16	0.0	0.21
ε	0.16	0.0	0.21

a. Prediction errors on the interest rate are in units of percentage points. Root-mean square errors as a proportion of the average interest rate are 6.3 and 12.5 percent, respectively.

tory factors also appear to have had significant effects on both monetary and intervention policies at various times.

In-sample forecasting experiments provide a useful picture of the reasonableness of the specification and the dynamic behavior of the model. Table 18.2 presents the mean squared errors of static forecasts (column 1) and the mean and root-mean-square errors of the dynamic forecasts (columns 2 and 3) made with the model during the entire (1964–1977) sample period.[25] Since the model is expressed in terms of the logarithms of the variables, the mean and root-mean-square errors in table 18.2 are automatically expressed as proportions of the actual value of each endogenous variable. The mean error for the interest rate, however, is in units of percent.

As Table 18.2 indicates, the in-sample forecasting results for the model are good. The root-mean-square errors of the one-period forecasts range from 0.16 percent for the effective exchange rate and the Canadian dollar value of the US dollar (θ) to 2.7 and 3.5 percent for imports and exports, respectively. The larger forecasting error on exports is partly a result of the fact that the linear identity has been approximated by a log-linear equation. The dynamic forecasting experiments are also very encouraging, in that the model shows no systematic tendency to over- or underpredict any variable and the root-mean-square errors are in most cases only slightly larger than those of the static forecasts.

Table 18.3
Canada: characteristic roots of the model

Characteristic root	Asymptotic standard error of root	Damping period (quarters)	Period of cycle (quarters)
−2.781	0.57	0.4	–
−0.584	0.127	1.7	–
−1.362	0.31	0.7	–
−0.008	0.002	124.9	–
−0.013	0.001	79.3	–
−0.499 ± 0.297i	0.081, 0.125	2.0	21.1
−0.061 ± 0.005i	0.018, 0.011	16.3	–

Table 18.3 presents the characteristic roots of the model linearized about the sample means of the variables. All of the real roots are significantly less than zero, as are the real parts of the two complex eigenvalues. Thus the estimated model is locally stable. The two complex roots provide evidence that the model generates at least one endogenous cycle. The first complex root implies a cycle of about five years that is significant at the 5 percent level. This cycle is highly damped; its amplitude falls by 63 percent in about ten months. The second complex root implies an extremely long cycle which, however, is not significantly different from zero and appears to be nothing more than a statistical artifact.

We also calculated the partial derivatives of the characteristic roots with respect to the parameters of the model.[26] There is no behavioral parameter for which a change in value of one standard error could move either of the two smaller eigenvalues from negative to positive. Nor is there any reasonable change in a systematic policy response parameter that would significantly affect the stability of the system. Finally, the complex part of the sixth eigenvalue (which yields the only significant cycle) also has very small partial derivatives with respect to the parameters of the policy reaction functions. These results have two implications. First, our estimated model of the Canadian economy exhibits strong local stability. Second, although a moderate change in systematic policy responses may affect certain aspects of the model's dynamic behavior, it would be unlikely to result in an unstable system.

18.3 Conclusions

The estimation results of the model provide a substantial amount of information about the major channels by which international disturbances are transmitted to the Canadian economy. For example, our work suggests that a rise in foreign demand has a strong stimulative effect on Canadian real output (and hence also on exports). Indeed its impact on output is estimated to be stronger and more significant than that of a rise in demand by domestic residents, and this stimulative effect appears to operate regardless of the exchange rate regime that is in force. Second, movements in national price levels abroad are transmitted to the Canadian economy via their direct impact on the behavior of domestic price setters and the level of imports, though—as the results also indicate—this international linkage among price levels is mitigated, even in the short run, when the exchange rate is floating. The third, and perhaps most interesting, international transmission mechanism that has been uncovered by our empirical work results from monetary spillovers. Disequilibria in holdings of money balances in the other industrial countries that are included in our ROW sector appear to exert powerful spillover effects on the level of real output in Canada and on the effective exchange rate for the Canadian dollar. For example, if a tightening of monetary policies in the four other industrial countries included in our paper were to induce a 1 percent excess ROW demand for money balances, Canadian real output would initially fall by 0.14 percent, and the dollar would depreciate by 0.1 percent in effective terms. Taken together, these results point to several empirically significant channels through which economic aggregates are linked together internationally in the short run under both types of exchange rate regime.

Another general implication of our results concerns the extent to which the mechanisms that transmit short-run disturbances internationally differ depending on the type of exchange rate regime that is in force. In this context, we found that the adjustment of the effective exchange rate to deviations from the fixed par value was much more rapid than its adjustment to deviations of the Canadian price level from international purchasing power parity under a floating rate regime. Similarly, the authorities' intervention in the foreign exchange market responded strongly to deviations from the par value exchange rate, but in the flexible rate period the only systematic evidence appeared to be that of "leaning against the wind" with regard to the effective exchange rate. Most important, the channels by which foreign price disturbances influence the Canadian price level differ markedly under alternative exchange rate regimes. Our estimates of the adjustment parameters in the price and exchange rate equations confirm the familiar proposition that an increase in foreign prices will be transmitted more strongly to the Canadian price level when exchange rate is fixed than would be the case under a flexible rate regime, where the appreciation of the Canadian dollar (owing to commodity arbitrage) acts to dampen the effect of foreign inflation. Furthermore, the direct price linkages under a fixed rate system are reinforced by induced increases in money supply, as the authorities intervene in the foreign exchange market to keep the Canadian dollar near its par value.

Finally, the estimated reaction functions provide at least some tentative evidence that international disturbances are transmitted to the Canadian economy not only as a result of private sector behavior but also from feedback responses of the Canadian authorities. These results have interesting implications. Standard economic theory suggests that in the steady state an economy that is on a floating exchange rate regime will be immune from monetary disturbances abroad. Our estimates suggest, in contrast, not only that private sector adjustment creates strong short-run international interdependence among the industrial countries, but also that to the extent that foreign developments influence domestic policy responses, monetary disturbances abroad may affect the domestic economy even in the longer run. These results, tentative as they are, provide evidence of a high degree of linkage among the major industrial countries, which needs to be taken into account in theoretical and empirical analyses of adjustment under flexible exchange rates.

Appendix   Transitory Policy Responses and Dummy Variables

This appendix defines the nine variables that are assumed to give rise to transitory policy reactions on the part of the authorities in equations (6) and (8). These variables attempt to capture major events that temporarily affected the monetary and intervention responses of the authorities. A few of these variables also enter the behavioral equations of the private sector along with three additional dummy variables.

Money supply reaction function:

$z_1 = 1.0$ in 1970:II, zero otherwise. Dummy for quarter during which Canada changed from a fixed to a floating exchange rate (also in the exchange market intervention function).

$z_2 = 1.0$ from 1972:IV to 1973:III, zero otherwise. Transitory change in authorities' desired trend rate of monetary expansion during the collapse of the Bretton Woods par value system.

$z_3 = 1.0$ in 1975:IV, -1.0 in 1976:I, II, and zero elsewhere. Effect of national postal strike and its aftermath on the measured money stock.

$z_4 = 1.0$ from 1975:IV to 1976:III, zero elsewhere. Period of first publicly declared quantitive proximate monetary target in Canada.

Exchange market intervention function:

$z_5 = 1.0$ from 1966:I to 1966:IV, zero elsewhere. Effect of agreed ceiling on international reserves on intervention policy.

$z_6 = 1.0$ in 1968:I. Intervention to counter speculative outflow from Canada following the sterling devaluation of 1967:IV. (Also in imports equation.)

$z_7 = 1.0$ in 1968:III, zero elsewhere. Intervention to counter reflux of speculative capital that flowed out during 1968:I.

$z_8 = 1.0$ in 1971:IV and 1972:I, zero elsewhere. Effects of Smithsonian par value realignments and associated events.

$z_9 = 1.0$ in 1973:IV, zero elsewhere. Oil embargo. (Also in the exchange rate equation.)

Dummy variables in private sector equations:

$z_{10} = 1.0$ in 1971:III, zero elsewhere. First 90-day price freeze in the United States (price equation).

$z_{11} = 1.0$ from 1973:II to 1973:IV, zero elsewhere. Effect of upward adjustment in Winnipeg Agreement on interest rates. (Interest rate equation.)

$z_{12} = 1.0$ in 1976:I, II, zero elsewhere. Effect of heavy foreign borrowing by the provincial and federal governments on exchange rate. (Exchange rate equation.)

Notes

1. For earlier empirical work, see Rhomberg (1964), Girton and Roper (1977), Knight (1976), and Alexander and Haas (1979).

2. These include the Bank of Canada's RDX2, CANDIDE, QFM, and TRACE; and also the subsystem representing the Canadian economy in the Federal Reserve's multi-country model. See De Bever et al. (1979); and Berner et al. (1977).

3. The main advantages of this approach are (i) it permits mixed stock/flow models to be consistently specified; (ii) it permits us to estimate adjustment parameters even in cases in which the mean time lag of a response is short relative to the observation period; and (iii) it is possible to use the model to forecast for dates within the basic observation period.

4. The present model is designed to be an integral part of a five-country forecasting system in which most of these rest-of-the-world variables are endogenous. See Knight and Mathieson (1979).

5. All adjustment functions except that for the interest rate are specified in log-linear form. The real interest rate is defined as $r - D\ln p^*$, where $D\ln p^*$ is the anticipated inflation rate.

6. All real variables are defined as the corresponding nominal variables divided by the implicit deflator of GNP.

7. R is the value of reserves earned through past official intervention transactions. For a more detailed discussion see Knight (1976).

8. This trend growth rate ρ was estimated by regressing the logarithm of output on a time trend for the period 1964:II–1973:IV. Y_0 is the value of this regression in 1970:II when $t = 0$.

9. Since private expenditure includes purchases of foreign as well as domestic goods, it is necessary to include the relative price of foreign goods in the private sector's ex ante expenditure function. Under reasonably general assumptions, $p/\varepsilon p_f$ enters E with a negative sign.

10. The price elasticity of the physical volume of imports can be derived directly from the elasticity estimate in equation (3′) as $\beta_{15} + 1$ (see Knight, 1976).

11. The first and third terms of (5) correspond to the standard price formation equation that is employed in the literature on money and growth. See, for example, Hadjimichalakis (1971) and Goldman (1972).

12. In the short run, the authorities' target level of Canadian prices relative to foreign prices, α_8, need not equal the level that private domestic producers regard as the equilibrium price ratio of domestic and foreign goods [α_7 in equation (5)]. However, one would expect such a condition to hold in the steady state.

13. Let the degree of sterilization τ be defined as the percentage reduction that the monetary authorities make in their domestic assets in order to sterilize a 1% rise in their foreign exchange reserves. Then the relation between τ and λ_4 is

$$\tau \simeq \frac{R}{A} - \lambda_4 \frac{(R + A)}{A},$$

where R is the domestic currency equivalent of holdings of official foreign exchange reserves, A is the net domestic assets of the monetary authorities, and the money multiplier is assumed constant.

14. The private sector's money demand is assumed to be homogenous of degree one in prices, and this restriction is imposed throughout our model. The private sector can adjust its real money balances either through its effect on the nominal money supply (via λ_7) or by affecting the domestic price level.

15. If i is taken as the marginal product of capital (assumed constant), then the expression in parenthesis in the second term is the nominal return on physical capital.

16. In principle, an increase in official holdings of international reserves should depreciate the domestic currency. In practice, since intervention is undertaken on a daily basis, its direct effect on the exchange rate is unlikely to show up in quarterly data. Further, to the extent that the authorities lean against the wind in their exchange market intervention policy, depreciations of the domestic currency are often cor-

related, in practice, with official intervention *purchases* of foreign exchange. For these reasons, γ_{19} was set equal to zero in the estimated model.

17. The year 1970 was chosen because it was the base year for real GNP data obtained from the IMF's data banks.

18. For flow variables the differential $Dx(t)$ and the level $x(t)$ were obtained by integrating over the observation period and approximating by

$$\int_{t-1}^{t} Dx(s)\,ds \simeq \Delta x_t, \qquad \int_{t-1}^{t} x(s)\,ds \simeq \Gamma x_t,$$

where $Lx_t = x_{t-1}$, $\Delta = (1 - L)$, and $\Gamma = \frac{1}{2}(1 + L)$. Stock variables (which are measured at the end of the period) are approximated by

$$\int_{t-1}^{t} Dy(s)\,ds \simeq \Delta \Gamma y_t, \qquad \int_{t-1}^{t} y(s)\,ds \simeq \Gamma^2 y_t.$$

19. Following Wymer (1972), these data were transformed to remove a first-order moving-average process that results from the approximation.

20. Specifically, the time series for θ_0 equals the par value during periods of fixed exchange rates and the *market* price of the US dollar in domestic currency when par values are absent. Similarly, the time series for the authorities' desired level of the effective exchange rate equals the actual effective rate at times when par values are in force.

21. Identities were linearized by solving for the growth rate of the left-hand variable and then obtaining a first-order Taylor's series expansion about the sample means of the variables.

22. The term "t-ratio" is used here to denote the ratio of a parameter estimate to its asymptotic standard error and does not imply that this ratio has a Student's t-distribution. In a sufficiently large sample this ratio is significantly different from zero at the 5 percent level if it lies outside the interval ± 1.96 and significantly different from zero at the 1 percent level if it is outside the interval ± 2.58.

23. There are 17 β parameters, but β_2 and β_3 cannot be separately identified.

24. The value of λ_4 gives a "ball park" estimate for the degree of sterilization (τ in note 13). When evaluated at 1977: III the values of central bank assets are $\overline{M} = \$26.4$ billion, $\overline{R} = \$5.13$ billion, and $\overline{A} = \$6.9$ billion, giving $\tau \simeq 0.564$.

25. Static forecast errors are here defined as the root mean square of the residuals of the restricted reduced form during the sample period. These "one-period" forecasts are made using the *actual* values of all predetermined variables in each period, and the estimation procedure ensures that the mean error for such forecasts is always equal to zero. The dynamic forecasts are conditional on the calculated series for expected prices and exchange rates, but other predetermined variables take on their actual observed values in the first period only, and thereafter are generated by the model.

26. These results, which are not reported in detail here, are available from the authors on request.

References

Alexander, William E., and Richard D. Haas (1979). "A Model of Exchange Rates and Capital Flows: The Canadian Floating Rate Experience," *Journal of Money, Credit and Banking* 11(4), November, 467–82.

Artus, J. R. (1976). "Exchange Rate Stability and Managed Floating: The Experience of the Federal Republic of Germany," IMF *Staff Papers* 23(2), July, 321–33.

Berner, Richard, et al. (1977). "A Multi-Country Model of the International Influences on the U.S. Economy: Preliminary Results," US Federal Reserve, *International Finance Discussion Papers*, No. 115.

Buiter, Willem (1978). "Short-Run and Long-Run Effects of External Disturbances under a Floating Exchange Rate," *Economica* 45(170), August, 251–72.

Burmeister, Edwin, and S. J. Turnovsky (1976). "The Specification of Adaptive Expectations in Continuous Time Dynamic Economic Models" *Econometrica* 44(5), September, 879–905.

De Bever, et al. (1979). "Dynamic Properties of Four Canadian Macroeconometric Models: A Collaborative Research Project," *Canadian Journal of Economics* 7(2), May, 133–94.

Dornbusch, R. (1976). "Expectations and Exchange Rate Dynamics," *Journal of Political Economy* 84(6), December, 1161–76.

Dugay, Pierre (1978). "Une Analyse du Modele a Forme Reduite et son Application au Canada," Banque du Canada, *Raport Technique* 15.

Girton, Lance, and Don Roper (1977). "A Monetary Model of Exchange Market Pressure Applied to the Postwar Canadian Experience," *American Economic Review* 67, September, 537–48.

Goldman, S. M. (1972). "Hyperinflation and the Rate of Growth of the Money Supply," *Journal of Economic Theory*, October.

Goldstein, Morris, Mohsin S. Khan, and Lawrence H. Officer (1980). "Prices of Tradable and Nontradable Goods in the Demand for Total Imports," *Review of Economics and Statistics* 62(2), May, 190–99.

Gordon, R. J. (1977). "World Inflation and Monetary Accommodation in Eight Countries," *Brookings Papers on Economic Activity* 2, 409–68.

Hadjimichalakis, M. G. (1971). "Equilibrium and Disequilibrium Growth with Money—the Tobin Model," *Review of Economic Studies* 38(116), October, 457–79.

Johnson, Harry G. (1958). "Towards a General Theory of the Balance of Payments," in *International Trade and Economic Growth*, London: George Allen and Unwin, pp. 153–68.

Jump, G. V., and T. A. Wilson (1975). "Macroeconomic Effects of the Energy Crisis 1974–75," *Canadian Public Policy* I(1), Winter, 30–8.

Knight, Malcolm D. (1976). "Output, Prices and the Floating Exchange Rate in Canada: A Monetary Approach," IMF, unpublished.

Knight, Malcolm D, and Donald J. Mathieson (1979). "Model of an Industrial Country Under Fixed and Flexible Exchange Rates," in John Martin and Alasdair Smith (eds.), *Trade and Payments Adjustment Under Flexible Exchange Rates*, Macmillan.

Knight, Malcolm D., and Clifford R. Wymer (1978). "A Macroeconomic Model of the United Kingdom," IMF *Staff papers* 25(4), December, 742–77.

Mathieson, D. J. (1977). "The Impact of Monetary and Fiscal Policy under Flexible Exchange Rates and Alternative Expectations Structures," IMF *Staff Papers*, 24(3), November, 535–68.

Poole, William (1978). "Burnsian Monetary Policy: Eight Years of Progress?", American Finance Association, *Papers and Proceedings*, 34(2), May, 473–84.

Rhomberg, R. (1964). "A Model of the Canadian Economy under Fixed and Fluctuating Exchange Rates," *Journal of Political Economy* 32(2), May.

Tatom, John A. (1979). "Energy Prices and Capital Formation: 1972–1977," Federal Reserve Bank of St. Louis, *Review*, 61(5), May, 2–9.

Waverman, L. (1975). "The Two-Price System in Energy: Subsidies Forgotten," *Canadian Public Policy* I(1), Winter, 76–88.

Wymer, C. R. (1972). "Econometric Estimation of Stochastic Differential Equation Systems," *Econometrica*.

List of Contributors

Jagdeep S. Bhandari
Department of Economics
Southern Illinois University
Carbondale, IL

John F. O. Bilson
Graduate School of Business
University of Chicago
Chicago, IL

William H. Branson
Woodrow Wilson School of Public
and International Affairs
Princeton University
Princeton, NJ

Willem H. Buiter
Department of Economics
University of Bristol
Bristol, United Kingdom

Victor A. Canto
Department of Finance
University of Southern California
Los Angeles, CA

Michael R. Darby
Department of Economics
University of California at Los Angeles
Los Angeles, CA

Alan V. Deardorff
Department of Economics
University of Michigan
Ann Arbor, MI

Rudiger Dornbusch
Department of Economics
Massachusetts Institute of Technology
Cambridge, MA

Jeffrey A. Frankel
Department of Economics
University of California at Berkeley
Berkeley, CA

Jacob A. Frenkel
Department of Economics
University of Chicago
Chicago, IL

Dale W. Henderson
International Finance Section
Federal Reserve Board
Washington, DC

Bryce Hool
Department of Economics
State University of New York at
Stony Brook
Stony Brook, NY

Malcolm D. Knight
Research Department
IMF
Washington, DC

Pentti J. K. Kouri
Department of Economics
New York University
New York, NY

Paul Krugman
Sloan School of Management
Massachusetts Institute of Technology
Cambridge, MA

Jay H. Levin
Department of Economics
Wayne State University
Detroit, MI

Donald J. Mathieson
Research Department
IMF
Washington, DC

Marc A. Miles
Department of Economics
Rutgers University
New Brunswick, NJ

Douglas D. Purvis
Department of Economics
Queens University
Kingston, Ontario, Canada

Bluford H. Putnam
Department of Finance
New York University
New York, NY

J. David Richardson
Department of Economics
University of Wisconsin at Madison
Madison, WI

Jeffrey Sachs
Department of Economics
Harvard University
Cambridge, MA

Robert M. Stern
Department of Economics
University of Michigan
Ann Arbor, MI

Stephen J. Turnovsky
Department of Economics
University of Illinois
Champaign, IL

Douglas G. Waldo
Department of Economics
University of Florida
Gainesville, FL

Willard E. Witte
Department of Economics
Indiana University
Bloomington, IN

Index

Acceleration equation
  OPEC balance of payments, 183
  supply-demand model, 129
Appreciation of currency. *See also specific
  currency*
  and current account surpluses, 60
  and inflation, 47
  jointly floating currency area, 333–335,
    338
  monetarist model, 88
  monetary approach, 46
  Mundell-Fleming model, 52, 54
  and relative income, 49
  supply constrained economies, 416
  supply-demand model, 118, 126, 128
  wealth, domestic, increases in, 96
Arbitrage
  foreign exchange market, 118
  supply constrained economies, 409
Asset market model, 32, 84–86, 385
  assumptions of, 85
  dollar depreciation, 86
  equilibrium model, 199–200, 204–205
  Eurodollar market, 375–376
  Eurodollar market under fixed exchange
    rates, 362–365
  Eurodollar market under flexible
    exchange rates, 370–371
  expectations and exchange rates, 17
  flexible exchange rates, 86, 313–318,
    370–371
  implied regression coefficients of
    competing equations, 103
  interdependence under flexible exchange
    rates, 313–318
  jointly floating currency area, 333
  monetary approach (*see* Monetary
    approach)

Mundell-Fleming model, 52
OPEC policies, 193
organized asset markets, 10
portfolio-balance model (*see* Portfolio-
  balance model)
supply-demand model compared, 117
Asset price determination, 5. *See also*
  Prices
  national price indices compared, 28,
    32
  volatility of prices, 28
Asset substitutability
  Mundell-Dornbusch model, 254, 255
Auction markets, 10

Balance of payments. *See also specific
  country*
  announcement effect of unexpected
    figures, 96
  equity claims to capital (*see* Equity claims
    to capital)
  international transmission models (*see*
    Mark III model; Mark IV model)
  J-curve problem (*see* J-curve problem)
  model of energy, flexible exchange rate,
    201, 205
  Mundell-Fleming model, 51, 53, 54
  and oil price increases, 186, 205
  supply-demand model (*see* Supply-
    demand model)
Balance of trade. *See* Goods markets
Beggar thy neighbor policy, 193
  interdependence under flexible exchange
    rates, 325
  jointly floating currency area, 330, 336
Belgium, 341
Bickerdike-Robinson-Machlup model
  supply-demand model compared, 124

Bond portfolios. *See also* Portfolio-
balance model
allocation between countries, 96
and domestic wealth increases, 96
monetarist model, 87–88
perfect capital mobility, 86
perfect substitutability, 86, 96, 101, 258
Borrowing in foreign currency
supply-demand model, 151–154
Bundesbank Eurodollar transaction. *See*
Eurodollar market

Canada
appreciation of currency, 523–524
characteristics roots of model, 522
errors of in-sample forecasts of model,
521
fixed exchange rates, 509, 523–524
flexible exchange rates, 509, 523–524
foreign demand and Canadian real
output, 523
interdependence of industrial countries,
524
international transmission models (*see*
Mark III model; Mark IV model)
leaning against the wind, 523
model of international disturbances
transmission, 500–513
parameter estimates for model, 513–522
price levels, transmission of, 523
private sector adjustments, 524
spillover of disequilibrium, 503–504, 523
tariffs (*see* Tariffs)
Capital
equity claims to (*see* Equity claims to
capital)
long-run labor-capital ratio, 207
oil prices and capital accumulation, 192
oil prices and intensity decline, 208, 212
Capital accounts
current account interaction with, supply-
demand model, 124
and exchange rate, 118–119
financing through short-term capital
flows, 76–77
invoicing and current accounts, 385–386
Capital mobility
asset market model, 84
current account imbalances, financing of,
73–75
cyclical variations stabilized by, 76–77
financing of capital accounts through,
76–77

fixed rates and perfect mobility, 251
Fleming-Mundell model, 341
flexible exchange rates, 341
freedom of capital movements, 76–77
interdependence of countries, 341
and interest rate policy, 75–76
jointly floating currency area, 334, 342
money-market equilibrium and fiscal
policy, 255
Mundell-Dornbusch model, 254–255
perfect capital mobility, 84, 86, 89, 251
portfolio-balance model equation, 98
short-term, elimination of, 76
supply constrained economies, 409
supply-demand model, 117–118
Central banks
intervention in foreign exchange markets,
312
once-and-for-all sale of foreign exchange,
122–123, 133–134
Commodities markets. *See* Goods markets
Commodities prices. *See* Prices
Consumer goods. *See* Goods markets
Consumer price indices, 9–11
and appreciation of currency, 47
and nominal money balances, 259
and wages, 203, 216
Corden formula, 479, 492, 496
Cost of living indices
average absolute monthly percentage, 29
oil and nonoil goods, 226
purchasing power parities, 29–30
Currency. *See also specific currency*
appreciation (*see* Appreciation of
currency)
depreciation (*see* Depreciation of
currency)
devaluation (*see* Devaluation of currency)
invoice currency (*see* Invoicing)
portfolio substitution (*see* Currency
substitution model)
Currency substitution model
anticipated component of monetary
policy, 164, 166
demand for real balances, 159–160
determination of exchange rates, 164–167
elasticity of substitution equal to two,
165–167
empirical studies, 167–170
global perspective, 157–158
market clearing prices, 161–162
monetary model with rational expectations, 158–159

perfect substitution, 165–166
spot exchange rate variances, 169
unanticipated component of monetary
  policy, 164–166
unitary elasticity of substitution, 165–167
usefulness of theory, 172
volatility of exchange rates, 170–171
Current accounts. *See also specific country*
announcement effect of unexpected
  figures, 96
and appreciation of currency, 60
balances as GNP percent, 73
capital account interaction with, supply-
  demand model, 124
deficits and exchange rates, 93, 95
and depreciation of currency, 60
and dollar depreciation, 93
Dutch disease, 239–240
and exchange rates, 385–386, 400
and foreign exchange markets, 96
imbalances, and shifts in wealth, 61
imbalances, financing of, 74–75
and interest rate policy, 74
invoicing and capital accounts, 385–386,
  400
J-curve, 384, 386
monetary model and oil prices, 95
money-market equilibrium (*see* Money-
  market equilibrium)
Mundell-Fleming model, 52–53, 55–56
news, effect of on exchange rate, 386
and oil prices, 95, 222
and oil production, 239–240
supply-demand model, 118, 126
and unanticipated depreciation, 75
Cyclical variables
capital flows promoting stability, 76–77
and exchange rates, 60
flexible exchange rates, 402
interest rates, 72
and intervention, 70

Deindustrialization
defined, 242
Dutch disease (*see* Dutch disease)
oil price shock, 224
Demand determined output
Mundell-Fleming model, 51–53, 56
Demand for money. *See* Supply and
  demand for money
Denmark, 341
Depreciation of currency. *See also*
  specific currency

anticipated and unanticipated, 15, 18,
  56, 58–59
Bickerdike-Robinson-Machlup model,
  124
and current account surpluses, 60, 75
and cyclical expansion, 60
expectation of in Mundell-Fleming model.
  54
and interest rates, 18, 49, 70, 75
jointly floating currency area, 337, 340
monetarist model, 88
monetary approach, 46–47
Mundell-Fleming model, 52, 54
nonzero expected rate of depreciation, 89
and oil prices, 216
overshooting model, 89
portfolio-balance model and intervention,
  105
and risk premium, 68
and spot exchange rate, 15
supply constrained economies, 404, 416
supply-demand model, 118, 124, 126, 128
unanticipated depreciation, 56, 58–59
wages, effect on, 203
Design of exchange rate and payments
  system, 75
Deutsche mark
appreciation and portfolio diversification,
  64
appreciation in 1978, 95
depreciation, 1979–1980, 95
Eurodollar market (*see* Eurodollar
  market)
exchange rates (*see specific exchange rate*)
intervention and unanticipated depreciation, 70
and oil prices, 95
OPEC investment in, 182–185
and portfolio diversification, 63–64
portfolio model, and unanticipated
  appreciation, 61
risk-premium model and appreciation
  of, 66
Devaluation of currency
jointly floating currency area, 331, 333
and tariffs, 494–498
Disinflation
dynamic adjustment, 234–235
and oil shock, 230
DM/dollar exchange rates. *See* Dollar/DM
  exchange rates
DM/franc exchange rates. *See* Franc/DM
  exchange rates

DM/pound exchange rates. *See* Pound/
DM exchange rates
Dollar
appreciation in 1979–1980, 95
asset market model of depreciation, 86
current account deficit and depreciation,
93
Eurodollar market (*see* Eurodollar
market)
IMF's nominal and real effective
exchange rates, 48
interest rates and exchange rates, 16, 93
intervention and unanticipated depreciation, 68
monetary model and depreciation, 92
1978 depreciation, 93
oil prices and demand for, 95
OPEC spending (*see* OPEC)
overvaluation in the 1960s, 76
unanticipated depreciation, 58
Dollar, Canadian. *See* Canada
Dollar/DM exchange rates, 6
efficiency of foreign exchange market, 7ff
and empirical studies of monetary model,
92
forward rates and the cost of living, 12–13
and inflation rates, 10–11
monetary approach, 50
overshooting model, 94
portfolio-balance model, 99–100
predicted and realized percentage, 10–11
purchasing power parities, 26, 29
spot rates and the cost of living, 12–13
synthesis of monetary and portfolio-
balance equations, 104
unanticipated depreciation, 59–60
and wholesale price indices, 29
Dollar/franc exchange rates, 6
efficiency of foreign exchange, 7
purchasing power parities, 26
Dollar/pound exchange rates, 6
efficiency of foreign exchange, 7
purchasing power parities, 26
Dollar/yen exchange rates
unanticipated depreciation, 59, 60
Dornbusch version of Mundell model. *See*
Mundell-Dornbusch model
Durable asset prices and future expectations, 10
Dutch disease
current account balance, 239–240
defined, 222
oil price increases, 222–223, 235–237

and OPEC, 215
United Kingdom, 223

Efficient markets. *See* Foreign exchange
market
Employment
classical unemployment, 409, 411, 414
and German intervention, 70
and interest rate differentials, 72
international transmission models (*see*
Mark III model; Mark IV model)
jointly floating currency area, 342
long-run capital-labor ratio, 207
Mundell-Fleming model, 52, 55
nontraded goods, effect of, 223
oil price or discovery shock, 224
oil prices and labor market equilibrium,
202–203, 205, 212, 215–216
real wages and unemployment, 216
supply constrained labor markets, 403
Energy prices. *See* Oil prices
England. *See* United Kingdom
Equilibrium and disequilibrium charac-
terizations, 402
Equity claims to capital
balance of payments and, 194, 196
flexible model of energy, 201
perfect substitutability in portfolios, 199
and wealth, 206–207
Equity markets, function of, 192
Eurobanks. *See* Eurodollar market
Eurocurrency market. *See* Eurodollar
market
Eurodollar market
asset demands, 374–376
asset demands under fixed exchange
rates, 362–365
asset demands under flexible exchange
rates, 370, 371
equilibrium conditions, 355, 357, 358, 374
fixed exchange rate model, 360–366
flexible exchange rate model, 367–374
goods markets, 375–377
goods markets under fixed exchange
rates, 365–366
goods markets under flexible exchange
rates, 371–374
interest on required reserves, 359
interest rates, 352–355
model of economic interactions, 351–359
reserve requirements on deposits, 350–351,
358–359, 374–375, 377
stabilization of home output, 376–377

European Monetary System, 4, 27
  interdependence of members, 341
Exchange rate. *See also*, *e.g.*, Fixed
  exchange rate; Flexible exchange rate
  asset price determination, 5
  fiscal policy (*see* Fiscal policy)
  interest rates and, 4, 5, 15, 17–18, 24
  monetary policy (*see* Monetary policy)
  and prices, 5
  tariffs (*see* Tariffs)
Expectations as to exchange rates
  asset market model, 17
  current exchange rate, 11, 13
  interdependence under flexible exchange
    rates, 318–323
  jointly floating currency area, 331–332
  market anticipation of changes, 187–189
  Mundell-Fleming model, 51
  and OPEC spending, 189
  rational expectations, 163–164 (*see also*
    Rational expectations model)
  and spot exchange rate, 162
  static expectations, 262
Exports. *See* Goods markets

Federal Reserve Eurodollar transactions.
  See Eurodollar market
Fiscal policy
  assumptions concerning, 261
  exchange rates, effect on, 251
  fixed and flexible rates, 251
  increase in public spending and rational
    expectations, 273, 274
  international transmission models (*see*
    Mark III model; Mark IV model)
  jointly floating currency area (*see* Jointly
    floating currency area)
  long-run effects under open-economy
    model, 277–281
  model of flexible exchange rates and
    monetary policy, 258–262
  and money-market equilibrium, 257, 258
  Mundell-Dornbusch model, 253–254
  open-economy model and static expecta-
    tions, 264
  supply constrained economies (*see*
    Supply constrained economies)
Fixed exchange rate, 286. *See also specific
  country*
  domestic monetary disturbance, 305–306
  domestic monetary disturbance in small
    open economy, 300
  Eurodollar market model, 360–366

fiscal policy, 251
flexible exchange rate compared, 304–306
foreign disturbances, 305–306
monetary policy, 251
nominal exchange rates, 75
optimal intervention policy, 307
perfect capital mobility, 251
stability properties of, 304–306
Fleming-Mundell model
  and capital mobility, 341
  jointly floating currency area compared,
    336, 341
Flexible exchange rate, 67–75, 86, 286.
  See also specific country
  asset market model, 86
  capital mobility, 341
  and current accounts, 385–386, 400
  domestic disturbances, 305–306
  domestic monetary disturbance in small
    open economy, 301
  domestic policy, 318–325
  Eurodollar market model, 367–374
  fiscal policy, 251
  fixed exchange rate compared, 304–306
  foreign disturbances, 305, 306
  foreign reactions to domestic policy, 318,
    321–325
  interdependence under, 312–325
  international transmission models (*see*
    Mark III model; Mark IV model)
  jointly floating currency area (*see* Jointly
    floating currency area)
  model of energy prices and two-country
    growth, 194–196, 204–206, 218
  model of fiscal and monetary policy,
    258–262
  monetary policy, 251
  necessity for, 76
  optimal intervention policy, 307
  perfectly flexible rate, 307
  portfolio diversification, 61
  price interactions, 312–313, 323–325
    (*see also* Prices)
  small open economy, 304
  stability properties of, 304–306
  synchronous cyclical movements, 402
  tariffs (*see* Tariffs)
  variability of, 84
  volatility of, 158
Flexible-price monetary model. *See*
  Monetarist model
Floating exchange rates. *See* Flexible
  exchange rate

Flow model
 assumptions of, 85
 implied regression coefficients of
  competing equations, 103
Foreign exchange market
 arbitrage, 118
 and current accounts, 96
 efficiency of, 5–9, 32, 157, 193
 intermediation, 118
 intervention in (see Intervention)
 supply and demand (see Supply and
  demand for money)
 supply constrained economies model,
  408
 supply-demand model (see Supply-
  demand model)
Foreign investment. See Investment
Forward exchange contract, 385
 invoicing and, 386, 391–392
Forward exchange rate
 average absolute monthly percentage,
  28
 and future spot exchange rate, 6, 10
 and spot rate, 13, 18
 volatility of, 32
Franc/DM exchange rates
 purchasing power parities, 26
Franc/dollar exchange rates. See Dollar/
 franc exchange rates
France, 341
 international transmission models (see
  Mark III model; Mark IV model)
Future spot exchange rate
 and forward exchange rate, 6, 10

Germany
 capital account surplus, 64
 current account balances, 66
 current account balances as percent of
  GNP, 74
 deutsche mark (see Deutsche mark)
 direct investment and portfolio investment deficit, 64
 Eurodollar deposits (see Eurodollar
  market)
 European Monetary System, 341
 imports by compared to OPEC imports,
  181
 interest rate differentials of U.S.
  compared, 71–72
 interest rates and monetary models, 92
 international transmission models (see
  Mark III model; Mark IV model)

 intervention, determinants of, 69–70
 monetary growth, 92
 net government borrowing, 66
 OPEC balance of payments, 182–184
 tariffs (see Tariffs)
 U.S./German government debt, 66
Gold prices
 and future expectations, 31
 futures, 13–15
 spot, 13, 15
 volatility of, 13–14
Goods markets
 Canadian model (see Canada)
 and cost of living, 226
 deficits in trade balance, 25
 employment and nontraded goods, 223
 Eurodollar market, 375–377
 Eurodollar market under fixed exchange
  rates, 365–366
 Eurodollar market under flexible
  exchange rates 371–374
 hedging (see Hedging)
 industrial countries vs. OPEC, 181
 inflation and interest rates, 72
 interdependence under flexible exchange
  rates, 313–318
 international transmission models (see
  Mark III model; Mark IV model)
 invoicing (see Invoicing)
 jointly floating currency area, 332–333,
  338–339
 monetarist model, 88
 nonoil and oil goods, 226, 241
 nontraded goods, effect of, 223
 oil as intermediate good, 223, 226, 241
 and oil prices, 185–186, 211, 222–223, 240
 and oil quantity shock, 226–228, 240
 overshooting model, 89
 supply constrained economies, 404, 409,
  411, 415–416
 supply-demand model (see Supply-
  demand model)
 tariffs (see Tariffs)
Government spending. See Fiscal policy
Grassman's rule, 384–386, 389–400
Gross national product
 current account balances as percent of,
  73

Hedging
 and invoicing, 384, 391–392, 400
 portfolio diversification, 392
Household model, 204

consumption equilibrium, 207
and oil prices, 196–198, 204, 211
output market equilibrium, 200, 205

Imports. *See* Goods markets
Income
actual, 226
and discovery of domestic oil reserves,
  230
international transmission models (*see*
  Mark III model; Mark IV model)
jointly floating currency area stabilization, 334–341
oil prices and quantity, effect of, 226, 227
oil production and prices, effect of, 241
permanent, 226
real, 226
stability of fixed vs. flexible exchange
  rates, 306
supply constrained economies, 404,
  415–416
Industrialization. *See* Deindustrialization
Inflation
and appreciation of currency, 47
Canadian model (*see* Canada)
disinflation (*see* Disinflation)
dollar/DM exchange rate, 10–11
expectation of and currency cost, 55
and German intervention, 70
import prices and interest rates, 72
interdependence under flexible exchange
  rates, 318–325
and interest rates, 17–18, 70, 72
and invoicing, 393, 396
monetarist model, 88
monetary model, 93
news, 19
and nominal effective exchange rates, 48
and nominal money supply, 226
and oil price shock, 224
supply constrained economies (*see* Supply
  constrained economies)
supply-demand model of inflation/balance
  of payments equilibrium, 135
Information. *See also* News
efficient markets theory, 157
and exchange rates, 11
and future expectations, 10
prices and monetary model with rational
  expectations, 159
Interdependence of industrial countries
Canadian model, 524
and capital mobility, 341

European Monetary System members,
  341
and flexible exchange rates, 312–325
  (*see also* Jointly floating currency area)
Interest rates
anticipated changes in, 5
and capital flows, 75–76
and current account imbalances, 74
cyclical variables, 72
demand for money and nominal interest
  rates, 259
and depreciation of currency, 18, 49, 70
domestic rate of interest, 226
and empirical studies of monetary model,
  92
equilibrium of capital in Mundell-
  Fleming model, 54
estimates of determinants of international
  differentials, 71
Eurodollar deposits (*see* Eurodollar
  market)
and exchange rates, 4–5, 15, 17–18, 24
exchange rates and one-month rate
  differential, 20–21
exchange rates and twelve-month rate
  differential, 22–23
foreign disturbances and foreign rates,
  341
foreign exchange value of domestic
  currency, 17
and import prices, 72
and inflation, 32, 70, 72
and inflationary expectations, 17–18
international transmission models (*see*
  Mark III model; Mark IV model)
and intervention, 73, 75
jointly floating currency area, 333–334,
  340
liquidity preference theory, 117
long-term rates, 49
monetarist model, 88
and monetary approach, 46, 49
Mundell-Fleming model, 51–52, 56
and news, 19
overshooting model, 89–90
and risk premium, 67
and spot exchange rate, 17, 24
stabilization of exchange rates, 74
unanticipated changes in, 5, 32, 58, 60
and unanticipated depreciation, 75
and value of dollar, 93
Intermediation in foreign exchange
  market, 118

International Monetary Fund
Articles of Agreement, 4
effective exchange rate of, 48
International Standard Industrial
Classification
categories of world industry, 475–476
International transmission of monetary
disturbances
Mark III model (*see* Mark III model)
Mark IV model (*see* Mark IV model)
Intervention, 68, 312. *See also specific
country*
cyclical variables, 70
fixed exchange rate (*see* Fixed exchange
rate)
flexible exchange rate (*see* Flexible
exchange rate)
and interest rates, 73, 75
leaning against the wind (*see* Leaning
against the wind)
leaning with the wind (*see* Leaning with
the wind)
optimal intervention, 286–287
optimal intervention in small open
economy, 289, 296–304, 306–307
portfolio-balance model of depreciation,
105
stable intervention defined, 294
stable intervention in small open
economy, 295–296, 298–299
and unanticipated depreciation, 68, 70
unstable intervention defined, 294
unstable intervention in small open
economy, 294–295, 297–298
Investment
and oil price increases, 192, 198–199,
204, 212
portfolio diversification, 63–64
Invoicing
capital accounts, 385–386
currency choice, 390–400
current accounts, 385–386, 400
forward exchange contracts, 385–386,
391–392
Grassman's rule, 384–386, 389–400
and hedging, 384, 391–392, 400
indifference curve, 392–399
and inflation, 393, 396
international markets, 389
market power, 398–399
optimizing model of invoicing decision,
387
practices, 384, 389

purchasing power parities, 389
risk aversion, 392, 395, 398, 400
separation theorem, 387, 389
Italy, 341
international transmission models (*see*
Mark III model; Mark IV model)

J-curve problem
Mark IV international transmission
model, 428
supply-demand model, 142
Japan
current account balances as percent
of GNP, 74
interest rate differentials of U.S.
compared, 71–72
international transmission models (*see*
Mark III model; Mark IV model)
intervention, determinants of, 69–70
tariffs (*see* Tariffs)
Jointly floating currency area. *See also*
Interdependence of industrial countries,
and flexible exchange rates
appreciation of currency, 333–335, 338
asset market model, 333
beggar thy neighbor policy, 330, 336
capital mobility, 342
depreciation of currency, 337, 340
devaluation of currency, 331, 333
expectations as to exchange rate, 331–
332
fiscal expansion and contraction, 330,
333–341
Fleming-Mundell model compared, 336,
341
goods market equilibrium, 333, 338–339
income, 334–341
interest rates, 333–334, 340
labor movements, 342
model, 329–332
perfect capital mobility, 334
stabilization policy, 333–338

Labor. *See* Employment
Leaning against the wind, 288
Canada, 523
domestic monetary disturbance in small
open economy, 301
foreign monetary disturbance in small
open economy, 303
optimal intervention in small open
economy, 304
optimal intervention policy, 306

Leaning with the wind, 289
   domestic monetary disturbance in small
      open economy, 301
   foreign output demand disturbance in
      small open economy, 302
   foreign output supply disturbance in
      small open economy, 303
   optimal intervention in small open
      economy, 304
   optimal intervention policy, 306
Liquidity preference theory of interest
      rate determination, 117
Luxembourg, 341

Machlup. See Bickerdike-Robinson-
   Machlup model
Macroeconomic shocks of supply
   constained economies. See Supply
   constrained economies
Manufacturing. See also Goods markets
   deindustrialization (see Deindustrial-
      ization)
   demise of manufacturing sector, 223
   Dutch disease (see Dutch disease)
   invoicing (see Invoicing)
   nonoil goods defined, 241–242
   oil price or discovery, effect of, 222–223,
      240
Mark III model
   described, 427–428, 430, 468
   simulation version (see Mark LV model)
Mark IV model
   asset substitution channel, 431
   balance of payments, 430–431
   base dynamic simulation, 436
   British money shock experiments, 459,
      466
   channels of transmission, 431, 436
   described, 428, 430–431, 436, 468
   domestic effects of real government
      spending shocks, 428
   export shocks, 431
   flexible exchange rate, 428
   foreign price levels, 431
   German money shock experiments,
      458–459, 466
   government spending, 431
   income, 430–431
   international transmission models (see
      Mark III model; Mark IV model)
   J-curve phenomenon and import demand
      inelasticity, 428
   monetary linkages with U.S., 427–428

money supply shocks, 431
   nominal interest rates, 431
   oil prices, 431
   pegged exchange rates, 427–428
   results of simulations, 468
   standard errors of estimate, 432–433, 436
   summary of structure, 429–430
   U.S. money shock experiments, 436, 443,
      450–451, 458–459, 466
   unemployment, 431
Modigliani consumption function, 96
Monetarist model, 86–89
   anticipated and unanticipated distur-
      bances, 89
   assumptions of, 85
   empirical studies, 92
   equation, 101
   equation of exchange rate determination,
      88
   implied regression coefficients of com-
      peting equations, 103
Monetary approach, 47–50
   assumptions of, 85
   criticism of, 117
   currency substitution model (see Currency
      substitution model)
   current accounts and oil prices, 95
   described, 46, 86
   and dollar depreciation, 92
   empirical studies, 92–93
   equation of money demand function, 87
   flexible price monetary model (see Mone-
      tarist model)
   implied regression coefficients of com-
      peting equations, 103
   inflation and currency appreciation, 47
   monetarist model (see Monetarist model)
   overshooting model (see Overshooting
      model)
   regression equations, 48–50
   sticky price monetary model (see
      Overshooting model)
   synthesis of portfolio-balance and
      monetary equations, 101–105
   usefulness of theory, 51
Monetary disinflation. See Disinflation
Monetary policy
   disinflation (see Disinflation)
   domestic policy, 318–325
   fixed exchanged rate (see Fixed exchange
      rate)
   flexible exchange rate (see Flexible
      exchange rate)

Monetary policy (*cont.*)
  foreign reactions to domestic policy, 318,
    321–325
  intervention (*see* Intervention)
  jointly floating currency area (*see* Jointly
    floating currency area)
  long-run effects under open-economy
    model, 277–281
  model of flexible exchange rates and
    fiscal policy, 258–262
  and oil shocks, 224, 242–243
  prices and policy interdependence (*see*
    Prices)
Money. *See* Currency
Money demand or supply. *See* Supply and
  demand for money
Money-market equilibrium. *See also*
  Open-economy model
  adjustment with flexible price of domestic
    output, 274–283
  and exchange rate, 256–258
  fiscal policy and perfect capital mobility,
    255
  fiscal policy effects, 257–258, 277–281
  flow equilibrium, 256
  instantaneous equilibrium, 256
  long-run effects of monetary and fiscal
    policy, 277–281
  long-run equilibrium, 256, 265, 269
  open-market purchase and rational
    expectations, 272
  public spending increase and rational
    expectations, 273
  rational expectations, 270–274
  rational expectations and flexible
    domestic price level, 281–283
  short-run effect of open-market purchase,
    265, 268
  short-run equilibrium under static expec-
    tations, 273
  static expectations and open-economy
    model, 264
Mundell model, 89–90, 251
  open-economy model version, 262
Mundell-Dornbusch model, 252
  asset substitutability, 254–255
  capital mobility, 254–255
  criticism of, 251
  fiscal policy effects, 253–254
  money-market equilibrium and exchange
    rates, 256
  open-economy model compared, 262–274
  and portfolio-balance model, 255, 257

Mundell-Fleming model, 51–55
  extended model, 51–52
  news form test, 56–60

Neo-Keynesian open-economy model. *See*
  Open-economy model
Netherlands, 341
  international transmission models (*see*
    Mark III model; Mark IV model)
  tariffs (*see* Tariffs)
News
  and aggregate price levels, 27
  asset price determination, 28
  current accounts and exchange rates, 386
  exchange rate determination, 18–19, 24,
    32
  inflationary expectations, 19
  interest rate changes, 19
  Mundell-Fleming model, 52, 55–60
  risk-premium model, 67

Official intervention. *See* Intervention
Oil as intermediate good, 223, 226, 241
Oil consumption and oil prices, 187
Oil discovery shock. *See* Oil quantity
  shock
Oil prices. *See also* OPEC
  balance of payments, 186, 201, 205
  capital accumulation, 192
  capital intensity decline, 208, 212
  comparative statics, 206–209
  and consumption of oil, 187
  and current accounts, 95, 222
  deindustralization, 224
  and depreciation of currency, 216
  deutsche mark, effect on, 95
  and disinflation, 230
  domestic production of energy, 213–214
    (*see also* Oil quantity shock)
  Dutch disease, 222–223, 235–237
  dynamic adjustment, 240
  employment, effect of oil shock on, 224
  equilibrium effect of increase in, 210–216
  and exchange rates, 179
  and goods markets, 185, 211, 222–223,
    240
  household model, 196, 197, 198, 204, 211
  income, effect on, 226, 227, 241
  increase, effect of, 179, 185–187, 191,
    221–222, 230, 232–233
  inflation, acceleration of, 224
  interdependence under flexible exchange
    rates, 325

international transmission models (*see* Mark III model; Mark IV model)
investment model of firm, 198–199, 204, 212
labor market equilibrium, 202, 203, 205, 212, 215–216
long-run comparative statics, 232
macroeconomic analysis, 191–192, 216–218, 225–229
manufacturing, effect on, 222–223, 240
model of two-country growth and flexible exchange rates, 194–196, 204–206, 218
monetary policy adjustment, 224, 242–243
and money supply and demand, 196
OPEC savings and consumption decision, 201–202
perfect foresight assumption, 193, 196
real price of energy, 195, 211
shocks, 222, 233–234
simulation of price setting, 207, 209
small economy analysis, 185, 192
supply and demand for dollars, 95
and wages, 211
wealth, equilibrium distribution of, 206–207, 209, 211–212
and yen, 95
Oil production and income derived from, 226
Oil production, domestic. *See* Oil quantity shock
Oil quantity shock, 222
actual oil production, 226
anticipated increase in production, 227
current account balance, 239–240
deindustrialization, 224
discovery of domestic oil reserves, 230, 237–239
and disinflation, 230
dynamic adjustment, 233–234, 240
employment, effect on, 224
and goods markets, 227–228, 240
gross price elasticities of demand, 227, 230
income, effect on, 226, 227, 241
long-run comparative statics, 230, 233
manufacturing, effect on, 240
monetary policy adjustment, 242–243
and trade balance, 226
unanticipated increase in production, 227
OPEC. *See also* Oil prices
asset market model, 193
balance of payments, 182–184
consumption and savings decision, 201–202, 205, 209, 211–212

consumption decisions and oil prices, 195
deutsche mark, investment in, 182, 184–185
dollar, investment in, 185
Dutch disease, 215
expectations as to exchange rates and spending by, 189
expenditure by, 180–181, 183
expenditures and balance of payments, 184–185
formation of cartel, 221
global effect of policies, 193
import preferences, 189
imports, 181
interdependence under flexible exchange rates, 325
investment preferences, 189
output market equilibrium, 200
wages, 203
wealth distribution and oil prices (*see* Oil prices)
Open-economy model, 262. *See also* Money-market equilibrium
adjustment with fixed price of domestic output, 262
adjustment with flexible price of domestic output 274–283
equilibrium with rational expectations, 271
long-run effects of monetary and fiscal policy, 277–281
rational expectations, 270–274, 281–283
small open economy (*see* Small open economy model)
stability under static expectations, 268–270
static expectations, 262–270, 274–277
static expectations and flexible price of domestic output, 274–277
Organisation for Economonic Co-operation and Development, 56
Output market equilibrium, 200, 205
Overshooting model, 89–92
anticipated and unanticipated monetary disturbances, 92
assumptions of, 85
empirical studies, 92
equation of exchange rate determination, 91
estimation of monetary exchange rate equation, 94
implied regression coefficients of competing equations, 103

Overshooting model (*cont.*)
nonzero expected rate of depreciation, 89
transitory and permanent monetary
disturbances, 91

Payments deficit. *See* Balance of payments
Pegged exchange rates, 3, 76
international transmission models (*see*
Mark III model; Mark IV model)
Perfect foresight assumption, 193
Perfect substitutability of bonds. *See*
Portfolio-balance model
Portfolio-balance model, 61–66, 93–101
assumptions of, 85
capital inflow and outflow, 98
defined, 86
and deutsche mark appreciation, 63–64
diversification of portfolios, 63–64
domestic small country model, 101
equations, 96–99, 101
estimation of equations, 100
flexible exchange rates, 61
foreign small country model, 101
imperfect asset substitutability, 61
implied regression coefficients of
competing equations, 103
intervention and currency depreciation,
105
macroeconomic models, 97–98
money demands and wealth, 61
and Mundell-Dornbusch model, 255, 257
perfect substitutability, 101
portfolio-diversification model described,
64–65
preferred local habitat, 99
and rational expectations model, 97
realized means and variances of real
returns, 61–63
risk-premium model, 65
small country assumption, 98
synthesis of monetary and portfolio-
balance equations, 101–102, 104–105
uniform asset preferences, 97, 101
Portfolio diversification. *See also*
Portfolio-balance model
bond portfolios (*see* Bond portfolios)
hedging, 392
and Tobin tax proposal, 77
Pound/DM exchange rates
purchasing power parities, 26
Pound/dollar exchange rates (*see* Dollar/
pound exchange rates)
Predictability of exchange rates, 10–11, 15

unanticipated changes, 24
unpredictability of, 402
Preferred local habitat model, 85
Prices
asset market interdependence under
flexible exchange rates, 313–318
average absolute monthly percentage
changes, 29
consumer price index (*see* Consumer price
indices)
and exchange rates, 5, 25–26, 46, 49
expectation interdependence under
flexible exchange rates, 318–323
and future expectations, 10
goods market interdependence under
flexible exchange rates, 313–318
inflation interdependence under flexible
exchange rates, 318–325
information and monetary model with
rational expectations, 159
and interest rates, long-term, 49
international transmission models (*see*
Mark III model; Mark IV model)
and monetary approach, 49
Mundell-Fleming model, 51
and news, 27
oil and nonoil goods, 226 (*see also* Goods
markets; Oil prices)
OPEC and policy interdependence, 325
predictability of, 15
purchasing power parities, 32
stability of fixed vs. flexible exchange
rates, 306
supply and demand interdependence
under flexible exchange rates, 61,
318–323
tariffs (*see* Tariffs)
time series properties of exchange rates,
27
unpredictability, 10
volatility, 10
volatility of aggregate price indices, 27
wage-price guidelines (*see* Wage-price
guidelines)
Productivity/technology trends. *See*
Technology/productivity trends
Public spending. *See* Fiscal policy
Purchasing power parities
and commodity price adjustment, 32
deviations from, 30
Europe, 26, 27
and invoicing, 389
monetarist model, 87–88

monetary approach to exchange, 46
Mundell-Fleming model, 52, 55
overshooting model, 91
rational expectations model, 90
U.S., 26–27
Purchasing power parity doctrine, 25, 27,
  32
excessive exchange rate, 28

Rational expectations model, 18, 157
currency substitution model (*see* Currency
  substitution model)
market expectations of exchange rate
  changes, 188–189
monetarist model, 88
Mundell-Fleming model, 52, 55–56
overshooting model, 90–91
and portfolio-balance model, 97
purchasing power parities, 90
and spot exchange rate, 162–164
and supply-demand model, 154
Relative income and currency appreciation,
  49
Reserve requirements on Eurodollar
  deposits (*see* Eurodollar market)
Risk aversion in invoicing (*see* Invoicing)
Risk-premium model, 65–67
Robinson. *See* Bickerdike-Robinson-
  Machlup model

Securities. *See* Portfolio-balance model
Services defined, 241–242
Simulation version of Mark III model. *See*
  Mark IV model
Small country model, 85
Small open economy model, 287–292
domestic monetary disturbance, 299–301
fixed exchange rate, 300
flexible exchange rate, 301, 304
foreign monetary disturbance, 302–303
foreign output demand disturbance,
  301–302
foreign output supply disturbance, 303
intervention, optimal, 289, 296–304,
  306–307
intervention, stable, 295–296
intervention, unstable, 294–299
leaning against the wind, 301, 303, 304
leaning with the wind, 301–304
rational expectations systems, 292
Snake agreement, 27
Spot exchange rate
average absolute monthly percentage, 28

currency substitutions, 169
and depreciation of currency, 15
and expected future exchange rate, 162
and forward exchange rates, 13, 18
and interest rates, 17, 24
and news, 18
tax on, proposed, 76–77
volatility of, 32
Stabilization of jointly floating currency
  area. *See* Jointly floating currency area
Stable intervention. *See* Intervention
Stagflation, 402
Sticky price monetary model. *See* Overshooting model
Stock market indices
mean absolute monthly percentage, 28
and volatility of exchange rates, 30
Stocks and money-market equilibrium. *See*
  Money-market equilibrium
Substitutability of currencies. *See* Currency
  substitution model
Supply and demand for money. *See also*
  Supply-demand model
Bickerdike-Robinson-Machlup model,
  124
Canadian model (*see* Canada)
classical money demand theory, 159
domestic monetary disturbance in small
  open economy, 299–301
domestic wealth, increases in, 96
Eurodollar market (*see* Eurodollar
  market)
foreign exchange market model, 117
foreign monetary disturbance in small
  open economy, 302–303
foreign output demand disturbance in
  small open economy, 301–302
foreign output supply disturbance in
  small open economy, 303
and inflation rate, 226
interdependence under flexible exchange
  rates, 318–323
and interest rates, 259
international transmission models (*see*
  Mark III model; Mark IV model)
jointly floating currency area (*see* Jointly
  floating currency area)
monetarist model, 88, 116
monetary model equation, 87
and oil prices, 95, 196
overshooting model, 89–90
rational expectations model, 90
and wealth, 259

Supply constrained economies, 403
  appreciation of currency, 416
  arbitrage, 409
  capital movements, 409
  central value version of model, 409, 411
  cleanly floating exchange rates, 414–415
  defined, 408–409
  depreciation of currency, 404, 416
  fiscal policy, 404, 415–416
  flexible exchange rates, 403
  goods markets, 404, 409, 411, 415–416
  incomes policies, 404, 415–416
  insulation of regions, 403, 414–415
  model, 404–408
  policy and output elasticities, 412–414
  rationing of households, 409–411, 414
  rationing repercussions, 415
  supply-side policies, 415
  technology/productivity trends, 404,
    415–416
  transmission of shocks, 403, 415
  wage-price guidelines, 404, 415
Supply-demand model
  acceleration equation, 129
  acceleration hypothesis, 118, 126
  anticipated disturbances in foreign
    exchanges, 139–141
  appreciation of currency, 118, 126, 128
  asset demand functions, 120
  Bickerdike-Robinson-Machlup model
    compared, 124
  borrowing in foreign currency, 151–154
  capital accounts and current accounts,
    124
  capital flows, 117–118
  comparative dynamic responses, 130–135
  comparison of models, 117
  current account surplus and deficit, 126
  current accounts, 118, 124, 126
  decline in foreign demand for domestic
    assets, 130–131
  depreciation of currency, 118, 126, 128
  domestic demand for foreign currency,
    119
  dynamic partial equilibrium model, 142
  dynamic response with multiple equilibria,
    132
  equilibrium of foreign exchange market,
    118, 120
  foreign demand for domestic currency,
    119
  foreign residents not holding domestic
    assets, 124, 126
  general equilibrium condition, 128–130
  inflation equilibrium with balance of
    payments, 135
  J-curve problem, 142
  linear approximations, 142–151
  momentary equilibrium in foreign
    exchange market, 120
  multiple equilibria and dynamic instability,
    127–128
  once-and-for-all sales, 122–123, 133–134
  permanent increase in domestic demand
    for foreign goods, 134–135
  rational expectations equilibrium, 154
  rational speculation in foreign exchanges,
    135–137
  short-run equilibrium in foreign exchange
    market, 118–119
  short-run equilibrium with no intervention,
    120
  unanticipated disturbances in, 137–138
  unanticipated disturbances in foreign
    exchanges, 139
Supply-side policies in supply constrained
  economies, 415

Tariffs
  Canada, currency devaluation and, 496
  Canada, protection measures in 1976,
    482–483, 493
  categories of world industry, 476
  conceptual framework of model, 475,
    477–478
  Corden formula, 479, 492, 496
  and devaluation of currency, 494–498
  exchange rate exogeneity, 479
  exchange rate flexibility, 493, 498
  exports, effect on, 493
  foreign tariff exogeneity, 479–480
  general equilibrium model, 472–472,
    493
  Germany, currency devaluation and, 496
  Germany, protection measures in 1976,
    484–485, 493
  imperfect substitutability of domestic and
    foreign goods, 492–493, 497
  Japan, currency devaluation and, 497
  Japan, protection measures in 1976, 487
  model of world production and trade,
    474–475
  Netherlands, currency devaluation and,
    497
  Netherlands, protection measures in 1976,
    488–489, 492–493

nontraded goods, effective protection of, 480–481
price exogeneity, 478–479
protection afforded by, 472–473, 498
ranking of industries, 493, 496–498
structure of protection in 1976, 481, 492–493
traded goods, 481
U.S., currency devaluation and, 497
U.S., protection measures in 1976, 490–491, 496
Taxation, 76–77
Technology/productivity trends
supply constrained economies, 404, 415–416
Tobin tax proposal, 76–77
Tobin's q, 192–193
asset market equilibrium, 200
Trade balances. *See* Goods markets
Trade barriers
nontariff, 27
Treasury Eurodollar transactions. *See* Eurodollar market

Uniform preference model, assumptions of, 85
United Kingdom
current account balances as percent of GNP, 74
Dutch disease, 223
international transmission models (*see* Mark III model; Mark IV model)
United States
current account balances and GNP percentage, 73–74
current account balances and official intervention, 68
current account balances and real interest differentials, 74
Eurodollar deposits (*see* Eurodollar market)
German/U.S. government debt, 66
imports by compared to OPEC imports, 181
interest rate differentials of Germany and Japan compared, 71–72
international transmission models (*see* Mark III model; Mark IV model)
monetary growth, 92–93
OPEC balance of payments, 182–183
tariffs (*see* Tariffs)
Unstable intervention. *See* Intervention

Volatility of aggregate price indices, 27
Volatility of exchange rates, 10, 32, 402
currency substitution model, 170–171
empirical studies, 171
flexible exchange rates, 158
spot exchange rates, 31
and stock market indices, 30
Volatility of gold prices, 13

Wage-price guidelines, 402
supply constrained economies, 404, 415
Wages
and consumer price index, 216
and exchange rate policy, 203
and oil prices, 211
OPEC wages, 203
unemployment and real wages, 216
Wealth
and appreciation of currency, 96
and demand for money, 259
and equity claims to capital, 206–207
and money demand, 61
oil prices and equilibrium distribution of, 206–207, 209, 211–212
risk-premium model, 65
and supply and demand for money, 96
transfer from foreign to domestic residents, 96
Wholesale price index
average absolute monthly percentage, 29
purchasing power parities, 29–30

Yen
appreciation, 1978, 95
depreciation, 1979–1980, 95
and oil prices, 95
Yen/dollar exchange rates (*see* Dollar/yen exchange rates)